POLITICS IN STATES AND COMMUNITIES

POLITICS IN

STATES
AND
COMMUNITIES

Thomas R. Dye

PRENTICE-HALL, INC.,
Englewood Cliffs, New Jersey

Thomas R. Dye
POLITICS IN STATES AND COMMUNITIES

Library of Congress Catalog Card Number: 69–10724

Current printing (last digit):
10   9   8   7   6   5   4

PRINTED IN THE UNITED STATES OF AMERICA

Prentice-Hall International, Inc., LONDON
Prentice-Hall of Australia, Pty. Ltd., SYDNEY
Prentice-Hall of Canada, Ltd., TORONTO
Prentice-Hall of India Private Ltd., NEW DELHI
Prentice-Hall of Japan, Inc., TOKYO

To JOANN

FOREWORD

If this book has a theme, it is that states and communities in America play an important role in the political life of the nation. State and local governments do more than merely provide certain services such as education, road building, or fire protection. They also perform a vital political function by helping to resolve conflicts of interest in American society. The concern of this book is with "politics," that is, conflicts over public policy in American states and communities and the structures and processes designed to manage these conflicts.

This book not only attempts to *describe* politics and public policy in American states and communities, but, more importantly, it attempts to *explain* differences that are encountered from state to state and community to community by means of comparative analysis. In the past the phrase "comparative government" applied to the study of foreign governments, but the American states and communities provide an excellent opportunity for genuine comparative study. By that we mean the comparison of political institutions and behavior from state to state and community to community for the purpose of identifying and explaining existing similarities or differences. Only by comparing politics and public policies in different states and communities can we arrive at any explanation of political life.

No longer is the field of state and local government a "lost world" to students of politics. Today, some of the most intellectually exciting and theoretically significant research in political science is focused on American states and communities. This book tries to summarize the results of recent systematic, comparative research in political science and incorporate these results into a comprehensive analysis of politics in states and communities.

The author of a textbook is deeply indebted to the research scholars whose labors produce the insight and understanding that a text tries to convey to its readers. There is no way to adequately express this indebtedness. A glance at these chapters will reveal some particularly heavy reliance on the work of James A. Robinson, Robert H. Salisbury, Joseph A. Schlesinger, Diel Wright, Kenneth N. Vines, Herbert Jacob, Harmon Zeigler, Austin Ranney, Lester W. Milbrath, Robert S. Friedman, Daniel J. Elazar, Lewis A. Froman, Jr., Edward C. Banfield, James Q. Wilson, John C. Bollens, Henry J. Schmandt, Oliver P. Williams, Duane Lockard, Charles R. Adrian, John H. Kessel, Daniel Grant, Robert C. Wood, Herbert Kaufman, Charles Press, Aaron Wildavsky, Peter Bachrach, Charles Gilbert, Brett W. Hawkins, Floyd Hunter, Robert A. Dahl, Raymond Wolfinger, Robert E. Agger, Heinz Eulau, Thomas J. Anton, M. Kent Jennings, Ira Sharkansky, Matthew Holden, Gilbert Steiner, and James E. Anderson.

I am more than usually indebted to the staff of Prentice-Hall, Inc., for their assistance in the preparation of this volume. In fact, it was the prompting of Samuel H. Gore of Prentice-Hall which got this work underway in the first place.

Finally, I am indebted to Maureen Morris McIntosh for many things, including her very real contributions to this volume.

THOMAS R. DYE

Florida State University
November 1968

CONTENTS

ix

THE POLITICS OF WELFARE, HEALTH, AND HOUSING

THE POLITICS OF BUDGETING AND TAXATION

INDEX

POLITICS IN STATES AND COMMUNITIES

1

POLITICS IN

STATES AND COMMUNITIES

States and Communities in American Political Life

Although states and communities in America bear the major responsibility for the nation's domestic affairs, the spotlight of national attention is usually on political events in Washington. Important issues of economic prosperity, international peace, and military preparedness must be resolved by the national government, but in such fields as education, law enforcement, crime prevention, welfare, health and hospitals, highways, housing, urban renewal, sanitation, water supply, sewage disposal, transportation, public utilities, and many others, the combined efforts of states and communities far exceed the efforts of the national government. DeTocqueville, a French political scientist who described American government over a century ago, observed that the real government of the United States was not found in the nation's capital: "The federal government scarcely interferes in any but foreign affairs . . . the governments of the states in reality direct society in America." The powers of the federal government have grown immeasurably since DeTocqueville's time, yet states and communities continue to do most of the "governing" in domestic affairs.

Although the national government spends more money than all states and communities combined, over three-fourths of the national government's expenditures go for the cost of past, present, and future wars. Thus, if we

1

TABLE 1.1

A COMPARISON OF FEDERAL, STATE, AND LOCAL EXPENDITURES
FOR ALL DOMESTIC PROGRAMS

| | Public expenditures (in millions of dollars) | | | Percent of domestic spending | |
| | Federal | | State-local | | |
	Total	Domestic*		Federal	State-local
1956	75,991	21,688	43,152	33.4	66.6
1960	97,284	36,828	60,999	37.6	62.4
1962	113,428	41,052	70,118	37.0	63.0
1964	126,569	47,928	80,579	37.2	62.8
1966	143,022	58,025	94,906	37.9	62.1

*Domestic spending excludes expenditures for defense, foreign relations, space, veterans benefits, and interest on general debt (which was created primarily by defense spending). Total federal spending includes trust/fund expenditures, such as social security.
Source: U.S. Bureau of the Census, Statistical Abstract.

subtract the costs of defense and defense related items from federal government expenditures, we find that federal expenditure for domestic affairs is quite modest. If only domestic spending is considered, states and communities spend twice as much as the federal government. As the President's Commission on Intergovernmental Relations pointed out:

> The states and their subdivisions bear directly more than two-thirds of the growing fiscal burden of domestic government. In recent years their activities have been increasing faster than the nondefense activities of the national government.[1]

War, depression, and international tension have directed so much public interest toward Washington that it seems the only government in America is the federal government. Public apathy towards state and local government is widespread. The news media emphasize national politics, rather than state or community politics. Voters show a greater interest in national elections than in state and local elections. We can expect 60 to 65 per cent of the nation's eligible voters to turn out in a presidential election, but average turnout in gubernatorial elections in nonpresidential years is closer to 50 per cent, and municipal elections often attract fewer than one-third of the eligible voters. Undoubtedly, the fact that the news media and the voters concentrate on national rather than state and local affairs indicates the great importance of peace and prosperity to most Americans. State

[1] Advisory Commission on Intergovernmental Relations, *Report* (Washington: Government Printing Office, 1955), p. 36.

and community governments can not cope with the issues of prosperity and depression, war and peace, yet their role in American government is vital.

States and communities in America operate the world's largest public school system and highway network. They operate most of the nation's judicial, welfare, police, health, correctional, and recreational facilities. Most regulation of industry, banking, commerce, utilities, labor, and protection of public safety is in the hands of state and local governments. Their programs in conservation, sanitation, social work, housing, and urban planning are vital to the day-to-day lives of all Americans. Even when the national government is involved in these programs, states and communities must decide whether to participate in national programs, and if they participate, they must administer the programs within their jurisdictions. Despite the glamour of national politics, states and communities carry on the greatest volume of public business, settle the greatest number of political conflicts, make the majority of policy decisions, and direct the bulk of public programs. They have the major responsibility for maintaining domestic law and order, for educating the children, for moving Americans from place to place, and for caring for the poor and the ill. They regulate the provision of water, gas, electric, and other public utilities, share in the

TABLE 1.2

STATE AND LOCAL GOVERNMENT EXPENDITURES BY FUNCTION

	1932	1942	1955	1960	1965
Total	8,403	10,914	40,375	60,999	86,962
Education	2,311	2,526	11,907	18,719	28,971
Highways	1,741	1,490	6,452	9,428	12,221
Welfare	444	1,225	3,168	4,404	6,315
Health	107	159	471	559	836
Hospitals	349	432	2,053	3,235	4,525
Police protection	318	394	1,229	1,857	2,549
Local fire protection	210	236	694	995	1,306
Natural resources	165	214	793	1,189	1,730
Sanitation and sewage	223	229	1,142	1,727	2,360
Housing and urban renewal	0	236	499	858	1,250
Local parks and recreation	147	128	509	770	11,040
Financial administration } General control }	470	578	1,452	2,113	{ 1,267 { 1,506
Interest	741	565	838	1,670	2,490
Other	539	718	2,517	4,351	6,524
Utilities and liquor stores	518	1,106	3,886	5,088	7,058
Insurance trusts	120	617	2,764	4,031	4,950

Source: U.S. Bureau of the Census, Statistical Abstract.

regulation of insurance and banking enterprise, regulate the use of land, and supervise the sale and ownership of property. Their courts settle by far the greatest number of civil and criminal cases. In short, states and communities are by no means unimportant political systems.

Education. Education is the most important responsibility of state and local governments. As Table 1.2 suggests, education is the most costly of all state-local functions. In 1966 nearly 50 million students attended public, primary and secondary education facilities; they were taught by nearly 2 million teachers; and the expenditures on their behalf exceeded $25 billion. States and communities are responsible for decisions about what should be taught in the public schools, how much should be spent on the education of each child, how many children should be in each classroom, how much teachers should be paid, how responsibilities in education should be divided between state and local governments, what qualifications teachers must have, what types and rates of taxes shall be levied for education, and many other decisions which affect the life of every child in America. Support for higher education, including funds for state colleges and universities, is the most rapidly increasing expenditure of state governments. The promise of equal access to a college degree for all qualified students is proving to be a heavy burden on states and communities. The federal government is currently spending over $2.5 billion per year on education; but this is less than 10 per cent of the total state and local expenditures for education.

Transportation. Transportation—more particularly highways—is the second most costly function of state and local governments. There are over 2 million miles of surface roads in America, and state and local expenditures for highways total more than $12 billion annually. There are nearly 90 million registered motor vehicles in the nation, almost one for every two persons. States and communities must make decisions about the allocation of money for streets and highways, sources of funds for highway revenue, the extent of gasoline and motor vehicle taxation, the regulation of traffic on the highways, the location of highways, the determination of construction policies, the division of responsibility between state and local for highway financing administration, the division of highway funds between rural and urban areas, and other important issues in highway politics. While the federal government is deeply involved in highway construction, federal grants for highways amount to less than 30 per cent of state-local expenditures for highways.

Health and welfare. States and communities continue to carry the heaviest burdens in the field of health and welfare—despite an extensive system of federal grants-in-aid for this purpose—and spend about twice as much as the federal government. States and communities must make decisions about participation in federal programs, and allocate responsibilities among themselves for health and welfare programs. Within the broad outlines of federal policy, states and communities decide the amount of money appropriated for health and welfare purposes, the benefits to be paid to recipients, the rules of eligibility, and the means by which the programs will be administered. States and communities may choose to grant assistance beyond the limits supported by the national government, or they may choose to have no welfare programs at all. Moreover, states and communities must maintain institutions for the care of persons who are so destitute, alone, or ill that federal payments are not sufficient. These are the state orphanages, homes for the aged, and state and county hospitals and homes for the physically and mentally ill.

Crime. States and communities have the principal responsibility for public safety in America. Crime is increasing at a much greater rate than the population. Major riots have been reported recently in all the major cities. The federal government, through the Federal Bureau of Investigation, has limited jurisdiction over certain crimes, such as kidnapping, bank robbery, and espionage. State police have important highway safety responsibilities and cooperate with local authorities in the apprehension of criminals. But community police forces continue to be the principal instrument of law enforcement and public safety. Local governments employ over a quarter of a million policemen in the United States today, and approximately the same number of firemen. The sheriff and his deputies are still the principal enforcement and arresting officers in rural counties. States and communities also have the principal responsibility for maintaining prisons and correctional institutions. Each year, over 2 million Americans are prisoners in jails, police stations, juvenile homes, or penitentiaries. More than 90 per cent of these prisoners are at state and local rather than federal institutions.

Civil rights. The national government has defined a national system of civil rights, but these rights cannot become realities without the support of state and local authorities. States and communities must deal directly with racial problems, such as desegregation in the public schools, job discrimination, and the existence of segregated housing patterns or ghettos in the cities. They must deal with the consequences of racial tension, including violence. Some states have gone much further than the federal government in guaranteeing civil rights, for example, by bussing students out of segregated neighborhoods to avoid de facto segregation in the schools. Other states and communities have resisted federal attempts to desegregate their public schools, hospitals, and recreation facilities.

Physical environment. Local governments have the principal responsibility for our physical environment. They must plan streets, parks, commercial, residential, and industrial areas, and provide essential public utilities for the community. The waste materials of human beings—rubbish, garbage, and sewage—exceed one ton every day per person. The task of disposal is an immense one; the problem is not only collecting it, but finding ways to dispose of it. If it is incinerated, it contributes to air pollution, and if it is carried off into streams, rivers, or lakes it contributes to water pollution. Thus, communities are largely responsible for two of the nation's most pressing problems—air and water pollution.

Taxation. To pay for these programs, states and communities must make important decisions about taxation: they must decide about levels of taxation and what tax burdens their citizens can carry. They must determine what reliance shall be placed upon income, sales, or property taxation. States and communities must raise nearly $100 billion per year and at the same time compete with each other to attract industry and commerce.

While it is true that the decisions of states and communities are at times heavily influenced by decisions made at the national level, states and communities continue to bear the major responsibility for policy-making and finance in domestic affairs. States and communities are important political systems with the legal authority, money, manpower, policies and programs which touch the lives of all Americans.

A Political Approach to States and Communities

States and communities do more than provide services such as education, highways, and police protection. They also play an important role in managing conflicts of interest in American society. It is appropriate for a book on "politics" in states and communities to consider important conflicts in American life, for "Politics arises out of conflicts, and it consists of the activities—for example, reasonable discussion, empassioned oratory, balloting, and street fighting—by which conflict is carried on." [2] The concern of this book is therefore with "politics," that is, conflicts over public policy in American states and communities, and the structures and processes designed to manage these conflicts.

There are various approaches to the study of state and local government. Many books emphasize basic structure, organization, and practice of government; other books suggest that the key to understanding lies in the mastery of the constituional relationships between national, state, and local governments; still other books concentrate on the administration of state and local governments. No one denies that the organizational, constitutional, or administrative aspects of state and local government are important, but the really critical problems facing American communities, such as education, welfare, racial hatred, slum housing, financial crises, and transportation, cannot be solved through organizational reform, constitu-

[2] Edward C. Banfield and James Q. Wilson, *City Politics* (Cambridge: Harvard–M.I.T. Press, 1963), p. 7.

tional change, or administrative efficiency. The obstacles to the solution of these problems are primarily *political* in character; that is, people have different ideas about what should be done, or if anything should be done at all. Only when everyone agrees on a solution can the problem be entrusted to lawyers, accountants, or technicians. In American politics, this agreement seldom exists. Even if there is "only one way to pave a street," political questions remain, "Whose street shall be paved?" "Who will get the paving contract?" "Who will bear the cost?" "Why not build a school gym instead of paving the street?"

The management of conflict in society is one of the basic purposes of government. The Founding Fathers were very much aware that the control of "factions" was the principal function of government. Moreover, they defined faction as a number of citizens united by common interests that oppose the interests of a number of other citizens. James Madison thought that regulating such conflict was "the principal task of modern legislation." [3] To paraphrase Madison, the management of conflict is a principal task of state and local government.

A political approach to states and communities does not ignore the organization of state and local government, the constitutional limitations upon them, or their administrative problems, for the principal responsibility for managing conflict falls upon government institutions. Governments manage conflict by establishing and enforcing general rules by which conflict is to be carried on, by arranging compromises and balancing interests in public policy, and by imposing settlements which the parties in the disputes must accept. In other words, governments must lay down "the rules of the game" in political activity; they must make decisions which allocate values among competing interests, and then see that these decisions are carried out. The organization of a government, its constitutional limitations, and the administrative arrangements under which it operates all vitally affect the way it performs political functions. In considering the constitutional, organizational, and administrative aspects of state and local government, we should focus our attention on their impact on political questions.

A Comparative Approach to States and Communities

The task of political science is not only to *describe* politics and public policy in American states and communities, but, more importantly, to *explain* differences encountered from state to state and community to community by means of comparative analysis. We want to know "what" is happening in American politics, but we also want to know "why" it is happening. In the past, the phrase "comparative government" applied to the study of

[3] James Madison, *The Federalist,* No. 10.

foreign governments, but American states and communities provide an excellent opportunity for genuine comparative study, that is, the comparison of political institutions and behavior from state to state and community to community for the purposes of identifying or explaining the similarities or differences which are found. Studies which merely describe governmental agencies or political events, without identifying or explaining their similarities or differences, cannot really contribute to the explanation of politics and public affairs. Even the most insightful descriptions of political events do not provide explanations of their significance that rise above the level of hunches. Professor Roy MacCridis explains that comparative study "entails the comparison of variables against the background of uniformity either actual or analytical for the purposes of discovering causal factors that account for variations." [4] Comparison, in other words, is a vital part of explanation. Only by comparing politics and public policy in different states and communities with different socio-economic and political environments can we arrive at any comprehensive explanations of political life. Comparative analysis can help us answer the question "why."

The American states provide an excellent opportunity for applying comparative analysis. These 50 separate political systems share a common institutional framework and cultural background. All states operate under written constitutions, which divide authority between executive, legislative, and judicial branches. The structure and operations of these branches are quite similar from state to state. All states function within the common framework of the American federal system. All states share a national language, national symbols, and a national history. Thus, important institutional and cultural factors can be treated as constants in comparative study, which make it easier to isolate causal factors in politics and public affairs. Comparative analysis of foreign political systems is very difficult because it is necessary to isolate the factors which cause differences in governmental systems or policy outcomes from the environmental differences which exist in the geography, climate, language, economy, history, religion, and so on. In contrast, when one focuses upon the American states, many environmental variables are held constant, and the influence of a single set of social or political conditions can be more clearly observed.

Of course, American states and communities are not entirely alike, in their social and economic environments, the nature of their political systems, or their public policies. These differences, however, are important assets in comparative study because they enable us to search for relationships between different socio-economic environments, political system characteristics, and policy outcomes. For example, if differences among states and communities in educational policies are closely associated with

[4] Roy C. MacCridis, *The Study of Comparative Government* (New York: Doubleday & Co., 1955), p. 2.

differences in social or economic environments or in party systems, then we may assume that socio-environments or party systems help explain educational policies.

Let us conceive of states and communities as *political systems.* We can think of public policies and programs as outcomes that result from *forces* brought to bear upon a *system* causing it to make particular *responses.* The explanation of politics and public policy, therefore, would involve an examination of relationships between social and economic inputs (forces), political system characteristics (systems), and policy outcomes (responses). These relationships can be diagrammed, as in Figure 1.1. This particular model assumes that the social and economic environment of a state or a community helps to determine the nature of its political system. The *political system* is that group of interrelated structures and processes which serve to allocate values authoritatively within the state or community. This

FIGURE 1.1

A MODEL FOR THE ANALYSIS OF STATE POLITICAL SYSTEMS

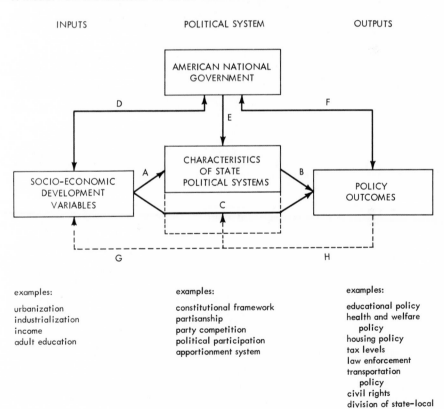

INPUTS	POLITICAL SYSTEM	OUTPUTS

examples:

urbanization
industrialization
income
adult education

examples:

constitutional framework
partisanship
party competition
political participation
apportionment system

examples:

educational policy
health and welfare
 policy
housing policy
tax levels
law enforcement
transportation
 policy
civil rights
division of state-local
 responsibilities

group includes not only state and local governments, but also political parties, interest groups, electoral systems, power structures, and other institutions and activities that help to transform political demands into public policy. Policy outcomes are viewed as the value commitments of the political system, and as such, they are the chief output of that system. They are authoritative decisions about education, welfare, health, taxation law enforcement, and so on, which require the support of society. Any political system absorbs a variety of often conflicting demands; to transform these demands into public policies (outputs), it must arrange settlements, compromise interests, and resolve conflict.

American states and communities can be studied as political systems, and this "systems model" can help to explain their operation. However, they are also *subsystems* in the larger "American political system," heavily influenced by the activities of the national government. The actions of the national government can affect public policies in the states (for example, federal grants-in-aid affect state welfare programs), help to shape state political systems (for example, Supreme Court decisions declaring malapportionment unconstitutional result in state legislative reapportionment), and influence socio-economic conditions in the states (for example, defense contracts can stimulate economic growth). We cannot really consider state and local politics as being separate from national politics. Throughout this volume we will consider the impact of federal activities on states and communities.

The systems model of political life helps to focus our attention on several important questions:

1. What are the significant environmental conditions which affect politics? What are the significant characteristics of political systems? What are the significant elements of public policy?
2. How do environmental conditions affect the character of political systems? (Linkage A)
3. How does the character of political systems affect policy outcomes? (Linkage B)
4. How do environmental conditions affect policy outcomes? (Linkage C)
5. How do the activities of the national government affect socio-economic conditions in the states, the character of state politics, and public policies in the states? (Linkages D, E, F)
6. How do public policies affect, through feedback, both environmental conditions and the character of the political system? (Linkages E and H)

Let us use the systems model to pose some specific questions about state politics, by way of example. What effect does urbanization have on the level of party competition in the states? What effect does industrialization have on Democratic or Republican party success in the states? How do income levels affect spending for public education? Do states with well educated adult populations support spending for higher education to a greater degree than states with less educated adult populations? Do two party states have more generous welfare programs than one party states? Do states with low voter participation have more conservative tax policies than states with higher voter participation? Do federal programs operate to reduce inequalities among the states in educational opportunities? These are the kinds of questions that a comparative approach will enable us to answer.

There are marked differences among the states in social and economic environments. Income levels among the states vary a great deal: in 1960 the median family income in Connecticut was 2½ times what it was in Mississippi. States differ in their rural and urban composition: over 85 per cent of New Jersey residents lived in urban areas, while 65 per cent of North Dakota residents lived in rural areas. States also differ in what people do to earn their living: only 1 per cent of the labor force in Massachusetts was engaged in agriculture in contrast to 33 per cent in North Dakota. Educational levels vary markedly. Kentucky adults averaged only an eighth grade education, while adults in seven states averaged more than 12 years of schooling. In other words, some states are urban, industrial, high income states with well educated adult populations; other states are rural, agricultural, low income states with poorly educated adult populations. There is sufficient variation among the states in these environmental conditions to permit us to examine their effect on political systems and public policies.

Despite uniformity in constitutional framework, the political systems of the 50 states are remarkably varied. The comparative strength of the Republican and Democratic parties obviously differs. States can also be differentiated by the level of interparty competition and by the strength and functions of their party organizations. In some states, conflict between rural and urban interests dominate state politics, while in other states conflict among regions or between legislature and governor, liberal and conservative, or labor and management may dominate. Another basis of comparison is the level of political participation among the voters. In some states, the legislature makes the crucial decisions about public policy, while in others the legislature simply rubberstamps the decisions of a strong governor, an influential party leader, or powerful interest groups. In some states political alignments follow party lines, while in others, they reflect factional rivalries, competition among powerful interest groups, or conflicts between liberals and conservatives or labor and industry. In short, state political systems can be quite different from one another. We are interested in what social and economic conditions create these differences in state political systems, and the effect of different political systems on public policies and programs.

There are marked differences in state programs and policies in many fields, such as education, health and welfare, highways, public safety, and taxation. For example, per pupil education expenditures in New York are over 2½ times what they are in Mississippi; average monthly welfare benefits in Connecticut are three times as much as they are in Arkansas; per capita expenditures for highways in Wyoming are four times higher than in New Jersey; per capita taxes in California are over twice as high as in South Carolina; Nevada provides three times the number of policemen per person that South Dakota provides. These very significant differences among the states in a wide variety of policy outcomes present both an opportunity and a challenge for comparative study.

Settings for State Politics

State politics are often affected by unique historical circumstances. Louisiana is distinctive because of its French-Spanish colonial background, and the continuing influence of this background on its politics today. For nine years Texas was an independent republic (1836-45) before it was annexed as a state by Congress. California was the scene of a great gold rush in 1849. Eleven southern states were involved in a bloody war against the federal government from 1861 to 1865. Hawaii has a unique history and culture, combining the influence of Polynesian, Chinese, Japanese, and hoalie civilizations. Alaska's rugged climate and geography and physical isolation set it apart. Wisconsin and Minnesota reflect the Scandinavian influences of their settlers. The states of the deep south—South Carolina, Georgia, Alabama, Mississippi, Louisiana—still reflect their plantation cultures. Life in Florida is more tourist oriented than anywhere else. Michigan is noted for its automobile industry, Pennsylvania for its steel industry, California for movie productions, and West Virginia for its depleted coal mines. Nevada is most conspicuous for its legalized gambling and liberal divorce laws.

These unique historical and cultural settings help to shape state political systems and public policies; however, students of state politics must search for social and economic conditions that appear most influential in shaping state politics over time in all the states. Despite the uniqueness of history and culture in many of our states, we must still search for generalizations which will help to explain why state governments do what they do. Since it is impossible to consider all the environmental conditions that might influence state politics, we must focus our attention on a limited number of environmental variables.

Economic development is one of the most influential environmental variables affecting state politics. Economic development is defined here to include four closely related components: urbanization, industrialization, income, and education. Economic development involves, first of all, indus-

FIGURE 1.2

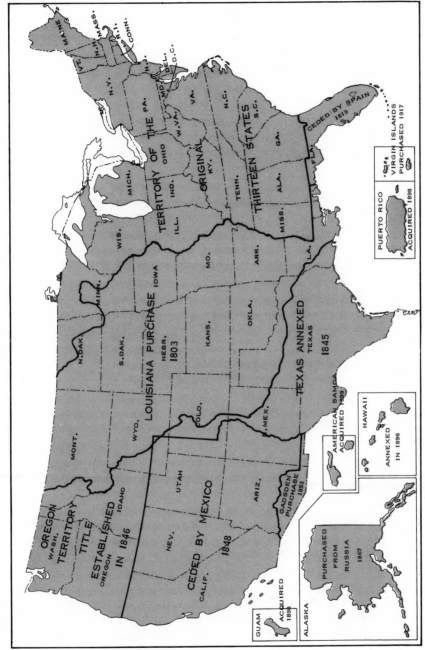

SOURCE: U.S. Bureau of the Census, *U.S. Census of Population, 1960.*

trialization. America's transformation from an agricultural to an industrial society is perhaps the most prominent development in its history. As late as 1870, over 53 per cent of America's work force was engaged in agriculture, forestry, or fisheries. Only 17 per cent of the work force was directly engaged in manufacturing, and less than 30 per cent was engaged in supporting economic activities: transportation and public utilities, finance, wholesale retail trade, and service activities including government. By 1900 these proportions had changed: 38 per cent of the work force was in primary economic activities—agriculture, forestry, and fisheries; 22 per cent in direct manufacturing activity; and 40 per cent in supporting activities. The history of the twentieth century describes the declining role of primary activities and the increase in manufacturing and in trade, finance, and service activities, which become important as the economy matures. By 1960 only 7 per cent of the labor force in America was employed in agriculture, forestry, and fisheries, while 27 per cent was employed in manufacturing, and 66 per cent in supporting activities.

Yet not all the states share the same high level of industrial activity that characterizes the nation as a whole. In 1960, 63.1 per cent of the population of North Dakota was in nonagricultural employment, while in Connecticut, Massachusetts, New Jersey, New York, and Rhode Island, nonagricultural employment accounted for over 98 per cent of the work force. Figure 1.3 shows the distribution of the states according to their degree of industrialization. Because of the industrial character of the nation as a whole, the distribution of states along this measure is heavily skewed toward nonagricultural employment.

Most economists have come to regard urbanization as an integral part of economic development. Industrial activities require the concentration of people in urban centers, whereas agricultural activities spread population over larger land areas. It is possible for a population center to grow without industrialization, but industrialization requires urbanization. A common definition of urbanization is the percentage of population living in urban areas, that is, in incorporated cities of 2500 or more or the urban fringe of cities of 50,000 or more. This is the standard Census Bureau definition. In 1790 the urban population of the United States was only 5.1 per cent of the total population. By 1900 this figure had grown to 39.7 per cent, and in 1960, 69.9 per cent of the population lived in urban areas. Yet here again not all the states share this high degree of urbanization. Alaska has the smallest proportion of urban residents of any state in the nation (37.9 per cent), and New Jersey has the highest proportion (88.6 per cent). The distribution of states according to the percentage of their population living in urban areas is shown in Figure 1.3.

Most economists treat rising income as a basic component of economic development. An industrial economy means increased worker productivity

FIGURE 1.3

ECONOMIC DEVELOPMENT IN THE FIFTY STATES

I. INDUSTRIALIZATION

				18	11
			11	Ariz.	Alaska
			Ala.	Calif.	Conn.
		5	Ga.	Colo.	Md.
	3	Ark.	Kans.	Del.	Mass.
1	Iowa	Idaho	Mo.	Fla.	Mich.
N.D.	Miss.	Ky.	N.C.	Hawaii	N.H.
S.D.	Neb.	Minn.	Okla.	Ill.	N.J.
		Mont.	S.C.	Ind.	N.Y.
			Tenn.	La.	Ohio
			Vt.	Me.	Pa.
			Wis.	Nev.	R.I.
			Wyo.	N.M.	
				Ore.	
				Tex.	
				Utah	
				Va.	
				Wash.	
				W.Va.	

Number of States

61–75   76–80   81–85   86–90   91–95   96–100

One Minus the Percentage of the Work Force in Agriculture, Fisheries and Forestry

III. INCOME

				17	14
		13	Ariz.	Calif.
		Fla.	Colo.	Conn.
		Ga.	Idaho	Del.
	4	Ky.	Ind.	Hawaii
1	Ala.	La.	Iowa	Ill.
Miss.	Ark.	Me.	Kans.	Md.
	S.C.	Neb.	Minn.	Mass.
	Tenn.	N.C.	Mo.	Mich.
		N.D.	Mont.	N.J.
		Okla.	N.H.	Nev.
		S.D.	N.M.	N.Y.
		Tex.	Ore.	Ohio
		Vt.	Pa.	Wash.
		W.Va.	R.I.	Wis.
			Utah	
			Va.	
			Wyo.	

						1
						Alaska

Number of States

2,000– 3,000– 4,000– 5,000– 6,000– 7,000
2,999   3,999   4,999   5,999   6,999

Median Family Income in Dollars, 1959

II. URBANIZATION

			11	12	
	10	Del.	Ariz.
5	6	Ala.	Ind.	Colo.
Alaska	Ark.	Ga.	Kans.	Conn.
Miss.	Idaho	Iowa	La.	Fla.
N.D.	Ky.	Me.	Minn.	Hawaii
S.D.	N.C.	Mont.	Mo.	Md.
Vt.	S.C.	Neb.	N.M.	Mich.
	W.Va.	N.H.	Okla.	Nev.
		Tenn.	Ore.	Ohio
		Va.	Wash.	Pa.
		Wyo.	Wis.	Tex.
				Utah

						6
						Calif.
						Ill.
						Mass.
						N.J.
						N.Y.
						R.I.

Number of States

30–39   40–49   50–59   60–69   70–79   80–89

Percentage of the Population Living in Urban Areas

IV. EDUCATION

		17		
8		Fla.	13	
Ark.		Ill.	Ariz.	
Ky.	5	Ind.	Conn.	
La.	Ala.	Md.	Del.	7
Miss.	Ga.	Mich.	Hawaii	Alaska
N.C.	N.D.	Minn.	Idaho	Calif.
S.C.	Mo.	N.H.	Iowa	Colo.
Tenn.	Va.	N.J.	Kans.	Nev.
W.Va.		N.Y.	Mass.	Utah
		Ohio	Me.	Wash.
		Okla.	Mont.	Wyo.
		Pa.	Neb.	
		R.I.	N.M.	
		S.D.	Ore.	
		Tex.		
		Vt.		
		Wis.		

Number of States

8–8.9   9–9.9   10–10.9   11–11.9   12–12.9

Median School Year Completed by Population, Age 25 and Over

in the creation of surplus wealth. Median family income in the U.S. grew from $1231 in 1939 to $5660 in 1959. This wealth was not evenly distributed throughout the states. Median family income in 1959 in Mississippi was $2884 while median family income in Connecticut was $6887— over 2½ times as much. Figure 1.3 shows the distribution in the 50 states according to median family income in 1959 (the most recent year for which accurate census figures on median family income are available).

An economically developed society requires educated, rather than uneducated, workers. Many economists have asserted that economic growth involves an upgrading of the quality in the work force, the development of professional managerial skills, and an increase in the volume of research. These developments obviously involve a general increase in the educational levels of the adult population. In 1940 the median school year completed by the adult population of the United States was 8.6. By 1960 the median school year had advanced to 10.6. This generally high level of educational attainment did not prevail uniformly throughout the states. Median school year completed by a population over 25 years of age in Kentucky was only 8.7, while the median school year completed in Utah was 12.2.

The extent to which economic development—urbanization, industrialization, income, and education—affects the politics of the states is an important question, which we will return to again and again in the chapters that follow.

The Constitutional Framework of State Government

Probably no other people in the world are more devoted than the American people to the idea of written constitutions. This devotion has deep roots in American national traditions. In 1215 a group of English Lords forced King John to sign a document, later known as the Magna Carta, which guaranteed them certain feudal rights, and set a precedent for constitutional government. Although the British political tradition eventually rejected the formal written constitutions, the idea of a written constitution was strongly reinforced by the experience in the American colonies. The American colonies were legally established by charters given to companies establishing settlements here. These charters became more elaborate as the colonial ventures succeeded, and the habit of depending upon a written code for the regulation of governmental organization and operation became strongly entrenched in the American colonies.

The charters, or "constitutions," were granted by royal action, either by recognizing proprietary rights as in Maryland, Delaware, and Pennsylvania, or by granting royal commissions to companies to establish governments, as in Virginia, Massachusetts, New Hampshire, New York, New Jersey,

Georgia, and North and South Carolina. Only in Connecticut and Rhode Island was there much popular participation in early constitution-making. In these two colonies, royal charters were granted directly to the colonists themselves, who participated in drawing up the charter for the submission to the Crown. The important point is that these charters, whatever their origin, were present in all of the colonies and that many political traditions and expectations grew up around them. All the colonies and charters were subject to royal control. Colonists looked to these charters for protection against British interference in colonial affairs. This was particularly true in Connecticut and Rhode Island, which were organized along popular principles with elected governors and legislatures whose acts were not subjected to a royal governor's veto, nor sent to England for approval. The political importance of these early charters is illustrated by the conflict over the Fundamental Orders of Connecticut. In 1685, King James issued an order for the repeal of Connecticut's charter. The colony offered its submission, and in 1687 Sir Edmund Androse went to Hartford and in the name of the Crown declared the government dissolved. The charter was not surrendered, however, but secreted in an oak tree, which is now displayed for sightseers. Immediately after the English revolution of 1688, people returned to exercising all the powers of the original charter. Succeeding British monarchs silently permitted this without struggle or resistance. After the Declaration of Independence, new constitutions were written in 11 colonies; Connecticut retained her charter as the fundamental law until 1818, and Rhode Island kept her charter until 1842. The colonial experience, together with the earlier English heritage, had firmly implanted the tradition of written constitutions.

Constitutions govern governments. They prescribe the essential structure and organization of government, and they distribute powers among the various branches of government. Constitutions both authorize governments to exercise power and place prohibitions on the exercise of governmental power. Constitutions provide for stability and continuity in government by providing for terms of offices and for orderly replacement of political leaders. They provide the opportunity for orderly change. Since constitutions govern the activities of governments themselves, they are considered more fundamental than the ordinary laws and statutes passed by governments. State *constitutions* take precedence over any state *law* in conflict with them. Since constitutions are more fundamental than ordinary law, they cannot be changed by the routine methods employed to amend ordinary laws. Amendments generally require some extraordinary legislative procedures together with popular referendum.

State constitutions take precedence over state law, but they are subordinate to the U.S. Constitution and the laws of the United States. The United

TABLE 1.3

GENERAL INFORMATION ON STATE CONSTITUTIONS

State or other jurisdiction	Number of constitutions	Dates of adoption	Effective date of present constitution	Estimated length (number of words)	Number of amendments Proposed	Adopted
Alabama	6	1819; 1861; 1865; 1868; 1875; 1901	1901	80,000	367	212
Alaska	1	1956	1959	12,000	–	–
Arizona	1	1912	1912	15,000	108	50
Arkansas	5	1836; 1861; 1864; 1868; 1874	1874	21,500	(a)	59
California	2	1849; 1879	1879	70,000	600	350
Colorado	1	1876	1876	15,000	(a)	64
Connecticut	1	1818(b)	1818	6,750	(a)	57(c)
Delaware	4	1776; 1792; 1831; 1897	1897	20,000	(a)	80(d)
Florida	5	1839; 1861; 1865; 1868; 1887	1887	14,500	176	117
Georgia	8	1777; 1789; 1798; 1861; 1865; 1868; 1877; 1945	1945	30,000	85	26
Hawaii	1	1950	1959	14,670	8	5(e)
Idaho	1	1889	1890	14,000	102	68
Illinois	3	1818; 1848; 1870	1870	15,000	30	13
Indiana	2	1816; 1851	1851	7,816	47	20
Iowa	2	1846; 1857	1857	11,000	(a)	21
Kansas	1	1859	1861	8,052	73	45(f)
Kentucky	4	1792; 1799; 1850; 1891	1891	21,500	40	18
Louisiana	10	1812; 1845; 1852; 1861; 1864; 1868; 1879; 1898; 1913; 1921	1921	227,000	566	439
Maine	1	1820	1820	12,438	107	89
Maryland	4	1776; 1851; 1864; 1867	1867	15,445	133	108
Massachusetts	1	1780	1780	11,361	98	81
Michigan	4	1835; 1850; 1908; 1963	1964	19,203	–	–
Minnesota	1	1858	1858	14,986	178	90
Mississippi	4	1817; 1832; 1869; 1890	1890	15,302	104	35
Missouri	4	1820; 1865; 1875; 1945	1945	40,000	26	13
Montana	1	1889	1889	22,000	46	30
Nebraska	2	1866; 1875	1875	16,550	147	94
Nevada	1	1864	1864	15,840	97	56
New Hampshire	2	1776; 1784(g)	1784	8,700	105	41(g)
New Jersey	3	1776; 1844; 1947	1947	12,500	9	6
New Mexico	1	1911	1912	22,400	130	55
New York	6	1777; 1801; 1821; 1846; 1868; 1894	1894	45,000	174	133
North Carolina	2	1776; 1868	1868	14,000	(a)	(a)
North Dakota	1	1889	1889	20,000	(a)	76
Ohio	2	1802; 1851	1851	10,700	162	88
Oklahoma	1	1907	1907	36,412	135	49
Oregon	1	1859	1859	21,982	249	111
Pennsylvania	4	1776; 1790; 1838; 1873	1873	15,092	92	62
Puerto Rico	1	1952	1952	9,000	5	5

18

State or other jurisdiction	Number of constitutions	Dates of adoption	Effective date of present constitution	Estimated length (number of words)	Number of amendments Proposed	Number of amendments Adopted
Rhode Island	1	1843(b)	1843	6,780	70	36
South Carolina	6	1776; 1778; 1790; 1865; 1868; 1895	1895	30,000	364	251
South Dakota	1	1889	1889	25,000	132	71
Tennessee	3	1796; 1835; 1870	1870	8,220	24	10
Texas	5	1845; 1861; 1866; 1869; 1876	1876	35,000	247	154
Utah	1	1896	1896	20,500	(a)	33
Vermont	3	1777; 1786; 1793	1793	4,840	193	44
Virginia	5	1776; 1830; 1851; 1868; 1902	1902	23,101	98	92
Washington	1	1889	1889	28,235	(a)	39
West Virginia	2	1863; 1872	1872	22,000	61	36
Wisconsin	1	1848	1848	10,717	99	66(h)
Wyoming	1	1890	1890	15,000	48	25

(a) Data not available.
(b) Colonial Charters with some alterations, in Connecticut (1662) and Rhode Island (1663), served as the first constitutions for these states.
(c) In 1955, 47 earlier amendments were recodified and incorporated in the constitution. Amendment I, adopted prior to 1955, was incorporated in the constitution in 1961. Nine amendments have been adopted since 1955.
(d) Figure does not include amendments of a local nature.
(e) Three amendments adopted in June, 1959 in accordance with Public Law 86-3, 86th Congress, providing for Hawaii's admission.
(f) If a single proposition amends more than one section of the constitution, it may not be counted as more than a single amendment.
(g) The constitution of 1784 was extensively amended, rearranged and clarified in 1793. Figures show proposals and adoptions since 1793.
(h) Including two amendments subsequently held invalid by the Wisconsin Supreme Court.
Source: Book of the States, 1964-1965 (Chicago: The Council of State Governments, 1964), p. 12.

States Constitution mentions state constitutions only once, and it does so to assert the supremacy of the U.S. Constitution and the laws and treaties of the United States. Article VI states:

> This constitution, and the laws of the United States which shall be made in pursuance thereof; and all treaties made, or which shall be made, under the authority of the United States, shall be the supreme law of the land; and the judge in every state shall be bound thereby, anything in the constitution or laws of any state to the contrary notwithstanding.

State constitutions cover a wide variety of subject matter. They range in age from Massachusetts (1780) to Michigan's new constitution of 1964. Their length varies from 6650 words (Rhode Island) to a lengthy 350,000 words (Louisiana). Some of the newer state constitutions are yet unamended, while the California constitution has been amended 350 times and the Louisiana constitution 450 times as of 1965. Yet despite these variations state constitutions have many common features.

All state constitutions have preambles, most of which begin with "We the people," as one might expect. In contrast to our Founding Fathers and their unholy belief in separation of church and state, most state constitutions make specific reference to divine authority. For example: "We the people of the state of Arizona, grateful to almighty God for our liberties, do ordain this constitution . . ."; "We the people of the state of New Jersey, grateful to almighty God for the civil and religious liberties which he hath so long permitted us to enjoy . . .". Several state constitutions are in probable violation of the First Amendment of the U.S. Constitution prohibiting the "establishment of religion": Massachusetts insists that "all persons should worship the Supreme Being"; Delaware that "all persons should assemble to public worship"; and several states prohibit "nonbelievers" from holding public office.

All state constitutions have a bill of rights, which asserts the basic freedoms of speech, press, religion, and assembly. There are frequent references to basic procedural rights, such as the writ of habeas corpus, trial by jury, protection against double jeopardy and self-incrimination, prohibitions against ex post facto laws, imprisonment for debt, unreasonable searches and seizures, and excessive bail. Frequently one finds in the state constitutions interesting "rights," which are not found in the national Constitution. The right of private clubs and fraternal organizations to sell alcoholic beverages is specifically enumerated in the Oregon constitution. Management interests have incorporated a "right to work" provision barring union shops in the Florida constitution.

All state constitutions reflect the American political tradition of separation of powers, with separate legislative, executive, and judicial articles establishing these separate branches of government. Generally, however, state constitutions emphasize legislative power over executive power. The historical explanation for this is that governors were appointed by the king in most colonies and the early constitutions reflected the colonists' distaste for executive authority. Yet the fact that constitutions are usually written by legislatures, legislative commissions, or constitutional conventions which resemble legislatures may also explain why legislative power is emphasized. Finally, the curtailment of executive power may reflect the desires of important interest groups in the states, who would prefer to deal with independent boards and commissions in the executive branch rather than a strong governor. (See Chapter 6 for further discussion of this point.)

Whether the reasons are historical or political, the executive branches of most state governments are weakened and divided by state constitutions. Executive powers are divided between the governor and many separately elected executive officers—attorney general, secretary of state, treasurer, auditor, lieutenant governor, state school superintendent, and others. State constitutions also curtail executive authority by establishing a multitude of boards or commissions to head executive departments. Membership on these boards and commissions is generally for long overlapping terms, which are not co-extensive with the term of the governor. In 37 states, governors have a four year term of office, but in 22 of these, the governor is not allowed to succeed himself. The remaining states have two year terms. (See Chapter 6.)

Only Nebraska's constitution provides for a unicameral legislature. All other state legislatures are divided into an upper and lower chamber—making a total of 99 state legislative bodies. In many states the basis for apportioning these bodies is set forth in the state constitution. However, since the guarantee of the U.S. Constitution that no state shall deny to any person the "equal protection of the laws" takes precedence over state constitutions, malapportionment embodied in a state constitution is no more acceptable to federal courts than malapportionment by state law. (See Chapter 5.)

Unlike the U.S. Congress, state legislatures do not need specific constitutional delegations of power to pass particular kinds of laws. Congress must justify every law it passes as part of its enumerated powers, according to Article I, Section 8 of the Constitution; but the states originated as governments of general sovereignty, and therefore did not need to enumerate their powers. Yet as state constitutions have grown more lengthy and complex, thus giving state courts greater opportunity to limit legislative power, the practice of inserting constitutional authorization for specific state programs has grown. In other words, although state legislatures have *general* rather than *enumerated* powers, the practice of specific constitutional authorization for state power has grown as a safeguard against court interpretations limiting legislative authority.

On the whole, state courts are far more likely to find the acts of state legislatures to violate the state's constitution, than the Supreme Court is to find the acts of Congress in violation of the U.S. Constitution. Lengthy constitutions with an abundance of detail invite litigation in the courts and the nullification of legislation. Lengthy, complex state constitutions, then, are a source of political strength for state courts. Supposedly, it is not the wisdom of legislation, but its constitutionality that concerns the courts. But obviously the power to interpret state constitutions gives the courts a great deal of political power. As Duane Lockard notes, there are many instances of court invalidation of legislation because of the "we–don't–think–it–is–a–good–idea" rule.[5]

All state constitutions have articles on suffrage and elections. These pro-

[5] Duane Lockard, *The Politics of State and Local Government* (New York: The Macmillan Company, 1963), p. 88.

visions set the times of elections and the qualifications for voting and office holding. (See Chapter 3 for further discussion.)

All state constitutions have articles on taxation and finance. These articles often place severe restrictions and limitations upon the taxing power of state and local governments. They reflect a distrust of state legislatures, and testify to the political power of interest groups seeking to avoid taxation. State constitutions generally provide that state taxation shall be uniform and equal upon the same classes of subjects. The power of municipalities to collect taxes is also set forth in restricted terms. Certain classes of property may be exempted from taxation: property devoted to religious, educational, or charitable purposes; municipal and public property; certain agricultural and forest land; public utilities; and even "homesteads," that is, low priced owner-occupied homes. Some state constitutions exempt new industries from certain kinds of taxation in order to stimulate industrial growth.

Another common limitation on taxing and spending powers of state governments is the constitutional earmarking of certain state revenues for specific programs. For example, constitutional provisions may require that all gasoline taxes be spent for highway purposes. Approximately half of all state revenues cannot be used for other than earmarked purposes. Some states have gone so far as to specify particular tax rates in their constitutions.

Debt limitations represent another constitutional restriction on fiscal powers. All but five states have constitutional limitations on debt. Some constitutions prevent a state from contracting any debt at all, requiring it to operate officially in the black each year. Other constitutions set specific dollar limits, usually very low sums, on the amount of debt that can be incurred. This forces many states to resort to constitutional amendment when they wish to borrow money for specific purposes. More commonly, however, it means that states must issue "revenue bonds" for specific projects, which are backed by revenue produced by the project rather than the general tax revenues of the state. Since these revenues are less secure, they carry a higher interest rate; thus, states are forced to pay higher interest rates simply because of their constitutional limitations on debt. State constitutions also limit the debt of local governments: it may not exceed a certain percentage of the property tax base; the purposes for which local government debt may be incurred are limited; bond referendums must be submitted for approval of the local electorate. These provisions also force local governments to finance specific projects on a revenue basis at higher cost, rather than through obligations on general tax and revenues. In general, constitutional limitations on debt force both state and local governments to devise ingenious methods of working their way out of their fiscal straitjacket.

Typical state constitutions will also have provisions on education, highways, natural resources, corporations, and public utilities. Many of these provisions go into great detail about regulation, administration, and financial management—details which would ordinarily be left to legislatures if voters and organized interests had much confidence in them. Many interest groups are not satisfied with writing their preferences into law, but seek instead to write their preferences into state constitutions. The result is that many constitutions contain a wide range of guarantees and prohibitions to protect interests powerful enough to push their way into the fundamental law of the state. Their preferences are thus protected from ordinary legislative majorities; therefore, extraordinary procedures of constitutional amendment are required to alter this protection.

All state constitutions provide for revision by amendment, but the difficulty of amending constitutions varies widely. Fourteen states require a constitutional amendment to be passed by not one but two successive legislatures, in addition to being submitted to the electorate for its approval in a referendum. In the states requiring only one legislative session to propose an amendment, only eight permit a constitutional amendment to be proposed by a simple majority vote; the remainder requires either a two-thirds or a three-fifths vote. Every state except Delaware requires constitutional amendments proposed by the legislature to be submitted to the voters for approval in a referendum. Six states require an approval by a majority of all voters participating in the general election, rather than a majority of those voting on the amendment. This presents a genuine obstacle to ratification of constitutional amendments, since voter interest and participation in the choice of candidates is generally greater than interest or participation in constitutional amendments. The most common means of amending state constitutions is to provide for approval by a two-thirds vote in the legislature and then by a majority of the people voting on it in the next election. In all but four states—Indiana, New Jersey, North Dakota, and Vermont—constitutions can also be changed by calling a constitutional convention. This is a very cumbersome procedure, although it can result in more extensive rewriting than the process of single amendments would achieve. Generally, the legislature must first submit to the voters the issue of calling a convention; if the voters approve, the convention must convene, draw up its revisions, and submit its revisions again to the electorate in a referendum. In recent years, conventions have been held in Michigan, Missouri, Pennsylvania, and New York.

All state constitutions have provisions regarding the organization and powers of local governments. Local governments are really subdivisions of state governments; they are not legally independent governmental bodies. State constitutions generally describe the organization of counties, cities, towns, townships, boroughs, school districts, and special districts. They may

TABLE 1.4

AMENDING STATE CONSTITUTIONS

State	Legislative vote required for proposal	Approval by two sessions	Ratification by electorate
Alabama	3/5	No	MA
Alaska	2/3	No	MA
Arizona	Maj.	No	MA
Arkansas	Maj.	No	MA
California	2/3	No	MA
Colorado	2/3	No	MA
Connecticut	2/3	Yes	MA
Delaware	2/3	Yes	None
Florida	3/5	No	MA
Georgia	2/3	No	MA
Hawaii	(f)	(f)	MA
Idaho	2/3	No	MA
Illinois	2/3	No	ME
Indiana	Maj.	Yes	MA
Iowa	Maj.	Yes	MA
Kansas	2/3	No	MA
Kentucky	3/5	No	MA
Louisiana	2/3	No	MA
Maine	2/3	No	MA
Maryland	3/5	No	MA
Massachusetts	Maj.	Yes	MA
Michigan	2/3	No	MA
Minnesota	Maj.	No	ME
Mississippi	2/3	No	ME
Missouri	Maj.	No	MA
Montana	2/3	No	MA
Nebraska	3/5	No	MA
Nevada	Maj.	Yes	MA
New Hampshire	(a)		
New Jersey	(b)	(b)	ME
New Mexico	Maj.(c)	No	MA(c)
New York	Maj.	Yes	MA
North Carolina	3/5	No	MA
North Dakota	Maj.	No	MA
Ohio	3/5	No	MA
Oklahoma	Maj.	No	ME
Oregon	Maj.	No	MA
Pennsylvania	Maj.	Yes	MA
Rhode Island	Maj.	Yes	3/5MA
South Carolina	2/3	Yes	MA
South Dakota	Maj.	No	MA
Tennessee	(d)	Yes	ME
Texas	2/3	No	MA
Utah	2/3	No	MA

State	Legislative vote required for proposal	Approval by two sessions	Ratification by electorate
Vermont	(e)	Yes	MA
Virginia	Maj.	Yes	MA
Washington	2/3	No	MA
West Virginia	2/3	No	MA
Wisconsin	Maj.	Yes	MA
Wyoming	2/3	No	ME

Key: MA—Majority vote on Amendment; ME—Majority vote in election.
(a) No provision for proposal of amendments by legislature. Constitution amended only by constitutional convention.
(b) Three-fifths of all members of each house; or majority of all members of each house for two successive sessions.
(c) Amendments dealing with certain sections on elective franchise and education must be proposed by 3/4 vote of the legislature and ratified by 3/4 vote of the electorate and 2/3 vote in each county.
(d) Majority members elected, first passage; 2/3 members elected, second passage.
(e) Two-thirds vote Senate, majority vote House, first passage; majority both houses, second passage. Since 1910, amendments may be submitted only at 10-year intervals.
(f) Approval at two successive sessions required if votes in each house are majority but less than 2/3.
Source: Book of the States, 1964-1965 (Chicago: The council of State Governments, 1964).

delegate responsibilities to them for public safety, police, fire, sanitation, sewage and refuse disposal, hospitals, streets, and public health. State constitutions may establish tax and debt limits for local governments, describe the kinds of taxes they may levy, and prescribe a way in which their funds may be spent. In the absence of constitutional provisions governing local governments, these subordinate units must rely upon state legislatures for their organization and powers. In recent years there has been a movement toward greater home rule for communities. More than half the states have provided for some semblance of home rule, which removes some of the internal affairs of communities from the intervention of state legislatures. Of course, when a "home rule" charter is granted to a community by an act of the legislature, it can be readily withdrawn or revised by the legislature. But when the authorization for municipal home rule is part of the state's constitution, it is somewhat less subject to state legislative intervention. Legislative home rule is a less secure grant of power to communities than constitutional home rule. There is still much opposition to home rule for communities. Rural interests may hesitate to relinquish their influence over city governments. Legislators elected from cities may prefer to exercise local power themselves through special legislation rather than grant power over communities to mayors and councils. (See Chapter 8 for further discussion.)

The Politics of State Constitutions

The U.S. Constitution is a relatively brief document, which sets forth the fundamental structure of the government and the important limitations placed upon its power. It is simple and brief; it leaves to the Congress, the President, and the courts the power to determine public policy. But very few state constitutions are simple or brief, and most of them set forth many details of public policy. As Duane Lockard notes, the California constitution limits the power of the legislature with regard to setting time limits on the length of wrestling matches.[6] The Georgia constitution announces a $250,000 reward for the first person to strike oil in the state. Louisiana's constitution proclaims Huey Long's birthday an annual state holiday. Such constitutional detail makes the need for amendment quite frequent. Unlike the U.S. Constitution, state constitutions are too detailed and specific to permit much change through interpretation. Hence, most existing constitutions have been amended many times, and there few elections are held in which voters are not asked to vote on constitutional amendments.

What is the political significance of these constitutional restraints on state power? Duane Lockard explains:

> Substantially, the reason the complexity is important is that it allots an advantage to some contestants in the political process and a handicap for others. By inviting litigation the wealth of detail plays into the hands of those who want to prevent a particular law from going into effect, and although a legislative majority may have approved it, and the governor's signature may be authentic, there are always possibilities that the courts can be persuaded to invalidate a law on grounds that some minute aspect of constitutional procedure was not properly complied with. If so, dissenters to a law may carry the day, and the legislation be cancelled, for it may be impossible to mount once again the necessary peak of interest that pushed through the legislation in the first place. At least, delay of from one to two years is likely since re-enactment must wait until the next legislative session.[7]

Thus, it appears that lengthy detailed constitutions tend to strengthen the position of conservative interests, those who wish to preserve the status quo. As we have already noted, it also tends to strengthen the role of the courts, since an abundance of constitutional detail leads to decision-making through court litigation.

Professor Lewis A. Froman has argued convincingly that lengthy and detailed state constitutions reflect the strength of organized interest groups in the states.[8] He reasons that in states where interest groups are stronger, a

---

[6] Lockard, *The Politics of State and Local Government*, p. 84.

[7] *Ibid.*, pp. 85-86.

[8] Lewis A. Froman, "Some Effects of Interest Group Strength in State Politics," *American Political Science Review*, 60 (December, 1966), 952-62.

larger number of special privileges and advantages will be granted in state constitutions. The stronger the interest groups in the state, the greater the length of the state constitution, the greater the number of proposed amendments, and the greater the number of amendments adopted. To test his theory about state constitutions, he used the judgments of political scientists about which states had strong, moderately strong, or weak interest groups, and then compared the constitutions of each of these three groups of states. The results are shown in Table 1.5. States with strong interest groups tend to have long constitutions, which deal directly with questions of public policy (labor practices, regulation of utilities, transportation problems, and so on). Typically interest groups press for constitutional provisions to protect their interests because they are unwilling to trust future legislatures in matters of public policy. Thus, strong interest group states are likely to have lengthy constitutions, which, among other things, specify public utility tariffs and charges, limit the taxing powers of the states and communities, place restrictions on state debt, specify the duties and powers of public service commissions and the regulation of utilities, set forth regulations on insurance companies, specify the hours and duties of local government officials, set the salaries of the state and local officeholders, exempt certain industries from taxation, regulate school systems, and so on. He concludes that constitutions are one of the means by which advantages and disadvantages are distributed in political systems, and that the strength of interest groups in gaining special constitutional advantages can be observed in the length of state constitutions and in amending activity.

Important political interests are at stake in constitutional revision. Legis-

TABLE 1.5

RELATIONSHIPS BETWEEN STRENGTH OF INTEREST GROUPS
AND THREE DEPENDENT VARIABLES

Strength of interest groups	Average length of constitution	N^1	Average no. of proposed amendments per year	N^2	Average no. of adopted amendments per year	N^3
Strong	33,233	24	2.97	19	1.58	22
Moderate	17,985	14	1.14	12	.76	14
Weak	14,828	7	.68	5	.41	7

[1] Alaska and Hawaii are excluded from this table. In addition, Idaho, New Hampshire, and North Dakota were not classified by strength of interest groups.
[2] Arkansas, Colorado, Connecticut, Delaware, Iowa, Michigan, North Carolina, Utah, and Washington are excluded for lack of data.
[3] Michigan and North Carolina are excluded for lack of data.
Source: Lewis A. Froman, Jr., "Some Effect of Interest Group Strength in State Politics," *American Political Science Review,* 60 (December 1966), 956.

latures are understandably hesitant about calling constitutional conventions. A "runaway" convention may rearrange the balance of political power in the state. It may strengthen the governor at the expense of the legislature, establish new bases for legislative apportionment, authorize new taxes, eliminate the earmarking of certain revenues, or allocate greater power over urban affairs to cities. In other words, a constitutional convention may seriously alter the status quo. Interest groups which presently enjoy special privileges or exemptions from taxation in the state constitution have reason to fear a constitutional convention. They may stress the expense involved in such a convention or the danger that "radical reformers" may foist their dangerous ideas upon an unsuspecting public. Taxpayer groups may fear that constitutional limitations on taxing powers may be removed. Public officials may be concerned that their offices will be abolished. In other words, constitutional revision is a political thicket which discourages all but the most courageous of men.

Reform interests—good government groups, the League of Women Voters, and political science professors—argue that the constitution and the structure of state and local government should be simple, brief, and understandable. It should permit the legislature and governor to make public policy. It should allocate power to the governor and the legislature commensurate with their responsibilities, and it should enable the voters to hold elected officials clearly accountable for public policy decisions. It should permit local governmental consolidation and community home rule. The need for frequent amendment should be eliminated.

These ideas are not received with enthusiasm by organized interests in the states, but they do appeal to many voters. The idea of successful constitutional revision appeals to an ambitious governor with aspirations to higher office. A favorite device for constitutional revision is the establishment of a constitutional revision commission. A typical commission is created by an act of a legislature, and its membership usually includes legislators, executive officials, and prominent citizens. Legislatures generally prefer such a commission to a constitutional convention, because a commission can only study and report to a legislature on the changes it deems necessary. Such recommendations are usually handled like regular constitutional amendments, although they may be more sweeping than ordinary amendments.

Of course, reform interests have not yet succeeded in simplifying state constitutions or in eliminating the special privileges and exemptions contained in them. However, there appears to be a slight trend toward shorter constitutions. The new constitutions in Hawaii, Alaska, and Michigan are somewhat shorter and more streamlined than the average state constitution. All of them tended to strengthen the executive. Yet, the new Michigan constitution is still a very conservative document. It prevents the legislature from levying more than a 4 per cent sales tax, and prohibits it from levying any graduated income tax. Democratic party delegates to that convention voted overwhelmingly against final passage of the new constitution, but it won voter approval in the state-wide referendum despite Democratic opposition. In summary, there is not much hope that state constitutions will be simplified in the foreseeable future, or that special exemptions and privileges will be eliminated.

2

STATES, COMMUNITIES, AND AMERICAN FEDERALISM

The Structure of American Federalism

In deciding in 1869 that a state had no constitutional right to secede from the union, Chief Justice Salmon P. Chase described the legal character of American federalism:

> The preservation of the states and the maintenance of their governments, are as much within the design and care of the constitution as the preservation of the union and the maintenance of the national government. The constitution, in all of its provisions, looks to an indestructible union, composed of indestructible states.[1]

What is meant by "an indestructible union, composed of indestructible states"? The American federal union is an indissoluble partnership between the states and the national government. The Constitution of the United States divided power between two separate authorities, the nation and the states, each of which was to be supreme in its own jurisdiction. Both the nation and the states were allowed to enforce their laws through their own officials and courts directly on individuals. Legally, neither the Congress nor any single state or group of states could determine for itself whose authority was legitimate in a disputed area, nor could either level of gov-

[1] Texas v. White, 7 Wallace 700 (1869).

30

ernment change the constitutional division of power without the approval of the other. The Constitution itself was the only legal source of authority for the division of powers between states and the nation. American federalism differs from a "decentralized" political system in that the central government is not constitutionally authorized to determine itself the extent to which powers are to be exercised by the states. The national government has no legal authority to alter or abolish the power of the states. At the same time, American federalism differs from a "confederation" of states in which the national government is dependent upon the states for its power. The American federal system is a strong national government, coupled with a strong state government, in which authority and power are shared, constitutionally and practically.

The framework of American federalism is determined by: (1) the powers delegated by the constitution to the national government; (2) the constitutional guarantees given to the states; (3) the powers denied by the Constitution to the national government and to the states; (4) the constitutional provisions giving the states a role in the composition of the national government; (5) the subsequent interpretation of these constitutional provisions by the courts; (6) the practices that evolved for the settlement of disputes between the nation and the states.

Article I, Section 8 of the U.S. Constitution lists 18 grants of delegated power to Congress, including authority over matters of war and foreign affairs, the power to declare war, raise armies, equip navies, establish uniform rules for naturalization, and so on. Another series of delegated powers are related to control of the economy, including the power to coin money, to control its value, and to regulate foreign and interstate commerce. The national government has been given independent powers of taxation "to pay the debts and provide for the common defense and general welfare of the United States." It has the power to establish its own court system, to decide cases arising under the Constitution and the laws and treaties of the U.S. and cases involving certain kinds of parties. The national government was given the authority to grant copyright patents, establish post offices, enact bankruptcy laws, punish counterfeiting, punish crimes committed on the high seas, and govern the District of Columbia. Finally, after 17 grants of express power, came the power "to make all laws which shall be necessary and proper for carrying into execution the foregoing powers, and all other powers vested by this constitution in the government of the United States or in any department or officer thereof."

These delegated powers, when coupled with the National Supremacy Clause of Article VI, insured a powerful national government. The National Supremacy Clause was quite specific regarding the relationship between national government and the states. In questions involving the Constitution or the laws or treaties of the U.S.:

> This constitution, and the laws of the United States which shall be made
> in pursuance thereof; and all treaties made or which shall be made under
> the authority of the United States shall be the supreme law of the land;
> and the judges in every state shall be bound thereby, anything in the con-
> stitution or laws of any state to the contrary notwithstanding.

Despite these broad grants of power to the national government, the
states retained a great deal of authority over the lives of their citizens. The
constitutional provision specifically guaranteeing or limiting state powers
are outlined in Table 2.1. The 10th Amendment reaffirmed the idea that
the national government had only certain delegated powers and that all
powers not delegated to it were retained by the states:

> The powers not delegated to the United States by the constitution, nor
> prohibited by it to the states, are reserved to the states respectively, or
> to the people.

The states retained control over the ownership and use of property; the regulation of offenses against persons and property (criminal law and civil
law); the regulation of marriage and divorce; the control of business, labor,
farming, trades, and professions; the provision of education, welfare,
health, hospitals, and other social welfare activities; and provision of highways, roads, canals and other public works. The states retained full authority over the organization and control of local government units. Finally, the states, like the federal government, possessed the power to tax
and spend for the general welfare.

The Constitution denies some powers to both national and state governments; these denials generally safeguard individual rights. Both nation and
states were forbidden to pass ex post facto laws or bills of attainder. The
first eight amendments to the Constitution, "the Bill of Rights," originally
applied to the federal government, but the 14th Amendment, passed by
Congress in 1866, provided that the states must also adhere to fundamental
guarantees of individual liberty. "No state shall make or enforce any law
which shall abridge the privileges or immunities of the citizens of the United
States; nor shall any state deprive any person of life, liberty or property
without due process of law; nor deny to any person within its jurisdiction
equal protection of the laws."

Some powers were denied only to the states, generally as a safeguard to
national unity, including the powers to coin money, enter into treaties with
foreign powers, interfere with the obligations of contracts, levy duties on
imports or exports without congressional consent, maintain military forces
in peacetime, engage in war, or enter into compacts with foreign nations
or other states. These limitations are outlined in Table 2.1.

The states also play an important role in the composition of the national
government. U.S. representatives must be apportioned among the states

TABLE 2.1

FEDERAL CONSTITUTIONAL PROVISIONS
SPECIFICALLY LIMITING OR GUARANTEEING STATE POWERS

Guarantees to states	Limits on states
A. State integrity and sovereignty	
No division or consolidation of states without state legislative consent (IV-2)[a]	States cannot enter into treaties, alliances, or confederations (I-10)
Republican form of government (IV-2)	No separate coinage (I-10)
Protection against invasion (IV-2)	No grants of titles of nobility (I-10)
Protection against domestic violence on application of proper state authorities (IV-2)	No interstate or foreign compacts without Congressional consent (I-10)
Powers not delegated to the U.S. by the Constitution, nor prohibited by it to the states, are reserved to the states (Amendment X)	U.S. Constitution, all laws and treaties made under it to be supreme law of the land, binding on every state (VI)
	Slavery forbidden (Amendment XIII)
States cannot be sued by citizens of another state or a foreign nation (Amendment XI)	All state legislative, executive, and judicial officers, and state Representatives in Congress to be bound by U.S. Constitution (VI)
	No abridgement of privileges and immunities of the U.S. Citizens (Amendment XIV)
	Reduction of representation in U.S. House of Representatives for denial of franchise to citizens (Amendment XIV)
	No payment of debts incurred in aid of insurrection or rebellion against U.S. or for emancipation of slaves (Amendment XIV)
	No abridgement of right to vote on account of race, color, or previous condition of servitude (Amendment XV)
	Popular election of Senators (Amendment XVII)
	No abridgement of right to vote on account of sex (Amendment XIX)
	No poll taxes in federal elections (Amendment XXIV)

a. Numbers in parentheses refer to the Article and Section of the Constitution containing the provision.
Source: Daniel J. Elazar, *American Federalism: A View from the States* (New York: Thomas Y. Crowell, 1966), pp. 40-45.

Guarantees to states	Limits on states

B. Military affairs and defense

Guarantees to states	Limits on states
Power to maintain militia and appoint militia officers (I-8, Amendment II)	No letters of marque and reprisal (I-10)
	No maintenance of standing military forces in peacetime without Congress's consent (I-10)
	No engaging in war without Congress's consent, except to repel invasion (I-10)

C. Commerce and taxation

Guarantees to states	Limits on states
Equal apportionment of federal direct taxes (I-2, 9)	No levying of duties on vessels of sister states (I-9)
No federal export duties (I-9)	No legal tender other than gold or silver (I-10)
No preferential treatment for ports of one state (I-9)	No impairment of obligations of contracts (I-10)
Reciprocal full faith and credit among states for public acts, records, and judicial proceedings (IV-1)	No levying of import or export duties without consent of Congress except reasonable inspection fees (I-10)
Reciprocal privileges and immunities for citizens of the several states (IV-2)	No tonnage duties without Congress's consent (I-10)
Intoxicating liquor may not be imported into states where its sale or use is prohibited (Amendment XXI-2)	

D. Administration of justice

Guarantees to states	Limits on states
Federal criminal trials to be held in state where crime was committed (III-2)[b]	No bills of attainder (I-10)
	No ex post facto laws (I-10)
Extradition for crimes (IV-2)	U.S. Supreme Court has original jurisdiction over all cases in which a state shall be a party (III-2)
Federal criminal juries to be chosen from states and district in which crime was committed (Amendment VI)[b]	
Federal judicial power to extend to controversies between two or more states, a state or citizens of another state when state is plaintiff, and between foreign nation or its citizens with original jurisdiction vested in the Supreme Court (III-2)	Judges in every state bounded by U.S. Constitution and all laws and treaties made under it, notwithstanding the constitutions or laws of any state (VI)
	No denial of life, liberty, or property without due process of law (Amendment XIV)
	No denial of equal protection of state laws to persons within its limits (Amendment XIV)

---

b. This provision insures the integrity of the state's common law in federal cases.

according to their population every ten years. Governors have the authority to fill vacancies in Congress, and every state must have at least one representative regardless of population. The Senate of the United States is composed of two senators from each state regardless of the state's population. The times, places, and manner of holding elections for Congress are determined by the states. The President is chosen by electors, allotted to each state on the basis of its senators and representatives. Amendments to the U.S. Constitution must be ratified by three-fourths of the states. Qualifications for voting in national elections are determined by the states, as long as they do not deny the right to vote on the basis of race or sex or the payment of poll taxes. The states' role in the composition of the national government is outlined in Table 2.2.

The Evolution of American Federalism

The importance of formal constitutional arrangements should not be underestimated; however, the American federal system is a product of more than formal constitutional provisions. It is also shaped by the interpretations placed upon constitutional principles and the way in which disputes over state and national authority have been resolved.

The real meaning of American federalism has emerged in the heat of political conflict between states and nation. In the formulative days of the new Republic, Chief Justice John Marshall, who presided over the Supreme Court from 1801 to 1835, became a major architect of American federalism. Under John Marshall, the Supreme Court assumed the role of arbiter in disputes between state and national authority. It was under John Marshall that the Supreme Court assumed the power to interpret the U.S. Constitution authoritatively. Nothing in the Constitution explicitly vested the Supreme Court with the power to render authoritative interpretations of the Constitution; from time to time Congress, the President, and the states have laid claim to this power. But John Marshall argued forcefully that Article III of the Constitution, which says that "the judicial power of the United States shall be vested in one Supreme Court," made the Court the final arbiter in conflicts over the meaning of the Constitution. Marshall argued that the "the judicial power" historically meant the power to interpret the meaning of the law, and since the Constitution was the supreme *law* of the land, it was the legitimate duty of the Supreme Court to interpret that law. This meant that the Supreme Court assumed the role of umpire of the federal system and referee of conflicts between nation and states. The Court, under John Marshall, would rule on whether Congress could charter a national bank under its "implied powers," whether a state could interfere with Congress in the exercise of one of its implied powers, and whether nation or states could regulate the navigable streams of America.

TABLE 2.2

FEDERAL CONSTITUTIONAL PROVISIONS SPECIFICALLY GIVING THE
STATES A ROLE IN THE COMPOSITION OF THE NATIONAL GOVERNMENT

Guarantees to states	Limits on states
A. National Legislature	
Members of House of Representatives chosen by people of several states based on those qualified to vote for most numerous house of state legislature (I-2)	Representatives must be 25 years old and citizens of the U.S. for 7 years (I-2)
Representatives must be inhabitants of states from which they are elected at time of election (I-2)	Senators must be 30 years old and citizens of the U.S. for 9 years (I-3)
Representatives to be apportioned among the states according to population every ten years (I-2)	Congress may make or alter regulations as to the times, places, and manner of holding elections for Senators and Representatives (I-4)
State executive has authority to fill vacancies (I-2)	Each House shall be the judge of the elections, returns, and qualifications of its own members, punish its members for disorderly behavior and expel a member by two-thirds vote (I-5)
Each state shall have at least one Representative (I-2)	
Senate shall be composed of two Senators from each state. (I-3) chosen by the people qualified to vote for the most numerous house of the state legislature (Amendment XVII) with vacancies to be filled as prescribed by state legislation (Amendment XVII)	Basis for apportionment of representation in House of Representatives may be reduced proportionate to state deprivation of the right to vote of otherwise qualified citizens (Amendment XIV-2)
Senators must be inhabitants of the states from which they are chosen at time of election (I-3)	States cannot be represented by persons who have taken an oath to support Constitution and since engaged in insurrection, without express consent of two-thirds of Congress (Amendment XIV-3)
Times, places, and manner of holding elections for Senators and Representatives shall be prescribed for each state by its legislature (I-4)	
No state to be deprived of equal representation in the Senate without its consent (V)	

Guarantees to states	Limits on states

B. National executive

To be selected by the electors of the several states with each state allotted a number of electors equal to the total number of its Senators and Representatives (II–1)	Congress may determine the time of choosing electors and a uniform day on which they shall cast their votes (II-1)
Each state to have one vote if Presidential election is decided in House of Representatives (II-1)	
Approval of Presidential appointees by the Senate as Congress shall prescribe (II-2)	

C. Amendment of constitution

Amendments must be ratified by three-fourths of the states (V)	
Amendments must be proposed by two-thirds of the states (V)	

D. Voting rights

	Cannot be denied or abridged on grounds of race, color, or previous condition of servitude (Amendment XV-1)
	Cannot be denied or abridged on account of sex (Amendment XIX-1)
	No poll tax may be levied as requirement to vote in federal elections (Amendment XXIV)

E. Foreign affairs

Treaties must be ratified by two-thirds of Senate (II-2)	Treaties binding on states as supreme law of the land (VI)
Appointment of foreign service officers subjected to Senate confirmation (II-2)	

F. Military affairs and defense

Power to appoint the officers of and train the militia when not in federal service reserved to the states (I-8)	Congress may provide for organizing, arming, and disciplining the militia when it is not in federal service and for governing it when it is (I-8)

It was during the Marshall Era that the constitutional battlegrounds—the Commerce Clause, the National Supremacy Clause, the taxing power, the Necessary and Proper Clause, the 10th Amendment—were marked off. These constitutional battlegrounds have remained the major foci of disputes over American federalism ever since.

The fact that the referee of disputes between state and national authority has been the *national* Supreme Court has had a profound influence on the development of American federalism. Since the Supreme Court is a national institution, organized and staffed by national authority, one might say that in disputes between nation and states, one of the members of the two contending teams is also serving as umpire.

Constitutionally speaking, then, there is really no limitation on national as against state authority *if* all three branches of the national government— the Congress, the President, and the Court—act together to override state authority. The Constitution and the laws of the United States "made in pursuance thereof" are the supreme laws of the land "anything in the constitution or laws of any state to the contrary notwithstanding." And the Supreme Court, a national institution, through its "judicial power" interprets the Constitution and decides what laws are "made in pursuance thereof." Thus, the Marshall Court paved the way for the development of national power.

Chief Justice John Marshall was also responsible for making the Necessary and Proper Clause the most significant grant of constitutional power to the national government. Political conflict over the scope of national power arose before the new republic had been in operation for a year. In 1790, Alexander Hamilton, as Secretary of the Treasury, proposed the establishment of a national bank. Congress acted on Hamilton's suggestion in 1791, establishing a national bank to serve as a depository for national money and to facilitate federal borrowing. Jeffersonians considered the national bank dangerous centralization in government, and objected that the power to establish a national bank was nowhere to be found in the enumerated powers of Congress. Thomas Jefferson contended that Congress had no constitutional authority to establish a bank because a bank was not "indispensably necessary" in carrying out its delegated functions. Hamilton replied that Congress could easily deduce the power to establish a bank from grants of authority in the Constitution relating to currency and other aspects of national finance, backed by the clause authorizing Congress "to make all laws which will be necessary and proper for carrying into execution the foregoing powers." Jefferson interpreted the word "necessary" to mean "indispensable," but Hamilton argued that the national government had the right to choose the manner and means of performing its delegated functions and was not restricted to employing only those means considered indispensable in the performance of its functions. The question eventually reached the Supreme Court in 1819 when Maryland levied a tax on the national bank and the bank refused to pay it. In the case of McCulloch *v.* Maryland, Chief Justice John Marshall accepted the broader Hamiltonian version of the necessary and proper clause:

> This government is acknowledged by all to be one of enumerated powers. The principle that it can exercise only the powers granted to it is now universally admitted. But·the question respecting the extent of the powers actually granted is perpetually arising and will probably continue to arise as long as our system shall exist . . . The powers of the government are limited, and its powers are not to be transcended. But we think the sound construction of the Constitution must allow the national legislature that discretion with respect to the means by which the powers it confers are to be carried into execution, which will enable that body to perform the high duties assigned to it in a manner most beneficial to the people. Let the end be legitimate, let it be within the scope of the Constitution, and all means which are appropriate, which are plainly adopted to that end, which are not prohibited but consistent with the letter and the spirit of the Constitution, are constitutional.[2]

The McCulloch case firmly established the principle that the Necessary and Proper Clause gives Congress the right to choose its means for carrying out the enumerated powers of the national government. Even the Jeffersonians found themselves invoking the Necessary and Proper Clause to support the annexation of Louisiana in 1803. Today Congress can devise programs, create agencies, and establish national laws on the basis of long chains of reasoning from the most meager phrases of the constitutional text because of the broad interpretation of the Necessary and Proper Clause. The Supreme Court has generally, although not universally, acceded to broad exercises of congressional power under the Necessary and Proper Clause.

Another major contribution of the Marshall Court was its interpretation of the National Supremacy Clause. In McCulloch *v.* Maryland, the Court held Maryland's tax on the national bank to be unconstitutional on the grounds that the state tax interfered with a national activity, which was being carried out under the Constitution and laws "made in pursuance thereof." Maryland's state taxing law was declared unconstitutional because it conflicted with the federal law establishing the national bank. From Marshall's time to the present, the National Supremacy Clause has meant that states could not refuse to obey federal laws. States have no right to disobey or resist the application of valid federal laws.

Of course it was one thing to announce that the state had no constitutional right to resist federal authority, but it was quite another thing to establish this principle as a political reality. In the famous Virginia and Kentucky Resolutions, the early Jeffersonians devised a doctrine of state "interposition" to resist enforcement of the national government's Alien

[2] McCulloch *v.* Maryland, 4 Wheaton 316 (1819).

and Sedition Acts of 1798 which were passed by a Federalist Congress. The Jeffersonians argued, rightly no doubt, that the Alien and Sedition Acts violated the Constitution's guarantees of free speech and press. But the "interposition" argument went on to assert that when the national government acted "unconstitutionally" in the eyes of the state, the state was empowered to "interpose" itself between its people and the operation of an unconstitutional federal law. Since the Jeffersonians captured the Presidency in 1800, and a Jeffersonian Congress repealed the Alien and Sedition Acts in 1801, the interposition argument in the Kentucky and Virginia Resolutions was never formally challenged in the courts.

The Civil War was, of course, the greatest crisis of the American federal system. Did a state have the right to oppose national law to the point of secession? In the years preceding the Civil War, John C. Calhoun argued that the Constitution was a compact made by the *states* in a sovereign capacity rather than by the *people* in their national capacity. Calhoun contended that the federal government was an agent of the states, that the states retained their sovereignty in this compact, and that the federal government must not violate the compact, under the penalty of state nullification or even secession. Calhoun's doctrine was embodied in the Constitution of the Confederacy, which begins with the words "We, the people of the Confederate States, each state acting in its sovereign and independent character, in order to form a permanent federal government . . ." This wording contrasts with the preamble of the United States Constitution, "We the people of the United States, in order to form a more perfect union . . ." The difference emphasizes Calhoun's thesis that the central government should be an agency of the states rather than of the people.

The issue was decided in the nation's bloodiest war. What was decided on the battlefield between 1861 and 1865 was confirmed by the Supreme Court in 1869: "Ours is an indestructible union, composed of indestructible states." [3] Yet the states' rights doctrines, and political disputes over the character of American federalism, did not disappear with Lee's surrender at Appomattox. The 13th, 14th, and 15th Amendments, passed by the Reconstruction Congress, were clearly aimed at limiting state power in the interests of individual freedom. The 13th Amendment eliminated slavery in the states; the 15th Amendment prevented states from discriminating against Negroes in the right to vote; and the 14th Amendment declared that: "No State shall make or enforce any law which shall abridge the privileges or immunities of citizens of the United States; nor shall any state deprive any person of life, liberty, or property without due process of law; nor deny to any person within its jurisdiction the equal protection of the laws." These amendments delegated to Congress the power to secure

[3] Texas *v*. White, 7 Wallace 700 (1869).

their enforcement. Yet for several generations these amendments were narrowly construed and added little, if anything, to national power. By tacit agreement, after the southern states demonstrated their continued political importance in the disputed presidential election of 1876, the federal government refrained from using its power to enforce these civil rights. But beginning slowly in the 1920's, the Supreme Court began to build a national system of civil rights based upon the 14th Amendment. In early cases, the Court held that the 14th Amendment prevented states from interfering with free speech, free press, or religious practices. But not until 1952, in the Supreme Court's desegregation decision in Brown v. the Board of Education in Topeka, Kansas, did the court begin to call for the full assertion of national authority on behalf of civil rights.[4] When the court decided that the 14th Amendment prohibited the states from segregating the races in public schools, it was asserting national authority over deeply held beliefs and long standing practices in many of the states.

The Supreme Court's use of the 14th Amendment to insure a national system of civil rights supported by the power of the federal government is an important step in the evolution of the American federal system. Of course, the controversy over federally imposed desegregation in the southern states renewed the debate over state's rights versus national authority. The vigorous resistance of southern states to desegregation in the decade following Brown v. the Board of Education testified to the continued strength of the states in the American federal system. Despite the clear mandate of the Supreme Court, the southern states succeeded avoiding all but token integration for more than ten years.[5] Yet only occasionally did resistance take the form of "interposition." Governor Faubus used the Arkansas National Guard to prevent the desegregation of Little Rock Central High School in 1957, but this "interposition" was ended quickly when President Eisenhower ordered the National Guard removed and sent units of the United States Army to enforce national authority. In 1962, President Kennedy took similar action when Governor Ross Barnett of Mississippi personally barred the entry of a Negro student to the University of Mississippi, despite a federal court order requiring his admission. Governor George Wallace of Alabama "stood in the doorway" to prevent desegregation but left his post at the doorway several hours later when federal marshals arrived. These actions failed to alter the principle of national supremacy in the American political system.

The growth of national power under the Interstate Commerce Clause is also an important development in the evolution of American federalism. The industrial revolution in America created a national economy with a

[4] Brown v. Board of Education of Topeka, Kansas, 347 U.S. 483 (1954).
[5] See Chapter 13, "Civil Rights and Public Order."

nationwide network of transportation and communication and the potential for national economic depressions. In response to the growth of the national economy, Congress progressively widened the definition of "interstate commerce" to include the regulation of interstate transportation (particularly the railroads) and of communication (particularly telephone and telegraph). Industrialization created interstate businesses, which could only be regulated by the national government; this was recognized in the passage of the Sherman Anti-Trust Act in 1890. Yet for a time, the Supreme Court placed obstacles in the way of national authority over the economy, and by so doing created a "crisis" in American federalism. For many years, the Court narrowly construed interstate commerce to mean only the movement of goods and services across state lines, and until the late 1930's, the Supreme Court insisted that agriculture, mining, manufacturing, and labor relations were outside of the reach of the delegated powers of the national government. But when confronted with the depression of the 1930's and the threat of presidential attack on the membership of the Court itself, the Court yielded. In National Labor Relations Board v. Jones and Laughlin Steel Corporation in 1937, the Court recognized the principle that production and distribution of goods and services for a national market could be regulated by Congress under the Interstate Commerce Clause.[6] The effect was to give the national government effective control over the national economy, and today few economic affairs are not within the reach of congressional power.

Controversy between national and state authority continues over the question of "federal pre-emption." In an early case of Cooley v. the Board of Wardens, the Supreme Court asserted that the states could exercise some powers over the Interstate Commerce Clause, as long as the matter was essentially local in nature, Congress had not acted directly on it, and the state action did not burden or interfere with interstate commerce.[7] But the Supreme Court has also held that when Congress enacts legislation in a delegated field, the effect is to preclude the states from exercising concurrent powers over this field, even when state law does not conflict with federal laws. This doctrine of "federal pre-emption" has struck down state laws in labor relations, taxation, and the regulation of "subversive activity."[8] Of course Congress can stipulate that a statute does not bar supplemental state laws; for example, in the Taft-Hartley Act, Congress specifically gave the states the power to outlaw union shops even in industries affecting interstate commerce. Generally, however, the federal courts will not allow state legislation in an area of concurrent jurisdiction after Congress acts in that field.

[6] National Labor Relations Board v. Jones and Laughlin Steel Corporation, 301 U.S. 1 (1937).

[7] Cooley v. Board of Wardens, 12 Howard 299 (1852).

[8] Pennsylvania v. Nelson, 350 U.S. 497 (1956).

National–State Relations: The "New Federalism"

A common view of American federalism is that it resembles a layer cake with local governments at the base, state governments in the middle, and the national government at the top. This view suggests that the state and local governments are "closer" to the people than the national government. The implication of such an image is that the federal government does not serve the people directly, and that governmental activities in the American system are parceled out either to the states or communities, or to the national government.[9]

While the layer cake theory of federalism with its separation of national and state powers has been very popular, there is ample evidence that in practice American federalism never really operated in this fashion.[10] American federalism has been characterized by far more cooperation, coordination, and sharing of responsibilities than by separation. At all times in our history, the national government and the states have shared powers. Today both are active in agriculture, aviation, civil defense, education, employment security, highways, housing and urban renewal, natural resources and conservation, public health and welfare—to name just a few fields in which nation and states share responsibilites.

Professor Morton Grodzins challenged the layer cake view of American federalism:

> A far more accurate image is the rainbow or marble cake, characterized by an inseparable mingling of differently colored ingredients, the colors appearing in vertical and diagonal strands and unexpected whorls. The colors are mixed in the marble cake, so functions are mixed in the American federal system.[11]

The Constitution provides for important concurrent powers to be exercised by both the national government and the states; perhaps the most important of these is the power to tax and spend for the general welfare. Actually, it is very difficult to identify programs of the national government in which states and communities do not participate or state and local programs in which the national government does not participate. Even in matters of national defense, which are thought to be wholly national con-

[9] In a modern political context, Senator Barry Goldwater, in his widely read, *The Conscience of a Conservative,* argues that: "The Constitution, I repeat, draws a sharp and clear line between federal jurisdiction and state jurisdiction. The federal government's failure to recognize that line has been a crushing blow to the principles of limited government. Barry Goldwater, *The Conscience of a Conservative* (Newark: MacFadden Books, 1960), p. 30.

[10] See Daniel J. Elazar, *The American Partnership: Inter-governmental Cooperation in Nineteenth-Century United States* (Chicago: University of Chicago Press, 1962).

[11] Morton Grodzins, "The Federal System," The American Assembly, *Goals for Americans* (Englewood Cliffs, N.J.: Prentice-Hall, Inc., 1960), p. 265.

cerns, state and local governments play a role. State national guard units remain under the command of state governors until they are called into the service of the United States. The selective service drafts men to serve in the military forces of the U.S., but the actual administration is left largely to local draft boards. Civil defense activities are largely administered by state and local officials. In the area of local law enforcement, which is commonly thought to be a community responsibility, police officers have considerable contact with the Federal Bureau of Investigation, including access to fingerprint files, the reporting service, and the FBI's famous national academy for training in law enforcement. Whatever the field of government activity, federal-state-local relations are usually characterized by frequent conferences, joint planning, continuous consultation, exchange of facilities and information, and awareness of common efforts on behalf of the public. As for the myth that the national government is not very "close" to the people, in terms of proximity, communication, and the provision of direct services, one may simply consult a local telephone directory to see how many *local* phone numbers are listed under "the United States Government." Even modest size communities have extensive listings under the Departments of Agriculture, Commerce, Justice, and the Interior, the Weather Bureau, Federal Bureau of Investigation, Federal Aviation Agency, General Services Administration, Social Security Administration, the Internal Revenue Service, and of course, the Post Office. Often federal listings outnumber state or local government listings.

In practice, then, federalism has come to mean the sharing of power between the nation and the states, rather than a sharp separation between national and state responsibilities. This idea of sharing powers and responsibilities of government in a wide variety of program areas has come to be called the "New Federalism" or "Cooperative Federalism."

How did this "New Federalism" come about? It is possible to argue that cooperative federalism was practiced in the earliest days of the republic. The first Congress of the United States in the famous Northwest Ordinance, providing for the government of the territories to the west of the Appalachian mountains, authorized grants of federal land for the establishment of public schools, and by so doing, showed a concern for an area "reserved" to the states by the Constitution. Again, in 1863 in the Morrill Land Grant Act, Congress provided grants of land to the states to promote higher education. But many commentators feel that the date 1913, when the 16th Amendment gave the federal government the power to tax incomes directly, was the beginning of a new era in American federalism. Congress had been given the power to tax and spend for the general welfare in Article I of the Constitution. But the 16th Amendment helped to shift the balance of financial power from the states to Washington, when it gave Congress the power to tax the incomes of corporations and individuals on a progressive basis. The income tax gave the federal government the power to raise large sums of money, which it proceeded to spend for the general welfare as well as for defense. It is no coincidence that the first major grant-in-aid programs (agricultural extension in 1914, highways in 1916, vocational education in 1917, and public health in 1918) all came shortly after the inauguration of the federal income tax. Many right-wing commentators have recognized the financial power that the progressive income tax has given the national government, and they have frequently proposed its elimination.

The federal "grant-in-aid" has become the principal instrument of the new cooperative federalism. It should be noted that there is no general grant of power to the national government in the Constitution to protect and advance the public health, safety, welfare, or morals. Thus, the national government may not enact laws dealing directly with housing, streets, zoning, schools, health, police protection, fire fighting, crime, vice, and so on, simply because such a law might contribute to the general welfare. However, it may *tax* or *borrow* or *spend money* for welfare purposes, even though it has no power in the Constitution to regulate welfare activities directly. This is a subtle distinction, but it is an important one. For example, Congress cannot outlaw billboards on highways, because billboard regulation is not among the enumerated powers of Congress in the U.S. Constitution. But the federal government, through its power to tax and spend, can provide financial assistance to the states to build highways and then pass a law threatening to withdraw financial aid, if the states do not outlaw billboards themselves. Thus, the federal government can involve itself in highways and even billboard regulation through its taxing power and financial resources, even though these fields are "reserved" to the states.

The great depression of the 1930's brought pressure upon the national government to use its tax and spending powers in a wide variety of areas formerly reserved to states and communities. The Federal government initiated grant-in-aid programs to states and communities for public assistance, unemployment compensation, employment services, child welfare, public housing, urban renewal, and so on; it also expanded federal grant-in-aid programs in highways, vocational education, and rehabilitation. The inadequacy of state and local revenue systems to meet the financial crisis created by the depression contributed significantly to the development of cooperative federalism. States and communities called upon the superior taxing powers of the national government to assist them in many fields, in which the federal government had not previously involved itself.

Federal grants-in-aid to state and local governments have expanded rapidly since the great depression. Table 2.3 shows the record of federal grants to states and communities from 1932 to 1968. Not only have fed-

TABLE 2.3

FEDERAL GRANTS TO STATES AND COMMUNITIES, 1932-1966

Year	Total federal grants in millions	Federal grants as percent of state-local revenue
1932	232	2.9
1938	800	7.2
1942	858	6.5
1950	2,486	9.7
1955	3,131	8.3
1960	6,974	11.6
1962	7,871	11.3
1965	11,029	12.5
1967	15,366	14.0
1968	17,439	15.0

Source: U.S. Bureau of the Census, *Statistical Abstract.*

eral grants to states and communities expanded rapidly in terms of dollar amounts, but also states and communities have come to rely upon the national government for an ever increasing share of their total revenues. Table 2.4 shows the major program areas of federal grants-in-aid to states and communities. A detailed listing of federal grant-in-aid programs is provided at the end of this chapter (see Table 2.8.) The variety of federal grant programs is truly astounding.

Whenever the national government contributes financially to state or local programs, state and local officials are left with less freedom of choice than they would have otherwise. Federal grants-in-aid are invariably accompanied by federal standards or "guidelines," which must be adhered to if states and communities are to receive their federal money. The national government gives money to states and communities only if they are willing to meet conditions specified by Congress. Often Congress delegates to federal agencies the power to establish the "conditions" that are attached to grants. For example, Congress specifies that states and communities receiving federal welfare money must comply with a great variety of rules and regulations: they must establish a merit system for welfare employees, which is approved by Washington; matching monies must be provided by states and communities; welfare aid must be distributed in money rather than distribution of goods and services; procedures for appeal by applicants denied relief must be provided; the program must apply uniformly throughout the state; requirements for eligibility must meet federal standards, and reams of reports must be filed in Washington. Federal regulations in all grant-in-aid programs are designed to insure compliance with minimum national standards, but they are bound to annoy state and local officials. Sometimes protests from state and local communities are loud enough to induce Congress to yield to local views.

No state is required to accept a federal grant-in-aid. Thus, states are not required to meet federal standards or guidelines, which are set forth as conditions for federal aid; states and communities have the alternative of rejecting the federal money, and they have sometimes done so. But it is very difficult for states and communities to resist the pressure to accept federal money. It is sometimes said that states are "bribed and black-mailed" into federal grant-in-aid programs. They are "bribed" by the temptation of much needed federal money, and they are "blackmailed" by the thought that other states and communities will get the federal money if they do not, money contributed in part by their own citizens through federal taxation.

In short, through the power to tax and spend for the general welfare, and through "conditions" attached to federal grants-in-aid, the national government has come to exercise great powers in many areas originally "reserved" to the states—highways, welfare, education, housing, natural

TABLE 2.4

FEDERAL GRANTS-IN-AID TO STATES AND COMMUNITIES
BY PROGRAM IN 1966

Program	Federal grants	Percent of all federal grants
All programs	13,087	100.0
Agriculture	541	4.1
Natural resources	284	2.2
Highways	3,998	30.5
Commerce and transportation	215	1.6
Public housing	236	1.8
Urban renewal	330	2.5
Urban planning	38	0.3
Urban transportation	32	0.2
Economic opportunity	822	6.3
Milk, lunch, and food stamp	358	2.7
Disaster relief	150	1.1
Health & hospitals	326	2.5
Pollution control	85	0.6
Welfare	3,726	28.5
Employment	702	5.4
Education	1,025	7.8
General government	109	0.8
Other	110	0.8

Source: U.S. Bureau of the Census, *Statistical Abstract.*

resources, employment, health, and so on. Of course, federal grants-in-aid have enabled many states and communities to provide necessary and desirable services that they could not have afforded had it not been for federal aid. Federal guidelines have often improved standards of administration, personnel policies, and fiscal practices in states and communities. More importantly, federal guidelines have helped to insure that states and communities will not engage in racial discrimination in federally aided programs. However, many commentators are genuinely apprehensive that the states have surrendered many of their powers to the national government in return for federal money. They argue that the role of states and communities in the American federal system has been weakened significantly by the conditions attached to federal grant-in-aid programs. (We shall return to this problem again in Chapter 17.)

The Continued Vitality of the States

What is the impact of the growth of national power on state government? Does an increase in the power of the national government necessarily mean a reduction in the power of the states?

A common view of our American federal system portrays national and state power as the opposite ends of the seesaw—if national powers are increased, then state powers must decline. Many people believe that the growth of national power has curtailed the powers of states and communities, but all available evidence contradicts this belief. National power has expanded over the years, but so has the power of states and communities. States and communities have vastly expanded their activities and responsibilities in many areas, which affect the day-to-day lives of all Americans. As V.O. Key has observed:

> ... the paradoxical conclusion emerges that, as the prophets of doom proclaimed the passing of the states during the ferment of the New Deal, state governments were expanding their staffs, and enlarging the scope of their activities, spending more and more money, and in general enjoying a boom as such things go in governmental circles.[12]

Despite increases in national power, states and communities have continued to bear the major responsibility for the nation's domestic affairs. States and communities perform more services, employ more people, spend more money, and have a greater impact in the lives of their citizens than they have ever had before. They are not dying, but growing and expanding. All talk of weakness, helplessness, and ineffectiveness of state and community government conflicts with the available evidence.

[12] V. O. Key, Jr., *American State Politics: An Introduction* (New York: Alfred A. Knopf, Inc., 1956), p. 7.

It is interesting to compare the relatively low proportion of federal, in contrast to state and local expenditures, for specific domestic programs. Table 2.5 shows that the federal government spent over $4 billion for educational programs in 1966, but this is far less than the $33 billion spent by state and local governments for education. In the same year, the federal government spent about $4 billion for highway construction, a major cooperative program, but federal grants amounted to less than 30 per cent of state-local expenditures' for highways. Even in the realm of housing and urban renewal, where the federal stimulus is most important, federal grants amounted to only about half of the total state-local expenditures. States and communities continue to spend far more than the federal government for health, hospitals, and public welfare, despite an extensive system of federal grants-in-aid for these purposes.

There are very few instances of an expansion of federal power at the expense of existing state operations. Generally, federal involvement in a program area has served to stimulate the states and communities to exercise their own powers and to encourage an expansion of state and community activity in the same field. The stimulus provided by federal grant-in-aid programs has not only meant greater state and community expenditure of funds, but also an increase in the number and quality of personnel involved—state–local civilian employment is almost three times larger than federal civilian employment.

The vitality of our state and local governments in America is also revealed in public attitudes towards these governments. Most Americans seem to be cognizant of the effect of state and local governments on their lives. A national survey revealed that most Americans feel that local governments have "some" or "great" effect on their daily lives, in similar per-

TABLE 2.5

FEDERAL, STATE AND LOCAL GOVERNMENTAL EXPENDITURE
BY SELECTED FUNCTION, 1966
(figures in millions of dollars)

	Federal	State and local
Education	$4,564	$33,287
Highways	4,078	12,770
Natural resources	8,480	2,039
Health and hospitals	2,775	5,910
Welfare	3,787	6,757
Housing and urban renewal	1,616	1,406

Source: U.S. Bureau of the Census, *Statistical Abstract*.

TABLE 2.6

PUBLIC ATTITUDES TOWARD LOCAL AND NATIONAL GOVERNMENT

Estimated degree of impact of national
and local governments on daily life

	National government	Local government
Great effect	41%	35%
Some effect	44	53
No effect	11	10
Other, don't know, etc.	4	2
	100	100

"On the whole, do the activities of the national or
local government tend to improve conditions in this
area, or would we be better off without them?"

	National government	Local government
Yes, tend to improve	74%	69%
Sometimes improve, sometimes not	18	23
Better off without them	3	4
Other, don't know, etc.	5	4
	100	100

Sense of understanding of issues

	National and international	Local
Very well	7%	21%
Moderately well	38	44
Not so well	37	23
Not at all	14	10
Depends, other, don't know, etc.	4	2
	100	100

"If you made an effort to change a proposed law or
regulation you considered very unjust or harmful,
how likely is it that you would succeed?"

	Local regulation	National law
Very likely or moderately likely	28%	11%
Somewhat unlikely	15	18
Not at all likely, impossible	25	36
Likely only if other joined in	25	24
Other, don't know	6	9
	100	100

Source: Original unpublished data from survey by Gabriel A. Almond and Sidney
Verba, *The Civic Culture* (Boston: Little, Brown, & Co., 1963). Table from analysis
by Robert A. Dahl, *Pluralist Democracy in the United States* (Chicago: Rand
McNally & Co. , 1967), pp. 198-201.

centages to those recorded concerning the national government (see Table 2.6). Moreover, the percentages of Americans who felt that local governments "tend to improve conditions in this area" was very high. Very few Americans felt that they would be "better off without them."

More importantly, perhaps, it is interesting to note that Americans look upon local governments as more manageable and more responsive to individual desires than the national government. The number of people who said that they understood "local issues in this town or part of the country very well" was three times as large as the number who said they understood "the important national and international issues facing the country." Moreover, when asked whether they felt they could change a proposed law or regulation which they considered "very unjust or harmful," 28 per cent felt that their efforts were likely to succeed at the local level but only 11 per cent considered success likely at the national level. In other words, most Americans feel more capable of understanding and affecting local issues than national issues.

Public confidence in state and local government is very high. A Gallup poll of January 1967 revealed that most Americans believe that state governments spend taxpayers' dollars "more wisely" than the federal government. This preference for state spending over federal spending was evidenced in all segments of the population, although the proportion of support for federal spending was slightly higher among Democrats, Catholics, Easterners, low income earners, and big city dwellers. Public opinion appears to support the notion that states and communities are better at spending money, even if the federal government is better at collecting it. Of course, public opinion may or may not be "right" about which level of government spends money "more wisely," but the confidence expressed in state government is itself a source of power for the states in their relations with the national government. (See Table 2.7.)

Finally, there is ample evidence that the states are not completely powerless in confrontations with national authority. The most common example of state resistance to national authority is, of course, the resistance of southern states to desegregation. For more than ten years after the Supreme Court's desegregation decision in Brown v. Topeka, 11 states successfully resisted all but token desegregation. Even today most southern school districts, which desire to do so, can still maintain substantially segregated schools. (See Chapter 13 for further discussion.)

Interstate Relations

The U.S. Constitution provides that "full faith and credit shall be given in each state to the public acts, records, and judicial proceedings of every other state." As more Americans move from state to state, it becomes in-

TABLE 2.7

GOVERNMENT SPENDING

Question: "Which do you think spends the taxpayer's dollar more wisely—the State government or the Federal Government?"

(in percent)

	January 1967 State	Federal	Neither	No opinion
National	49	18	17	16
Sex				
Men	52	18	19	11
Women	47	16	16	21
Education				
College	57	19	18	6
High school	51	17	16	16
Grade school	40	18	18	24
Occupation				
Professional and				
business	56	15	17	12
White collar	52	20	16	12
Farmers	59	6	20	15
Manual	45	21	16	18
Age				
21 to 29 years	49	23	14	14
30 to 49 years	49	17	17	17
50 and over	49	15	19	17
Religion				
Protestant	52	15	16	17
Catholic	44	24	18	14
Jewish	X	X	X	X
Politics				
Republican	60	11	17	12
Democrat	46	21	14	19
Independent	44	19	22	15
Region				
East	37	27	19	17
Midwest	54	16	18	12
South	58	10	14	18
West	46	16	19	19
Income				
$10,000 and over	53	18	18	11
$7,000 and over	50	18	19	13
$5,000 to $6,999	54	19	14	13
$3,000 to $4,999	44	16	16	24
Under $3,000	44	15	18	23
Community size				
1,000,000 and				
over	36	24	19	21
500,000 and over	41	23	17	19
50,000 to 499,999	46	19	18	17
2,500 to 49,999	57	13	14	16
Under 2,500, rural	56	12	19	13

Source: *Congressional Record*, February 15, 1967.

creasingly important that the states recognize each other's legal instruments. This constitutional clause is intended to protect the rights of individuals who move from one state to another, and it is also intended to prevent individuals from evading their legal responsibilities by crossing state lines. Courts in Illinois must recognize decisions made by courts in Michigan. Contracts entered into in New York may be enforced in Florida. Corporations chartered in Delaware should be permitted to do business in North Dakota. One of the more serious problems in interstate relations today is the failure of the states to meet their obligations under the full faith and credit clause in the area of domestic relations, including divorce, alimony, child support, and custody of children. Nevada's divorce laws are quite liberal, and one need only live in that state six weeks in order to establish residence. When Mr. Williams left North Carolina to go to Reno to obtain a divorce, then married and returned home to North Carolina, his home state convicted him of bigamy and refused to recognize his Nevada divorce. The Supreme Court said that Mr. Williams had not established a bonafide residence in Nevada and the Nevada court had no jurisdiction over his divorce.[13] This decision opened the door to challenging the validity of divorces granted by other states where the divorce had been preceded only by temporary residence. States have also begun to evade the intent of the full faith and credit clause in cases involving alimony payments, child support, and custody of children. The result is now a complex and confused situation in domestic relations law.

The Constituion also states: "The citizens of each state shall be entitled to all privileges and immunities of citizens in the several states." Apparently the Founding Fathers thought that no state should discriminate against citizens from another state in favor of its own citizens. To do so would seriously jeopardize national unity. This clause also implies that citizens of any state may move freely about the country and settle where they like, with the assurance that as newcomers they will not be subjected to unreasonable discrimination. The newcomer should not be subject to discriminatory taxation, he should be permitted to engage in lawful occupations under the same conditions as other citizens of the state, he should not be prevented from acquiring and using property, or denied equal protection of the laws, or refused access to the courts. However, states have managed to compromise this constitutional guarantee in several important ways. States establish residence requirements for voting and holding office, which prevent newcomers from exercising the same rights as older residents. States often require periods of residence as a prerequisite for holding a state job or for admission into professional practice such as law, medicine, and so on. States discriminate against out-of-state students in the tuition charged in public schools and colleges.

13 Williams v. North Carolina, 325 U.S. 226 (1945).

The Constitution also provides that: "A person charged in any state with treason, felony, or other crime who shall flee from justice and be found in another state, shall on the demand of the executive authority from the state from which he fled, be delivered up, to be removed to the state having jurisdiction of the crime." In other words, the Constitution requires governors to extradite fugitives from another state's justice. But the Supreme Court conceded that it has no power to compel the governor of a state to fulfill this constitutional obligation. Governors have not always honored requests for extradition, but since no state wants to harbor criminals of another state, extradition is seldom refused. Among reasons advanced for the occasional refusals are (1) the individual has become a law abiding citizen in his new state; (2) a northern governor did not approve of the conditions in Georgia chain gangs; (3) a Negro returned to a southern state would not receive a fair trial; (4) the governor did not believe that there was sufficient evidence against the fugitive to warrant his conviction in the first place.

The Constitution provides that "No state shall without the consent of Congress . . . enter into any agreement or compact with another state." Over 100 interstate compacts now serve a wide variety of interests, such as interstate water resources; conservation of natural resources, including oil, wild life, fisheries; the control of floods; the development of interstate toll highways; the coordination of civil defense measures, the reciprocal supervision of parolees; the coordination of welfare and institutional care programs; the administration of interstate metropolitan areas; and the resolution of interstate tax conflicts. In practice, Congress has little to do with these compacts; the Supreme Court has held that congressional consent is required only if the compact encroaches upon some federal power. Only once did Congress refuse consent to an interstate compact. In 1947 Congress refused to authorize a regional agreement between southern governors for the establishment of the Southern Regional Education Board. This Board was to plan a regional program for higher education in the southern states, but the congressional debates centered upon segregation in southern colleges and universities. When Congress failed to give its consent, the southern states formed the Board anyhow, and its constitutionality has never been challenged in the courts. One of the most notable interstate compacts is the Port of New York Authority which was established by New York and New Jersey in 1921. The Port Authority is a giant organization which operates a wide variety of port and transportation enterprises. A new pattern of interstate compacts was established with the Delaware Basin River Compact in 1961. This compact included Delaware, New York, New Jersey, and Pennsylvania, and, in a new departure, the U.S. Government. This was the first interstate compact in which the federal government itself became a signatory and a party to the compact. The Delaware River Basin Commission is authorized to deal with water resource problems in the Delaware River, in hopes to resolve long conflicts between the four states over the use of water in the river.

States are not supposed to make war on each other, although they did so from 1861 to 1865. They are supposed to take their conflicts to the Supreme Court. The constitution gives the Supreme Court the power to settle all cases involving two or more states. In recent years the Supreme Court has heard disputes between states over boundaries, the diversion of water, fishing rights, and the disposal of sewage and garbage.

Politics of Federalism

In the early 1950's the issue of national versus state authority was raised in a contest over the control of "tidelands oil," that is, offshore oil wells. The nation's major oil companies objected strenuously to national control of submerged offshore oil deposits; they argued vigorously on behalf of the right of states to regulate the use of these important natural resources. Professor Robert J. Harris has described the controversy as follows:

> The solicitude of the oil companies for states' rights is hardly based on convictions derived from political theory, but rather from fears that federal ownership may result in the cancellation or modification of state leases favorable to their interests, their knowledge that they can successfully cope with state regulatory agencies, and uncertainty concerning their ability to control the federal agency.[14]

The tidelands oil controversy ended in victory for the states' rights advocates, that is, the oil companies. Yet, the controversy poses some interesting questions about the politics of federalism. What political interests are likely to support the rights of states in contrast to national authority? Are arguments over states' rights versus national authority merely sham arguments which hide deeper political cleavages?

Debate over federalism can never be removed from the political context in which it takes place. The concept of federalism itself was born in the political environment that surrounded the Constitutional Convention. Federalism was a political compromise between those "anti-federalists" who wanted to retain the full sovereignty of the individual states by not allowing the national government to act directly on individuals, and those "federalists" who wanted a strong national government capable of acting directly on individuals. It was a political compromise, which eased the way to reconciliation of the interests of the larger and smaller states. It stifled the objections of many small farmers, "Jefferson's men," and others, who would later form the Democratic Party, to a national government with real

[14] Robert J. Harris, "States' Rights and Vested Interests," *Journal of Politics,* 15 (November, 1954), 457-71.

power. For the conservatives, or "Hamilton's men," and those who would later form the Federalist Party, the most important aspect of federalism was that it removed political power from the states where democratic tendencies were most marked and where, sometimes, small farmers captured control from the "men of principle and property." The federal principle itself was counted upon to operate as a bulwark against majority rule and as a safeguard of the rights of property. But the Founding Fathers knew that they could not abolish the states without incurring the terrible wrath of the Democrats, who stood for decentralized government and the retention of political power in the states. In fact, without the Bill of Rights, which were then limitations on the power of the *national* government, the Constitution would never have been ratified by the state legislatures. It scraped by only with the slimmest of majorities in several states anyhow, amidst heated political conflict between Democrats and Federalists.

The Jeffersonians continued to criticize the national government and to argue in favor of a strict interpretation of its powers. When the Federalists passed the Alien and Sedition Acts of 1798 to stifle newspaper criticism of the new government by Jeffersonian newspaper editors, Jeffersonians responded with the most extreme states' rights arguments, that is, the doctrines of "nullification" and "interposition." Yet, when Jefferson himself became President in 1801, he seemingly reversed his earlier position of strict interpretation of national power and proceeded to purchase the Louisiana territory, even though there was no expressed authorization in the Constitution to do so. Later, the New England states, long the backbone of the Federalist Party, threatened to secede from the Union because of harm suffered by shipping interests in the War of 1812 against England. Thus, even in the early days of the American Republic, the shifting position of the Federalists and Democrats over the question of states' rights and national authority suggests that the question of federalism is not wholly divorced from the question of which political interests are stronger in Washington and which political interests are stronger in the states.

Certainly the issue of slavery was at the heart of the debate between the right of secession and the indissolubility of the Union. John C. Calhoun's well reasoned defense of states' rights was written in behalf of the political interests of his native South Carolina, and the South. While slavery, and the economic life of the South that depended upon this institution, was at the heart of the conflict between the states, the debate was conducted over such matters as whether the Constitution had been created by the people as citizens of the United States or by the people as citizens of their respective states. The central government, according to Calhoun, was an agent of the states and must not violate the compact made by the states— that is, the Constitution—under the penalty of state nullification or even secession.

The Civil War brought about the overthrow of the institution of slavery, and it added immeasurably to national power. It produced three constitutional amendments preventing *state* interference or discrimination in the sphere of human freedom and civil and political rights. But the states' rights argument was to remain a potent one. The great rhetoric of John C. Calhoun was to be used by every interest that felt itself threatened by action in the national arena.

Interests that constituted a majority at the national level continued to assert the supremacy of the national government and to extol the virtues of national regulation. Interests that were minorities in national politics, but composed local or statewide majorities in one or more states, continued to see merit in the preservation of the rights of states.

The states' rights argument has been most vigorously defended in recent years by the southern states seeking to preserve segregation of the races. So closely tied was the states' rights argument with the question of segregation that it became almost synonymous with bigotry, prejudice, and racial hatred. Yet the right to "interpose" state sovereignty and "nullify" federal laws has been claimed at one time or another by states in every section of the country. On the eve of the Civil War, many northern states affirmed their right to interpose themselves between federal fugitive slave laws and the immorality of returning escaped Negroes to the bonds of slavery. Yet in recent years the states' rights argument became a thin cover for the advocacy of white supremacy in the South. The southern states wished to remain free from the national enforcement of civil rights, and the assertion of states' rights became a means to keep the Negro "in his place." States' rights became the antithesis of civil rights. The Supreme Court's desegregation decision in Brown *v.* the Board of Education in Topeka, Kansas prompted 100 southern congressmen to draw up the "Southern Manifesto" in March of 1956, which bitterly attacked the Supreme Court for "the clear abuse of judicial power" that "encroaches upon the reserved rights of the states and the people." It even commended the motives of "those states which have declared the intention to resist forced integration by any lawful means." The southern argument for states' rights was clearly designed to cover up the racial issue. With Alabama and Virginia in the lead, many southern states drafted their own declarations of "interposition." Of course, the federal courts quickly disposed of the doctrine of "interposition" as they had done so many times in the past: "The conclusion is clear that interposition is not a constitutional doctrine. If taken seriously, it is illegal defiance of constitutional authority." [15]

States' rights have also been argued by conservative and rural political interests, which oppose big government and big spending and do not feel the necessity of extensive public services in education, health, welfare, hous-

[15] Bush *v.* New Orleans School Board, 364 U.S. 500 (1960).

TABLE 2.8

FEDERAL AID TO STATE AND LOCAL GOVERNMENTS
(Expenditures in millions of dollars)

Agency and program	1967 actual	1968 estimate	1969 estimate
National defense:			
Executive Office of the President: Office of Emergency Planning—Federal contributions to State and local planning	0.4	0.3	*
Department of Defense—Military:			
Civil defense shelters and financial assistance	25.7	25.1	29.5
Construction of Army National Guard centers	.7	2.0	3.0
Total, national defense	26.8	27.4	32.5
International affairs and finance:			
Department of State: East-West Cultural and Technical Interchange Center	6.6	5.8	5.3
Agriculture and agricultural resources:			
Department of Agriculture:			
Commodity Credit Corporation and Consumer and Marketing Service: Removal of surplus agricultural commodities and value of commodities donated	278.4	420.8	444.3
Rural water and waste disposal facilities	11.1	27.0	33.8
Rural housing for domestic farm labor	8.6	3.8	5.0
Resource conservation and development	1.1	1.5	.9
Agricultural Research Service: Grants for basic scientific research	2.3	2.1	1.9
Agricultural experiment stations	54.9	56.1	62.4
Cooperative agricultural extension service	89.4	86.2	93.9
Payments to States, territories, and possessions, Consumer and Marketing Service	1.8	1.8	1.8
Commodity Credit Corporation: Grants for research	.3	.2	.1
Total, agriculture and agricultural resources	448.0	599.4	644.0
Natural resources:			
Department of Agriculture:			
Watershed protection and flood prevention	71.8	77.2	68.5
Grants for forest protection, utilization, and basic scientific research	18.8	18.4	18.3
National forest and grassland funds; payments to States and counties (shared revenue)	42.9	44.6	47.7
Department of Defense—Civil: Corps of Engineers:			
Payment to California, flood control	12.1	25.7	69.1
Payments to States, Flood Control Act of 1954 (shared revenue)	2.4	2.5	2.5
Department of the Interior:			
Water pollution control	99.0	139.8	190.9
Payments to States and counties from grazing receipts, grasslands, and sales of public lands (shared revenue)	1.0	.9	1.0
Bureau of Indian Affairs: Resources management	.9	1.0	1.1

FEDERAL AID TO STATE AND LOCAL GOVERNMENTS (Continued)
(Expenditures in millions of dollars)

Agency and program	1967 actual	1968 estimate	1969 estimate
Natural resources (Continued)			
Department of the Interior (Continued)			
Bureau of Reclamation:			
Grants	.1	.1	
Payments to Arizona, Nevada, and Klamath restoration area (shared revenue)	.7	.7	.8
Office of Water Resources Research	5.8	7.9	9.3
Office of Saline Water		1.8	3.3
Payments from grant lands: Oregon, California, and Coos and Douglas Counties (shared revenue)	21.2	22.4	22.5
Mineral Leasing Act payments (shared revenue)	48.4	50.0	50.2
Bureau of Mines:			
Mine drainage and solid waste disposal	0.2	0.1	0.2
Aid for commercial fisheries	2.7	5.6	5.9
Payment to Alaska from Pribilof Island fund (shared revenue)	.3	.3	.1
Fish and wildlife restoration and management	22.5	25.4	31.6
Wildlife refuge fund and grasslands payments (shared revenue)	1.2	1.0	1.1
Land and water conservation grants	22.2	56.3	74.5
Preservation of historic properties	*	.3	.7
Department of State: Pacific Halibut Commission		.2	.2
Federal Power Commission: Payments to States (shared revenue)	.1	.1	.1
Tennessee Valley Authority: Payments in lieu of taxes (shared revenue)	11.9	13.1	14.8
Water Resources Council	1.6	2.4	2.7
Total, natural resources	387.7	497.9	617.0
Commerce and transportation:			
Funds appropriated to the President: Public works acceleration	19.4	12.0	
Department of Commerce:			
State marine schools	.4	.4	.4
Office of State Technical Services	1.2	5.1	5.2
Economic development assistance	19.8	109.8	150.6
Appalachian development	58.8	139.5	232.8
Department of Transportation:			
Chamizal Memorial Highway		1.0	5.4
Forest and public lands highways	37.3		
Highway beautification	24.3	79.7	81.2
Highway safety	.8	26.2	70.0
Federal-aid highways (trust fund)	3,965.9	4,206.1	4,187.4
Federal Aviation Administration: Federal-aid airport program	64.1	58.0	73.0
Total, commerce and transportation	4,192.2	4,637.8	4,806.0

59

Agency and program	1967 actual	1968 estimate	1969 estimate
Housing and community development:			
Funds appropriated to the President: Alaska mortgage indemnity grants	2.6		
Department of Housing and Urban Development:			
Alaska housing			1.0
Low-income housing	2.3	1.8	3.8
Low-rent public housing program	245.6	283.5	337.9
Urban planning grants	21.8	31.0	46.0
Open space land and urban beautification	19.1	60.0	60.0
Grants for basic water and sewer facilities	5.7	90.0	130.0
Grants for neighborhood facilities	.8	15.0	32.0
Model city grants		22.4	241.6
Urban renewal	370.4	500.0	700.0
Urban transportation assistance	42.1	98.3	150.0
Metropolitan development incentive grants			3.0
Other aids for urban renewal and community facilities		1.0	8.2
National Capital region:			
Federal payments to District of Columbia	58.0	70.0	80.2
Washington Metropolitan Area Transit Authority		1.0	18.0
Dulles sewer project		11.2	.8
Total, housing and community development	768.3	1,185.2	1,812.5
Health, labor, and welfare:			
Funds appropriated to the President:			
Disaster relief	52.6	44.5	34.8
Office of Economic Opportunity:			
Community action programs:			
Head Start	287.3	293.5	294.0
Local initiative	220.6	301.4	314.0
Other	154.2	179.6	196.4
Work and training programs:			
School year and summer	129.6	172.9	156.6
Comprehensive employment	141.1	207.3	406.8
Special impact		15.4	21.9
Work experience program	117.6	101.9	36.2
Department of Agriculture:			
Special milk and school lunch	302.1	319.0	344.8
Food stamp	106.0	168.8	223.5
Department of Health, Education, and Welfare:			
Hospital construction	204.9	217.8	212.0
(Portion to private, nonprofit institutions)	(91.3)	(104.2)	(95.4)
Health manpower	31.6	130.3	172.4
Comprehensive health planning and services	*	72.0	110.0
Regional medical programs	3.0	13.7	34.6
National Institutes of Health	1.6	1.6	1.6
Mental health	11.0	49.6	57.4
Health services	19.0	65.9	17.1
Disease prevention and environmental health	89.2	76.6	19.4

FEDERAL AID TO STATE AND LOCAL GOVERNMENTS (Continued)
(Expenditures in millions of dollars)

Agency and program	1967 actual	1968 estimate	1969 estimate
Health, labor, and welfare (Continued)			
Department of Health, Education, and Welfare (Continued)			
Maternal and child welfare	178.7	214.1	248.7
Public assistance:			
Medical assistance	1,173.0	1,761.0	2,121.6
Work incentives (training and child care)		13.9	113.8
Income maintenance payments	2,610.1	2,976.0	2,960.9
Social services for welfare recipients	392.0	460.2	589.3
Juvenile delinquency			20.0
Vocational rehabilitation	185.5	280.1	341.0
Mental retardation			8.7
Administration on Aging	3.5	7.1	16.1
Department of Labor:			
Manpower development and training activities	22.1	60.2	58.2
Grants to States for administration of employment security programs (trust fund)	535.8	567.0	609.3
Development of labor mobility	1.8	1.8	1.8
Equal Opportunity Commission	.1	.8	.9
Total, health, labor, and welfare	6,973.8	8,774.1	9,744.3
Education:			
Department of Health, Education, and Welfare:			
Assistance to schools in federally affected areas	417.4	341.2	381.9
Elementary and secondary educational activities	1,364.4	1,473.0	1,404.4
Higher education activities (including land-grant colleges)	187.4	247.0	174.2
Vocational education	232.8	255.1	249.8
Arts and humanities educational activities	.4	.5	.3
Grants for library services and construction	57.4	84.8	94.8
Training teachers of the handicapped	*	12.0	21.5
Community services and National Teacher Corps	7.0	10.0	11.5
Civil rights educational activities	3.3	4.7	7.0
Teaching of the blind and deaf	1.0	1.2	1.3
Educational television facilities	7.9	6.7	8.2
Education professions development			7.5
Department of the Interior: Bureau of Indian Affairs:			
Education and welfare services	10.8	11.4	14.8
National Foundation on the Arts and Humanities	8.9	14.3	21.0
Total, education	2,298.7	2,461.9	2,398.2
Veterans benefits and services:			
Veterans Administration:			
Aid to State homes	8.8	9.3	10.0
Grants for construction of State nursing homes	.1	2.4	3.0
Administrative expenses	1.1	1.7	1.8
Total, veterans benefits and services	9.9	13.4	14.8

61

FEDERAL AID TO STATE AND LOCAL GOVERNMENTS (Continued)
(Expenditures in millions of dollars)

Agency and program	1967 actual	1968 estimate	1969 estimate
General government:			
Civil Service Commission: Intergovernmental personnel assistance			12.0
Funds appropriated to the President: Transitional grants to Alaska	*		
Department of the Interior:			
Grants to territories	25.9	37.0	51.4
Internal revenue collections, Virgin Islands (shared revenue)	11.1	12.4	12.5
Department of Justice:			
Law enforcement assistance:			
Education and training	1.6	2.7	5.6
Other	1.1	4.0	8.1
Crime prevention and control		9.4	36.9
Treasury Department:			
Tax collections for Puerto Rico (shared revenue)	59.3	65.0	67.0
Bureau of Customs: Refunds, transfers and expenses of operation, Puerto Rico and the Virgin Islands (trust fund shared revenue)	27.5	28.7	29.1
General Services Administration: Hospital facilities in the District of Columbia		*	
President's Crime Commissions	.8	*	
American Revolution Bicentennial Commission		.1	.2
Total, general government	127.3	159.4	222.8
Total, grants-in-aid and shared revenue	15,239.5	18,362.3	20,297.3

* Less than $500 thousand.

ing and transportation, or urban renewal. They are joined by powerful economic interests, who resist federal regulatory activity and who prefer to be regulated, if at all, by the states. Their argument for states' rights may stem from the fact that the states may be incapable of effectively regulating national economic enterprise, and the states' rights argument may be merely a way of avoiding *any* effective regulations. Often their arguments against the activities of the national government are really arguments against governmental activities in general.

In contrast, urban interests, low income groups, Negroes, ethnic groups, and labor organizations frequently turn to the national government for help. States' rights arguments have little appeal to these groups, which are important in the national electorate, but do not constitute majorities in the large number of sparsely settled states of New England, the Midwest, the Rocky Mountains, and the South. They are heavily concentrated in the large, urban, industrial states—states that are of critical importance in presidential elections, and hence must be reckoned with by the national parties. Since these interests are unable to gain satisfaction at one level of government, they naturally turn to another in an effort to better their fortunes.

Certainly, conservative business interests have been strongly opposed to centralization in Washington and have been consistent defenders of state powers. State governments appear to be more susceptible than the federal government to powerful economic interests. States and communities are not in a very good position to regulate a business or corporation that is national in organization and scope. States and communities compete with one another to attract business and industry. The success of their efforts often depends on whether they can offer a "favorable climate" for business. This means that in addition to the availability of transportation, land, and a skilled labor force, states and communities attempt to provide a "favorable" tax structure, with correspondingly low levels of expenditure for public services not deemed essential by business interests. Moreover, states and communities that are in competition with one another cannot afford regulatory systems which are inimical to business interests. In contrast the national government does not face these competitive pressures. It is coextensive with the economy, and it can avoid being divided and ruled by economic interests. It is capable of regulating the economy on behalf of interests other than those of business. Consequently, those who identify with business interests are likely to invoke the slogan of states' rights and eulogize the virtue of government that is "closer to the people."

President Eisenhower's unsuccessful attempt to "return" some federal powers to the states provides an interesting example of the politics of federalism. Eisenhower established a Joint Federal State Action Committee in 1957 to consider the reallocation of responsibilities between the national government and the states and the returning to the states of as many activities as they were willing to handle. The President's appointees were distinguished men, including three cabinet members, the director of the Bureau of the Budget and ten governors; it had an excellent staff and worked seriously at its job for more than two years. The result was a total failure to "return" any powers to the states. It produced only two recommendations on minor federal grant programs—vocational education and sewage and water pollution control. These programs accounted for only 2 per cent of all federal grants to the states in 1957, an amount of less than $80 million. Yet even these modest recommendations were set aside when the affected interest groups converged on Washington. State departments of education, professional associations, and others with an interest in vocational education succeeded in preventing any cuts in federal aid for vocational education. The nation's mayors, the American Municipal Association, and various conservation, wildlife, and sportsmen's associations asked for more, not less, federal aid for sewage treatment. In the end, not a single recommendation of the President's committee was ever put into effect. Even the states themselves failed to support the President's effort to "return" programs to them. Many state officials wanted the federal government to continue to share in the cost of these programs. One commentator noted that some governors "would rather have the states' rights issue to talk about, than to solve."

3

PARTICIPATION
IN STATE POLITICS

The Nature of Political Participation

Popular participation in the political system is the very definition of democracy. There are many ways that individuals can participate in politics. They may run for, and win, public office; participate in marches, demonstrations, and sit-ins; make financial contributions to political candidates or causes; attend political meetings, speeches, and rallies; write letters to public officials or to newspapers; belong to organizations that support or oppose particular candidates or take stands on public issues; wear a political button or place a bumper sticker on a car; attempt to influence friends while discussing candidates or issues; vote in elections; or merely follow an issue or campaign in the mass media. This listing probably constitutes a ranking of the forms of political participation in their ascending order of frequency. Only a small proportion of the population ever runs for office or participates in demonstrations, while a much larger proportion votes in elections and follows campaigns in newspapers or on television.

The first activities listed involve greater expenditure of time and energy and require greater personal commitment than the more common activities. Less than 1 per cent of the American adult population runs for public office. Only about 5 per cent are ever active in parties and campaigns, and about 10 per cent make financial contributions. About one-third of the population belongs to organizations that could be classified as interest groups, and only a few more ever try to convince their friends to vote for a certain candidate. About 65 per cent of the American people will vote in a hard fought presidential campaign; but far fewer vote in state and local elections. Fully one-third of the population is politically apathetic: they do not vote at all, and they are largely unaware of the political life of the nation.

Voting in the States

Voting is the central form of popular participation in a democracy. Voting requires an individual to make not one, but two decisions. He must choose between rival parties or candidates, and he must choose whether or not to cast his vote at all. This latter decision is just as important as his selection of parties or candidates, because his selection is not effective if he fails to vote. Decisions about whether or not to vote can clearly influence the outcome of elections, yet nonvoting is widespread. Presidential elections inspire about two-thirds of the voting age population to go to the polls, while elections to statewide offices turn out less than half of the eligible voters. State elections held in nonpresidential years inspire even fewer voters, and only a very small minority cast votes in local elections held at times other than national or statewide elections. The idea behind "off-year" elections was to separate state and local issues from matters of national concern. Such off-year elections may succeed in insulating state and local politics from national trends, but they also reduce significantly the number of voters participating in state and local elections.

There is a great deal of variation among the states in voter participation rates. The average turnout in gubernatorial elections from 1954 to 1964 ranged from a low of 4.2 per cent of the voting population in Mississippi, to a high of 79.1 per cent in West Virginia. Voter participation is significantly related to income and educational levels. Participation is notably higher in states with higher median family incomes and well educated adult populations. The states with the lowest turnouts are the deep South states; the next lowest turnouts are found in the border states. Midwestern, New England, and Mountain states rank very high in voter turnout. The urban industrial states, with large metropolitan populations, tend to cluster around the middle of the rankings.

Region, income, and education levels are not the only variables affecting voter turnout. Voter participation is also affected by the exclusion of Negroes through social, political, and economic barriers; by the exclusion of less educated groups through literacy tests and complicated registration procedures; and by the exclusion of highly mobile people through residence requirements. Voter participation rates of the states are also affected by racial composition: Negroes vote less often than whites even when legal

FIGURE 3.1

DISTRIBUTION OF STATES BY LEVEL OF VOTER PARTICIPATION

Gubernatorial, 1960–66

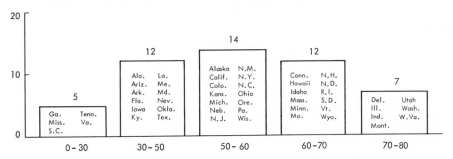

Average Percentage of Voting Age Population Casting Votes, 1960–66

Congressional, 1962

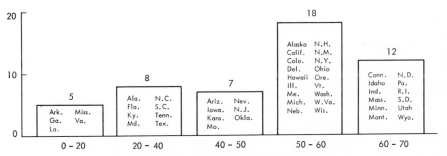

Percentage of Voting Age Population Casting Votes, 1962

Congressional, 1966

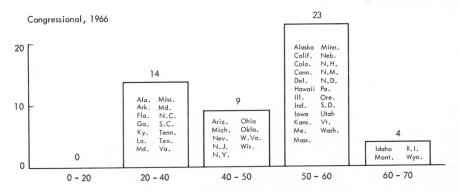

Percentage of Voting Age Population Casting Votes, 1966

TABLE 3.1

POLITICAL PARTICIPATION: PERCENTAGES OF RESPONDENTS IN A
PRESIDENTIAL ELECTION WHO ENGAGED IN TYPES OF
POLITICAL ACTIVITY

	Northeast	Midwest	Far west	South
Vote	85	81	80	57
Talk others into voting a certain way	28	30	30	25
Wear a button or put sticker on car	18	17	17	10
Give money to candidate or party	13	10	10	6
Attend political meetings	7	8	5	6
Join political club	4	3	2	1.7
Work for a party	3	4	1.7	2.5

Source: Lester W. Milbrath, "Political Participation in the States," *Politics in the
American States,* Herbert Jacob and Kenneth Vines, eds. (Boston: Little, Brown,
and Co., 1965), p. 35.

barriers are eliminated. Turnout figures are also affected by the laws of
the states, which define registration procedures, voting hours, absentee
ballot rules, and so on.

Voter participation rates can also be affected by the degree of interparty competition in a state. The more vigorous the competition between
the parties, the greater the interest of citizens in elections, and the larger
the voter turnout. Lester Milbrath reasons that: "When parties and candidates compete vigorously, they make news and are given a large play via
the mass media. Thus a setting of competitive politics tends to have a
greater amount of political stimuli available in the environment than does
a setting with weak competition . . . people tend to follow a close election
with more interest. Furthermore, in a close contest they are more likely
to perceive that their votes count, and thus, they are more likely to cast
them. An additional factor is that when parties are fighting in a close contest, their workers tend to spend more time and energy campaigning and
getting out the vote." [1]

Finally, voter behavior in some states defies systematic explanation.
West Virginia has experienced considerable poverty in recent years—its
adult educational level is one of the lowest in the nation and its registration and voting laws are similar to those of most states. Yet West Virginia
voters insist upon going to the polls in large numbers. Perhaps in Appalachia politics are one form of recreation, in an otherwise drab environment.

Accurate state-by-state figures on the percentage of persons who engage

[1] Lester Milbrath, "Political Participation in the States," *Politics in the American
States,* Herbert Jacob and Kenneth Vines, eds. (Boston: Little, Brown and Company,
1966), p. 50.

in political activities other than voting are not really available. A few years ago the Survey Research Center of the University of Michigan gathered regional figures based upon a public opinion survey for several types of political activities. These percentages are shown in Table 3.1. The survey figures on voting are obviously inflated. Official figures show that in 1956 the nationwide turnout was 60.1 per cent, yet Table 3.1 shows turnout percentages in three régions above 80 per cent. This suggests that respondents will lie about whether they have voted or not in an interview situation, or that opinion surveys seldom include nonvoters, or both. But Table 3.1 does show that voting is the most popular form of participation, and that the frequency of other types of political activities declines with the time and energy required. It also shows that the South has fewer voters, proselytizers, button wearers, and contributors than other regions, but like other regions, it has a small minority of political activists.

Who Votes and Who Doesn't

Nonvoting does not occur uniformly throughout all segments of the population. National surveys conducted by the University of Michigan's Survey Research Center produced the following percentages for nonvoting for various groups in a presidential election:

Group Characteristic	Per Cent Nonvoting
Education	
Grade school	33
High school	19
College	10
Occupation	
Professional and managerial	12
Other white collar	16
Skilled and unskilled	22
Unskilled	32
Farm	23
Community	
Metropolitan area	18
Towns and cities	22
Rural areas	23
Race	
White	19
Negro	46
Labor	
Union	23
Nonunion	20
Religion	
Protestant	24
Catholic	15

The exact percentages as listed may change from one election to another, but the general pattern remains very stable. Nonvoting is associated with lower educational levels, unskilled occupations, rural living, nonmembership in organizations, and the especially deprived status in which large numbers of Negroes find themselves. High voter turnout is related to college education; professional, managerial, or other white collar occupations; metropolitan residence; and membership in voluntary associations. On the whole, Catholics and Jews vote more frequently than Protestants. Although these figures pertain only to voting, other forms of participation follow substantially the same pattern.

Nonvoting is sometimes viewed as a reflection of "alienation" from the political system. Political alienation involves a feeling that voting and other forms of participation are useless, that nothing is really decided by an election, and that the individual cannot personally influence the outcome of political events. The fact that nonvoting occurs most frequently among those at the bottom of the income, occupation, and education ladder in America tends to substantiate this view. Alienation occurs more frequently among those groups who have not shared in the general affluence of society. This interpretation is discouraging for those who cherish the democratic ideal, because it suggests that not all groups in society place a high value on democratic institutions.

Voting and the Law

The only mention of voting requirements in the Constitution of the United States as it was originally adopted is in Article I: "The electors in each state shall have the qualifications requisite for electors for the most numerous branch of the state legislature." Of course, "electors" (voters) for the most numerous branch of the state legislature are determined by *state* laws and constitutions. The effect of this constitutional provision was to leave to the states the power to determine who is eligible to vote in both state and federal elections. The constitutional power of the states to determine voter qualifications remains substantially in effect today, subject only to the provisions of the 14th, 19th, and 24th Amendments to the Constitution, which prohibit the states from using race, sex, or poll taxes as a qualification for voting.

Early in American history, the states chose to enact very restrictive voter eligibility standards: suffrage was limited to males over 21 years of age, who resided in the voting district for a certain period and owned a considerable amount of land or received a large income from other investments. So great was the fear that "the common man" would use his franchise to attack the rights of property, that only about 120,000 persons out of 2 million were permitted to vote in the 1780's. Men of property felt that only other men of property had sufficient "stake in society" to exercise their franchise in a "responsible" fashion—that is, use their franchise to elect men who would protect private property. But Jeffersonian and Jacksonian principles of democracy, including confidence in the reason and integrity of the common man, spread rapidly in the new Republic. Soon property qualifications were eliminated and suffrage was extended to great masses of people.

All 50 states have decided that only citizens should be permitted to vote. Aliens were permitted to vote in many states in the 19th century, but after World War I, open immigration was curtailed at the national level and all states made citizenship a requirement for voting.

All states have an age requirement. Forty-six states have adopted a minimum voting age of 21; Georgia and Kentucky have reduced minimum age to 18, Alaska to 19, and Hawaii to 20. The question of lowering the voting age from 21 to 18 will doubtless continue to be raised in the states as long as young men of that age are required to fight in the nation's wars. Georgia was the first state to reduce the voting age to 18—in 1943 when men 18 years old were being drafted for military service. The Georgia experience suggests that younger voters behave in much the same fashion as older voters: there is no evidence that lowering the voting age had any significant impact on the politics of that state. One result of 18 year old voters is that college campuses become a favorite platform for political candidates. Campus politics in many states are largely "mock" politics, in which the candidates take relatively little interest; but real votes are at stake on Georgia campuses, and politicians tend to have a greater respect for student political activity.

All states also have a residence requirement for voting. The required period of residence varies considerably from state to state, with one year of residence in the state and 90 days in the county voting district as an average period. Six states (Idaho, Kansas, Maine, Michigan, Minnesota, Nevada, Oregon) have the very modest requirement of only six months' residence in the state and 30 days in the county. At the other extreme, Alabama, Mississippi, and South Carolina appear reluctant to extend the vote to "outsiders." They require two years in the state and one year in the county before becoming eligible to vote. It is estimated that residence requirements disenfranchise 3 to 5 per cent of the population. They are particularly troublesome to mobile young people, and these requirements will become more troublesome as the population becomes increasingly mobile. Even if residence requirements could be justified in state and local elections on the grounds that the new arrival does not understand state and local issues, there is little justification for residence requirements in

TABLE 3.2

ELECTION LAWS IN THE STATES

State	1964 Presidential turnout	Age	Residence	Presidential voting for new residents	Presidential voting for former residents	Literacy test
Alabama	34.1	21	1 yr.	No	No	Yes
Alaska	40.0	19	1 yr.	No	No	No
Arizona	54.6	21	1 yr.	Yes	Yes	Yes
Arkansas	50.1	21	1 yr.	No	No	No
California	62.7	21	1 yr.	Yes	No	Yes
Colorado	67.1	21	1 yr.	Yes	No	No
Connecticut	71.7	21	1 yr.	Yes	Yes	Yes
Delaware	70.2	21	1 yr.	No	No	Yes
Florida	49.9	21	1 yr.	No	No	No
Georgia	39.4	18	1 yr.	No	No	Yes
Hawaii	53.4	20	1 yr.	No	No	Yes
Idaho	75.3	21	6 mo.	Yes	No	No
Illinois	72.9	21	1 yr.	Yes	No	No
Indiana	73.3	21	6 mo.	No	No	No
Iowa	72.0	21	6 mo.	No	No	No
Kansas	63.8	21	6 mo.	Yes	No	No
Kentucky	52.6	18	1 yr.	No	No	No
Louisiana	47.1	21	1 yr.	No	No	Yes
Maine	65.0	21	6 mo.	Yes	No	Yes
Maryland	56.6	21	1 yr.	No	Yes	No
Massachusetts	67.1	21	1 yr.	Yes	No	Yes
Michigan	68.8	21	6 mo.	No	No	No
Minnesota	76.3	21	6 mo.	No	No	No
Mississippi	33.2	21	2 yrs.	No	No	Yes
Missouri	62.9	21	1 yr.	Yes	No	No
Montana	69.5	21	1 yr.	No	No	No
Nebraska	63.2	21	6 mo.	Yes	No	No
Nevada	54.5	21	6 mo.	No	No	No
New Hampshire	72.9	21	6 mo.	No	No	Yes
New Jersey	67.2	21	6 mo.	Yes	Yes	No
New Mexico	63.6	21	1 yr.	No	No	No
New York	61.9	21	1 yr.	No	No	Yes
North Carolina	52.2	21	1 yr.	No	No	Yes
North Dakota	67.3	21	1 yr.	No	No	No
Ohio	66.5	21	1 yr.	Yes	No	No
Oklahoma	62.4	21	6 mo.	No	No	Yes
Oregon	67.1	21	6 mo.	Yes	No	Yes
Pennsylvania	65.0	21	1 yr.	No	No	No
Rhode Island	66.3	21	1 yr.	No	No	No
South Carolina	38.5	21	1 yr.	No	No	Yes
South Dakota	72.6	21	1 yr.	No	No	No
Tennessee	51.2	21	1 yr.	No	No	No
Texas	44.0	21	1 yr.	No	No	No
Utah	77.0	21	1 yr.	No	No	No
Vermont	67.8	21	1 yr.	No	Yes	No

State	1964 Presidential turnout	Age	Residence	Presidential voting for new residents	Presidential voting for former residents	Literacy test
Virginia	40.9	21	1 yr.	No	No	No
Washington	64.6	21	1 yr.	No	No	Yes
West Virginia	74.5	21	1 yr.	No	No	No
Wisconsin	70.5	21	1 yr.	Yes	Yes	No
Wyoming	69.9	21	1 yr.	No	Yes	Yes

presidential elections. Fifteen states now permit new residents to vote for the President, before they are eligible to vote for state and local officials. Seven states permit former residents to vote in presidential elections if they are not yet eligible to vote in their new state of residence.

All but four states (Alaska, Arkansas, North Dakota, Texas) have established a system of voting registration. Presumably, registration helps to prevent fraud and multiple voting in elections. Registration may be either permanent (once a voter is on a registration list, he remains there until he leaves the district), or periodic (voters must reregister at periodic intervals ranging from one to ten years). Some states will accept a record of having voted sometime during the registration period as a substitute for reregistration. This system requires no initiative on the part of the voter in keeping his name on the list of eligibles. As a matter of practice, registration lists are usually out of date whether registration is permanent or periodic. Persons who have died or moved away can always be found on registration lists, and the opportunity for fraud may be just as prevalent under registration as it would be without any registration. It is quite common in Philadelphia for registered voters to outnumber the population in many city wards, and on occasion, the number of votes cast in a ward have exceeded its population.

Registration procedures can be employed to facilitate or to hinder voting. In many localities registration is deliberately made inconvenient. It may require a trip to the county courthouse, registration forms may be deliberately complicated, or literacy tests may be required. In contrast, many communities have adopted mobile registration systems, where registrars canvass door to door or booths are established conveniently in shopping centers on well publicized days preceding elections.

Nineteen states require literacy tests. The Civil Rights Act of 1964 requires that literacy tests be given in writing and that a sixth grade education shall be a presumption of literacy. The Voting Rights Act of 1965 authorizes the Attorney General to suspend such tests in counties where there is evidence that they were used for racial discrimination. The argument on behalf of literacy tests is that the ability to read is a prerequisite to good judgment in elections. But opponents of literacy tests argue that there is no real evidence that illiterates have poorer judgments than literates, nor is there any way of establishing what constitutes "good judgment." They also argue that the opportunity to participate in government is the right of all men, whether literate or not. Finally, literacy may no longer be as important in making political judgments now that most voters get their information from television.

Securing the Right to Vote

It is difficult to imagine a clearer or more specific guarantee of individual liberty than that contained in the 15th Amendment: "The right of the citizens of the United States to vote shall not be denied or abridged by the United States or any state on account of race, color, or previous condition of servitude." The object of this amendment, passed by the Reconstruction Congress and adopted in 1870, was to extend suffrage to former Negro slaves and prohibit voter discrimination on the basis of race. The 15th Amendment also gives Congress the power to enforce Negro voting rights "by appropriate legislation." Thus, the states retained their right to determine voter qualifications, *so long as they do not practice racial discrimination*, and Congress was given the power to pass legislation insuring Negro voting rights.

It is a tribute to the ingenuity of southern statesmen that they were able to defeat the purpose of this amendment for almost a century. While social and economic pressures and threats of violence succeeded in intimidating many thousands of would-be voters, most southern statesmen preferred more "legal" methods of disenfranchisement.

For many years the most effective means of banning Negro voting was a technique known as the "white primary." So strong was the Democratic party throughout the South that the Democratic nomination for public office was tantamount to election. This meant that *primary* elections to chose the Democratic nominee were the only elections in which real choices were made. If Negroes were prevented from voting in Democratic primaries they could be effectively disenfranchised. Thus southern leaders resorted to the simple device of declaring the Democratic party in southern states a private club and ruling that only white persons could participate in its elections, that is, in *primary* elections. Negroes would be free to vote in "official," general elections, but all whites tacitly agreed to support the Democratic, or "white man's" party, in general elections, regardless of their differences in the primary. Not until 1944, in Smith v. Allright, did the Supreme Court declare this practice unconstitutional: "When primaries become part of the machinery in choosing officials, state and national, as they have here, the same tests to determine the character of discrimination . . . should be applied to the primary as are applied to the general election." [2] The white primary was declared to be a violation of the 15th Amendment.

Negro voting in the South increased substantially after World War II. From an estimated 5 per cent of voting age Negroes registered in southern states in the 1940's, Negro registration rose to an estimated 20 per cent in 1952, 25 per cent in 1956, 28 per cent in 1960, and 39 per cent in 1964. This last figure is a little more than half of the comparable figure for white registration in the South. However, most of this increase in Negro registration occurred in urban areas of the South. Prior to 1965, in hundreds of rural counties throughout the South, no Negroes had ever been permitted to vote. Despite the 15th Amendment, local registrars in the South succeeded in barring Negro registration by means of an endless variety of obstacles, delays, and frustrations. Application forms for registration were lengthy and complicated; even a minor error would lead to rejection, like underlining rather than circling in the "Mr.-Mrs.-Miss" set of choices as instructed. Literacy tests were the most common form of disenfranchisement. Many a Negro college graduate failed to interpret "properly" the complex legal documents that were part of his test. Moreover, many tests required the applicant to demonstrate to the registrar "a reasonable understanding of the duties and obligations of citizenship under the constitutional form of government." In the unlikely event that a Negro succeeded in passing such tests, he would then be required to convince the registrar that he was of "good character," and that he had paid his poll taxes. Often the law requires that an applicant's name be published in the newspaper for two weeks. Needless to say, white applicants for voter registration were seldom asked to go through these lengthy procedures.

The Civil Rights Act of 1964 made it unlawful for registrars to apply unequal standards in registration procedures, or to reject applications because of immaterial errors. It required that literacy tests be in writing and made a sixth grade education a presumption of literacy. The 24th Amendment to the Constitution was ratified in 1964, making poll taxes unconstitutional as a requirement for voting in national elections. In 1965 the Supreme Court declared poll taxes unconstitutional in state and local elections as well.[3] Yet in Selma, Alabama, in early 1965, civil rights organizations effectively demonstrated that local registrars were still keeping large numbers of Negroes off the voting rolls. Registrars closed their offices for all but a few hours every month, placed limits on the number of applications processed, went

[2] Smith v. Allright, 321 U.S. 649 (1944).
[3] Harper v. Virginia State Board of Elections, 383 U.S. 663 (1966).

out to lunch when Negro applicants appeared, delayed months before processing Negro applications, and discovered a variety of other methods to keep Negroes disenfranchised. It became apparent that a registrar who wanted to keep Negroes from voting could always find a way to do so if he tried hard enough, regardless of the law.

In response to the Selma episode, Congress enacted a strong Voting Rights Act in 1965 designed to fulfill the 15th Amendment's promise that the right to vote shall not be denied because of race. The Act applied to any state or county, where (1) the literacy test or similar qualifying device was enforced as of November 1, 1964, and (2) fewer than 50 per cent of voting age residents either were registered or cast ballots in the 1964 presidential election. In these areas, the Attorney General upon evidence of voter discrimination was empowered to replace local registrars with federal registrars, abolish literacy tests, and register voters under simplified federal procedures. Opponents of the new law argue that it interfered with the historic right of states to determine voter qualifications. Article I of the Constitution declares that "the electors in every state shall have the qualifications requisite for electors in the most numerous branch of the state legislature." However, a constitutional amendment by definition takes precedence over earlier language in a constitution. The 15th Amendment prohibited racial discrimination in voting and gave Congress the power to enforce this prohibition "by appropriate legislation." In 1966 the Supreme Court took notice of the long history of discrimination by southern voting registrars and upheld the Voting Rights Act of 1965 as "appropriate legislation" in the fight against voter discrimination.[4]

Thus far, federal registrars have been sent to only a small number of southern counties. Many southern counties which had previously discriminated in voting registration hurried to sign up Negro voters just to avoid the imposition of federal registrars. The Negro vote is now very important in the South. President Johnson's plurality in 1964 was smaller than the Negro vote in four southern states—Arkansas, Tennessee, Virginia, and Florida. This suggests that without Negro votes those four states might have ended up in the Goldwater column.

However, it is important to remember that the Negro is still a minority in every state in the Union, and that he goes to the polls only half as frequently as whites. Unless the Negro wins some white support, he cannot achieve success at the polls. In any election in which Negroes and whites divide strictly along racial lines, the Negro will suffer heavy defeat. In Georgia, for example, even if Negroes vote solidly for a particular candidate, that candidate must also win more than one-third of the white vote in order to achieve victory.

[4] South Carolina v. Katzenbach, 383 U.S. 301 (1966).

□

TABLE 3.3

THE NEGRO POTENTIAL FOR ELECTORAL INFLUENCE IN THE SOUTH

	Voting age population (in thousands)	Negro population (in thousands)	Negro percent voting age population
Alabama	1,834	841	45.9
Arkansas	1,043	192	18.4
Florida	3,088	464	15.0
Georgia	2,410	610	25.3
Louisiana	1,804	511	28.3
Mississippi	1,171	420	35.9
North Carolina	2,557	535	20.9
South Carolina	1,266	371	29.3
Tennessee	2,093	312	14.9
Texas	5,534	639	11.5
Virginia	2,313	432	18.8

Source: U.S. Bureau of the Census, *Statistical Abstract.*

Interest Groups in Political Life

Membership in a political interest group is an important form of political participation, and interest group activity is an important aspect of political life.[5] Political interest groups arise when individuals with a common interest decide that by banding together and by consolidating their strength, they can exercise more influence over public policy than they could as individuals acting alone. The impulse toward organization and collective action is particularly strong in a society of great size and complexity. As societies become more urban and industrial, individual action in politics gives way to collective action by giant organizations of businessmen, farmers, professionals, laborers, as well as racial, religious, and ideological groups. As Earl Latham explained: "Organization represents concentrated power, and concentrated power can exercise dominating influence when it encounters power which is diffused and not concentrated and therefore weaker." [6]

Groups may be highly organized into formal organizations with offices and professional staffs within the state capitals of every state: the National

[5] See Harmon Zeigler, *Interest Groups in American Society* (Englewood Cliffs, N.J.: Prentice-Hall, Inc., 1964).

[6] Earl Latham, "The Group Basis of Politics," *American Political Science Review*, 46 (June, 1952), 387.

Association of Manufacturers, the AFL-CIO, and the National Education Association are examples of highly organized interest groups that operate in every state. Other groups have little formal organization and have been unable to organize themselves very effectively for political action: an example of such a group would be American consumers. Political interest groups may be organized around occupational or economic interests (for example, the American Farm Bureau Federation, the National Association of Real Estate Boards, the United States Chamber of Commerce), or on racial or religious bases (for example, the National Association for the Advancement of Colored People, National Council of Churches, the Anti-Defamation League of B'nai B'rith), or around shared experiences, (for example, the American Legion, the Veterans of Foreign Wars, the League of Women Voters, Automobile Association of America), or around ideological positions (for example, Americans for Democratic Action, Americans for Constitutional Action).

Many scholars believe that economic interests tend to exercise more influence in American politics than noneconomic interests. Nearly 175 years ago, James Madison in *The Federalist,* No. 10, spoke about the power of "a land interest, a manufacturing interest, a mercantile interest, a moneyed interest, and many lesser interests" in the new American nation. But certainly the proliferation of active noneconomic groups in America, from the American Legion to the League of Women Voters to the National Society for the Prevention of Cruelty to Animals, testifies to the importance of organization in all phases of political life. Particularly active at the state level are the businesses subject to extensive regulation by state governments. The truckers, railroads, and liquor interests are consistently found to be among the most highly organized groups in state capitals. State chapters of the National Education Association are active in state capitals, presenting the demands of educational administrators and teachers. Even local governments and local government officials organize themselves to present their demands at state capitals.

It is very difficult to get a comprehensive picture of interest group activity in state capitals. Many organizations, business, legal firms, and individuals engage in interest group activity of one kind or another, and it is difficult to keep track of their varied activities. Many states require the registration of "lobbyists" and the submission of reports about their membership and finances. These laws do not restrain lobbying (that would probably violate the First Amendment freedom to "petition the government for redress of grievances"). Rather they are meant to spotlight the activities of lobbyists. However, many hundreds of lobbyists never register under the pretext that they are not *really* lobbyists, but instead, businesses, public relations firms, lawyers, researchers, or educational people. Thus, only the larger, formal, organized interest groups are officially registered as lobbyists in the states.

For example, the following list of organizations that were active in the Pennsylvania legislature greatly underestimated the extent of interest group activity:

Pennsylvania Motor Truck Federation
Pennsylvania Nurses Association
Pennsylvania Bankers Association
Pennsylvania Grange
Pennsylvania Hotels Association
Chiefs of Police Association
Pennsylvania Health Council
Pennsylvania Mental Health Inc.
Pennsylvania Economy League Inc.
Pennsylvania Bar Association
Association of Colleges and Universities
Pennsylvania Educational Association (NEA)
Federation of Women's Clubs

AFL-CIO
Pennsylvania Medical Society (AMA)
Pennsylvania State Chamber of Commerce
Council of General Contractors
Pennsylvania State School Directors
Congress of Parents and Teachers
Pennsylvania Electric Association
League of Cities
League of Women Voters
Pennsylvania Pharmaceutical Association
Pennsylvania Gas Association
Pennsylvania Farm Bureau Federation

A list of formal organizations excludes individual businesses that engage in interest group activity; the Pennsylvania Railroad, for example, is one of the most influential interests in Pennsylvania politics and maintains full time professional representation in the state capitol. Many smaller businesses maintain part time lobbyists or contract with law firms that specialize in representing businesses in government. These lobbyists and business representatives help to sell their company's services or products to government agencies, handle their company's relations with administrative and regulatory agencies, and attempt to influence legislation in which their company has an interest. In almost every state, there are hundreds of professional organizations, from accountants to undertakers, and most of these have engaged in lobbying activity from time to time. State chapters of the National Education Association and the American Medical Association are perhaps the most influential of these professional groups. In addition to the activities of the AFL-CIO, individual labor unions—United Automobile Workers, United Steel Workers, International Association of Machinists, International Brotherhood of Teamsters, United Mine Workers, and so on— are also active in state capitols on behalf of working men and women. American farmers generally have a number of trade associations speaking for them in specialized fields—cattlemen, sheepmen, poultry producers, and citrus growers, for example—and three organizations attempt to speak for all farmers at both the state and national level—the American Farm Bureau Federation, the National Grange, and the National Farmers Union.

One way to assess interest group activity is to ask state legislators what groups, if any, they perceive as being powerful in state politics. This was

TABLE 3.4

INTEREST GROUPS IN FOUR STATES MOST FREQUENTLY MENTIONED
BY STATE LEGISLATORS

California	*New Jersey*
California Teachers Association	New Jersey Education Association
AFL-CIO	Chamber of Commerce
California Farm Bureau	AFL-CIO
California Medical Association	New Jersey Municipal League
League of California Cities	New Jersey Taxpayer Association
Chamber of Commerce	New Jersey Manufacturer's Association
PTA(s)	League of Women Voters
League of Women Voters	New Jersey Farm Bureau
California State Grange	PTA(s)
Legislative Committee	
California Taxpayers Association	

Ohio	*Tennessee*
Ohio Farm Bureau	Tennessee Education Association
Ohio Education Association	Tennessee Municipal League
Chamber of Commerce	Tennessee Manufacturer's Association
Ohio State Grange	Tennessee County Services Association
AFL-CIO	Tennessee Farm Bureau
Ohio Manufacturer's Association	"Trading Stamps"
Ohio Council of Retail Merchants	AFL-CIO
Ohio Medical Association	Tennessee Taxpayers Association
League of Women Voters	PTA(s)
PTA(s)	

Source: John Wahlke, et. al., *The Legislative System* (New York: John Wiley, 1962), p. 318-319.

the approach of authors of *The Legislative System*. In the course of their interviews, California state legislators referred to 56 specific organizations; New Jersey legislators named 38 or more organizations; Ohio legislators mentioned 60 organizations; and Tennessee lawmakers mentioned 40 organizations.[7] Some of the more frequently mentioned interest groups are listed in Table 3.4. Thus, there seems to be little doubt that most elected officials are aware of extensive organized interest group activity.

There is also considerable agreement among the state legislators about which types of interest groups are most powerful. Business interests were named in the *Legislative System* study as "most powerful groups" more

[7] John C. Wahlke, *et al.*, *The Legislative System* (New York: John Wiley & Sons, Inc., 1962), pp. 311–42.

often than any other interests in all four states. Educational interests rank second in three states and tie for third in the fourth, and labor interests rank third in all four states. Agricultural interests, government interests, (the associations of city, county, and township governments and government employee associations), ethnic and demographic interests, and religious, charitable, and civic interests were given some mention as powerful interests.

Functions and Tactics of Interest Groups

Both interest groups and political parties organize individuals to make claims upon government, but these two forms of political organizations differ in several respects. An interest group seeks to influence specific policies of government—it does not seek to achieve control over government as a whole. A political party concentrates on winning public office in elections and is somewhat less concerned with policy questions. An interest group does not ordinarily run candidates for public office under its own banner, although it may give influential support to candidates running under a party banner. Finally, the basic function of a political party in a two party system is to organize a *majority* of persons for the purpose of governing. In contrast, an interest group gives political expression to the interests of *minority* groups.

In a democracy, where decisions are made by majority rule, it is particularly important that minorities have a means of expressing themselves. Organized interest group activity offers a form of protection for minorities when the faint preferences of a majority threaten the vital interest of a minority. The threatened minority can be expected to engage in intense political activity and, in so doing, ward off the threat to its vital interest. In short, interest group activity can function to represent intensity of feelings in minorities and to blunt the effects of majoritarianism.

Interest groups are also essential in representing interests that are not geographically defined in American society. The formal structure of American government does not recognize functional interest groupings—such as businessmen, laborers, farmers, Negroes, Catholics, and so on—but territorial divisions instead—such as cities, counties, legislative districts, and states. Interest groups supplement the formal system of territorial representation in American government by providing for an internal system of functional representation.

Interest groups also function to stimulate interest and participation in politics among their members. They often pressure candidates to clarify their stands on issues in an election, and they perform an important information and education function for public officials and citizens alike.

Interest group techniques are as varied as the imaginations of their leaders. Groups are attempting to advance their interests when a liquor firm sends a case of bourbon to a state legislator; when the John Birch Society distributes its books to public school children; when the League of Women Voters distributes biographies of political candidates; when an insurance company argues before a state insurance commission that insurance rates must be increased; when the National Educational Association provides state legislators with information comparing teachers' salaries in the 50 states; when railroads ask state highway departments to place weight limitations upon trucks; when the American Civil Liberties Union supplies lawyers for civil rights demonstrators; or when theatre owners testify in legislative committee hearings against the adoption of daylight savings time. Let us try to classify the many techniques of interest groups under three major headings—public relations, electioneering, and lobbying.

Most people think of interest group tactics as direct attempts to influence decision-makers, but these groups spend more of their time, energy, and resources in general public relations activities than anything else. The purpose of a continuing public relations campaign is to create an environment favorable to the interest group and its program. It is hoped that a reservoir of public good will can be established, which can be relied on later when a critical issue arises. Generally, business interests have a distinct advantage over nonbusiness interests in public relations. Business interests already have at their disposal public relations skills of their advertising departments. The cost of business public relations campaigns can be regarded as tax deductible, operating costs.

Electioneering is a common practice among interest groups. If a candidate who is already favorably inclined toward a particular interest can be elected, the group is reassured that its interests will be protected once he has taken office. On the whole, it is a good strategy for interest groups to remain in the background during campaigns—making monetary contributions to their favorite candidates, offering their public relations skills to them, or exorting their own members to support them. Political campaigns are very expensive, and it is always difficult for a candidate to find enough money to finance his campaign. This is true for officeholders seeking reelection as well as new contenders. It is perfectly legal for an interest group to make a large contribution to a candidate's campaign fund. Ordinarily, a respectable lobbyist would not be so crude as to exact any specific pledges from a candidate in exchange for a campaign contribution. He simply makes a contribution and lets the candidate figure out what he should do when in office to assure further contributions for his next campaign.

It is considered bad taste for an interest group to make a campaign contribution to a state legislator at the very time that a bill in which the group is interested is being considered. However, interest group activity in state capitals may be somewhat cruder—if not actually corrupt—than interest group activity in Washington. In interviewing lobbyists and legislators in Washington, Lester Milbrath found that they considered state lobbying much more corrupt than national lobbying:[8] "Lobbying is very different before state legislators; it is much more individualistic. Maybe this is the reason they have more bribery in state legislatures than in Congress." "In the state legislatures, lobbying is definitely on a lower plane. The lobbyists are loose and hand out money and favors quite freely." "Lobbying at the state level is cruder, more basic, and more obvious." "Lobbying at the state level is faster and more freewheeling and less visible; that is why it is more open to corruption."

Needless to say, it is difficult to document such activity. However, it seems reasonable to believe that state legislators are more subject to the pressures and appeals of organized interest groups than congressmen. State legislators meet less often and for shorter periods of time than Congress, and consequently, most state legislatures have not developed the formal and informal rules governing their behavior that exist in the U.S. Congress. State legislators are less likely to assume the "professional" attitude that characterizes many congressmen; state legislators are more likely to regard their legislative careers as secondary aspects of their lives. Moreover, state legislators make less money than congressmen, and therefore may be more vulnerable to the appeals of interest groups offering financial support.

"Lobbying" is defined as any communication, by someone acting on behalf of a group, directed at a government decision maker with the hope of influencing his decision. Direct persuasion is usually more than just a matter of argument or emotional appeal to the lawmaker. Often it involves the communication of useful technical and political information. Many public officials are required to vote on, or decide about, hundreds of questions each year. It is impossible for them to be fully informed about the wide variety of the bills and issues they face. Consequently, many decision makers come to depend upon the skilled lobbyists to provide technical information about matters requiring action and to inform them of the policy preferences of important segments of the population. A state legislator or administrator may call upon the Chamber of Commerce, the AFL-CIO, or the National Education Association to inform him about the views of businessmen, labor, or teachers on a particular issue.

---

[8] Lester Milbrath, *The Washington Lobbyists* (Chicago: Rand McNally & Co., 1963), pp. 241–43; also cited by Harmon Zeigler, "Interest Groups in the States," *Politics in the American States,* Herbert Jacob and Kenneth Vines, eds. (Boston: Little, Brown and Company, 1965), p. 104.

A Case of Pressure Politics: The Railroads versus the Truckers

A classic example of pressure politics was the dispute in Pennsylvania in the early 1950's over the weight limitations on trucks.[9] The weight load a truck may carry is a matter of state law. For many years Pennsylvania had one of the lowest permissible truck weights in the country. For three-quarters of a century, the Pennsylvania Railroad had virtually undisputed power in Pennsylvania. This did not result so much from bribery or overt pressure, as from a widespread feeling that "what is good for the Pennsylvania Railroad, is good for Pennsylvania." But the accelerated growth of the trucking industry after World War II created serious competition for the railroads. By the 1950's the truckers had become a sizable political force in their own right. Pennsylvania is the keystone state in east-west traffic in the nation, and the weight limitation seriously affected truck transportation. Democratic victories in the early 1950's encouraged the truckers to believe that the time had arrived for raising the permissible truck weights. Democratic legislators in Pennsylvania generally owe very little to the Pennsylvania Railroad, since "the Pennsy" had long been a bulwark of the Republican party in that state.

The "Pennsy," sensing that the truckers were about to make their move, formed an Eastern Railroads President's Conference and hired a professional public relations firm to plan and execute a countercampaign against the truckers. Carl Bryor and Associates, Inc. planned a grassroots campaign of suspicion and resentment against heavy trucks that travel the roads. The campaign tried to take advantage of motorists' hostility toward large trucks and to emphasize the theme that large trucks are destroying the roads and taxpayers are forced to pay for these damages. Bryor insisted that the railroads remain in the background in his public relations campaign and used other groups—motorists, property owners, taxpayers, farmers, or women's groups—to circulate their anti-truck propaganda. Shortly after the Bryor firm was hired, the following articles appeared in national magazines: *Everybody's Digest* contained an article entitled "The Giants That Wreck Our Highways." The message: "Heavy trucks are making their runs on your tax dollars." *The Reader's Digest* contained an article entitled "The Rape of Our Roads." The message: "Overloaded trucks are breaking up our highways faster than we can find money to repair them." *Harper's* contained an article entitled "Our Roads are Going to Pot." Its message: "Trucks have apparently been a large factor in hastening highway destruction." *The Saturday Evening Post*'s article, entitled "Are Trucks Destroying Our Highways?" contained the message: "Giant trailer rigs, some weighing close to

<hr>

[9] The following case study is taken from Andrew Hacker, "Pressure Politics in Pennsylvania: The Truckers v. The Railroads," *The Uses of Power,* Alan F. Westin, ed. (New York: Harcourt, Brace & World, Inc., 1962).

80 tons, speed overland by night hitting back roads to dodge weight inspectors." *Argosy* contained an article entitled, "Hell on Wheels," and its message was: "Gunning his big trailer-truck up to 60, often driving 24 hours without a rest, breaking the law, and risking his life, Butch Watson is typical of the tough breed of gypsy truckers."

The Bryor organization took credit for these articles, saying that they were better than straight advertising since readers suspect that the advertiser has some self-serving ax to grind. Readers are more likely to accept ideas they find in news stories or feature articles.

The trucking industry, however, had its own resources. The Pennsylvania Motor Truck Federation had members in every Pennsylvania county, and these owners or operators of trucking firms were relatively wealthy men, who were often prominent locally and could exert influence on the legislators throughout the state. The federation collected a large war chest from its members and proceeded to make generous campaign contributions to Democrats and Republicans alike. The federation was nonpartisan in its cultivation of votes, and news of its generosity toward candidates spread rapidly. One state legislator wrote to the Federation: "I am again a candidate for the legislature. What, if any, assistance can I expect from your association? I can assure you that I do not forget my friends." Needless to say, the Federation saw to it that this aspiring legislator's campaign fund was generously increased. The truckers invested a great deal of money throughout the state, but this expenditure would be more than recouped by the new profits that would result from increasing the weight limit.

While the Bryor organization was recruiting support of the automobile association, business groups, and county and township officials, and placing articles and stories attacking the truckers, the Pennsylvania legislature was considering its bill to raise truck rates. The Pennsylvania Motor Truck Association had done an effective lobbying job with legislators. Despite the climate of opinion created by the antitruck messages, the Pennsylvania legislators paid their campaign debt to the truckers by voting through the increase in weight limits. Both houses of the legislature gave large majorities to the bill and the scene quickly shifted to the office of Governor John S. Fine. He had the power to veto the bill, and in Pennsylvania, the legislature seldom overrides a governor's veto. The Governor, a Republican, was more in debt to the Pennsylvania Railroad than he was to the truckers. He took the unusual step of holding a public hearing, which 100 individuals from 94 organizations attended. Speaking against the bill were representatives from Pennsylvania Federation of Women's Clubs, the Keystone Auto Club, the Pittsburgh Auto Club, the Brotherhood of Railway Trainmen, the Brotherhood of Locomotive Firemen and Engineers, the Brotherhood of Railroad Conductors, the United Mine Workers, the Pennsylvania Grange, the Association of Township Supervisors, and of course, the Associated Railroads of Pennsylvania. Speaking for the bill were 24 persons representing the Teamsters Union, the major gasoline companies, the Automobile Industry, the Cement Industry, several construction unions, and the Pennsylvania Motor Truck Association.

To the dismay of the truckers, Governor Fine vetoed the bill. The truckers immediately proceeded to launch a devastating counterattack. At very modest expense, they secured the services of Miss Sonya Saroyan, a disgruntled employee of the Bryor firm, who defected to the enemy's camp and brought with her a complete file of the antitruck campaign. Armed with the Saroyan documents, the Pennsylvania Motor Truck Association and 37 trucking firms sued the Eastern Railroad Presidents' Conference, 31 railroads, and Carl Bryor and Associates for the sum of $250 million. Counsel for the truckers claimed that the railroads, in alliance with Bryor, had conspired to put the truckers out of the long-haul freight business in violation of the Sherman and Clayton antitrust laws. The truckers contended that the railroads, by means of a public relations campaign and the corruption of public officials, had caused them to lose the good will of their customers and the general public. The complete record of the Bryor activity was exposed. It was also argued that the railroads and Bryor had tried to damage the truckers by securing, through illegitimate means, statutory restrictions that would do them economic harm. The railroads were also accused of using unfair techniques to exert political pressure.

The railroads, in their defense, contended that they had retained Bryor to give them expert assistance in effectively exercising their rights under the First Amendment. The Association of Railroads, just like any other group, has the constitutional rights of free speech and petition. Free speech, they argued, gave them the right to point out the shortcomings of the trucking industry. As for working through other groups and publications instead of conducting the antitruck campaign in the name of the railroads, they argued that these organizations and publications agreed with the railroad position of their own free will. Railroad money and Bryor talent, in short, only subsidized groups that favored the railroad cause. The railroads claimed that the whole controversy was a political rather than an economic one. The entire campaign was one of political persuasion: bringing one's case to the general public is a legitimate and time-honored practice. Moreover, they argued that the application of pressure on lawmakers and executive officials was a necessary and desirable component of the democratic process.

The case reached the Supreme Court in 1961. In a unanimous opinion, Justice Hugo Black supported the position of the railroads:

> In a representative democracy such as this, these branches of government act on behalf of the people, and to a very large extent, the whole concept of representation depends upon the ability of the people to make

their wishes known to their representatives. . . . It is neither unusual nor illegal for people to seek action on laws in the hope that they may bring about an advantage to themselves and a disadvantage to their competitors. . . . Indeed it is quite probably people with just such a hope of personal advantage who provide much of the information upon which governments must act. . . . We have restored what seems to have been the true nature of the case—a "no holds barred" fight between two industries both of which are seeking a profitable source of income. Inherent in such fights, which are commonplace in the halls of legislative bodies, is the possibility, and in many instances even the probability, that one group or the other will get hurt by the arguments that are made. In this particular instance, each group appeared to have utilized all the political powers it could muster in an attempt to bring about the passage of laws that would help it or injure the other. But the contest itself appears to have been conducted along the lines normally accepted in our political system, except to the extent that each group has deliberately deceived the public and public officials.[10]

In the meantime, even before the case was decided, Pennsylvania elected a new governor, George Leader, a Democrat. The railroads did not support Leader in his campaign for the governorship, but instead gave their customary heavy support to the Republican candidate. Again, the legislature passed a bill raising truck weights, but this time the governor signed the bill into law.

Interest Groups in the States: A Comparative View

How can states be compared in terms of the strength of their interest groups? Some measure of "strength" must be developed by which the states can be ranked. But it is very difficult to measure the "strength" of interest groups, since this is a function of many factors including size, resources, organization, leadership, prestige, unity or "cohesion," and "access" (contacts) to decision makers. Thus, a strictly objective measure of interest group strength in each state is exceedingly difficult to obtain. However, some years ago the American Political Science Association sent questionnaires to political scientists located in several states, asking them to judge whether interest groups in their respective states were strong, moderately strong, or weak.[11] These judgments by political scientists are open to challenge, but they are probably the best available estimate of interest group strength in the states.

Harmon Zeigler used this "classification" to show that states with stronger interest groups are also more likely to be (1) one party states in contrast to competitive two party states, (2) states in which parties in the

---

[10] Hacker, *The Uses of Power*, p. 365.
[11] Belle Zeller, ed., *American State Legislatures* (New York: Thomas Y. Crowell Company, 1954), pp. 190–91.

TABLE 3.5

THE STRENGTH OF PRESSURE GROUPS IN VARYING POLITICAL
AND ECONOMIC SITUATIONS

Social conditions	Types of pressure system[a]		
	Strong[b]	Moderate[c]	Weak [d]
Party competition	(24 states)	(14 states)	(7 states)
One-party	33.3%	0%	0%
Modified one-party	37.5%	42.8%	0
Two party	29.1%	57.1%	100.0%
Cohesion of parties in legislature			
Weak cohesion	75.0%	14.2%	0%
Moderate cohesion	12.5%	35.7%	14.2%
Strong cohesion	12.5%	50.0%	85.7%
Socio-economic variables			
Urban	58.6%	65.1%	73.3%
Per capita income	$1900	$2335	$2450
Industrialization index	88.8	92.8	94.0

a. Alaska, Hawaii, Idaho, New Hampshire, and North Dakota are not classified
or included.
b. Alabama, Arizona, Arkansas, California, Florida, Georgia, Iowa, Kentucky,
Louisiana, Maine, Michigan, Minnesota, Mississippi, Montana, Nebraska, New
Mexico, North Carolina, Oklahoma, Oregon, South Carolina, Tennessee, Texas,
Washington, Wisconsin.
c. Delaware, Illinois, Kansas, Maryland, Massachusetts, Nevada, New York,
Ohio, Pennsylvania, South Dakota, Utah, Vermont, Virginia, West Virginia.
d. Colorado, Connecticut, Indiana, Missouri, New Jersey, Rhode Island,
Wyoming.
Source: Harmon Zeigler, "Interest Groups in the American States," Herbert
Jacob and Kenneth Vines, eds., Politics in the American States (Boston:
Little, Brown, & Co., 1965), p. 114.

legislature show little cohesion or unity, (3) states that are poor, rural, and
agricultural in character.[12] Zeigler notes that states that are wealthy, urban,
and industrial have *more* interest groups, but it is in these states that interest groups are more likely to balance each other and less likely to dominate
the political scene. Poor, rural, agricultural states may have *fewer* interest
groups, but it is in these states with relatively backward economies that
strong interest groups exercise considerable power over public policy.

Zeigler also identified several "pressure group patterns" in the states.[13]
The first pattern, "an alliance of dominant groups" was the typical pattern
in rural, agricultural states with one party politics and weak legislative

[12] Harmon Zeigler, Politics in the American States.
[13] Ibid., pp. 117–28.

unity among the parties. This pattern was descriptive of the southern states and of nonsouthern states without industrial economies, such as Maine.

> A good sample of this pattern is Maine, of which Lockhard writes: 'In few American states are the reins of government more openly or more completely in the hands of a few leaders of economic interest groups than in Maine.' Specifically, power, timber, and manufacturing —the big three—have proven to be the catalysts for much of the controversy in the state. While other interests occasionally voice demands, the big three clearly outdistance any rivals in political activity and power. Certainly the key position of these interests in the economy of the state contributes to their crucial position in the decision making process of the state. Over three-fourths of the state is woodland and most of this land is owned by a handful of timber companies and paper manufacturers. These interests, combined with power companies and textile and shoe manufacturers, are able—in so far as their well-being is directly involved—to 'control Maine politics.' [14]

A second pattern of "a single dominant interest" is found in rural nonindustrial states, but states with two party politics and moderate legislative unity, such as Montana. About Montana, Zeigler writes:

> In a state in which the extraction of minerals is the major nonagricultural source of personal income, Anaconda is the largest employer. While 'the company,' as it is known in Montana, began its operations in mining for copper, it now owns mills, aluminum companies, railroads, fabricating plants, and forests. The enormity of the Anaconda empire is described by Thomas Paine: 'Its strength rests not only in its wealth and resources, but also with its elaborate network of relationships with key citizens, banks, legal firms, and business organizations throughout the state. Rare is that unit of local government—county, city, or school district—that does not have among its official family an associate, in some capacity, of the Anaconda Company.' In addition, Anaconda controlled, until 1959, a chain of newspapers with a combined circulation greater than that of all the other daily papers in the state . . .
> The conflict in the state seemed to be structured around the company rather than the political parties. Wheeler writes: 'In the 1911–1912 legislature the Democrats controlled the House, the Republicans controlled the Senate, and the company controlled both . . .
> As its newspapers became concerned with its growing public image, it is not surprising that Anaconda in recent years has tended to remain as quiet as possible, confining itself to blocking adverse legislation and reducing its efforts to influencing the electoral process.[15]

The position of Anaconda in Montana is not much different than the position of oil companies in Texas or Dupont in Delaware. Of course, there

---

[14] *Ibid.,* p. 118.

[15] *Ibid.,* pp. 119–20; quotation from Thomas Paine, "Under the Copper Dome: Politics in Montana," Frank Jonas, *Western Politics* (Salt Lake City: University of Utah Press, 1961), pp. 197–98; quotation from Burton K. Wheeler with Paul Healy, *Yankee from the West* (Garden City: Doubleday & Company, Inc., 1962), p. 821.

is a difference between reputation for control and actual control of public policy. No doubt the reputation for control exceeds the actual control that these interests exercise over public policy. Undoubtedly, in large areas of state policy, these dominant groups have little interest and exercise little influence.

A third pattern described by Zeigler was that in which there is a "conflict between two dominant groups." This pattern is found in a nondiversified industrial economy with strong two party politics and legislative unity within the parties. Michigan is a prime example of this bipolar interest group pattern. Joseph LaPalombara writes: ". . . No major issues of policy (taxation, social legislation, labor legislation, and so on) are likely to be decided in Michigan, without the intervention, within their respective parties and before agencies of government, of automotive labor, and automotive management." [16] The United Automobile Workers Union is deeply involved in the affairs of the Democratic party, while the automobile manufacturers are deeply involved in the Republican party. In other words, labor and management in Michigan each have "their" political parties.

Another pattern of interest group activity was described by Zeigler as the "triumph of many interests." This pattern is found in urban states with industrial economies but relatively weak political parties. Party loyalty has never been strong in California, with many legislators and voters crossing party lines in their political activity. The lack of any effective and disciplined party organization in California paved the way for interest groups to exercise relatively unchecked influence in California politics. No one interest group dominated California politics, but especially during the "lobby era" of 1942–53, the initiation of public policy appeared to be largely the responsibility of organized groups in that state. The railroads, especially Southern Pacific, the California State Brewers Institute, the race tracks, motion pictures, citrus growers, airplane manufacturers, insurance companies, utilities, and a host of other interests maintained large offices in Sacramento, financially supported many state legislators, and largely dominated legislative affairs.

In states with strong party systems, one usually finds that interest groups are vigorous and active, but dependent upon parties for access to governmental decision makers. Strong parties appear to act as a check upon interest group influence. Interest groups must channel their contributions to candidates through the party organization, and as a consequence, candidates feel more in debt to their parties. Interest groups direct their appeals not to individual legislators so much as to party leaders. While the parties in such states come to represent coalitions of interest groups, the interven-

---

[16] Joseph LaPalombara, *Guide to Michigan Politics* (East Lansing: Michigan State University Press, 1960), p. 104; also cited by Zeigler, *Politics in the American States,* p. 123.

tion of parties appears to free candidates and officeholders from direct dependence upon interest groups.

What is the impact of interest groups on the structure of state government? Lewis A. Froman used the same classification of states by interest group strength that Zeigler employed in an interesting attempt to answer this question.[17] He found that the stronger the interest groups, the greater the number of state elected officials, and the greater the likelihood that state agencies would be headed by elected rather than appointed officials. He concluded that states with stronger interest groups are better able to isolate government agencies and officials from executive and legislative influence than states with weaker interest groups. Interest groups strive to isolate administrative agencies from the governor and the legislature in order to strengthen their own influence with these agencies. By weakening gubernatorial and legislative control over state administration, interest groups feel that they are more likely to be successful in exercising influence in administrative agencies.

[17] Lewis A. Froman, "Some Effects of Interest Group Strength in State Politics," *American Political Science Review,* 60 (December, 1966), 952-62.

4

PARTIES IN
STATE POLITICS

Parties in the Fifty States

Federalism has had a profound effect on the organization of American parties. Decentralization of power is the most important characteristic of American party organizations. These organizations are built around important public offices at the federal, state, and local level. Organizationally, the Democratic and Republican parties consist of a National Committee; a House and Senate party conference; various national clubs, such as Young Democrats and Young Republicans, and Democratic and Republican Women's Federations; and 50 state parties, which in turn are composed of state committees and county and city organizations. This structure is tied together very loosely. State parties are not very responsive to national direction, and in most states, city and county organizations operate quite independently of the state committees. State committees are generally involved in important statewide elections—governors, U.S. Senators, and Congressmen in the smaller states. City and county committees are generally responsible for county and municipal offices, state legislative seats, and congressional seats in the larger states. The Democratic and Republican national committees exist primarily for the purpose of holding national conventions every four years to select the presidential candidate. Since each level of party organization has "its own fish to fry," each operates quite independently of the other levels.

State parties are by no means merely local representatives of national firms. In fact, the national Democratic and Republican parties are often described as confederations of 50 distinct party organizations. National committees are meetings of state party organizations, not a board of directors that can dictate policy to the state parties. Both the Republican and Democratic National Committees consist of one man and one woman from every state party organization, together with representatives from the territories, and in the case of the Republicans, some "bonus" members awarded to states that voted Republican in recent elections. These national committees have relatively little power other than determining the city where the national convention will meet. National committees have no control over state party organizations. Even Democratic and Republican National Chairmen usually confine their activities to managing presidential campaigns and raising the necessary money to pay presidential campaign bills. In short, the political machinery of the national parties is quite separate from the machinery of state and local party organizations.

It is not surprising in the American system of federalism—where only the President and Vice President have *national* constituencies, and senators, congressmen, governors, state legislators, county and municipal officials all have *local* constituencies—that the American parties would be decentralized in their organization. Parties function to capture control of public office for their nominees, and most elective offices in the American political system are chosen by state and local constituencies rather than national constituencies. (One might say *all* elected offices in the U.S. are chosen by state or local constituencies, since the President and Vice President are really elected by the electoral votes of the states rather than the popular vote of the nation.) Elections in the U.S. are regulated and administered mainly by the 50 states, rather than the national government.

Party affairs are largely governed by the laws of the states. Each state sets forth the conditions that an organization must meet in order to qualify as a political party and to get its candidates' names printed on the official election ballots. Each state sets the qualifications for membership in a party, and the right to vote in the party's primary election. State laws determine the number, method of selection, and duties of various party officials, committees, and conventions. The states, rather than the parties themselves, decide how the parties shall go about nominating candidates for public office. Most states require that party nominations be made by direct primaries, but several states still nominate by party caucuses or conventions. Most states also attempt to regulate party finances, although with little success.

Since party organizations in the states are relatively autonomous from the national Democratic and Republican parties, we can expect a great deal of variation in party systems from state to state. First of all, the comparative strength of the Republican and Democratic parties obviously differs from state to state. States can also be differentiated by the level of interparty competition and by the strengths and functions of their party organizations. In some states, party conflict is very important, while in other states political alignments tend to reflect factional rivalries, competition among powerful interest groups, or conflict between liberals and conservatives or labor and industry. Some states can be characterized as one party states, while in other states more competitive situations exist. In some states, the Republican and Democratic parties offer substantially different policy positions on education, welfare, taxation, highways, and other important public issues. In other states, it is more difficult to distinguish a clear party position on these issues. In some states, the Democratic and Republican parties represent separate social and economic groups in the states: the Democratic party may be composed of central city, low income, ethnic, and racial constituencies, while the Republican party represents middle class, suburban, small town, and rural constituencies. However, in other states both parties may attempt to represent the same groups, and it is then difficult to detect any socio-economic differences between Democrats and Republicans.

The wide range of differences between state party systems means that state party organizations with the same party label may be quite different from one another. Often, state Democratic parties are further apart on policy matters from each other than from Republicans. The Minnesota and Mississippi Democratic parties, for example, have little in common except the party label. Variations in state Republican parties may be just as great: certainly the New York and Arizona Republicans are quite different from one another, not to mention the new Alabama Republicans. Each of these Republican and Democratic state parties is more a product of its statewide constituency than of any national Democratic or Republican organization. State parties are more inclined to fit their programs to popular demands within their states than to offer significantly different policy alternatives derived from national party differences. Democratic and Republican parties within a state are competing in the same vote market, and hence their policy positions have more in common with each other than with those of their counterparts in different states. In short, parties in each state tailor their policies to local conditions.

In this chapter we will endeavor not only to describe the structure and activities of state party systems, but also to compare state party systems and identify some of the causes and consequences of variations among the states.

One Party and Two Party States

Interparty competition has received a great deal of attention from political scientists studying state politics. Many political scientists have contended that competitive, responsible parties are necessary for effective democratic control of government in modern society.[1] The ideal party system is said to be one in which competitive parties present alternative programs in election campaigns, and the party winning the majority of votes captures all the power it needs to write its program into law. Moreover, in the ideal party system, the party's elected officials act cohesively, so the voters can hold the party collectively responsible for public affairs at the end of its term of public office. The key to this ideal party system is the existence of competitive parties, which are roughly balanced in strength.

The degree of party competition among the states varies a great deal. In the past, the Republican party in the deep southern states was practically nonexistent, and even today, despite the recent Republican upsurge in the South, the Republican party frequently fails to run candidates for governor, U.S. Senator, Congress, and the state legislature. Even though these southern states may be competitive in presidential elections, Democrats have continued to win state office by wide margins and dominate southern state legislatures by heavy majorities. The party systems in these states have been termed "one party Democratic." Republican domination in the midwestern and upper New England states has never been so complete that it warants the designation of a "one party system."

There are several important differences between one party states and two party states. Voters in two party states use party labels to help them identify the politics of candidates. The fact that a candidate runs under a Republican or Democratic label does not guarantee his stand on every public issue, but it indicates with which broad coalition in American politics a candidate has associated himself. Party labels carry meaning for most voters, even though individual candidates may be "disloyal" to their party on occasion. At the very least, a party label in a two party state tells more about a candidate's politics than a strange name on a ballot, with no party affiliation indicated.

A party label in a competitive state is a very conspicuous attribute of a candidate. One party states may have important "liberal" or "conservative" factions of some durability. But in two party states, the party label can be seen by every voter on election day. A party label is not so obscure as an alignment with a faction. Most students of state politics feel that it is more difficult to hold factions responsible. Factions are even more fluid, and change personality and policies more frequently than parties. Even in Lou-

---

[1] See Austin Ranney, *The Doctrine of Responsible Party Government* (Urbana: University of Illinois Press, 1954).

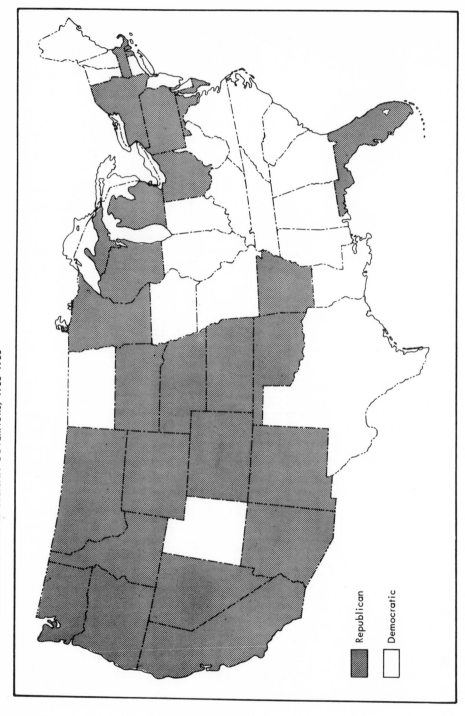

FIGURE 4.1 DEMOCRATIC AND REPUBLICAN GOVERNORS, 1966–1968

Republican

Democratic

isiana, which has one of the more durable, bifactional systems among the one party states, observers have felt that factionalism was "considerably inferior to two party politics." [2] V. O. Key argues that southern factional systems obscure politics for most voters and permit conservative interests to manipulate the voters.[3] A large number of people who have very little knowledge about the policies or memberships of various factions are easily misled. This does not mean that many voters are not confused about party policies in competitive states or that competitive parties can always hold their legislators responsible, but it does mean that party competition is more likely to clarify things for the voter than factional politics. Even if policy differences between the parties are vague, there is at least an "in-party" and an "out-party," which can be identified at election time. Finally, in one party states, and even in states with limited competition, the minority party often fails to run candidates for many offices. Under these circumstances, the party out of office is unable to perform the important role of criticizing officeholders. The existence of a competitive party *outside* of government, a party that has a real chance of replacing officeholders at the next election, can help to make officeholders more aware of their responsibilities to the voters. In a competitive two party system, the party out of power has the strongest kind of incentive for exposing the weaknesses of the ruling party.

In recent years political scientists have developed various ways of measuring interparty competition in the states. Figure 4.2 shows the distribution of the 50 states by levels of interparty competition in lower and upper houses of state legislatures and in governors' elections. This distribution of states by level of party competition focuses upon *state* offices and not upon a state's congressional delegation, its U.S. Senators, or its vote in presidential elections. Other students of state politics have included a wider range of offices in their measures of party competition, but these measures of party competition are directly related to the study of *state* government. Note that Figure 4.2 deals with the proportion of success achieved by the *majority* party in each state, regardless of whether the majority party is Democratic or Republican. Competition for control of lower houses of state legislatures was highest in Pennsylvania and Illinois over a ten year period, and lowest in Arkansas, Alabama, Louisiana, Mississippi, and South Carolina. In state senates, competition was high in New Jersey and Michigan, and low in Alabama, Arkansas, Louisiana, Mississippi, South Carolina, and Texas. Gubernatorial competition was highest in Illinois, Delaware, Wyoming, Mas-

[2] Alan P. Sindler, "Bifactional Rivalry as an Alternative to Two-Party Competition in Louisiana," *American Political Science Review,* 46 (1955), 641.

[3] V. O. Key, Jr. *Southern Poltics in State and Nation* (New York: Alfred A. Knopf, Inc., 1949).

FIGURE 4.2

DISTRIBUTION OF STATES BY LEVEL OF INTERPARTY COMPETITION, 1962–1966

Lower Houses

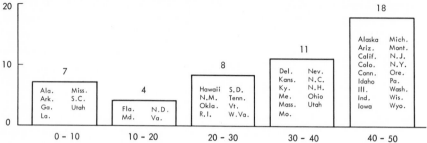

One Minus the Percentage of Seats Held by the Majority Party, 1962-1966

Upper Houses

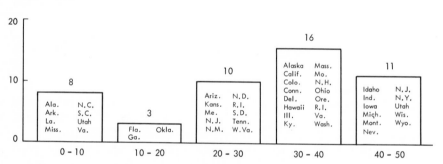

One Minus the Percentage of Seats Held by the Majority Party, 1962-1966

Governors

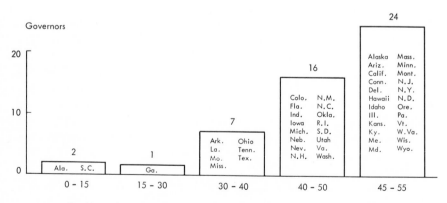

One Minus the Average Margin of Victory in Gubernatorial Elections, 1962-1966

sachusetts, Montana, New York, Michigan, New Jersey, and Minnesota, and lowest in Alabama and South Carolina.

Why do some states have competitive two party systems and others do not? Slavery and the subsequent status of the Negro in society had a great deal to do with one-partyism in the South.[4] A majority of white southerners were Democrats before the civil war, and the Republican party was founded to resist the spread of slavery. A Republican President wrote the Emancipation Proclamation and a Republican Congress wrote the 13th, 14th, and 15th Amendments and supervised the military occupation of the South. Also, one-partyism is characteristic of political systems in which large numbers of people are united in opposition to a perceived serious threat. One overriding sentiment in the South, which united both rich and poor, farmers and laborers, and all other groups of southern whites, was the desire to keep Negroes "in their place." One-partyism helped to exclude Negroes from effective political participation. Whites would handle their own squabbles within the Democratic party primary and unite behind the "white man's party" in the general election.

But this explanation, while helpful in understanding southern politics, fails to explain the lack of effective party competition in many states outside the South. Party competition also appears to be closely related to socio-economic conditions in the states. Party competition is greater in those urban, industrial states in which separate socio-economic groups reside. Rural agricultural states with homogeneous populations do not provide enough social division to support well organized, disciplined and competitive parties. Nationally, the Democratic party receives a disproportionate amount of support from Catholics and Jews; Negroes; less educated, lower income groups; younger people; skilled, semiskilled, and unskilled workers; union members; and big city residents. The Republican party receives disproportionate support from Protestants; whites; well educated, higher income groups; older people; professional, managerial, and other white collar workers; nonunion members; and rural and small town residents. It is not surprising, then, that competitive states tend to be those urban and industrial states with heterogeneous populations.

In large states, such as New York, Pennsylvania, and Illinois, the parties are first divided along rural-urban lines, and within urban areas, they are further divided on socio-economic bases. Republicans dominate in rural areas and in the wealthier urban areas (upper middle class suburbs and several "silk stocking" districts in the cities). Democratic districts are found predominantly in the less wealthy, urban areas of the state. A similar pattern emerges if occupational, religious, or racial characteristics are considered. Republican districts within urban areas prove to be the districts

[4] See V. O. Key, *Southern Politics in State and Nation.*

TABLE 4.1

SOCIO-ECONOMIC DEVELOPMENT AND PARTY CONTROL
OF STATE LEGISLATURES, 1954-62

| | Indices of economic development (Figures are mean scores) | | | |
	Urbanization	Industrialization	Income	Education
One party democratic: Over 70% both houses Democratic (16 states)[a]	55.2%	90.3%	$4448	9.5 yrs.
Democratic dominant: Over 50% both houses Democratic (12 states)[b]	69.3	93.3	6037	11.5
Divided: One house over 50% Democratic, one house Over 50% Republican (4 states)[c]	78.0	96.5	6578	11.5
Republican dominant: Over 50% both houses Republican (12 states)[d]	64.5	90.6	5762	10.9
One party Republican: Over 70% both houses Republican (4 states)[e]	44.5	82.1	4840	10.6

a. Alabama, Arkansas, Florida, Georgia, Kentucky, Louisiana, Maryland, Mississippi, New Mexico, North Carolina, Oklahoma, South Carolina, Tennessee, Texas, Virginia, West Virginia.
b. Alaska, Arizona, California, Colorado, Delaware, Hawaii, Massachusetts, Missouri, Montana, Oregon, Rhode Island, Washington.
c. Connecticut, Nevada, New Jersey, Utah.
d. Idaho, Illinois, Indiana, Kansas, Michigan, New Hampshire, New York, Ohio, Pennsylvania, South Dakota, Wisconsin, Wyoming.
e. Iowa, Maine, North Dakota, Vermont.
Source: U. S. Bureau of the Census, *Statistical Abstract.*

with greater concentrations of professional, managerial, sales, and clerical jobs. Republican candidates fare badly among Negro voters. The Democrats dominate in the ethnic districts with southern and eastern European, Irish, and Catholic voters. These are frequently the big city, mining, and mill districts. The Republicans draw heavily in the Anglo-Saxon, northern and western European, Protestant districts of these states. A high degree of party competition results from these socio-economic conditions within a state's electorate. In contrast, the less competitive states—for example,

Maine, Iowa, Vermont, New Hampshire, North and South Dakota—are more homogeneous in their social composition.

What difference does it make in public policy whether a state has competitive or noncompetitive parties? Do states with a competitive party system differ in their approach to education, welfare, health, taxation, or highways from states with noncompetitive party systems? This is not an easy question to answer. Since competitive states tend to be wealthy, urban, industrial states, and noncompetitive states poorer, rural, agricultural states, it is difficult to sort out the effects of party competition from these other socio-economic variables. Several scholars have asserted that a competitive party system leads to more liberal education, welfare, and taxation policies and that one-partyism strengthens conservative views; however, available evidence suggests that interparty competition does not play a really influential role in determining public policies in these fields. As we shall see in later chapters, education, welfare, taxation, and highway programs appear to be more closely related to socio-economic factors in the states than to the degree of party competition itself. However, as we have already observed, a lack of party competition can seriously affect the degree of popular control over state government and the ability of individuals to hold public officials responsible for the state of public affairs. Also, as we observed in Chapter 3, the lack of party competition appears to reduce voter participation in state politics.

The "ideal" party model, with its emphasis on responsibility, unity, and discipline may be ill suited to a complex, pluralistic society such as the United States. A large nation with many diverse interests might not be accommodated by a two party system in which the parties were highly centralized and disciplined. It is the relative irresponsibility of our parties, and the generality and ambiguity of their party platforms, that makes compromise possible in this nation. Neither party is so different from the other that members of the losing party will fail to support candidates of the winning party after they are elected to office. Austin Ranney has argued that an increase in responsibility, discipline, and unity in American parties might destroy the system rather than improve it: "To the extent that this [party irresponsibility] is an accurate description of our present national party system, it results, not from any mere organizational deficiency in our national party machinery, but rather from the diversity and multiplicity of our interest groups and the heterogeneity and complexity of the political conflict they express. As long as the basic nature of the American community remains the same, therefore, centralizing and disciplining our national parties would very likely result in a multiple party rather than a two party system." [5]

[5] See Austin Ranney, *The Doctrine of Responsible Party Government.*

TABLE 4.2

GOVERNORSHIPS AND STATE LEGISLATIVE CHAMBERS CONTROLLED
BY DEMOCRATS AND REPUBLICANS, 1954-1966

	Upper houses			Lower houses			Governorships	
	Dem.	*Rep.*	*Tie*	*Dem.*	*Rep.*	*Tie*	*Dem.*	*Rep.*
1966	29	18	1	25	22	1	24	26
1964	34	12	2	39	9	0	33	17
1962	28	20	0	27	20	1	33	17
1960	30	18	0	31	17	0	34	16
1958	31	17	0	28	9	1	35	15
1956	25	21	2	28	20	0	31	19
1954	20	25	1	26	20	0	27	21

Source: U.S. Bureau of the Census, *Statistical Abstract of the United States,
1966*, pp. 379-380.

Republican and Democratic Party Fortunes in the States

In recent years the Democratic party has dominated American state politics. Table 4.2 shows the number of upper and lower houses in state legislatures controlled by Democrats from 1954 through 1966, and the number of Democratic and Republican governors during that period. The Democratic party has fared very well in state senates; only in the 1954–1956 session did it control fewer senates than the Republican party. The Democratic party's control of lower houses has been even more pronounced: Democrats never controlled fewer than 25 lower houses at any time and have controlled as many as 39. Until 1966 the Democratic party also had success in controlling governors' chairs. Republican victories in 1966 gave the GOP a majority of governorships for the first time in over a decade. This majority was increased in 1968.

Because of these Democratic successes, any distribution of states according to the degree of Democratic or Republican party success will be skewed toward the Democratic party. Figure 4.3 shows the distribution of states by Democratic and Republican control of lower houses, upper houses, and governors' chairs between 1962 and 1966. Note that this distribution takes into account only *state* offices, not the state's congressional delegation, its United States Senators, or its vote in presidential elections. A state's political coloration in national politics may be quite different from its statewide political affiliations. In 1964, five Democratic states of the Old Confederacy—Alabama, Georgia, Louisiana, Mississippi, and South Carolina—voted for Republican presidential candidate Barry Goldwater, largely on the basis of his vote against the Civil Rights Act of 1964. Yet in these states, over 90 per cent of both houses of the legislature are

FIGURE 4.3

DISTRIBUTION OF STATES BY DEMOCRATIC AND REPUBLICAN CONTROL OF STATE
GOVERNMENT, 1962–1966

Lower Houses

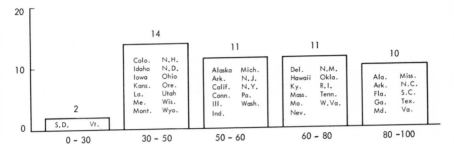

Percentage of Total Seats Held by Democrats, 1962–1966

Upper Houses

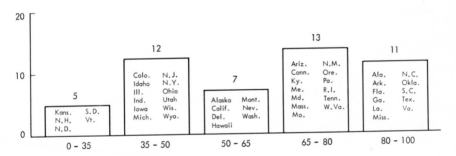

Percentage of Total Seats Held by Democrats, 1962–1966

Governors

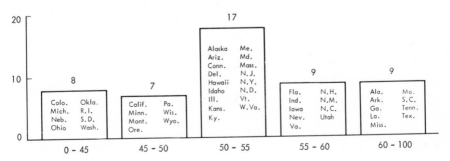

Average Democratic Percentage in Votes for Governor, 1962 –1966

Democratic, and with the exception of Georgia, Democratic gubernatorial nominees have received little opposition in general elections. In Goldwater's home state of Arizona, Democrats controlled over 70 per cent of the seats in the legislature in recent years. It is important to remember, therefore, that these measures of Democratic and Republican success deal with state rather than national politics.

Historically, southern states have accounted for much of the Democratic party's strength in state politics, while midwestern and New England states accounted for much of the Republican party's victories. It is not really surprising that this regional factor is reflected in Democratic and Republican party successes. The Republican party was founded in 1854 to resist the spread of slavery, which, at the time, was the principal labor source in the southern region. The Civil War was the deepest political cleavage in American history; 17 states fought for the Union and 11 states for the Confederacy. A Republican President wrote the Emancipation Proclamation, led the union to victory in the war against the Confederacy, and presided over the military occupation of the southern states. Of course, the Civil War ended a century ago, but these party identifications linger on in state politics as a product of the way in which individuals acquire party affiliations from their parents. A few individuals change party affiliation, as a result of changes in their social or economic position in life or a move to another community. But massive party switches take place only under crises circumstances, such as the Civil War, the great Depression, or, perhaps, the Civil Rights Act of 1964.

Democratic and Republican states differ significantly with respect to income and educational levels. Democratic states tend to have lower income and educational levels than Republican states. This relationship between Democratic success and state politics in lower income and educational levels depends upon the 11 southern states, which are both Democratic and at the bottom of state rankings on income and education. If we remove the 11 southern states, we find that there is really no relationship in the 39 nonsouthern states between Democratic or Republican party success and urbanization or income or education. There is, however, a significant relationship between Democratic success and industrialization in nonsouthern states: an increase in industrialization leads to an increase in Democratic success.[6]

Perhaps the most noteworthy trend in party fortunes in recent years has been the rise of Republican party strength in a number of southern and border states. Table 4.3 reveals the increasing success of the Republican party in the South in presidential voting, gubernatorial voting, and state legislative representation. Prior to the Eisenhower years, both southern

[6] Thomas R. Dye, *Politics, Economics, and the Public* (Chicago: Rand McNally & Co., 1966), p. 53.

and border states merited the phrase, "the solid South." Eisenhower made the original inroads into the solid South by carrying Texas, Virginia, and Florida. Yet for a while, it did not appear that these isolated Republican victories in presidential elections would result in any significant Republican inroads in state capitals. When Barry Goldwater cast his vote against the Civil Rights Act of 1964, Republican party fortunes soared in the deep South states with heavy segregationist voting. While it is true that a majority of both Republicans and Democrats in Congress supported the Civil Rights Act, many deep South voters held the Democratic party responsible since the Act was passed by a Democratic Congress with the support of a Democratic President. Goldwater won electoral votes of 5 deep South states—Alabama, Georgia, Louisiana, Mississippi, and South Carolina—largely on the basis of the still dominant segregationist voting blocks in these states. And Johnson's margin of victory in Florida, Virginia, Tennessee, and Arkansas was quite slim. In fact, his margin of victory in these four states was smaller than the estimated Negro vote in these states, thus lending some support to the theory that increased Negro voting in the South was partially responsible for Johnson's showing there. However, it should be noted that Johnson carried six of the 11 southern states, and all border states.

The increasing Republicanism of the South is not confined to a single presidential election, but appears to extend to state offices as well. Republicans have dramatically increased their representation in southern state legislatures in recent years, and several Republicans have been elected to important statewide offices. Republican Howard "Bo" Callaway won a plurality of votes in the Georgia gubernatorial election in 1966, although he failed to win a majority, and as prescribed by the state constitution in such cases, the Georgia legislature picked the winner—a segregationist Democrat, Lester Maddox. Republican Claude Kirk was elected governor of Florida in 1966, and Republican Winthrop Rockefeller was elected governor of Arkansas. The Republican gains in the South reflect the region's increasing disenchantment with the policies of the federal government and with the federal government itself. Despite the South's traditional ties to the Democratic party, the apparent conservatism of the Republican party in recent years appeals to many southern votes. It is interesting that successful Democratic candidates in the deep South have been those candidates who have succeeded in projecting an even more conservative, segregationist, and anti-federal government image than their Republican opponents. Thus, Wallace of Alabama and Maddox of Georgia have kept their states Democratic by disassociating themselves and their state parties from the national Democratic party. The lot of "national Democrats" in the South is not a happy one. In Georgia in 1966, faced with a choice between segregationist Democrat Lester Maddox, and segregationist Republican

Howard Callaway, both openly hostile to the Johnson administration and the national government, many "national Democrats" were forced to write in the name of Ellis Arnold, a Georgia moderate. This write-in vote denied both candidates a majority, but the Democratic legislature proceeded to pick Lester Maddox as governor, thus frustrating the write-in movement.

In the 1968 Presidential election the deep South states of Alabama, Arkansas, Georgia, Louisiana, and Mississippi deserted the Republican and Democratic parties to support third-party candidate George C. Wallace. Of the 1964 Goldwater states in the south only South Carolina stayed with the GOP. In 1968 Nixon won five of the eleven southern states, Wallace won five, and Humphrey took one (Texas).

A less dramatic change in party fortunes in the states has been the rise

TABLE 4.3

THE RISE OF REPUBLICANISM IN THE SOUTH

	Presidential voting				Vote for governor		
	1944	1956	1964	1968	1954-56	1964-66	1968
Southern states							
Alabama	D81.3	D56.5	R69.5	W66	D73.4	D63.4	—
Arkansas	D70.0	D52.5	D56.1	W40	D80.6	R54.3	R51.0
Florida	D70.3	R57.2	D51.1	R40	D73.7	R55.1	—
Georgia	D81.7	D66.4	R54.1	W42	D100.0	R47.4*	—
Louisiana	D80.6	R53.3	R56.8	W48	D100.0	D60.7	—
Mississippi	D88.0	D58.2	R87.1	W64	D100.0	D61.9	—
North Carolina	D66.7	D50.7	D56.2	R40	D67.0	D56.6	D51.7
South Carolina	D87.6	D45.4	R58.9	R38	D100.0	D58.2	—
Tennessee	D60.4	R49.2	D55.5	R39	D87.2	D80.2	—
Texas	D71.3	R55.3	D63.5	D41	D78.4	D72.8	D56.5
Virginia	D62.4	R55.4	D53.5	R43	D54.8	D47.9	—
Border states							
Delaware	D54.4	R63.7	D60.9	R45	R52.0	D51.4	R51.5
Kentucky	D54.5	R54.3	D64.0	R44	D58.0	D50.7	—
Maryland	D51.9	R60.0	D65.5	D43	D54.5	R49.6	—
Missouri	D51.4	D50.1	D64.0	R46	D52.1	D62.1	D61.1
Oklahoma	D55.1	R55.1	D55.7	R47	D58.7	R55.7	—
West Virginia	D54.9	R54.1	D67.9	D50	R53.9	D54.9	R50.9

*Republican candidate Howard Calloway won the popular vote but failed to obtain the necessary majority; Democratic candidate Lester Maddox was elected by the state legislature.

Source: U.S. Bureau of the Census, *Statistical Abstract 1967*, p. 366, 375.

of Democratic party strength in a number of formerly solid Republican states in the Midwest and New England. Iowa and North Dakota have elected several Democratic governors in recent years; Kansas elected Democrat Robert Docking in 1966; Maine elected Democratic governor Kenneth M. Curtis in 1966; New Hampshire elected a Democratic governor in 1962, 1964, and 1966, and so did Vermont.

The rise of Republicanism in the South and the improvement of Democratic party fortunes in the Midwest and New England suggest that American state politics are becoming more competitive over time. What explanation would be offered for this apparent increase of party competition in the states? All of the states, including those in the South, Midwest, and New England, are becoming increasingly urban and industrial, and as we have already seen, increasing urbanization, industrialization, income, and education is associated with increasing party competition. Certainly population migration has also had a great deal to do with the increase in competitive politics in the states. An ever increasing number of Americans are moving about the nation, and these "newcomers" in every region and state tend to speed the erosion of regional culture, including the political culture. In 1960, the Bureau of Census found that 12 per cent of the population had moved to one state from another since 1955. Large numbers of southern Negroes have moved to big cities in both the North and the South. At the same time the South has experienced an influx of many northern whites, who can provide a foundation for a Republican party as well as a national Democratic party in the South.

National Tides and State Politics

National political tides have an important bearing on party fortunes in states and communities. National issues, personalities, and party loyalties will affect voting for state and local offices, particularly in presidential election years. Of course, one way of trying to insulate state elections from national influences is to hold state elections at times other than the dates of national elections. Twenty-four states elect their governors in off-years, that is, years in which no presidential election takes place. Fourteen states elect their governors for two year terms in even-numbered years and alternate gubernatorial elections between presidential years and off-years. Twelve states elect their governors for four year terms in presidential years, and theoretically, these states are most subject to national tides in their gubernatorial politics. It is difficult to measure the effect of a President's "coattails" in state politics. Eisenhower did not appear to help Republican officeholders in the states in 1956, yet in 1958, without Eisenhower at the head of the Republican ticket, Republicans fared even worse. In 1960, the Kennedy-Nixon battle was so close that no national trends are apparent,

TABLE 4.4

GOVERNORSHIPS WON BY DEMOCRATS AND REPUBLICANS

Eisenhower v. Stevenson 1956		Off-year 1958		Kennedy v. Nixon 1960		Off-year 1962		Johnson v. Goldwater 1964		Off-year 1966		Nixon v. Humphrey 1968	
Dem	*Rep*	*Dem*	*Rep*	*Dem*	*Rep*	*Dem*	*Rep*	*Dem*	*Rep*	*Dem*	*Rep*	*Dem*	*Rep*
17	14	30	9	16	12	25	14	18	8	13	24	8	13

although Kennedy helped many local Democratic candidates in big city, Catholic areas. Johnson was influential in sweeping many state and local candidates into office in 1964 (although it may have been that Goldwater was influential in keeping many Republican candidates out of office). Republicans fared much better in the off-years, 1962 and 1966, when Johnson was not a candidate (and Goldwater was not leading the Republican ticket). Nixon appeared to help GOP candidates for governor in 1968.

On the whole, states that vote Democratic in presidential elections tend to vote Democratic in gubernatorial elections, and of course, there is a correlation between Republican voting in presidential and gubernatorial elections.[7] Prior to 1964, southern states not only elected Democrats to their state houses but also provided electoral votes for Democratic presidential candidates. Midwestern and New England states tended to vote for Republican presidential as well as gubernatorial candidates. Thus, a state's partisan preferences in national and state politics are not totally divorced. However, it is possible to identify those states that are more Democratic in presidential elections than in gubernatorial elections, and those states that are more Democratic in gubernatorial elections than presidential elections. Certainly the southern states have been more Democratic in gubernatorial than in presidential elections—this was true even before the Goldwater candidacy in 1964. Interestingly, fewer states have been more Democratic in presidential than in gubernatorial elections; however, New York and California have treated Republican gubernatorial candidates better than Republican presidential aspirants.

Democrats and Republicans—What's the Difference?

It is sometimes difficult to define the meaning of party labels in state politics. The Democratic and Republican party organizations in the 50 states are devoid of any common ideology and very often lacking in clear

[7] See M. Kent Jennings and Richard G. Niemi, "Party Identification at Multiple Levels of Government," *American Journal of Sociology,* 72 (July, 1966), 86–101.

and consistent policy positions. The Democratic and Republican parties within a state are competing in the same vote market, and hence, both must tailor their policies to local conditions.

Does this mean that there are no real differences between Republican and Democratic parties in the states? Certainly at the national level, it is not difficult to see the different coalitions of groups that compose the Democratic and Republican parties. While the moderate viewpoints of American parties insure that major social groups are seldom wholly within one party or the other, differences between the Democratic and Republican parties at the national level are revealed by different proportions of votes given by major groups in the electorate to the Democratic and Republican parties.[8] The Democratic party receives a disproportionate amount of support from Catholics and Jews; Negroes; lower educational and income groups; younger people; skilled, semi-skilled, and unskilled laborers; union members; and big city residents. The Republican party receives disproportionate support from Protestants; whites; higher educational and income groups; older people; professional, managerial, and other white collar workers; non-union members; and rural and small-town residents.

The differing group bases of the Democratic and Republican parties at the national level is reflected in the policy positions of Democratic and Republican leaders. Herbert J. McCloskey and his associates presented a series of policy questions to over 3000 delegates at the Democratic and Republican national convention.[9] McCloskey found that there were substantial differences between Democrats and Republicans on important public issues including public ownership of natural resources, government regulation of economy, equalitarianism, tax policy, and foreign policy. McCloskey concluded:

> Although it has received wide currency, especially among Europeans, the belief that the two American parties are identical in principle and doctrine has little foundation in fact. Examination of the opinions of Democratic and Republican leaders shows them to be distinct communities of co-believers who diverge sharply on many important issues. Their disagreements, furthermore, conform to an image familiar to most observers and are generally consistent with differences turned up by studies of congressional rollcalls. Republican and Democratic leaders stand furthest apart on issues that grow out of their group identification and support—out of the managerial, proprietary, and high status connections of the one, and the labor, minority, low status, and intellectual connections of these other.[10]

[8] See Fred I. Greenstein, *The American Party System and the American People* (Englewood Cliffs, N.J.: Prentice-Hall, Inc., 1965).

[9] Herbert J. McCloskey, *et al.*, "Issue Conflict and Consensus Among Leaders and Followers," *American Political Science Review*, 54 (1960), 426.

[10] *Ibid.*, p. 426.

McCloskey went on to identify the different policy positions of his Democratic and Republican leaders:

> Democratic leaders typically display the strongest urge to elevate the lowborn, the uneducated, the deprived minorities, and the poor in general; they are more disposed to employ the nation's collective power to advance humanitarian and social welfare goals (for example, social security, immigration, racial integration, a higher minimum wage, and public education). They are more critical of wealth and big business and more eager to bring them under regulation. Theirs is the greater faith in the wisdom of using legislation for redistributing the national product and for furnishing social services on a wide scale. Of the two groups of leaders, the Democrats are the more "progressively" oriented toward social reform and experimentation. Republican leaders, while not uniformly differentiated from their opponents, subscribe in greater measure to the simple practices of individualism, laissez faire, and national independence. They prefer to overcome humanity's misfortunes by relying upon personal effort, private incentives, frugality, hard work, responsibility, self denial (for both men and government), and the strengthening rather than the diminution of the economic and status distinctions that are the "natural" rewards of the differences of human character and fortunes.[11]

These differences between the Democratic and Republican parties at the national level can be observed in the politics of some states but not in others. Certainly, differences between the Democratic and Republican parties in the large, urban, industrial states tend to resemble the differences between the national Democratic and Republican parties. William J. Keefe reported that Democratic and Republican parties in the Pennsylvania and Illinois state legislatures differed substantially in questions involving labor, minorities, social legislation, and the role of government in the economy.[12] On the other hand, the Democratic party in the southern states has *not* typically represented the "lowborn, the uneducated, the deprived minorities, and the poor in general," nor has it advocated the use of national power to advance racial integration. While it is true that the Democratic party in the southern states has supported national efforts to redistribute wealth and furnish social services on a national scale, one suspects that the southern Democrats have done so for the very practical reason that the southern states stand to gain the most by such redistribution. Nor has the Republican party in New York always conformed to the symbols and practices of individualism and laissez faire to the same extent as the national Republican party. New York Republicans have rather consistently supported humanitarian and social welfare measures at both the state and

---

[11] *Ibid.*, p. 428.

[12] William J. Keefe, "Comparative Study of the Role of Political Parties in State Legislatures," *Western Political Quarterly*, 9 (1956), 535–41.

national level. In short, the national images of the Democratic and Republican parties are not always the images that these parties reflect in the politics of individual states.

State Republican and Democratic parties resemble the national Republican and Democratic parties only in those states where each party represents separate socio-economic constituencies. Party conflict over policy questions is most frequent in those states in which the Democratic party represents central city, low income, ethnic, and racial constituencies, and the Republican party represents middle class, suburban, small town, and rural constituencies.[13] In these larger, urban, industrialized states, the Democratic and Republican parties will tend to disagree over taxation and appropriations, welfare, education, and regulation of business and labor— that is, the major social and economic controversies that divide the national parties.

In contrast, state parties do not necessarily reflect national party differences in homogeneous states, where there are no major social divisions in the electorate. For example, the Democratic party does not fully reflect the views of labor groups, Catholic voters, racial and ethnic minorities, in those midwestern and New England states that do not have large numbers of these kinds of voters. In these states the Democratic party will tend to be atypical of the national Democratic party and will tend to represent the attitudes of small town and rural residents, farmers, and shopkeepers. Similarly, the Republican party in New York cannot afford the image of a party devoted to the interests of white, Protestant, middle class, small town, rural people. New York's large number of Catholics and Jews, ethnic groups, Negroes and Puerto Ricans, low income, urban dwellers make the New York state Republican party something different from the national Republican party. The Democratic party in southern states has not been associated with urban, ethnic, or racial minorities; quite the contrary, it has been the party of the "establishment." The fact that the national Democratic party has been associated at various times with the aspirations of minorities in America, including the Negro, has caused quite a bit of confusion and frustration among the ranks of traditional southern Democrats. "I am a *Georgia* Democrat" is a common phrase by which Georgia Democrats disassociate themselves with the national image of their party. In the long run, the influence of mass communication, and the concentration of attention on national affairs, may cause state parties to reflect increasingly the views of the national parties.

13 See Thomas A. Flinn, "Party Responsibility in the States: Some Causal Factors," *American Political Science Review*, 58 (1964), 60–71; Duncan MacRae, Jr., "The Relation Between Roll Call Votes and Constituencies in the Massachusetts House of Representatives," *American Political Science Review*, 46 (1952), 1046–55; and Thomas R. Dye, "A Comparison of Constituency Influences in the Upper and Lower Chambers of a State Legislature," *Western Political Quarterly*, 14 (1961), 473–80.

State Party Organizations

State party organizations generally consist of a "state committee," a "state chairman," and perhaps a small office staff working at the state capitol. Democratic and Republican state committees vary from state to state in composition, organization, and functions; they are generally controlled by state law. Membership on the "state committee" may range from about a dozen up to several hundred. The members may be chosen through party primaries or by state party conventions. Generally, representation on state committees is allocated to counties, but occasionally other units of government are recognized in state party organization. A "state party chairman" generally serves at the head of the state committee; state chairmen are generally selected by the state committee, but their selection is often dictated by the party's candidate for governor.

State committees are supposed to direct the campaigns for important statewide elections—governors and U.S. Senators, and Congressmen in the smaller states. They are supposed to serve as central coordinating agencies for these election campaigns and to serve as the party's principal fund-raising organization in the state. However, the role of the state committee very often depends upon the preferences of the party's statewide candidates regarding the handling of their campaigns. Often candidates have their own campaign organizations to plan and execute campaign strategy. State party organizations may or may not play an effective role in the candidate's campaign, depending upon the candidate's preferences. State committees are not very responsive to the direction of the national committee, and in most states, city and county party organizations operate quite independently of the state committees. In other words, there is no real hierarchy of authority in state party systems. As V. O. Key explained: "The party organization is sometimes regarded as a hierarchy, based upon the precinct executive, and capped by the national committee, but it may be more accurately described as a system of layers of organization. Each successive layer—county or city, state, national—has an independent concern about elections in its geographical jurisdiction. Yet each higher level of organization, to accomplish its ends, must obtain the collaboration of the lower layer or layers of organization. That collaboration comes about, to the extent that it does come about, through a sense of common cause rather than by the exercise of command." [14]

Party organizations at the city and county level are probably the most cohesive organizations within the parties. The nation's 3000 Republican

---

[14] V. O. Key, Jr., *Politics, Parties, and Pressure Groups* (New York: Thomas Y. Crowell Company, 1964), p. 316; see also Austin Ranney, "Parties in State Politics," *Politics in the American States,* Herbert Jacob and Kenneth Vines, eds. (Boston: Little, Brown and Co., 1965).

and 3000 Democratic county chairmen probably constitute the most important building blocks in party organization in America. City and county party officers and committees are chosen locally and cannot be removed by any higher party authority. City and county committees are elected by the voters in their constituency, and they cannot be removed by state committees or national committees of their party, even if they decide to campaign for the opposition party. For example, many Democratic party officials in the South openly campaigned for Goldwater in 1964, yet there was nothing the state or national Democratic party organizations could do about it. In short, authority is not concentrated in any single statewide organization, but is divided among many city and county party organizations.

State party organizations have also been weakened by our system of primary elections for determining the party's nominee for statewide office. State party organizations were very powerful in the 19th century, when state party conventions made the nominations for statewide office. But with the advent of the primary system, support from party leaders was no longer a prerequisite for a party nomination, and anyone who wished to run for governor, senator, or other statewide offices could organize a group of supporters to place his name on the party's primary ballot. The state party organization may give an "official" endorsement to a candidate in the primary, but such an endorsement may or may not carry weight with the party's rank and file voters.

Thus, in most states, city and county, rather than state, party organizations are the most effective level of organization. City machines and bosses are discussed at length in Chapter 9, together with the reform movements which have attempted to counter their power. There are very few *statewide* machines headed by *state* bosses that command the loyalties of their county chairmen and direct party affairs from a statewide perspective. Ed Crump, from Memphis, Tennessee, was said to manage governors and legislators in the same way he managed mayors. Huey Long's organization in Louisiana in the 1920's and 1930's and the Harry Byrd organization in Virginia from the 1930's to the 1960's could be classified as statewide machines. They were tightly disciplined party organizations, held together and motivated by a desire for tangible benefits rather than by principle or ideology. They established a system of rewards and punishments in which votes were obtained by trading off social services, patronage jobs, and petty favors; these were, in turn, paid for by kickbacks from public contractors, bribes from holders of business franchises, contributions from persons with an interest in specific public policies, and other proceeds from the sale of government benefits. It is not a coincidence that most statewide machines developed in the poor rural states, particularly in the South. It is in these states, with their rural economies, lower family income, and poorly educated work forces, that patronage looks most attractive, and local pork barrel projects are most important. "Ole Gene" Talmadge found that Georgia's county chairmen could be bought relatively cheaply; all that was required was a firm grip on the state highway department, which acted as the chief dispenser of patronage and pork in the Talmadge organization. It is also in the poorer, rural states where demagoguery can be an important instrument of power, supplementing the use of patronage and pork. A demagogue plays upon racial and religious prejudice and fear to attract uneducated masses to his cause. However, statewide political machines are highly exceptional, and on the whole, state party organizations are quite decentralized. (See Chapter 9 for further discussion.)

5

LEGISLATORS

IN STATE POLITICS*

Functions of State Legislatures

If you were to ask state legislators what the job of the legislature is, they might say: "Our job is to pass laws," or "We have to represent the people," or "We have to make policy." All of the answers are correct. But none by itself tells the whole story of the role of the legislature in state politics.

It is true that, from a legal viewpoint, the function of state legislatures is to "pass laws," that is, the enactment of statutory law. In the early 1950's, American state legislators considered about 25,000 bills a year, but by the 1960's, this figure had grown to over 50,000. The total number of state legislative enactments grew from approximately 15,000 to over 35,000 in that same 10 year period.[1] As our society grows more complex and becomes increasingly urban and industrial, the need for formal statutory control seems to grow. Legislatures in urban industrial states will enact more than 1000 laws in a legislative session, while legislatures in rural agricultural states will enact fewer than 500.

* Parts of this chapter are adapted from Thomas R. Dye, "State Legislative Politics," in *Politics in the American States,* Herbert Jacob and Kenneth Vines, eds. (Boston: Little, Brown and Co., 1965).

[1] Council on State Governments, *Book of the States.* Published biennially by the Council of State Governments, Chicago.

The range of subject matter of bills considered by a legislature is enormous. A legislature may consider the authorization of a billion dollars of state spending, or it may debate the expansion of the hunting season on raccoons, or it may increase teachers' salaries, or it may argue over an appropriate color for automobile license plates. Obviously, these considerations range from the trivial to the vital; yet every bill that comes into the legislature is important to someone. In addition to the enactment of statutory law, legislatures share in the process of state constitutional revision, approve many of the governor's appointments, establish U.S. congressional districts, and consider amendments to the U.S. Constitution. But perhaps their single most important legal function is the passage of the appropriation and tax measures in the state budget. No state monies may be spent without a legislative appropriation, and it is difficult to think of any governmental action that does not involve some financial expenditure. Potentially, a legislature can control any activity of the state government through its power over appropriations, but as a practical matter, this legal power over fiscal affairs does not amount to political control.

From a political viewpoint, the function of state legislatures is to resolve conflicts over public policy. But it is misleading to say merely that the legislature "makes policy." Obviously, the legislature is not the only group that helps to make policy. The governor, the courts, executive agencies, interest groups, the press, political parties, and many other groups of individuals share in the making of public policy. How, then, do we distinguish the role of the legislature from that of other groups? For example, does the legislature merely "rubber stamp" the decisions of a strong governor or of the influential leaders of powerful interest groups? Or are legislatures themselves an important part of the process of proposing and deciding public policy? Does the legislature merely referee political struggles between organized interests in the state, recording the terms of surrender, compromises, or conquests in the form of statutes, or does the legislature exercise independent influence over policy? Are legislatures "initiators" of public policy, or do they merely express public sentiment in favor of or in opposition to policies initiated by others? These are the critical questions about the function of legislatures in state politics.

It is true, from the point of view of representation, that the legislature functions to "represent the people." But the question remains, "How does a state legislature go about representing the people?" Do legislators simply "mirror" the views of their constituents or do they exercise independent judgment in determining policy judgments? Do legislators follow public opinion, or do they try to educate the people about the public issues and change their opinion before the next election? And exactly who are "the people" the legislator represents? Does the legislator represent the views of the state's population, his own constituents, or particular groups within his constituency? How does he respond to the appeals of the governor, in-fluential party leaders, or important interest groups in his state? Does he vote along party lines to uphold the party platform with which he is affili-ated, or does he ignore party labels in legislative issues? What role do liberal or conservative ideologies play in determining a state legislator's behavior. In short, in "representing the people," does a legislator reflect the views of his state, his constituency, groups within his constituency, his party, or his own conscience? We hope in this chapter to explore some of of the forces influencing the way in which legislatures "represent the people."

The Making of a State Legislator

People need not be physically represented in a legislature in order for their interests to be recognized. State legislators are not "representative" of the population of their states in the sense of being typical cross-sections of them. On the contrary, state legislators are generally selected from the better educated, more prestigiously employed, middle class segments of the population. Yet our system of popular elections requires these legislators to "represent" the interests of their constituents, even though they do not share the same social background as their constituents.

However, evidence indicates that legislators generally mirror their con-stituents in certain "birthright" characteristics—race, religion, ethnic, and national background. In a thorough study of the Pennsylvania state legis-lature, for example, Frank Sorauf found that religious composition of con-stituencies had a distinct impact on both Democratic and Republican can-didates.[2] Protestant candidates came from Protestant districts, and Catho-lics tended to win in Catholic districts. These religious differences parallel ethnic differences. Catholic candidates seldom won in the Protestant "Bible Belt" counties of Pennsylvania, nor did Lutherans or Presbyterians win in the Irish and Italian wards of Philadelphia. Another characteristic, to which a district demands the conformity of its legislator, is race. The small number of Negro state legislators throughout the nation all come from pre-dominantly Negro districts, and Negro districts still dominated by white political leadership are threatening to end that domination. Predominantly Negro districts in Atlanta, Georgia, have elected eight representatives and two state senators to the Georgia General Assembly.

Legislators are far less mobile than the population as a whole. They tend to have deep roots in their constituencies. In 1957, 83 per cent of the state legislators of New Jersey had been born in the district they repre-sented or had lived there over 30 years; in Tennessee this figure was 76

[2] Frank J. Sorauf, *Party and Representation* (New York: Atherton Press, 1963), pp. 89–94.

per cent, and in Ohio it was 88 per cent.[3] Legislators are also "joiners." Participation in a wide variety of public activity means that a candidate has at least a modest circle of friends, that he is a "good mixer," and that he is known for his interest in the community. Religion and sports are particularly good areas for participation, as they provide a favorable local image for the legislator, which can be used as a springboard to office. The record of group activity of most legislators indicates that they have many points of contact with their constituents.

Although voters seem to want candidates to be typical of themselves in religion, race, and ethnic background, they want legislators who are atypical, in regard to education, occupation and social status. More than three-fourths of the nation's state legislators have been to college, a striking contrast to the educational level of the total population. Legislators are also concentrated in the more prestigious occupations. A great majority of legislators are either engaged in the professions, or they are proprietors, managers, or officials of business concerns. Among state legislators, farmers are overrepresented, and those employed by business are the largest single occupational group. Legislators are frequently among the middle-class groups, for whom politics is an avenue of upward mobility—they are the "local boys who made good." [4] Many of them are among the "second rung" elite in social circles, rather than the established wealthy. Although the sons and grandsons of distinguished, wealthy families are increasingly entering presidential and gubernatorial politics in the states, they seldom run for the state legislature.

The occupation of state legislator is part time, with a salary that does not provide full support. Legislators, therefore, must have occupations with flexible work responsibility. The lawyer, the farmer, and the business owner can adjust his work to the legislative schedule, but the office manager cannot. The overrepresented occupations are those involving extensive public contact—for example, the lawyer, insurance agent, farm implement dealer, tavern owner, and even undertaker, who establish in their business a wide circle of friends necessary for political success. In short, the legislator's occupation should provide free time, public contacts, and social respectability.

The overrepresentation of lawyers among state legislators is particularly marked. It is sometimes argued that the lawyer brings a special kind of skill to politics. The lawyer's occupation is the representation of clients, so he makes no great change in occupation when he moves from representing clients in private practice to representing constituents in the legislature. A lawyer is trained to deal with public policy as it is reflected in

[3] John C. Wahlke, et al., The Legislative System (New York: John Wiley & Sons, Inc., 1962), p. 488.

[4] Sorauf, Party and Representation, p. 91.

TABLE 5.1

SOCIAL BACKGROUND OF STATE LEGISLATORS, SELECTED STATES

	Per cent college graduate	Per cent professional, managerial or sales	Per cent farmers and farm laborers	Per cent Catholic
California				
Population	10	48	2	22
Legislators (1957)	54	86	13	17
New Jersey				
Population	8	45	1	37
Legislators (1957)	63	92	2	36
Ohio				
Population	7	40	3	18
Legislators (1957)	58	88	10	23
Tennessee				
Population	5	35	10	1
Legislators (1957)	46	84	13	2
Pennsylvania				
Population	6	39	2	27
Legislators (1958)	32	76	5	34
Georgia				
Population	6	35	8	0.9
Legislators (1961)	57	78	22	0.4
Wisconsin				
Population	7	37	11	29
Legislators (1953)	40	68	22	33

Sources: Figures are derived from the following: John C. Wahlke, *et al., The Legislative System*, pp. 486-91; Frank J. Sorauf, *Party and Representation*, pp. 69-71; *The Wisconsin Blue Book 1954; Georgia Official and Statistical Register 1961;* National Council of Churches of Christ, *Churches and Church Membership in the U.S.* (New York: 1956); U.S. Bureau of Census, *U.S. Census of Population 1960*, "United States Summary" PC1 (1)-1C (Washington: U.S. Government Printing Office, 1962).

the statute books, so he may be reasonably familiar with public policy before entering the legislature. Also, service in the legislature can help a lawyer's private practice, through free public advertising and opportunities to make contacts with potential clients.[5]

The state legislature is a convenient starting place for a political career. About one-half of the state legislators in the nation had never served in public office before their election to the legislature, and a greater percentage of new members are in the lower rather than upper chambers. The other

[5] Joseph A. Schlesinger, "Lawyers and American Politics," *Midwest Journal of Political Science,* 1 (1957), 26–39; David Derge, "The Lawyer as Decision-Maker in American State Legislatures," *Journal of Politics,* 21 (1959), 408–33.

half had only limited experience on city councils, county commissions, and school boards. The record of turnover of state legislators suggests that returning to office is not particularly important to many of them. Thus, in many ways the state legislatures appear "amateurish" in comparison with Congress, for example, where turnover is low and members acquire more parliamentary skills. The high turnover clearly is not a product of competition for the job; only a very small proportion of state legislators are rejected at the polls. Most simply do not seek re-election and quit because of dissatisfactions: "Being in the legislature has hurt my law practice and cost me money"; "Anyway you look at it, the job means a sacrifice to you, your home, and your business"; "It's a nervous life"; "The more service a man has, the more enemies he makes." [6]

Why does a legislator decide to run for office in the first place? It is next to impossible to determine the real motivations of political office seekers—they seldom know themselves. Legislators will usually describe their motivations in highly idealistic terms: "I felt that I could do the community a service"; "I considered it a civic duty." [7] Only seldom are the reasons for candidacy expressed in personal terms: "Oh, I just think it's lots of fun." Occasionally a state legislator admits that legislative service is an alternative to unemployment. Gregariousness and the desire to socialize no doubt contribute to the reasons for some office seekers. Politics can have a special lure of its own: "It gets into your blood and you like it." Particular issues may mobilize a political career but ideological involvement occupies a relatively unimportant place in a candidate's motives. Activity in organizations that are deeply involved in politics often leads to candidacy: "When I decided to run, I was quite active in the union."

An individual faces two important obstacles when he decides to run for the state legislature: the primary and the general election. His seat in the legislature depends on how much competition he meets in these elections. First let us consider competition in the primary elections. Available evidence indicates that more than half of the nation's state legislators are unopposed for their party's nomination in primary elections. Many legislators who do face primary competition have only token opposition. V. O. Key has shown most primary competition occurs in a party's "sure" districts, some competition occurs in "close" districts, and there is a distinct shortage of candidates in districts where the party's chances are poor.[8] In other words, primary competition is greater where the likelihood of victory in the general election is greater. Exceptions to this generalization are found in

---

[6] Quotations from state legislators interviewed by Wahlke, *et. al.*, *The Legislative System*, pp. 95–134.

[7] *Ibid.*

[8] V. O. Key, Jr., *American State Politics*, pp. 171–81.

districts where the incumbent legislator is so strong that he discourages prospective competitors, even though chances for success in the general election may be good.

The culmination of the recruitment process is in the general election, yet in many legislative constituencies one party is so entrenched that the voters have little real choice at the general election. In many one party states, the minority party is so weak that it fails to run candidates for many legislative seats. In the southern and border states where the legislatures are heavily Democratic, there often is no competition in the general election for legislative seats. (Of course, in these states primary competition in the majority party is frequent.) More seats are contested in states with close two party competition, but even in a hotly contested state such as Pennsylvania, nominations to the state legislature occasionally will not be filled, because of a collapse in local party organization in certain districts. "Competition" implies more than a name filed under the opposition party label. Generally a competitive election is one in which the winning candidate wins by something less than 2–1. In light of this more realistic definition of competition, the absence of truly competitive politics in state legislative elections is striking. Even in Pennsylvania, over half of the state legislators are elected by margins in excess of 2–1.[9] Similar findings are reported for competitive Massachusetts and Michigan.[10]

Legislators Represent People, not Trees or Acres

A great deal of political conflict in recent years has centered around the question of inequality of representation or "malapportionment." Malapportionment is claimed when there are different numbers of people in districts that have the same number of representatives in the legislature. For example, if one legislator represents a district of 10,000 inhabitants and another, a district of 40,000, it is said that the right to vote in the larger district is worth only one-fourth of what it is in the smaller district. Hence, inequality of representation exists. Until recently, malapportionment of state legislatures was quite widespread. In many state legislative chambers the ratio of the largest to the smallest district exceeded 100 to 1. And this malapportionment almost invariably discriminated against urban areas. David and Eisenberg compared the "value" of the vote cast for a state legislator in rural and urban areas in every state, and their study clearly shows

[9] Sorauf, *Party and Representation*, p. 117.
[10] Duncan MacRae, "The Relation Between Roll-Call Votes and Constituencies in the Massachusetts House of Representatives," *American Political Science Review*, 46 (1952), 1046–55; Robert W. Becker, *et al.*, "Correlates of Legislative Voting," *Midwest Journal of Political Science*, 6 (1962), 384–96.

TABLE 5.2

RELATIVE VALUES OF A VOTE FOR STATE LEGISLATORS,
NATIONAL AVERAGES FOR COUNTIES BY SIZE, 1910-60

Categories of counties by population size	1910	1930	1950	1960
Under 25,000	1.13	1.31	1.41	1.71
25,000 to 99,999	1.03	1.09	1.14	1.23
100,000 to 499,999	.91	.84	.83	.81
500,000 and Over	.81	.74	.78	.76

Source: Paul T. David and Ralph Eisenberg, *Devaluation of the Urban and Suburban Vote,* Bureau of Public Administration, University of Virginia, 1961, p. 8.

that the urban counties in the nation were underrepresented in American state legislatures.[11] Furthermore, prior to 1962 it did not seem that the situation was improving.

How did urban underrepresentation come about? The task of districting a state generally falls upon the legislature itself. One explanation attributes urban underrepresentation to our rural heritage: districts drawn when our nation was overwhelmingly rural remained because of rural distrust of growing city populations. Entrenched rural and small town interests were reluctant to surrender control to city populations, with their large blocs of ethnic, laboring, Catholic, and Negro voters. Often defenses of rural over-representation are made on the grounds that rural and small town people are "better" or "safer" citizens than big city voters. In addition, there is always a natural reluctance of legislative bodies to perform major surgery on themselves; to expect a legislature to redistrict itself is to expect legislators to threaten their own seats. In 1961 Tennessee and Alabama had not reapportioned their legislature in 60 years. In many cases, however, urban underrepresentation was a product of political compromises made in constitutional conventions—compromises similar to those made in the Convention of 1787 which made the U.S. House of Representatives representative of population and the U.S. Senate representative of the states regardless of their population. Many state constitutions based representa-

[11] David and Eisenberg first compute the average size of the constituency of a single member in each state. Actual constituencies were then compared to this average constituency; the "value" of a vote was the ratio of a real constituency to the average constituency in the state. For example, in a constituency twice the size of the state average, the value of a vote is .50; in a constituency half the size of the state average, the value of a vote is 2.0. The average value of a vote in rural and urban areas can be compared in this manner both within a single state and between states. See *Devaluation of the Urban and Suburban Vote,* p. 2.

tion, particularly in the upper chamber, upon some unit of government within the state (usually the county), rather than population.

But ever since March, 1962, when the Supreme Court decided Baker v. Carr, reapportionment has been a chief topic of concern and activity for all state legislatures. For many years, federal courts avoided the distasteful task of compelling legislative reapportionment, by asserting that this was a legislative rather than a judicial task. Urban populations were told by the courts that their remedy was to elect a legislature that would reapportion itself—a worthless prescription, of course, since electing a legislature was the very thing urban populations could not do. The position of the federal courts changed radically after the Supreme Court held that inequalities in state apportionment laws denied citizens the "equal protection of the laws" guaranteed them in the 14th Amendment and that the federal courts could grant relief from these inequalities.[12] Reaction to the decision was immediate and widespread. Urban voters throughout the nation petitioned federal courts to order legislative reapportionment, and federal courts found themselves struggling with the mathematics of this task. The federal courts have shown a tendency to invalidate any apportionment scheme in which a legislative district deviated in population from the average district by more than 15 per cent. State after state was induced to reapportion its legislature under the threat of judicial intervention. Federal courts generally allow legislators enough time to reapportion themselves, but token reapportionment is found unacceptable. The courts threatened to bar legislative elections by districts, in states which failed to meet constitutional standards of reapportionment. However, the Supreme Court is not willing to declare null and void the enactments of malapportioned legislatures, nor, in the case of Georgia, was the Court prepared to prevent the election of the governor by a malapportioned legislature, when no candidate received a popular majority in the general election, and the state constitution provided for legislative selection of the governor in this event.[13] In addition to requiring legislative apportionment on a population basis, the Supreme Court required population equality in congressional districting by state legislatures [14] and the unit system of voting for governor.[15] The philosophy underlying all of these decisions was expressed by the Court: "The conception of political equality from the Declaration of Independence to Lincoln's Gettysburg address, to the 14th, 15th, 17th, and 19th Amendments can mean only one thing—one person, one vote." [16]

In 1964 the Supreme Court, in Reynolds v. Sims,[17] decided that *both*

[12] *Baker vs. Carr,* 369 U.S. 186 (1962).
[13] *Fortson vs. Morris,* 385 U.S. 231 (1966).
[14] *Westberry vs. Sanders,* 84 S. Ct. 526 (1964).
[15] *Gray vs. Sanders,* 83 S. Ct. 801 (1963).
[16] *Ibid.,* p. 809.
[17] *Reynolds vs. Sims,* 84 S. Ct. 1362 (1964).

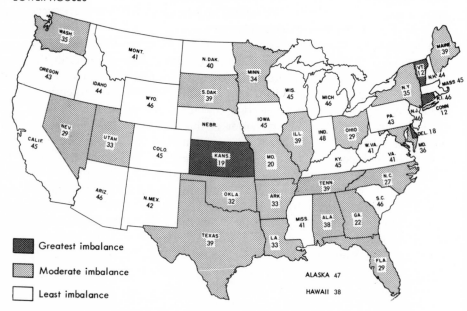

FIGURE 5.1

MALAPPORTIONMENT IN STATE LEGISLATURES, 1962

SENATES

WASH. 34
OREGON 48
MONT. 16
IDAHO 17
N. DAK. 32
MINN. 40
WIS. 48
MICH. 41
MAINE 47
VT. 47
N.H. 45
MASS 45
WYO. 24
S. DAK. 38
N.Y. 42
R.I.
CONN. 32
NEV. 8
NEBR. 44
IOWA 39
ILL. 29
IND. 40
OHIO 45
PA. 43
N.J. 19
DEL. 22
CALIF. 11
UTAH 21
COLO. 33
KANS. 48
MO. 48
W.VA. 47
VA. 41
MD. 14
KY. 47
ARIZ. 13
N. MEX. 14
OKLA. 44
ARK. 44
TENN. 44
N.C. 48
S.C. 23
MISS. 37
ALA. 28
GA. 48
TEXAS 30
LA. 33
FLA. 15

ALASKA 42

HAWAII 18

LOWER HOUSES

WASH. 35
OREGON 43
MONT. 41
N. DAK. 40
MINN. 34
WIS. 45
MICH. 46
MAINE 39
VT. 12
N.H. 44
MASS 45
IDAHO 44
WYO. 46
S. DAK. 39
N.Y. 35
R.I. 46
CONN. 12
NEV. 29
NEBR.
IOWA 45
ILL. 39
IND. 48
OHIO 29
PA. 43
N.J. 46
DEL. 18
CALIF. 45
UTAH 33
COLO. 45
KANS. 19
MO. 20
W.VA. 41
VA. 41
MD. 36
KY. 45
ARIZ. 46
N. MEX. 42
OKLA. 32
ARK. 33
TENN. 39
N.C. 27
S.C. 46
MISS. 41
ALA. 38
GA. 22
TEXAS 39
LA. 33
FLA. 29

ALASKA 47

HAWAII 38

■ Greatest imbalance

▨ Moderate imbalance

□ Least imbalance

(Figures represent percentage of state population which could elect a majority of legislators in each house.)

124

houses of a state legislature must be fairly apportioned according to population. This meant that the states could not have the system of representation found in Congress, where one house represents population and the other house represents a unit of government. The idea of bicameralism was originally based in part upon the advantages of having two separate systems of representation in a legislature. The *Federalist Papers* vigorously defended a second chamber capable of checking the popular majority represented in the lower chamber and protecting interests that might be threatened by that majority. But in the words of Chief Justice Earl Warren, writing for the Supreme Court: "Legislators represent people, not trees or acres. Legislators are elected by voters, not farms or cities or economic interests. . . . The complexities of societies and civilizations change, often with amazing rapidity. A nation once primarily rural in character becomes predominantly urban. Representation schemes, once fair and equitable, become archaic and outdated." [18]

As a result of these decisions, reapportionment has occurred in almost every state, and urban constituencies have achieved a greater voice in legislative affairs. What is the political impact of reapportionment? If the perceptions of the legislators themselves about conflict are to be accorded any weight, rural-urban conflict is not only discernible, but the most important conflict in American state legislatures. Rural-urban conflict was the only type of conflict rated "important" by over half the legislators interviewed in four separate states.[19] It seems safe to say that, in general, legislators from large, central cities and those from rural areas and small towns differ over the following: housing and welfare measures, aid for urban renewal and mass transit, the division of the state's tax dollar, state aids to schools, the location of highways, and the regulatory authority granted cities. In some southern states, urban legislators represent the "moderate" approach to race relations while segregationists remain strong in rural areas. According to the President's Commission on Intergovernmental Relations, the underrepresentation of urban areas in state legislatures causes cities to take their case to the federal government where they can obtain a fair hearing.[20] The rural character of state legislatures results in cities bypassing the states, by requesting direct federal-to-local grants-in-aid, such as federal public housing and urban renewal programs.

There is little doubt that reapportionment will bring about a change in legislative personnel at state capitals. But will reapportionment noticeably

[18] *Reynolds vs. Sims*, p. 1381.
[19] Wahlke, *The Legislative System*, p. 425.
[20] Commission on Intergovernmental Relations, *A Report to the President for Transmittal to the Congress* (Washington: U.S. Government Printing Office, 1955), p. 39.

affect the *content of policies* adopted by the states? This is a difficult question: so many variables other than urban underrepresentation affect the policies of a state that it is difficult to attribute particular policies to this factor. Some recent studies have shown that there is not much difference between the policies adopted by malapportioned legislatures and those adopted by fairly apportioned legislatures, in important areas in education, welfare, highways, expenditures and taxation.[21] Policies in these areas appear to be more a product of a state's economic resources rather than whether or not it was well apportioned. Rural voting blocs in state legislatures may remain important political forces because rural legislators have greater cohesion; this is, they stick together on major legislative issues. Rural constituencies are very homogeneous and rural voters think alike on many issues. In contrast, there is a great deal of conflict among urban groups.[22] Representatives of large cities and small cities are often at odds with each other in legislative debate. Moreover, within metropolitan areas there are many conflicts of interests between city and suburbs based upon the different types of persons living in each area. Crowded slum dwellers have different opinions about public policy than the inhabitants of suburban split levels on half acre lots. On some issues, we find a conservative coalition of suburban and rural legislators facing representatives of downtown areas.

What will be the effect of reapportionment on the political parties? Traditionally, urban underrepresentation hurt the Democratic party in those northern and eastern parts of the United States, where Democratic strength was heavily concentrated in urban areas, such as Michigan, Illinois, Ohio, and New Jersey. However, more recently the growth of suburbs and their underrepresentation in state legislatures has tended to hurt the Republican party. In New York, Pennsylvania, and Maryland particularly, the Republican suburbs were the most underrepresented areas of the state. Malapportionment also worked to the disadvantage of Republicans in those southern, southwestern and border states where rural votes traditionally supported the Democratic party. In many of these states the Republican party was strongest in the growing urban and suburban areas. In short, reapportionment may have little *net* effect on the parties nationwide, although it may upset longstanding balances of power between the parties in particular states.

---

[21] Herbert Jacob, "The Consequences of Malapportionment: A Note Of Caution," *Social Forces* (Winter, 1964), 246–61; Thomas R. Dye, "Malapportionment, a Public Policy in The States," *Journal of Politics,* 27 (August, 1965), 586–601.

[22] David Derge, "Metropolitan and Missouri Legislative Delegations," *American Political Science Review,* 52 (1958) 1052–65; Richard T. Frost, "On Derge's Metropolitan and Outstate Legislative Delegations," *American Political Science Review,* 53 (1959), 792–95.

Legislative Organization and Procedure

The formal rules and procedures by which state legislatures operate are designed primarily to make the legislative process fair and orderly. Without established customs, rules, and procedures it would be impossible for 50, 100, or 200 men to arrive at a collective decision about the thousands of items submitted to them at a legislative session. State legislatures follow a fairly standard pattern in the formal process of making laws. Table 5.3 below provides a brief description of some of the more important procedural steps in lawmaking.

What are the political consequences of the legislative procedures described in Table 5.3? Obviously, it is a very difficult process for a bill to become a law—legislative procedures offer many opportunities to defeat legislation. Formal rules and procedures of state legislatures lend themselves easily to those who would delay or obstruct legislation. Table 5.3 illustrates the deliberative function of legislatures and the consequent procedural advantages given to "conservative" forces; that is, those who would defend the *status quo*. Moreover, these procedures imply that the legislature is structured for deliberation, destruction, and delay in decision making, rather than speed and innovation. This suggests that the legislature functions as an arbiter, rather than an initiator, of public policy, since its procedures are designed to maximize deliberation, even at the expense of granting advantage to those who oppose change.

Partly to counteract the impact of formal rules and procedures, legislatures have developed a number of informal "rules of the game." These unwritten rules are not merely quaint and curious folkways. They support the purposes and functions of the legislature by helping to maintain the working consensus among legislators so essential to legislative output. Some rules contribute to the legislative task by promoting group cohesion and solidarity. In the words of legislators themselves: "Support another member's local bill if it doesn't affect you or your district"; "Don't steal another's bill"; "Accept the author's amendments to a bill"; "Don't make personal attacks on other members." [23] Other informal rules promote predictability of behavior: "Keep your word"; "Don't conceal the real purpose of bills or amendments"; "Notify in advance if you cannot keep an amendment." Other rules try to put limits on inter-personal conflict: "Be willing to compromise"; "Accept half a loaf"; "Respect the seniority system"; "Respect committee jurisdiction." Finally, other rules are designed to expedite legislative business: "Don't talk too much, fight unnecessarily, introduce too many bills and amendments, point out the absence of a quorum, or be too political."

[23] Quotations from state legislators interviewed by Wahlke, *The Legislative System*, pp. 146–61.

TABLE 5.3

SUMMARY OF LEGISLATIVE PROCEDURE FOR BILL PASSAGE

1.	*Introduction of bill*	One or more members file bill with Clerk or presiding officer who gives it a number and refers it to a committee. This constitutes the first reading.
2.	*Committee hearings*	Important bills may be given public hearings at which all interested persons or groups may testify. Committee may speed or delay hearings.
3.	*Committee report*	Committee meets in executive (closed) session. Bills may be amended or pigeonholed or reported favorably or unfavorably.
4.	*Bill placed on calendar*	Bills reported by committee are placed on calendar for floor consideration. Urgent or favorite bills may get priority by unanimous consent or informal maneuvering; other bills may be delayed, sometimes indefinitely.
5.	*Floor debate, amendment, vote*	The second reading of the bill before the entire chamber is usually accompanied by debate and perhaps amendments from the floor. Often the crucial vote is on an amendment or on second reading.
6.	*Third reading and passage*	Usually a bill is delayed one calendar day before it is brought to the floor for third reading. On third reading debate is not customary and amendments usually require unanimous consent. After final vote, bill is certified by presiding officer and sent to second house.
7.	*Referral to second chamber*	Bill is sent to second chamber where steps 1 through 6 must be repeated. Bills must pass both chambers in identical form before going to governor.
8.	*Conference committee*	If there are differences in wording in the bills passed by each house, one or the other house must accept the wording of the other house or request a conference committee. This committee is made up of members of both houses and it arrives at a single wording for the bill.
9.	*Vote on conference committee report*	Both houses must vote to approve conference committee wording of bill. Bills may be shuttled back and forth and eventually die for lack of agreement between both houses.

10.	*Governor's signature or veto*	An identical bill passed by both houses becomes law with the governor's signature. It may also become law without his signature after a certain lapse of time (e.g., 10 days) if the legislature is still in session. If the legislature has adjourned during this time, the governor's failure to sign is the same as a veto. A governor may formally veto a bill and return it to the house of origin for reconsideration. An unusual majority is generally required to override a veto.

A most important informal device is unanimous consent for the suspension of formal rules; this permits a legislature to consider bills not on the calendar, pass bills immediately without the necessary three readings, dispense with time-consuming formalities, permit nonmembers to speak, and otherwise alter procedure. Another informal rule is the practice in many states of passing bills that would affect only one area of a state without debate or opposition when the delegation in that area unanimously supports that bill.

Most of these rules are enforced by informal sanctions. The most frequently mentioned sanction involves obstructing the bills of errant legislators, by abstaining or voting against him; keeping his bills in committee; and amending his bills, or more personal sanctions, such as using the "silent treatment"; not trusting him; removing patronage and good committee assignments.[24] Other sanctions include denial of legislative courtesies and occasionally even overt demonstrations of displeasure, such as ridicule, hissing, or laughing. The observance of rules, however, is not obtained primarily through fear of sanction so much as the positive recognition by legislators of the usefulness of rules in helping the legislature perform its chores.

While it is most convenient to study legislative decision making by observing floor actions, particularly the division of ayes and nays, the floor is not the only locus of important legislative decisions. Many legislatures feel that committee work is essential to the legislative process. It is in committees that public hearings are held, policies completed and debated, legislation amended and compromised, and bills rushed to the floor or pigeonholed. The function of the committee system is to reduce legislative work to manageable proportions by providing for a division of labor among legislators. A typical legislative chamber may have between 20 and 30 standing committees, each of which consider all bills in a particular field, such as revenue, appropriations, highways, welfare, education, labor, judiciary, or local government. Committees may prevent a bill from coming to the floor for a vote by inaction ("pigeonholing"); however, 20 states require every committee to report on every bill referred to it either favor-

[24] *Ibid.*

ably or unfavorably. The political impact of the committee system is to provide still another opportunity for delay and obstruction by less than a majority of legislators, sometimes by a single committee chairman. Duane Lockard reports, "What a new legislator soon finds is that there is no choice but to depend on his colleagues to inform him about issues sent to their committees, and like it or not, he is reduced to following their advice unless he knows the subject well enough to have an opinion. It is a source of surprise to new members how many issues they are too ignorant to have an opinion about. . . ." [25]

Committees in state legislatures are not nearly so powerful as committees in Congress. Most state legislatures meet only a few months every other year, giving committees very little time for any careful review of the bills. Committees seldom have any staff assistance, legislative turnover is high, the seniority system is not as prevalent as it is in Congress, and committee members seldom acquire the experience and expertise that congressmen do. In most state legislatures, the rules committee does not have the power to determine what bills will reach the floor as does the Rules Committee of the House of Representatives. Of course, the fact that legislative committees are not great sources of power does not mean that they are never used as important instruments of party or gubernatorial control.

Role Playing in Legislatures

Roles are expectations about the kind of behavior people ought to exhibit. Expectations are placed upon a legislator by his fellow legislators, his party, the opposition party, the governor, his constituents, interest groups, his friends, as well as by himself.

Perhaps the most distinctive roles in the legislative process are those of the leadership. A typical legislative chamber has a presiding officer, a majority and minority floor leader, a number of committee chairmen, and a steering committee. These leaders perform functions similar to the functions of rules. First of all, leaders are expected to help make the legislative system stable and manageable. They are expected to maintain order, to know the rules and procedures, to follow the rules, and to show fairness and impartiality. Leaders are also expected to help focus the issues and resolve conflict, by presenting issues clearly, narrowing the alternatives, organizing public hearings, and promoting the party or administrative point of view on bills. The majority leader is supposed to "get the administrative program through," while the minority leader "tries to develop criticism," "find party issues," and "develop a constructive opposition." [26] Leaders

---

[25] Duane Lockard, *The Politics of State and Local Government,* (New York: The Macmillan Company, 1963), p. 28.

[26] Quotations from state legislators interviewed by Wahlke, *op. cit.,* pp. 170–90.

FIGURE 5.2

THE MANY ROLES OF A STATE LEGISLATOR

SOURCE: *The Atlanta Journal and Constitution,* January 23, 1966. Reproduced by permission.

are also expected to administer the legislature and expedite business. This includes "promoting teamwork," "being accessible," "cracking the whip in the interest of time and smooth operation," starting the sessions on time, keeping them on schedule, and distributing the workload. It involves communication, coordination, and liaison with the governor, the administrative departments, and the other chambers.

Another set of legislative roles that are commonly encountered and which makes important contributions to the legislative process are the "subject-matter experts." Unlike leadership roles, the roles of subject matter experts are not embodied in formal offices. The committee system introduces specialization into the legislature, and the seniority system places at the head of the committee those persons longest exposed to the information about the committee's subject matter. Thus, subject matter experts emerge among legislators in the fields of law, finance, education, agriculture, natural resources, local government, labor, transportation, and so on. There is some evidence to support the view that subject matter experts exercise more influence over bills within their fields than nonexperts.[27]

Still another way of describing characteristic behaviors in a legislature is to discover the legislators' orientations toward the expectations of constituents and party. Legislators have been classified as either "trustees" (those who are guided in legislative affairs solely by their personal conscience), "delegates" (those who are guided by instructions or wishes of their constituents), and "partisans" (those who look to the party leadership for guidance).[28] Despite the concern of many political scientists with the classic question of whether legislators should represent their party, their constituency, or their own conscience, few legislators actually exhibit in their behavior a firm commitment to any one of these. Most legislators when facing specific issues do not see any conflict between the wishes of their constituents, their party, or their own judgment. Even where such conflict is perceived, most legislators attempt to find a compromise between conflicting demands rather than choose one role or the other exclusively. One legislator even denied that such a question would ever arise: "A representative's judgment should arise from knowing the needs and wants of his district and state." [29] Of course, if legislators are asked how they make their decisions, they *claim* to be guided solely by their own conscience. But this is little more than a verbalism; it reflects a heroic image of the courageous defender of the public interest, who acts out of personal virtue and conviction regardless of the consequences.

Legislators might also be classified according to the way in which they see the legislative function—in other words, according to the expectations they place upon their own behavior. The *Legislative System* study found four types of self conceptions among legislators—the ritualist, the tribune, the inventor, and the broker.[30] The ritualist sees his job in a technical fashion as one of "making laws." The ritualist is concerned with the mechanics of legislative operations, parliamentary rules and routine, and committee work. The technical perfection of a law seems almost as important to him as its policy implication. The tribune perceives his role as the discoverer of popular needs and the defender of popular interests. He sees his task as one of understanding his constituents' problems, making himself available to them, and keeping track of public opinion. Only a few legisla-

[27] William Buchanan, *et. al.,* "The Legislator as Specialist," *Western Political Quarterly,* 13 (1960), 636–51.
[28] Sorauf, *Party and Representation,* pp. 121–46; and Wahlke, *op. cit.,* pp. 281–86.
[29] Sorauf, *op. cit.,* p. 125.
[30] The discussion which follows relies upon Wahlke, *op. cit.,* pp. 245–60.

tors consider themselves inventors. The inventor sees himself as the initiator and creator of public policy. He wants to see the legislature take the lead in solving important problems in his state—welfare, education, highways, taxes, and so on. The fact that few legislators even claim to approach their task in a creative manner is further evidence that legislators themselves realize that policy initiation has shifted from the legislature to the governor, executive agencies, and interest groups. The true inventors of legislatures are probably frustrated men, since seldom does the legislature do anything but respond to the governor, civil servants, or active pressure groups. Finally, some legislators see their role as that of referee or broker in the struggle between interest groups, constituencies, and executive agencies. The broker's task is to balance, to compromise, to arbitrate between conflicting interests. It is interesting that legislative leaders are more likely to see themselves in this role than nonleaders.

The roles mentioned here by no means exhaust the possibilities. In the words of a former Connecticut state senator:

> It is obvious of course that there is no such thing as the single perspective on the legislature; the member's conception of his own proper role determines how he sees the legislative process, and the illusions that members bring with them to the state capitol are by no means identical. Some see their task in terms of an idealized, if fuzzy, conception of a rational man whose task it is to mediate on all questions, resist all special interest pressures, and decide all issues on their "merits," regardless of the pressures brought to bear by anybody—even including constituents. Others see themselves as the chosen delegates of some special element in the society—farmers, laborers, insurance and real estate businesses, or the party organization—and they fully expect to act accordingly.[31]

Party Politics in State Legislatures

Many decisions made by state legislatures do not involve conflict, and most bills are enacted into law without a single negative vote. This does not mean, however, that the legislative chambers are free from conflict; unanimous bills are generally local bills or minor bills involving decisions that are not deeply divisive. What are the principal types of conflict which affect legislative decision making? If we can rely on the perceptions of legislators themselves about the types of conflict that consume their energies, then Table 5.4 is a valuable indicator of what types of conflict prevail in different states. Note that only rural-urban conflicts are rated as important by over half the legislators in all four states.

There are 96 partisan legislative chambers in the U.S.; Nebraska and Minnesota legislatures are elected on a nonpartisan ballot. In recent years,

[31] Lockard, *Politics of State and Local Government*, p. 280.

TABLE 5.4

CONFLICTS PERCEIVED AS IMPORTANT BY STATE LEGISLATORS IN FOUR STATES

Type of Conflict	Per cent declared "important," House and Senate							
	California		*New Jersey*		*Ohio*		*Tennessee*	
	H	*S*	*H*	*S*	*H*	*S*	*H*	*S*
Rural-urban	65	74	53	50	79	65	91	63
Party	26	26	96	85	49	59	23	17
Governor-legislature	18	24	76	70	36	38	89	96
Liberal-conservative	58	74	22	25	52	59	29	37
Labor-management	65	62	18	15	61	55	54	67
Regional	69	44	18	40	17	10	13	20

Source: John C. Wahlke, *et al., The Legislative System,* p. 425. (New York: John Wiley, 1962)

the Democratic party has dominated American state legislative politics. Table 5.5 shows the Democratic and Republican division of upper and lower houses in state legislatures from 1962 to 1966. In Chapter 4 we discussed what types of states are most likely to experience Democratic or Republican legislative control and the difference between competitive and noncompetitive party politics. Now let us consider the influence of parties in legislative decision making.

TABLE 5.5

DEMOCRATIC AND REPUBLICAN DIVISION OF STATE LEGISLATURES

State	Lower House						Upper House					
	1962		1964		1966		1962		1964		1966	
	Dem.	Rep.	Dem.	Rep.	Dem.	Rep.	Dem.	Rep.	Dem.	Rep.	Dem.	Rep.
Ala.	104	2	104	2	106	-	35	-	35	-	34	1
Alaska	20	20	30	10	15	25	15	5	17	3	6	14
Ariz.	48	32	45	35	27	33	24	4	26	2	14	16
Ark.	99	1	99	1	98	2	35	-	35	-	35	-
Calif.	52	28	49	31	42	38	27	13	27	13	21	19
Colo.	24	41	42	23	27	38	15	20	15	20	15	20
Conn.	110	184	111	183	117	60	23	13	23	13	25	11
Del.	24	11	30	5	12	23	10	7	13	5	9	9
Fla.	90	5	102	10	91	26	37	1	42	2	37	11
Ga.	203	2	198	7	183	22	52	2	44	9	46	7
Hawaii	40	11	39	12	39	12	15	10	16	9	15	10
Idaho	29	34	36	43	31	39	21	23	19	25	12	23
Ill.	87	90	118	59	78	99	23	35	25	33	21	37
Ind.	44	56	78	22	34	66	24	26	35	15	29	21
Iowa	29	79	101	23	35	89	12	38	34	25	31	28

	Lower House						Upper House					
	1962		1964		1966		1962		1964		1966	
State	Dem.	Rep.	Dem.	Rep.	Dem.	Rep.	Dem.	Rep.	Dem.	Rep.	Dem.	Rep.
Kans.	36	89	44	81	49	76	8	32	13	27	13·	27
Ky.	63	37	63	37	63	36	25	13	25	13	26	12
La.	101	-	103	2	103	2	39	-	39	-	39	-
Me.	41	110	81	70	56	95	5	29	29	5	9	25
Md.	117	25	117	25	118	24	22	7	22	7	35	8
Mass.	147	93	169	70	168	71	28	12	28	12	26	14
Mich.	52	58	72	38	55	55	11	23	23	15	18	20
Minn.	(X)	(X)	(X)	(X)	(X)	(X)	(X)	(X)	(X)	(X)	(X)	(X)
Miss.	122	-	122	-	120	2	52	-	52	-	51	1
Mo.	101	62	124	39	107	56	23	11	23	11	23	11
Mont.	37	57	56	38	40	64	35	21	32	24	30	25
Neb.	(X)	(X)	(X)	(X)	(X)	(X)	(X)	(X)	(X)	(X)	(X)	(X)
Nev.	25	12	25	12	21	19	8	9	9	9	11	9
N.H.	146	254	176½	223½	156	244	5	19	9	15	10	14
N.J.	27	33	27	33	41	19	6	15	6	15	19	10
N.M.	55	11	59	18	46	24	28	4	28	4	25	17
N.Y.	65	85	88	62	80	70	25	33	33	25	26	31
N.C.	99	21	106	14	94	26	48	2	49	1	43	7
N.D.	43	70	65	44	16	82	11	38	20	29	5	44
Ohio	49	88	62	75	37	62	13	20	16	16	10	23
Okla.	95	25	78	21	74	25	38	6	41	7	38	10
Ore.	31	29	28	32	22	38	21	9	19	11	19	11
Pa.	101	109	116	93	99	104	23	27	23	27	23	27
R.I.	75	25	76	24	68	32	27	19	30	15	35	15
S.C.	124	-	124	-	107	17	46	-	46	-	44	6
S.D.	17	58	30	45	12	63	9	26	16	18	6	29
Tenn.	78	21	75	24	59	39	27	6	25	8	25	8
Tex.	143	7	149	1	147	3	31	-	31	-	30	1
Utah.	30	34	39	30	10	59	12	13	15	12	7	21
Vt.	45	189	50	192	48	102	9	21	13	17	8	22
Va.	89	11	89	11	88	11	37	3	37	3	36	4
Wash.	51	48	60	39	44	55	32	17	32	17	29	20
W. Va.	76	24	91	9	65	35	23	9	27	7	25	9
Wis.	47	53	52	48	47	53	11	22	13	20	12	21
Wyo.	19	37	34	27	27	34	11	16	12	13	12	18

Source: U.S. Bureau of the Census, *Statistical Abstract of the United States 1967*, p. 376.

The influence of parties is by no means uniform throughout the states. First of all, it is obvious that parties in one party states do not exercise tight party discipline over the voting of legislators. But the extent of party influence in legislative decision-making varies even among the more or less competitive states. One common measure of party influence on voting is the percentage of nonunanimous roll call votes in which a majority of Democrats vote against the majority of Republicans. This is referred to as

TABLE 5.6

PARTY VOTING IN SELECTED LEGISLATURES ON NON-UNANIMOUS ROLL CALL VOTES

State	Per cent of nonunanimous roll calls with party majorities in disagreement		Years
	Senate	*House*	
Rhode Island	96	96	1931, '37, '51
Connecticut	90	83	1931–51
Massachusetts	82	87	1931, '37, '51*
New York	62	61	1947, '49*
Pennsylvania	64	81	1945*
Pennsylvania	34	43	1951
Pennsylvania	51	43	1957
Ohio	52	40	1949, '55, '57*
Illinois	53	54	1949*
New Hampshire	72	68	1931, '37, '51*
Washington	71	51	1945*
Kentucky	54	41	1944, '46*
Colorado	36	38	1941, '47*
Missouri	23	36	1945, '46*
California	20	32	1947, '49*
California	†	34	1957*
California	31	49	1959*

*In the starred years, percentages are based upon roll calls with at least 10 per cent of the members voting in the minority.
†Data not available.
Source: Malcolm Jewell, *The State Legislature* (New York: Random House, 1962), p. 52.

a "party vote." The compilations by the *Congressional Quarterly* show that congressional roll calls in which the two parties have been in opposition has averaged about 50 per cent in recent years. Table 5.6 suggests that party voting may be higher in the state legislatures of New York, Pennsylvania, Connecticut, Rhode Island, and Massachusetts than it is in Congress. Parties appear less influential in Colorado, Missouri, and California.

Another approach to determining the extent of party influence in legislatures is to ask legislators what they think the role of parties should be. Again, we find great differences in the perceived role of parties.[32] Over 90 per cent of New Jersey's legislators perceived "much" or "considerable" party influence. Ohio legislators were divided: 51 per cent perceived considerable party influence, while 31 per cent saw little or no party influence.

[32] Wahlke, *op. cit.*, p. 355.

In California and Tennessee, 40 and 57 per cent, respectively, felt that parties exercise little or no influence; only 6 and 21 per cent respectively perceived considerable party influence.

What factors distinguish those states in which the party significantly influences legislative decision making from those states in which it does not? First of all, parties appear to be more influential in states where there is a great deal of party competition. In terms of legislative behavior, one party states are really "no party" states. Since the one party states are the rural agricultural states, party voting appears related to urbanism and industrialization if all 50 states are considered; however, there are some urban industrial states in which party voting is not very frequent—California is a notable example. Actually, party influence appears strongest in those urban industrial states in which the parties represent separate social and economic constituencies. Party voting occurs in those two party states in which Democratic legislators represent central city, low income, ethnic, and racial constituencies, and Republican legislators represent middle class, suburban, small town, and rural constituencies. Party cohesion is weak in the states where party alignments do not coincide with socio-economic divisions of the population.

On what types of issues do the parties exercise great influence? Minor bills involving the licensing of water-well-drillers, beauticians, or barbers and such matters as the designation of an official state bird seldom divide the parties. In the urban industrial states, parties usually display greatest influence on issues involving taxation and appropriations, welfare, education, and the regulation of business and labor—major socio-economic controversies that divide our national parties. Party influence in budgetary matters is also apparent, since the budget often involves basic issues of social welfare and class interest on which parties in urban states were split. Another type of bill that is often the subject of party voting is one involving the party as an interest group. Parties often have an interest in bills proposing a transfer of power from an office controlled by one party to an office controlled by another, and bills proposing to create or abolish non-civil service jobs. Parties display a considerable interest in bills affecting the organization of local government, state administration, the civil service, registration and election laws, and legislative procedure.

What is the basis of party cohesion in the states where it exists? Is party cohesion a product of effective party organization and discipline? Or is it really a result of similarities in the constituents represented by each party? For example, is Democratic party cohesion in industrial states a result of party organization pressures? Or does it result from the fact that Democrats typically are elected from metropolitan centers with strong labor groups, many Catholic voters, racial ethnic minorities, and persons with few skills and poor education, and these constituency similarities really hold the Democratic legislators together? Could it be that Republican cohesion in these states is a product of the fact that Republicans typically represent middle class suburbs, small towns, and rural areas, and these types of constituencies have similar ideas about public policy?

Constituency Influence in Legislative Politics

It is unlikely that party organization and discipline alone is the cause of party voting, for organization and discipline can only be effective under certain conditions. The evidence seems to indicate that party influence is only effective where the parties represent separate and distinct socio-economic coalitions. Where the constituencies of a state are divided along socio-economic lines and where party divisions coincide with these constituency divisions, only then will party program and discipline be effective in shaping policy in legislative chambers.

Pennsylvania is an excellent example of a state in which Republican and Democratic legislative districts are clearly differentiated along socio-economic variables. The parties are first divided along rural-urban lines, and within urban areas they are further divided along lines of social and economic status. Republicans dominate in rural areas and in the wealthier urban areas (upper middle class suburbs and several "silk stocking" districts). Democratic districts are found predominantly in the less wealthy, urban areas of a state. Republican districts within urban areas prove to be the districts with the greater concentrations of professional, managerial, sales, and clerical jobs. Republican candidates fare badly among Negro voters. The Democrats dominate in districts with many blue collar workers, and tend to win legislative seats in southern and eastern European, Irish, Catholic districts, which are frequently the big-city mining or mill districts. The Republicans draw heavily in the Anglo-Saxon, northern and western European Protestant districts of the state. The same sort of party division of legislative districts has been documented in Massachusetts and Michigan.[33]

It is this division of constituencies that is really the basis of party influence in the legislatures of these states. Evidence to support this view is provided if we examine the voting behavior of legislators elected from districts *atypical* of districts which usually elect members of their party. Since rural and high-income urban districts in Pennsylvania generally elect Republicans, and low-income urban districts generally elect Democrats, "atypical" legislators are those Democrats elected from rural or wealthy districts and those Republicans elected from low-income, urban districts. Studies in Pennsylvania, Massachusetts, and Michigan of the voting behavior of atyp-

[33] MacRae, *American Political Science Review,* 46, pp. 1046-55; Becker, *Midwest Journal of Political Science,* 6, pp. 384-96.

ical representatives show that they tend to cross party lines much more frequently than representatives elected from districts typical of their party.[34] The threat to Democratic party cohesion in these states came from small bands of rural Democrats; insurgency within the Republican party came from urban Republican legislators. The fact that party cohesion breaks down among representatives elected by districts atypical of their party indicates that cohesion is really a function of constituency similarities rather than party organization and discipline. In short, to the extent that parties find their support in contrasting social and economic groups in a state, party responsibility in the legislature is the consequence.

The constituency basis of party voting has been studied in Pennsylvania, Michigan, Massachusetts, Ohio, and Kansas and appears to be operative in New York, Illinois and many other states.[35] In contrast, Washington presents an example of a state where party lines do not follow socio-economic differences, and as a consequence, party unity is lower despite attempts to organize the parties in the legislature.[36] Democratic party cohesion in that state is broken down by the existence of conservative and liberal wings, which roughly follow a rural-urban division. In California, too, the parties clearly do not follow rural-urban divisions within the state, and the result is the lack of party cohesion and influence in the legislature. Party voting is also low in Missouri, and there too, we do not find a clear rural-urban or socio-economic alignment of the parties.[37] Both parties win seats in rural and urban constituencies in approximately equal proportions.

To say that constituencies make themselves felt in legislative decision making is not to accept completely the image of a legislator as an errand boy, a delegate, or a "lackey." In fact, most legislators will say that they are guided by their conscience rather than their constituency. However, legislators themselves are seldom conscious of the many ways in which their constituency affects their behavior. The classic choice between their district's demands and personal judgment is really an artificial issue to most legislators. They are products of their constituency and they share its goals and values. Conflicts between their district's views and their own

[34] Thomas R. Dye, "A Comparison of Constituency Influences in the Upper and Lower Chambers of a State Legislature," *Western Political Quarterly*, 14 (1966), 473–80; Duncan MacRae, *op. cit.*, pp. 1046–55; Sorauf, *op. cit.*, pp. 133–46; Becker, *op. cit.*, pp. 384–96.

[35] For an analysis of voting patterns in the Ohio legislature, see Thomas A. Flinn, "Party Responsibility in the States: Some Causal Factors," *American Political Science Review*, 58 (1964), 60–71; for the Kansas legislature, see John Grumm, "A Factor Analysis of Legislative Voting," *Midwest Journal of Political Science*, 7 (1963), 336–56.

[36] Daniel M. Ogden, Jr., and Hugh A. Bone, *Washington Politics* (New York: New York University Press, 1960); also cited by Malcolm Jewell, *The State Legislature* (New York: Random House, Inc., 1962), p. 55.

[37] Robert H. Salisbury, *Missouri Politics and State Political Systems*, University of Missouri, Bureau of Governmental Research, 1959; also cited by Jewell, *op. cit.*, p. 59.

are rare. We have seen that legislators have deep roots in their constituencies—many organizational memberships, lifetime residency, shared religious and ethnic affiliations, for example. A legislator is so much "of" his constituency that he needs little direct prompting or supervision. As one discerning legislator commented: "Basically, you represent the thinking of the people who have gone through what you have gone through and who are what you are. You vote according to that. In other words, if you come from a suburb, you reflect the thinking of the people in the suburbs; if you are of depressed people, you reflect that. You represent the sum total of your background." [38]

Interest Groups in State Legislatures

The influence of organized groups in legislative decision making varies from state to state. In Chapter 3 of this volume the reader will find a discussion of interest groups in state politics and an analysis of their relative influence in the 50 states. One way to approach interest group activity in the legislative process is to ask legislators what groups, if any, they see as being powerful. This was the approach of the authors of *The Legislative System*. In the course of their interviews, California legislators referred to 56 specifically named organizations; New Jersey legislators named 38 formal organizations; Ohio legislators named 68 organizations; and Tennessee lawmakers mentioned 40 organizations.[39] Thus, there seems to be little doubt that most legislators are aware of considerable organized lobbying. There is also agreement among legislators about which types of interests are perceived as most powerful. Business interests were named as "most powerful groups" more often than any other interests in all four states. Educational interests are second in three states and tied for third in the other, and labor interests run third in all four states. Agriculture interests, government interests (associations of city, township, and county governments and government employee associations), ethnic and demographic interests, and religious, charitable, and civil interests were given some mention as powerful groups.

On what kinds of decisions are interest groups most likely to exercise influence? Party and constituency influence are most important on broad social and economic issues. But on narrower issues, parties are less likely to take a stand, and constituents are less likely to have either an interest or an opinion. The legislator is, therefore, freer to respond to the pleas of organized groups on highly specialized topics than he is on major issues of public interest. The absence of both party and constituency influence on certain types of issues contributes to the effectiveness of organized interests.

[38] Quotation from Wahlke, *op. cit.*, p. 253.
[39] *Ibid.*, pp. 311–42.

Economic interests, seeking to use the law to improve their competitive position, are a major source of group pressure on these specialized topics. Of course, these arguments are phrased in terms of "the public interest." As Malcolm Jewell reports in Kentucky: "Representatives of horse racing interests write that the introduction of dog racing would damage not only them but the state's way of life. The chiropractors are upset by a bill sponsored by the state medical association. Bank presidents wire to prevent a bill that would permit small loan companies to loan larger amounts. Florists and nurserymen want license laws to limit competition. Local dairies want legislation to guarantee orderly market practices and undercut methods used by chain stores." [40] Particularly active in lobbying are the businesses subject to extensive government regulation. The truckers, railroads, and liquor interests are consistently found to be among the most highly organized and active lobbyists in state capitals. Organized pressure also comes from associations of governments and associations of government employees. State chapters of the National Education Association (NEA) are persistent in presenting the demands of educational administrators and occasionally the demands of the dues-paying teachers as well.

Many legislators welcome the help of organized interests in lawmaking. They depend upon lobbyists to tell them the meaning of complex bills, to keep track of the bills as they move through the legislative maze, to testify at committee hearings, and to provide them with arguments justifying a stand against proposed legislation. Lobbyists also provide the legislator with political information; that is, with information about the groups that are likely to support and oppose particular pieces of legislation. Finally, lobbyists may be a source of campaign contributions for state legislators. Many legislators are hard put to find enough money to finance increasingly expensive campaigns. It is perfectly legal for an interest group to make a contribution. The shrewd lobbyist does not normally exact any specific pledges from a legislator on particular pieces of legislation in exchange for a campaign contribution. The lobbyist simply makes the contribution and relies on the good will that the contribution generates to help him in later legislative battles. It is considered bad taste for a lobbyist to make a campaign contribution at the very time that a bill in which the lobbyist is interested is up for a vote. Lobbying is largely unregulated except for registration requirements established by about half of the states.

The Governor in Legislative Decision Making

The responsibility for initiating major legislative programs in a state falls upon the governor. There is not much incentive for a governor to shirk this responsibility. In the eyes of the public the governor is responsible for

[40] Jewell, *op. cit.*, p. 70.

everything that happens in the state during his term of office, whether he has authority to do anything about it or not. The governor's legislative programs are presented to the legislature in various messages and in his budget. Through his power of policy initiation alone, the governor's impact on the legislature is considerable. The governor sets the agenda for public decision making; he largely determines what the business of the legislature will be in any session. Few major state undertakings ever get started without being initiated by the governor. In setting the agenda of legislative business, the governor frames the issues, determines their context, and decides their timing. By setting the agenda, the governor has a great deal to do with the outcome of issues. However, as influential as the governor can be through policy initiation alone, few governors seem to be content with the role of "initiator" and most interject themselves into the role of "arbiter" as well. In other words, not only do governors propose policy for the legislature, but they also attempt to influence the legislature in its deliberations over these proposals.

Governors have a variety of formal and informal powers, which enable them to involve themselves directly in legislative decisions.[41] Among the formal powers is the governor's right to call special sessions; by utilizing this power a governor can focus attention on an issue and intensify pressure on the legislature. Another formal power is the veto, which every governor has except in North Carolina. In 35 states, it requires a two-thirds vote to override a veto rather than a simple majority. The governor has an item veto on appropriations measures in 41 states. The closing days of any legislative session generally see a flurry of bills passed. A governor can exercise his veto on these measures after the legislature has adjourned, and for all practical purposes foreclose the opportunity of being overriden. Overriding vetoes is a difficult process, since the governor is seldom so weak that he cannot count on at least one-third of the legislature to sustain his veto. A 1947 study showed that there were 1253 vetoes by American state governors (about 5 per cent of the total bills passed), of which only 22 were overridden.[42] The mere threat of a veto can also operate to change the course of legislative action. The state constitution may limit or strengthen the governor's influence in the legislature by determining his frequency of election and ability to succeed himself. All things being equal, a governor with a four year term and an opportunity to succeed himself should be in a stronger position than a governor who faces an election every other year or one who cannot serve more than four years.

The governor has many informal powers at his disposal as well. The governor's office carries prestige in any state; no man becomes governor with-

[41] See Coleman B. Ransome, Jr., *The Office of Governor in the United States* (Tuscaloosa: University of Alabama Press, 1956).

[42] Frank W. Prescott, "The Executive Veto in American States," *Western Political Quarterly*, 3 (1950), 97–111.

out considerable political resources of one kind or another. It is natural that a governor will attempt to use his prestige and resourcefulness to influence legislatures. The governor is the most visible state official. His comments are more newsworthy than those of legislators. He is much more sought after for television, radio, and public appearances. As a consequence, he is able to focus public attention on issues that he considers important. There is no assurance that he will always be able to influence public opinion, but there is little doubt that he has ample opportunity to be heard. Skillfully used, the power of publicity can be more influential than any formal power. In addition, the governors of large urban states are invariably thrust into prominence in national politics. This added national prestige can be used to advantage with legislators, many of whom are anxious to rub shoulders with the great and near great on the American political scene.

Other informal powers stem from the governor's dominant role in his party. In states with competitive two-party systems, the program of the governor is likely to be identified in the public's mind as the program of his party. Legislators know that they carry the same party label into the next election. In some measure they will share with the governor the responsibility for the success or the failure of his program, because of their common party label. It may be sufficient for a governor in a competitive state to tell his party leaders in the legislature that he feels his prestige is at stake on a particular bill and he expects the support of the party faithful. So long as the governor's party has a majority in the legislature, the governor's role in the legislature is strengthened through his leadership of the party. Of course when a governor in a competitive two party state faces a legislature controlled by the opposition party, the fact that the governor's program is linked to the fortunes of his party operates to reduce his influence over the legislature rather than strengthen it.

In contrast to the situation in competitive two party states, the governor of the one party state cannot inspire either loyalty or opposition by virtue of party identification alone. Legislators run independently of the governor and have no political stake in the success of the governor's program. In the one party states where party appeals are themselves insufficient, the astute use of patronage and pork is indispensable in securing support for the governor's program. Pork can include construction contracts, roads, parks, hospitals, and other institutions, state insurance contracts, and innumerable other items. It is in the one party states, with their rural economies, lower family incomes, and poorly educated work forces, that state patronage jobs look most attractive and local pork barrel projects are most important. Robert Highsaw writes about the sources of gubernatorial influence in the one party South: "It is fairly standard practice now for executive leaders to make a careful tabulation of the legislative votes on gubernatorial programs and to tell dissenting legislators that if their attitudes and votes are not changed, they will get no more jobs for constituents, no more state aid for rural roads in their districts, no more favors done, which are the lifeblood of state legislators. The relationship is not subtle; it is direct, brutal, and it is effective." [43]

However, even in two party states, sanctions can only be effective against occasional errant legislators; they cannot be used effectively when the governor's opposition is widespread. The ultimate sanction, that of denying the party's renomination to an errant legislator or defeating him in the general election, is usually unavailable to a governor. Party machinery is localized; it responds to constituency demands, not the voice of the governor. So long as the recalcitrant legislator does not violate constituency expectations, his local party will probably renominate him and his constituency re-elect him.

The legislative influence of governors varies from state to state, and even varies over time and within states. A recent study of the success of governors in passing their legislative programs in a number of states produced the following rather interesting conclusions: [44] (1) Governors appear more successful in competitive two party states where they hold a small majority in the legislature than in one-party states where their party holds an overwhelming majority in the legislature. We might think that the more seats the governor had to spare, the more successful he would be, but this is not the case. Apparently the governor is better able to rally his boys around the flag when he has only a modest majority; when his party becomes an overwhelming majority, he has a more difficult time in organizing support within his own party. (2) A governor is more successful when he wins a large popular vote in the general election. However, the success of the governor in the legislature is more closely related to his showing in the primary election than in the general election. A governor who wins the primary election with little or no opposition seems to have more legislative success than a governor who meets major opposition in his own party's primary. Apparently strong opposition in the party's primary indicates factionalism within the party and the resulting inability of the governor to secure the support of party members in the legislature.

Legislatures in State Politics

At least two general propositions about the function of legislatures in state political systems seem to emerge from this discussion. First of all, it seems

[43] Robert B. Highsaw, "The Southern Governor—Challenge to the Strong Executive Theme," *Public Administration Review*, 2 (1960), p. 30.
[44] Sarah P. McCally, "The Governor and His Legislative Party," *American Political Science Review*, 60 (December, 1966), 923–42.

safe to say that most state legislatures function as "arbiters" of public policy rather than as "initiators." Policy initiation is the function of the governor, the bureaucrat, and the interest group. It is principally these elements that develop policy proposals in the first instance; legislatures are placed in the role of responding to the stimulus provided by these groups.

The structure of legislatures clearly reflects their deliberative function. Their rules and procedures and their leadership and committee systems do not lend themselves to policy initiation so much as they lend themselves to deliberation, discussion, and delay. The size and complexity of state government is the critical ingredient in policy formation. The state budget, for example, perhaps the single most important policy-making document, is drawn up by bureaucrats subordinate to the governor and modified by the governor before submission to the legislature. Legislatures make further modifications, but seldom do they undertake to rewrite an executive budget. Legislatures are still critical obstacles through which appropriation and revenue measures must pass; they are still the scenes of bloody battles over the ends for which public money is to be spent. Yet prior to legislative deliberation, the agenda for decision making has already been drawn up, the framework for conflict has already been established, and the issues have already been placed in particular bills. Sophisticated lawmakers are aware of their function as arbiters rather than initiators of public policy. As one of them put it: "We're the policy making body of the state government, and basically we should give leadership necessary to meet the problems the state faces. But in practice it comes from the executive branch." [45]

A second general proposition about legislatures is that they function to inject into public decision making a parochial influence. Legislatures function to represent locally organized interests, interests manifested in local, rather than statewide, constituencies. Legislators have deep roots in their local constituencies: they have the same religious and ethnic affiliations; they have lived among them for most of their lives; and they meet frequently in their businesses and clubs. The process of recruiting legislators is carried on at the local level. A governor may alienate a particular interest in his state and turn for support to other interests within his heterogeneous constituency. Legislators have no such options; their flexibility is limited by a more restricted and specialized constituency. State legislators clearly function to represent local interests in state politics. Precisely because the constituency of the legislature is territorially defined as many small segments of the state, the legislature will exhibit a parochial bias in decision making. By representing small segments of a state, each legislator represents a more homogeneous constituency than the governor who is chosen by the state at large. The legislator's constituents share a local environment, whether it be rich or poor, rural or urban, mining or manufac-

[45] Quotation from Wahlke, *op. cit.*, p. 255.

turing. As a result they are more likely to have roughly similar opinions on policy matters. The constituency influences on legislators are relatively clear, unmixed, and unambiguous. A governor on the other hand must please a wider, more heterogeneous constituency. No single local interest can dominate his judgment; he can balance one interest against another; he is free to represent widely shared interests throughout the state; and he is freer to direct himself to statewide problems and concerns.

6

GOVERNORS
IN STATE POLITICS

The Many Roles of a Governor

The governor is the central political figure in American state politics. In the eyes of many Americans, the governor is responsible for everything that happens in his state during his term of office, whether he has the authority or the capacity to do anything about it or not. Governors are expected to bring industry into their states, discourage riots in universities, prevent floods, raise teachers' salaries, keep taxes low, reduce unemployment, see that the state gets its fair share of defense contracts from Washington, remove "chiselers" from the welfare rolls, prevent violence in big cities, speed up highway construction, bring tourists into the state, and in some southern states, keep Negroes out of the public schools. These public expectations far exceed the formal authority given to governors in state constitutions. In many ways the expectations placed upon the governor resemble those placed upon the President. But few governors have the powers in state political systems that the President has in the national government. Like the President, the governor is expected to be his state's chief administrator, chief legislator, leader of his party, ceremonial head of his government, chief ambassador to other governments, and leader of public opinion.

As chief executive, he must try to achieve coordination within the state's bureaucracy, oversee the preparation of the state's budget, and supervise major state programs. He must resolve conflicts within his administration and troubleshoot where difficulties arise. He must be concerned with public scandal and endeavor to prevent it from becoming public, or act decisively to eliminate it if it does. The public will hold him responsible for any scandal in his administration whether he was a party to it or not. The public will hold him responsible for the financial structure of the state, whether it was he or his predecessors who were responsible for the state's debts.

Yet, as we shall see in this chapter, the formal administrative powers of a governor are severely restricted. Many of the governor's administrative agencies are headed by elected officials or independent boards or commissions, over which the governor has little or no control. His powers of appointment and removal are severely restricted by state constitutions. Despite a generation of recommendations by political scientists and public administrators that the governor's control over his administration should be strengthened, governors still do not have control over their administration that is commensurate with their responsibility for it.

As chief legislator, the governor is responsible for the major statewide legislative programs. There is a general public expectation that every governor will put forward some sort of legislative program, even a governor committed to a "caretaker" role. The governor largely determines what public issues will be considered by the legislature. By sending bills to the legislature, the governor is cast in the role of the "initiator" of public policy decisions. And if he wants to see his legislative proposals enacted into law, he must also persuade legislators to support them. In other words, he must also involve himself directly in legislative decisions and become an "arbiter" in public policy as well. Yet the governor has very few formal powers over legislation. He can call special sessions of the legislature, and he has the power to veto bills passed by the legislature (except in North Carolina where the governor has no veto power). In 35 states it requires a two-thirds vote to override a veto rather than a simple majority. Yet these formal powers do not by themselves make a governor a state's "chief legislator."

Governors also function as leaders of their party. The governor's office carries great prestige in any state, and no man becomes governor without considerable political resources of one kind or another. The program of the governor is likely to be identified in the public's mind as the program of its party. To some extent, everyone who runs for public office under the same party label as the governor has a stake in his success. Since all who run under the party's label share its common fortunes, and since its fortunes are often governed by the strength of its gubernatorial candidate, there will always be a tendency for loyal party members to support their governor. However, governors do not have the power to deny party nominations to recalcitrant legislators in their own party. Party nominations are determined at the local level in the American states. The governor has little formal authority over members of his own party.

Ceremonial duties occupy a great deal of a governor's time. Yet a governor is seldom able to mobilize the symbolic and ceremonial powers of his office on behalf of state goals in the same way that the President can mobilize the power of his office on behalf of national goals. Emotional ties to state government are not at all comparable to those associated with the national government, not even in the South.

The governor is the chief negotiator with other governments in the American federal system, a variation on the diplomatic role of the President. Governors must negotiate with their local governments on the division of state and local responsibilities for public programs, and with other state governments over coordinating highway development, water pollution, resource conservation, and reciprocity in state laws. Increasingly, governors must undertake responsibility for negotiation with the national government as well. The governor shares responsibility with United States Senators in seeing to it that his state receives a "fair share" of defense contracts, highway monies, educational monies, poverty funds, and so on.

Finally, the governor is a leader of public opinion in his state. He is the most visible of state officials. His comments on public affairs make news, and he is sought after for television, radio, and public appearances. He is able to focus public attention on issues he deems important. He may not always be able to win public opinion to his side, but at least he will be heard.

If the governor has little formal authority to deal with the complex problems of his state, what political resources are available to him to make the most of his leadership? How can he provide the leadership required for the development of the major state programs for education, welfare, highways, taxation, and so on? How can he control his administration, get his bills passed, and negotiate effectively with the federal government? Why is the governor a leader instead of a figurehead? How does he make his influence felt in questions of public policy?

Much of the rest of this chapter is an attempt to come to grips with these questions. But it is clear at the outset that the governor's real power rests upon his abilities at persuasion. His power depends upon his ability to persuade administrators over whom he has little authority, legislators who are jealous of their own powers, party leaders who are selected by local constituents, federal officials over whom the governor has little authority, and a public that thinks he has more authority than he really has. Professor Richard Neustadt has pointed out that even the President of the United States, whose authority over his subordinates is legally much greater than the authority of a governor over his subordinates, must depend upon the power of persuasion to get results. Neustadt reports that in 1952 President

Truman felt that General Eisenhower did not understand that executive powers depended upon persuasion: "He'll sit here," (Truman would remark tapping his desk for emphasis), "and he'll say 'Do this! Do that!' *and nothing will happen.* Poor Ike—it won't be a bit like the Army. He'll find it very frustrating. " [1] Neustadt further reports that Eisenhower indeed found it frustrating: "The President still feels," an Eisenhower aide remarked to me in 1958, "that when he has decided something that ought to be the end of it . . . and when it bounces back undone or done wrong, he tends to react with shocked surprise." [2] Eisenhower eventually realized that the power of persuasion was his most formidable power; Neustadt quotes him as saying "I sit here all day trying to persuade people to do things they ought to have the sense enough to do without my persuading them. . . . that's all the powers of the President amount to." [3] Certainly what is true about the Presidency is even more true about American state governors. Constituents expect more of him in relation to his formal powers than Americans expect of their President in relationship to his formal powers. Consequently, the role of a governor is, above all, that of a persuader—of his own administrators, state legislators, federal officials, party leaders, the press, and the public.

The Making of a Governor

As the central position in American state politics, the governorship is a much sought after office. The prestige of being called "governor" for the rest of one's life, and the opportunity to use the office as a steppingstone to the United States Senate, or even the Presidency or Vice Presidency of the United States, is extremely attractive to men of ambition in American politics. And so the office often attracts men of ability, despite the relatively low pay (salaries range from lows of $10,000 in Arkansas and North Dakota to $50,000 in New York for an average of $25,000; a governor is also provided a mansion and some expense funds in every state). The governor's office is the center of attention in state politics. It has gained in popularity and power in recent years, even though turnover in the office has been very high.

Duane Lockard writes: "The 'ideal' governor has the looks of Adonis, stamina of a marathon runner, a reputation for honesty and independence, political acumen of the highest order, ability to entertain and to educate, and the capacity to appear concerned with the problems of everyone, while remaining calm and collected in the midst of the political whirlwind." [4]

[1] Richard E. Neustadt, *Presidential Power* (New York: John Wiley & Sons, 1960).
[2] *Ibid.*
[3] *Ibid.*
[4] Duane Lockard, *The Politics of State and Local Government* (New York: The Macmillan Company, 1963), p. 365.

There are many types of governors, just as there are many different constituencies in the United States. The urbanity and concern for international affairs displayed by Governor Nelson Rockefeller is a totally different political style from the folksy, provincial approach of Governor Lester Maddox of Georgia. Many governors are the sons of families of great wealth, who have chosen public service as an outlet for their energies—the Roosevelts, the Harrimans, the Rockefellers, the Scrantons. Some are men with successful business careers behind them, such as Governor George Romney of Michigan, former President of American Motors. Others are men of the people, who have emphasized, or exaggerated, their humble beginnings—Huey Long of Louisiana, Al Smith of New York, Gene Talmadge of Georgia. Some promise to bring industry into their state as did Governor Winthrop Rockefeller of Arkansas; others promise to develop the state's educational system as did Governor Terry Sanford of North Carolina; others promise to improve the conditions of minority and labor groups as did Governor Soapy Williams of Michigan; others promise to resist federally imposed "race mixing" as did Governor George Wallace of Alabama; or to aid the farmer as did Orville Freeman of Minnesota; or to reduce state expenditures as did Governor Claude Kirk of Florida, and so on. Governors have been movie actors (Governor Ronald Reagan of California), restaurant owners (Governor Lester Maddox of Georgia), and even professional politicians (Governor David Lawrence of Pennsylvania). But the majority of governors have been lawyers by profession. (The predominance of lawyers in public office is explained in Chapter 5.) The advent of television has apparently increased the accent on youth and good looks among state governors. The median beginning age among governors has declined over the last few decades.

Historically, Presidents were chosen from among the ranks of America's state governors, particularly the governors of the larger states. But recently the importance of international affairs in American politics has detracted somewhat from the popular image of the governorship as a training ground for the Presidency. Governors tend to be associated with domestic rather than foreign policy questions. Men such as Nixon, Kennedy, Goldwater, and Johnson found the United States Senate a good place to promote their campaigns for presidential nominations. Long tenures in the office of the governor are a rarity. Governor Soapy Williams of Michigan was elected to six consecutive two year terms (1948–1960)—a political feat equaled only by Faubus of Arkansas, who was also elected for six consecutive two year terms (1954–1966).

Governors, unlike state legislators, usually come to their office with considerable experience in public affairs.[5] "Promotion" from a statewide elec-

---

[5] See Joseph A. Schlesinger, *How They Became Governor* (East Lansing: Michigan State University Press, 1957).

tive office, particularly lieutenant governor or attorney general, is the most well worn path to the governorship. For example, of the 50 governors holding office in 1965, 21 had previously served in a statewide elective office, including attorney general, lieutenant governor, public service commissioner, comptroller, secretary of state, and state auditor.[6] Experience in the state legislature was also quite common among these 50 governors— 21 had served in their state legislatures at some time before becoming governor. Eight of the 50 governors had been both legislators and holders of statewide elective office. Four governors had served in the state judiciary before assuming office. Eleven governors had experience in local government. Five governors had experience in Congress, and seven had experience in the executive branch of the national government. In fact, only five of the 50 governors had no prior experience in public office.

In recent years more governors have been Democrats than Republicans. Only in 1966 was this tide reversed, and the GOP held more governor's chairs than the Democratic Party (see Table 6.1).

TABLE 6.1

DEMOCRATIC AND REPUBLICAN MARGINS IN ELECTIONS
FOR GOVERNOR 1958-1968

	1958	1960	1962	1964	1966	1968
Alabama	D-88.4	- - - - -	D-96.3	- - - - -	D-63.4	- - - - -
Alaska	D-59.6	- - - - -	D-52.3	- - - - -	R-50.0	- - - - -
Arizona	R-55.1	R-59.3	R-54.8	D-53.2	R-53.8	R59.2
Arkansas	D-82.5	D-69.2	D-73.3	D-57.0	R-54.3	R51.0
California	D-59.7	- - - - -	D-51.9	- - - - -	R-57.6	- - - - -
Colorado	D-58.4	- - - - -	R-56.7	- - - - -	R-54.0	- - - - -
Connecticut	D-62.3	- - - - -	D-53.2	- - - - -	D-55.7	- - - - -
Delaware	- - - - -	D-51.7	- - - - -	D-51.4	- - - - -	R51.5
Florida	- - - - -	D-59.8	- - - - -	D-56.1	R-55.1	- - - - -
Georgia	D-100.0	- - - - -	D-100.0	- - - - -	R-47.4*	- - - - -
Hawaii	R-51.1	- - - - -	D-58.3	- - - - -	D-51.1	- - - - -
Idaho	R-51.0	- - - - -	R-54.6	- - - - -	R-41.4	- - - - -
Illinois	- - - - -	D-55.5	- - - - -	D-51.9	- - - - -	R51.1
Indiana	- - - - -	D-50.4	- - - - -	D-56.2	- - - - -	R52.8
Iowa	D-54.1	R-52.1	D-52.6	D-68.0	D-55.3	R54.0
Kansas	D-56.5	R-56.0	R-53.4	R-50.9	D-54.8	D52.2
Kentucky	- - - - -	D-60.6	- - - - -	D-50.7	- - - - -	R51.2
Louisiana	- - - - -	D-80.5	D-60.7	D-60.7	- - - - -	- - - - -
Maine	D-52.0	R-52.7	R-50.1	- - - - -	D-53.1	- - - - -
Maryland	D-63.6	- - - - -	D-55.7	- - - - -	R-49.6	- - - - -
Massachusetts	D-56.2	R-52.9	D-49.9	R-50.3	R-62.6	- - - - -
Michigan	D-53.0	D-50.6	R-51.4	R-55.9	R-60.5	- - - - -
Minnesota	D-56.8	R-50.6	D-49.7	- - - - -	R-52.6	- - - - -

[6] Council of State Governments, *Book of the States.*

	1958	1960	1962	1964	1966	1968
Mississippi	-----	D-100.0	-----	D-61.9	-----	D65.0
Missouri	-----	D-58.0	-----	D-62.1	-----	D61.1
Montana	-----	R-55.1	-----	R-51.3	-----	D53.6
Nebraska	D-50.2	D-52.3	D-52.2	D-60.0	R-61.5	-----
Nevada	D-59.9	-----	D-66.8	-----	R-52.2	-----
New Hampshire	R-51.7	R-55.5	D-58.9	D-66.8	D-54.0	R52.4
New Jersey	D-57.6	-----	D-50.4	D-57.4	D-57.4	-----
New Mexico	D-50.5	R-52.0	D-53.0	D-60.2	R-51.7	R50.5
New York	R-54.7	-----	D-53.1	D-60.2	R-54.6	-----
North Carolina	-----	D-54.4	-----	D-56.6	-----	D51.7
North Dakota	R-53.1	D-49.4	D-50.4	D-55.7	-----	D54.7
Ohio	D-56.9	-----	R-58.9	-----	R-62.2	-----
Oklahoma	D-74.1	-----	R-55.3	-----	R-55.7	-----
Oregon	R-55.3	-----	R-54.2	-----	R-55.3	-----
Pennsylvania	D-50.8	-----	R-55.4	-----	R-52.1	-----
Rhode Island	R-50.9	D-56.9	R-50.1	R-61.1	R-63.3	D51.7
South Carolina	D-100.0	-----	D-100.0	-----	D-58.2	-----
South Dakota	D-51.4	R-50.7	R-56.1	R-51.7	R-57.7	R57.6
Tennessee	D-57.5	-----	D-50.8	-----	D-81.2	-----
Texas	D-88.1	D-72.8	D-54.0	D-73.8	D-72.8	D56.5
Utah	-----	R-52.7	-----	D-57.0	-----	D68.6
Vermont	R-50.3	R-56.4	D-50.6	D-64.9	D-57.7	R55.0
Virginia	D-63.2	-----	D-63.8	D-47.9	D-47.9	-----
Washington	-----	D-51.3	-----	R-55.8	-----	R53.2
West Virginia	-----	D-54.0	-----	D-54.9	-----	R50.9
Wisconsin	D-53.6	D-51.6	D-50.4	R-50.6	R-53.5	R52.6
Wyoming	D-48.9	-----	R-54.5	-----	R-54.3	-----

* Republican candidate Howard Calloway won the popular vote but failed to obtain the necessary majority; Democratic candidate Lester Maddox was elected by the state legislature.

Source: U.S. Bureau of the Census *Statistical Abstract 1967*, p. 366, 375, updated.

Executive Power in State Government

Frequently we speak of "strong" and "weak" governors. Yet it is difficult to compare the power of one governor with that of another. To do so, one must examine the constitutional position of the governor, his powers of appointment and removal over state officials, his ability or inability to succeed himself, his powers over the state budget, his legislative influence, his position in his own party and its position in state politics, and his influence over interest groups and public opinion in the state.

Let us examine first of all the governor's constitutional position in state government. In many ways the organization of American state government resembles political thinking of 100 or 200 years ago. This colonial experience emphasized "fear of the executive" and resulted in state constitutional restrictions on a governor's term of office, his ability to succeed himself, his control over appointments and removals, the proliferation of separate boards and commissions to govern particular state programs, and long overlapping terms for the members of these boards and commissions. The Jacksonian era of "popular democracy" brought with it the idea that the way to insure popular control of state government was to elect separately as many state officials as possible. The Reform movement of the late 19th and early 20th century led to merit systems and civil service boards, which further curtailed the governor's power of appointment.[7] Not all of these trends were experienced uniformly by all 50 states, and there are considerable variations from state to state in the powers that governors have over the state executive branch. Figure 6.1 is an example of a "weak" executive type of state administrative organization. Many important state offices are governed by boards or commissions whose members may be appointed by the governor with the consent of the state senate but for long overlapping terms, which reduces the governor's influence over members of these boards and commissions. Figure 6.2 is an example of a "strong" executive type of state government organization. Only the governor and lieutenant governor and legislature are elected directly by the people. The governor appoints the heads of all major state agencies for a term that is coterminous with his own.

Fortunately, the trend toward separately elected officials and independent boards and commissions appears to be on the wane. In recent years, "administrative efficiency" has emerged as the central theme in state government reorganization proposals. Since World War II, reorganization proposals have generally emphasized a reduction in the number of departments, more functional integration of state programs, and more power in the governor's office. Yet even though the trend may be toward more streamlined state government organization, it is clear that separately elected officials and independent boards and officials will be around for a long time. Political parties and public officials develop a stake in the continued existence of separately elected public offices; separately elected offices provide more party nominations for the party faithful. Moreover, as we observed in Chapter 3, many interest groups prefer to be governed by boards and commissions that are independent of executive authority. They feel they have more influence over independent boards than those which come directly under a governor's authority. There is often the assumption that boards and commissions enable divergent interests to be represented in the governing of state agencies. Groups are thereby permitted to have a voice in state programs in which they are interested.

Another component of a governor's influence is his ability or inability to succeed himself in office. Turnover in governor's offices is quite high: 16 states have a two year term for the office of governor, and 34 states

---

[7] For a description of the Reform Movement in state and local government see Chapter 9.

"WEAK" EXECUTIVE TYPE OF STATE ADMINISTRATIVE ORGANIZATION

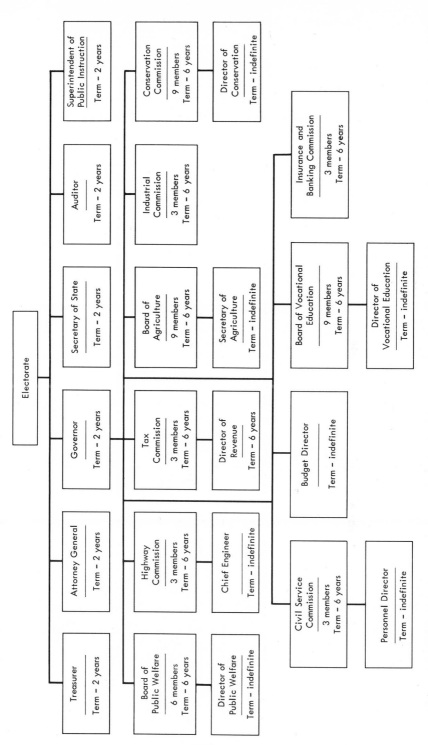

SOURCE: Frederic A. Ogg and P. Orman Ray, *Introduction to American Government*, 13th ed. by William H. Young (New York: Appleton-Century-Crofts, 1966), pp. 772–73. Reproduced by permission of the publisher.

FIGURE 6.2

"STRONG" EXECUTIVE TYPE OF STATE ADMINISTRATIVE ORGANIZATION

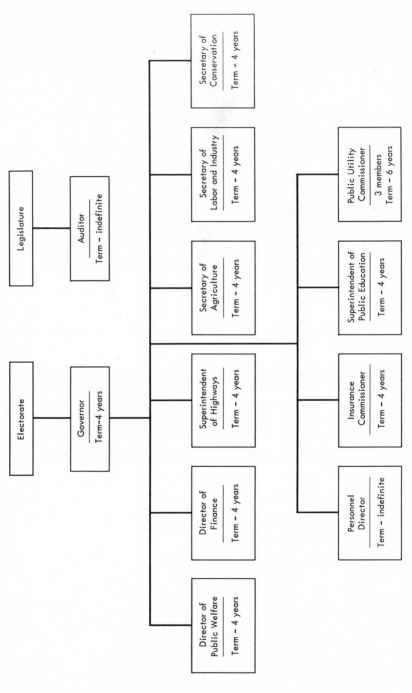

SOURCE: Frederic A. Ogg and P. Orman Ray, *Introduction to American Government*, 13th ed. by William H. Young (New York: Appleton-Century-Crofts, 1966), pp. 772–73. Reproduced by permission of the publisher.

have a four year term. However, about half the states providing for a four year term forbid the incumbent to succeed himself. Turnover figures suggest that minor elected state officials have longer tenures in office than governors. Apparently a typical secretary of state, state treasurer, or state auditor can expect to stay in office longer than the governor (lieutenant governor and attorney general are positions of high turnover like the governor), and this long tenure for minor elected officials further reduces the governor's control over them.

Joseph A. Schlesinger has ranked the states according to the power that a governor derives from his tenure in office.[8] Governors with the highest "tenure power" are those who are elected for a four year term and are permitted to succeed themselves indefinitely. Eleven states fall into this category (see Table 6.2). Governors with the lowest "tenure power" are those who have only two year terms and are permitted only one re-election (New Mexico and South Dakota). The 22nd Amendment to the U.S. Constitution suggests that most Americans believe in restricting executive tenure at the presidential level, and a majority of states have similar restrictions on their governors. However, these constitutional restrictions can

TABLE 6.2

TENURE PROVISIONS FOR GOVERNORS

Four year term, no restrictions on re-election:

California	Illinois	Nevada
Colorado	Massachusetts	New York
Connecticut	Michigan	North Dakota
Hawaii	Minnesota	Utah
Idaho	Montana	Washington
		Wyoming

Four year term, restricted to two terms:

Alaska	Maryland	Ohio
Delaware	Missouri	Oklahoma
Louisiana	Nebraska	Oregon
Maine	New Jersey	

Four year term, consecutive re-election prohibited:

Alabama	Mississippi	Tennessee
Florida	North Carolina	Virginia
Georgia	Pennsylvania	West Virginia
Indiana	South Carolina	
Kentucky		

Two year term, no restrictions on re-election:

Arizona	New Hampshire	Wisconsin
Arkansas	Rhode Island	
Iowa	Texas	
Kansas	Vermont	

Two year term, restricted to two terms:

New Mexico	South Dakota

[8] Joseph A. Schlesinger, "The Politics of the Executive," *Politics in the American States*, Herbert Jacob and Kenneth Vines, eds. (Boston: Little, Brown and Co., 1965).

be circumvented by a very powerful governor. When Governor Wallace of Alabama was restricted by his state's constitution to a single four year term, his wife ran in his place, with Wallace openly avowing that if she were elected he would run the state. Apparently the voters of Alabama were quite willing to accept this arrangement despite the obvious circumvention of the Alabama Constitution; Lurleen Wallace won an overwhelming victory at the polls. A similar circumvention of constitutional intent on the governor's tenure occurred in the 1930's, when "Ma" and "Pa" Ferguson alternately governed the state of Texas.

The Governor's Managerial Powers

Perhaps the most important managerial power is the power to appoint subordinate officials. Personal appointment of subordinates does not guarantee their responsibility, but there is a greater likelihood that an official appointed by a governor will be someone whose values coincide with those of the governor. Of course a governor is subject to many different pressures in exercising his appointing power; often he must pay off political debts or win the support of a political faction by his selection. Salary limitations and the shortness of tenure make it exceedingly difficult to find capable men for positions of high responsibility in state government. But it is safe to infer that a governor who can name his major department heads is stronger than a governor who cannot. As we have already seen, many department heads in state government are popularly elected, and many departments are headed by elected or appointed boards or commissions over whom the governor has relatively little control.

Joseph M. Schlesinger has undertaken to compare the governors' appointive powers in all 50 states. Taking 16 major governmental functions in every state, he scored each according to the relative influence, in formal terms, which the governor has over the appointment of the head of each agency handling these functions.[9] If the governor can appoint an agency head without the need for legislative confirmation, this gives him strong appointive power. The need for legislative confirmation by one or both houses reduces the governor's formal appointive power; and of course, if an agency head is appointed by a separate board rather than the governor, this further reduces his appointive power. Finally, if an agency head is separately elected by the people, the governor has no formal authority over his appointment. Schlesinger classified the fifty states according to the degree to which the governor had formal appointive powers within the executive branch of government (see Table 6.3). The governor of Ten-

[9] These functions are finance, agriculture, attorney general, auditor, budget officer, conservation, comptroller, education, health, highways, insurance, labor, secretary of state, tax commissioner, treasurer, and welfare.

TABLE 6.3

APPOINTIVE POWERS OF GOVERNORS

Very Strong	Strong	Moderate
Tennessee	Michigan	Iowa
New Jersey	Vermont	New Mexico
Pennsylvania	Missouri	Utah
Maryland	Ohio	Rhode Island
New York	Oregon	California
Idaho	Minnesota	Nebraska
Indiana	Washington	Alabama
Virginia	Connecticut	Arizona
Illinois	Kentucky	Wyoming

Weak	Very Weak	
Nevada	Alaska	Texas
Arkansas	Maine	South Carolina
Kansas	Mississippi	Delaware
Louisiana	New Hampshire	Oklahoma
Montana	Massachusetts	North Dakota
Wisconsin	Georgia	Colorado
South Dakota		
Florida		
North Carolina		

nessee had the strongest appointive power and governor of Colorado the weakest. States that have had major constitutional revisions in recent years, such as New Jersey, New York, and Tennessee, rate high. This is a reflection of the extent of management reform in these states. The reason why Tennessee ranks so high is that its governor is the only elected officer (with the exception of three public utilities commissioners), and most of the other major positions in state government are filled by him without the need for legislative approval. However, even in Tennessee, the secretary of state, treasurer, and comptroller are chosen by the legislature rather than the governor. At the other extreme, Colorado's governor has weak appointive powers not only because Colorado's secretary of state, attorney general, treasurer, and auditor are popularly elected, but also because major departments, such as agriculture, labor, health, and so on are headed by civil service appointees. North Dakota's governor has weak appointive powers because, in addition to the usual elective offices, the tax commissioner, and commissioner of agriculture, labor, and insurance are also elected positions.

Restrictions on a governor's power of appointment are further complicated by restrictions on his power of removal. A common statutory or constitutional provision dealing with the governor's removal states that removal must be "for cause only"; that is, the governor must provide a clearcut statement of charges and an opportunity for an open hearing to the employee he is trying to oust. This process is often unpleasant, and governors seek to avoid it, unless they have strong evidence of incompetence, fraud, or mismanagement. When a governor's removal powers are limited "for cause only," it is next to impossible to remove a subordinate for policy differences. Of course a governor may request an officeholder to resign, even when the governor's removal power is limited, and such a request may be honored by the officeholder in preference to continued unhappy relationships with the governor's office or in fear of the governor's ability to mobilize public opinion against him. As a final resort, a determined governor with influence in the legislature can always oust an official by a legislative act, which abolishes the office or agency the official heads and replaces it with another; this device is sometimes called a "ripper bill."

Certain elected state officials, notably the lieutenant governor and attorney general, often use their positions to advance their own candidacy for the governorship or U.S. Senate, thus creating further problems for a governor, particularly when their ambitions are in competition with his own. Lieutenant governors, of course, have few substantive duties in state government, other than the ceremonial one of presiding over the state senate. But the attorney general has more influence—his legal opinions have great importance for a governor's program. Governors are often bound by statute to conform to the attorney general's legal opinion in interpreting state laws and constitutions.

The governor's control over patronage is another potential source of executive power in state government. A governor can win the support of party chairmen throughout the state by providing them with jobs to dispense to "deserving" party workers. This provides prestige and power to party chairmen within their communities, and they are expected to return the favor by supporting the governor. Patronage jobs are particularly important in depressed economies. In the one party states of the South, for example, with their rural economies, lower family incomes, and poorly educated work forces, state jobs look most attractive. But Frank Sorauf reports that patronage jobs in urban industrial economies are insecure and unattractive, at best "short term desperation job alternatives." [10] A large number of state jobs on highways and public works are lower paid, menial positions, which are not very attractive in a wealthy state. Other state jobs require specialized skills and training and do not lend themselves to patronage appointments. Patronage has declined in recent years in importance not only as a product of economic development, but also as a result of the growth of civil service systems. A great expansion of state civil service systems occurred after 1936, as a result of the requirement of the federal

[10] Frank J. Sorauf, "State Patronage in a Rural County," *American Political Science Review,* 50 (1956), 1046.

Social Security Act of that year that states participating in national grants under that law must install civil service systems for employees in the federally aided public assistance, insurance, and health programs. Civil service coverage is now required in state agencies financed even in part by federal grants-in-aid. This national requirement inspired many states to extend civil service coverage to a large number of their own employees. Today more than half of all state employees are under civil service.

Civil service systems, particularly those administered by independent civil service commissions, significantly reduce executive control over program administration. There is a persistent tendency for civil service systems to be routine, mechanical, and unimaginative. Job classification schemes, to which recruitment, qualifications, and pay scales are closely tied, become so rigid with time that executives have little flexibility in recruiting really talented people to state government. Executives whose authority to promote, hire, and fire their employees is severely curtailed can hardly be expected to obtain maximum effort and cooperation from their employees. The Michigan Civil Service Commission, for example, is independent of both the governor and the legislature; it is established in the state constitution, and even its budget is guaranteed by a constitutional amendment that it must receive 1 per cent of the administrative payroll of the state for its operating expenses. Even the public administration experts, who originally supported the civil service movement and the removal of state jobs from the governor's authority, are beginning to recommend that the power over personnel administration be returned to the governor.

The Governor's Fiscal Powers

The state budget is the most important policy document in state government. The governor's control over the state budget is perhaps his most formidable power. While the legislature must enact the state budget into law, and no state monies may be spent without a legislative appropriation, in practice the greatest amount of control over state government rests with the governor and his budget staff. The governor has full responsibility for the preparation of the budget and its submission to the legislature in a majority of states, but in some states he shares this responsibility with a civil service appointee or an appointee of someone other than himself, and in other states he shares the power to prepare the budget with popularly elected officials or members of the legislature (see Table 6.4).

Budget-making involves bringing together the requests of all existing state agencies, calculating the costs of new state programs, estimating the probable income of the state, and evaluating these costs and income estimates in the light of program and policy objectives. The final budget document is submitted to the legislature for its adoption as an appropriations

TABLE 6.4

BUDGET POWERS OF GOVERNORS

	Full Responsibility	
Alabama	Minnesota	Oregon
Arkansas	Missouri	Pennsylvania
California	Montana	South Dakota
Georgia	Nebraska	Tennessee
Illinois	Nevada	Utah
Iowa	New Hampshire	Virginia
Kentucky	New Jersey	Washington
Maryland	New York	Wisconsin
Massachusetts	Ohio	Wyoming
Michigan	Oklahoma	
	Responsibility Shared with Appointee	
Colorado	Louisiana	North Carolina
Connecticut	Maine	Rhode Island
Kansas	New Mexico	Indiana
	Responsibility Shared With Elected Official	
Arizona	Idaho	South Carolina
Vermont	Mississippi	Texas
Delaware	North Dakota	West Virginia
Florida		

measure. No state monies can be spent without a legislative appropriation, and the legislature can make any alterations in the state budget that it sees fit. Potentially, then, a legislature can control any activity of the state government through its power over appropriations, but as a practical matter, the legislature seldom reviews every item of the governor's budget. In practice, budgets tend to reflect the views of those responsible for their preparation, namely, the governor. Thomas Anton summarizes the role of state agencies, budget officers, governors, and legislatures in budget-making as follows: "A peek into the decision making black box in most states, I submit, would probably reveal a system in which operating agency heads consistently request more funds, executive and/or legislative reviewers consistently reduce agency requests, governors consistently pursue balanced budgets at higher expenditure levels, and legislatures consistently approve higher appropriations while engaging in frequent disputes with the governor over revenues." [11]

The pressure for budget increases comes from the request of agency officials. Most agency officials feel compelled to ask for more money each year. According to Anton, requesting an increase in funds "affirms the

[11] Thomas J. Anton, "Roles and Symbols in the Determination of State Expenditures," *Midwest Journal of Political Science,* 11 (February, 1967), 36; see also Thomas J. Anton, *The Politics of State Expenditure in Illinois* (Urbana: University of Illinois Press, 1966).

significance and protects the status of agency employees, assures clientele groups that new and higher standards of service are being pursued aggressively," [12] and gives the governor's office and the legislature something to cut that will not affect existing programs. The governor's budget staff generally recognizes the built-in pressure to expand budgets. The budget staff see themselves as "cutters." As Allen Schick describes it: "The agencies, anticipating a cut, overestimate their needs and pad the budget, while the budget office, in the conviction that the budget is padded, make deep cuts in the agency's estimates." [13] Agencies press for budgetary expansion with better programs in mind, while the governor's budget staff tries to reduce expenditures with cost cutting in mind.

While most states have executive budget systems, and the governor is responsible for the activities of his budgetary staff, the governor's actual control over state spending is limited in many ways. First of all, it is quite common to "earmark" in state constitutions and laws certain funds for particular purposes, such as gasoline taxes for highways. The earmarking device provides certain agencies with an independent source of income, thus reducing the governor's control over operations. In addition, Anton writes: "The governor will probably come to his position without any direct experience in dealing with state finance. His own inexperience will thus provide a sharp contrast to the wisdom of the old hands who occupy administrative and legislative positions of influence, and who will probably regard the governor as an outsider—a "new boy" come to meddle in their affairs. Moreover, since the average length of service for most governors is less than five years, the old hands can constantly think of the "new boy" as someone who is likely to be gone from the scene far in advance of their own departure." [14] It is not easy for a governor to master the "constitutional limitations, marvelously incoherent divisions of financial accountability, incomprehensible budget documents, and worst of all, an intricate maze of general funds, special funds, revolving funds, loan funds, trust funds, federal funds, local funds, all conspired to shroud the state's financial situation in mystery." [15]

Governors have little influence over many items of state spending. Over 50 per cent of state finances come from special "earmarked" funds. What is left, "general fund expenditures," are also largely committed to existing state programs, particularly welfare and education. Governors typically campaign on platforms stressing both increased service and increased economy. Once in office, however, they typically find it impossible to accomplish both and very difficult to accomplish either one. Often new pro-

---

[12] *Ibid.,* p. 29.
[13] Allen Schick, "Control Patterns in State Budget Execution," *Public Administration Review,* 24 (1964), 99.
[14] Anton, *Midwest Journal of Political Science,* p. 32.
[15] *Ibid.,* p. 33.

grams planned by a governor must be put aside, because money must be found to educate more students who are entitled to an education under existing programs; or money must be found to pay the welfare costs of additional clients who are entitled to care under existing programs; or money must be found to raise the salaries of state personnel who are adminstering existing programs. The result is that social and economic conditions really "determine" expenditures and governors have little flexibility in budget-making. Anton feels that governors must focus most of their attention on revenue, which typically must be increased just to keep pace with existing programs. "Governors may be regarded as 'money providers' or as 'budget balancers'; only infrequently can they be viewed as 'decision makers' in the determination of state expenditures." [16] (See Chapter 17 for further discussion.)

The Governor's Legislative Powers

The responsibility for initiating major statewide legislative programs falls upon the governor. The governor's programs are presented to the legislature in various governor's messages and in his budget. Much of the governor's power over the legislature stems from his power as party leader of public opinion. However, the governor's veto power is a source of formal authority over legislature and deserves special attention. Joseph M. Schlesinger notes that governor's veto powers can vary in several ways.[17] Only in North Carolina does the governor have no veto power at all. In some states, the veto power is restricted by giving the governor only a short time to consider a bill after it has passed the legislature, by permitting a simple majority of legislative members to override the veto, or by requiring vetoed bills to reappear at the next legislative session. In other states governors have the added power of the item veto, they are given longer periods of time to consider a bill, and a two-thirds vote of both houses of the legislature is required to override a veto rather than a simple majority. Thus, it is possible to rank states according to the strength of the governor's veto; this is done in Table 6.5.

Since we have already discussed the governor's power over the legislature in Chapter 4, let us turn to a consideration of the legislature's power over executive departments. Professor Deil S. Wright asked 933 department and agency heads from all 50 states a series of questions about legislative versus gubernatorial influence in their departments.[18] One question asked the agency heads to judge whether the governor or the legislature exercised greater control over the affairs of his department. As Table 6.6

[16] *Ibid.,* p. 34.

[17] Schlesinger, *Politics in the American States,* pp. 227–28.

[18] Deil S. Wright, "Executive Leadership in State Administration," *Midwest Journal of Political Science,* 11 (February, 1967), 1–26.

TABLE 6.5

THE GOVERNORS' VETO POWERS

Very strong	Strong	Medium	Weak
Alabama	Arizona	Arkansas	Indiana
California	Georgia	Connecticut	North Carolina
Colorado	Idaho	Florida	Rhode Island
Delaware	Illinois	Iowa	Tenessee
Louisiana	Kansas	Kentucky	West Virginia
Massachusetts	Michigan	Maine	
Missouri	Minnesota	Maryland	
Montana	New Mexico	Mississippi	
New Jersey	North Dakota	Nebraska	
New York	Oregon	Nevada	
Oklahoma	South Dakota	New Hampshire	
Pennsylvania	Texas	Ohio	
Virginia	Utah	South Carolina	
	Washington	Vermont	
	Wisconsin		
	Wyoming		

Source: F.W. Prescott, "The Executive Veto in American states," *Western Political Quarterly*, 3 (1950), 98-112.

indicates, more agency heads felt that the legislature exercised greater control over their departments than the governor. Agency heads also felt that the legislature was more likely to reduce their budget requests than the governor, and that the governor was more sympathetic to the goals of their agency than the legislature. Agency heads generally preferred gubernatorial control to control by the legislature, but many agency heads seemed to prefer independence from either direct gubernatorial or direct legislative control.

Wright also found that state executives are generally disposed to respond in favor of enlarging their own programs and those of the state government generally. Table 6.7 documents their attitudes toward expansion of state services and expenditures. Almost one-third felt that their agency's expenditures should be increased by more than 15 per cent. Only one-fourth of the agency heads interviewed felt their own programs did not need expansion.

The Powers of Governors: A Comparative View

It is possible to combine several of the measures of the governor's formal powers into a combined index of governor's powers in all 50 states. In Table 6.8, Joseph A. Schlesinger has combined four measures of the governor's strength already presented: his tenure potential, his appointive

TABLE 6.6

ATTITUDES OF AMERICAN STATE EXECUTIVES ON POLITICAL
RELATIONSHIPS*

	Percentages** (N=933)
Who Exercises Greater Control Over Your Agency's Affairs?	
Governor	32
Each About the Same	22
Legislature	44
Other and N.A.	2
	100
Who Has The Greater Tendency To Reduce Budget Requests?	
Governor	25
Legislature	60
Other and N.A.	15
	100
Who Is More Sympathetic To The Goals Of Your Agency?	
Governor	55
Each About the Same	14
Legislature	20
Other and N.A.	11
	100
What Type Of Control Do You Prefer?	
Governor	42
Independent Commission	28
Legislature	24
Other and N.A.	5
	100

*For the source of data and the survey instrument containing the precise wording
of the questions see: Deil S. Wright and Richard L. McAnaw, "American State
Administrators: Study Code and Marginal Tabulations for the State Administrative
Officials Questionnaire," (Iowa City, Iowa: Department of Political Science and
Institute of Public Affairs, January, 1965), mimeographed, 40 pp.
**Tabled percentages may not add to 100 because of rounding.
Source: Deil S. Wright, "Executive Leadership in State Administration," *Midwest
Journal of Political Science*, II (February, 1967), *p* 4.

powers, his budgetary powers, and his veto powers. Schlesinger's rankings
of the formal power of governors suggest that it is the urban industrial
states that require strong executive government. The large urban industrial
states—New York, Illinois, New Jersey, Pennsylvania, and California—
all rate near the top in formal gubernatorial powers. States at the bottom
of the rankings tend to be the smaller, rural, agricultural states. Apparently size, urbanization, and industrialization increase the complexity of
state administration and the need for formal gubernatorial powers. This
does not necessarily mean, as Schlesinger points out, that within the context

TABLE 6.7

ATTITUDES OF AMERICAN STATE EXECUTIVES ON EXPANSION OF STATE
AND OWN AGENCY'S SERVICES AND EXPENDITURES

Attitude toward degree of expansion	Overall expansion of state services and expenditures	Expansion of own agency services and expenditures
	(percentages; number of cases in parentheses)	
No Expansion	30	24
Expand 0-5 Per Cent	7	8
Expand 5-10 Per Cent	19	16
Expand 10-15 Per Cent	16	16
Expand 15 Plus Per Cent	18	31
Other and N.A.	10	6
Total	100 (933)	100 (933)

Source: Deil S. Wright, "Executive Leadership in State Administration," *Midwest Journal of Political Science,* Vol. 11 (February, 1967), p. 18.

of their own states the governors of Mississippi and North Dakota do not have as much influence as the governors of New York and Illinois. It means only that the governors of New York and Illinois need more formal powers to control the large complex bureaucracies in those states. Within their own borders, the governors of Mississippi and North Dakota are still central figures in their state's political system. We have already observed that minor jobs, contracts, and patronage provide governors of small, rural, agricultural states with more power than the governors of urban, industrial states. These small favors are less important in urban, industrial states where the governors require formal hierarchical controls.

It is also interesting to observe that the governor's formal powers are greatest in the states with the highest party competition.

The Governor as Political Leader

The governor is the most visible figure in state politics. He commands the attention of press, radio, and television. He has a greater opportunity than any other state official to exercise leadership by persuasion. An attractive governor who is skillful in public relations can command support from administrators, legislators, local officials, and party leaders through public appeals to their constituents. Politicians must respect the governor's greater access to the communications media and hence to the minds of their constituents. An effective governor not only understands the broad range of issues facing his state but is also able to speak clearly and per-

TABLE 6.8

A COMBINED INDEX OF THE FORMAL POWERS OF THE GOVERNORS

	Budget powers	Appointive powers	Tenure potential	Veto powers	Total index
New York	5	5	5	4	19
Illinois	5	5	5	3	18
New Jersey	5	5	4	4	18
Pennsylvania	5	5	3	4	17
Virginia	5	5	3	4	17
Washington	5	4	5	3	17
California	5	3	5	4	17
Maryland	5	5	4	2	16
Missouri	5	4	3	4	16
Oregon	5	4	4	3	16
Utah	5	3	5	3	16
Wyoming	5	3	5	3	16
Montana	5	2	5	4	16
Alabama	5	3	3	4	15
Connecticut	4	4	5	2	15
Ohio	5	4	4	2	15
Tennessee	5	5	3	1	14
Kentucky	5	4	3	2	14
Michigan	5	4	2	3	14
Minnesota	5	4	2	3	14
Nevada	5	2	5	2	14
Colorado	4	1	5	4	14
Idaho	1	5	5	3	14
Louisiana	4	2	3	4	13
Oklahoma	5	1	3	4	13
Iowa	5	3	2	2	12
Nebraska	5	3	2	2	12
Wisconsin	5	2	2	3	12
Georgia	5	1	3	3	12
Massachusetts	5	1	2	4	12
Indiana	3	5	3	1	12
Arkansas	5	2	2	2	11
South Dakota	5	2	1	3	11
New Mexico	4	3	1	3	11
Kansas	4	2	2	3	11
Maine	4	1	4	2	11
New Hampshire	5	1	2	2	10
Rhode Island	4	3	2	1	10
North Carolina	4	2	3	1	10
Vermont	2	4	2	2	10
Arizona	2	3	2	3	10
Delaware	1	1	4	4	10
West Virginia	1	3	3	1	8
Florida	1	2	3	2	8
Mississippi	1	1	3	2	7
South Carolina	1	1	3	2	7

	Budget powers	Appointive powers	Tenure potential	Veto powers	Total index
Texas	1	1	2	3	7
North Dakota	1	1	2	3	7

Source: Joseph M. Schlesinger, "Politics of the Executive," in *Politics in the American States*, eds. Herbert Jacob and Kenneth Vines (New York: Little, Brown, & Co., 1965), p. 229. Note: Schlesinger index is based on figures for 1962-63.

suasively about them. A governor's reputation as a leader, however, stems not only from what he says but also from what he does. His reputation must include a capacity to decide issues and to persist in his decision once it is made. A reputation for backing down, for avoiding situations that involve him in public conflict, or for wavering in the face of momentary pressures invite the governor's adversaries to ignore or oppose him. A sense of insecurity or weakness can damage a governor's power more than any constitutional limitation. A governor can also increase his influence by developing a reputation for punishing his adversaries and rewarding his supporters. Once his reputation as an effective leader is established, cooperation is often forthcoming in anticipation of the governor's reaction. As Duane Lockard points out: "Reputations may be intangible and based upon gossip and rumor, but they may nevertheless be the foundation of gubernatorial power or weakness." [19]

Governors are also the recognized leaders of their state parties. In a majority of states, it is the governor who picks the state party chairman and who is consulted in questions of party platform, campaign tactics, nominations for party office, and party finances. Governors are generally leading spokesmen for their state parties at national party conventions. On the whole, governors play a much more prominent role in national convention politics than congressmen, mayors, or other party officials.

The amount of power which a governor derives from his position as party leader varies from state to state according to the strength, cohesion, and discipline of the state parties. A few governors have been able to build strong party organization in their states and have gained power through partisan appeal. In urban, industrial states, where party lines reflect socioeconomic, religious, and ethnic divisions, the governor can exercise great power by an appeal to party loyalty. Given the absence of divided government, a governor can win support by telling his party leaders that he feels that his prestige and the prestige of the party is at stake on a particular measure and that he expects the support of the party faithful. Of course when a governor in a competitive two party state faces a legislature controlled by the opposition party, an outright partisan appeal is likely to reduce rather than to increase his influence in the legislature. Where a gov-

[19] Lockard, *Politics of State and Local Government*, p. 371.

ernor's party is not in firm control of the state's political scene, a nonpartisan approach may strengthen the governor's influence.

Of course in one party states, particularly in the South and the Midwest, the party mechanism is not really an effective instrument of gubernatorial power. Governors in one party states must rely upon personal organizations or factional support. As we observed earlier, one party states are really no-party states. The Governor must negotiate with individuals and factions in the legislature on an issue by issue basis to accomplish his program.

There are at least three limitations to the power that a governor derives from his role as party leader. First of all, a governor cannot deny party renomination to disloyal members. City and county leaders and state legislators hold their position by their own efforts and owe the governor nothing. Party machinery is localized; it responds to constituency demands, not the voice of the governor. Secondly, the frequency of divided control, where the governor faces the legislature dominated by the opposition party, requires him to bargain with individuals and groups in the opposition party. If he has acquired a reputation for being too "partisan" in his approach to state programs, he will find it difficult to win over the necessary support of opposition party members. Finally, the use of patronage may make as many enemies as friends. An old political maxim states that, "For every one patronage appointment, you make 9 enemies and 1 ingrate."

Governors of the populous, urban states occupy prominent roles in national politics. This added national prestige can be useful with politicians who are anxious to rub shoulders with the great and near great on the American political scene. In recent years, however, governors have had to give way to U.S. Senators in presidential politics. In both 1960 and 1964, none of the presidential or vice presidential candidates of either party had ever been a governor. Undoubtedly, part of the reason lies in the increasing importance of foreign policy issues in contrast to domestic issues where governors had their experience. Austin Ranney provides another explanation:

"The reason for the new political vulnerability of governors is plain:

> Most state governments . . . now face enormously increased demands for more and better schools, highways, welfare, recreational facilities and so on—but most face them armed with very inadequate revenue sources. Consequently, most large two party states are in perpetual financial crisis. The governor is to a great extent the most visible state official and therefore, the logical scapegoat to the state's apparent inability to solve its problems. It is he who must press for new taxes or announce the curtailment of services—neither of which makes for political popularity. Thus, when the voters wish to express their annoyance with high taxes or inadequate services, the governor is the natural target.[20]

[20] Austin Ranney, "Parties in State Politics," *Politics in the American States,* Herbert Jacob and Kenneth Vines, eds. (Boston: Little, Brown and Co., 1965), p. 91.

Other Executive Offices

The lieutenant governor's office in many states is looked upon as a campaign platform for the governorship. Lieutenant governors are said to have a two or four year head start for the top job. The lieutenant governor's formal duties are comparable to the Vice President of the United States; in other words, lieutenant governors have relatively little to do. The two basic functions of the office are to serve in direct line of succession to the governor and replace him in the event of a vacancy in that office, and to be the presiding officer of the state senate. Since lieutenant governors generally have political ambitions of their own, they seldom make good "assistant governors" who will submerge their own interests for the success of the governor's administration. Unlike the vice president, lieutenant governors are separately elected and are sometimes members of the governor's opposition party. Some efforts have been made to reduce the boredom of the lieutenant governor's office by assigning him membership on various boards and commissions. Lieutenant governors are frequently members of pardon and parole boards, boards of education, and so on. Thirty-nine states have separately elected lieutenant governors.

The office of attorney general has more real powers and responsibilities than that of lieutenant governor. Attorneys general are elected in 42 states, appointed by the supreme court in Tennessee, by the legislature in Maine, and by the governor in Alaska, Hawaii, New Hampshire, New Jersey, Pennsylvania, and Wyoming. The attorney general is the chief legal counsel for the state. He represents the state in any suits to which it is a party. He acts as legal counsel for the governor and for other state executive officials.

TABLE 6.9

NUMBER OF STATES WITH ELECTED EXECUTIVE OFFICIALS

Governor	50		
Attorney General	42	University Regents	7
State Treasurer	40	Mining Commissioner	5
Secretary of State	39	Tax Commission	3
Lieutenant Governor	38	Highway Commissioner	2
State Auditor	30	Board of Equalization	1
Superintendent of Education	26	Printer	1
Public Utilities Commission	14	Railroad Commission	1
Agriculture Commission	11	Fish and Game Commission	1
Controller	10	Corporation Commission	1
Board of Education	10	Commissioner of Charities	1
Insurance Commissioner	8	Secretary of Internal Affairs	1
Land Commissioner	8	Adjutant and Inspector General	1

The legal business of state agencies is subject to his supervision. The source of the attorney general's power comes from his quasi-judicial duty of rendering formal written opinions in response to requests from the governor, state agencies, or other public officials, regarding the legality and constitutionality of their acts. His opinions have the power of law in state affairs unless they are successfully challenged in court. The governor and other state officials are generally obliged to conform to the attorney general's legal opinion until a court specifies otherwise. He renders authoritative interpretations of state constitutions, laws, city ordinances, and administrative rulings.

The attorney general also has substantial law enforcement powers. Thirty-eight states allow the attorney general to initiate criminal proceedings on his own motion, and nearly all states assign him responsibility for handling criminal cases on appeal to higher state courts or to federal courts. In some states the attorney general has supervisory powers over law enforcement throughout the state. The California constitution, for example, gives the attorney general supervisory powers over all district attorneys and sheriffs in the state.

Forty states have elected treasurers, and treasurers in other states are appointed by either the governor or the legislature. Treasurers are custodians of state funds: collecting taxes; acting as paymaster for the state; and administering the investment of state funds. The principal job of the treasurer is to make payments on departmental requisitions for payrolls and for checks to be issued to those who have furnished the state with goods or services. Generally, the department's requests for checks must be accompanied by a voucher showing the proper legislative authority for such payment. Generally requests for payment must also be accompanied by a statement from the auditor or comptroller's office that legislative appropriations are available for such payment. Thus the treasurer's office works in close relation to another executive office of importance: that of auditor or comptroller. The principal duty of the office of state "auditor" is that of insuring the legislature that expenditures and investment of state funds have been made in accordance with the law. This function is known as a "post audit" and occurs after state expenditures have been made. The primary duty of the office of the state "comptroller" is to insure that a prospective departmental expenditure is in accordance with the law and does not exceed the appropriations made by the legislature. This "pre-audit" occurs before any expenditure is made by the treasurer. Public administration experts consider the comptroller's job of pre-audit to be an executive function, and they urge that the comptroller be appointed by the governor. On the other hand, the job of post-audit is essentially a legislative check on the executive, and students of public administration generally feel that the auditor should be elected or appointed by the legislature.

However, there is still some confusion in state organizations about the separate functions of auditors and comptrollers—some auditors do "pre-auditing" and some comptrollers do "post-auditing."

Another interesting state office is that of secretary of state. Thirty-nine states elect secretaries of state and they are appointed by the governor in seven states and by the legislature in three. Only Hawaii does not have a secretary of state. Like the lieutenant governor, the secretary of state has very little to keep him busy. He is the chief custodian of state records and, in the case of several states, "keeper of the great seal of the commonwealth." He keeps many state documents filed in his office, including corporation papers. He also supervises the preparation of ballots and certifies election results for the state. The keeping of documents and the supervision of elections does not involve much discretionary power, since these activities are closely regulated by law.

7

COURTS, CRIME,

AND CORRECTIONAL POLICY

Politics and the Judicial Process

Courts are "political" institutions because they attempt to resolve conflicts among men. Like legislative and executive institutions, courts make public policy in the process of resolving conflict. Some of the nation's most important policy decisions have been made by courts rather than legislative or executive bodies. In recent years the federal courts have taken the lead in eliminating segregation in public life, insuring the separation of church and state, defining relationships between individuals and law enforcers, and guaranteeing individual voters an equal voice in government. These are just a few of the important policy decisions made by courts—policy decisions that are just as significant to all Americans as those made by Congress or the President. Courts, then, are deeply involved in policy making, and they are an important part of the political system in America. Sooner or later in American politics, most important policy questions reach the courts. Interests that are unsuccessful in the legislative and executive branches of government usually turn to the courts in a final effort to win their arguments. All manner of political controversy are brought to the courts—election disputes, rivalries between governmental agencies, disputes over the meaning of laws and constitutions, and so on.[1]

[1] For a discussion of courts as political institutions see Herbert Jacob, *Justice in America* (Boston: Little, Brown and Co., 1965); Henry J. Abraham, *The Judicial Process* (New York: Oxford University Press, 1962).

In resolving conflict and deciding about public policy, courts function very much like other government agencies. However, the *style* of judicial decision making differs significantly from legislative or executive decision making. First of all, courts rarely initiate policy decisions. Rather, they wait until a case involving a policy question they must decide is brought to them. However, the vast majority of cases brought before courts do not involve important policy issues. Much court activity involves the enforcement of existing public policy. Courts punish criminals, enforce contracts, and award damages to the victims of injuries. Most of these decisions are based upon established law. Only occasionally are important policy questions brought to the court. This "passive" character of the judicial process restricts the policy initiative of judges; neither legislators nor executives suffer from such restrictions. In defining the judicial process, Carl Brent Swisher observed that a court "determines the facts involved in particular controversies brought before it, relates the facts to the relevant law, settles the controversies in terms of the law, and more or less incidentally makes new law through the process of decision." [2]

Courts also differ from other government agencies in that *access* to them is governed by a special set of requirements. An interested individual or group must have an attorney and sufficient money to bear the expense of the court suit. Courts must accept "jurisdiction," which means that a dispute must meet judicial criteria of a "case" or the courts cannot settle it. A case must involve two disputing parties, one of which must have incurred some real damages as a result of the action or inaction of the other. For example, an individual who objects to the state welfare program cannot take his objections to a court unless he can show that the program inflicted some direct personal or property damage on him.

The *procedures* under which judges and other participants in the judicial process operate are also quite different from procedures in legislative or executive branches of government. Facts and arguments must be presented to the courts in the manner specified. Generally these communications are quite formal, and legal skills are generally required to provide written briefs or oral arguments that meet the technical specifications of the courts. While an interest group may hire a public relations firm to pressure a legislature, they must hire a law firm to put their arguments into a legal context. Decorum in courtrooms is rigorously enforced in order to convey a sense of dignity; seldom do legislatures or executive offices function with the same degree of decorum.

Courts must direct their decisions to *specific cases*. While higher courts sometimes depart from particular cases and announce general policy positions, most courts refrain from general policy statements and limit their decision to the particular circumstances of a case. Rarely do the courts

---

[2] Carl B. Swisher, "The Supreme Court and the Moment of Truth," *American Political Science Review*, 54 (December, 1960), 879.

announce a comprehensive policy in the way the legislature does when it enacts a law. Of course, the implication of a court's decision in a particular case is that future cases of the same nature will be decided the same way. This implication amounts to a policy statement; however, it is not as comprehensive as a legislative policy pronouncement, because future cases with only slightly different circumstances might be decided differently.

Perhaps the most important distinction between judicial decision making and decision making in other branches of government is that judges must not appear to permit political consideration to affect their decisions. Judges must not appear to base their decisions on partisan considerations, to bargain, or to compromise in decision making. Legislators and governors may base their decisions on party platforms or on their estimate of what will win in the next election, but such considerations are not supposed to influence judges. The *appearance of objectivity* in judicial decision making gives courts a measure of prestige that other governmental institutions lack. While it is true that judges have fewer direct ties with political organizations than legislators or governors, they are, of course, subject to social, economic, and political pressures just as other men are. Judges hold socioeconomic and political views just as everyone else, and they would be less than human if these views did not affect their decisions; but it is important that a large portion of the American public perceive judges as unaffected by personal considerations. Court decisions become more acceptable to the public if they believe that the courts have dispensed unbiased justice.

The distinctive features of the judicial process—its passive appearance, special rules of access, specialized legal procedures, decorum, focus on particular cases, and appearance of objectivity in decision making—help to provide essential support for judicial decisions and thus enable the courts to play an influential role in the political system. These distinctive features help to "legitimize" the decisions reached by the courts; that is, they help to win popular acceptance of these decisions.

Legal traditions are influential in court decisions. English common law has vitally affected the law of all of our states except Louisiana, which was influenced by the Napoleonic Code. English common law developed in the 13th century through the decisions of judges who applied their notions of justice to specific cases. This body of judge-made law grew over the centuries and is still the foundation of our legal system today. Legislated statutes take precedence over common law, but the common law is applied by the courts where no statutory provisions are relevant. The degree to which statutory law has replaced common law varies among the states according to the comprehensiveness of state statutes and codes. Common law covers both criminal and civil law, although for the most part, the common law of crimes has been replaced by comprehensive criminal codes in the states.

The Structure of Court Systems

State courts are generally organized into a hierarchy similar to that shown in Figure 7.1. The courts of a state constitute a single, integrated judicial system; even city courts, traffic courts, and justices of the peace are part of the state judicial system.

At the lowest level are minor courts presided over by justices of the

FIGURE 7.1

THE STRUCTURE OF STATE AND LOCAL COURTS

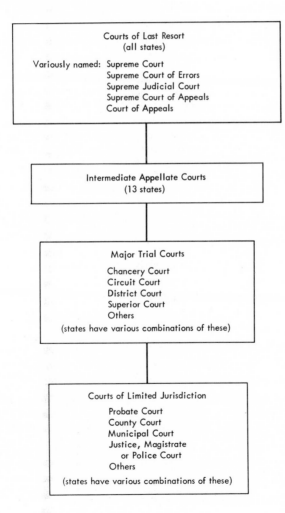

peace, magistrates, or police judges, who frequently have little formal training. These courts are concerned principally with traffic cases, small claims, and misdemeanors, although they may hold preliminary hearings to determine whether a person accused of a felony shall be held in jail or placed under bond. These grassroot courts have often bred distrust for the law because of their incompetence, their reliance upon the fee system, or their direct links with partisan politics.[3] Many justices of the peace have no training in the law.[4] There are frequent complaints about collusion between justices of the peace and local police in the maintenance of "speed traps" for collecting heavy fines from out-of-town motorists. Many "J.P.'s" are paid on a fee basis, which means that the J.P. is paid for the number of convictions he obtains; this has led to the cynical observation that "J.P." signifies "judgment for the plaintiff."

Kenneth N. Vines comments on the links between minor courts and party politics in the states:

> In many areas, partcularly in those states with partisan elective methods of judicial selection, or where the judiciary is appointed by the governor, judicial office at the county and municipal level is one of the most important sources of patronage existent for the political parties. A careful study of the selection of judges in Chicago has shown how closely local judges are sometimes joined to the activities of political parties. Chicago judges recognized the need for taking time to maintain good party relations, for securing endorsement of party leaders to secure the judicial nomination, and on occasion were responding to political pressures that were brought to bear when important cases occur in which party influentials were interested. Often judges campaigned for judicial office and contributed to political campaign funds in order to hold their judgeships.[5]

Major trial courts of general jurisdiction—sometimes called district courts, circuit courts, superior courts, chancery courts, county courts, or common pleas courts—handle major civil and criminal cases arising out of statutes, common law, and state constitutions. The geographic jurisdiction of these courts is usually the county or city; there are about 1500 major trial courts in the United States. Juries are used in these courts, and judges are generally qualified in the law. These courts handle criminal cases involving felonies and important civil suits. Almost all cases decided

[3] See Arthur T. Vanderbilt, *The Challenge of Law Reform* (Princeton: Princeton University Press, 1955).

[4] On the other hand, Henry J. Abraham quotes a Philadelphia Chief Magistrate as saying: "A law degree doesn't make a magistrate more qualified. Living with people is more essential than going to a law library to find out what it's all about . . . If you take Purdon's law books away from them (lawyers), they're out of business." Abraham, *The Judicial Process*, p. 130.

[5] Kenneth N. Vines, "Courts as Political and Governmental Agencies," *Politics in the American States,* Herbert Jacob and Kenneth Vines, eds. (Boston: Little, Brown and Co., 1965).

by state courts originate in these major trial courts; trial courts make the initial decision in cases carried to appellate and supreme courts and may also handle some appeals from minor courts. Although trial courts are courts of original jurisdiction rather than appeal courts, for most individuals, they are the courts of last resort. It has been estimated that not more than 5 per cent of the cases decided in major trial courts are ever appealed.[6] However, it is probable that most cases involving major policy questions are appealed to higher courts.

Every state has a court of last resort, which is generally called the supreme court. These courts consist of three to nine judges, and most of their work is devoted to cases on appeal from major trial courts, although some states grant original jurisdiction to supreme courts in special types of cases. Since they consider questions of law rather than questions of fact, they sit without a jury. State supreme courts are the most important and visible judicial bodies in the states. Their decisions are written, published, and distributed like the decisions of the U.S. Supreme Court. Judges can express their views in majority opinions, dissenting opinions, or concurring opinions. These courts get the most controversial cases and those with the most at stake, since these cases are most likely to be appealed all the way to the state's highest court. To relieve supreme courts of heavy case burdens, 14 of the more populous states maintain intermediate courts of appeal between trial courts and courts of last resort.

There is no appeal from state supreme courts, except to the U.S. Supreme Court on federal constitutional grounds. This means that state supreme courts have the final word in the interpretation of state constitutions and laws. These courts seldom hesitate to exercise judicial review over state legislative acts.

Special courts can always be found in addition to those already mentioned, notably in large cities. These specialized courts may handle domestic relations, juvenile delinquency, the probation of wills, small claims, and so on. It is interesting to note that many of the more populous urban states have created very complex court structures with many specialized types of courts. Kenneth Vines contrasts the simplicity of Wyoming's court structure with the complexity of New York's:[7]

Wyoming	*New York*
Supreme Court	Courts of Appeals
District Courts	Appellate Divisions of Supreme Court
Justice Courts	Appellate Terms of Supreme Court
	Supreme Courts
	Courts of Claims

[6] Council of State Governments, *Trial Courts of General Jurisdiction in the Forty-Eight States* (Chicago, 1951), p. 6; also cited by Kenneth Vines, *op. cit.,* p. 243.
[7] Vines, *op. cit.,* p. 245.

Surrogate's Courts
Courts of General Sessions
Children's Courts
County Courts
Domestic Relations Courts
City Courts
Municipal Courts
Magistrate Courts
District Courts
Justice Courts
Police Justice Courts
Traffic Courts
Recorders Courts
Police Courts
Courts of Special Sessions

The complexity of New York's court system reflects the character and problems of the modern, industrial, urban state.

The Making of a Judge

Political debate over methods of selecting judges in the states has been carried on for many years. In writing the federal Constitution, the Founding Fathers reflected conservative views in establishing an independent judiciary, whose members were appointed by the President for life terms and were not subject to direct popular control. Jacksonian views of popular election were strong in the states, however, and today a majority of judges are directly elected by the people on partisan or nonpartisan ballots. Table 7.1 shows the several ways in which judges are selected. Thirty-four states elect their judges, about half in partisan elections and the other half in nonpartisan elections in which candidates for the bench do not carry party labels. In five states, judges are chosen by their legislatures, and in seven states, they are appointed by the governor. Six states have adopted the "Missouri Plan," in which governors appoint judges on the recommendations of a select committee, and after the judge has been in office for a year or more, the voters are given the opportunity to retain or oust the appointed judge.

The argument for selecting judges by appointment rests upon the value of judicial independence and isolation from direct political involvement. Critics of the elective method feel that it forces judges into political relationships and compromises their independence on the bench. This is particularly true if judicial elections are held on a partisan rather than a nonpartisan ballot, where judges must secure nomination with the support of party leaders. Moreover, it is argued that voters are not able to evaluate "legal" qualifications—knowledge of the law, judicial temperament, skill in the court room, and so on. Hence, judges should be appointed rather than elected by voters. Attorneys, bar associations, and judges themselves pre-

TABLE 7.1

METHODS OF JUDICIAL SELECTION IN THE STATES

Partisan election	Election by legislature	Nonpartisan election	Appointment	Missouri plan*
Alabama	Connecticut†	Alaska	Delaware	Alaska
Arkansas	Rhode Island	Arizona	Hawaii	California
Colorado	South Carolina	California	Maine	Iowa
Florida	Vermont	Idaho	Maryland	Kansas
Georgia	Virginia	Michigan	Massachusetts	Missouri
Illinois		Minnesota	New Hampshire	Nebraska
Indiana		Montana	New Jersey	
Iowa		Nebraska		
Kansas		Nevada		
Kentucky		North Carolina		
Louisiana		Ohio		
Mississippi		Oregon		
Missouri		South Dakota		
New Mexico		Tennessee		
New York		Utah		
North Carolina		Washington		
Oklahoma		Wisconsin		
Pennsylvania		Wyoming		
Texas				
West Virginia				

*Several Missouri plan states select some judges according to the Missouri plan, other judges by election.
†Formally by legislature, actually by nomination of the governor.
Source: Kenneth W. Vines, "Courts as Political and Governmental Agencies," Herbert Jacob and Kenneth Vines, eds., *Politics in the American States* (Boston: Little, Brown & Co., 1965), p. 269.

fer an appointive method in which they are given the opportunity to screen candidates and evaluate legal qualifications prior to appointment.

In contrast, supporters of an elective judiciary stress the importance of popular control over judges. If American voters are competent to select legislators and governors, why should they not select judges as well? William J. Keefe argues that elected, partisan judges better reflect society's values:

> The judgments of the courts reflect not only the established body of substantive law but also reflect in their opinions the changed economic conditions and social mores of our times. Therefore, it is to be hoped that a judge's political affiliation, which cannot help but have a substantial impact on his decisions, should be representative of the party which elects him. Any system which makes more remote the influence of the free electorate on those who hold high office should be discarded.[8]

[8] William J. Keefe, "Judges and Politics: The Pennsylvania Plan of Judge Selection," *University of Pittsburgh Law Review* (May, 1959), p. 628.

Actually it is not possible to "take judges out of politics." Selection by appointment or by the Missouri plan removes the selection of judges from *party* politics, but simply places the selection in different political hands. Instead of party leaders, the governor or the bar association become the principal actors in judicial selection. Party leaders are assumed to be familiar with the wishes of attorneys. It is not clear which influence leads to "better" judges, or whether "better" judges are those more sensitive to community values or more trained in legal procedures. Interestingly, states with competitive two party systems are not necessarily the same states that select their judges through partisan elections. Some of the competitive states appoint as well as elect their judges.

Although a majority of states elect their judges, in practice many judges come to the bench in elective states through the appointment procedure. The apparent paradox comes about because even in elective states, governors generally have the power to make interim judicial appointments, when a judgeship is vacant because of the retirement or death of a judge between elections. An interim-appointed judge must seek election at the next regular election, but by that time he has acquired the prestige and status of a judge, and he is unlikely to be defeated by an outsider. Kenneth Vines has surmised that many members of the judiciary in elective states deliberately resign before the end of their term, if they are not seeking re-election, in order to give the governor the opportunity to fill the post by appointment.[9] It is interesting to note that over half of the supreme court judges in states which elect their judiciary come to the bench initially by means of appointment. In practice, then, the elective system of judicial selection is greatly compromised by the appointment of judges to fill unexpired terms.

Another feature of the elective system of judicial selection, which often escapes attention, is that few incumbent judges are ever defeated in running for re-election. Figures compiled by Kenneth Vines (for several states) suggest that the majority of judges seeking re-election are unopposed by anyone on the ballot and that fewer than 10 per cent of the judges seeking re-election are ever defeated.[10] This suggests that even in states with elective systems of judicial selection, judges are still separated from the normal political recruitment process. Judges enjoy more stability and independence from popular control than do legislators or governors.

The Missouri plan is an interesting attempt to combine the elective and appointive systems of selection. The Missouri plan calls for a select committee of judges, attorneys, and laymen to make nominations for judicial vacancies. The governor appoints one of the committee's nominees to office. After the judge has served at least one year, his name is placed on

[9] Vines, *op. cit.,* p. 263.
[10] Vines, *op. cit.,* p. 266.

a nonpartisan ballot without any other name in opposition. "Shall judge (the name of the judge is inserted) of the (the name of the court is inserted) be retained in office. Yes _____ No _____." If the voters vote "yes," the judge is then entitled to a full term of office. If the voters vote "no," the governor must select another name from those submitted by his nominating committee, and repeat the whole process. In practice, a judge is seldom defeated under the Missouri plan, for the same reasons that make it difficult to defeat an incumbent judge (see preceding discussion). Moreover, since "you can't beat somebody with nobody," running under the referendum feature of the Missouri plan is the equivalent of being unopposed. The effect is to place judicial selection in the hands of the judges or attorneys who compose the nominating committee and the governor, with only a semblance of voter participation. Reformers argue that the plan removes judges from politics, and spares the electorate the problem of voting on judicial candidates when they know little about their professional qualifications.

Republicans have fared better in capturing judgeships than in winning legislative seats or governors' chairs. Stuart Nagel reports that Republicans outnumber Democrats almost two to one in judicial posts.[11] Of course, the one party Democratic states have Democratic judges just as one party Republican states have Republican judges; but Republicans do surprisingly well in winning judgeships in the competitive states, proportionately much better than Republican candidates for the legislature or governorship in these states. Kenneth Vines reports that about half of the judges selected in nonpartisan elections refuse to identify themselves with a political party, as do nearly three-fourths of the judges selected under the Missouri plan.[12] Judges selected in partisan elections, of course, usually do not hesitate to identify themselves as Republicans or Democrats.

The Politics of Prosecution

Prosecution is part of the political process. Legislatures and governors enact policy, but its enforcement depends upon the decisions of prosecutors as well as judges. Political pressures are most obvious in the enforcement of controversial policies—gambling laws, Sunday closing laws, liquor rules, laws against prostitution, and other laws that are contrary to the interests of significant segments of the population. But prosecution also involves decision making about the allocation of law enforcement resources to different types of offenses—traffic violations, juvenile delinquency, auto theft, assault, burglary, larceny, and robbery. Decisions must be made about

[11] Stuart Nagel, "Unequal Party Representation in State Supreme Courts," *Journal of the American Judicature Society,* 44 (1961) 62–65.
[12] Vines, *op. cit.,* p. 275.

what sections of the city should be most vigorously protected and what segments of the population will be most closely watched. The public prosecutor, sometimes called the district attorney (D.A.) or State's attorney, is at the center of diverse pressures concerning law enforcement.

The political nature of the prosecutor's job is suggested by the frequency with which this job leads to higher political office. Prosecuting attorney is often a steppingstone to state and federal judgeships, congressional seats, and even the governorship. An ambitious D.A., concerned with his political future, may seek to build a reputation as a crusader against crime and vice, while at the same time maintaining the support and friendship of important interests in the community. The political power of the prosecutor stems from his discretion in deciding (1) whether or not to prosecute in criminal cases, and (2) whether prosecution will be on more-serious or less-serious charges. Prosecutors are elective in every state, except Rhode Island, Connecticut, Delaware, and New Jersey.

Kenneth Vines describes some of the discretionary powers of the prosecutor:

> The important points at which criminal procedures against persons may either be dropped or carried through by the prosecutor begin with actual arrest and the possibility of police discharge after arrest. Next, failure to issue an affidavit showing the cause of arrest may also result in dropping charges. A flexible weapon in the hands of the prosecutor is a device of "nolle prosequi" or "nol-pros.".... a case is "nol-pros." whenever an arrest has been made and a charge issued but the prosecutor feels that adequate proof is lacking or for some other reason he feels that the case should not be pressed.... Even when a person is indicted for a crime, the consequences of conviction may be considerably mitigated by a decision of the prosecutor to allow a guilty plea, possibly with a lesser charge than the one originally contemplated, or on a promise of a lighter sentence. Even if an individual is convicted, the prosecutor may play a role in allowing him to seek bench parole with all of the attendant advantages that a respite for the conviction may bring.[13]

Herbert Jacob has documented the extent of discretion in the criminal prosecution in New Orleans.[14] Nearly half of all offenses were dismissed by the prosecutor. An additional 5 per cent were permitted to plead guilty on reduced charges; 40 per cent of the defendants apparently felt it was to their advantage to plead guilty on the original charge; only 10 per cent pleaded innocent and went to trial. In short, the prosecutor is a central figure in the judicial process, and his power makes him an important political figure in the community.

[13] Vines, op. cit., p. 251.
[14] Herbert Jacob, "Politics and Criminal Prosecution in New Orleans," in Kenneth Vines and Herbert Jacob, Studies in Judicial Politics, Tulane Studies in Political Science, Vol. VIII (New Orleans: Tulane University, 1963).

Judicial Decision Making

Conflict in state supreme courts, as measured by the number of divided opinions, is much less frequent than in the U.S. Supreme Court. Dissenting votes are reported on more than half of all U.S. Supreme Court decisions, but state judges dissent in very few cases. The Council of State Governments reports that the rate of dissent in the state supreme courts is less than 10 per cent in more than half of the states.[15] In only five states is the rate of dissent more than 15 per cent—California, Indiana, Louisiana, Michigan, and Pennsylvania. Public disagreement is somewhat more frequent in competitive party states where judges of both parties are represented on the court.

The infrequency of dissenting opinions may obscure a great deal of conflict in state courts. Supreme Court justices write dissenting opinions in order to keep alive a point of view that may serve as a basis for a majority decision by a later court. Well-written dissenting opinions on the U.S. Supreme Court attract the attention of scholars, judges, attorneys, and law students throughout the nation. They can have an important impact on legal thinking even though they represent a minority view on the court. But seldom do state supreme courts attract enough attention to merit the writing of dissenting opinions. At the state level many judges feel that dissenting opinions are useless. Moreover, many judges feel that a lack of unanimity damages judicial prestige, and may tend to destroy the myth of certainty within the law.

A great deal of judicial decision making involves economic interests. Kenneth Vines reports that in 1961–62, economic interests were directly represented in 37 per cent of the cases before the Louisiana Supreme Court, 45 per cent of the cases before the Pennsylvania Supreme Court, and 59 per cent of the cases before the Idaho Supreme Court.[16] A large number of cases involving economic interests result from the important role of the states in the allocation of economic resources. All states regulate public utilities, including water, electrical companies, gas companies, and public transportation companies. The insurance industry is state regulated. Labor relations and workmen's compensation cases are frequently found in state courts. Litigation over natural resources, real estate, small business regulations, gas, oil, lumber, and mining, alcoholic beverage control, racing, and gambling all reflect the importance of state regulation in these fields.

Judges are also called upon to make decisions in political controversies—disputes over elections, appointments to government positions, and juris-

---

[15] Council of State Governments, *Workload of State Courts of Last Resort* (Chicago, 1962).

[16] Vines, *op. cit.*, p. 272.

dictional squabbles between governments. These cases may constitute 5 to 10 per cent of the workload of the courts.

What is the impact of the party affiliation of the judges in court decision making? Party affiliation probably has little impact in decisions in lower trial courts, where much of the litigation has little to do with policy making. But at least two studies have shown party affiliation to be an important influence on state supreme court decision making.[17] Stuart Nagel found that Democratic judges differed from Republican judges by deciding more frequently:

1. For the defense in criminal cases;
2. For the administrative agency in business regulation cases;
3. For the claimant in unemployment compensation;
4. For finding a constitutional violation in criminal cases;
5. For the government in tax cases;
6. For the tenant in landlord-tenant cases;
7. For the consumer in sale-of-goods cases;
8. For the injured in motor vehicle cases;
9. For the employee in employee injury cases.

These decisions suggest that Democratic judges were more in sympathy with the consumer, the workingman, and the defendant in criminal cases, and less in sympathy with business and utilities seeking to avoid public regulation. These are the kinds of attitudes that we might expect Democrats to express, although there is no evidence that the party itself influences these judges. Rather it is likely that the judges' social, economic, and political views influence both his decisions on the court and his decision to affiliate with the Democratic or Republican party. Sidney Ulmer traced the influence of party affiliation on judges' decisions in the Michigan Supreme Court, particularly in workmen's compensation and contributory negligence cases involving attitudes toward labor. He found that Democratic judges are more likely to hold with the workingman in these cases, while Republican judges are more likely to decide in favor of the company.

What is the effect of social and ethnic group membership on judges' decisions? Judges, like other decision makers, generally belong to higher social and economic groups; white, Anglo-Saxon Protestants are disproportionately represented among state judges. Stuart Nagel found that judges who were members of ethnic minority groups in America were more likely to decide—(1) for the defense in criminal cases, (2) for finding a violation in criminal constitutional cases, and (3) for the wife in divorce cases

---

[17] Stuart Nagel, "Political Party Affiliation and Judges' Decisions," *American Political Science Association,* 55 (1961), 843–51; and Sidney Ulmer, "The Political Party Variable on the Michigan Supreme Court," *Journal of Public Law,* 11 (1962), 352–62.

—than judges with white, Anglo-Saxon backgrounds.[18] He also found a difference in the decisions of Catholic and non-Catholic judges. Catholic judges tended to decide: (1) for the defense in criminal cases, (2) for the administrative agency in business regulation cases, (3) for the wife in divorce settlement cases, (4) for the debtor in debtor-creditor cases, and (5) for the employee in employee injury cases. Nagel's studies suggest that party influence in judicial selection, with its tendency to grant representation to religious and ethnic groups in proportion to their electoral influence, may help to bring about decisions that reflect popular values.

Kenneth Vines has documented the influence of social and political views in race relations cases.[19] As one might expect, he found that southern state supreme courts were much less likely to find in favor of Negro claims than federal district courts handling the same claims. He also found that supreme courts in border states, those on the periphery of the deep South, were more favorable toward Negroes in race relations decisions than supreme courts in the deep South. From 1954–1963, the average percentage of cases in which favorable decisions were rendered for Negroes in Alabama, Arkansas, Georgia, Louisiana, Mississippi, and South Carolina was 29 per cent; the average for Florida, North Carolina, Tennessee, Texas, and Virginia during these same years was 37 per cent. Georgia and Florida appear to be exceptions to the general proposition that the supreme courts reflect the prevailing social views in the state. Although racial attitudes in Florida are considered moderate by southern standards, the Florida Supreme Court compiled a very "anti-Negro" record, deciding for Negroes in less than 10 per cent of the cases, a record exceeded only by the Alabama Supreme Court. In contrast, in Georgia, a deep South state, the supreme court decided more than half of its race relations cases in favor of Negro claims. Southern supreme court judges are also prone to be more conservative than nonsouthern judges in areas outside of race relations.

On the whole, courts tend to be very conservative political bodies. Judicial activism on behalf of social reform in the U.S. Supreme Court is a relatively recent phenomenon. Historically, the Supreme Court was considered a bastion of conservatism, and state courts continue to be viewed as very conservative institutions. Doubtlessly, the heavy reliance that courts place on precedents in decision making is partly responsible for the conservatism of court decisions. The recent liberal posture of the U.S. Supreme Court has required it to overturn many earlier precedents; state courts feel more bound by earlier precedents than the U.S. Supreme Court and consequently are committed to a more conservative posture. Yet re-

[18] Stuart Nagel, "Ethnic Affiliation and Judicial Propensities," *Journal of Politics,* 24 (1962), 92–110.

[19] Kenneth N. Vines, "Southern State Supreme Courts and Race Relations," *Western Political Quarterly,* 18 (1965), 5–18.

liance upon precedents cannot be the whole explanation of judicial conservatism, because state judges appear to evidence conservative attitudes even when they are off the bench. Stuart Nagel reports that not only do the judges evidence a great deal of conservatism in their off-the-bench views, but also conservatism seems to make a difference in case decisions.[20] When Nagel compared judges with conservative off-the-bench attitudes to judges having liberal attitudes, the two groups differed significantly. Judges with higher liberal scores decided more frequently: (1) for the defense in criminal cases, (2) for the administrative agency in business regulation cases, (3) for the injured party in motor vehicle accident cases, and (4) for the employee in employee injury cases. In other words, conservative judges were more likely to find for the state in criminal cases, against the state in business regulation cases, and in favor of insurance companies and employers in cases brought against them.

In summary, judicial decision making is influenced by interest group activity, political party affiliation, social and ethnic ties, religious affiliations, and the liberal and conservative views of judges. This does not mean that "judicial impartiality" is nonexistent, or that judges are as free as legislators or governors to write their social and political views into the law. Judges participate in the game of politics as players as well as umpires, but they are limited by the rules of the game, the decisions of legislatures and governors, and public expectations about the way judges ought to behave.

Crime in the States

Crime rates are the subject of a great deal of popular discussion. Very often they are employed to express the degree of social disorganization or even the effectiveness of law enforcement agencies. Crime rates are based upon the Federal Bureau of Investigation's *Uniform Crime Reports,* but the FBI reports are based on figures supplied by state and local police agencies. The FBI has succeeded in establishing a uniform classification of the number of serious crimes per 100,000 people that are known to the police—murder and non-negligent manslaughter, robbery, aggravated assault, burglary, larceny, and theft, including auto theft. But record keeping is still a problem, and one should be cautious in interpreting official crime rates. They are really a function of several factors: the diligence of police in detecting crime, the adequacy of the reporting system tabulating crime, and the amount of crime itself. Yet the evidence seems inescapable that crime in the United States is increasing at a rapid pace. The greatest increase in crime rates occurs in nonviolent crimes—burglary, larceny, theft

[20] Stuart Nagel, "Off-the-Bench Judicial Attitudes," *Judicial Decision-Making,* Glendon Schubert, ed. (Glencoe: The Free Press, 1963).

TABLE 7.2

CRIME RATES IN THE UNITED STATES
OFFENSES KNOWN TO THE POLICE
(*rates per 100,000 population*)

	1960	1961	1962	1963	1964	1965
Murder and						
non-negligent manslaughter	5.0	4.7	4.5	4.5	4.8	5.1
Forcible rape	9.2	9.0	9.1	9.0	10.7	11.6
Robbery	51.6	50.0	51.1	53.0	58.4	61.4
Aggravated assault	82.5	82.2	84.9	88.6	101.8	106.6
Burglary	465.5	474.9	489.7	527.4	580.4	605.3
Larceny	271.4	277.9	296.6	330.9	368.2	393.3
Auto theft	179.2	179.9	193.4	212.1	242.0	251.0
Total crimes against person	148.3	154.9	149.6	155.1	175.7	184.7
Total crimes against property	916.1	932.7	979.7	1,070.4	1,190.6	1,249.6

Source: FBI, *Uniform Crime Reports*, 1966.

—and lesser increases are found in crimes involving violence against the person—murder and non-negligent manslaughter and robbery.

Crime rates are related to urbanization and economic development in the states.[21] The nation's highest crime rates are in Nevada and California, and its lowest are in North Dakota and Mississippi. Generally, the urban, industrial, high income states have higher crime rates than the rural, agricultural, low income states. Urbanization and economic development involves certain social complications: a certain degree of unemployment seems inevitable; the transition from rural to urban life creates many social problems; social isolation and hostility are frequent byproducts; traditional value systems and social control are undermined and not immediately replaced by other values and institutions. All of these traditions are associated with crime. Figure 7.2 shows the relationship between urbanization and crime rates in the states. Nevada is the most deviant state; it has a much higher crime rate than its degree of urbanization would suggest.

Crime rates in Nevada suggest that crime is related to gambling. Nevada has the most permissive gambling laws of any state in the nation. A total of 25 states reported revenue from gambling or parimutuel betting in 1961. The highest amount was, of course, reported in Nevada, which received about a quarter of its state revenue from gambling taxes. Twenty-five states reported no revenue from gambling taxes. Gambling and parimutuel betting is found more frequently in the urban, industrial states than in the

[21] See Thomas R. Dye, *Politics, Economics, and the Public* (Chicago: Rand McNally & Co., 1966), pp. 219–22.

FIGURE 7.2

THE FIFTY STATES ARRANGED ACCORDING TO URBANIZATION AND CRIME RATES

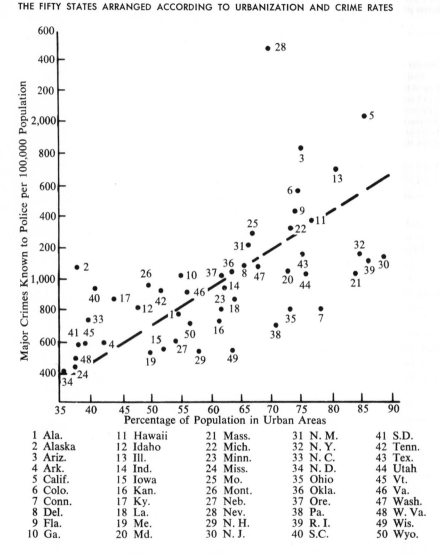

SOURCE: Thomas R. Dye, *Politics, Economics, and the Public* (Chicago: Rand McNally & Co., 1966), p. 221. Reproduced by permission.

rural, agricultural states. Since both gambling and crime rates are associated with urbanization and industrialization, it is difficult to say whether or not gambling itself brings about an increase in the crime rate, or whether the association between the two is merely a product of the fact that they both occur in urban, industrial states. Nevada's extraordinarily high crime rate, however, suggests that gambling does contribute to an increase in crime.

Police statistics vastly understate the real amount of crime. Citizens do not report many crimes to the police. In 1965 the National Opinion Research Center of the University of Chicago asked a national sample of individuals whether they or any member of their household had been a victim of crime during the past year. This survey revealed that the actual amount of crime is several times greater than that reported by the FBI. As Table 7.3 shows, there are twice as many crimes committed as reported to the police. The number of forcible rapes was more than 3½ times the number reported, burglaries three times, aggravated assaults and larcenies more than double, and robbery 50 per cent greater than the reported rate. Only auto theft statistics were reasonably accurate, indicating that most people call the police when their cars are stolen.

Interviewees gave a variety of reasons for their failure to report crime to the police. The most common reason was the feeling that police could not be effective in dealing with the crime. This is a serious comment about police protection in America today. Other reasons included the feeling that the crime was "a private matter" or that the victim did not want to harm the offender. Fear of reprisal was mentioned much less frequently, usually in cases of assaults and family crimes.

TABLE 7.3

A COMPARISON OF SURVEY DATA ON CRIME WITH FBI UNIFORM CRIME REPORTS
(rates per 100,000 population)

	NORC survey data 1965-66	FBI rate for individuals 1965
Murder and non-negligent manslaughter	3.0	5.1
Forcible rape	42.5	11.6
Robbery	94.0	61.4
Aggravated assault	218.3	106.6
Burglary	949.1	299.6
Larceny	606.5	267.4
Auto theft	206.2	226.0
Total crimes against person	357.8	184.7
Total crimes against property	1,761.8	793.0

Source: National Opinion Research Center, "Criminal Victimization in the United States," President's Commission on Law Enforcement and Administration of Justice, *Report* (Washington: Government Printing Office, 1967).

Police Protection in the States

State, county, and municipal government are all directly involved in law enforcement. Every state has a central law enforcement agency, sometimes called the state police, state troopers, state highway patrol, and even Texas Rangers. At one time, state governors had only the National Guard at their disposal to back up local law enforcement efforts, but the coming of the automobile and intercity highway traffic led to the establishment in every state of a centralized police system. In addition to patrolling the state's highways, these centralized agencies now provide expert aid and service for local police officers and strengthen law enforcement in sparsely populated regions. Three-quarters of the states have given their central police agencies full law enforcement authority in addition to highway duties: they may quell riots, cooperate with local authorities in the apprehension of criminals, or even intervene when local authorities are unable or unwilling to enforce the law. The size and influence of these agencies varies from state to state. State police range in number from two dozen in Nevada and Alaska to over 3000 in California. On the whole, however, state police forces constitute a very small proportion of the total law enforcement effort in America. Law enforcement in the nation is principally a local responsibility.

Historically, the county sheriff has been the keystone of law enforcement in the United States. He and his deputies are still the principal enforcement and arresting officers in the rural counties and in the unincorporated fringe areas of many urban counties. In addition, the sheriff serves as an executive agent for county and state courts in both civil and criminal matters, and he maintains the county jail for the retention of persons whose trials or sentences are pending or who are serving short terms of punishment. The sheriff's office is a political one; in every state except Rhode Island he is an elected official. Very often the office of sheriff is a lucrative one. Antiquated fee systems exist in many states in which a sheriff collects a fee for every order, process, warrant, or arrest in which he is involved. Small fortunes can be made by "diligent" sheriffs in one term of office. Constables are elected in most states to perform many of the same functions of sheriffs for rural townships or other subdivisions of the county. Reliance upon the sheriff's office for law enforcement is a characteristic of rural states. Since municipal police forces usually assume the sheriff's law enforcement duties within the boundaries of municipalities, the sheriff's office has seriously atrophied in most urban states; often he is reduced to a process server for the courts.

Urban police departments are the most important instruments of law enforcement and public safety in the nation today. About two-thirds of the nation's population live in municipalities and depend upon municipal police for their protection. City policemen vastly outnumber all other state and county law enforcement officers combined. The urban police department does more than merely enforce the law; it engages in a wide range of activities for social control.

Urban, industrial states employ more policemen than rural, farm states.[22] We have already seen that urbanization brings about increases in crime rates, so it is not surprising that urbanization also requires an increase in police protection. Urbanization, crime rates, and police protection are all interrelated. But even if urbanization has stabilized, there is still a significant relationship between crime rates and police protection. An increase in the crime rate leads to an increase in police protection.

TABLE 7.4

CRIME AND PUNISHMENT IN THE STATES

Crime rates 1965 per 10,000		Police protection 1966 per 10,000		Prison population 1965 per 10,000	
1. Calif.	254.2	1. Nev.	45.1	1. Mass.	23.1
2. Nev.	239.6	2. N.Y.	30.6	2. Nev.	21.4
3. Okla.	233.4	3. N.J.	26.6	3. Ga.	18.9
4. Fla.	201.1	4. Md.	26.3	4. Md.	17.6
5. Ariz.	193.5	5. Fla.	25.7	5. Colo.	15.6
6. Hawaii	189.0	6. Calif.	25.6	6. N. M.	15.3
7. Mich.	173.5	7. Ariz.	23.2	7. Fla.	15.0
8. Md.	171.8	8. Ill.	22.7	8. Tex.	13.3
9. Alaska	171.0	9. R.I.	22.6	9. Ala.	12.8
10. Ill.	161.3	10. Mass.	21.9	10. Ariz.	12.8
11. N.Y.	160.8	11. Conn.	21.1	11. Kans.	12.8
12. Mo.	160.3	12. Mo.	20.8	12. Okla.	12.1
13. Colo.	154.5	13. Hawaii	20.5	13. La.	11.8
14. N. M.	151.4	14. Del.	20.4	14. Ohio	11.7
15. Mass.	150.7	15. La.	20.4	15. Va.	11.4
16. Oreg.	148.7	16. Pa.	20.2	16. Calif.	11.3
17. R.I.	141.8	17. Wisc.	19.7	17. Oreg.	11.3
18. Tex.	140.4	18. Wyo.	19.5	18. Wash.	11.2
19. N.J.	139.7	19. Mich.	19.0	19. Ark.	11.0
20. Utah	136.4	20. Oreg.	18.8	20. N.C.	10.9
21. Wash.	136.4	21. Colo.	18.6	21. N.Y.	10.4
22. Del.	128.8	22. N.H.	18.1	22. Wyo.	10.2
23. Ind.	121.8	23. Idaho	17.2	23. S.C.	9.7
24. Ga.	120.0	24. Mont.	17.1	24. Ind.	9.6
25. La.	118.4	25. N.M.	16.9	25. Mich.	9.4
26. Tenn.	118.4	26. Wash.	16.2	26. Ky.	9.2
27. Conn.	117.5	27. Tex.	16.1	27. Miss.	9.2
28. Va.	115.9	28. Utah	16.1	28. Tenn.	9.0
29. Minn.	115.0	29. Ga.	15.8	29. Mont.	8.6

[22] Dye, *op. cit.*, pp. 223–26.

Crime rates 1965 per 10,000		Police protection 1966 per 10,000		Prison population 1965 per 10,000	
30. S.C.	109.7	30. Va.	15.8	30. S. Dak.	8.4
31. Mont.	108.3	31. Ind.	15.6	31. Ill.	8.3
32. Ala.	106.8	32. Ohio	15.6	32. Mo.	8.1
33. Ohio	103.9	33. Okla.	15.4	33. Neb.	8.1
34. Wyo.	100.2	34. Alaska	15.3	34. W. Va.	8.0
35. Kans.	99.7	35. Kans.	15.3	35. Iowa	7.9
36. N.C.	98.0	36. Nebr.	15.3	36. N.J.	7.9
37. Pa.	96.9	37. Tenn.	14.6	37. Utah	7.8
38. Idaho	92.7	38. Ala.	14.4	38. Hawaii	7.2
39. Nebr.	85.1	39. Me.	14.4	39. Idaho	7.2
40. Ark.	74.0	40. Minn.	14.2	40. Me.	7.1
41. Ky.	74.0	41. Miss.	14.2	41. Wis.	7.1
42. Wisc.	73.8	42. S. Dak.	14.1	42. Vt.	6.8
43. Iowa	70.7	43. Ky.	13.8	43. Conn.	6.5
44. Miss.	69.1	44. N.C.	13.6	44. Del.	6.5
45. Me.	68.0	45. S.C.	13.6	45. Pa.	6.3
46. S. Dak.	63.2	46. Iowa	13.3	46. Minn.	5.2
47. N.H.	61.1	47. Vt.	13.2	47. R.I.	3.6
48. Vt.	57.9	48. N. Dak.	11.4	48. N.H.	3.4
49. W. Va.	52.9	49. Ark.	11.3	49. N. Dak.	3.3
50. N. Dak.	50.2	50. W. Va.	10.5	50. Alaska	- - -

Source: U.S. Bureau of the Census *Statistical Abstract 1967*, p. 151, 165.

State Correctional Policies

Correctional policies vary enormously among the states. States differ in the number of persons committed to prison, correctional expenditures per capita, the care and treatment provided offenders, the policies governing the parole of the prisoners, the number of executions carried out, and in many other aspects of penology. Perhaps the explanation for the wide range of state policies in correction lies in the deep division among the American people concerning correctional philosophy. At least four separate theories of crime and punishment compete for pre-eminence in guiding correctional policies.[23] First, there is the ancient Judaeo-Christian idea of holding the individual responsible for his guilty acts and compelling him to pay a debt to society. Another philosophy argues that punishment should be sure, speedy, and commensurate with the crime, and sufficiently conspicuous to deter others from committing crime. Still another consideration in correctional policy is that of protecting the public from lawbreakers or habitual criminals by segregating these people behind prison walls. Finally, there is the theory that criminals are partly or entirely victims of social circumstance beyond their control, and that society owes them comprehensive treatment in reform and rehabilitation.

[23] See Daniel Glaser, *The Effectiveness of a Prison and Parole System* (Indianapolis and New York: Bobbs-Merrill Co., 1964).

Over two million Americans each year are prisoners in a jail, police station, or juvenile home or penitentiary. The vast majority are released within one year. There are however, about a quarter of a million inmates in state and federal prisons in the United States. These prisoners are serving time for serious offenses: 90 per cent had a record of crime before they committed the act which led to their current imprisonment. About 115,000 of these are released each year, only to be replaced by an even larger number of prisoners. For, despite increased emphasis on rehabilitation, the prison population of the United States increases yearly. New prisons, costing $10,000 to $15,000 yearly for each inmate, are regularly constructed. Psychological and other treatment facilities have been added to prison services, so that the annual cost of operating a correctional system now exceeds $2000 per inmate. But penologist Daniel Glaser points out: "Unfortunately, there is no convincing evidence that this investment reduces what criminologists call 'recidivism,' the offender's return to crime." [24] In short, there is no evidence that correctional policies in the states meet any of the goals of society—retribution, protection of the public, deterrence of crime, or rehabilitation for the criminal.

The prisoner populations of the states, even on a population basis, differ significantly. New Hampshire, Rhode Island, Massachusetts, and North Dakota imprisoned about three persons per 10,000 population in 1961, while Alabama imprisoned 16, Georgia 17, and Maryland 18 per 10,000 population. In short, per capita prison populations vary by as much as 600 per cent among the states. Differences among the states in prisoner population may be partly explained by the difference in crime rates: there is a slight relationship between the two.[25] However, prisoner populations also represent differences in sentences and parole policies. The fact that the statistical probability of a person landing in a state penitentiary is six times greater in some states than in others is more than a result of differences in crime rates. It also reflects differences among the states in correctional philosophy. Available evidence indicates that states with well educated, adult populations have fewer prisoners in relation to their size than states with poorly educated, adult populations. We might conclude that educated populations are more successful in staying out of jail, or that the correctional philosophy of states with educated populations is more lenient in sentencing and parole, or both.

About 60 per cent of all prisoner releases come about by means of parole. Modern penology, with its concern for reform and rehabilitation, appears to favor parole releases rather than unconditional releases.[26] The function of parole and post-release supervision is: (1) to procure informa-

[24] Glaser, *op. cit.*, p. 4.
[25] Dye, *op. cit.*, pp. 226–32.
[26] Glaser, *op. cit.*, chaps. 16, 17.

tion on the parolees' post-prison conduct, and (2) to facilitate and graduate the transition between the prison and complete freedom. These functions are presumably oriented toward protecting the public and rehabilitating the offender. But states differ substantially in their use of parole: in some states, 90 per cent of all releases come about because of parole, while in other states, parole is granted to less than 30 per cent of all prisoners. Generally, urban, industrial states with higher income and educational levels release higher proportion of prisoners on parole than rural farm states, with lower income and educational characteristics.

One of the more heated debates in correctional policy today concerns capital punishment. As of 1967, the death policy had been abolished in 13 states.[27] Of the states retaining the death penalty, most specified electrocution as the method of execution, several specified the gas chamber or hanging, and Utah permitted either shooting or hanging. However, many of these states have not actually executed anyone for some time. Bills to abolish the death penalty are currently being considered by many states. In 1966 Colorado voters defeated an abolition referendum by a 2 to 1 margin. Opponents of the death penalty argue that nations and states that have abolished the death penalty do not have higher homicide rates, and hence there is no concrete evidence that the death penalty discourages crime. They also contend that the death penalty is applied unequally. There are tens of thousands of homicides each year, yet only an average of ten persons are executed annually for their crime. A large proportion of those who have been executed are poor, uneducated, and nonwhite. Yet there is a strong sense of justice among many Americans that demands retribution for heinous crimes—a life for a life. A mere jail sentence for a multiple murderer or rapist murderer seems unjust compared to the damage inflicted upon society and the victims. In most cases, a life sentence means less than ten years in prison, under the current parole and probation policies of many states. Convicted murderers have been set free, and some have killed again. Public opinion polls continue to support the death penalty, although opponents have been gaining supporters over time.

[27] Alaska, Hawaii, Iowa, Maine, Michigan, Minnesota, New York, North Dakota, Oregon, Rhode Island, Vermont, West Virginia, and Wisconsin (although in Michigan, New York, North Dakota, Rhode Island, and Vermont, there were provisions for certain serious exceptions, for example, killing a prison guard).

8

COMMUNITY

POLITICAL SYSTEMS

Communities as Settings for Politics

American communities come in different shapes and sizes, and community politics come in a variety of styles. Generalizing about community politics is perhaps even more difficult than generalizing about American state politics. There are over 18,000 municipalities in America, 18,000 townships, 3000 counties, and a host of other school districts and special districts. Cities range in size from less than 100 persons to New York's eight million. Two-thirds of the American people live in urban units of local government known as "municipalities," including "cities," "boroughs," "villages," or "towns." Other Americans are served by county or township governments. Moreover, there are 212 metropolitan areas in the United States; these are clusterings of people and governments around a core city of 50,000 or more persons. These metropolitan areas are as small as Meriden, Connecticut, with few local governments and only 52,000 persons, or as large as the New York area with 600 local governments and 11 million people. In short, one may conceive of community political systems as rural counties, country towns, villages, cities of all sizes, or even sprawling metropolitan areas.

Community political systems serve two principal functions. One is that of supplying goods and services—for example, police protection or sewage disposal—that are not supplied by private enterprise. This is the "service" function. The other function is the "political" one, that of managing conflict over public policy. Of course, the "political" and the "service" functions of local governments are often indistinguishable in practice. A mayor who intervenes in a dispute about the location of a park is managing a local government service, namely recreation, at the same time that he is managing political conflict about whose neighborhood should get the most benefit from the new park. In the day-to-day administration of the service functions of local government, officials must decide a variety of political questions. Where are the facilities to be located? Often the question is where *not* to locate facilities, since many neighborhoods avoid having public facilities for fear that they will displace families, attract "undesirables," or depress local property values. How are public services to be paid for? Which agency or official will be in charge of a particular service? What policies or practices will govern the provision of this service? What level of service will be provided? What will the budget for the service be?

Occasionally, students are led to believe that local governments should be less "political" than state or national governments. Many people feel that it would be best to eliminate "politics" from local government. Historically, this attitude arose in conjunction with the municipal reform movement of the Progressive Era.[1] The reform movement involved a preference for nonpartisan elections, city-manager government, and an "antiseptic," "no-party" style of local government, devoid of stigma of "politics." A city without politics appealed to many idealists who were disenchanted with boss rule. Perhaps another incentive for banishing politics from communities has been the distaste that many people have for conflict. Conflict is psychologically discomforting, and arouses strong, unpleasant emotions. Often associated with these feelings is a belief that there is always a "right" answer to public questions, that conflict is unnecessary, and that reasonable men can arrive at the right answer by thought and discussion. It is a belief that differences of opinion are not really legitimate, that the pursuit of special interests is immoral, and that all men should devote themselves to the public interest. Such beliefs force many politicians to *claim* that their decisions are based solely on efficiency, economy, or service considerations, even when the real grounds are to satisfy the political demands of individuals or groups.

The politician who responds to political considerations, in contrast to service considerations, is not necessarily sacrificing the welfare of his community. It is not necessarily true that the community is best served by treating the service function of government as if it were more important or

---

[1] See Richard Hofstadter, *The Age of Reform* (New York: Alfred A. Knopf, Inc., 1955); Lorin Peterson, *The Day of the Mugwump* (New York: Random House, Inc., 1961).

more worthy of government attention than the political one. A politician who undertakes to arrange political compromises and balance competing interests in a community is performing a very important function. James Madison once said that regulating conflict among people with diverse interests was "the principal task of modern legislation." [2] Certainly, a politician who attempts to win votes by satisfying the demands of competing interests in a community is helping to resolve conflict in an orderly fashion, reduce tension, and make life a little more bearable. Helping people with different incomes, occupations, skin colors, religious beliefs, and styles of living to live together in a reasonably peaceful fashion is a vital task.

Interestingly enough, even though James Madison shared a distaste for conflict, he had long ago given up the notion of eliminating "politics" from public life. He pointed out that this could only be done by "destroying liberty," or by "giving to every citizen the same opinions, the same passions, and the same interests." The former method he thought "unwise" and the latter "impracticable."

Edward C. Banfield and James Q. Wilson in their important study, *City Politics,* echo Madison's political philosophy in the contemporary community setting:

> Whether one likes it or not, politics, like sex, cannot be abolished. It can sometimes be repressed by denying people the opportunity to practice it, but it cannot be done away with because it is in the nature of man to disagree and to contend. We are not saying that politics arise solely from the selfish desire of some to have their way, although that is certainly one source of it. The fact is even in a society of altruists or angels there would be politics, for some would conceive of the common good in one way, and some in another, and (assuming the uncertainties that prevail in this world) some would think one course of action more prudent, and some would think another.
>
> Whether it is generally desirable to try to repress conflict may also be doubted . . . to repress it is to discourage or prevent some people from asserting their needs, wants, and interests. One can imagine a political system in which there is no struggle because people in disagreement know that their efforts to exercise influence would have no effect upon events. In such a case, politics is absent but also the conditions of progress.
>
> Where there exists conflict that threatens the existence of the good health of the society, the political function should certainly take precedence over the service one. In some cities race and class conflict has this dangerous character. To govern New York, Chicago, or Los Angeles, by the canons of efficiency—of efficiency *simply*—might lead to an accumulation of restless tension that would eventually erupt in meaningless, individual acts of violence, in some irrational mass movement, or perhaps in the slow imperceptible weakening of the social bonds. Politics is, among other things, a way of converting the restless, hostile impulses of individuals

[2] James Madison, *The Federalist,* No. 10.

into a fairly stable social product (albeit perhaps a revolution!) and in doing so, of giving these impulses moral significance.[3]

Government is only an imperfect instrument for managing conflict in society. Government tries to lay down certain "rules of the game" in political activity; it tries to make decisions among competing interests, and it tries to see that these decisions are carried out. Yet governments often fail in these tasks. The rules of the game are sometimes violated by those who have never accepted them in the first place or those who feel they have not won enough games to merit their continued adherence to the rules. Riots in Watts, Newark, Detroit, Harlem, Cleveland, Chicago, Buffalo, and almost every other major city in America provide ample evidence that the rules often break down, that conflict cannot always be resolved peacefully, that governments do not always succeed in getting their laws obeyed. Yet how can governments really serve as a manager of conflict in the sense of an impartial referee? For governments are only men—men who are themselves members of the community and who have the same diverse interests as their constituents. How can men act impartially on behalf of public good? James Madison was aware of this paradox:

> No man should be allowed to be a judge in his own cause, because his interests would certainly bias his judgment, and, not improbably, corrupt his integrity. With equal, nay with greater reason, a group of men are unfit to be both judges and parties at the same time; what are many of the most important acts of legislation, or so many judicial determinations, not concerning the rights of a single person, but concerning the rights of large bodies of citizens? And what are the different classes of legislators but advocates and parties to the causes which they determine? [4]

Is Madison overly cynical? Does he shut his eyes to the notion of the "enlightened statesman" who can be entrusted to serve the public without regard to his own interests?

> It is vain to say that enlightened statesmen will be able to adjust these clashing interests, and render them all subservient to the public good. Enlightened statesmen will not always be at the helm, nor, in many cases, can such an adjustment be made at all, without taking into view indirect and remote considerations, which one party may find in disregarding the rights of another for the good of the whole.[5]

Thus, another complication arises in attempting to find a way to manage conflict in communities—the imperfect nature of government itself. Conflicts must be managed, but how can we devise a human institution that can stand above partisanship and resolve conflicts impartially?

[3] Edward C. Banfield and James Q. Wilson, *City Politics* (Cambridge: Harvard-M.I.T. Press, 1963), pp. 20–21.
[4] James Madison, *Federalist,* No. 10, p. 56.
[5] *Ibid.,* p. 57.

Variety in Community Politics

There is great variety in community political systems. The politics of some communities are dominated by individuals, families, or cliques, while the politics of other communities are dominated by large, formal organizations —the press, business firms, city bureaucracies, civic associations, Negro or ethnic groups, or labor unions. Small town politics are more likely to be characterized by individual or family friendships and associations rather than organized interest groups. There seems to be less conflict in small town politics, at least on the surface. Meetings of the village council are dull and meaningless, decisions are usually unanimous, only occasionally do citizens drop by to make a request of the council. Perhaps the intimacy of small town life makes harmony, or at least the appearance of it, almost indispensable. Where people have frequent face-to-face contacts and nearly everyone is related to everyone else, bitter controversies must be avoided if life is to be at all pleasant. Perhaps there is more homogeneity or like-mindedness among people in a small town: class cleavages may not be as deep, and there are few minority groups. Small towns may be agricultural towns or one-industry towns, where nearly everyone has a stake in the dominant economic enterprise. In contrast, large cities often have diverse and competing economic activities, antagonisms between labor and management, and large minority and ethnic populations. In the relatively small and homogeneous community, it is easier to develop shared ideas of the common good or "what is good for the community." There are fewer large organizations with rival interests, and therefore less need for the "balancing" of competing interests. Individuals can act as individuals in politics rather than as representatives of large organizations. On the other hand, in larger cities and metropolitan areas, participation of individuals in politics is probably less important, as large organizations overshadow the activities of individuals and pre-empt the political field for themselves.

The classic style of big city organization politics is the "machine" model. These are tightly disciplined party organizations, held together and motivated by a desire for tangible benefits rather than by principle or ideology, and staffed by professional politicians. These urban party organizations have been dubbed "machines" and their leaders "bosses." Big city machines won notoriety in the era of the muckrakers and have remained the focus of attention ever since. However, rural county courthouses often house political machines that make big city organizations look like church socials: Judge Leander Perez of Plaquemines County, Louisiana once won an election by a margin of 3465 votes to 3, a feat unequaled by any city boss in history. Yet for a long time the machine has been the major instrument for regulating conflict and maintaining order in the nation's major cities. There can be no doubt that America's cities thrived, prospered, and grew under boss rule. The machine was like a large brokerage organization, obtaining votes from the poor and recent immigrants in return for social services, patronage, and petty favors. To get the money to pay for these votes, it traded city contracts, protection, and privileges to business interests, who paid for them in cash. The machine helped to centralize power; it could "get things done in city hall." It humanized and personalized assistance to the indigent. It was a source of upward social mobility for Irish, Italian, and other immigrants to whom upward mobility was denied in private enterprise.

In many ways the urban machine served the very rich and the very poor. The middle class was excluded, and much of the opposition to the machine has come from this group. The middle class was largely responsible for introducing another style of community politics—the reform or "good government" style. The good government movement was concerned largely with efficiency, economy, and saving the tax dollars of the middle class; it offered very little to the low income, low status elements of the large metropolis. As the middle class grew in power in American cities, many aspects of machine politics began to go out of style. Today good government is more likely to be supported by the white middle class voters than by Negroes or the poor. The good government movement included nonpartisan elections, municipal home rule, the short ballot, centralized municipal administration, and a professional city manager. It promoted the belief that government should be honest, impartial, efficient, and operated by professional administrators directly responsible to the citizens, and that the institutions of government should be structured to bring "good" people into control. It deplored boss rule, machines, and partisan politics.

While the good government movement has been important in America's large cities, its real successes came in the suburbs of the nation's large metropolitan areas. The suburban style of politics is neither the folksy, individualistic, "friends and neighbors" style of small-town politics, nor the highly organized, conflict ridden style of the big city. It is based on the conviction that good government comes in small packages and that the best government is the one closest to home. Suburban politics might be characterized as an incomplete attempt to recreate in the large metropolis an ideal of small town grass roots democracy. Economically, the suburbanite retains his association with the city, but politically, he can enter the civic life of a small community, where a man is no longer a face in the crowd, but a citizen whose votes count and whose opinions make a difference. Suburban life provides an escape from the central city with its corrupt politics and complex diversity of interests. Yet the suburbanite is not altogether willing to go back to rural living; for he demands high quality schools, water supply, sewage and refuse disposal, and other modern, urban services.

Another way of characterizing community politics is to distinguish be-

FIGURE 8.1

LOCAL GOVERNMENTS IN THE STATES

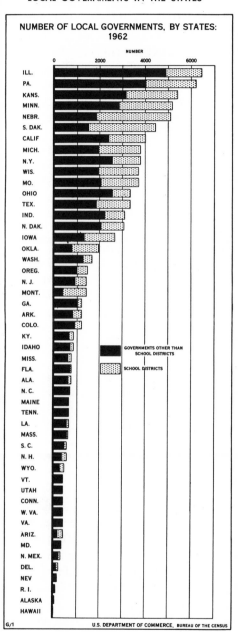

NUMBER OF LOCAL GOVERNMENTS, BY STATES: 1962

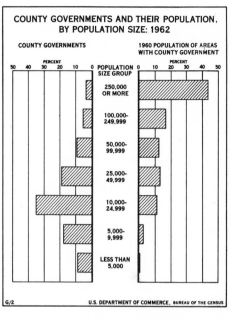

COUNTY GOVERNMENTS AND THEIR POPULATION, BY POPULATION SIZE: 1962

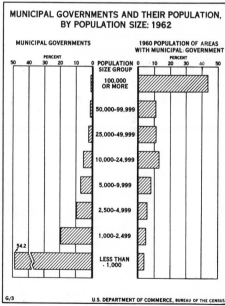

MUNICIPAL GOVERNMENTS AND THEIR POPULATION, BY POPULATION SIZE: 1962

SOURCE: U.S. Bureau of the Census, *Census of Governments, 1962.*

tween the "pluralist" and "elitist" models of community power. "Pluralist" communities are those in which there are many competing interests and structures of power. These competing interests tend to balance each other in policy making, and interests that exercise influence over certain kinds of policies do not necessarily have influence on others kinds of policies. In pluralist communities, there is no single interest or elite which dominates decision making in all policy areas—there is considerable competition among interest groups, and influential community leaders are not united by any common interests and do not act in unison. In short, pluralist communities are those in which competition, fluidity, access, and equality characterize political activity. On the other hand, "elitist" communities are those in which power is concentrated in the hands of a very small portion of the population. In elitist communities, decision makers are *not* typical or representative of the people at large; rather they are usually people who have control over the economic resources of a community, which gives them a dominant position in community politics. Thus, a single "elite" is influential in many different kinds of decisions, and members of this elite share an interest in maintaining the status quo. Such an elite is not really subject to much control by the masses of people, who are largely uninformed and apathetic about community affairs. The elitist model of community politics stresses the concentration of power in the hands of business leaders, who influence political events in many subtle ways.

Finally, metropolitan areas provide another kind of setting for "community" politics. A metropolitan area is a community in the sense that its residents are economically interdependent, but the political system of metropolitan areas is highly fragmented, and conflict, rather than cooperation, often characterizes relations between city and suburban governments. (The following chapters will examine all types of community political systems in more detail.)

Communities as Governmental Units

Local government is not mentioned in the U.S. Constitution. Although we regard the American federal system as a mixture of federal, state, and *local* governments, from a constitutional point of view, local governments are really a part of state governments. Communities have no constitutional right to self-government: all of their governmental powers legally flow from state governments. Local governments—cities, townships, counties, special districts, and school districts—are creatures of the states, subject to the obligations, privileges, powers, and restrictions that state governments impose upon them. The state, either through its constitution or its laws, may create or destroy any or all units of local government. To the extent that local governments can collect taxes, regulate their citizens, provide services, they are actually exercising *state* powers delegated to them by the state in either its constitution or its laws.

All states, with the exception of Alaska, Connecticut, and Rhode Island have organized *county* governments. Connecticut abolished its eight counties in 1960. In Louisiana, counties are called "parishes." It is difficult to generalize about the powers of counties. The average population served by a county government is 52,135, but Hinsdale County, Colorado had only 208 inhabitants in 1960, while Los Angeles County, California had more than six million. The legal powers, organization, and officers of counties also vary a great deal.

Perhaps it would be best to begin a description of county government by distinguishing between rural and urban counties. Obviously there is a great deal of difference between Los Angeles County with six million people, Cook County, Chicago with 5.1 million, and Wayne County, Detroit with 2.7 million, and the more than 800 rural counties in the nation with populations of 10,000 or less. Traditionally, the rural county was the most important unit of local government: it handled such essential matters as law enforcement, courts, schools, roads, elections, poor relief, and the legal recording of property deeds, mortgages, wills, and marriages. Rural communities competed with each other for the location of the county seat, because the community named as county seat won social and political prestige, county jobs, a county fair, and preferential treatment in county roads and public buildings. Moreover, many rural dwellers identify themselves as "coming from" a particular county. The county seat attracted retail business: farm markets were generally located in county seats, where a farmer could transact both public and private business. Rural county government provided an arena for a folksy, provincial, individualistic, "friends and neighbors," type of politics. Rural county government was the province of laymen and amateurs rather than experts or professionals. Decision making was personalized and informal. Often rural counties resemble urban coun-

TABLE 8.1

LOCAL GOVERNMENTS IN THE UNITED STATES

	1962	1957	1952
Counties	3,043	3,050	3,052
Municipalities	17,997	17,215	16,807
Townships	17,144	17,198	17,202
School districts	34,678	50,454	67,355
Special districts	18.323	14,424	12,340
Total	91,185	102,341	116,756

Source: U.S. Bureau of the Census, *Census of Governments, 1962.*

ties about as much as the old-fashioned country store resembles a modern supermarket.

Although county governments differ markedly in their organization, they generally have: (1) a governing body variously called the "county commissioners," "county board," "board of supervisors," or even "judges," which is composed of anywhere from three to 50 elected members; (2) a number of separately elected officials with countywide jurisdictions, such as sheriff, county attorney, auditor, recorder, coroner, assessor, judge, treasurer, engineer, and so on; (3) a large number of special boards or commissions which have authority over various functions, such as the county welfare board, county tax equalization committee, the hospital board, library board, the civil service commission, and so on, whose members may be elected or appointed by the county commissioners or may even include the county commissioners in an ex officio capacity; and (4) an appointed county bureaucracy in roads, health, welfare, libraries, schools, and so on.

Typically county officials have the following duties: [6]

> *Sheriff:* maintains jail; furnishes police protection in unincorporated areas; carries out orders of the county court.
>
> *Auditor:* maintains financial records and tax rolls; authorizes payment of county obligations.
>
> *County attorney:* serves as chief prosecuting attorney; conducts criminal investigations and prosecutes law violators.
>
> *Coroner:* conducts medical investigations to determine cause of death; maintains county morgue.
>
> *Treasurer:* collects, disburses, and maintains county funds, and makes county fiscal reports.
>
> *Clerk:* registers and records legal documents including deeds, mortgages, plats, marriages, divorces, births; certifies election returns.
>
> *Assessor:* determines value of all taxable property in the county.

The many separately elected county officials and the surplus of independent boards and commissions in county government are generally considered an obstacle to the emergence of strong executive leadership at the county level. The ability of county governments to assume more important functions and responsibilities, particularly in urban areas, probably hinges upon a reorganization of county government to provide for stronger executive leadership.

County government in urban areas is acquiring many of the responsibilities of city governments, and urban counties are increasingly adopting more streamlined, manager types of government organization. Urban counties may provide recreation, flood control, water supply, sewage disposal,

[6] G. Theodore Mitau, *State and Local Government* (New York: Charles Scribner's Sons, 1966), p. 383.

library services, airport facilities, countywide police and fire protection, and other urban services. Urban counties may provide these traditional "city services" to the unincorporated areas of the county, that is, to the areas not within the boundaries of cities, and occasionally to cities as well. Table 8.2 shows the extent to which urban counties have undertaken to provide urban services to their residents, particularly the suburban fringe areas of larger cities. (See Chapter 9 for further discussion of the future of county government in metropolitan areas.)

County governments can only exercise those powers delegated to them by state laws or constitutions. Even the organization of county government is determined by state law. Some states have enacted "home rule" laws under which counties might operate more independently and even provide more streamlined, manager type governmental structures. Yet, to date, very few counties have undertaken to reorganize themselves. The large number of elected county officials, the "courthouse gangs," county employees, and party organizations, which use county jobs for patronage, all tend to obstruct the reorganization of county government. Only gradually have county managers been introduced into the structure of urban counties.

Another interesting unit of local government is the "township" or "town," which is found in about half of the states—the northern states from New England to the Midwest. Southern and western states have made little use of this unit of government. Townships are subdivisions of counties and perform many of the functions of county governments at a grass-

TABLE 8.2

PERCENTAGE OF COUNTIES OVER 100,000 POPULATION PROVIDING SERVICES TO ENTIRE COUNTY AND TO UNINCORPORATED AREAS

Service	Percent of counties providing services to	
	Entire county	Unincorporated areas
Police	33.0	68.8
Fire	5.4	24.4
Street construction	20.4	50.7
Street lighting	1.4	17.6
Recreation	21.3	37.5
Parks	33.0	42.9
Garbage collection	2.3	12.7
Public housing	1.4	6.8
Libraries	28.9	45.2
None	23.5	4.1
Not reporting	19.0	6.8

Source: *Municipal Year Book, 1962*, p. 64.

roots level—schools, elections, road repair, tax administration, fire protection, and even law enforcement through local justices of the peace. Townships are unincorporated, which means they do not have charters from state governments guaranteeing their political independence or authorizing them to provide many municipal services. The jurisdiction of townships may extend over many square miles of sparsely populated rural territory. About 40 million people, or one-fifth of the U.S. population live under township governments today.

Township governments vary considerably in their powers and organization. Perhaps it would be best to classify them as "towns," "rural townships," and "urban townships." In the New England states, the "town" is a significant unit of local government, with long traditions and deep roots in the political philosophy of the people of the region. In fact, the New England "town meeting" is often cited by political philosophers as the ideal form of *direct* democracy as distinguished from *representative* democracy. For the town meeting was, and to some extent still is, the central institution of "town" government. The New England town included a village and all of its surrounding farms. The town meeting was open to all eligible voters; it was generally an important social as well as political event. The town meeting would levy taxes, make appropriations, determine policy and elect officers for the year. Between town meetings, a board of selected men, "selectmen," would supervise the activities of the town—schools, health, roads, care of the poor, and so on. Other officers included town clerk, tax assessors and collectors, justices of the peace, constables, road commissioners, and school board members. Although the ideal of direct democracy is still alive in many smaller New England towns, in the large towns, the pure democracy of the town meeting has given way to a representative system, in which town meeting members are elected prior to the town meeting. Moreover, much of the determination of the towns' financial affairs, previously decided at town meetings, has now been given over to the "selectmen," and many towns have appointed town managers to supervise the day-to-day administration of town services.

Rural townships outside of New England have lost much of their vitality in recent years. The school district consolidation movement (see Chapter 14) has centralized the control of public schools at the county level or in school districts, which span villages and townships. Population decline in America's rural areas has made it difficult for many rural *counties* to operate effectively, let alone smaller rural *townships*. Township government seldom has the financial resources to provide the level of public services that even rural dwellers now insist upon. As communities grow, they incorporate themselves into cities and remove valuable property from the tax roll of the township. Cities, unlike townships, are usually authorized by state governments to choose among various forms of government organization, levy higher taxes, spend more money, and provide a higher level of public service.

Some urban townships appear to have a brighter future as units of government than rural townships. This is particularly true in certain suburban areas of larger cities where metropolitan growth has enveloped township governments. Some states, Pennsylvania for example, have authorized urban townships to exercise many· of the powers and provide many of the services previously reserved to city governments. While these urban townships are not incorporated, they often function very much as if they were cities. Of course by not incorporating, they risk the possibility of being annexed by nearby cities, since ordinarily only a municipal charter can guarantee political independence.

Cities as "Municipal Corporations"

Nearly 70 per cent of the American people live in cities. Legally speaking, cities are "municipal corporations," which have received charters from state governments setting forth their boundaries, governmental powers and functions, structure and organization, methods of finance, and powers to elect and appoint officers and employees. The municipal charter is intended to grant the powers of local self-government to a community. Of course, the powers of self-government granted by a municipal charter are not unlimited. A state can change a charter or take it away altogether, as it sees fit. Cities, like other local governments, have only the powers that state laws and constitutions grant them. They are still subdivisions of the state. And, of course, state laws operate within the boundaries of cities. In fact, municipal corporations are generally responsible for the enforcement of state law within their boundaries. But they also have the additional power to make local laws, "ordinances," which operate only within their boundaries. But perhaps the most serious limitation on the powers of cities is the fact that American courts have insisted upon interpreting the powers granted in charters very narrowly. The classic statement of this principle of restrictive interpretation of municipal powers was made by John F. Dillon over 50 years ago and is now well known as "Dillon's rule":

> It is a general and undisputed proposition of law that a municipal corporation possesses and can exercise the following powers, and no others: first, those granted in express words; second, those necessarily or fairly implied in or incident to the powers expressly granted; third, those essential to the accomplishment of the declared objects and purposes of the corporation—not simply convenient, but indispensable. Any fair, reasonable, substantial doubt concerning the existence of power is resolved by the courts against a corporation, and the power is denied.[7]

[7] John F. Dillon, *Commentaries on the Laws of Municipal Corporations,* 5th ed., (Boston: 1911), p. 448.

As Banfield and Wilson point out, "This means that a city cannot operate a peanut stand at the city zoo without first getting the state legislature to pass an enabling law, unless, per chance, the city's charter or some previously enacted law unmistakably covers the sale of peanuts." [8]

The restrictive interpretation of the powers of cities leads to rather lengthy city charters, since nearly everything a city does must have specific legal authorization in the city charter. The city charter of New York, for example is several hundred pages long. City charters must cover in detail such matters as boundaries, structure of government, ordinance making powers, finances, contracts, purchasing, bonds, courts, municipal elections, property assessments, zoning laws and building codes, licenses, franchises, law enforcement, education, health, streets, parks, public utilities, and on and on. Since any proposed change in the powers, organization, or responsibilities of cities requires an act of a state legislature amending the city's charter, state legislatures are intimately involved in local legislation. This practice of narrowly interpreting city charters may appear awkward, but its effect is to increase the power of courts and state legislators in city affairs. Courts acquire power from their ability to interpret complex city charters; and state legislators with city constituencies acquire power through the practice of granting a local legislator the courtesy of accepting his views on local legislation that affects only his constituency.

State legislative control over cities is most firmly entrenched in *special act* charters. These charters are specially drawn for the cities named in them. Cities under special act charters remain directly under legislative control, and specific legislative approval for that city and that city alone must be obtained for any change in its government or service activities. Such charters give rise to local acts dealing with small details of city government in a specially named city, for example, "that Fall River be authorized to appropriate money for the purchase of uniforms for the park police and watershed guards of said city." [9] Under special act charters, laws that apply to one city do not necessarily apply to others.

Municipal reformers, with the political support of the city official, have long argued that *special act* charters place the city at the mercy of political forces outside of the city, particularly rural-dominated legislatures; lead to legislative logrolling among the delegations from several cities in a state; and consume a large amount of state legislatures' time, which ought to be concerned with statewide rather than local legislation. Agitation against special act charters has led many states to outlaw them by constitutional amendment. In their place, *general act* charters usually classify cities according to their size and then apply municipal laws to all cities in each size classification. Thus, a state's municipal law may apply to all

[8] Banfield and Wilson, *City Politics*, p. 65.
[9] Banfield and Wilson, *op. cit.*, p. 66.

cities of less than 10,000 people, another law to all cities with populations of 10–25,000, another to cities with 25–50,000 people, and so on. These general act charters make it difficult to interfere in the activities of a particular city without affecting the activities of all cities of a similar size category. Yet in practice there are often exceptions and modifications to general act legislation. For example, since legislators know the populations of their cities, they can select size categories for municipal law that apply to only one city. The Pennsylvania legislature can pass laws for cities of over 1 million, aware that only Philadelphia falls into this category, and for cities of 500,000 to 1 million, aware that only Pittsburgh falls into this category.

Optional charter laws provide cities with some choice in the structure and organization of their governments. Such laws generally offer a choice of governmental forms: strong mayor and weak council, weak mayor and strong council, commission, city manager, or some modification of these.

Home rule charters are designed to give cities the power to adopt governmental forms and provide municipal services, as they see fit, without state legislative interference. Home rule charters may be given to cities by state constitutions or by legislative enactments; legislative home rule is considered less secure since a legislature could retract the grant if it wished to do so. Beginning with Missouri in 1875, more than half the states have included in their constitutions provisions for the issuance of home rule charters. About two-thirds of the nation's cities with populations over 200,000 have some form of home rule.

The intended effect of home rule is to reverse "Dillon's rule" and enable cities to "exercise all legislative powers not prohibited by law or by charter." In other words, instead of preventing a city from doing anything not specifically authorized, home rule permits the city to do anything not specifically prohibited. The theory of home rule grants sweeping powers to cities; however, in practice, home rule has not brought self-government to cities. Home rule provisions in state constitutions range from those that grant considerable power and discretion over local affairs, to provisions that are so useless that no city has ever made use of them. (Pennsylvania adopted a constitutional amendment providing for home rule for cities in 1922, but not until 1951, when Philadelphia adopted a home rule charter, did any city make use of it.) First of all, these constitutional provisions may be too cumbersome or vague for effective implementation. In some states, cities feel that it is easier to use the general law charters, particularly if they provide for optional forms of government, than to use the cumbersome procedures for obtaining home rule. Another important limitation on home rule is the distinction between "self-enforcing" and "non-self-enforcing," or "permissive," home rule provisions in state constitutions.

Non-self-enforcing home rule provisions merely permit the state legislature to grant home rule to its cities; cities cannot acquire home rule without legislative action. Only about a dozen states have "self-enforcing" home rule provisions, which enable cities to bypass the state legislature and adopt home rule for themselves. (Missouri's original constitutional home rule amendment was a self-enforcing type.) Finally, home rule may be limited by court interpretations of the language of the constitutional provisions granting power to home rule in cities. Constitutional provisions may grant to home rule cities the power to make "all laws and ordinances relating to municipal concerns" (Michigan), or the "powers of local self-government" (Ohio), or all powers "in respect to municipal affairs" (California).[10] Of course, ordinances passed under home rule authority cannot be in conflict with state law. Courts must distinguish between municipal and statewide concerns. In cases where doubt exists, legal traditions of municipal law require that courts resolve the doubt in favor of the state and against local powers of home rule. State legislatures can intervene in local affairs in home rule cities by simply deciding that a particular matter is of statewide concern.

The politics of home rule often pits reform groups, city mayors, and administrators against state legislators and large municipal taxpayers. State legislators are generally wary of giving up their authority over cities. Rural legislators have little reason to support city home rule, and even city legislators seldom welcome proposals to give up their authority over local bills. Sometimes city employees with good access to the legislature will oppose giving a mayor or city manager too much control over their employment. Taxpayer groups may fear that home rule will give the city the ability to increase taxes. Local bills may be pictured as a distraction to legislators by reformers, but many legislators enjoy the power that it brings them in local affairs and welcome the opportunity to perform legislative services for their constituents. And so, even with reapportionment adding to the number of urban legislators, the League of Women Voters, good government groups, and mayors may still be frustrated in their attempts to achieve genuine home rule for American cities.

Courts figure prominently in municipal politics. This is because of the subordinate position of the municipal corporation in the hierarchy of governments, and legal traditions, such as Dillon's rule, which narrowly interpret the power of local governments. The power of courts over municipal affairs grants leverage to defenders of the status quo in any political battle at the local level. Not only must proponents of a new municipal law or municipal service win the battle over whether a city *ought* to pass the new law or provide the new service, but also they must win the legal battle over

---

[10] See Duane Lockard, *The Politics of State and Local Government* (New York: The Macmillan Co., 1963), p. 124.

whether the city *can* pass the law or provide the service. As Duane Lockard explained:

> Limitations and uncertainties abound and doubts about the validity of local enactments can always be raised. The costs and delays of litigation challenging the authority of a city to undertake new services or regulatory action, therefore, constitute a major political force in municipal government. The city attorney (or the corporation council, as he is often called) becomes a key official and often a very negative force, for his reputation is at stake every time the city undertakes an action that may be successfully challenged in the courts. He recommends cautiously as indeed both his professional training and the facts of the law incline him to do.[11]

Not only must the city obey the federal constitution, but it is also subject to the restraints of the state constitution, state laws, its municipal charter, and of course, Dillon's rule. The result is to greatly strengthen courts, attorneys, and defenders of the status quo.

Forms of City Government

American city government comes in three structural packages. There are some adaptations and variations from city to city, but generally one can classify the form of city government as mayor-council, commission, or council-manager.

The nation's largest cities tend to function under the mayor-council plan. Figure 8.2 shows the structure of the mayor-council government. This is the oldest form of American city government and is designed in the American tradition of separation of powers between legislature and executive. One may also establish subcategories of "strong" or "weak" mayor forms of mayor-council government. A strong mayor is one who is the undisputed master of the executive agencies of city government and who has substantial legislative powers in the form of budget making, vetoes, and the opportunity to propose legislation. Only Boston and Cleveland, among the nation's largest cities, make the mayor the sole elected official among city executive officers; it is common in other cities for the mayor to share budgetary and administrative powers with other elected officials. In New York, an eight member board of estimate (mayor, council president, comptroller, and five borough presidents) draw up the city's budget. In Chicago, a council committee prepares the budget. Minneapolis is perhaps the prime example of a weak mayor system: voters elect a library board, the parks board, a board of estimate and taxation, 13 aldermen, a treasurer, and a comptroller; the council, not the mayor, appoints the city attorney, city engineer, city assessor, and city clerk; the mayor makes only one major

[11] Lockard, *op. cit.*, p. 131.

FIGURE 8.2

MAYOR-COUNCIL FORM

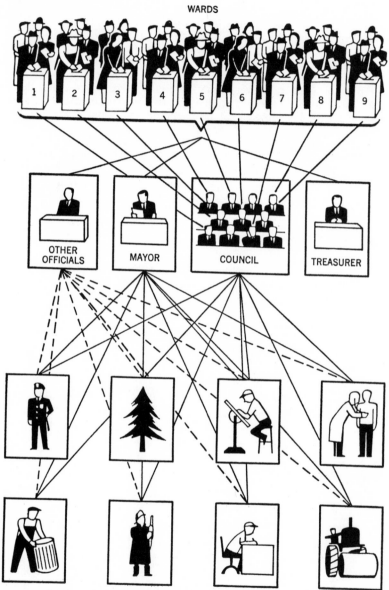

appointment—the city chief of police. Yet many mayors, by virtue of their prestige, persuasive abilities, or role as party leader, have been able to overcome most of the weaknesses of their formal office. Mayor Daley of Chicago must deal with a 50 member city council, a wide variety of independent boards and agencies like the Park District, Board of Education, and Housing Authority, a large legislative delegation, and various lesser elected officials. Yet Mayor Daley is the undisputed center of political influence in Chicago.

In recent years, large cities have been adding to the formal powers of their chief executives. Cities have augmented the mayor's role by providing him with direction over budgeting, purchasing, and personnel controls, and independent boards and commissions and individual councilmen have relinquished administrative control over city departments in many cities. Moreover, many cities have strengthened the mayor's position by providing him with a chief administrative officer, "CAO," to handle important staff and administrative duties of supervising city departments and providing central management services.

The commission form of city government gives both legislative and executive powers to a small body, usually consisting of five members (see Figure 8.3). The commission form originated at the beginning of the century as a reform movement, designed to end a system of divided responsibility between mayor and council. One of the commission members is nominally the mayor, but he has no more formal powers than his fellow commissioners. The board of commissioners is directly responsible for the operation of city departments and agencies. In practice, one commission member will become responsible for the management of a specific department, such as finance, public works, or public safety. As long as the councilmen are in agreement over policy, there are few problems; but when commissioners differ among themselves and develop separate spheres of influence in city government, city government becomes a multiheaded monster, totally lacking in coordination. The results of a commission form of government were generally so disastrous that the reform movement abandoned its early support of this form of government in favor of the council-manager plan. Memphis, Portland, St. Paul, Omaha, and Jersey City are principal cities that still operate under this plan. Even Galveston, the birthplace of the commission plan in 1901, abandoned it in 1960, in favor of the council-manager plan.

The council-manager form of government revived the distinction between legislative "policy-making" and executive "administration" in city government. Policy making responsibility is vested in an elected council, and administration is assigned to an appointed, professional administrator, known as a manager (see Figure 8.4). The council chooses the manager and he is responsible to them. All departments of the city government operate

FIGURE 8.3

COMMISSION FORM

SOURCE: National Municipal League. Reproduced by permission.

FIGURE 8.4

COUNCIL-MANAGER FORM

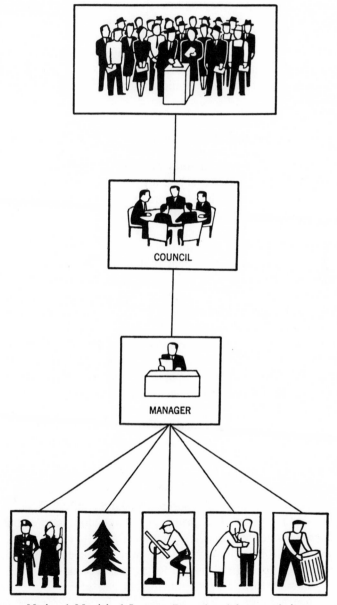

SOURCE: National Municipal League. Reproduced by permission.

under the direction of the manager, who has the power to hire and fire personnel within the limits set by the merit system. The council's role in administration is limited to selecting and dismissing the city manager. The plan is based on the idea that policy making and administration are separate functions, and that the principal task of city government is to provide the highest level of services at the lowest possible cost—utilities, streets, fire, police protection, health, welfare, recreation, and so on. Hence, a professionally trained, career oriented administrator is given direct control over city departments.

Socio-economic Environment and the Structure of City Government

We shall return to the political roles of mayors, managers, and councils in the next chapter, but let us examine for a moment the social, economic, and political forces shaping the structure of city government: that is, the conditions associated with the selection of one of the principal forms of government.

First of all, city manager government is closely associated with the size of cities. Large cities show a distinct preference for the more "political" form of mayor-council government in contrast to the more "efficient" form of council-manager government. Only four of the nation's 21 cities with more than 500,000 people have council-manager government: Dallas, San Antonio, San Diego, and Cincinnati. All other major cities have the mayor-council form of government. The council-manager and commission forms of government are most popular in the middle-sized cities—cities with populations of 10,000–250,000 people. Probably, cities with less than 10,000 persons do not have sufficient resources to justify hiring a trained professional city manager, nor in all probability, do they have the administrative problems requiring his expertise. Thus, small cities, like large cities, tend to rely upon mayor-council government, although probably for different reasons.

If the lack of resources and the absence of complex administrative problems in small cities explains the absence of council-manager government in these cities, what explains its absence in larger cities? A common explanation is that the political environment of large cities is so complex, with many competing interests, that these cities require strong political leadership, which can arbitrate struggles for power, arrange compromises, and be directly responsible to the people for policy decisions. A large city requires a "political" form of government that can arbitrate the conflicting claims of diverse interests. This implies that in smaller cities there are fewer competing interests, more acceptance of a common public interest, and less division over community policy. A professional city manager would have less difficulty in accepting cues about correct behavior in a small city than in a large city with a complex social and political structure. A single interest is more likely to dominate politics in a small city; therefore, such a city requires a professional administrator rather than a political negotiator. The question is whether or not political skill or administrative expertise is more important in a city, and there is reason to believe that larger cities require political skills more than professional administration. Growing cities face more administrative and technical problems than cities whose population is stable. There is a strong relationship between population *growth* and council-manager government. A rapidly growing city faces many administrative problems in providing streets, sewers, and the many other services required by an expanding population. This creates a demand for a professional administrator. In contrast, the mayor-council form of government is associated with cities having relatively stable populations, in which administrative and technical problems are not quite so pressing, and political conflict is more likely to be well defined and persistent.

Council-manager cities tend to be middle class cities. Cities with large proportions of working class residents, low income families, Negroes, and

FIGURE 8.5

GOVERNMENTAL FORM AND SIZE OF CITY

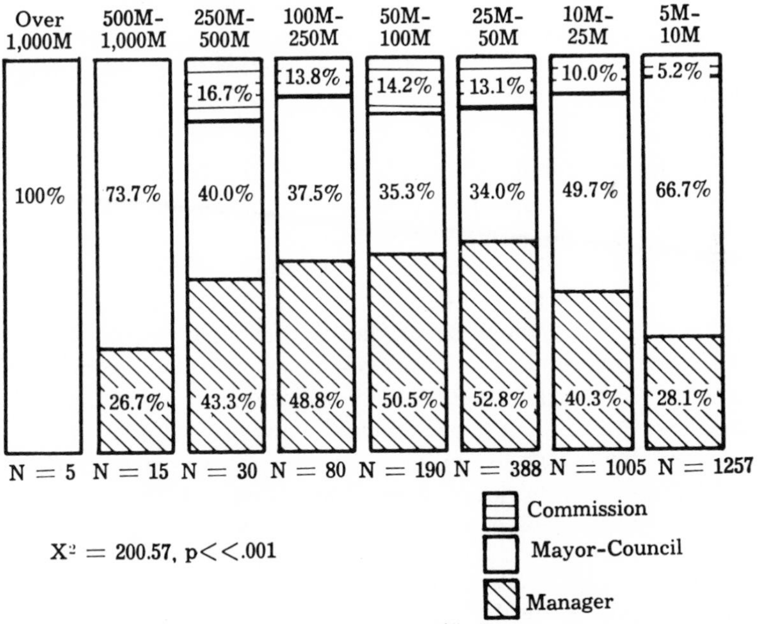

Over 1,000M	500M– 1,000M	250M– 500M	100M– 250M	50M– 100M	25M– 50M	10M– 25M	5M– 10M
		16.7%	13.8%	14.2%	13.1%	10.0%	5.2%
100%	73.7%	40.0%	37.5%	35.3%	34.0%	49.7%	66.7%
	26.7%	43.3%	48.8%	50.5%	52.8%	40.3%	28.1%
N = 5	N = 15	N = 30	N = 80	N = 190	N = 388	N = 1005	N = 1257

$X^2 = 200.57$, p<<.001

▤ Commission
☐ Mayor-Council
▨ Manager

SOURCE: John H. Kessel, "Governmental Structure and Political Environment," *American Political Science Review*, 56 (September, 1962), 616. Reproduced by permission.

FIGURE 8.6

GOVERNMENTAL FORM AND CITY GROWTH RATE

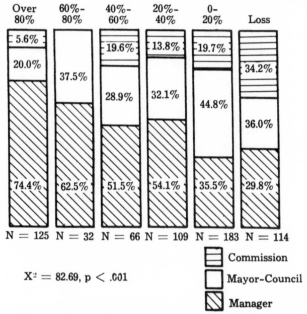

SOURCE: John H. Kessel, "Governmental Structure and Political Environment," *American Political Science Review*, 56 (September, 1962), 616. Reproduced by permission.

ethnic minorities are unlikely to adopt council-manager government. Schnore and Alfred have presented conclusive evidence, for 300 suburbs in 25 large metropolitan areas, that communities with council-manager government have a smaller proportion of nonwhites, foreign born, and persons over 65 years of age, a larger proportion of white collar workers, with a high school education or better, and tend to grow more rapidly in population than communities with mayor-council or commission forms of government.[12] In a study of the Chicago area, a ranking of 74 suburban cities, according to the median value of homes, shows that 18 of the 20 cities with the highest home values had council-manager government, whereas none of the 31 cities with the lowest home values had it.[13] Figure 8.7 shows a decrease in manager government associated with an increase in foreign

[12] Leo F. Schnore and Robert R. Alford, "Forms of Government and Socioeconomic Characteristics of Suburbs," *Administrative Science Quarterly* (June, 1963), pp. 1–17.

[13] Edgar L. Sherbenov, "Class, Participation, and the Council-Manager Plan," *Public Administration Review* (Summer, 1961), pp. 131–35.

born population of a city. Figure 8.7 also shows the relationship between form of government and principal economic function: there is a decreasing use of the manager plan, according to the principal economic activity, in the following order: personnel services, retail, finance, professional, public administration, wholesale, transportation, diversified industry, and manufacturing. Figure 8.8 pertains only to middle-sized cities with populations between 25,000 and 250,000; thus, these findings are not merely a product of the intervening effect of size of city. The white collar employees in personnel services, retail store, and financial establishments, as well as professional people and public administrators, appear to prefer manager government more than blue collar workers in wholesale trade, transportation, diversified industry, and manufacturing. Blue collar workers appear to prefer a mayor-council system which provides political channels for the expression of their interests.

Why is it that middle class communities prefer the manager form of government while working class communities prefer a mayor-council gov-

FIGURE 8.7

GOVERNMENTAL FORM AND MINORITY GROUPS

(*Percent foreign-born in city population*)

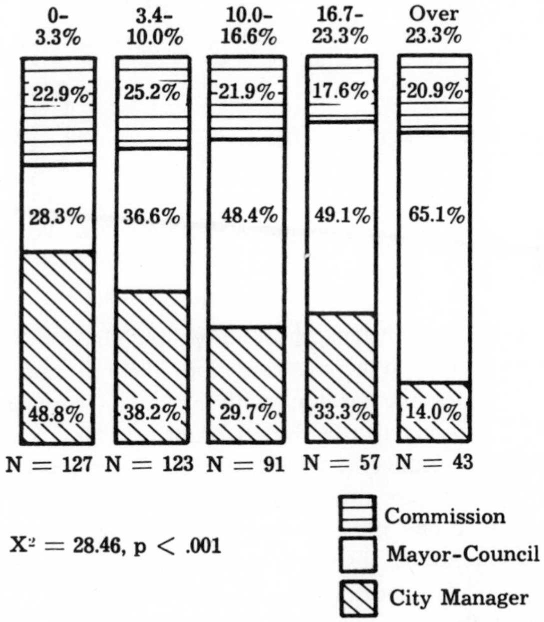

0– 3.3%	3.4– 10.0%	10.0– 16.6%	16.7– 23.3%	Over 23.3%
22.9%	25.2%	21.9%	17.6%	20.9%
28.3%	36.6%	48.4%	49.1%	65.1%
48.8%	38.2%	29.7%	33.3%	14.0%
N = 127	N = 123	N = 91	N = 57	N = 43

$X^2 = 28.46$, p $< .001$

Commission
Mayor-Council
City Manager

SOURCE: John H. Kessel, "Governmental Structure and Political Environment," *American Political Science Review*, 56 (September, 1962), 618. Reproduced by permission.

FIGURE 8.8

GOVERNMENTAL FORM AND ECONOMIC BASE

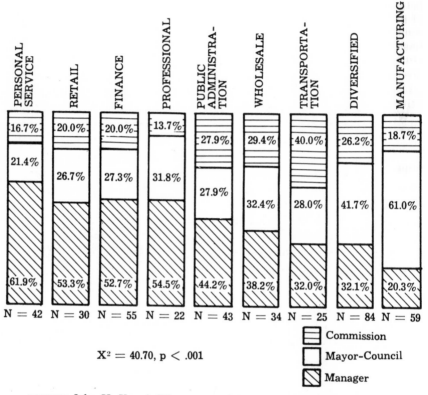

$X^2 = 40.70, p < .001$

Commission

Mayor-Council

Manager

SOURCE: John H. Kessel, "Governmental Structure and Political Environment," *American Political Science Review*, 56 (September, 1962), 619. Reproduced by permission.

ernment? Middle class citizens, those in white collar jobs with good educations and reasonably high incomes, are more likely to want government conducted in a businesslike fashion, with a council serving as a board of directors and a city manager as the president of a "municipal corporation." They are primarily concerned with efficiency, honesty, and saving their tax dollars. These values are not necessarily shared by labor, low status, low income, ethnic and minority groups, which may prefer a government that grants small favors, dispenses patronage jobs, awards representation and "recognition" to minority groups, and can be held directly responsible by the voters at election time. In a campaign for city-manager government, one usually finds business leaders, newspapers, and civic associations supporting the plan, and labor unions and minority group organizations far less enthusiastic. Party organizations and professional politicians can usually be expected to oppose this plan. Its support generally comes from white collar, high income, well educated, white neighborhoods, and its opposition from low income, blue collar, Negro and ethnic neighborhoods.

Communities with well-organized competitive party systems are less likely to have council-manager government than one party communities or communities in which the formal party organization is weak. States with the highest percentages of medium-sized cities with manager plans are Virginia, North Carolina, California, Texas, and Florida; in contrast, states with the highest percentages of mayor-council plans are Indiana, Connecticut, and Ohio. The former states are either one party states or, in the case of California, states with relatively weak party organizations. The states with mayor-council cities are competitive two party states. It is sometimes argued that the introduction of the manager plan decreases party activity in communities, but it is also true that the presence of strong party organizations may be a significant factor in the defeat of manager plans. Thus, manager government may depress party activity, or strong parties may kill off manager government, or both; but whatever the case, manager government appears incompatible with strong partisan politics in a community. Thus, social, economic, and political forces influence the structure of city government.

9

PARTICIPATION IN COMMUNITY POLITICS

Voters

The influence of the voter is felt not only on election day, but on every day that elected officials act to win his support or avoid his displeasure. The successful political leader is always concerned with what the voter will think.

Voter turnout in local elections is substantially lower than state or national elections. While two-thirds of the nation's eligible voters can be expected to cast ballots in a presidential election, voter turnouts of 30–50 per cent are all that can be expected in local elections, even in the nation's largest cities. Low voter turnout is another conservative influence on local government. A low turnout generally means that people at lower social economic levels have not participated: the lower the turnout, the more overrepresented are the higher socio-economic groups. Because of this disproportionate representation of higher socio-economic groups, we can expect local officials to be disproportionately concerned with the attitudes of middle class voters in contrast to lower class nonvoters.

Nonpartisanship depresses voter turnout quite substantially. The *Municipal Yearbook* reports that the median voter turnout for partisan cities was 50 per cent, while the median voter turnout for nonpartisan cities was only 30 per cent (see Table 9.1). This suggests that nonpartisanship increases the influence of middle class voters in city government, since it is fair to assume that the decrease in voter turnout from partisan to nonpartisan elections occurs primarily among working class voters. Partisan campaigns heighten voter turnout, in part because of the greater interest they generate and in part because of the role of party workers in getting out the vote. The

TABLE 9.1

PER CENT OF ADULTS VOTING IN CITIES OVER 25,000

	No. of cities reporting	Lower quartile	Median	Upper quartile	No. of cities reporting	Lower quartile	Median	Upper quartile
	All city elections				Held concurrently with state or national elections			
Form of election								
Partisan	109	37	50	57	31	47	51	65
Nonpartisan	350	21	30	43	32	31	43	59
Form of government								
Mayor-council	137	38	50	57	31	47	51	65
Commission	41	29	38	47	3	28	33	61
Counsil-manager	281	20	27	39	29	29	43	60
Population group								
Over 500,000	15	26	39	47	2	46	–	47
250,000 to 500,000	25	21	37	48	4	45	56	76
100,000 to 250,000	54	24	32	50	9	30	50	55
50,000 to 100,000	124	21	33	51	17	20	51	62
25,000 to 50,000	243	23	33	47	31	35	47	64
All cities over 25,000	461	22	33	48	63	35	50	62
	Held concurrently with other local elections*				Held independently of any other election			
Form of election								
Partisan	22	48	53	58	56	26	41	53
Nonpartisan	65	27	35	47	246	19	27	39
Form of government								
Mayor-council	28	40	50	55	78	34	44	56
Commission	5	28	57	71	32	28	38	47
Council-manager	54	26	35	47	193	18	23	32
Population group								
Over 500,000	7	33	39	50	5	19	20	39
250,000 to 500,000	5	24	35	54	16	18	34	41
100,000 to 250,000	9	31	46	50	36	21	29	46
50,000 to 100,000	24	30	51	55	82	20	29	44
25,000 to 50,000	42	28	41	50	164	20	29	41
All cities over 25,000	87	29	44	51	303	20	29	41

*Excluding cities also holding election concurrently with state or national election.

Source: *Municipal Year Book, 1963*, p. 83.

difference in voter turnout in partisan and nonpartisan, local elections is an important comment on the role of parties in stimulating political participation.

Voter participation in local government can be further reduced by holding municipal elections at odd times of the year, when no other state or national elections are being held. A common rationale for holding municipal elections at times other than state or national elections is to separate local issues from state or national questions, but the real effect of scheduling local elections independently is to reduce further voter turnout and to increase the influence of middle class groups, which vote regularly.

Voter turnout in municipal elections is greater in large than in small cities. Voter turnout in cities with a mayor-council form of government is much higher than in cities with a council-manager plan. In summary, nonpartisanship, council-manager government, and separate municipal elections—all part of the municipal "reform" movement—operate to reduce voter turnout and probably strengthen the influence of middle class voters at the polls.

As we know, party voting is closely related to income, occupation, education, religion, race, and ethnic origin. Sample surveys and election studies at the state and national level demonstrate repeatedly that the Republican party draws its voter strength from high income, well educated, white collar, Anglo-Saxon, Protestant, and suburban and small town residents; and in contrast, the Democratic party draws its strength from low income, poorly educated, blue collar, Negro, Catholic, Jewish, and ethnic populations living in larger cities. There is reason to believe that these socio-economic divisions are influential in partisan elections at the local level as well. Of course the "class" theory of voting in American politics is subject to many important exceptions. At the national level, there are large numbers of voters, whose socio-economic backgrounds would indicate a tendency to the Democratic party, who regularly vote Republican; and vice versa. For this reason, we can only state that lower socio-economic groups "tend to" vote Democratic, that "by and large" they support Democratic candidates, and that "on the whole" they prefer the Democratic ticket.

In Chapter 11, "Metropolitics: Cities and Suburbs," we will observe that the nation's large, central cities tend to be Democratic, while their suburbs are normally Republican. Only one of the nation's ten largest cities has elected a Republican mayor in the last decade: Mayor Lindsay's startling victory in New York City in 1965 attracted nationwide attention and suggested that normally Democratic city voters can become disenchanted with "politics as usual" at city hall. The growing racial problem in the nation's central cities may also threaten the Democratic party's winning urban coalition. Working class whites in large cities may increasingly turn to the Republican party for protection against Negro "inroads." Yet major voting blocs tend to retain their attachments to parties with great tenacity, and the white "backlash" in major cities may not represent any permanent party realignment.

Studies of voting behavior in Philadelphia and its surrounding suburbs in the early 1960's supports the view that socio-economic divisions that are important in national politics also operate in local partisan elections.[1] Within the city of Philadelphia, Democratic and Republican party voting for mayor, district attorney, and other local offices was closely correlated with income, education, occupation, and race. Likewise, outside of Philadelphia, in suburban Delaware County, Republican and Democratic party strength was correlated with income, occupation, and educational levels among suburban communities. In short, class cleavages could be observed in voting patterns in both the city and the suburbs. While Democrats dominated city politics and Republicans suburban politics, in both city and suburb, party voting correlated with socio-economic divisions.

The relationships between class and party voting, however, seem to vary according to the size of the city. Masters and Wright report that laborers in small Michigan cities were less likely to vote Democratic than were laborers in large cities.[2] V. O. Key, in *Public Opinion and American Democracy*, reports that blue collar and white collar workers differ more

TABLE 9.2

DEMOCRATIC PRESIDENTIAL PERCENTAGES IN TEN MAJOR CITIES

	1936	1940	1944	1948	1952	1956	1960	1964
Baltimore	68.3	64.0	59.2	53.3	51.7	44.2	63.9	76.0
Boston	69.9	63.3	62.3	69.2	59.6	53.8	74.7	86.4
Chicago	66.9	58.5	61.4	58.6	54.4	49.0	63.6	63.2
Cleveland	76.5	69.9	67.9	61.8	59.9	54.6	70.9	82.8
Detroit	68.9	63.0	65.0	59.6	60.5	61.8	71.0	80.0
Milwaukee	82.1	64.1	61.7	59.4	51.5	47.3	61.8	70.0
New York	75.4	61.2	61.6	51.1*	55.4	51.0	62.8	73.2
Philadelphia	62.1	60.0	58.9	49.2*	58.4	57.1	68.1	73.7
Pittsburgh	70.7	61.6	60.8	60.1	56.1	52.3	67.0	74.7
St. Louis	67.0	58.1	60.4	64.3	62.0	61.0	66.6	77.7

*The Progressive party of Henry Wallace polled 13.5% in New York City and 2.4% in Philadelphia.
Source: Adapted from Richard M. Scammon (ed.), *America Votes, A Handbook of Contemporary American Election Statistics*, Vol. IV (Pittsburgh, 1962).

[1] See Oliver P. Williams, Harold Herman, Charles S. Liebman, and Thomas R. Dye, *Suburban Differences and Metropolitan Policies* (Philadelphia: University of Pennsylvania Press, 1964).

[2] Nicholas A. Masters and Deil S. Wright, "Trends and Variations in the Two-Party Vote: The Case of Michigan," *American Political Science Review*, 53 (December, 1958), 1078–90.

over policy questions in large metropolitan areas than in smaller cities.[3] In smaller cities, the blue collar workers tended to adopt attitudes similar to the white collar workers, which suggests that class cleavages are not as important in smaller cities as in larger metropolitan areas, and hence Democratic and Republican voting is less likely to correlate with socio-economic class position.[4]

Voters also influence local government through referenda. Referenda voting is an important aspect of local politics—an aspect not found at the national level. City charters frequently require that referenda be held on all proposals to increase indebtedness or to increase property taxation. These referenda votes provide us with an excellent opportunity to examine the factors influencing voter attitudes toward local government and to test some theories about voting behavior on local issues.

One theory is that a voter in local referenda will try to maximize his family income, by weighing the benefits that will come to him from a bond issue against the amount of the tax that will fall on him as a result of the expenditure.[5] This theory assumes that voters act rationally in pursuit of their own narrowly conceived self-interest: if the estimated benefit from a bond issue is more than the estimated cost, he votes for the expenditure, but if it is less, he votes against it. One problem connected with this theory is that voters seldom know whether a public expenditure proposal will benefit them or not. Usually ballots in municipal referenda do not specify precisely *which* streets are to be paved or *where* a bridge is to be built. Even if a facility is to serve a whole city (for example, a zoo, civic center, or county hospital), it is difficult for the voter to judge what benefits he will derive from the expenditure or to estimate the amount of the tax that will result from the expenditure. In other words, the voter is told on the ballot that the anticipated cost of a public undertaking may be "$12 million for street improvements," but he does not know how much of an increase in the tax rate would result or what this means to his total tax bill. Yet the theory that voters will try to maximize their economic self-interest deserves examination.

One would certainly expect voters who would have no tax levied upon them from passage of an expenditure proposal to vote affirmatively, even if they will derive only trivial benefits. Non-property owners, having noth-

---

[3] V. O. Key, Jr., *Public Opinion and American Democracy* (New York: Alfred A. Knopf, 1961), pp. 116–18.

[4] See also Edward C. Banfield and James Q. Wilson, *City Politics* (Cambridge: Harvard-M.I.T. Press, 1963), chap. 16.

[5] The following discussion of voter behavior on referenda relies heavily upon James Q. Wilson and Edward C. Banfield, "Public Regardingness as a Value Premise in Voting Behavior," *American Political Science Review,* 58 (December, 1964), 876–87; see also Raymond E. Wolfinger and John Field, "Political Ethos and the Structure of City Government," *American Political Science Review,* 60 (June, 1966), 306–26.

ing to lose by the expenditure and something to gain, however small, can be expected to favor the passage of bond and expenditure referenda. (Renters seldom realize that landlords will pass the tax increase on to them in higher rent.) Property owners should be far less willing to favor municipal expenditure proposals. Banfield and Wilson examined returns on 35 expenditure proposals, voted in 20 separate elections in seven cities, and their findings give strong support to the theory that property owners and non-property owners differ consistently over municipal expenditure proposals. The voters in non-homeowning districts almost invariably supported all expenditure proposals (see Table 9.3). Support for expenditure proposals consistently declined with increases in homeownership (see Figure 9.1). Homeowners show a greater distaste for public expenditures that are financed from property taxes than non-homeowners.

Up to this point, the Banfield and Wilson findings tend to support the theory that voters in municipal referenda act rationally in pursuit of their own economic self-interest. However, Banfield and Wilson came up with some very interesting, contrasting findings when they examined the voting behavior of large and small property owners. One might suppose that the

TABLE 9.3

REFERENDA VOTING BEHAVIOR OF FOUR MAJOR ECONOMIC GROUPS, COOK COUNTY, ILLINOIS

Group	Percent "yes" vote	
	County hospital	Welfare building
High income homeowners		
Winnetka	64	76
Wilmette	55	70
Lincolnwood	47	64
Middle income homeowners		
Lansing	30	54
Bellwood	21	55
Brookfield	22	51
Middle income renters		
Chicago ward 44	65	71
Chicago ward 48	61	72
Chicago ward 49	64	74
Low income renters		
Chicago ward 2	88	73
Chicago ward 3	87	76
Chicago ward 27	87	78

Source: James Q. Wilson and Edward C. Banfield, "Public Regardingness as a Value Premise in Voting Behavior," *American Political Science Review*, vol. 58 (December, 1964), p. 878.

FIGURE 9.1

THE RELATIONSHIP BETWEEN VOTING "YES" FOR SEWER FACILITIES AND
HOME OWNERSHIP IN CHICAGO

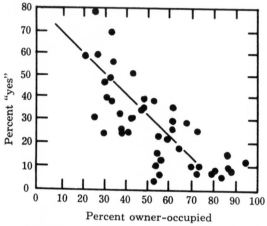

SOURCE: James Q. Wilson and Edward C. Banfield, "Public Regardingness as a Value Premise in Voting Behavior," *American Political Science Review,* 58 (December, 1964), 885.

more property a voter has, the less likely he is to favor public expenditures that increase his tax rate, since the more property he owns, the higher his tax bill. The owner of a $30,000 home, for example, probably gets no more benefit from a new city zoo than does the owner of a $10,000 one, yet his share of the tax increase is three times as much. Moreover, since many municipal health and welfare facilities will probably never be used by high income families, these families have added reason to oppose such facilities, if they are acting solely on behalf of their own economic self-interest. However, these expectations are not borne out by the voting returns. Banfield and Wilson found that the higher the family income and value of their property, the greater the support for public expenditures in municipal referenda: that is, higher income groups and the owners of more valuable property can usually be counted upon to support rather than oppose public expenditures—in contrast to lower income families and owners of less valuable property.

One explanation of the greater willingness of the high-income groups to support public expenditures rests upon the marginal utility theory of money. The richer a man is, the smaller the sacrifice that an additional dollar of taxation represents to him. Poor homeowners simply cannot afford additional dollars of taxation, even though their tax may be smaller than that levied upon more wealthy homeowners. But Banfield and Wilson offer another explanation: that support for public expenditures is a function of a "public-regarding" ethic, which is rooted in class and ethnic group subculture. Banfield and Wilson argue effectively that "public-regardingness," in contrast to "private-regardingness," is part of the middle class, white, Anglo-Saxon, Protestant subculture in America. The public-regarding voter has a conception of the public interest, which inspires him to support measures that benefit the whole community, whether or not they produce specific rewards for himself. In contrast, private-regarding voters—lower income, working class, Irish, Italian, Polish and other eastern European, white voters—tend to vote against public expenditures that do not directly benefit them. Negroes are much more likely to support public expenditures than low income whites; both Negro renters and homeowners are more favorable to all proposals than white ethnic voters, although Negro homeowners are somewhat less enthusiastic than Negro renters. Jews tend to support public expenditures as much as upper income Anglo-Saxon homeowners (see Table 9.4). The middle class conception of "the public interest" caused upper income, white, Anglo-Saxon homeowners to vote *against* veterans' bonuses and other proposals they regard as serving special interests rather than the entire community. Banfield and Wilson summarize their public-regardingness theory as follows:

> Each subcultural group, we think, has a more or less distinctive notion of how much a citizen ought to sacrifice for the sake of the community, as well as of what the welfare of the community has constituted; in a word, each has its own idea of what justice requires and of the im-

TABLE 9.4

PERCENTAGE OF VARIOUS "ETHNIC" PRECINCTS VOTING "YES" ON
SELECTED EXPENDITURES IN CHICAGO

Ethnic group and number of precincts	Co. hosp. (6/57)	Percent voting "yes" on:			
		Vet's bonus (11/58)	Urban renewal (4/62)	City hall (5/62)	School (4/59)
Low income renters	(%)	(%)	(%)	(%)	(%)
Negro (22)	84.9	80.2	88.6	82.3	97.8
Irish (6)	61.3	55.3	45.7	46.3	79.4
Polish (26)	60.1	54.6	57.1	53.8	81.8
Middle income home owners					
Negro (13)	66.8	54.9	69.6	49.8	88.9
Irish (6)	54.6	44.1	22.0	27.2	64.2
Polish (38)	47.4	40.0	14.6	15.2	58.3

Source: James Q. Wilson and Edward C. Banfield, "Public Regardingness as a Value Premise in Voting Behavior," *American Political Science Review*, 58 (December, 1964), 884.

portance of acting justly. According to this hypothesis, the voter is presumed to act rationally; the ends he seeks are not always verily self-interested ones, however. On the contrary, depending upon his income and ethnic status they are more or less public-regarded.[6]

Whether one accepts Banfield and Wilson's explanation or not,[7] their findings are important: (1) non-homeowners give greater support to proposals for public spending than homeowners; (2) among homeowners, wealthy families support public expenditures more than middle or low income families; (3) white Anglo-Saxon Protestants, Negroes, and Jews tend to support public expenditures more than Irish, Italian, Polish, or other eastern European ethnic voters. It is also interesting to note that the alliance between white, Anglo-Saxon Protestants and Negroes in support of public expenditures collapses in elections for public officials. Upper income, white, Anglo-Saxon Protestants vote overwhelmingly for Republican candidates for partisan offices and "good government" candidates in nonpartisan elections. Negroes, who are allied with white, Anglo-Saxon Protestants on expenditure referenda, vote strongly for Democratic candidates for partisan offices and against "good government" candidates in nonpartisan elections. In elections for public office, Negroes are more frequently aligned with low income, white, ethnic voters.

Managers and Councils

When council-manager government was first introduced as part of the municipal reform movement, managers were expressly forbidden to participate in community "politics." Early supporters of manager government believed in the separation of "politics" from "administration." "Politics," not only partisanship but policymaking as well, should be the exclusive domain of the elected city council. The classic statement of the separation of policy making from administration was delivered in 1927 by Leonard White:

> It ought to be possible in this country to separate politics from administration. Sound administration can develop and continue only if this separation can be achieved. For a century they have been confused, with evil results beyond measure. The managers have an unparalleled opportunity and a deep obligation to teach the American people by their perception and conduct that their job is to administer the affairs of the city with integrity and efficiency and loyalty to the council, without participating in or allowing their work to be affected by contending programs or partisans. Their duties with regard to the policy of the city are properly restricted to recommendations to the council and to supplying information to citizens upon request. They have a duty on their own initiative

[6] Wilson and Banfield, "Public Regardingness," p. 885.
[7] The explanation is disputed by Wolfinger and Field, *American Political Science Review*.

to keep the city informed on the administrative program and achieve-ments, they can hardly go beyond this to dabble in public advocacy of an unsettled policy.[8]

This belief in the separation of policy making from administration was in-tended to produce the "nonpolitical," efficient, and economical government, which middle class supporters of the reform movement valued so highly. Popular control of government was to be guaranteed by making the man-ager's tenure completely dependent upon the will of the elected council.

The idea that policy making could be separated from administration was slow to die. Managers themselves, in meetings and publications of the International City Managers Association, discussed their role in policy making for many years. The first code of ethics of the ICMA stated flatly that "no manager should take an active part in politics." [9] Managers agreed that they should stay out of partisan politics and election cam-paigns, but there was a great deal of debate about the role of managers in community policy making. Not until 1938 did the managers revise their code of ethics to recognize their role in policy leadership: ". . . [the city manager] encourages positive decisions on policy by the council instead of passive acceptance of his recommendations." [10]

By 1940, even political scientists who believed that policy making and administration *ought* to be separate, had come to the conclusion that in practice it was not. In one of the first comprehensive studies of city-man-ager government, Stone, Price, and Stone, noted that:

> It is generally impossible for a city manager to escape being a leader in matters of policy, for it is an essential part of his administrative job to make recommendations. The most important municipal policy is em-bodied in the budget, and the city manager, of course, must prepare and propose the budget. The city manager's recommendation on an important policy, even if he makes it in an executive session of the council, is usually a matter of common knowledge.[11]

While it is recognized that managers participate in policy making, their style of participation differs from that of elected political leaders. Generally, a city manager does not wish to *appear* to be a policy maker even when he is. He seeks to have others present his policy proposals to the commu-nity, and he avoids the brasher methods of policy promotion. Like any successful politician, he tries to avoid taking public stands on the more

[8] Leonard D. White, *The City Manager* (Chicago: University of Chicago Press, 1927), p. 301; also reprinted in Edward C. Banfield, *Urban Government: A Reader in Administration and Politics* (Glencoe: Free Press, 1961).

[9] See Harold A. Stone, Don K. Price, and Kathryn H. Stone, *City Manager Gov-ernment in the United States* (Chicago: Public Administration Service, 1940).

[10] See Charles R. Adrian "Leadership and Decision-Making in Manager Cities," *Public Administration Review*, 18 (Summer, 1958), 208–13.

[11] Stone, Price, and Stone, *City Manager Government*.

controversial issues facing the community. His dependence upon the council for his job prevents him from being too extreme in policy promotion. Managers can push their councils, but can seldom fight them with any success. Open disputes between the manager and his council are usually resolved by the dismissal of the manager. Managers who assume strong policy leadership roles have shorter tenures than those who do not.

In his study of council-manager politics in three Michigan communities, Charles Adrian observed that managers often assumed leadership of policy proposals that originated in city departments (for example, the police department on parking policies), advisory groups (for example, the planning commission's urban renewal plans), citizens' groups (for example, citizens seeking to prevent the breakdown of public transportation), or private enterprise (for example, downtown merchants interested in off-street parking). As Adrian explained:

> There appeared to be a psychological advantage to the manager if he could place himself in the position of defending a policy developed by these individuals or groups. He would take a strong stand, but would use protective coloration of saying, 'Professional planners tell me. . . .' He would, in other words, take a public position of *leadership* in policy matters, but preferred to attribute policy *innovation* to technical experts or citizens groups.[12]

Yet even though managers were providing leadership for their communities, they went to great pains to avoid the public appearance of being the tail that wags the dog—that is, the appearance of making policy for the city council rather than merely executing it.

Contrary to orthodox theory, Adrian found that councilmen did not serve as either general policy innovators or general policy leaders. Councilmen found it politically dangerous to be too closely associated with particular issues. Policy leadership subjected a councilman to greater public attention and scrutiny and the risk of defeat, if the issue turned out to be a controversial one. In other words, there was danger in leadership and relative safety in conformity and anonymity. When councilmen did take a stand on public issues, they were more likely to oppose a proposal than to support one. Most of the opposition was aimed at expanded public services or increased expenditures. Adrian describes a typical response of the council to a community problem, as follows:

> When the bus companies came to the councils from time to time asking for fare increases, each councilman would deplore the trend toward higher fares and poorer service, but since the only discernible alternative to refusing the rate increase was a discontinuance of service, almost all councilmen voted in favor of the request. In each of the cities, study committees of lay citizens were appointed to seek solutions to the bus

[12] Charles R. Adrian, *Public Administration Review,* p. 210.

problem. . . . In each case, the council gratefully, and with little discussion, accepted the proposed solutions.[13]

Adrian concludes that the role of the council was one of a largely passive body, granting or withholding its approval in the name of the community, when presented with proposals from a leadership outside of itself. The outside leadership consisted of a manager, city departments, the planning commission, citizens groups, or private enterprise.

Adrian concludes:

> It might be noted that the important policy and leadership role of the manager, of his administration, and of leaders of nonofficial groups differs from the patterns intended in the original theory of the council-manager plan. That theory assumed that able, respected leaders of the community would be willing to serve on councils and would take responsibility for policy decisions in government as they did in their businesses. While the typical councilman in the three city study gave the impression of being a sufficiently competent person, it seemed clear enough that he was not willing to assume a leadership role under circumstances where he might thereby be planted in controversy. The politician in the council manager's city, though he may be an amateur, thus follows the traditional practice of American politicians and seeks to avoid taking sides in closely matched battles.[14]

Undoubtedly, managers are much more happy and secure in their jobs in communities where there is little or no conflict and few controversial issues—usually small communities with homogeneous, middle class populations. This is why manager government itself is found more frequently in such communities, than in larger communities with deeper socio-economic cleavages. The tenure of managers, and indeed the tenure of the council-manager system itself, is more secure in communities devoted to economic growth and communities concerned with providing a high level of public services. In a city concerned with "managing" conflicting political interests, there is often too much instability for a manager to survive for long. In a strictly "caretaker" community, a trained professional manager may be an unnecessary luxury. Occasionally, caretaker communities will appoint a local resident or "amateur," perhaps a former city clerk or city engineer, to the position of city manager. (The ICMA has never adopted any certification practices or official standards for the training and education of a city manager.)

The typical councilman is a local businessman, well respected in his community, and active in civic organizations. He is more likely to be a small businessman with many contacts among his constituents—retail merchants, real estate dealers, insurance agents, and so on; seldom\ do execu-

[13] Charles R. Adrian, *op. cit.*, p. 212.
[14] Charles R. Adrian, *op. cit.*, p. 212.

tives of large corporations concern themselves with local affairs, although they may encourage lower management personnel to do so. In other words, councilmen are recruited from lower middle class groups in a ·community and not from the community's leading men in industry or finance. Councilmen serve because of the prestige it gives them or because of the free advertising and public contacts for their businesses. With the exception of a few very large cities, the pay of councilmen is very nominal. The councilman's job is a part time one; it is a "community service," which he undertakes in addition to his occupation or business. The low rate of pay is a deliberate attempt to discourage candidates who are interested in the salary alone. This is supposed to get "better men" into the office; but of course, the effect is to restrict opportunities for working men and lower income groups, who cannot afford to spend their time in jobs without pay.

City councils in larger cities may be quite different from councils in smaller cities. First of all, they are likely to have more members; moreover, members are more likely to be elected by wards rather than at-large. Since the pay is higher and the opportunity for political advancement is greater in a large city council, one is more likely to find lawyers and professional politicians on these councils than on the councils of smaller cities. Since there is more conflict in larger communities, there is more likelihood of open disputes and divided votes at council meetings. In contrast, council meetings in smaller communities are likely to be very dull affairs, with most decisions being made unanimously. Any disagreement or factionalism is not likely to be expressed openly at council meetings, but resolved prior to an official meeting, through consultation and discussion.

Increasingly, city managers are coming to their profession after graduate training in public administration at the university level. An increasing number of cities are taking university graduates as interns and administrative assistants to city managers, and after a few years they become city managers. About three-quarters of all city manager appointments are made from outside of the city, and only about one-quarter are local residents, which indicates the professionalization of city management. The turnover rate among the nation's city managers is about 7.5 per cent per year. In recent years the average tenure of managers who resigned or were removed from office during the year has been about 5 years.[15]

Mayors

Today, more than ever before, the nation's cities need forceful, imaginative leadership. The nation's major domestic problems—race relations, poverty, slum housing, violence, transportation, poor schools, urban blight—are concentrated in cities. Mayors are in the "hot seat" of American politics;

[15] *Municipal Yearbook,* 1963, p. 519.

they must deal directly with these pressing issues. No other elected official in the American federal system must deal face-to-face, eyeball-to-eyeball with these problems, in quite the same fashion as mayors. Next to the Presidency, the office of mayor in a big city may be the most challenging job in American politics.

The challenges facing big city mayors are enormous; however, their powers to deal with these challenges are restricted on every side. Executive power in major cities is often fragmented among a variety of elected officials—city treasurer, city clerk, city comptroller, the district attorney, and so on. The mayor may also be required to share power over municipal affairs with county officials. Many city agencies and functions are outside of the mayor's formal authority: independent boards and commissions often govern important city departments—for example, the board of education, board of health, zoning appeals board, planning commission, civil service board, library board, park commission, sewage and water board, and so on. Even if the mayor is permitted to appoint the members of the boards and commissions, they are often appointed for a fixed term, and the mayor cannot remove them. The mayor's power over the affairs of the city may also be affected by the many public authorities and special district governments operating within the city, including the public housing authority, urban renewal authority, community action agency (poverty program), sewage and water authority, a mass transit authority, port authority, and so on. Traditionally school districts have been outside the authority of the mayor or city government. The mayor's powers over city finances may even be restricted—he may share budget making powers with a board of estimate, and powers over expenditures with an elected comptroller or treasurer. Civil service regulations and independent civil service boards can greatly hamper the mayor's control over his own bureaucrats.

Of course the method of selecting the mayor also influences his powers

TABLE 9.5

TERM OF OFFICE OF MAYORS IN CITIES OVER 5,000

| Form of government | Percent of reporting cities | | | |
	One year	Two years	Three years	Four years
Mayor-council	2.9	54.2	1.0	41.7
Commission	3.9	19.3	6.4	67.0
Council-manager	21.3	54.6	2.3	24.0
All cities	10.3	51.4	2.0	35.9[1]

[1]An additional 3 per cent of reporting cities have five or six year terms for mayors.
Source: *Municipal Year Book*, 1966, p. 92

TABLE 9.6

METHOD OF SELECTION AND VOTING POWERS OF MAYORS IN CITIES OVER 5,000

Form of Government	Percent of reporting cities			Percent of directly elected mayor voting		
	Directly elected	Selected by council	Councilman with highest vote	On all issues	In case of tie	No voting power
Mayor-council	95.3	4.1	0.6	12.9	65.8	21.3
Commission	76.6	22.6	0.8	94.2	4.1	1.7
Council-manager	51.0	48.0	1.0	47.8	47.6	4.6
All cities	76.0	23.2	0.8	28.7	56.0	15.3

Source: *Municipal Year Book*, 1966, p. 91.

over city affairs. Nearly a quarter of the nation's mayors are not directly elected by the people of their cities. These mayors are selected by their city councils or commissions, and generally have little more power than other councilmen or commissioners. Their job is generally ceremonial: they crown beauty queens, dedicate parks, lay corner stones, and lead parades. Mayors may be elected for anything from one to six years, but the two year term is most common in American cities.

The mayor's legislative powers also vary widely. Of course in all cities he has the right to submit messages to the council and to recommend policy. These recommendations will carry whatever prestige the mayor possesses in the community. In cities where the mayor is chosen by the council, he almost always has voting power equal to other council members, and more than one-quarter of the mayors who are elected directly have the power to cast a vote on all issues coming before the council. Most mayors preside over meetings of the city council, and this gives them an opportunity to cast votes in case of a tie. Less than one-fifth of the nation's mayors have no voting powers at all on city councils. The veto power over municipal ordinances is another source of legislative strength for the mayor. Almost one-half of the directly elected mayors, however, have no veto power, one-quarter may veto only selected items (usually appropriations). Only one-quarter of the nation's mayors have full veto powers over their councils. Mayors in mayor-council governments are more likely to have veto powers than mayors in commission or council-manager cities (see Table 9.7).

The formal distinction between "strong mayors" and "weak mayors" is made on the basis of their powers of administration. The weak mayor has very limited appointing powers and even more limited removing powers. He has little control over separately elected boards and commissions or separately elected offices, such as clerk, treasurer, tax assessor, comptroller, and attorney. The council rather than the mayor often appoints the key administrative officers. No single individual has the complete responsibility for law enforcement or coordinating city administration.

One summary of the mayor's difficulties with "good government," civil service, fragmented authority, state interference, and suburban opposition was presented in *The Exploding Metropolis:*

> One of the biggest threats to his leadership, indeed, is too much 'good government.' The big problem at the city hall is no longer honesty, or even simple efficiency. The fight for these virtues is a continuous one, of course, and Lucifer is always lurking in the hall, but most big city governments have become reasonably honest and efficient. Today the big problem is not good housekeeping: it is whether the mayor can provide the aggressive leadership and the positive programs without which no big city has a prayer. . . .
>
> The mayor is hemmed in. As he strives to exercise policy leadership, his power is challenged on all sides. In his own house the staff experts and the civil service bureaucrats threaten to nibble him to death in their efforts to increase their own authority. Then there are the public 'authorities.' Some are single purpose authorities—like the city housing authorities, and the sewer districts; some, like the Port of New York Authority, handle a whole range of functions. They are eminently useful institutions, but however efficient they may be, they are virtually laws unto themselves and they have severely limited the mayor's ability to rule in his own house and, more important, his ability to plan for long range development.
>
> The power struggle also goes on between the mayor and state legislature, which has a controlling voice in the city's fiscal affairs, but whose membership is apportioned in favor of the rural areas. It is the rare mayor who need not make frequent trips to the state capitol for additional funds, and the legislature is usually unsympathetic. . . .
>
> There is the continuing struggle between the mayor and the suburbs, whose people, the big city firmly believes, are welching on their obligations to the city. The mayor must win the cooperation of his suburban

TABLE 9.7

VETO POWERS OF MAYORS IN CITIES OVER 5,000

Form of government	Percent of reporting cities where mayor may		
	Veto all measures	Veto selected items	No veto
Mayor-council	33.5	32.9	33.6
Commission	4.4	3.8	91.8
Council-manager	11.4	18.6	70.4
All cities	25.2	26.6	48.2

Source: *Municipal Year Book,* 1963, p. 161.

counterparts if he is to do anything at all about the city's most pressing problems—e.g., the traffic mess—and the going is grim.[16]

Only occasionally will mayors create issues themselves or initiate pet projects. Several mayors have taken the initiative on urban renewal—rebuilding a city is a very dramatic way of illustrating one's achievements in office. Typically new programs or new issues are first raised by large public or private organizations in the community.[17] The planning commission, for example, may propose that the city embark upon a program for mass transit. City departments may notify the mayor that it is time to build a new sewage disposal plant, or that new policemen must be hired, or that water rates must be increased. Citizens groups, like the Chamber of Commerce, may propose that the city build a new civic auditorium. Downtown merchants may suggest that the city build new parking facilities. Newspapers play a very important role in initiating new programs and in creating public issues. Editors believe, rightly or wrongly, that public crusades help to sell newspapers, and they bring many issues to the attention of mayors and decision-makers as well as their readers.

The role of mayors is to watch the maneuvers of the prime-moving organizations with critical attention. As Banfield and Wilson explain:

> They (mayors) know well enough what is going on behind the scenes and they know approximately how many—if any—votes the organizations may be able to swing. Usually they wait as long as possible before making a decision. They know that as long as they do nothing they are probably safe, and anyway, they want to allow time for public opinion to form. When a magazine writer suggested to Mayor Richard Daley of Chicago that the mayor had never in his whole life committed himself to anything whatsoever until he absolutely had to, the mayor laughed. 'That's a pretty good way to be, don't you think? Pretty good way to run any business.' [18]

What happens when a mayor is unable to overcome the fragmentation of authority in a city? What happens when there is no party organization that can "get things done at city hall," and there is no strong charismatic leader who possesses the charm or salesmanship to "put things across" to the community? Banfield and Wilson provide an excellent summary as to how this decentralization of authority is overcome:

1. To a large extent it is *not* overcome; many things are not done because it is impossible to secure the collaboration of all those whose collaboration is needed.

[16] Seymour Freedgood, "New Strength in City Hall," *The Exploding Metropolis* (New York: Doubleday & Co., 1958), pp. 66–67.
[17] See Banfield and Wilson, *City Politics,* chap. 2.
[18] *Ibid.,* p. 30.

2. When overcome at all, it is overcome on an ad hoc basis; the mayor, for example, must consider anew with each issue how to get the eight votes he needs in council.

3. Widespread indifference and apathy among the voters mitigates the effect of decentralization of authority to them.

4. The mass communications media are fairly effective in overcoming by salesmanship such decentralization of authority to the voters as remains; causes with strong newspaper support and with big budgets for TV advertising are usually approved at the polls.

5. The devices of salesmanship are extensively used. It was in Los Angeles that the mayor scolded Khrushchev to his face in public while Khrushchev was the city's guest (a stunt like this would not have been resorted to by Mayor Daley of Chicago, whose machine makes salesmanship unnecessary).

6. Measures are frequently compromised so as to 'give something to everybody' in order to get them accepted.[19]

In summary, most mayors do not have the formal authority sufficient to deal with the many challenges facing city government. The successful mayor must rely chiefly upon his own personal qualities of leadership: his powers to persuade, to organize, to promote, to sell, to publicize, to compromise, to bargain, and to "get things done." The mayor's role is not usually to initiate proposals for new programs or to create public issues. Nor is his primary concern the administration of existing programs, although he must always seek to avoid scandal and gross mismanagement, which would give his administration a bad public "image." He must rely upon other public agencies, planners, citizens groups, and private enterprise to propose new programs, and he can usually rely upon his department heads and other key subordinates to supervise the day-to-day administration of city government. The mayor is primarily a promoter of public policy: his role is to promote, publicize, organize, and finance the projects that others suggest.

Planners

Professional planners are playing an increasingly important role in community decision making. The modern city planning movement was given its impetus in the 1920's, when Secretary of Commerce Herbert Hoover approved a Standard City Planning Enabling Act, by Edward Bassett, Alfred Bettman, and several other founders of the planning movement. Within a few years this act had been adopted by most of the states, and cities throughout the nation began establishing official planning commissions. By 1963, 90 per cent of the cities with populations of 10,000 or more reported that they had official planning agencies, although only about

[19] *Ibid.,* p. 111.

one-third of these cities employed a full time professional planner. Nearly all cities with populations over 100,000 employ full time professional planners.[20]

Early city planners were concerned primarily with the physical development of the city and the use of land.[21] They concentrated on writing zoning laws, preparing "subdivision regulations" governing the division of large plots of land into smaller ones, laying out public streets, and choosing the location of parks, public building sites, public utilities, and other public facilities.

Early city planning dealt almost exclusively with topics that could be shown on a map. Planners were trained primarily as engineers or landscape architects. Planners were expected to prepare a "master plan," or overall blueprint, for the physical development of the community. The master plan is a set of maps, information, and policy statements intended to serve as guides for both public and private decision makers. The master plan shows recommendations for:

> The most desirable use of land within the municipality for residential, recreational, commercial, industrial, and other purposes; for the most desirable density of population in several parts of the municipality; for a system of thoroughfares, parks, bridges, streets, and other public ways; for airports, parks, playgrounds, and other public grounds; for general location, relocation, and extent of public utilities and terminals, whether publicly or privately owned, for water, sewage, light, power, transit, and other purposes; and for the extent and location of public housing projects.[22]

In recent years, the definition of planning has been broadened to include more than physical and land use planning. Today, planners stress the interrelatedness of urban life and argue that planning is a continuing activity, which attempts to anticipate human needs and goals, to prepare for them and guide them into desirable patterns, and to influence and shape public policy to serve the community's needs and goals most effectively.[23] In addition to land use and physical development considerations, planners now direct their attention to population projections, economic conditions, social patterns, life styles, cultural developments, education, transportation, and beautification. The phrase "comprehensive planning" has largely replaced the earlier term "master plan," in recognition of the new emphasis on planning as a continuing activity. Obviously this extended definition of

---

[20] *Municipal Yearbook*, 1963, p. 324.

[21] For an introduction to city planning, see Donald H. Webster, *Urban Planning and Municipal Public Policy* (New York: Harper & Row, Publishers, 1955).

[22] General Statutes of Connecticut (1949 Revision), Title 8, Chapter 45; cited by John C. Bollens and Henry J. Schmandt, *The Metropolis* (New York: Harper & Row, Publishers, 1965), p. 279.

[23] See Bollens and Schmandt, *The Metropolis*, chap. 10.

planning plunges the planner deep into the political life of the community.

What formal powers do planners have to influence community policy? The master plan itself is not legally binding on anyone. Only insofar as the mayor and council see fit to adopt and incorporate into law recommendations made in the plan do they have any legal effect. Planners are legally powerless to effectuate their plan themselves—they must rely on its appeal to policy makers. Mayors and councils can simply file the master plan away and forget it. However, cities which choose to implement comprehensive planning and guide physical development by law have a variety of legal tools available to them: zoning ordinances, subdivision regulations, an official map, building and construction codes, locational decisions on public facilities and buildings, and a capital improvement program. Planning agencies often have an important role in all of these activities, even though the principal responsibility for these tools of implementation rests with the mayor and council.

Planning commissions usually prepare the zoning ordinance and map for the approval of the council. The zoning ordinance divides the community into districts for the purpose of regulating the use and development of land and buildings. Zoning originated as an attempt to separate residential areas from commercial and industrial activity, thereby protecting residential property values. The zoning ordinance divides the community into residential, commercial, and industrial zones, and perhaps subdivisions within each zone, such as "light industrial" and "heavy industrial," or "single family residential" and "multi-family residential." Owners of land in each zone must use their land in conformity with the zoning ordinance; however, exceptions are made for persons who have used the land in a certain way before the adoption of the zoning ordinance. An ordinance cannot prevent a person from using the land as he has done in the past; thus zoning laws can only influence land use if they are passed prior to the development of a community. Many rapidly expanding suburban communities pass zoning ordinances too late—after commercial and industrial establishments are strung out along highways, ideal industrial land is covered with houses, good park and recreational land has been sold for other purposes, and so on. Zoning ordinances also contain regulations on the size and height of buildings, set-back lines, and the like. Once adopted, the zoning ordinance is enforced by the building commissioner or another public official, not the planning agency.

Since the planning commission prepares the zoning ordinance as well as the master plan, the ordinance is expected to conform with the plan. In many communities, the role of the planning commission is strengthened by the requirement that a city council must submit all proposed changes in the zoning ordinance to the planning commission for their recommendation before any council action. The council may ignore the recommendations of the planning commission and rezone areas as they see fit; nevertheless, the requirement that the planning commission review requests for zoning changes doubtlessly contributes to their influence in community development.

Another means of implementing the master plan is subdivision regulations, which govern the way in which land is divided into smaller lots and made ready for improvements. Subdivision regulations, together with the zoning ordinance, may specify the minimum size of lots, the standards to be followed by real estate developers in laying out new streets, and the improvements developers must provide, such as sewers, water mains, and sidewalks. Often planning commissions are given direct responsibility for the enforcement of subdivision regulations. Builders and developers must submit their proposed "plans" for subdividing land and for improvements to the planning commission for approval before deeds can be recorded.

The planning commission also prepares the official map of the city for enactment by the council. The official map shows proposed, as well as existing, streets, water mains, public utilities, and the like. Presumably no one is permitted to build any structures on land that appears as a street or other public facility on the official map. Many cities require the council to submit to the planning commission for their recommendation any proposed action that affects the plan of streets or the subdivision plan and any proposed acquisition or sale of city real estate. Here again the recommendation of the planning commission may be ignored by the council, but at least the planners must be listened to.

Finally, comprehensive planning can be implemented through a planned capital improvement program. This program is simply the planned schedule of public projects by the city—new public buildings, parks, streets, and so on. Many larger cities instruct their planning commissions to prepare a long range capital improvement program for a five or ten year period. Of course, the council may choose to ignore the planning commission's long range capital improvement program in their decisions about capital expenditures, but at least the planning commission will have expressed its opinions about major capital investments.

The federal government has strengthened the position of planning commissions by requiring planning as a prerequisite to receiving federal money for public housing, urban renewal, airports, sewage systems, highways, recreation and open space facilities, and even hospitals. The Housing Act of 1949 required cities to undertake extensive planning in housing and urban renewal projects and the federal government agreed to pay much of the cost of this planning. The Housing Act of 1954 went even further and required cities to adopt a "workable program" and a "comprehensive plan" as a prerequisite to federal housing and urban renewal grants. A "workable program" was defined to include adequate zoning and subdivision control ordinances, building and construction codes, and other land use policies, which would help prevent the spread of urban blight to new areas and rehabilitate and conserve those areas that could still be restored. A requirement for "comprehensive planning" included the preparation of a long range plan and a capital improvement program. At the same time, federal grants were offered to communities for participation in citywide or regional planning programs. Presumably the federal government's interest in community planning stems from its desire to see that its grant money is not wasted. Local planning makes it easier for federal agencies to evaluate the impact of their own grants on total community development. These federal requirements for planning greatly strengthened the influence of planners at the local level: without planning, a community would be deprived of federal money in a wide variety of grant-in-aid programs, and much of the cost of planning is paid for by federal planning grants anyhow. The result is that very few communities today are without planning agencies.

The formal role of planners is advisory, but they can have a substantial influence on community policy. In smaller cities, planners may be preoccupied with the day-to-day administration of the zoning and subdivision control ordinances. They may have insufficient time or staff resources to engage in genuine long range comprehensive planning. In larger cities, the planning staff may be the only agency that has a really comprehensive view of community development. Although they may not have the power to "decide" about public policy, they can "initiate" policy discussion through their plans, proposals, and recommendations. The planners can project the image of the city of the future and thereby establish the agenda of community decision making. Their plans can initiate public discussion over the goals and values to be implemented in the community. The master plan can be a tool for mobilizing public interest in community development.

There are, of course, serious limitations on the influence of planners. First of all, most of the important decisions in community development are made by private enterprise rather than by government. Real estate interests, developers, builders, and property owners make most of the key decisions shaping the development of the community. The most important influence on their decisions is not the actions of government, but the economics of the marketplace. There is very little evidence that *any* governmental tools—planning, zoning, subdivision control, or capital programming, and so on—can overcome market forces. Property owners will find a way to make the most profitable use of their land, the ideals of the planners notwithstanding. Secondly, the planners can only advise policy makers, they are just one voice among many attempting to influence public decisions about land use and physical development. As Norton Long explains:

> This work of art, the master plan, once adopted becomes holy writ to be defended by an amateur lay board of hopefully high civic prestige, spurred on and kept to the mark by a professional staff of planners. The battle is fought along lines of piecemeal engagements as the facts of power, the pressure of economics, and the haste of the populous force a patchwork desecration of the architect's pretty rendering of green and white lines and dots. Like the WCTU, the proponents of planning find it is one thing to achieve the noble experiment in law, another in the drinking habits of sinful men. In both cases bootlegging represents the recrudescence of rugged individualism. People want their prohibition and their liquor, too. The same is true of planning.[24]

Norton Long goes on to point out that historically planning was part of the municipal reform movement. Planners generally showed the anti-political bias of the reform movement and were deeply suspicious and distrustful of political leaders. Their maps and charts were drawn with little regard to political realities; "If one were to insist that it was as much the planner's business to face the facts of political feasibility as to face the facts of economics or topography, he would be regarded as an agent of the devil if not the tempter himself." [25] Yet today many planners are coming to realize that plans are policies and policies spell politics. There is no doubt that planning will reflect politics; the only question is whose politics it will reflect. What values and whose values will become part of the comprehensive plan?

Recognition of the political nature of planning has brought about a gradual shift in the organization of city planning agencies. Historically, planning agencies were semi-independent commissions, whose members were appointed from outside of the government for long terms. Ordinarily the mayor could not remove the commissioners. Sometimes their recommendations regarding changes in the zoning and subdivision ordinances or the capital budget could not be overridden by council, except by a two-thirds or three-quarters vote. This semi-independent status for planning commissions reflected the reform movement's desire to remove planning from "politics."

Recently, the trend has been to organize planning agencies as part of the city government, directly responsible to the mayor or council. Organizing planners as staff to the mayor and council is expected to make them more sensitive to community values as they are expressed in the political process. Norton Long has commented: "This change will both compel political realism and enrich the end systems of the planners by forcing them

---

[24] Norton Long, "Planning and Politics in Urban Development," *Journal of The American Institute of Planners,* 25 (November, 1959), 167.
[25] *Ibid.,* p. 167.

to understand the politician's prospectives and incentives, and it will jeopardize the planner's capacity to take the long and detached view. Realism will not be an unmixed blessing, though it is essential to get a sufficient range of values into the planner's thinking." [26] Professor Long also believes that more realistic, political planning will be taken more seriously than the elegant but utopian planning of past years.

There is some evidence to suggest that the best plans often are jeopardized when they reach the political arena. In a study of capital programming in Philadelphia, Professors Brown and Gilbert compared the capital expenditures *proposed* in the city's planning commission's capital program

FIGURE 9.2

CAPITAL FUNDS ACTUALLY SPENT BY THE CITY COUNCIL COMPARED TO FUNDS
SCHEDULED IN THE PREVIOUS YEAR BY THE PLANNING COMMISSION IN
PHILADELPHIA

(Percentage Deviations: Denominator is the Previous Year, Numerator the Actual Budget Adopted)

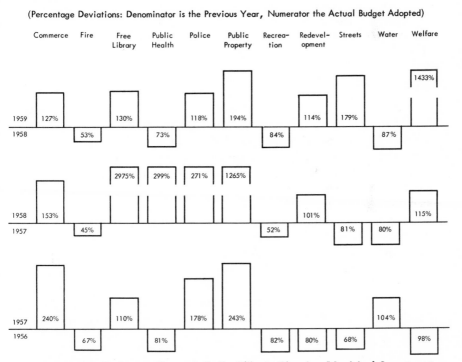

SOURCE: W. H. Brown, Jr., and C. E. Gilbert, *Planning Municipal Investment* (Philadelphia: University of Pennsylvania Press, 1961), p. 177. Reproduced by permission.

[26] *Ibid.*, p. 169.

with the *actual* capital expenditures authorized by the city council.[27] The results are shown in Figure 9.2. The deviations between the planning commission's capital program and the council's capital budget range up to 2975 per cent! The authors point out that some of this deviation resulted from unexpected availability of land and other economic factors. However, they acknowledge that political considerations had a very dramatic effect upon the capital budget. These vast differences between the planners' capital program and the city's actual capital budget suggest the instability of planning.

Interest Groups

Interest group activity may be more influential in community politics than in state or national political affairs. Since the arena of local politics is smaller, the activities of organized interest groups may be more obvious at the local level. As one local councilman was once quoted:

> Pressure groups are probably more important in local government than they are nationally or in the state, because they are right here. You see them and they see you, and what you do affects them. It's not like in Washington, where half the time a businessman doesn't really know what the result will be for him.[28]

A study of interest group activity in 23 city councils in the San Francisco Bay area discovered that only 16 per cent of the 115 councilmen interviewed were unable to name any groups or organizations as "influential" in their city.[29] Twenty-three per cent named one organization as "influential" and 61 per cent named two or more groups as influential in their community. Fourteen per cent were able to name as many as five influential groups. The median number of groups seen as influential by these councilmen was 2.4. The median number of active groups perceived by state legislators in the four state legislative system study were as follows: California —1.15; New Jersey—1.28; Ohio—.90; Tennessee—.89.[30] In other words, local councilmen in the San Francisco Bay area perceived more group activity at the local level than legislators in four states perceived at the state level!

At the local level, interest groups frequently assume the form of "civic associations." Few communities are too small to have at least one or two

---

[27] W. H. Brown, Jr. and C. E. Gilbert, *Planning Municipal Investment* (Philadelphia: University of Pennsylvania Press, 1961).

[28] Betty Zisk, Heinz Eulau, and Kenneth Prewitt, "City Councilmen and the Group Struggle," *Journal of Politics,* Vol. 27 (August, 1965), p. 633.

[29] *Ibid.,* pp. 618–46.

[30] John C. Wahlke, et. al., *The Legislative System* (New York: John Wiley & Sons, Inc., 1962), pp. 311–42.

associations devoted to civic well-being, and larger cities may have hundreds of these organizations. In the San Francisco Bay area study of local councilmen, 94 per cent of the councilmen who perceived group activity at the local level named civic associations (service clubs, citizens commissions, improvement associations) as the most influential groups or organizations, which were active and appeared before the council.[31] Only 28 per cent of these councilmen named economic groups (merchants, realtors, unions, and so on) and 21 per cent named taxpayer associations and reform groups. Actually these results do not mean that economic interests or taxpayer associations are less active than civic associations, but probably that civic associations are the predominant style of organized interest group activity at the local level, and that businessmen, reform groups, taxpayer associations, merchants, service clubs, developers, and so on, all organize themselves into civic associations for action at the local level. Civic associations generally make their appeals in terms of "the welfare of the community," "the public interest," "civic responsibility," "making Janesville a better place to live." In other words, civic associations claim to be community-serving rather than self-serving. Many local civic associations can be classified as "good government" groups who seek to implement the program of the municipal reform movement—council-manager government, civil service, home rule, nonpartisan elections, and efficiency and economy in government. (The reform movement is described in greater detail in Chapter 10.) Good government civic associations are not seeking specific material inducements for their members; they are really seeking to promote a middle class ethic of government. Members belong to these groups as a hobby, because of the sense of prestige and civic participation they derive from membership. Occasionally, of course, participation in civic associations can be a steppingstone to local office. The League of Women Voters is occasionally classified as a good government group, although its principal interest is participation per se, rather than any particular program of civic action. The League is nonpartisan, and its traditional activity is to prepare a set of questions on current issues, which it submits to candidates whose responses are then circulated throughout the community. When the League does occasionally endorse certain policies, their aims are usually similar to those of reform groups.

Another form of civic association is a neighborhood improvement association, generally composed of businessmen or residents who are interested in safeguarding the value of their property. They may be interested in zoning laws because they do not want unsightly trailer parks located nearby; they may insist on stop signs to make the streets safer for their children; or they want potholes repaired immediately; or they want an extra policeman to patrol their neighborhood. They are also concerned with keeping tax

[31] Betty Zisk, et. al., *Journal of Politics,* p. 632.

rates low and with keeping a close watch on property assessments. Often, improvement associations lead the fight to keep "undesirables" out of the neighborhood, whose presence, they fear, will reduce property value. This type of endeavor is usually directed against Negroes, but depending on the "purity" of the neighborhood may also be directed at other ethnic groups or simply "the kinds of people who build cheaper homes on smaller lots." Since there is little empirical evidence that property values are really affected by the presence of Negroes or other ethnic group members, it is probably safe to say that the real objectives of neighborhood improvement associations in these sorts of campaigns is to maintain the social and economic homogeneity of the neighborhood.

Organized taxpayer groups generally stand for lower taxes and fewer governmental activities and services. Their most enthusiastic support comes from the community's larger taxpayers, generally the businessmen with large investments in commercial or industrial property in the community.

Business interests may be the most influential of all group interests in community politics. (See Chapter 11 for a detailed discussion of the role of businessmen and economic interests.) Many businessmen or "economic notables" occupy an important role in the structure of community decision-making or "the power structure." Business interests are also represented in local politics by organized groups: the Chamber of Commerce and the Junior Chamber of Commerce, or "Jaycees," are found in nearly every community, representing the general views of men in business. The program of the Chamber of Commerce is likely to be more general in nature than interests of particular sectors of the business community—banks, utilities, contractors, real estate developers, downtown merchants, or bar and club owners. The Chamber or the Jaycees can be expected to support lower taxes and more economy and efficiency in government operations. They are also active "promoters" of community growth and business activity. They can be expected to back civic improvements, so long as it does not raise the tax rate too much. "Service to the community" creates a "favorable image": which the Chamber and businessmen are anxious to cultivate. As the Vice President for Civic Affairs and Real Estate of a large department store once explained to Professors Banfield and Wilson:

> Obviously a business of the stature I hope ours has should present a good face to the public . . . should be for constant improvement to the public. All through the years this business has tried to achieve the feeling among the public that we are just a nice, fine, wonderful organization, and whatever it takes to achieve that, we are interested in. What it takes is to be just a plain, honest, good citizen—and fostering the kinds of things that are good for *everyone*.[32]

[32] Banfield and Wilson, *City Politics,* p. 268.

Generally, the active members of the Chamber of Commerce or the Jaycees are younger businessmen in the community who are still on their way "up" in business. Owners of larger businesses, banks, utilities—the "big men" in the community—are more likely to function informally in the community's power structure than to take an overt role in organized interest group activity. Because Chamber and Jaycee leaders are likely to come from a wide variety of business concerns, from banks to insurance companies to real estate agencies, it is easier for them to agree on a program of "boosterism" and a variety of civic happenings, than it is for them to pursue specific policy objectives that might divide the business community.

The so-called "service clubs"—the Lions, Kiwanis, Rotarians, and others—are basically for businessmen. Their interests are likely be more social than political, but their service projects often involve them in political activity and their meetings provide an excellent opportunity for speech making by political candidates.

The businesses most active in community affairs are those most directly affected by policies of local government, such as department stores, banks, utilities, contractors, real estate operators, bar and club owners, and television and newspaper interests.

Banks often own, or hold the mortgages on, downtown business property. They have an interest in maintaining business, commercial, and industrial property values. Banks are also interested in the growth and prosperity of the city as a whole, particularly large business enterprises who are their primary customers. Bankers are influential because they decide who is able to borrow money in a community and under what conditions. Banks are directly involved in local governments in financing municipal bond issues for public works, school buildings, and so on, and in pledging financial backing for urban renewal projects. Banks are also influential in land development, for they must provide the financial backing for real estate developers, contractors, businesses, and home buyers; hence they are interested in business regulation, taxation, zoning, and housing.

Public utility companies may be primarily concerned with *state* agencies that determine rates and services, but they are also active in community politics. They must work closely with streets and public works departments. They generally favor policies which would increase the city's population and income. They are generally advocates of city planning and land use control because they benefit from steady and predictable urban growth. They are particularly interested in community policies to attract large industries that would be heavy users of electricity, gas, water, and other utility services. Finally, utilities must guard against proposals to place utilities under public ownership.

Contractors are vitally interested in city government because the city has the power of inspection over all kinds of construction. Local governments enforce building, plumbing, electric, and other codes, which are of great interest to contractors. Some contractors, particularly road-grading and surfacing companies, depend on public contracts and they are vitally concerned with both city policy and the personnel who administer this policy. While municipal contracts are generally required by law to be given to the "low bidder" among "responsible" contractors, definitions about what is or is not a "low bid," and who is or who is not a "responsible" contractor make it important for contractors to maintain close and friendly relationships with municipal officials.

Real estate developers are particularly interested in planning, zoning, and subdivision control regulations and urban renewal programs. (Urban renewal programs are discussed at length in Chapter 16.) The success of urban renewal depends upon participation of private developers and re-developers. When land is cleared, that portion of it which is not used for public housing or civic improvements is placed on the open market. At this point the ideas of city planners about beautiful, clean, low cost hous-ing, scenic open spaces, and artistic and cultural amenities must face the economic realities of the marketplace. The land must be sold for as high a price as possible, in order to reduce the city's local dollar contribution to the project. It must be sold quickly in order to get the land back on the city's tax rolls. Successful renewal projects generally secure the support of the city's developers before they are even begun. This means that big city mayors, whether they be Democrats or Republicans, must be on speak-ing terms with developers and real estate interests. Private developers gen-erally show greater enthusiasm for renewal projects that result in high rent apartments, office buildings, stores, or new industrial plants. They are usually cool to low or moderate priced housing. A mayor must have a great deal of charm, political skill, and economic sense to develop renewal projects that will appeal to his constituents, meet federal standards, and be economically feasible.

Support for urban renewal can be expected from mayors who seek to dramatize their contribution to the city's development, downtown merchants who wish to preserve their investments, and businessmen and developers who want to acquire downtown land at good prices. Opposition to re-newal often comes from slum dwellers themselves, who are pushed from their homes and are "relocated" by renewal projects.[33] Long waiting lists for public housing mean that only a small percentage of relocated residents will find room in public housing projects; most will be forced to pay higher rents elsewhere in the city. Landlords who control slum property may lose

---

[33] For a critical view of urban renewal, see Martin Anderson, *The Federal Bull-dozer* (Cambridge: Harvard University Press, 1964); and William G. Grigsby, "Housing and Urban Renewal: Elusive Goals," *Annals of the American Academy of Political and Social Science,* 352 (March, 1964), 107–18.

a lucrative source of income through urban renewal. And urban renewal has been called "Negro removal" by Negro leaders, who charge that urban renewal is being used to displace Negroes from low cost housing in central city areas in favor of high income apartment developments, which house mostly white, middle class residents.[34]

Newspapers are an important force in community politics.[35] The influence of the press would be relatively minor if its opinions were limited to its editorial pages. The influence of the press arises from its power to decide what is "news," thereby focusing public attention on the events and issues that are of interest to the press. Newspapermen must first decide what proportion of space in the paper will be devoted to local news in contrast to state, national, and international news. A big city paper may give local news about the same amount of space that it gives to national or foreign news. Suburban or small town papers, which operate within the circulation area of a large metropolitan daily, may give a greater proportion of the news space to local events than to national and international affairs. Crime and corruption in government are favorite targets for the press. Editors believe that civic crusades, and the exposure of crime and corruption, help sell newspapers. Moreover, many editors and newspapermen believe they have a civic responsibility to use the power of the press to protect the public. In the absence of crime or corruption, newspapers may turn to crusades on behalf of civic improvements—a city auditorium, a cultural center, and the like.

The politics of newspapers can be understood in part by some insight into the economics of the newspaper business. While it is true that, on occasion, some newspapers make financial sacrifices in order to defend the public interest as they see it, in the long run, newspapers are businesses and they must consider profit and loss statements like any other business. Only occasionally can a wealthy newspaper owner ignore business considerations and run his paper at a loss. Newspapers get two-thirds of their revenue from advertising. The daily circulation of newspapers is at an all time high, but in recent years the newspapers' percentage of all advertising dollars has declined in the face of stiff competition from television. At the same time the cost of newsprint and labor has risen steadily. Many big city daily newspapers have either merged or gone out of business in recent years because of a lack of sufficient advertising revenue to offset increasing costs; it was not a lack of readers that brought about their collapse. Moreover, it is important to know that downtown department stores provide the largest source of advertising revenue. Big city newspapers have been hurt by the

34 For a close case study of urban renewal in Chicago, see Peter Rossi and Robert A. Dentler, *The Politics of Urban Renewal*, (Glencoe: Free Press, 1961).

35 See Banfield and Wilson, *City Politics*, chap. 21; and Morris Janowitz, *The Community Press in an Urban Setting* (Glencoe: Free Press, 1954).

flight of the middle class to the suburbs and the declining role of downtown department stores in retail sales in the metropolitan area. In metropolitan affairs, one can expect big city newspapers to support the position of downtown interests. This means support for urban renewal, mass transit, downtown parking, and other pro-central city policies in metropolitan affairs. On the other hand, suburban daily and weekly newspapers are supported by the advertising from suburban shopping centers, and they can be expected to take a pro-suburban position on metropolitan issues.

Newspapers are more influential among middle class populations than among working class, ethnic, or Negro populations. This is a product of differences in reading habits and educational levels between these groups. Newspapers are more influential in the absence of strong party organizations, which would compete with newspapers as channels of communication to the voters. Nonpartisanship, lengthy ballots, numerous referenda, all contribute to the influence of newspapers. Any situation that tends to obscure candidates or issues to the voter contributes to the power of newspapers, since the voter is obliged to rely upon them for information. Newspapers doubtlessly have more influence in local than in state or national politics, because of: (1) the relative importance in local politics of middle class groups who read newspapers, (2) the relative obscurity of local politics to the voter in his reliance upon newspapers for information about local affairs, and (3) the relative weakening of party affiliations in local politics.

On the whole, labor unions are much less active or influential at the local level than at the state or national level.[36] It is at the state and national level that the economic and regulatory issues that vitally affect labor are resolved. Economic prosperity, social security, minimum wages, fair labor standards, and protection of the rights to organize and bargain collectively are all issues determined primarily at the state or national level. Occasionally unions will become interested in police involvement in strikes and picketing at the local level, or they will become aroused by a local judge who enjoins them from striking or picketing. Unions become most intimately involved in local politics when they undertake to represent municipal employees. The American Federation of State, County, and Municipal Employees, the International Association of Fire Fighters, and the American Federation of Teachers, all AFL-CIO unions, are directly concerned with organization and collective bargaining in public employment. In addition, certain other unions, such as the Transport Workers Union, were organized to bargain on behalf of both public and private employees. In the absence of union representation, public employees may form "professional associations," such as the Fraternal Order of Police and, of course, the National Education Association, which do not engage in collective bargaining in the strictest sense but do attempt to represent their members.

[36] See Banfield and Wilson, *City Politics,* chap. 19.

Labor unions in America are principally concerned with "bread and butter" matters—better wages, hours, benefits, and job tenure. They are also concerned with protecting the right to organize, to bargain collectively, and to strike, for these are the tools which labor unions require in order to achieve their economic objectives. Municipal employee unions are more influential in large cities where fragmentation of authority and public acceptance of union activity encourage unions to assert their employees' interests. In New York City, for example, associations of teachers, policemen, firemen, transit workers, social workers, sanitation workers, and so on, have great political significance. Employee work stoppages and other forms of protest occur frequently, even though state law prohibits strikes of municipal employees.

Finally, any listing of influential interest groups in local politics should include the community's churches and church related organizations. Ministers, priests, rabbis, and leaders of religious lay groups are frequent participants in community decision making. The Catholic church, and its many lay organizations, is vitally concerned with the operations of parochial schools. Protestant ministerial associations in large cities may be concerned with public health, welfare, housing, and other social problems. Ministers and church congregations in small towns may be concerned with the enforcement of blue laws, limitations on liquor sales, prohibitions on horse racing and gambling, and other public policies relative to "vice" and public morality. In recent years, Catholic groups have also led the opposition to the distribution of birth control information and devices at city hospitals and public health clinics.

Robert H. Salisbury summarizes interest group politics in St. Louis as follows:

> St. Louis ... displays two broad configurations of interest. On one side are the locally oriented labor unions, Negroes, neighborhood businessmen, and lower income people generally. This grouping focuses its attention primarily on the specific bread and butter issues of jobs, stop signs, spot zoning, and the like, and exhibits a sharp antipathy toward any suggestion of increase of tax rates. Downtown business interests and the middle and upper middle residents, on the other hand, are primarily interested in broader policy questions—economic growth, urban renewal—and their approach to problems of fiscal solvency is more sympathetic to the needs for more tax revenue.[37]

[37] Robert H. Salisbury, "St. Louis Politics: Relationships Among Interests, Parties and Government Structure," *Western Political Quarterly*, 13 (June, 1960), 498–507.

10

STYLES OF
COMMUNITY POLITICS

Machines and Bosses

Machine politics may be going out of style, but something resembling machine politics still exists in Chicago, Pittsburgh, Philadelphia, and a number of other cities. Party organizations in most cities tend to be better organized, more cohesive, and better disciplined than state or national party organizations. Tightly disciplined party organizations, held together and motivated by a desire for tangible benefits rather than by principle or ideology, and staffed by professional politicians emerged in the nation's large cities early in the 19th century. The machine style of city politics has historical importance: between the Civil War and the New Deal, every big city had a machine at one time or another, and it is sometimes easier to understand the character of city politics today by knowing what went on in years past. But a more important reason for examining the machine style of politics is to understand the style of political organization and activity that employs personal and material inducements to control behavior. These kinds of inducements will always be important in politics, and the big city machine serves the prototype of a style of politics, in which ideologies and issues are secondary and personal friendships, favors, jobs, and material rewards are primary.

The political machine was essentially a large brokerage organization. It was a business organization, devoid of ideologies and issues, whose business it was to get votes and control elections, by trading off social services, patronage, and petty favors to the urban masses, particularly the poor and the recent immigrants. To get the money to pay for these social services and favors, it traded off city contracts, protection, and privileges to business interests, which paid off in cash. Like other brokerage organizations, a great many middle men came between the cash paid for a franchise for a trolley line or a construction contract and a Christmas turkey sent by the ward chairman to the Widow O'Leary. But the machine worked. It performed many important and social functions for the city.[1]

First of all, it personalized government. With keen social intuition, the machine recognized the voter as a man, generally living in a neighborhood, who had specific personal problems and wants. The machine politician avoided abstract and remote public issues or ideologies, and concentrated instead on the personal problems and needs of his constituents. Lincoln Steffens once quoted a Boston ward leader:

> I think that there's got to be in every ward somebody that any bloke can come to—no matter what he's done—and get help. Help, you understand; none of your law and justice, but help.[2]

The machine provided individual attention and recognition. As Tammany Hall boss, George Washington Plunkitt, the philosopher king of old style machine politics, explained:

> I know every man, woman, and child in the 15th district, except them that's been born this summer—and I know some of them, too. I know what they like and what they don't like, what they are strong at and what they are weak in, and I reach them by approachin' at the right side. For instance, here's how I gather in the young men. I hear of a young feller that's proud of his voice, thinks that he can sing fine. I ask him to come around to Washington Hall and join our Glee Club. Then there's the feller that likes rowin' on the river, the young feller that makes a name as a waltzer on his block, the young feller that's handy with his dukes—I rope them all in by givin' them opportunities to show themselves off. I don't trouble them with political arguments. I just study human nature and act accordin'.[3]

The machine also performed functions of a welfare agency:

> What tells in holdin' your grip on your district is to go right down among the poor families and help them in the different ways they need help. I've got a regular system for this. If there's a fire in Ninth, Tenth, or

---

[1] See Robert K. Merton, *Social Theory and Social Structure* (Glencoe: Free Press, 1957), pp. 71–81.

[2] Lincoln Steffens, *Autobiography* (New York: Harcourt, Brace & World, Inc., 1931) p. 618; also cited by Merton, *op. cit.*, p. 74.

[3] William L. Riordan, *Plunkitt of Tammany Hall* (New York: McClure, Phillips & Co., 1905), p. 46.

Eleventh Avenue, for example, any hour of the day or night, I'm usually there with some of my election district captains as soon as the fire engines. If a family is burned out I don't ask whether they are Republicans or Democrats, and I don't refer them to the Charity Organization Society, which would investigate their case in a month or two and decide they were worthy of help about the time they are dead from starvation. I just get quarters for them, buy clothes for them if their clothes were burned up, and fix them up till they get things runnin' again. It's philanthropy, but it's politics, too—mighty good politics. Who can tell how many votes one of these fires bring me? The poor are the most grateful people in the world, and let me tell you, they have more friends in their neighborhoods than the rich have in theirs.[4]

The machine also functioned as an employment agency. In the absence of government unemployment insurance or a federal employment service, patronage was an effective political tool, particularly in hard times. Not only were city jobs at the disposal of the machine, but the machine also had its business contacts:

Another thing, I can always get a job for a deservin' man. I make it a point to keep on the track of jobs, and it seldom happens that I don't have a few up my sleeve ready for use. I know every big employer in the district and in the whole city, for that matter, and they ain't in the habit of sayin' no to me when I ask them for a job.[5]

Banfield and Wilson argue effectively that it was not so much the petty favors and patronage that won votes among urban dwellers, so much as the sense of friendship and humanity that characterized the "machine" and its "boss." [6] The free turkeys and bushels of coal were really only tokens of this friendship. As Jane Addams, the famous settlement house worker, explained: "On the whole, the gifts and favors were taken quite simply as evidence of genuine loving kindness. The alderman is really elected because he is a good friend and neighbor. He is corrupt, of course, but he is not elected because he is corrupt, but rather in spite of it. His standard suits his constituents. He exemplifies and exaggerates the popular type of a good man. He has attained what his constituents secretly long for." [7]

The machine also played an important role in educating recent immigrants and assimilating them into American life.[8] Machine politics provided

[4] *Ibid.*, p. 52.

[5] *Ibid.*, p. 53.

[6] Edward C. Banfield and James Q. Wilson, *City Politics* (Cambridge: Harvard-M.I.T. Press, 1963), chap. 9.

[7] Jane Addams, *Democracy and Social Ethics* (New York: 1902), p. 254; also cited by Banfield and Wilson, *op. cit.*, p. 118.

[8] See Elmer E. Cornwell, Jr., "Bosses, Machines, and Ethnic Groups," *Annals of the American Academy of Political and Social Science* (May, 1964), pp. 27–39.

a means of upward social mobility for ethnic group members, which was not open to them in businesses or professions. City machines sometimes met immigrants at dockside and led them in groups through naturalization and voter registration procedures. Machines did not keep out people with "funny" sounding names, but instead went out of its way to put these names on ballots. Politics. became a way "up" for the bright sons of Irish and Italian immigrants.

Finally, for the businessman, particularly public utilities and construction companies with government contracts, the machine provided the necessary franchises, rights of way, contracts, and privileges. As Lincoln Steffens wrote: "You cannot build or operate a railroad, or a street railway, gas, water, or power company, develop and operate a mine, or cut forests or timber on a large scale, or run any privileged business, without corrupting or joining in the corruption of government." [9] The machine also provided the essential protection from police interference, which is required by illicit businesses, particularly gambling. In short, the machine helped to centralize power in large cities. It could "get things done at city hall."

Political analysts frequently remark that the day of the political machine has passed, and that big city political organizations have radically altered their style of operation. Federal and state welfare agencies now provide the basic welfare services that the bosses used to provide. Large scale immigration has stopped, and there are fewer people requiring the kinds of services once provided by the machine. Patronage jobs do not look as attractive in an affluent economy, and today civil service examinations cover most governmental jobs anyhow. In many ways the urban machine served the very rich and the very poor. The middle class was excluded, and much of the opposition to the machine came from the middle class. As the middle class grew in American society (today white collar workers outnumber blue collar workers), opposition to the machine has grown in every city. Middle class voters supported reform movements and good government crusades, which often succeeded in replacing the machine with professional city managers, civil service, reorganized city government, and city administrations pledged to eliminate corruption and exercise economy and efficiency in government.

Big city party organizations continue to thrive, although in a somewhat modified form. Party organizations such as those led by Mayor Richard J. Daley in Chicago, William Green in Philadelphia, David Lawrence in Pittsburgh, and Carmine DeSapio in New York all survived through the 1960's because they continued to perform important political and social functions in their communities. In a system of "fragmented" government in the nation's large cities, these party organizations continue to play an important part in organizing power: that is to say, in "getting things done at

[9] Lincoln Steffens, *Autobiography*, p. 168.

city hall." [10] A centralized, well disciplined party organization helps to overcome the dispersion of power one finds in a normal structure of a big city government, with its maze of authorities, boards, commissions, agencies, and separately elected officials.

Mayor Richard J. Daley of Chicago is perhaps the closest thing to the old style political boss still operating in the nation's large cities. In Chicago, few others understand so well the labyrinths of formal and informal power, the complex structure of federal, state, and local government and public opinion in Chicago as the mayor. Daley has served three four-year terms as mayor of Chicago beginning in 1955; he remains the captain of his old 11th ward Democratic committee; and he is chairman of the Cook County Democratic committee. He picks candidates' slates, runs the patronage machinery, and works his will on nearly all of the 50 submissive aldermen who comprise Chicago's city council. Illinois Democratic governors must be responsive to his wishes and Chicago's nine member delegation to the US House of Representatives also acts promptly on Daley's recommendations. The Cook County Democratic delegation to the Illinois legislature is firmly in his hands.

Chicago has had bosses before. There was "Big Bill" Thompson (1915–23, 1927–31), a Republican who left a safe deposit box stuffed with $1.5 million in cash when he died. There was Democrat Ed Kelley (1933–47), who used his powers mostly to throw public projects to his personal and political pal, contractor Pat Nash. Chicago has also had reform mayors; one of these was Democrat Martin Kennelley (1947–55), whose good intentions were frustrated by a lack of political acumen and who was unseated by Daley in 1955.

Daley, a Roman Catholic, was born in the impoverished Bridgeport district of Chicago near the stockyards. He sold newspapers on the street as a boy and worked in the stockyards. He worked his way up to clerk in the stockyards office and then went at night to the law school at DePauw University. He was appointed secretary to the city council at 25, and has remained on the public payroll for the next 40 years. He still lives with his large family in his old city neighborhood. In 1936, when a state legislator from Daley's district died, Democratic boss Ed Kelley and ward leader Jake Arvey gave the job to Daley, who gradually worked his way up in the Kelley-Arvey machine. When Adlai Stevenson became Governor of Illinois in 1949 he rewarded the Chicago machine by making Daley the State Revenue Director. But more important to Daley's political power, he was also made county clerk for Cook County, which placed him in charge of all the voting machinery in the county and many patronage jobs. Daley's

---

[10] For an excellent description of the functions of Mayor Daley's political organization in Chicago, see Edward C. Banfield, *Political Influence* (Glencoe: Free Press, 1961).

old teacher, Boss Jake Arvey, always felt that a boss should be a "behind-the-scenes operator" and should not run for public office himself, but Daley broke with his old boss Arvey to run for mayor against a Republican reform candidate, who charged scandal and corruption in Chicago in the Democratic government. Daley replied: "If I am elected I will embrace mercy, love, charity, and walk humbly with my God." When he was elected, one commentator observed: "Chicago ain't ready for reform!" From his base in Chicago, Daley quickly made himself the unchallenged leader of Illinois Democrats. Adlai Stevenson was not a "machine" Illinois Democrat, and Daley always remained somewhat cool towards Stevenson, but was a staunch supporter of Senator John F. Kennedy. Daley was a key supporter and consultant in Kennedy's race for the presidential nomination. On election day, 1960, Daley's machine in Chicago gave Kennedy a margin of 450,000 votes, giving the crucial state of Illinois to Kennedy, who lost the rest of the state so badly that his statewide edge was only 9000 votes. Daley was unworried about later charges of voting irregularities in Chicago.

Like other big city mayors, Daley's biggest problem today is race relations. Chicago's Negroes compose nearly a third of the city's population and half of the public school pupils. Daley remains close to many older Negro leaders whose support he has always courted, but he is not very close to younger, more militant Negro leaders like Negro comedian Dick Gregory of Chicago. Many younger Negroes refer to Daley's urban renewal and slum clearance programs as "Negro removal." Many white residents of Chicago have become upset by what they consider Daley's "concessions" to Negroes. Yet Daley is the classic style of the political broker, who continues to try to arrange compromises and win support from both Negroes and whites.

Unlike older bosses, Daley has maintained a progressive image. He has not tolerated much corruption in office, and he has kept a tight reign on gambling, prostitution, and organized crime. He brought in the nation's leading criminologist, University of California Professor Orlando W. Wilson, to clean up and revitalize the city police force, which he did, although he was later criticized by Negro leaders because of his strict enforcement policies. Daley also inaugurated many reforms, including an executive budget for the city, an extended merit system, a new zoning and housing code, and many other organizational improvements. Although a big city Democrat, Daley earnestly solicited the support of prominent businessmen for city projects. He has sought and won a great deal of newspaper support and has even appealed with success to civic leaders and good government associations.

As a political broker, Daley is seldom the initiator of public policy. His approach to policy questions is more like that of an arbitrator between competing interests. When political controversies develop, Daley often waits at the sidelines without committing himself, in the hope that public opinion will soon "crystallize" behind a particular course of action. Once the community is behind a project—and this determination Daley makes himself after lengthy consultations with his political advisors—he then awards his stamp of approval. This suggests that in policy matters many political "bosses" are not so much bosses as referees among interested individuals and groups. The boss is really "apolitical" when it comes to policy matters. He is really more concerned with resolving conflict and maintaining his position and organization than he is with the outcome of public policy decisions.

Machine politics will remain with us as long as there is an unmet need to personalize the operations of government, and as long as individuals need services that the formal machinery of government cannot provide. Machine politics will remain as long as people place little or no value on their vote, or more precisely, as long as they place a lower value on their vote than they do on the things a machine can offer them in exchange for it. Voters who are indifferent to issues and candidates, and there are still many of these, and who put little value on their vote can be easily induced to trade it for the small favors that the party organization can offer. And urban party organizations continue to perform important welfare duties, employment services, and petty favors. A recent survey of precinct politicians in a New Jersey county revealed the following list of services: [11]

1. Help poor people to get work;
2. Help deserving people to get jobs on a highway crew, police force, or fire department or in state positions;
3. Show people how to get their social security benefits, welfare, and unemployment compensation;
4. Help citizens with problems like rent gouging, unfair labor practices, zoning, or unfair assessments;
5. Help one's precinct to get a needed traffic light, more parking space, or more policemen;
6. Run clambakes or other get togethers for interested people even though no political campaign is involved;
7. Help people who are in difficulty with the law;
8. Help newcomers to this county to get adjusted and get places to live and work;
9. Work with some of the other party's people to reduce the friction and keep the campaign from getting too rough;
10. Help boys with military service problems with advice on the best way to serve.

It is unlikely that these kinds of services will ever go out of style completely. A certain amount of machine politics will be found in every city.

[11] Richard T. Frost, "Stability and Change in Local Politics," *Public Opinion Quarterly*, 25 (Summer, 1961) 231–32.

Reformers and Dogooders

A reform style of politics appeared in the United States shortly after the Civil War to battle the "bosses." Beginning in 1869, scathing editorials in the *New York Times* and cartoons by Thomas Nast in *Harper's Weekly* attacked the "Tammany Society" in New York City, a political organization that controlled the local Democratic organization. William M. Tweed was President of the Board of Supervisors of New York County, and undisputed boss of "Tammany Hall," as the New York County Democratic committee was called, after its old meeting place on 14th Street. This early reform movement achieved temporary success under the brilliant leadership of Samuel J. Tilden, who succeeded in driving the "Tweed Ring" out of office and went on in 1876 to be the only presidential candidate ever to win a majority of popular votes and then be denied the Presidency through the operation of the electoral college. George William Curtis, editor of *Harper's Weekly,* E. L. Godkin, editor of the *Nation,* and Senator Carl Schurz of Missouri laid the foundations for a style of reform politics that continues to have great influence in American cities.[12]

Early municipal reform is closely linked to the progressive movement in American politics. Leaders, such as Robert M. LaFollette of Wisconsin, Hiram Johnson of California, Gifford Pinchot of Pennsylvania, and Charles Evans Hughes of New York backed municipal reform at the local level as well as the direct primary and direct election of senators and women's suffrage at the national level. In 1912 social worker Jane Addams, who labored in the slums and settlement houses in New York, sang "Onward Christian Soldiers" at the Progressive party convention in 1912, which nominated Teddy Roosevelt for President. Lincoln Steffens wrote in *The Shame of the Cities* ". . . St. Louis exemplified boodle; Minneapolis, police graft; Pittsburgh, a political industrial machine; and Philadelphia (the worst city in the country), general civic corruption." [13] The National Municipal League was formed in 1900 by representatives of 15 reform citizens associations throughout the country.

From its beginning, reform politics was strongly supported by the native middle class, Anglo-Saxon, Protestant, old residents of cities whose political ethos was very different than that which the new immigrants brought with them. The immigrant, the machine that relied upon his vote, and the businessman who relied upon the machine for street railway and other utility franchises had formed an alliance in the 19th century, which had displaced the native, old family, yankee elite that had traditionally dominated north-

---

[12] See Richard J. Hofstadter, *The Age of Reform* (New York: Alfred A. Knopf, Inc., 1955); Lorin Peterson, *The Day of the Mugwump* (New York: Random House, Inc., 1961).

[13] Lincoln Steffens, *The Shame of the Cities* (Sagamore Press, 1957), p. 10.

ern cities. This middle class elite fought to recapture control of local government through the municipal reform movement.

Richard Hofstader described the social, ideological, and political clash between the new immigrants and the Anglo-Saxon, Protestant, middle class in the *Age of Reform:*

> Out of the clash between the needs of the immigrants and the sentiments of the natives, there emerged two thoroughly different systems of political ethics . . . one, founded upon the indigenous yankee–Protestant political traditions, and upon middle class life, assumed and demanded the constant, disinterested activity of the citizen in public affairs, argued that political life ought to be run to a greater degree than it was in accordance to general principles, abstract laws, apart from and superior to personal needs, and expressed a common feeling that government should be in good part an effort to moralize the lives of individuals, while economic life should be intimately related to the stimulation and development of individual character. The other system, founded upon the European background of the immigrants, upon their unfamiliarity with independent political action, their familiarity with hierarchy and authority, and upon the urgent needs that so often grew out of their migration, took for granted that the political life of the individual would arise out of family needs, interpreted political and civic relations, chiefly in terms of personal obligations, and placed strong personal loyalties above allegiance to abstract codes of law or morals.[14]

This conflict can still be observed today in American politics. Machine politicians cater to ethnic groups, Negroes, recent immigrants to the city, ethnic minorities, and other working class and lower class elements of the city. The reform politician appeals to the middle class, the third generation American who has acquired an education, a good job, and owns his own home. It is no coincidence that Mayor Daley of Chicago was born of Irish immigrant parents behind the stockyards, while reform Mayor Joe Clark of Philadelphia (later U.S. Senator) was a "Philadelphia gentleman" and scion of one of the city's oldest families. In an interesting study entitled *The LaGuardia Years, Machine and Reform Politics in New York City,* Charles Garrett notes that "the good government advocates of this period came mainly from the professional and business classes. They tended to be native Americans of the older sort, Protestant, well-to-do, and well educated." [15] The middle class is largely Republican in its politics, and many of the early middle class municipal reformers were independent or progressive Republicans. Some of the early municipal reformers were mugwumps —Republicans who supported Democrat Grover Cleveland, a reform governor of New York. While today's reformers may be either Republicans or Democrats, there may be a slight tendency for reformers to be Republicans

---

[14] Hofstadter, *The Age of Reform.*
[15] Charles Garrett, *The LaGuardia Years: Machine and Reform Politics in New York City* (New Brunswick, N.J.: Rutgers University Press, 1961), pp. 20–21.

by conviction. Today machine politics is closely identified with the Democratic party. While reform Democrats are active in many cities, the importance of big-city Democratic party organizations in the Democratic party at the state and national levels often makes reformers feel unwelcome.

Reform politics includes a belief that there is a "public interest" that should prevail over competing, partial interests in a city. The idea of balancing competing interests or compromising public policy is not part of the reformers' view of political life. Rather, the reform ethos includes a belief that there is a "right" answer to public questions, which "reasonable men" can arrive at by thought and discussion. Conflict and indeed even "politics" is viewed as distasteful. Since reasonable men can agree upon the public interest, municipal government is really a technical and administrative problem rather than a political one. City government should be placed in the hands of those who are best qualified, by training, ability, and devotion to public service, to manage public business. These best qualified men can decide on policy and then leave a separate activity of administration to professional experts. Any interference by special interests in the policies or administration of the best qualified people would be viewed as corruption.

Banfield and Wilson cite an example of cities where reform politics holds sway:

> An example is Winnetka, a suburb of Chicago, the residents of which are almost all upper middle class, Anglo-Saxon Protestants. Winnetkans are in fundamental agreement on the kind of local government they want: it must provide excellent schools, parks, libraries, and other community services, and it must provide them with businesslike efficiency and perfect honesty. Politics, in the sense of a competitive struggle for office or for private advantage, does not exist. No one offers himself as a candidate for office. Instead, the civic associations agree upon a slate of those 'best qualified to serve,' which the voters ratify as a matter of course. Members of the city council leave 'administration' entirely in the hands of the city manager. That the Winnetka style of local government reflects the middle class ethos and is not a mere historical accident may be seen from the fact that the same style exists in other similarly constituted communities. For example, Scarsdale, New York, although about a thousand miles from Winnetka, follows the same practice of 'tapping' those 'best qualified to serve.' [16]

The objectives of the reform movement were:

1. The elimination of corruption in public office, and the recruitment of "good men" (educated, upper income men who were successful in private business or professions) to replace "politicians" (men who were no more successful than their constituents in private life and who were dependent upon public office for their principal source of income).

[16] Banfield and Wilson, *City Politics*, p. 140.

2. The provision of means by which party machinery could be bypassed in nominations and elections. This meant nomination by petition, and the initiative, recall, and referendum. (Reformers were not really sure about the necessity of this item; it was left to local option in the model city charter.)

3. The reorganization of local government to eliminate many separately elected offices (the "short ballot" movement) in order to simplify the voter's task and focus responsibility for the conduct of public affairs on a small number of top elected officials.

4. The strengthening of executive leadership in city government—longer terms for mayors, subordination of departments and commissions to a chief executive, and an executive budget combined with modern financial practices.

5. The replacement of patronage appointments with the merit system of civil service.

6. The separation of local politics from state and national politics by home rule charters and the holding of local elections at times when there were no state and national elections.

7. The elimination of parties from local politics by nonpartisan elections. (The effect of nonpartisanship is described below in more detail.)

8. The establishment of the council-manager form of government, and the separation of "politics" from the "business" of municipal government.

All of these objectives are interrelated. Ideally, a "reformed city" would be one with a council-manager form of government, nonpartisan election for mayor and council, a home rule charter, a short ballot, a modern budgeting and financial system, a civil service personnel system, initiative, recall, and referendum systems, and "good men" at the helm. Later, the reform movement added comprehensive city planning to its list of objectives —official planning agencies with professional planners authorized to prepare a master plan of future development for the city. The National Municipal League incorporated its program of reform into a *Model City Charter* which continues to be the standard manual of municipal reform.[17] There is reason to believe that the early reformers also opposed immigration (which was very logical, of course, since the immigrant was the backbone of machine politics). Many persons active in municipal reform at the time also supported the passage of the Immigration Act of 1921 reducing immigration to a trickle and establishing quotas heavily weighted in favor of Anglo-Saxon Protestant immigrants and against southern and eastern European Catholic immigrants. One of the most effective of the early municipal reformers was Richard S. Childs, an advertising executive who took up municipal reform as a hobby. He started a National Short Ballot organization and is often credited with inventing the council-manager form of government. He used his advertising skills to sell city-manager government

[17] National Municipal League, *Model City Charter* (Chicago: National Municipal League, 1961).

with the popular symbols of big business—"economy and efficiency, businesslike government, municipal corporation, professional management, just like a corporation with its board of directors."

Andrew D. White, first president of Cornell University, summarized early reform thinking when he wrote in 1890:

> What is this evil theory? It is simply that the city is a political body; that its interior affairs have to do with national political parties and issues. My fundamental contention is that a city is a corporation; that as a city it has nothing whatever to do with general political interests; that party political names and duties are utterly out of place there. The questions in a city are not political questions. They have reference to the laying out of streets; to the erection of buildings; to sanitary arrangements, sewerage, water supply, gas supply, electrical supply; to the control of franchises and the like; and to provisions for the public health and comfort in parks, boulevards, libraries, and museums. The work of a city being the creation and control of the city property, it should logically be managed as a piece of property by those who have created it, or a real substantial part in it, and who can therefore feel strongly their duty to it. Under our theory that a city is a political body, a crowd of illiterate peasants, freshly raked in from Irish bogs, or Bohemian mines, or Italian robber nests, may exercise virtual control.[18]

Reform movements can assume a variety of forms. Professor James Q. Wilson has identified five types of reform movements in big city politics: citizens associations, candidate screening committees, independent local parties, "blue ribbon" leadership factions, and intraparty reform clubs.[19] Citizens associations operate outside of party structures as voluntary associations, often with paid staffs and researchers. These associations scrutinize local government structure, programs, and expenditures and recommend changes and reforms. Ordinarily, they do not endorse candidates, participate in election campaigns, or take sides in controversial policy questions. The Pennsylvania Economy League, the Chicago Civic Confederation, New York's Citizens Budget Commission, and the Detroit Citizens League are examples of extraparty, policy oriented, citizens committees that are active in reform efforts. The League of Women Voters is probably the largest organization of this kind. At the state and national level, the Committee for Economic Development (CED) plays a somewhat similar role. These citizens associations claim to provide "objective" information about taxes, expenditures, services, and administration. This information

---

[18] Andrew D. White, "The Government of American Cities," in *Forum* (1890); reprinted in Edward C. Banfield, *Urban Government: A Reader in Administration and Politics* (Glencoe: Free Press, 1961).

[19] James Q. Wilson, "Politics and Reform in American Cities" in *American Government Annual 1962–63* (New York: Holt, Rinehart, & Winston, Inc., 1962); see also James Q. Wilson, *The Amateur Democrat* (Chicago: University of Chicago Press, 1963).

generally stresses the need for economy and efficiency, lower taxes, or streamlined administration.

A second type of reform movement is the candidate screening committee, which also operates outside of the political parties and recommends or evaluates candidates for public office. These committees are probably more effective in nonpartisan cities or cities in which party organizations are weak than in cities with strong two party systems. These committees may be informal groups of the most influential businessmen, lawyers, and publishers, who in the absence of parties actually select a candidate for mayor and raise funds for his campaign.

Occasionally reform movements assume the form of an independent local party. Reform parties, however, usually do not last very long. Since they are committed to "reform," they are prevented by their principles from offering jobs or other material inducements to maintain the continued, disciplined support of their party workers. They must rely upon social and ideological rewards and their supporters often grow tired of these intangible satisfactions. New York City's Fusion Party was successful in electing three reform mayors in this century—Seth Low, 1901, John Purroy Mitchel, 1913, and Fiorello LaGuardia, 1933—but in each case, success depended upon an alliance with Republicans, an alliance that always collapsed shortly after victory was achieved. Although most independent reform parties are heavily saturated with middle class business elements, the liberal party of New York provides an interesting contrast. The Liberal Party has had considerable success at the polls and has operated successfully over many years. While it is committed to many reform ideals, it has the strong support of the International Ladies Garment Workers Union and is liberal rather than conservative on most national policy issues. Wilson lists as other examples of independent good government parties the City Charter Committee in Cincinnati, the Citizens Association in Kansas City, the San Francisco Volunteers for Better Government, the San Antonio Good Government League, the Phoenix Charter Government Committee, the Minneapolis Citizens Organized for Responsible Government, the Independent Voters of Illinois (Chicago), and the Cambridge (Mass.) Civic Association.

Blue ribbon leadership factions operate within existing party organizations. A "blue ribbon" candidate is usually a man with high integrity, high professional achievement, and devotion to public service. He may be related to a distinguished old family or be a wealthy and successful businessman with a record of statesmanlike participation in public affairs, and although a loyal party member, have no personal identification with local machines or professional politicians. Reform came to Philadelphia in 1951 in the form of blue ribbon Democratic party leadership of Joseph S. Clark and Richardson Dilworth. Philadelphia had been ruled by a Republican machine from 1884 to 1951, a machine which had been rocked regularly by scandals and flagrant corruption. The disorganized and dispirited Democratic party organization sought an alliance with attractive reformers from Philadelphia's upper crust. The shrewd Democratic party leader, James Finnegan, who was later to become National Democratic Party Chairman under Adlai Stevenson, forged a coalition between Democratic politicians and reformers, which defeated the Republican machine in 1951. Blueblood socialite, Joseph Clark, was elected mayor; Richardson Dilworth, a flamboyant and emotional war hero, whose family rested on the outskirts of the city's old society, was elected district attorney; and James Finnegan himself was elected president of the city council. The campaign was based on an anticorruption, "throw the rascals out" platform, and attracted many young liberals, idealists, and reformers to the Democratic party. Yet almost immediately after Clark's victory, the latent tension between blue ribbon office holders and Democratic party leaders became evident. Clark succeeded in winning a new home rule city charter, inaugurated a civil service system, and began to eliminate patronage jobs from the city administration. Democratic politicians, who had waited since 1884 to capture control of Philadelphia, wanted jobs, not reform. For a while, Jim Finnegan mediated conflict between reformers and party leaders, but he was replaced in 1953 as Democratic Party Chairman by Congressman William Green, a man who had little use for reform or reformers. Although Mayor Clark denied many patronage jobs to Green's regular party organization, the Democrats captured the governorship of Pennsylvania in 1954, and put at the disposal of the regular organization in Philadelphia a large supply of patronage jobs from the administration of Governor George Leader. Green immediately set about to construct one of the most efficient machines in American politics with this supply of state jobs. In an era when big city machines were supposed to be dying, Green created a new one in Philadelphia.[20]

Dilworth replaced Clark as Mayor in 1955, and Clark left city politics to go off to Washington as a United States Senator. While Clark had successfully resisted machine inroads into his reform administration, Dilworth was unable to do so. Green succeeded in recruiting many of the old Republican ward chairmen into his own organization (remember, professional politicians are motivated by material rewards, not ideologies or issues). An amazed Richardson Dilworth, looking around city hall one day, exclaimed: "I seem to see the same faces in the corridors here that I saw eight years ago." Gradually the Green machine took control of the Dilworth administration, and although the Green machine had the power to replace Dilworth on the Democratic party ticket in 1959, it permitted him to be re-elected Mayor based on his promise of noninterference in machine affairs. In 1963

[20] See James Reichley, *The Art of Government: Reform and Organization Politics in Philadelphia* (New York: Fund for the Republic, 1959).

the machine placed in office its own mayor, James H. Tate, although the machine was weakened by the death of Boss Green. Interestingly, the regular Democratic organization split with Tate in 1967 (it was thought that his administration had been so uninspiring that he could not be re-elected), but Tate defeated the organization endorsed candidate in the Democratic primary and went on to defeat a Republican reform candidate in the general election.

While the reform spirit gradually wilted in Philadelphia, and the material rewards of machine politics have proven very effective in the long run, many reforms introduced by the Clark administration remain in Philadelphia today. Urban renewal and public housing took giant steps forward under the Clark administration. Comprehensive city planning was introduced and became an important influence in the city's development. A new, home rule city charter streamlined the city government, and the city's financial system was completely overhauled. With the exception of civil service, the reforms of the Clark administration have not been undone. Yet, the Philadelphia experience also suggests that reform cannot be sustained without a permanent, disciplined organization, the kind of organization that reformers themselves find distasteful. It is exceptionally difficult to maintain a permanent reform movement in a big city with partisan elections and a large, lower income, ethnic electorate, committed to traditional party allegiances and attracted by the material rewards which the machine can offer.

Another type of reform politics is the intraparty club, which seeks to capture the regular party organization from within.[21] Reform clubs have been surprisingly effective in California and New York in defeating regular party organizations in intraparty primary battles. The California Democratic Council (CDC) was created in 1953 to bring together the growing club movement in California. The CDC has been dominated by liberal clubs in California cities; the CDC is regarded as the voice of the issue-oriented liberal wing of the California Democratic Party. The New York Committee for Democratic Voters (CDV) was formed in 1959 under the sponsorship of several prominent New York liberal Democrats including Senator Herbert Lehman and Mrs. Eleanor Roosevelt. The CDV helped raise funds for many local reform clubs in New York. In 1961 the Village Independent Democrats, a reform club in Greenwich Village in New York, won nationwide attention by defeating New York County Democratic Chairman, Carmine DeSapio, in his bid for re-election to the county Democratic committee.

Club members are "amateurs" in contrast to the professional politicians who constitute the regular party organizations. The Manhattan Reformers, which defeated DeSapio, were mostly young (under 40) people with middle

[21] See Wilson, *The Amateur Democrat.*

class backgrounds. Over half were Jewish, and practically all of the members were "liberals." Many of them were brought into politics by Adlai Stevenson's candidacy for the Presidency in 1952 and 1956. These amateurs are generally aware of the failures of reform in the past and they generally believe that effective reform can only come through capturing party machinery in primary elections. Like early reformers, these amateurs are more motivated by the ideological and social rewards of mixing in politics than the professional party worker. They differ from early reformers not only in their desire to capture party machinery, but also in their interest in national issues and their belief that local, state, and national issues are interrelated. Rather than remove politics from local government, they wish to see local governments and local party organizations much more issue-oriented.

The Future Style of City Politics

Boss Plunkitt once observed that "reform administrations never succeed themselves." [22] Plunkitt realized that the emotional fervor of reform could arouse the public to "throw the rascals out" in moments of righteous reform, but he was confident that, in the long run, organization politics, with its reliance upon personal and material rewards, could outlast the emotional appeal of reform. Reform administrations, he felt, would come and go, but the machine would remain to govern the city with only occasional interruptions. Yet these interruptions occurred with increased frequency in the 20th century. The machine style of politics still exists, but it has declined noticeably in recent years. City government is vastly more honest, efficient, and democratic than it was a generation ago.

Several factors are generally cited as contributing to the decline of machine politics:

1. The decline in immigration and the gradual assimilation of white ethnic groups—Irish, Italians, Germans, Poles, Slavs;
2. Federal social welfare programs, which undercut the machine's role in welfare work—unemployment insurance, workmen's compensation, social security, and public assistance have ended the party's monopoly of welfare services;
3. Rising levels of prosperity and higher educational levels which make the traditional rewards of the machine less attractive;
4. The spread of middle class values about honesty, efficiency, and good government, which inhibit party organizations in purchases, contracts, and vote-buying, and other cruder forms of municipal corruption. The more successful machine today, like Daley's in Chicago, have had to reform themselves in order to maintain a good public image;
5. Reforms such as nonpartisanship, better voting procedures, city-manager government, and—most important of all—civil service,

[22] William Riordan, *Plunkitt of Tammany Hall.*

which has weakened the party's role in municipal elections and administration.

Edwin O'Connor, in an interesting novel *The Last Hurrah,* based upon the life of Mayor Curley of Boston, describes the defeat of Boss Skeffington in his bid for re-election as Mayor:

> Well, of course, the old boss was strong simply because he held all the cards. If anybody wanted anything—jobs, favors, cash, he could only go to the boss, the local leader. What Roosevelt did was to take the handouts out of the local hands. A few little things like social security, unemployment insurance, and the like—that's what shifted the gears, Sport. No need now to depend on the boss for everything; the federal government is getting into the act . . . the old timers would still string along with the boss, of course, because that's the way they always did things. But what about the kids coming along? Did you ever stop to think, Sport, about the *age* of the people around (Boss Skeffington)? I wouldn't mind betting that it didn't exactly look like a youth movement . . . and what about the kids? To begin with, they were one step further away from the old country; he didn't have the old emotional appeal for them. You know, the racial spokesman kind of thing. For another, a lot of them have been educated away from home. They didn't know much about Skeffington, and they didn't much care.[23]

Patronage was once very useful in maintaining a party organization, attracting voters, financing the party, insuring favorable government actions for party requests, and maintaining discipline within the party's ranks, yet Frank Sorauf has commented on the declining usefulness of patronage in an era of economic prosperity and high levels of employment: "While low pay and chronic job insecurity plague the patronage job holder, private employment has become progressively more attractive with rising wage levels, union protections and securities, unemployment compensation, pension plans, and fringe benefits. Viewed by most Americans as a short term desperation job alternative, the patronage position has lost considerable value as a political incentive." [24] Sorauf also notes that patronage runs contrary to the prevailing values of the growing middle class in America: "Patronage is also losing its respectability. Its ethic—the naked political quid pro quo—no longer seems to many a natural and reasonable ingredient in politics . . . the mores of the middle class and image of civic virtue instilled by public education extolled the unfettered, independent voter, rather than the patronage seeking party liner . . . briefly, patronage has fallen into public disfavor for appearing to approach an outright political payoff, with the result that its usefulness to the parties has diminished." [25]

[23] Edwin O'Connor, *The Last Hurrah* (Boston: Little, Brown and Co., 1956), pp. 374–75.
[24] Frank J. Sorauf, "State Patronage in a Rural County," *American Political Science Review,* Vol. 50 (1956), 1046–1056.
[25] *Ibid.,* p. 1055.

Nonpartisanship

The nonpartisan ballot was the most widely adopted reform ever put forward to curb the machines and insure an "antiseptic," "no party" style of politics. Nearly two-thirds of America's cities use the nonpartisan ballot to elect local officials. Reformers felt that nonpartisanship would take the "politics" out of local government and raise the caliber of candidates for elected offices. They believed that nonpartisanship would resrict local campaigning to local issues, and thereby rule out extraneous state issues from local elections. They also believed that, by eliminating party labels, local campaigns would emphasize the qualifications of the individual candidates rather than their party affiliations.

Nonpartisanship is found in large as well as small cities. Party labels have been removed from local elections in Detroit, Los Angeles, Boston, Cincinnati, Cleveland, Milwaukee, San Francisco, Seattle, and even Chicago. Nonpartisanship is even more widespread than council-manager government. However, there is a tendency for these two forms to be related; 84 per cent of all council-manager cities have nonpartisan ballots, while only 49 per cent of all mayor-council cities are nonpartisan (see Table 10.1). While nonpartisan cities are found in both one party and two party states, there is some tendency for competitive two party states to have a smaller percentage of nonpartisan cities than one party Democratic or Republican states. Table 10.2, by Phillips Cutwright, shows that 56 per cent of the

TABLE 10.1

NONPARTISANSHIP IN AMERICAN CITIES

Form of government	Number of cities reporting	Percent partisan	Percent nonpartisan
Mayor-council	1,533	51	49
Commission	241	37	63
Council-manager	1,165	16	84
Town meeting	13	46	54
Rep. town meeting	17	24	76
Population			
Over 500,000	20	40	60
250,000–500,000	30	23	77
100,000–250,000	79	38	62
50,000–100,000	194	32	68
25,000– 50,000	400	30	70
10,000– 25,000	1,010	38	62
5,000– 10,000	1,237	38	62
All cities over 5,000	2,970	36	64

Source: *Municipal Year Book, 1964*, p. 88.

TABLE 10.2

STATE PARTY SYSTEMS, COMMUNITY CLEAVAGE, AND NONPARTISANSHIP

State party system	Percent nonpartisan	Number of cities[2]
Competitive states[1]	56	280
Democratic states	74	115
Republican states	86	85
Total	65	480
Religious composition[3]		
High Catholic	56	225
Low Catholic	73	255
Manufacturing levels		
High manufacturing employment	56	218
Low manufacturing employment	73	262

[1]Competitive States: California, Colorado, Connecticut, Delaware, Illinois, Indiana, Kentucky, Massachusetts, Idaho, Michigan, Maryland, Montana, Missouri, New Mexico, New York, Nevada, Ohio, Pennsylvania, Vermont, Washington, West Virginia, Wyoming.

[2]All incorporated cities with 25,000 inhabitants in 1950.

[3]From U.S. Department of Commerce, *Religious Bodies, 1936*, Vol. 1 (Washington: U.S. Government Printing Office, 1941).

Source: Adapted from figures presented in Phillips Cutright, "Nonpartisan Electoral Systems in American Cities," *Comparative Studies in Society and History* (January, 1963).

cities in competitive states have nonpartisan ballots, compared to 74 per cent of the cities in Democratic states and 86 per cent of the cities in Republican states. The nonpartisan ballot is also more likely to be adopted in homogeneous middle class cities, where there is less social cleavage and smaller proportions of working class and ethnic group members. Cutright reports that there is a tendency for cities with large Catholic populations to retain the partisan ballot; there is also a tendency for cities with heavy factory employment to prefer partisan over nonpartisan elections.[26] However, Cutright's findings are subject to many exceptions: Chicago, Detroit, and Boston are located in competitive party states and have large working class populations, large Catholic populations, and deep social cleavages— yet they are officially nonpartisan cities.

To what extent has nonpartisanship succeeded in removing "politics" from local government? Of course, if "politics" is defined as conflict over public policy, then "politics" has certainly not disappeared with the elimination of party labels. There is no evidence that eliminating party ballots can reduce the level of community conflict. If we define "politics" to mean "partisanship," that is *party* politics, then nonpartisanship may have re-

[26] Phillips Cutright, "Nonpartisan Electoral Systems in American Cities," *Comparative Studies in Society and History* (January, 1963), pp. 212–26.

moved some party influences from local government, although the evidence is by no means clear on this point.

Apparently several types of political systems can be found in nonpartisan cities.[27] First of all, in some nonpartisan cities, parties continue to operate effectively behind the scenes in local affairs. In Chicago, for example, it is said that the city council is composed of 47 nonpartisan Democrats and three nonpartisan Republicans. Chicago is nonpartisan only in the sense that party affiliations are not printed on the ballot. Denver, Seattle, Cincinnati, and Kansas City have also been cited as nonpartisan cities, in which the parties continue to play a vital role in local elections.

Another type of nonpartisan political system is one in which the major parties are inactive, but other formal organizations function very much like parties. Frequently these organizations are civic organizations led by newspapers or business firms. Occasionally, liberal or labor groups arise to challenge middle class civic associations. These organizations may "slate" candidates, manage their campaigns, and even exercise some influence over them while they are in office. These organizations are not usually as permanent as parties, but they may operate as clearly identifiable political entities over a number of years. Cities with these "local parties" include San Francisco, Detroit, Dallas, Fort Worth, and Cambridge, Massachusetts. Many of these local party systems are indirectly related to the national parties. In a Massachusetts city, J. Lieper Freeman found that the "progressives," and the "nonpartisans" who opposed each other consistently in local elections were largely Democrats and Republicans in disguise.[28] There was a high correlation between voting for progressives in local elections and Democrats in national elections, and between nonpartisans in local elections and Republicans in national elections. Williams and Adrian studied four nonpartisan Michigan cities and found identifiable blocks of candidates and a high correlation between party identification and voting for a particular local slate.[29] Salisbury and Black testify that, after the adoption of nonpartisanship in Des Moines in 1949, party organizations ceased to play an active role in campaigns, but there continued to be significant relationships between party identification and voting for particular slates of candidates in local nonpartisan elections.[30]

[27] The following discussion relies upon Charles Adrian, "A Typology of Non-Partisan Elections," *Western Political Quarterly,* 12 (June, 1959). 449–58; see also Banfield and Wilson, *City Politics,* chap. 12.

[28] J. Lieper Freeman, "Local Party Systems: Theoretical Considerations and a Case Analysis," *American Journal of Sociology,* Vol. 64 (1958).

[29] Oliver P. Williams and Charles R. Adrian, "The Insulation of Local Politics Under the Non-Partisan Ballot," *American Political Science Review,* 53 (1959), 1052–63.

[30] Robert Salisbury and Gordon Black, "Class and Party in Partisan and Non-Partisan Elections," *American Political Science Review,* 57 (September, 1963), 587–97.

A third type of nonpartisan political system is one in which the Democratic and Republican parties play no role at all and in which there are no local parties or slate making associations. This is the most common type of nonpartisanship in small cities. Individual candidates select themselves, collect their own money, and create their own temporary campaign organizations. Voting does not correlate highly with party identification, but instead tends to follow a "friends and neighbors" pattern, rather than socio-economic or partisan lines.

Does nonpartisanship increase Republican influence in city government? It is sometimes argued that the removal of party designations from local elections hurts Democrats by disengaging their traditional support from urban voters—the low income, labor, ethnic, and Negro groups that traditionally vote the Democratic ticket. Moreover, the well educated, high income groups and interests that are normally Republican and have a natural edge in organization, communication, and prestige in the absence of parties have better chances for victory in nonpartisan elections. Republicans also have better turnout records in nonpartisan elections.[31] All of this may help to explain why many cities that are heavily Democratic in state and national elections elect mayors and councilmen who are somewhat more conservative. Eugene Lee found that the decline in voter turnout in local (nonpartisan) elections, in contrast to national (partisan) elections, is greatest in Democratic precincts and least in Republican precincts.[32] In other words, Democratic voters are less likely than Republican voters to cast ballots when the familiar party labels do not appear on the ballot and when a local Democratic organization does not prod them to the polls. Williams and Adrian conclude: "A nonpartisan election leads to an increased voice in local affairs for persons who normally vote Republican." [33]

It seems safe to conclude that a minority party member has a better chance of winning against a majority party member in a nonpartisan election than in a partisan election. And since the Democratic party is the majority party in most of the nation's large and middle size cities, nonpartisan elections probably make it easier for Republicans to win municipal office.

Does nonpartisanship result in "better qualified" candidates winning public office? Of course the answer to this question depends upon one's definition of better qualified. Nonpartisanship may result in more high income "respectable," white, Anglo-Saxon Protestants, with prestige jobs, running for public office. Minority group candidates are disadvantaged by nonpartisanship, for several reasons. First of all, as we have already observed, non-

[31] See Charles E. Gilbert, "Some Aspects of Nonpartisan Elections in Large Cities," *Midwest Journal of Political Science,* 6 (November, 1962), 346–54.

[32] Eugene C. Lee, *Nonpartisan Politics* (Berkeley: University of California Press, 1960).

[33] Williams and Adrian, *American Political Science Review,* p. 1063.

partisanship reduces the turnout of labor, low income, ethnic, Democratic voters, and consequently, increases the influence of well educated, high income, white, Anglo-Saxon Protestant Republican voters, who continue to come to the polls in nonpartisan elections. In addition, nonpartisanship means the recruitment of candidates will be left to civic associations, or ad hoc groups of one kind or another, rather than Democratic or Republican party organizations. This difference in recruitment and endorsement practices tends to give an advantage to middle class, white, Protestant candidates. Candidates from minority groups are rarely put forward and endorsed by newspapers and influential civic associations. They seldom receive the kind of public attention in private life that would make their names well known enough to place on a ballot, nor do they have the organizational ties or memberships that would bring them to the attention of civic associations which are recruiting in nonpartisan elections. In contrast, in partisan big city politics, being a member of a minority group may be a positive advantage. Parties traditionally try to "balance the ticket" with candidates who represent minority groups or ethnic groups, in rough proportion to their voting strength. This practice of having a balanced party ticket with Irish, Italian, Polish, Jewish and Negro names on the ballot is thought to add strength to the entire party ticket, since voters will be asked to vote for the party ticket rather than the individual candidates. Eugene C. Lee reports that the "typical" nonpartisan councilman is a registered Republican, 45 to 50 years old, who has a professional, managerial, or sales occupation and lives in the "better part of town." [34] He is likely to be a Protestant, a Mason, a member of the Chamber of Commerce, member of a Veterans Group, and have lived in the city for a long time, and to have made his mark in the Community Chest, the Red Cross, or some other civic or welfare association. Of course, there are exceptions to this generalization about nonpartisan candidates. Certainly, in nonpartisan Boston, one is more likely to encounter Irish or Italian Democrats on the city council than yankee Republicans.

Banfield and Wilson observed that the influence of newspapers in city politics is strengthened by nonpartisan elections. Newspapers are particularly important to the election of candidates in nonpartisan cities, where voters do not have party organizations to keep them informed about candidates. "You can't tell the players without a score card," a newspaperman remarked happily, "and we sell the score cards."

Nonpartisanship contributes to the re-election of incumbent councilmen, particularly when nonpartisanship is combined with at-large elections. Incumbents are more likely to have a name which is known to the voters. Gilbert and Clague found that in Chicago and Pittsburgh, with their ma-

---

[34] Lee, *Nonpartisan Politics,* p. 170.

chine style of politics, incumbent councilmen were easily re-elected.[35] However, incumbent councilmen in all other partisan cities were not re-elected as often as incumbents in nonpartisan cities. Moreover, incumbent councilmen running at-large in the city were more likely to be re-elected than incumbent councilmen running from districts. This suggests that it is difficult to hold public officials accountable in a nonpartisan election. The voter does not have the opportunity to hear organized criticisms of incumbent office holders from an opposition party. When the only challenge to an incumbent officeholder is an unknown name on the ballot, he is more likely to be re-elected than if he is challenged by a candidate backed by an opposition party. The higher rates of re-election in nonpartisan systems suggest that accountability is harder to achieve where party labels are absent.

What is the effect of nonpartisan elections on public policy? Nonpartisanship probably encourages the avoidance of issues in local elections and puts a premium on personal publicity. It is generally to the advantage of any candidate to avoid controversial questions and, therefore, important issues. Candidates generally utter bland generalities and try to differentiate themselves from other candidates on the basis of personality, integrity, or experience. A nonpartisan candidate has no obligation to support his party's position on public issues or to accept responsibility for decisions made by a mayor or other public officeholder who shares the same party label.

Policy Styles in Local Government

Community political systems have been classified according to their governmental structure and political style, but we can also classify them according to the types of policies their citizens and officials expect of them. Oliver P. Williams has suggested a typology of four different policy roles for local government: 1) promoting economic growth; 2) providing or securing life's amenities; 3) maintaining traditional public services, that is, a caretaker role; and 4) arbitrating among conflicting interests.[36]

A community whose major policy concern is the promotion of economic growth is interested in population expansion, industrial development, commercial activities, total wealth, and the like. This type of community is prepared to enact zoning regulations, reduce tax assessments, develop industrial parks, install utilities, and do whatever else may be required to attract business and industry and promote production. These policies may be most vigorously endorsed by business and commercial interests that have a stake in the community's growth, but the appeal of these policies is much broader.

[35] Charles E. Gilbert and Christopher Clague, "Electoral Participation and Electoral Systems in Large Cities," *Journal of Politics*, 24 (1962), 323–30.

[36] The following discussion relies upon Oliver P. Williams, "A Typology for Comparative Local Government," *Midwest Journal of Political Science*, 5 (May, 1961), 150–64.

A growing, thriving community infects its many residents with a certain pride that gives them a feeling of being a part of community progress. Of course it is the merchant, the chamber of commerce, the banker, the newspaper editor, and the city official who see each new resident as a potential customer, taxpayer, or contributor to the growth of their business enterprise. To aid in economic growth, a city should have a good reputation. This means politics should be conducted in a low key, the image of stability and regularity in city finances should be assured, and friendliness toward business should be the prevailing attitude of city officials.

The major policy concern of other communities is providing and securing life's amenities; that is, preserving a certain "way of life" that is highly valued by the residents and safeguarding and improving the advantages of the city as a place to live. "Amenity" communities are less concerned with economic growth and more concerned with providing the comforts of life for their citizens. Policies accent the home environment rather than the working environment—the citizen as consumer rather than producer. Laws stress safety, slowness, quiet, beauty, convenience, and restfulness. The rights of pedestrians and children take precedence over the claims of commerce. Neighborhoods are defended by rigid zoning laws and building codes, open space is guarded, traffic routed around the city, and noise and smoke curtailed. Population growth is not particularly welcome. Heavy industry is excluded. Since the costs of such policies are quite high, and these policies discourage business and industrial tax bases, amenity communities must have residential populations with above average incomes. Middle and upper income residential suburbs in large metropolitan areas are likely to be amenity communities. Amenities may also become the major concern of the traditional small town that is threatened by engulfment from a nearby, major urban complex. Such a small town may not have the middle class homogeneity of the exclusive suburb, but its amenities may not require the costly expenditures required in a suburb. Because the growth of the town was slow, necessary capital investments for amenities were amortized over a very long time. A sudden population influx threatens the way of life of the community and the cost of maintaining that way of life.

A caretaker government, on the other hand is expected to provide minimum public services in the community, and nothing more. Caretaker government is limited government, where extreme conservative views toward the role of government can be effectively realized. "Freedom" and "self reliance of the individual" are preferred over government programs of any kind. The overriding policy consideration is keeping the costs of government low. Tax increases are hardly ever justified. Nothing new is ever tried. Pressing public problems are passed onto higher levels of government (the county, state, or federal government) or given to private groups or charities (the chamber of commerce, the churches, or the Salvation Army), or they are ignored. Caretaker policies are often preferred by farmers, small merchants, and home owners who can barely afford the home they are buying and do not want to pay taxes for amenities of any kind.

A fourth type of local government role suggested by Williams is that of arbitrator between conflicting interests. Strictly speaking, this is not a policy role because emphasis is placed upon process of decision making rather than the substance of governmental action. An arbiter government is primarily concerned with managing conflict among competing interests and finding workable compromises that can be enacted into public policy. An arbiter government is more likely to be found in a heterogeneous community, where social and economic cleavages create demands for different policies, rather than in a homogeneous community, where there is substantial agreement on the proper policies for government to follow. Arbiter governments frequently exist in larger cities, and they are generally preferred by minority groups. As we have already observed, ethnic based, patronage oriented, political machines usually provide arbiter government. But such organizations are not confined to large cities; Williams himself describes an arbiter government in a middle size Michigan city. In an arbiter government, individual group access to decision making is more important than any substantive policy orientation.

Reform and Public Policy

What are the policy consequences of reform government? Other things being equal, do reformed cities pursue significantly different taxing and spending policies than unreformed cities? In an important study of taxing and spending in 200 American cities with populations of 50,000 or more,[37] Lineberry and Fowler found that reformed cities tended to tax and spend less than unreformed cities. Cities with manager governments and at-large council constituencies were less willing to spend money for public purposes than cities with mayor-council governments and ward constituencies. (However, cities with partisan elections did not tax or spend any more than cities with nonpartisan elections.) In short, reformism does save tax money.

Lineberry and Fowler also found that:

a. The more middle-class the city, measured by income, education, and occupation, the lower the general tax and spending levels.
b. The greater the home-ownership in a city, the lower the tax and spending levels.
c. The larger the percentage of religious and ethnic minorities in the population, the higher the city's taxes and expenditures.

[37] Robert L. Lineberry and Edmond P. Fowler, "Reformism and Public Policy in American Cities," *American Political Science Review*, LXI (September, 1967), 701–16.

What turned out to be an even more important finding in the Lineberry and Fowler study was the difference in *reponsiveness* of the two kinds of city governments to the socio-economic composition of their populations. Reformed cities (cities with manager governments, at-large constituencies, and nonpartisan elections) appeared to be unresponsive in tax and spending policies to differences in income, educational, occupational, religious, and ethnic characteristics of their populations. In contrast, unreformed cities (cities with mayor-council governments, ward constituencies, and partisan elections) reflected class, racial, and religious composition in their taxing and spending decisions.

Reformism tends to reduce the importance of class, home ownership, ethnicity, and religion in city politics. It tends to minimize the role which social conflicts play in public decision making. In contrast, mayor-council governments, ward constituencies, and partisan elections permit social cleavages to be reflected in city politics and public policy to be responsive to socio-economic factors.

11

METROPOLITICS:
CITIES AND SUBURBS

The Anatomy of a Metropolis

Two out of every three Americans live in 212 population clusters called metropolitan areas. The rapid growth of these population clusters in recent years is perhaps the most striking and significant social change occurring in America. Most of the nation's population increase is occurring in these metropolitan areas—the increase in metropolitan area population from 1950 to 1960 was 23.6 million, in contrast to a 4.4 million increase in the rest of the United States. Moreover, most of this increase in metropolitan population is occurring outside of the core cities in the nation's booming suburbs. The suburban population of the U.S., persons living in metropolitan areas but outside of the core city, grew by an amazing 48.5 per cent in a single decade, while the core cities grew only 10.8 per cent.

What is a metropolitan area? Briefly, a metropolitan area consists of a large central city of 50,000 or more persons together with the surrounding suburbs, which are socially and economically tied to the central city. The Census Bureau calls a metropolitan area a "Standard Metropolitan Statistical Area" (SMSA), and defines it as a city of 50,000 or more persons together with adjacent counties which have predominantly urban industrial populations with close ties to the central city.

Urban sociologists tell us that the very definition of metropolitan life

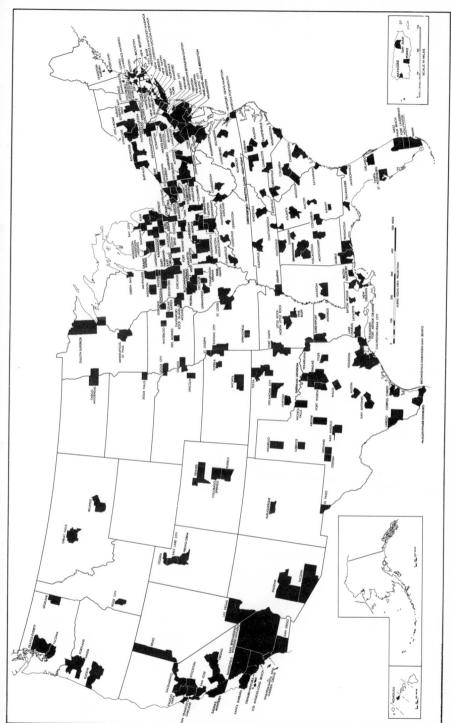

STANDARD METROPOLITAN STATISTICAL AREAS, JANUARY, 1968

SOURCE: U.S. Bureau of the Census.

involves *large numbers* of *different* types of people living *close together* who are socially and economically *dependent* upon one another.[1] *Numbers, density, heterogeneity,* and *interdependence* are said to be distinguishing characteristics of metropolitan life. It is not difficult to envision a metropolitan area as a large number of people living together; we can see these characteristics in metropolitan life from a map or an airplane window. But it is more difficult to understand the heterogeneity and interdependence of people living in metropolitan areas.

The modern economic system of the metropolis is based upon a highly specialized and complex division of labor. We are told that in the simple farm community, a dozen occupations exhausted the job opportunities available to men. An agricultural economy meant homogeneous employment opportunities; that is to say, nearly everyone was a farmer or was closely connected to and depended upon farming. But in the modern metropolis there are tens of thousands of different kinds of jobs. An industrial economy means highly specialized jobs and accounts for much of the heterogeneity in urban populations. There are wide differences between occupational worlds. It is on the basis of his job that the individual receives an income and his share of the goods and services available in life. Different jobs produce different levels of income, dress, and styles of living. The individual's job shapes the way he looks at the world and his evaluations of social and political events. In acquiring his job, he attains a certain level and type of education that also distinguishes him from those in other jobs with different educational requirements. Differences in educational level in turn produce a wide variety of differences and opinions, attitudes, and styles of living. Metropolitan living concentrates people with all of these different economic and occupational characteristics in a very few square miles. This is what is meant by heterogeneity in metropolitan life.

Ethnic and racial diversity are also present. A few decades ago opportunities for human betterment in the cities attracted immigrants from Ireland, Germany, Italy, Poland, and Russia; today, the city attracts Negroes, Puerto Ricans, and rural families. These newcomers to the metropolis bring with them different needs, attitudes, and ways of life. The "melting pot" tends to reduce some of this diversity over time, but the pot does not "melt" people immediately, and there always seem to be new arrivals.

People always differ in where they live and how they live. There is a certain uniformity to rural life; day-to-day family life on the farm is remarkably similar from one county to the next. But urban dwellers may live in apartments in the central city or in single family homes in the suburbs. Some urban dwellers choose a familistic style of life—raising two or more children in their own single family house, with the wife functioning

[1] See especially Scott Greer, *Governing the Metropolis* (New York: John Wiley & Sons, Inc., 1962).

as a homemaker. Others are less familistic—raising no children or a single child in a rented apartment with the wife holding down a job outside of the home.

The list of social, economic, and life style differences among the people in a metropolitan area is almost endless. Scott Greer writes, "The city is a maze, a social zoo, a mass of heterogeneous social types." [2] Moreover, urban sociologists tell us that people with different social, economic, and life style characteristics generally live in different parts of a metropolitan area. Physical separation of residences generally accompanies social and economic separation, and so there are "ghettos," "silk-stocking districts," "little Italys," middle class suburbs, and so on. This physical separation tends to emphasize and reinforce differences among people in a metropolitan area.

But another fundamental characteristic is interdependence. Rural living involves very little interdependence. While the traditional farm family was not wholly self-sufficient, its members were much less dependent upon the larger community for employment, goods, and services, than the modern metropolitan dweller.

In contrast, urban dwellers are highly dependent upon one another in their daily, economic, and social activities. Suburbanites, for example, rely upon the central city for food, clothing, newspapers, entertainment, hospitalization, and a host of other modern household needs. More importantly, they rely upon the central city for employment opportunities. Conversely, the central city relies upon the suburbs to supply its labor and management forces. Downtown merchants look to the entire metropolitan area for consumers. This interdependence involves an intricate web of economic and social relationships, a high degree of communication, and a great deal of daily physical interchange among residents, groups, and firms in a metropolitan area. Just as specialization produces diversity among men, it also produces interdependence and the need for coordinated human activity.

Suburbs account for most of the growth of America's metropolitan areas. In the last decade, more than 10 million Americans moved to the suburbs. Rows upon rows of "ranches," "split-levels," and "cape cods" now encircle our major cities as if to lay siege to them. No other sector of American life has grown so rapidly. Very few large *central cities* are growing in size; metropolitan areas are growing because their *suburbs* are growing (see Table 11.1). This suburbanization is due to technological advances in transportation—the automobile and the expressway. In the 19th century an industrial worker had to live within walking distance of his place of employment. This meant that the 19th century American city crowded large masses of people into relatively small central areas, often in tenement

[2] *Ibid.,* p. 5.

TABLE 11.1

POPULATION GROWTH IN CITIES AND SUBURBS
OF METROPOLITAN AREAS

	Total U.S. population	Metropolitan area	Central cities	Suburbs
1960				
Population (000)	179,993	111,886	57,360	54,526
Percent of total	100.0	62.3	31.9	30.3
1966				
Population (000)	195,857	123,773	58,518	65,255
Percent of total	100.0	63.2	29.9	33.3
Percentage Increase, 1960-1966	8.8	10.6	2.0	19.7

houses and other high density neighborhoods. But new modes of transportation—first the streetcar, then the private automobile, and now the expressway—eliminated the necessity of workers living close to their jobs. Now a man can spend his working hours in a central business district office or industrial plant and spend his evenings in a residential suburb many miles away. The same technology that led to the suburbanization of residences has also influenced commercial and industrial location. Originally industry was tied to waterways or railroads for access to supplies and markets. This dependence has been reduced by the development of motor truck transportation, the highway system, and the greater mobility of the labor force. Now many industries can locate in the suburbs, particularly light industries, which do not require extremely heavy bulk shipment that can only be handled by rail or water. When industry and people move to the suburbs, commerce follows. Giant suburban shopping centers have sprung up to compete with downtown stores. Thus, metropolitan areas are becoming decentralized over time as people, business, and industry spread themselves over the suburban landscape. As Lewis Mumford puts it: "The city has burst open and scattered its complex organs and organizations over the entire landscape." [3]

How far will the trend towards suburbanization go? There is good reason to believe that suburbanization will continue until America becomes one vast sprawling suburban development.[4] Jean Gottmann, a French geographer, has described a vast urban complex that stretches from New Hampshire to Virginia, where the suburbs of one metropolitan area blend with

[3] Lewis Mumford, *The City in History* (New York: Harcourt, Brace, & World, 1961), p. 34.
[4] Oscar Handlin and John Burchard, eds., *The Historian and the City* (Cambridge: Harvard-M.I.T. Press, 1963), p. 1.

FIGURE 11.2

THE MEGALOPOLIS

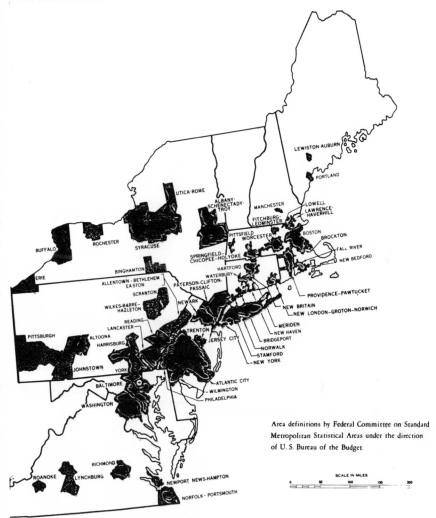

Area definitions by Federal Committee on Standard
Metropolitan Statistical Areas under the direction
of U. S. Bureau of the Budget.

SOURCE: U.S. Bureau of the Census.

the suburbs of another metropolitan area all along the northeastern coast
of the United States.[5] (See Fig. 11.2.)

Another characteristic of metropolitan areas is "fragmented" government. This is another result of suburbanization. Suburban development,

[5] Jean Gottmann, *Megalopolis: The Urbanized Northeastern Seaboard of the
United States* (New York: Twentieth Century Fund, 1961).

TABLE 11.2

LOCAL GOVERNMENTS IN METROPOLITAN AREAS

	Number of local governments
Total in 212 SMSA's*	18,442
Municipalities	4,144
Townships	2,573
Counties	310
Special districts	5,411
School districts	6,004
Total in selected SMSA's	
Chicago, Illinois	1,060
Philadelphia, Pennsylvania	963
Pittsburgh, Pennsylvania	806
New York, New York	555
St. Louis, Missouri	440
San Francisco-Oakland, Calif.	398
Portland, Oregon	374
Los Angeles, California	348
Seattle, Washington	281
Minneapolis-St. Paul, Minnesota	261
San Bernardino, California	250

*Standard Metropolitan Statistical Areas
Source: U.S. Bureau of the Census, *Census of Governments, 1962,* Vol. V., p. 3.

spreading out from central cities, generally ignored governmental boundaries and engulfed counties, townships, towns, and smaller cities. Twenty-six of 212 metropolitan areas even spread across state lines, and four metropolitan areas of the United States—Detroit, San Diego, El Paso, and Laredo—adjoin urban territory in Canada and Mexico. This suburbanization has meant that hundreds of governments may be operating in a single metropolitan area. Thus, while metropolitan areas are characterized by social and economic interdependence, and consequently require coordinating mechanisms, metropolitan government is generally "fragmented" into many smaller jurisdictions, none of which is capable of governing the entire metropolitan area in a unified fashion.

James Madison argues effectively that the source of political conflict is diversity among men.[6] Madison's insight into diversity as a source of political conflict is important in understanding metropolitan politics. Since a metropolitan area consists of a large number of different kinds of people living closely together, the problem of regulating conflict and maintaining order in a heterogenous metropolitan community assumes tremendous proportions. Persons with different occupations, income, and education levels

[6] *The Federalist,* Number 10.

are known to have different views on a wide variety of public issues. Persons well equipped to compete for jobs and income in a free market sometimes have different views about government housing and welfare programs than those not so well equipped. People at the bottom of the social ladder have a different view toward police, and government authority in general, than those on higher rungs. Persons who have a large investment in property view taxation in a different light from those who do not. Families with children have different ideas about school systems than those without children. And so it goes. Differences among men and the way they make their living, in their income and education levels, and the color of their skin, and the way they worship, and their style of living, and so on, are at the roots of political life in the metropolis.

Social, economic, and racial conflict can be observed at all levels of government, but at the metropolitan level, it is most obvious in the conflict that occurs between central cities and their suburbs. At the heart of city-suburban conflict are the differences in the kinds of people who live in cities and suburbs. And city-suburban conflict is at the heart of "the metropolitan problem"; that is, the failure to achieve metropolitanwide consensus on public policy questions affecting the entire metropolitan area and the failure to develop metropolitan government institutions. It is very difficult to arrive at metropolitanwide consensus about questions involving mass transit, highway construction, the sharing of welfare costs, tax burdens, water supply and sewage disposal problems, planning and zoning, housing policy (including the concentration of Negroes in central cities), and a host of other problems. We shall refer to the social, economic, and racial differences between city and suburb as "social distance." This social distance accounts for much conflict between cities and suburbs and constitutes the chief obstacle to the development of metropolitanwide policies and government institutions.

Of course, generalizing about cities and suburbs is a dangerous thing. While we will talk about some common characteristics of cities and suburbs, students are cautioned that individual suburbs may be quite different from one another, just as there are wide differences between social and economic groups living in central cities. Nonetheless, a clear perception of the social distance between cities and suburbs is important in understanding metropolitan politics.

Cities and suburbs can be differentiated, first of all, on the basis of occupation, income, and educational levels of their populations. The cultured class of an earlier era established "country" living as a symbol of affluence; widespread prosperity has made possible mass imitation of the aristocracy by an upwardly mobile middle class population. The occupational, education, and income characteristics of persons living in the suburbs of our nation's large metropolitan areas can be clearly differentiated

TABLE 11.3

SOCIAL, ECONOMIC, AND LIFE STYLE DIFFERENCES BETWEEN CITIES AND SUBURBS

	Average for United States	Average for 212 SMSA's	
		Central cities	Suburbs
White collar occupation (percent of work force)	41.1	45.9	50.3
Median family income	$5660	$5945	$7114
Families under $3000 (percent of all families)	21.4	17.6	9.9
Families over $10,000 (percent of all families)	15.1	16.6	24.1
Median school year completed	10.6	10.7	12.0
High school graduates (percent)	41.1	40.9	50.9
Nonwhite percentage	11.2	17.4	4.4
Foreign born percentage	5.4	8.8	6.4
Mobility (percent living in different county 5 years ago)	17.4	14.0	21.1
Fertility rate (children ever born per 1,000 females)	1,746	1,541	1,715
Families with children under 6 (percent of all families)	30.8	28.4	33.7
Females in labor force (percent of all females over 14)	34.5	39.6	34.1

from those of central city dwellers. The suburbs house the greater proportions of white collar employees, of college graduates, and of affluent families than any other sector in American life. Table 11.3 contrasts several common measures of social status for American central cities and suburbs. Status differentials in favor of suburbs are more pronounced in larger metropolitan areas; Leo Schnore reports that status differentials in smaller metropolitan areas are not as great as in larger areas, and sometimes even favor the city rather than the suburbs.[7] However, on the whole, suburban living reflects middle class values.[8] And, social differences between city and suburb are increasing rather than decreasing, as middle class Americans continue to flee from the central city to the suburbs, and lower income, occupational, and educational groups are concentrated in central cities.

Cities and suburbs can also be differentiated on the basis of "familism," or life style. Perhaps the most frequently mentioned reason for a move to

[7] Leo Schnore, "The Socio-economic Status of Cities and Suburbs," *American Sociological Review*, 28 (February, 1963), 76–85.
[8] See Robert C. Wood, *Suburbia: Its People and Their Politics* (New York: Houghton Mifflin Co., 1958).

the suburbs is "the kids." Family after family lists consideration to their young as the primary cause for their move to suburbia. The city is hardly the place for most child-centered amenities. A familistic or child-centered life style can be identified in certain social statistics. One measure is the "fertility ratio" or the number of children born per 1000 women from 15 to 44 years of age. Another measure is the percentage of women aged 14 or over who are in the work force. A large number of children per 1000 married females of childbearing age, together with a small proportion of women who work, suggest a family-centered environment. In addition, the single family, free-standing home is the *sine qua non* of familistic living in an affluent society. Cumulatively, these three life style measures are said to identify a familistic or child-centered way of life. Table 11.3 shows that: (1) there are proportionately more children in the suburbs than in the central cities; (2) a larger proportion of suburban mothers stay at home to take care of these children; and (3) a larger proportion of suburban families are housed in single family units. The nonfamilistic life style is characteristic of the central city where there are proportionately fewer children, more apartment living, and greater numbers of employed mothers. A familistic style of life in suburbia suggests the importance of the most fundamental of all child amenities—the school.

Again, it should be pointed out that the suburbs of smaller metropolitan areas are less differentiated from their central cities in terms of life style than the suburbs of larger metropolitan areas. Smaller cities seem to be able to support a familistic life style almost as well as their suburbs.

Perhaps the most important difference between cities and suburbs is their contrasting racial composition. Negro populations in most large cities are growing at a very rapid rate, partly from natural increases and partly from migration from the rural South. New arrivals go into Negro slums, which almost everywhere are located in the oldest part of the central city. The increases in nonwhite populations in large central cities in recent years has been truly astounding. Table 11.4 shows the increase in nonwhite populations of the 50 largest cities in the United States, from 1950 to 1960, together with changes in the white populations in these cities. The nonwhite population of New York, for example, increased 47 per cent in that decade. At the same time the white populations of these central cities have been fleeing to the suburbs. New York lost 7 per cent of its white population that decade. Very few large cities gained in white population. The result has been striking changes in the racial composition of central cities.

Many whites have fled to the suburbs to get away from heavy concentrations of Negroes in central cities. One reason why many suburbanites may want to remain politically separate from the central cities is that it might make it easier for them to resist "invasion" by Negroes. As Negroes gain majorities in central cities, they too, may resist metropolitan govern-

TABLE 11.4

NONWHITE POPULATION AS A PERCENT OF TOTAL POPULATION, 1950
AND 1960, AND PERCENT CHANGE IN WHITE AND NONWHITE POPULATION,
1950-1960, 50 LARGEST CITIES IN CONTINENTAL UNITED STATES.

Region and City	Percent nonwhite		Percent change, 1950-1960	
	1950	1960	White	Nonwhite
Northeast				
New York	9.8	14.7	- 6.7	47.2
Philadelphia	18.3	26.7	-13.3	41.2
Boston	5.3	9.8	-17.1	59.9
Pittsburgh	12.3	16.8	-15.3	22.3
Buffalo	6.5	13.8	-15.3	94.7
Newark	17.2	34.4	-26.8	84.2
Rochester	2.4	7.6	- 9.3	208.8
Jersey City	7.0	13.5	-14.1	77.8
North Central				
Chicago	14.1	23.6	-12.8	64.4
Detroit	16.4	29.2	-23.5	60.4
Cleveland	16.3	28.9	-18.6	69.3
St. Louis	18.0	28.8	-24.0	39.9
Milwaukee*	3.6	10.5	-10.1	185.5
Cincinnati*	15.6	22.0	- 9.4	39.4
Minneapolis	1.6	3.2	- 9.0	84.2
Indianapolis*	15.0	23.0	- 9.1	53.9
Kansas City*	12.3	19.3	-12.7	49.9
Columbus, O.*	12.5	19.0	- 2.4	58.8
Toledo*	8.3	13.5	- 7.1	59.4
St. Paul	2.0	3.0	- 0.3	49.8
Omaha*	6.7	10.0	0.4	54.7
Akron	8.7	13.1	0.7	58.7
Dayton*	14.1	22.8	-15.4	52.7
Wichita*	5.0	11.7	- 5.4	138.8
South				
Baltimore	23.8	35.0	-15.6	45.3
Houston*	21.1	26.0	8.1	42.1
Washington, D.C.	35.4	54.8	-33.3	47.3
Dallas*	13.2	18.7	4.9	59.2
New Orleans	32.0	37.4	1.2	28.6
San Antonio*	7.2	7.9	8.9	20.0
Memphis*	37.2	42.7	- 1.2	24.1
Atlanta*	36.6	46.6	-19.6	21.2
Louisville*	15.7	21.4	-17.1	21.6
Fort Worth*	13.1	17.3	2.4	40.0
Birmingham*	39.9	41.1	- 1.5	3.8
Oklahoma City*	9.3	13.8	- 0.9	54.9
Norfolk*	29.7	32.6	- 2.3	11.8
Miami	16.3	22.6	8.2	62.2
El Paso*	2.6	3.1	5.8	91.8
Tampa*	22.0	29.0	- 1.7	42.1
Tulsa	10.0	14.0	-16.1	22.0

Region and City	Percent nonwhite		Percent change, 1950-1960	
	1950	1960	White	Nonwhite
West				
Los Angeles	10.7	16.8	17.2	97.2
San Francisco	10.5	18.4	-12.9	66.8
San Diego*	5.5	8.5	46.9	135.1
Seattle*	5.8	9.8	- 3.5	69.5
Denver*	4.4	7.7	5.8	91.8
Phoenix*	6.2	8.4	- 2.3	34.6
Portland, Ore.*	3.5	5.7	- 5.4	57.6
Oakland	14.5	26.4	-17.7	73.9
Long Beach*	2.6	5.1	10.7	121.7

*Extensive annexations occurred during the 1950-1960 decade; data refer to populations within the 1950 boundaries at both dates.

mental consolidation in order to avoid dilution of their political power through merger with white suburbs. The restriction of suburban home sales to whites only and the generally higher costs of suburban homes and property have made it difficult or impossible for Negroes to follow whites to the suburbs in any significant number. The nonwhite percentage of all U.S. suburbs was 4.4 per cent in 1960 in contrast to a nonwhite percentage for all central cities of 17.4 per cent.

American life is becoming more, not less, segregated over time. These population statistics clearly show that America is building racial "ghettos" in its large central cities and surrounding them with white middle class suburbs. As the population exodus to the suburbs continues, cities are becoming increasingly bereft of their middle class, white, high income, tax paying populations. Increasingly, nonwhite, low income, low education, unskilled, nonfamilistic populations are being concentrated in the central cities. This means we have also concentrated the problems of these people in downtown areas—racial imbalance, crime, violence, inadequate education, poverty, slum housing, and so on. By moving to the suburbs, white middle class families not only separate themselves from Negroes and poor people, but they also place physical distance between themselves and the major social problems that confront metropolitan areas. This permits them, for the time being, to ignore problems of slum housing, poor schools, expanding welfare rolls, crime and juvenile delinquency, and rioting in the central cities.

Political Differences Between Cities and Suburbs

City and suburban social differences are reflected in divergent political patterns in cities and suburbs. Table 11.5 shows that, in general, large

TABLE 11.5

DEMOCRATIC AND REPUBLICAN PARTY VOTE IN CITIES AND SUBURBS IN PRESIDENTIAL ELECTIONS

	1956		1960		1964	
	Dem.	Rep.	Dem.	Rep.	Dem.	Rep.
New York City	51.0	49.0	62.8	37.2	73.2	26.8
Suburban counties						
Rockland	29.0	71.0	45.0	55.0	63.7	36.3
Westchester	27.8	72.2	43.2	56.8	62.0	38.0
Nassau	30.9	69.1	44.8	55.2	60.5	39.5
Suffolk	22.3	77.7	40.6	59.4	55.5	44.5
Chicago	49.0	51.0	63.6	36.4	71.0	29.0
Cook County outside of Chicago	27.7	72.3	40.9	59.1	52.1	47.9
Philadelphia	57.1	42.9	68.1	31.9	73.7	26.3
Suburban counties						
Bucks	39.1	60.9	45.7	54.3	60.6	39.4
Chester	29.7	70.3	36.2	63.8	54.1	45.9
Delaware	38.0	62.0	47.8	52.2	56.8	43.2
Montgomery	30.7	69.3	39.2	60.8	56.7	43.3
Detroit	61.8	38.2	71.0	29.0	80.0	20.0
Wayne Co. outside of Detroit	49.6	50.4	57.7	42.3	30.3	69.7
Pittsubrgh	52.3	47.7	67.0	33.0	74.7	25.3
Allegheny Co. outside of Pittsburgh	40.3	59.7	51.5	48.5	61.7	38.3
St. Louis	61.0	39.0	66.6	33.4	77.7	22.3
St. Louis Co.	46.9	44.1	51.3	48.7	61.3	38.7
San Francisco	48.0	52.0	57.8	42.8	71.2	28.8
Suburban counties						
Marin	33.8	65.2	42.5	57.5	61.7	38.3
San Mateo	38.8	61.2	48.0	52.0	64.3	35.7
Cleveland	54.6	45.4	70.9	29.1	82.8	17.2
Cuyahoga Co. outside of Cleveland	37.4	62.6	49.9	50.1	62.6	37.4
Minneapolis	48.3	51.7	52.3	47.7	65.6	34.4
Hennepin Co. outside of Minneapolis	38.6	61.4	44.5	55.5	55.1	44.9
Buffalo	42.3	57.7	64.9	35.1	79.7	20.3
Erie Co. outside of Buffalo	29.5	70.5	48.6	51.4	67.5	32.5
Milwaukee	47.3	52.7	61.8	38.2	70.0	30.0
Milwaukee Co. outside of Milwaukee	34.6	65.4	49.1	50.9	56.7	43.3
Cincinnati	37.5	62.5	50.4	49.6	62.0	38.0
Hamilton Co. outside of Cincinnati	28.3	71.7	39.4	60.6	57.7	42.3

Source: R.M. Scammon, *America Votes* (Washington: Government Affairs Institute, 1966).

cities are much more Democratic than their suburban rings, which are generally Republican. While temporary shifts may occur from one election to another, this general pattern of Democratic cities and Republican suburbs is likely to prevail for the foreseeable future. As long as the national Democratic party represents central city, low income, ethnic, labor, and racial constituencies, and the Republican party represents middle class, educated, managerial, white, Anglo-Saxon, Protestant constituencies, the political coloration of cities and suburbs is likely to be different. Persons who are leaving cities for the suburbs include a disproportionate number of Republicans. Their places in the cities are being taken by Negroes, Puerto Ricans, and poor whites, most of whom are normally Democratic in their politics.

There is, of course, the possibility that the conflict over race in central cities may drive a wedge in the Democratic party coalition between Negroes and white, low income, ethnic minorities. In some cities, where the Democratic party has consistently championed Negro interests, the Republican party has won "backlash" votes in low income, ethnic, working class wards among Italian, Polish, and Irish voters who normally cast Democratic votes. But "backlash" voting may not in the long run prove a solid basis for a Republican surge in the central cities. Another possible challenge to the Democratic cities–Republican suburbs pattern is the increasing affluence of ethnic, working class populations in America, which permits many of them to buy suburban homes and leave their central city neighborhoods. If these new suburbanites retain their ethnic and labor affiliations and traditions of Democratic party voting, they could make serious inroads into Republican party strength in the suburbs. However, while some low income, industrial suburbs regularly support the Democratic ticket, on the whole, the Republican suburban vote percentages have suffered very little from the vast increase in suburban population. In fact, suburban population explosion has saved the Republican party the slow death that it would have experienced if its appeal had been limited to the diminishing ranks of small town and rural voters.

These party differences suggest that for many years to come it will be difficult, if not impossible, to achieve the consolidation of metropolitan governments. Metropolitan consolidation schemes would place Democratic control of central cities in jeopardy, just as it may threaten Republican control of suburban counties. Political leaders, both Democratic and Republican, are not likely to view with favor any proposal that would substitute political insecurity for "a good thing." Republican party leaders outside central cities are just as well satisfied with a local one party system as are the Democrats of the central cities.

In commenting on city-suburban political differences, Edward C. Banfield also pointed out the following political problems raised by metropolitan government:

> It would be a mistake to suppose that the conflict lies altogether or even mainly between the two party organizations or among the professional politicians who have a stake in them. The party differences are important in themselves, but they reflect deeper but still more important differences.

Metropolitan government would mean the transfer of power over the central cities from the largely lower class Negro and Catholic elements who live in them to the largely middle-class, white, and Protestant elements who live in the suburbs . . .

The few Republicans of the central cities, and in general, the good government forces—in short, all those who want to weaken the Democratic machines—will favor adding the suburban vote to the central city vote wherever the suburbs are predominantly middle or upper class . . .

As the Negro tide rises in the central cities, many white Democrats begin to think of annexation and consolidation as ways to maintain a white (but alas, a Republican!) majority. Unless there is consolidation, some cities will probably have Negro mayors within the next 20 years. Negroes can be expected to oppose annexation and consolidation under these circumstances, of course.[9]

In other words, metropolitan government threatens the political status quo, where both Democrats and Republicans share political power. It threatens to replace this happy arrangement with a "winner take all" political system, which threatens both Democratic and Republican party interests in metropolitan areas.

City and suburban social differences are also reflected in the divergent public policies of city and suburban governments. First of all, there is some evidence that the child-centered character of suburban living produces higher educational expenditures in suburbs than in cities. Suburban parents with high hopes and plans for their children's occupational success tend to focus more concern upon the school system, and spend more money on it per pupil, than city residents (see Table 11.6). (Of course, in smaller metropolitan areas, where social and life style differences between city and suburb are slight, differences between city and suburb in educational expenditures are very slight and occasionally run opposite from the expected direction.)

Large central cities show substantially higher operating expenditures per capita than their suburbs. The maintenance of a large physical plant for the entire metropolitan area requires city residents to make higher per capita operating expenditures than those required for suburbanites. In addition, many living costs in suburban communities are shifted from public to private spending (private septic tanks instead of public sewers, private instead of public recreation, and so on). Differences in the public services provided by city and suburban governments are greatest in the area of police protection, recreation, and health. This reflects a concentration in the city of people who are likely to require these public services, in contrast to the suburbs.

The tax bill in suburbs may be slightly lower than in central cities. Taxes had much to do with the migration of the "pioneer" suburbanites, those

[9] Edward C. Banfield, "The Politics of Metropolitan Area Organizations," *Midwest Journal of Political Science*, 1 (May, 1957), 77–91.

TABLE 11.6

DIFFERENTIAL IN TAX AND EXPENDITURE POLICIES OF CITY AND
SUBURBAN GOVERNMENTS IN WISCONSIN BY URBANIZED AREA, 1960

| | Total operating school expenditures $ per pupil | Total operating munic- ipal expenditures $ per capita | Full value property tax rate (in mills) | | | | Indebtedness | |
			Total	Munic- ipal	School	County	$ per capita	$ per $1000 full value
Milwaukee area								
City	438	87	31.0	11.3	12.4	8.9	163	32
18 suburbs	590	67	26.7	4.0	13.2	9.1	189	28
Madison area								
City	441	75	25.9	9.9	11.7	4.4	223	40
7 suburbs	467	31	25.2	2.8	17.3	4.8	79	22
Green Bay area								
City	455	69	22.5	6.6	10.3	5.3	178	32
6 suburbs	405	34	20.0	4.4	9.8	5.8	55	11
Racine area								
City	401	62	24.9	7.5	13.4	3.8	204	40
5 suburbs	394	24	18.0	1.4	15.0	3.9	4	1
Kenosha area								
City	435	62	26.5	5.7	15.0	5.6	201	40
2 suburbs	365	12	22.2	.9	14.8	6.0	0	0

Source: Thomas R. Dye, "City-Suburban Social Distance and Public Policy",
Social Forces, 44 (September, 1965), 100-106.

who moved to the suburbs in the 1930's and 1940's. At that time, suburban
living offered a significant savings in property taxation over what were
thought to be heavy city taxes. But the tax advantage of the suburbs turned
out partly to be a "self-denying prophecy": the more people who fled to
the suburbs to avoid heavy taxes, the greater the demand for public services in these new suburban communities, and the higher suburban taxes
became to meet these new demands. Yet, the tax bill in most suburbs remains lower than in central cities. The difference in tax burden between
city and suburb would be even greater if suburbanities did not choose to
spend more per pupil in education than city residents, which produces
higher school taxes in the suburbs. The suburbs also manage to limit their
indebtedness more than cities, and most of the indebtedness incurred by the
suburbs is for school, rather than municipal, purposes.

Finally, it should be noted that policy differences between city and suburb in smaller metropolitan areas do not appear to be as great as policy differences in cities and suburbs in larger metropolitan areas. This corresponds to our earlier point that social and economic differences between city and suburb in smaller metropolitan areas are not as great as in larger metropolitan areas. Of course, it should also be remembered that all of these generalizations about cities and suburbs are, indeed, generalizations. Individual cities and suburbs can be found that do not conform to these national patterns.

The So-called Metropolitan Problem

The term "metropolitan problem" has been given to any situation requiring cooperation between city and suburban governments. And there is hardly any governmental activity that has not been identified as a metropolitan problem. Too often civic reformers have tended to limit the discussion of metropolitan problems to the technical problems of providing public services in a metropolis, such as water supply, sewage disposal, transportation, and fire and police protection. But metropolitan problems include all the major social and economic problems confronting American society. Poverty, racial hatred, slum housing, crime and juvenile delinquency, financial crisis—these problems may be "national" in scope, but they occur principally in the metropolis.[10] In short, the major social problems facing American society are also "metropolitan problems." Nor is it possible to argue convincingly that these major social, economic problems are problems of central cities rather than of the entire metropolitan area. John C. Bollens and Henry J. Schmandt in *The Metropolis* addressed themselves to this point very effectively:

> Some myopic defenders of suburbia go so far as to say that the major socio-economic problems of urban society are problems of the central city, not those of the total metropolitan community. Where but within the boundaries of the core city, they ask, does one find an abundance of racial strife, crime, blight of housing, and welfare recipients? Superficially, their logic may seem sound, since they are in general correct about the prevalent spatial location of these maladies. Although crime and other social problems exist in suburbia, their magnitude and extent are substantially less than in the central city. But why in an interdependent metropolitan community should the responsibility of suburbanites be any less than that of the central city dwellers? Certainly no one would think of contending that residents of higher income neighborhoods within the corporate limits of the city should be exempt from responsibility for its less fortunate districts. What logic then is there in

[10] Mitchel Gordon, *Sick Cities: The Psychology and Pathology of American Urban Life* (New York: The Macmillan Co., 1963), pp. 339–40.

believing that neighborhoods on the other side of a legal line can wash their hands of social disorders in these sections?

... No large community can hope to reap the benefits of industrialization and urbanization and yet escape their less desirable byproducts. The suburbanite and the central city resident share the responsibility for the total community and its problems. Neither can run fast enough to escape involvement sooner or later.[11]

Many scholars over the years have insisted that "the metropolitan problem" was essentially the problem of "fragmented" government—that is, the proliferation of governments in metropolitan areas and the lack of coordination of public programs.[12] The objective of the metropolitan reform movement of the last 30 years was to reorganize, consolidate, and enlarge government jurisdictions. The goal was to rid metropolitan areas of "ineffective multiple local jurisdictions" and "governments which do not coincide with the boundaries of the metropolis."

Many advantages were claimed for metropolitan governmental reorganization. First of all, the reorganization and consolidation of metropolitan governments was expected to bring about *improved public services* as a result of centralization. Consolidation of governments was expected to achieve many economies of large scale operations and enable government to provide specialized public services, which "fragmented" units of government could not provide. For example, larger water treatment plant facilities can deliver water at lower per gallon costs, and larger sewage disposal plants can handle sewage at a lower per gallon cost of disposal. An example of specialized public services that could be provided on a metropolitan-wide level were police crime laboratories, central record systems, and central communications systems, which cannot be provided by small suburban police forces. Robert Wood described the technical and administrative arguments for the metropolitan government consolidation as follows:

Technical specialist after technical specialist moves from one city to another, engaging in painstaking operations of conditions in his own proficiency, and solemnly proclaiming that no public health department would work properly without a clientele of at least 50,000 people; or that no zoning regulation made sense without reference to a master plan for the whole region; or that no police force could support a qualified laboratory until x number of precinct stations were in being to refer to sufficient quantity of cases to keep scientific technicians analyzing at optimum speed.[13]

[11] John C. Bollens and Henry J. Schmandt, *The Metropolis* (New York: Harper & Row, Publishers, 1965), pp. 249–50.

[12] See Luther Gulick, *The Metropolitan Problem and American Ideas* (New York: Alfred A. Knopf, Inc., 1962).

[13] Robert C. Wood, "A Division of Powers in Metropolitan Areas," *Area and Power*, Arthur Maass, ed. (Glencoe: Free Press, 1959), p. 59.

Secondly, it was argued that metropolitan consolidation would provide the necessary *coordination of public services* for the metropolis. Study after study reported that disease, crime, fire, traffic congestion, air pollution, water pollution, and so on, do not respect municipal boundary lines. The transportation problem is the most common example of a coordination problem. Traffic experts have pleaded for the development of a balanced transportation system in which mass transit carries many of the passengers currently travelling in private automobiles. Experience indicates that new expressways are congested during peak hours on the day that they are opened. Yet mass transit requires decisive public action by the entire metropolitan area. Metropolitan reformers have contended that the absence of metropolitan government has also contributed to the inability to solve traffic problems. Certainly, the city government is in a poor position to provide mass transit by itself without the support of the suburbanites who will be riding on it. And of course small suburban governments are totally inadequate to this task. The demonstrated inability of local government to deal with the transportation problem has shifted attention to Washington. Action in many metropolitan areas on mass transit has come to a near standstill, awaiting the helping hand of the federal government. It is argued by some that this sad state of affairs may not have come about if strong, metropolitanwide governments had been in existence that could have acted effectively to solve the mass transit problem at the local level.

The third major argument for metropolitan consolidation stresses the need to eliminate *inequalities in financial burdens* throughout the metropolitan area. Suburbanites who escaped many city taxes continue to add to the cities' traffic and parking problems, use city streets and parks, find employment in the cities, use city hospitals and cultural facilities, and so on. By concentrating the poor uneducated, unskilled minorities in central cities, we also saddle central cities with costly problems of public health and welfare, crime control, fire protection, slum clearance, and the like, all the social problems which are associated with poverty and discrimination. We concentrate these costly problems in cities at the same time that middle class, taxpaying individuals, taxpaying commercial enterprises, and taxpaying industries are moving into the suburbs. Thus, metropolitan governmental fragmentation often succeeds in segregating financial needs from resources.[14]

The financial crisis facing the central cities has resulted in their turning to Washington for financial support. Direct federal grants to cities began with the Housing Act of 1937, when the federal government initiated its financial support for public housing and urban renewal. There is now a truly staggering array of federal grant-in-aid programs for cities—for com-

[14] See Lyle C. Fitch, "Metropolitan Financial Problems," *Annals of the American Academy of Social and Political Science* (November, 1957), pp. 66–73.

munity facilities, sewage and water plants, urban planning, mass transit, urban beautification, air pollution control, schools and hospitals, ports, airports, and so on.

It might be argued that metropolitan government, by eliminating financial inequalities between cities and suburbs, may have reduced the dependence of city governments on federal handouts and enabled the metropolitan areas to solve at least some of their financial problems themselves.

It is also argued that metropolitan government would *clearly establish responsibility for metropolitanwide policy.* One of the consequences of "fragmented" government is the scattering of public authority and the decentralization of policy making in the metropolis.[15] This proliferation in the number of autonomous governmental units reduces the probability of developing a consensus on metropolitan policy. Each autonomous unit exercises a veto over metropolitan policy within its jurisdiction; it is often impossible to secure the unanimity required to achieve metropolitan consensus on any metropolitanwide problem. An opponent of any particular solution need only find, among the countless independent governmental bodies whose consent is required, one that can be induced to withhold its consent in order to obstruct action.

Fragmented government divides political power into many small units with limited jurisdiction. As a result, decisions on matters of general concern, such as improving mass transit or water pollution, may be binding on only a portion of the metropolitan area. The dispersion of power among a large number of governmental units makes it possible for each of them to reach decisions without concern for the possible spill-over effects, which may be harmful to other governments or residents of the metropolis.

Metropolitan leadership has no institutional means of implementing metropolitanwide policy proposals. There is no metropolitanwide government, with the legal authority or political relationship with a metropolitan constituency, capable of resolving metropolitan conflict, developing consensus in metropolitan policy, or implementing metropolitan projects. As a result, metropolitan leadership, what there is of it, must be content to transmit its proposals for metropolitànwide policy to a large number of separate governmental units, where its reception depends upon voluntary acceptance. Moreover, the decision of these independent units to accept a proposal is usually based on the *local* effect of the proposal rather than its impact upon the total metropolitan community. The proliferation of metropolitan governments, with a scattering of public authority and the overlapping of governmental jurisdictions, makes it extremely difficult even for the most conscientious citizen to hold public officials accountable for their decisions. Conscientious citizens have enough difficulty remaining reasonably

[15] See Robert C. Wood, *1400 Governments* (Cambridge: Harvard University Press, 1961).

knowledgeable about local, state and national affairs, without sorting through the maze of city, county, township, school district, authority, and special district governments, which operate in metropolitan areas. Metropolitan government, it is argued, could simplify and streamline government organization in the metropolis and make it easier for citizens to hold public officials accountable and responsible for their decisions.

The Case for "Fragmented" Government

So long as we view local government exclusively as a mechanism for providing municipal services, the "fragmented" character of metropolitan government will have appeared to be obsolete and in need of reform. Highway location, sewage systems, water systems, public utilities, mass transit, recreational facilities, law enforcement, and land use control would be among the particular services that would benefit by metropolitan consolidation.

But, the suburbanite does not look upon the efficient provision of public service as the *only* function of local government. Nor does he look upon "the optimum development of the metropolitan region" as a particularly compelling goal. Rather, there are a variety of social, political, and psychological values at stake in maintaining the existing "fragmented" system of local government.[16] First of all, the existence of separate and independent local governments for suburbs plays a vital rôle in developing and maintaining a sense of community identity. The suburbanite identifies his residential community by reference to the local political unit. He does not think of himself as a resident of the "New York metropolitan region," but rather as a resident of Scarsdale or Mineola. Even the existence of community problems, the existence of a governmental forum for their resolution, and the necessity to elect local officials heighten community involvement and identity. The suburban community, with a government small in scale and close to home, represents a partial escape from the anonymity of mass urban culture. The institutional apparatus of government helps the suburban community to differentiate itself from "the urban mass," by legislating differences in the size and design of buldings, neighborhood and subdivision plans, school policies, types and quality of public services, and tax expenditure levels.

The political advantages of a fragmented suburbia cannot easily be dismissed. The existence of many local governments provides additional forums for the airing of public grievances. People feel better when they can publicly voice their complaints against governments, regardless of the eventual outcome of their grievance. The additional points of access, pressure,

[16] Oliver P. Williams, Harold Herman, Charles S. Liebman, and Thomas R. Dye *Suburban Differences and Metropolitan Policies* (Philadelphia: University of Pennsylvania Press, 1965), chap. 8.

and control provided by a decentralized system of local government give added insurance that political demands will be heard and perhaps even acted upon. Opportunities for individual participation in the making of public policy are expanded in a decentralized governmental system.

Maintaining the suburb as an independent political community provides the individual with a sense of personal effectiveness in public affairs. The individual can feel a greater sense of manageability over the affairs of a small community. A smaller community helps relieve feelings of frustration and apathy, which people often feel in their relations with larger bureaucracies. The suburbanite feels that his vote, his opinion, and his political activity count for more in a small community. He clings to the idea of grass-roots democracy in an organizational society.

Political independence also allows the suburbanite to insulate himself from those whose standards and way of life he does not share. Persons who have strived to place physical distance between themselves and those with different cultures and life styles are unlikely to look with favor on attempts to remove or weaken identifiable boundaries between their communities and communities that are socially dissimilar. It is not necessarily the color of the Negro doctor who first moves into an all white suburb that "frightens" the suburbanite. It is the belief that he will be followed by other Negroes with "lower" cultural and economic standards. The cultural homogeneity which the suburbanite seeks for himself and his children is better protected when he can make use of the legal machinery of an independent government to maintain this homogeneity by excluding those who might change it. Of course, a suburban government cannot directly discriminate, but it can establish and enforce, through building, zoning, subdivision, and tax ordinances, specific standards which are high enough that they make it economically unlikely that a "disrupting" element could enter the community. These formal controls, together with informal pressures on builders, real estate firms, and others, can operate to preserve effectively the cultural uniformity valued so highly in the suburban community.

Fragmented government clearly offers a larger number of groups the opportunity to exercise influence over government policy. Groups that would be minorities in the metropolitan area as a whole can avail themselves of government position and enact diverse public policies. This applies to Negroes in the central city as well as white Anglo-Saxon Protestants in the suburbs. Fragmented government creates within the metropolitan area a wide range of government policies. Communities that prefer, for example, higher standards in their school system at higher costs have the opportunity to implement this preference. Communities that prefer higher levels of public service or one set of services over another or stricter enforcement of particular standards can achieve their goals under a decentralized governmental system. Communities that wish to get along with reduced public services in order to maximize funds available for private spending may do so.

One final argument might be advanced on behalf of independent suburbs. It may be that area-wide government would heighten conflicts between city and suburb by raising questions that could only be settled by bitter political struggles. Edward C. Banfield raised this point regarding metropolitan government, and he added:

> Conflict is not something to be avoided at all costs. It may be well, nevertheless, to consider if there are not decisive advantages in the organizational arrangements which now exist—arrangements which while handicapping or entirely frustrating some important undertakings also serve to insulate the opposed interests and to protect them from each other. In view of their differences, it may be well despite obvious disadvantages that the people in the central cities and suburbs live largely in separate political communities.[17]

"Solutions" to the Metropolitan Problem

Let us examine various strategies for metropolitan governmental consolidation, in the light of the previous discussion of the values involved in suburban independence and the need for coordinating governmental activity in metropolitan areas.

The most obvious method of achieving governmental consolidation in the metropolitan area would be for the central city to annex suburban areas. *Annexation* continues to win widespread acceptance as an integrative device in the nation's metropolitan areas. Between 1950 and 1960, over 6 million persons were annexed to central cities in metropolitan areas, more than the combined populations of a dozen states. Approximately three-fourths of the nation's 212 central cities succeeded in annexing some territory and people in that 10 year period; half of these major cities annexed more than 10 per cent of their 1960 populations.

Not all cities have been equally successful in annexation efforts. Sixty of the 212 central cities of metropolitan areas in the U.S. annexed no territory in the period from 1950–60, while Phoenix and Tucson nearly doubled the size of their central city populations through annexation. This variation in annexation success among central cities provides an excellent opportunity for comparative analysis of the conditions associated with successful metropolitan political integration.[18, 19]

It was expected that opposition to central city annexation would be

---

[17] Edward C. Banfield, *Midwest Journal of Political Science*, p. 91.

[18] For a thorough discussion of various approaches to metropolitan governmental integration, see Bobbens and Schmandt, *The Metropolis.*

[19] The following discussion of annexation activity relies upon Thomas R. Dye, "Urban Political Integration: Conditions Associated with Annexation in American Cities," *Midwest Journal of Political Science*, 8 (November, 1964), 430–46.

more intense in the larger metropolitan areas. The bigger the metropolis, the more one would expect that suburbanites would defend themselves against being "swallowed up" or "submerged" by the central city. Table 11.7 suggests that central cities in smaller urbanized areas experienced slightly more success in annexing people than cities in larger urbanized areas. Yet size does not appear to be the most influential factor affecting annexation success. Actually, the "age" of a city appears more influential than size in determining the success of annexation efforts. City boundary lines in "older" metropolitan areas are relatively more fixed than in "newer" areas. Perhaps the immobility of boundaries is a product of sheer age. Over time, persons and organizations adjust themselves to circumstances as they find them. The longer these adjustments have been in existence, the greater the discomfort, expense, and fear of unanticipated consequences associated with change.

Central cities with higher proportions of well educated, white collar, middle income, white persons are more successful in annexing their suburbs than cities with smaller proportions of these "middle class" attributes. Table 11.7 shows that annexation success is correlated with the education level of the central city population, and similar correlations can be obtained between annexation success and income, occupation, and racial composition. In general, cities with higher status populations, and fewer minority groups,

TABLE 11.7

CONDITIONS ASSOCIATED WITH ANNEXATION SUCCESS IN AMERICAN CITIES
(Figures are mean annexation success scores for cities in each category*)

Size of urbanized area in thousands					
50-80	81-115	116-160	161-240	241-500	over 500
15.0	9.4	13.8	13.0	9.0	11.1
Age: Number of decades since city population surpassed 50,000					
0	1-2	3-4	5-7		over 7
22.3	13.1	14.3	7.8		4.2
Education level of central city population median school year completed					
Less than					More than
9.8	9.8-10.2	10.2-10.8	10.8-11.4	11.4-12.0	12.0
3.8	6.4	11.8	12.2	18.9	20.1
City-suburban social distance on education index					
Favors city				Favors suburbs	
21.7 14.6 12.7				10.2 4.7 5.9	

*Annexation success scores are the percent of the 1960 central city population which was annexed to it between 1950 and 1960.
Source: Thomas R. Dye, "Urban Political Integration", *Midwest Journal of Political Science*, Vol. 8 (November, 1964), 430-446.

are able to annex more suburbanites than cities with lower status populations and larger minority groups. Actually, the important variable in annexation success, and probably other efforts at metropolitan consolidation, seems to be the *differential* in status between the central city and its surrounding suburbs. Social class distance favoring the suburbs appears to be a distinct barrier to successful annexation efforts by central cities. Cities are more likely to be successful in annexing persons where there is little social differential between city and suburb.

Three-quarters of the nation's 212 metropolitan areas lie entirely within a single county. From the standpoint of administration there is much to be said for *city-county consolidation*. It would make sense administratively to endow county governments with the powers of cities and to organize them to exercise these powers effectively. Yet, important political problems— problems in the allocation of influence over public decision making—remain formidable barriers to strong county government. Central city interests can be expected to demand representation on county boards on the basis of population, "one man, one vote," yet suburbanites are likely to fear that consolidation will give city residents a dominant voice in county affairs. Suburbanites may also fear that city-county consolidation may force them to pay higher taxes to help support the higher municipal costs of running the city. Suburbanites may not welcome uniform, countywide policies in taxation or zoning or any number of other policy areas. Suburbanites who have paid for their own wells and septic tanks will hardly welcome the opportunity to help pay for city water or sewer services. Suburbanites with well established, high quality public school systems may be unenthusiastic about integrating their schools with city schools in a countywide system, and so on. A variety of policy differences may exist between city and suburb, which will reflect themselves in any attempt to achieve city-county consolidation. Unless these political issues can be resolved in a responsible manner by political leaders who are willing to bargain and compromise, the prospect for city-county consolidation will not be great.

Another serious obstacle to city-county consolidation is that the typical county government organization is still unsuited to administering urban functions. Often the county has limited powers under state law (even more limited than cities), it may have numerous elected officials and a cumbersome and antiquated organization, and it may be unaccustomed to effective and efficient performance of the heavy responsibilities of metropolitan government. Before counties can be granted authority to provide urban services, they will probably have to be reorganized. Perhaps in the long run, we may see a slow transfer of functions from the city to the county in those metropolitan areas lying entirely within the single county. A gradual transfer of functions is less disturbing than the more drastic alternative of city-county consolidation. Functional consolidation involves the transfer of an activity, such as public health, sewage disposal, or water supply, previously performed by two or more municipal units, to the county level with no change in the general structure of relationships between cities and the county.

One of the more popular approaches to metropolitan integration is the creation of *special districts or authorities* charged with administrating a particular function or service on a metropolitanwide or at least intermunicipal level, such as a park, sewage, water, parking, airport, planning, or other district or authority. Because the special district or authority leaves the social and governmental status quo relatively undisturbed, important integrative demands are met with a minimum of resistance with this device. The autonomy of suburban communities is not really threatened, loyalties are not disturbed, political jobs are not lost, and the existing tax structure is left relatively intact. Special districts or authorities may be preferred by suburban political leaders, when they believe it will lessen the pressure for annexation by the central city. Special districts or authorities may also be able to incur additional debt, after existing units of government have already reached their tax and debt limits, Thus, special districts or authorities may be able to operate in an area wider than that of existing units of governments, and at the same time enable governments to evade tax or debt limits in financing a desired public service.

Yet, experience in cities that have relied heavily upon special districts or authorities has suggested that these devices may create as many problems as they solve. Many special districts and authorities are governed by a quasi-independent board or commission, which, once established, becomes largely immune from popular pressures for change. These agencies may be quite independent of other governmental jurisdictions in the metropolis; their concerns might be water, air or water pollution control, city planning and so on. Remoteness from popular control or close political responsibility often results in the professional administrators of these authorities exercising great power over their particular function. While authorities and special districts are supposed to be nonprofit, governmental agencies, they often act very much like private enterprises, concentrating their resources on those activities that produce revenue and ignoring equally important non-revenue producing responsibilities.[20] Independent authorities often borrow money, collect tolls and service charges, and otherwise control their own finances in a manner very much like a private business. While a local government has a clearly defined constituency in a position of ultimately sanctioning the actions of officials, the constituencies of special districts are usually other governmental bureaucracies. The determination of program, budget, and finance for authorities and special districts often follows a complicated and unseen route through executive and legislative branches of

20 See Wood, *1400 Governments,* chap. 4.

a variety of state and local government agencies. The structure of these districts and authorities usually confuse the voters and make it difficult for the average citizen to hold officials of these agencies responsible for their decisions. Moreover, since these special districts and authorities are usually created for a single purpose, they often come to define the public interest in terms of the promotion of their own particular function—recreation, mass transit, water, parks, and so on—without regard for other metropolitan concerns. This "single-mindedness" can lead to competition and conflict between authorities and other governmental agencies in the region. Sooner or later, the problem of coordinating the activities of these independent authorities of special districts arises. Thus, even from the point of view of administrative efficiency, it is not clear whether the special district or authority, with its maze of divided responsibility, in the long run reduces or compounds the problem of governmental coordination in the metropolis.

Perhaps the Port of New York Authority is the largest and best known metropolitan authority in the nation. Established by interstate compact in 1921, the Port of New York Authority is controlled by a 12 man board, appointed for long overlapping terms by the governors of New Jersey and New York. While the governors have a veto on the actions of the authority and the legislatures of the two states must authorize new undertakings, the Authority, nevertheless, has considerable independence. Governors rarely reverse a decision of the Authority and legislatures have proven unable to alter substantially policy decisions made by the Authority. The Port of New York Authority is a billion dollar business, which is financially independent and self sustaining; it operates airports, bridges, piers, tunnels, bus and freight terminals, and a heliport.

Duane Lockard has commented on the political independence of the New York Port Authority:

> Fiscal independence, a good reputation, and skillful management have made it a giant among the actors in New York metropolitan politics. Every municipal leader or interest group that has tangled with the authority is well aware of its potential. It has public status combined with freedom from some of the standard restraints (such as the necessity to levy taxes, get budget approval from a legislature, or have its leaders face the public for reelection) plus great economic resources with which to undertake impressive public-satisfying. The business community in general felt kindly toward the authority as a well rounded organization, and it has had warm support from the metropolitan newspapers as well. With these assets, its competitive position is formidable.[21]

Robert C. Wood has characterized the New York Port Authority as a "metropolitan giant," which is deeply involved with the politics of the New

[21] Duane Lockard, *The Politics of State and Local Government* (New York: The Macmillan Co., 1963), p. 522.

York region, but operates more as a private business than as a government responsible to a local constituency:

> Where the institution takes the form of a public corporation, its creation is formally designed to remove the program 'from politics,' yet political pressures do arise in the informal relations that are established between the corporation's executives and other public officials, influential groups and private individuals. In this instance, the officeholders are not seeking 'votes' in the usual sense. More likely they are cultivating 'public opinion' in such forms as favorable editorial comment, the assistance of a strategically placed bureaucrat, or the support of an influential civic leader. . . .
>
> As for the public corporations and authorities, their process of collecting revenues closely resembles that of a private corporation. The Port of New York Authority and the Tri-Borough Bridge and Tunnel Authority rely on user charges, fees paid by the individual consumer for their services. The consumer's payment is not always a completely free choice, given the nature of the facilities involved, but neither is it as completely mandatory as the charges imposed by the local special districts concerned with streetlighting, water distribution, public schools and refuse collection. Whatever the consumer's position, his patronage frees the corporations of having to depend upon general tax revenues. Because their activities are self-supporting, their objectives, programs, and operations are likely to be self-determined. Hence, in their behavior they are more closely akin to private enterprise than to other government agencies. . . .[22]

"Metro" Government

The American experience with federalism at the national level has prompted consideration of federated governmental structures for metropolitan areas. A "metro" government with authority to make metropolitanwide policy in selected fields might be combined with local control over functions that are "local" in character. Metropolitan federation, in one form or another and at one time or another, has been proposed for many major metropolitan regions in the nation. Yet, with the exception of Toronto, Miami, and Nashville, proposals for metropolitan federation have been consistently rejected by both voters and political leaders throughout the nation. While metropolitan federation promises many of the advantages of governmental consolidation listed earlier—administrative efficiency, economy of large-scale operation, the elimination of financial inequalities, and public accountability for metropolitanwide policy—it seriously threatens many of the social, political, and psychological values in the existing "fragmented" system of local government in the metropolis. Metropolitan federation also poses a problem discussed earlier, that of deciding what is a "metropolitan" problem. In order to allocate functions to a "metro" gov-

[22] Robert C. Wood, *1400 Governments*, pp. 120–22.

ernment in a federation arrangement, one must first determine what is a metropolitan problem, in which all the citizens of the area have a responsibility. Let us examine the metro governments of Toronto, Miami, and Nashville in more detail, and then identify sources of political opposition.

It is interesting to note that Toronto's metropolitan federation was *not* adopted by popular referendum in the area, but rather was imposed upon the area by the Province of Ontario.[23] The Municipality of Metropolitan Toronto was created in 1954 by the provincial government, after many years of fruitless negotiations over metropolitan federation between Toronto and its 12 suburbs. The Municipality of Metropolitan Toronto, the new metro government, was given authority over water supply, sewage services, major roads, police, school buildings, metropolitan planning, and mass transit. The metropolitan government is financed by proportional assessments on the tax of the local governments; these local governments retain their tax collecting duties. They also retain authority over fire protection, street maintenance, garbage collection, and more importantly, public schools. Metropolitan Toronto is governed by a Metropolitan Council of 25 members: 12 from the city, one from each of the 12 suburbs, and one outsider who serves as chairman. Notice that representation on the council is not accorded on the basis of population but rather on the basis of equality between cities and suburbs. Since city and suburban representation is evenly balanced on the council, the chairman has come to play an influential role in developing consensus on metropolitan policy.

Miami's metropolitan experiment, the first in the U.S., was approved by popular referendum in the area, but only by a bare majority of the 26 per cent of Dade County registered voters who voted on May 21, 1957.[24] They approved a Dade County home rule charter, under which the county government became in effect a metro government. The county government assumed a number of functions performed by the 26 local governments in the metropolitan area including sewage, water supply, transportation, traffic, central planning, and "those municipal functions which are susceptible to areawide control." All other municipal powers are reserved to the cities, although the county may set minimum performance standards. Vagueness in the charter over precisely what is an areawide problem has resulted in a great deal of court litigation over the powers of the metro government. The Miami metro plan included council-manager government for the county, to replace the traditional commission form of county

[23] This discussion relies upon Bollens and Schmandt, *The Metropolis*, pp. 477–88; see also Frank Smallwood, *Metro Toronto: A Decade Later* (Toronto: Bureau of Municipal Research, 1963).

[24] This discussion relies upon Edward Sofen, *The Miami Metropolitan Experiment* (Bloomington: University of Indiana Press, 1963); and Edward Sofen, "The Politics of Metropolitan Leadership: The Miami Experience," *Midwest Journal of Political Science,* 5 (February, 1961), 18–38.

government. The Dade County Commission consisted of five members elected at large; five by districts, and one from each city whose population exceeds 6000—Miami, Miami Beach, and Hialeah. Since its beginning, the Commission has been badly divided; the first county manager was forced to resign and controversy and court cases have surrounded the activities of the county. Miami Beach even attempted to secede from the metropolitan federation. Amendments to the charter that would have crippled the powers of the metro government were defeated at the polls by very slim margins. Opponents of metro included the Dade County League of Municipalities, municipal employees, labor unions, several mayors and elected officials, local chambers of commerce, and the press, with the exception of *The Miami Herald*. The cities of Miami Beach and Hialeah have been strongly opposed to the metro idea. Metro supporters have been concentrated among Miami's business and political leadership, including the Miami Chamber of Commerce, *The Miami Herald, The Miami News,* the League of Women Voters, and the Dade County legislators.

Edward Sofen explained the narrow victory of the "metro" idea in Miami in the following way:

> Greater Miami is unique in a number of ways; it is warm when almost every other place in the nation is cold—a fact which has attracted a constant influx of migrants from all over the nation ... Miami is almost wholly devoid of strongly organized political factions and strongly organized labor or minority groups. It is generally lacking in organized and consistent community leadership.
>
> Is there, perhaps, a high correlation between these "negative" or passive factors in the successful emergence of metropolitan government in Miami? The reply to this question must be in the affirmative. This seems certain for the following reasons. Miami with its 'every man for himself' type of politics in effect has a no party system and, consequently, was spared the kind of struggle that might have occurred if the fate of political parties had turned on the outcome of the move to create a metropolitan government. By contrast, certain other metropolitan areas, such as Cuyahoga County in the Cleveland area, with its more formal party structure, have reflected sharp divisions between the parties, as well as within the parties on the issue of metropolitanization. Metropolitan government has been rejected there.[25]

In short, Sofen seems to believe that the newspapers and the good government forces were able to prevail in Miami because of the heavy influx of "newcomers" and the absence of strongly entrenched parties or powerful interest groups.

The future of metropolitan Miami is by no means assured. The opposition of political officials is still very intense. Former Dade County Man-

[25] Edward Sofen, *op. cit.*, p. 20.

ager Irving McNayr complains of the "political opposition that municipal officials have placed in the path of almost every areawide endeavor attempted." [26]

In 1962, the voters of Nashville and Davidson County, Tennessee, approved a metro charter which consolidated the city and the county.[27] Following the defeat of a 1958 consolidation proposal, in which city residents voted three to two in favor of consolidation and suburban residents, three to two against it, the City of Nashville undertook a very aggressive annexation program in which suburban residents and industries were incorporated into the city without a referendum and probably against their will. Voter approval of the Nashville metro charter is a product of unique and interesting political circumstances in that area. Nashville politics was dominated by Mayor Ben West, an ardent champion of urban causes including reapportionment, urban renewal, and federal and state aid in cities. He headed a strong political organization which was reputedly maintained by the use of patronage. Like many city bosses, West was disliked and distrusted by newspapers, businessmen, and suburbanites. The *Nashville*

TABLE 11.8

VOTING FOR METROPOLITAN GOVERNMENT REORGANIZATION IN NASHVILLE, 1962

| | Within city | | | Percent Outside city | | | |
	Old city	Annexed area	Total	Unincorporated suburban area	Rural area	Incorporated suburban cities	Total
Number of precincts	42	27	69	53	20	6	79
Vote							
For reorganization	45.2	72.2	57.4	62.6	34.0	47.3	56.0
Against reorganization	54.8	27.8	42.6	37.4	66.0	52.7	44.0
Number of voters (=100%)	19,960	16,726	36,686	19,706	4,040	4,662	28,408

Source: Brett W. Hawkins, "Public Opinion and Metropolitan Reorganization in Nashville," *Journal of Politics,* 28 (May, 1966), p. 416.

[26] Quotation from Bollens and Schmandt, *The Metropolis,* p. 470; from Irving J. McNayr, "A Report of the County Manager to the Board of County Commissioners," Miami: September 25, 1962, pp. 5-7.

[27] This discussion relies upon Brett W. Hawkins, *Nashville Metro* (Nashville: University of Vanderbilt Press, 1966); and Brett W. Hawkins, "Public Opinion and Metropolitan Reorganization in Nashville," *Journal of Politics,* 28 (May, 1966), 408-18.

Tennesseean, long a political foe of Mayor West, portrayed the annexation as an assault on county residents and began a campaign to convince them that metro government would protect them from the evils of the West administration in the city. Unlike 1958 when West supported Metro government and it was presented to suburbanites as a city program, in 1962 it was presented as a means to abolish the city and eliminate Mayor Ben West! The city also passed an ordinance levying a $10 tax on all automobiles using the streets of Nashville for 30 days or more. This "green sticker law" raised a storm of protest among suburbanites as "taxation without representation," a storm that reached hurricane proportions when Mayor West ordered the police to arrest and jail suburbanites whose cars were found on the streets of Nashville without green stickers. Thus, pro-metro forces were able to present metropolitan government to suburbanites as an anticity proposal, which would cripple the city political machine and protect the suburbs from the green sticker tax and the threat of annexation.

While opposition to the 1958 proposal had come from the suburban and quasi-rural areas of Davidson county, opposition in 1962 was led by Mayor West, city councilmen, and city employees. Metro's proponents relied on a newspaper campaign to stigmatize the governmental status quo and to personalize the issue by attacking Mayor West. Metro's opponents hoped to use the well-oiled West political organization to obtain an overwhelming "no" vote in the city. They counted on a heavy "no" vote from the city's Negroes, who feared a dilution of their influence in a metropolitan-wide government. Lining up behind metro were the city's businessmen, Chamber of Commerce, the League of Women Voters, the *Nashville Tennesseean,* the Tennessee Taxpayers Association, the Citizens Committee for Better Government, and many suburban Jaycee and civic clubs. In addition to the mayor, city employees, particularly firemen and policemen, and the Davidson County Democratic party, opposition to Metro was expressed by many labor and Negro leaders in the city. The metro charter passed by a vote of 57 per cent in the suburbs and 56 per cent in the cities.

Professor Brett W. Hawkins in an interesting study, *Nashville Metro,* has analyzed the politics of successful metropolitan consolidation. He concludes that the political circumstances surrounding the adoption of Nashville Metro were unlike those in other areas:

> Certainly the annexation of 85,000 county residents helped metro's proponents to put the issue on a personal, barely relevent, nonrational basis —namely for or against Mayor West. The insertion of a 'devil,' moreover, simplified the task of selling a highly complicated government organization. It is certainly true, in any case, that the circumstances which pertained to Nashville from 1958–1962 have not been common to proposals for governmental reorganization in metropolitan areas. This in turn lends some support to Robert C. Woods' proposition that 'program expansion of

urban governments' not initiated from without the system, nor by highly mobilized elite groups is random—'the result of accident, not design.'[28]

The voting returns in the Nashville metro referendum clearly suggest that the aggressive, if not hostile, behavior of the city toward its suburbs contributed significantly, if not decisively, to the victory of metropolitan government. Voters who had been recently annexed to the city, that is, voters who had been most recently the victims of city "aggression," were most heavily in favor of reorganization. The second highest vote for reorganization came from voters in the unincorporated suburban areas, those who may have felt the greatest threat of further annexations. Incorporated suburbs and rural areas voted against reorganization, even though it was presented as an anti-city proposal. No doubt the voters in these areas are just as "anti-city" as other suburbanites, but apparently they did not feel any immediate threat from the city. In the old city, it appears that entrenched political organizations carried the day with an assist from Negro voters in turning out a substantial "no" vote on reorganization. The Hawkins research also indicated that voters who anticipate higher taxes with reorganization are more likely to oppose it than those who do not, that voters who are dissatisfied with public services are more likely to support reorganization than those who are not, that less knowledgeable voters are more likely to oppose reorganization than more knowledgeable voters.

The important lesson in the success of the Nashville Metro is that it succeeded *not* because of an absence of city-suburban conflict, but because many suburbanites and others who were hostile to the city administration perceived metro government as a means of attacking the city. A metro proposal, which failed when it was presented as a reform, economy, and efficiency proposal, was later successful when it was presented as a political proposal.

Bargaining and Metropolitan Decision Making

Since conflict, rather than coordination, characterizes many of the relations between city and suburb, it seems reasonable to use a decision making technique—bargaining—which is especially designed for conflict situations. Bargaining is made possible by the fact that conflict between city and suburbs, or even among suburbs, is necessarily of the "non-zero sum" type; that is, a gain for the city is not necessarily a loss for the suburbs, and vice versa. Bargaining can result in the formation of rewarding coalitions even between governments with totally different goals. It may be that coordinating efforts in the metropolis should be directed toward facilitating bargaining, rather than toward "solutions," which ignore the values

[28] Hawkins, *op. cit.*, p. 418.

of suburban living, threaten the existence of separate suburban communities, or disregard social and political differences between city and suburbs. Annexation may still be a feasible strategy in smaller metropolitan areas, as we suggested earlier, but in the larger metropolis, with well entrenched city and suburban governments, city-suburban bargaining may be the most realistic and the most rewarding approach to metropolitan governmental coordination.

Bargaining can be used in many different types of cooperative efforts in metropolitan governments.[29] Cooperation may take the form of *informal,* verbal understandings, or "gentlemen's agreements," which might involve, for example, the exchange of information on cases between welfare departments or cooperation among police departments in the apprehension of a law breaker, or an agreement among local fire departments to come to the assistance of each other in the event of a major fire. Cooperation may result in *formal,* interjurisdictional agreements among governments, perhaps to build and operate a major facility, such as a garbage incinerator or sewage treatment plant. Interjurisdictional agreements may provide for: (1) one government performing a service or providing a facility for one or more other governments on a contractual basis; (2) two or more governments performing a function jointly or operating a facility on a joint basis; or (3) two or more local governments agreeing to assist and supply mutual aid to each other in emergency situations.

One of the attractions of interjurisdictional agreements is that they provide a means for dealing with metropolitan problems on a voluntary basis while retaining local determination and control. Interjurisdictional agreements do not threaten the existence of communities or governments. They do not threaten the jobs of incumbent public officials. Yet at the same time they enable governments to achieve the economies and provide the specialized services that only a larger jurisdiction can make possible.

Interjurisdictional agreements are very common in metropolitan areas. Over 15 years ago, a study of interjurisdictional agreements in the Philadelphia Metropolitan Area revealed that 427 local governments in that metropolis were involved in 756 agreements.[30] Similar findings are reported for Cleveland, St. Louis, and Los Angeles.[31] Apparently, most metropolitan areas have developed a complex network of interjurisdictional relationships. Cooperative arrangements embrace a broad sweep of local services and facilities, including airports, jails, and other public buildings, fire protection, public health, law enforcement, library services, recreation, planning, refuse disposal, road maintenance, sewage disposal, tax assess-

[29] See Thomas R. Dye, "Metropolitan Integration by Bargaining Among Subareas," *American Behavioral Scientist,* Vol. 5 (May, 1962), 11.

[30] George C. Blair, *Interjurisdictional Agreements in Southeastern Pennsylvania* (Philadelphia: Fels Institute, University of Pennsylvania, 1960).

[31] See Bollens and Schmandt, *The Metropolis,* pp. 379–80.

ment and collection, welfare activities, and water supply. Agreements among school districts are also quite common, and many suburban communities have been able to reach agreement on the creation of joint school districts. Often central cities, which are locked in bitter combat with their suburbs over annexation, are still able to negotiate agreements with these same suburbs for water supply, sewage disposal, or fire protection. County governments have often negotiated agreements with one or more of their municipalities, in which the county government provides the tax collecting and assessment services, ambulance services, fire protection, street maintenance, and so on, all on a contractual basis. Of course, interjurisdictional agreements may be ended or renegotiated by the participating governments from time to time. These agreements are not necessarily permanent, and they depend upon the voluntary participation of the governments involved; this is both a weakness and a strength of the interjurisdictional agreement.

Interjurisdictional agreements are not a "cure all" for the problems in the metropolis. Often communities are unable to reach agreement with each other on common problems because of social, partisan, or policy differences. An interesting study of the pattern of interjurisdictional agreements in the Philadelphia metropolitan area revealed that agreements were influenced by social and economic differences between communities.[32] Adjacent communities similar to each other in social composition, party affiliation, and wealth were much more likely to negotiate interjurisdictional agreements than dissimilar adjacent communities. Social, economic, and partisan differences between adjacent communities were particularly influential factors in the decision to create a joint school district. Socially dissimilar communities are not likely to reach agreement on a joint school district, but social differences were not quite so important in the negotiation of police radio agreements.

Los Angeles County provides an interesting example of the extent to which contractual agreements between a county and its municipalities can be employed to provide urban services to communities that could not otherwise afford them. Los Angeles County has negotiated about 1500 agreements, involving all 76 municipalities in the county, for various packages of services ranging from as few as four to as many as 45.[33] The County supplies election services for all cities, tax assessment and collection for all but two cities, and the enforcement of health laws for all except three cities. The county also provides ambulance service, enforcement of various city ordinances, library services, street maintenance, various inspection services, law enforcement, fire protection, and so on, all on a contractual

---

[32] Thomas R. Dye, Oliver P. Williams, Harold Herman, and Charles Liebman, "Differentiation and Cooperation in a Metropolitan Area," *Midwest Journal of Political Science*, 7 (May, 1963), 145–55.

[33] The following discussion relies upon Bollens and Schmandt, *The Metropolis*, pp. 385–92.

basis. Municipalities within the county contract for a specific package from the county; the package of services which they buy can vary according to their own felt needs. These county-city contractual arrangements enable cities to avail themselves of the services of large well staffed, well equipped county departments at much less cost than the cost of maintaining these services for themselves. Additionally, these cities are spared the necessity of large capital investments for facilities like police and fire stations and large staffs of municipal employees. At the same time cities retain discretion about what services they wish to purchase in their package from the county. The county's rates for the services that it provides on a contractual basis are set at the full cost; and the county assesses costs on the basis of the services provided to each city, including a share of county administrative and overhead expenses.

Metropolitan councils are the newest form of cooperation in metropoli-

FIGURE 11.3

MUNICIPAL SERVICES PROVIDED TO CITIES BY LOS ANGELES COUNTY, 1964

Service	Number of Cities
Ambulance (emergency)	62
Building Inspection	31
Elections	76
Fire Protection	27
Health Ordinance Enforcement (city)	73
Law Enforcement	29
License Issuance (business)	11
Mobile Home and Trailer Park Inspection	45
Planning and Zoning	21
Prosecution (city)	43
Sewer Maintenance	29
Street Construction and Maintenance	29
Subdivision Final Map Check	71
Tax Assessment and Collection	74
Tree Trimming	20

SOURCE: John C. Bollens and Henry J. Schmandt, *The Metropolis* (New York: Harper & Row, Publishers, 1965), p. 390. Reproduced by permission.

tan areas. Metropolitan councils are voluntary associations of governments or government officials that provide an opportunity for study, discussion, and recommendations regarding common metropolitan problems. These metropolitan councils are not governments themselves; they have no power to implement decisions but must rely instead upon voluntary compliance by member governments. Metropolitan councils provide an arena where elected heads of metropolitan governments can come together regularly, discuss problems, make recommendations, and hopefully coordinate their activities. Metropolitan councils are in operation in Detroit (Supervisors Inter-County Committee), Washington, D.C. (Metropolitan Washington Council of Governments), New York (Metropolitan Regional Council), Philadelphia (Regional Conference of Elected Officials), Seattle (Puget Sound Government Conference), Salem, Oregon (Mid-Willamette Valley Council of Governments), San Francisco (Association of Bay Area Governments). Generally, metropolitan councils strive for unity in their decisions and recommendations, because their recommendations must be acted upon by member governments, who are unlikely to implement proposals they oppose. The result, for the most part, is that studies and recommendations of metropolitan councils are likely to be rather bland in character. It is very difficult for these councils to deal with the really divisive issues in the metropolis. Since councils have no authority to act upon metropolitan problems, they may be, in the words of Bollens and Schmandt, a "toothless tiger or—even worse—a protector of the inadequate status quo." [34]

[34] *Ibid.,* p. 392.

12

COMMUNITY
POWER STRUCTURES

Models of Community Power

Who runs this town? Do the elected public officials actually make the important decisions? Or is there a "power structure" in this community that really runs things? If so, who is in the power structure? Are public officials "errand boys" who carry out the orders of powerful men who operate "behind the scenes"? Or are community affairs decided by democratically elected officials acting openly in response to the wishes of many different individuals and groups? Is city government of the people, by the people, and for the people? Or is it a government run by a small "elite" with the "masses" of people largely apathetic and uninfluential in public affairs? Do people who make important decisions in business and finance also make the important decisions in urban renewal, public works, education, taxation, public charity, land development, and so on? Or are there different groups of people making decisions in each of these areas, with little or no overlap except for elected officials?

Social scientists have differed over the answers to these questions. Some social scientists, whom we shall refer to as "elitists," believe that power in American communities is concentrated in the hands of relatively few people, usually top business and financial leaders. They believe that this "elite" is subject to relatively little influence from the "masses" of people. Other social scientists, whom we shall refer to as "pluralists," believe that power is widely shared in American communities among many leadership groups, who represent segments of the community and who are held responsible by the people through elections and group participation. Interestingly, both elitists and pluralists seem to agree that decisions are made by small minorities in the community. The idea of direct, individual citizen participation in decision making has suffered with the coming of organizational society and high levels of urbanization and industrialization. Elitists describe a more monolithic structure of power, with a single leadership group making decisions on a variety of issues, while pluralists describe a polycentric structure of power, with different elite groups active in different issues and a great deal of competition, bargaining, and sharing of power among elites.

Let us summarize the points of conflict between elitist and pluralist models of community power. These points have been distilled from a large body of rapidly expanding literature on community power,[1] and they can provide us with a framework for further discussion.

Elitist thinking about community power appears to include the following ideas.

1. Power stems from roles within the social system of the community. Political power is inextricably bound together with social and economic power. Men of wealth and social position in the community will also be men of power.

2. Power is "structured"—that is, power relationships tend to persist over time. Issues and elections may come and go, but the same men will continue to exercise power in the community.

3. There is a reasonably clear and persistent distinction over time between those who exercise power (elite) and those who do not (mass).

4. This distinction is based primarily upon the unequal distribution of control over economic resources in the community. Business and financial leaders will compose the major part of the "elite." Elected public officials are largely "errand boys" who knowingly or unknowingly respond to the wishes of the dominant economic elite.

---

[1] This literature is becoming so voluminous that it seems appropriate to cite only some of the major summary pieces: Thomas J. Anton, "Power, Pluralism, and Local Politics," *Administrative Science Quarterly*, 7 (March, 1963), 425–57; Lawrence Herson, "In the Footsteps of Community Power," *American Political Science Review*, 55, (December, 1961), 817–31; Peter Bachrach and Morton S. Baratz, "Two Faces of Power", *American Political Science Review*, 56 (December, 1962), 947–53; Herbert Kaufman and Victor Jones, "The Mystery of Power," *Public Administration Review*, 14 (Summer 1954), 205–12; Nelson Polsby, *Community Power and Political Theory*, (New Haven: Yale University Press, 1963); Robert Presthus, *Men At The Top*, (New York: Oxford University Press, 1964); Robert Dahl, *Who Governs?* (New Haven: Yale University Press, 1961); Floyd Hunter, *Community Power Structure* (Chapel Hill: The University of North Carolina Press, 1953); Robert Agger, Daniel Goldrich, and Burt Swanson, *The Rulers and the Ruled* (New York: John Wiley & Sons, Inc., 1965); other citations are given in footnotes below.

5. The elite constitutes a very small proportion of the people in the community. They are not typical or representative of the people of the community in income, education, occupation, or ethnic background. They have higher incomes, better educations, and more prestigious occupations than the "masses," and they come from the culturally dominant ethnic group in America—the white, Anglo-Saxon Protestants.

6. There is considerable convergence of power at the "top" of the political system. A diagram of community power would take the shape of a pyramid.

7. Persons in the elite may disagree from time to time but they share a certain commonality of interests, particularly in support of the basic values that underly the social system itself.

8. The elite is subject to relatively little influence from the masses, even through elections or any other form of political activity. The masses are largely misinformed and apathetic, if not completely alienated, from the community's political system. Of course, the elite usually is benevolent and does not oppress the masses because of a sense of "high-mindedness" and "civic responsibility" and the need to avoid violence and revolution.

In contrast pluralist thinking involves the following notions.

1. Power is an attribute of individuals in their relationship with other individuals in the process of decision making. An individual has power to the extent that he can get another individual to do something he would not otherwise do, regardless of social position.

2. Power relationships do not necessarily persist over time. They are formed for a particular decision, and after this decision is made, they disappear, to be replaced by a different set of power relationships when the next decision is made.

3. There is no permanent distinction between "elites" and "masses." Individuals who participate in decisions at one point in time are not necessarily the same individuals who participate at some other time. Many individuals have the *opportunity* to exercise power, whether they choose to do so or not.

4. The distinction between those who participate in a decision and those who do not is based primarily upon the level of interest people have in that particular decision. Individuals can move in and out of the ranks of decision making, simply by becoming active or inactive in politics. Men of wealth and social position are often defeated on community issues by active, skillful leaders who win popular support.

5. Leadership is fluid and mobile. Access to decision making is based primarily upon acquiring the skills of leadership—information about issues, knowledge about democratic processes, skill, organization, and public relations, and so on. Wealth is an asset in politics, but it is only one of many kinds of assets.

6. There are multiple centers and bases of power within a community. Persons who exercise power in some kinds of decisions do not necessarily exercise power in other kinds of decisions. No single elite dominates decision making in all issue areas.

7. There is considerable competition among leaders. Community leaders are not united by any common interest. They seek many divergent policies. Community policy also represents bargains or compromises reached between competing leadership groups.

8. Individuals can participate and make their views felt, through their membership in organizations of many kinds. Elections are also important instruments of mass participation in political decisions. Leaders are constantly concerned with public opinion and often refer to it in decision making. Nonparticipation in elections or community affairs may be a product of popular satisfaction with the conduct of leaders.

While these statements describe "ideal" models of elite and pluralist communities, most "real" world communities will probably fall somewhere in between—that is, along a continuum from the monolithic elite model of power to a diffused and polycentric pluralist model. Many social scientists are neither confirmed "elitists" or "pluralists," but are aware that different structures and power may exist in different communities. Yet these ideal models of community power may be helpful in understanding the different ways in which community power can be structured. Later we shall suggest some social, economic, and political conditions that may be associated with elite or pluralist power configurations in American communities.

The Elite Model of Community Power

European social theory has long been at odds with democratic political writers about the existence and necessity of elites. Gaetano Mosca, in his book *The Ruling Class,* wrote, "In all societies . . . two classes of people appear—a class that rules and a class that is ruled." [2] For Mosca, elitism is explained by the nature of social organization. Organization inevitably results in the concentration of political power in the hands of a few. Organized power cannot be resisted by an unorganized majority, in which each individual ". . . stands alone before the totality of the organized minority. A hundred men acting uniformly in concert, with a common understanding, will triumph over a thousand men who are not in accord and can therefore be dealt with one by one." [3] Since organized power will prevail over individual effort in politics, sooner or later, organizations will come to be the more important actors in political life. And organizations cannot function

---

[2] Gaetano Mosca, *The Ruling Class* (New York: McGraw-Hill Book Co., 1939), p. 50.

[3] *Ibid.,* p. 51.

without leaders. In Robert Michels' words, "He who says organization, says oligarchy." [4] The masses are permanently incapable of running or controlling political organizations. They must cede that power to active, expert, and interested leadership groups. The idea that economic elites will tend to dominate in politics is also found in a great deal of social theory. Mosca wrote that the ruling class will possess ". . . some attribute real or apparent which is highly esteemed or very influential in the society in which they live." Needless to say, in a capitalist society, control over business and financial resources generally makes one "highly esteemed and very influential." Karl Marx made social scientists everywhere very much aware of the impact of economic power on political power.

One of the earliest studies of American communities, the classic study of Middletown, conducted by Robert and Helen Lynd in the middle 1920's and again in the mid 1930's, tended to confirm a great deal of elitist thinking about community power.[5] The Lynds found in Muncie, Indiana, a monolithic power structure dominated by the owners of the town's largest industry. Community power was firmly entrenched in the hands of the business class, centering on, but not limited to, the "X" family. The power of this group was based upon its control over the economic life in the city, particularly its ability to control the extension of credit. The city was run by a "small top group" of "wealthy local manufacturers, bankers, the local head managers of . . . national corporations with units in Middletown, and . . . one or two outstanding lawyers." Democratic procedures and governmental institutions were so much window-dressing for business control. The Lynds described the typical city official as a "man of meager calibre" and as "a man whom the inner business control group ignore economically and socially and use politically." Perhaps the most famous quote from the Lynds' study was a comment by a Middletown man made in 1935:

> "If I'm out of work, I go to the X plant; if I need money I go to the X bank, and if they don't like me I don't get it; my children go to the X college; when I get sick I go to the X hospital; I buy a building lot or house in the X subdivision; my wife goes downtown to buy X milk: I drink X beer, vote for X political parties, and get help from X charities; my boy goes to the X YMCA and my girl to their YWCA; I listen to the word of God in X subsidized churches; if I'm a Mason, I go to the X Masonic temple; I read the news from the X morning paper; and, if I'm rich enough, I travel via the X airport." [6]

W. Lloyd Warner, a noted sociologist, studied Morris, Illinois, in the 1940's, and he describes a somewhat similar power structure to that en-

[4] Robert Michels, *Political Parties* (Glencoe: Free Press, 1949).

[5] Robert S. Lynd and Helen M. Lynd, *Middletown* (New York: Harcourt Brace and World, Inc., 1929); and *Middletown in Transition* (New York: Harcourt Brace and World, Inc., 1937).

[6] *Middletown in Transition*, p. 74.

countered by the Lynds in Muncie.[7] About one-third of all of the city's workers had jobs in "the mill," which Warner says dominated the town:

> The economic and social force of the mill affects every part of the life of the community. Everyone recognizes its power. Politicians, hat in hand, wait upon Mr. Waddell, manager of The Mill, to find out what he thinks on such important questions as 'Shall the tax rate be increased to improve the education our young people are getting?'—'Shall the new minister be Mr. Jones or Mr. Smith?'—'Should the city support various civic and world enterprises?'—'Should new industries enter the town and possibly compete with The Mill for the town's available labor supply?' They want to know what Mr. Waddell thinks. Mr. Waddell usually lets them know.[8]

Sociologist August B. Hollingshead studied the same town (sociologists seem to prefer to disguise the names of towns they are studying: Warner called the town Jonesville while Hollingshead called it Elmtown) and his findings substantially confirmed those of Warner.[9]

One of the most influential studies of community politics was sociologist Floyd Hunter's, *Community Power Structure,* a study of Atlanta, Georgia.[10] According to Hunter, no one man or family or business dominated "Regional City" (a synonym for Atlanta), as might be true in a smaller town. Instead, Hunter described several tiers of influentials, with the most important community decisions reserved for a top layer of the business community. Admission to the innermost circle was based primarily on one's position in the business world. These top decision makers were not formally organized, but conferred informally and passed down decisions to government leaders, professional personnel, civic organizations, and other "front men." Hunter explained that the top power structure only concerned itself with major policy decisions; there were other substructures—economic, governmental, religious, educational, professional, civic, and cultural—which communicated and implemented the policies decided at the top level. These substructures:

> ... are subordinate, however, to the interests of the policy makers who operate in the economic sphere of community life in Regional City. The institutions of the family, church, state, education, and the like draw sustenance from economic institutional sources and are thereby subordinate to this particular institution more than any other.... Within the policy forming groups the economic interests are dominant.[11]

[7] W. Lloyd Warner, *et. al., Democracy in Jonesville* (New York: Harper & Row, Publishers, 1949).

[8] *Ibid.,* p. 101.

[9] August B. Hollingshead, *Elmtown's Youth* (New York: John Wiley & Sons, Inc., 1949).

[10] Floyd Hunter, *Community Power Structure* (Chapel Hill: University of North Carolina Press, 1953).

[11] *Ibid.,* p. 94.

Top power holders seldom operated openly. "Most of the top personnel in the power group are rarely seen in the meetings attended by the associational understructure personnel in Regional City." [12]

Hunter describes the process of community action as follows:

> If a project of major proportions were before the community for consideration—let us say a project aimed at building a new municipal auditorium—a policy committee would be formed. . . . Such a policy committee would more than likely grow out of a series of informal meetings, and it might be related to a project that has been on the discussion agenda of many associations for months or even years. But the time has arrived for action. Money must be raised through private subscription or taxation, a site selected, and contracts let. The time for a policy committee is propitious. The selection of the policy committee will fall largely to the men of power in the community. They will likely be businessmen in one or more of the large business establishments. Mutual choices will be agreed upon for committee membership. In the early stages of policy formulation there will be few men who make basic decisions. . . . Top ranking organizational and institutional personnel will then be selected by the original members to augment their numbers, i.e., the committee will be expanded. Civic associations and the formalized institutions will next be drawn into certain phases of planning and initiation of the projects on a communitywide basis. The newspapers will finally carry stories, the ministers will preach sermons, the associations will hear speeches regarding plans. This rather simply is the process, familiar to many, that goes on in getting any community project underway.[13]

Note that in Hunter's description of community decision making, decisions tend to flow *down* from top policy makers, composed primarily of business and financial leaders, to civic, professional, and cultural association leaders, religious and education leaders, and government officials, who implement the program; and the masses of people have little direct or indirect participation in the whole process. Policy does not go *up* from associational groupings or from the people themselves. "The top group of the power hierarchy has been isolated and defined as being comprised of policy makers. These men are drawn largely from the businessmen's class in Regional City. They form cliques or "crowds," as the term is more often used in the community, which formulate policy. Committees for the formulation of policy are commonplace, and on communitywide issues policy is channeled by a 'fluid committee structure' down to institutional, associational groupings through a lower level bureaucracy which executes policy." [14] According to Hunter, elected public officials are clearly part of the lower level institutional substructure, which "executes" policy rather than formu-

12 *Ibid.*, p. 90.
13 *Ibid.*, pp. 92–93.
14 *Ibid.*, p. 113.

lates it. Finally Hunter found that this whole power structure is held together by "common interests, mutual obligations, money, habit, delegated responsibilities, and in some cases, by coercion and force." [15]

Businessmen in Politics—An Alternative View

While Hunter describes the role of Atlanta's business elite as one of top policy making, a study of businessmen in big city politics by Peter B. Clark suggests that businessmen are used as prestigious "front men" for policies initiated by civic associations and governmental agencies.[16] Clark argues that big businessmen themselves almost never think up or suggest proposals. Rather, ideas for community action generally come from the professional staffs of various community organizations, for example, a professional hospital director, a civic association staff worker, the newspaper's city editor, or the heads of governmental agencies. Once an idea has been generated at the professional staff level, the next stage is to seek out top businessmen to lend their prestige to the project. As one enthusiastic staff man put it:

> "I've got a project now. One of the greatest things we can do for the central area. . . . I am not doing it alone. . . . I am sitting with it until I can present it to the proper man to handle it as *his* idea. I think so much of it that I've got to find the right guy to take credit for it. . . . The man I'm going to pick has to be president of his club . . . head of his business. That's 50, 70 per cent of the success of the project." [17]

A proposal's presentation to the public and submission to city government for ratification is the third stage in policy making. If the proposal has been well thought out in advance by the professional staff, and has the support and public backing of prominent businessmen, this final stage may be a mere formality. Only if organized opposition has developed in some influential segment of the community, and this opposition also has the support of some businessmen, will the mayor and council be faced with an important decision.

Business support for community projects is thought to be essential for several reasons. First of all, business support bestows great prestige on a proposal. The low prestige of municipal officials helps to explain why businessmen are needed to help put across any major community project. Moreover, middle class people, whose vote is relatively more important in local than in state or national politics, tend to respect the views of businessmen

[15] *Ibid.*

[16] Peter B. Clark, "Civic Leadership: The Symbols of Legitimacy." Paper delivered at the 1960 Annual Meeting of the American Political Science Association, New York, September, 1960; see also Peter B. Clark, *The Businessman as a Civic Leader* (Glencoe: Free Press, 1964).

[17] Clark, "Civic Leadership," p. 4.

more than the views of city officials. Peter Clark supplies a quotation from a Chicago attorney who had long been involved in civic affairs:

> "By and large, those with strong business backgrounds command greater respect ... than those with the same skills who don't have that background. And the same is true of a lawyer versus the president of General Motors. They both could say the same thing ... but the president would be listened to more. They transfer part of their business achievement into their public life." [18]

The views of businessmen are respected in part because the community's economic growth and continued prosperity are linked to business firms and the men who head them. Any suggestion from these men that a particular proposal might "hurt business" or "slow down the economy" must be taken seriously by a community that depends upon these businessmen for employment. Only occasionally will a business firm be required to issue a direct threat to the community that it will close down and move elsewhere in order to get its way in policy matters. While direct public threats like this are not infrequent, businessmen prefer to rely more on subtle hints that a particular policy might hurt the growth of business and employment. Business support is also sought to lend a "conservative" image to community proposals. Businessmen are expected to be sound guardians of the status quo. They are expected to oppose "radical," sweeping changes in governmental structure, tax programs, public services, and so on. Thus, the endorsement by these conservatives of any new program helps to assure the community that it does not represent any radical break with the past. For this reason, too, the support of businessmen from older established firms is often more valued than the support of businessmen from newer firms in the community.

In addition to considerations of respect and prestige, business support is also sought because so many community projects require financial investment—public works, urban renewal, schools, streets, auditoriums, hospitals, and so on—and banks and investment firms must be called in to underwrite the bond issues. Businessmen also have technical information which local governments, normally operating without much professional staff, cannot themselves provide. Finally, business support is often sought to disarm potentially influential businessmen who might provide opposition to a proposal if they are not consulted about it in its earliest stages.

In short Clark's argument is that businessmen do not initiate policy proposals, but business support is essential to their success. This means that big businessmen have a potential or actual veto over policy proposals. According to Clark, a businessman's power comes from his ability to grant or withhold the approval that others seek: "It is his capacity to withhold his

[18] *Ibid.,* p. 6.

approval and participation—even if participation means only his name on a letterhead—that constitutes the most significant basis of the big business-man's potential veto." [19]

Business support is especially vital on proposals involving great change in the community—programs like metropolitan area government, urban renewal, public housing, freeway construction, and other massive public works involving bond issues, condemnation of properties, increased tax burdens, and so on. The highest ranking businessmen in the community are needed for these kinds of undertakings. More routine governmental decisions—school, water, and park systems, for example—usually require less business support. The businessmen associated with these activities may come from smaller firms or the vice presidential level of larger firms.

The influence of businessmen can be felt even in matters in which they are not directly involved. Many government officials and civic organization workers admit that they anticipate the views of big businessmen in policy decisions even when businessmen are not directly consulted. Clark quotes a civic staff man who explained why a particular community project failed: "This thing wasn't done right. It was just announced. The power structure and the newspaper people weren't checked out. All hell broke loose." [20] Another staff man revealed both his style and his motives when he said: "My method of operation is to touch base early before I raise a question. I do my homework thoroughly to get the controversy out of it. Either revise it or throw it out. I have never proposed anything that hasn't been accepted. I don't want to propose anything that would fail." [21]

Big businessmen are not equally powerful in all cities. Nor are they equally powerful in all issues. Endorsement by big businessmen does not always guarantee success. It is not quite clear whether businessmen are "using" public officials to achieve the goals of business, or whether public officials are "using" business leaders to achieve their political goals. Mayor David Lawrence of Pittsburgh seldom undertook a major city project without the support of Richard K. Mellon, President of the Mellon Bank and Chairman of the Allegheny Conference on Community Development, a small group of top business leaders concerned with Pittsburgh's economy. Pittsburgh's dramatic "renaissance" of the 1950's was engineered and financed by the "Mellon Group," so much so that some commentators referred to Pittsburgh as "Mellon town." The Mellon group "used" the Lawrence administration to accomplish Pittsburgh's redevelopment. On the other hand, it could be said that Mayor Lawrence "used" the Mellon Group to help make his administration the most successful in the city's history. Lawrence was elected to four consecutive four-year terms as

19 *Ibid.*, p. 10.
20 *Ibid.*, p. 11.
21 *Ibid.*, p. 11.

mayor, an unprecedented accomplishment itself, and then was elected governor of Pennsylvania; these political successes could largely be attributed to the dramatic renaissance of the city, for which Lawrence took much of the credit.

Several studies have suggested interesting variations on the power elite model. Robert O. Schultze's study of Cibola (Ypsilanti, Michigan) describes shifts in the power structure in that community, resulting from the town's integration into a "national" economy and the appearance of absentee ownership and a new managerial class in the power structure.[22] Schultze contends that in an earlier era of the town's history, locally owned industries dominated the political and economic life of the community. But as local industrialists were replaced by the managers of large, national, absentee-owned corporations, the power structure became less concentrated. The managers of Cibola's plants had great potential for power within the community, but they were preoccupied with their relationships to their national firms and tended to neglect community affairs. The result was that political power came to rest in the hands of a group of middle class, local professionals and small businessmen. Delbert C. Miller described the power structure of Pacific City (Seattle, Washington) and compared it to an English city of comparable size.[23] His thesis is that power is related to whatever is highly valued by the community. Where the American power structure is largely business dominated, and employs government merely to ratify its decisions, the English power structure showed less business domination and greater deference to intellectuals and public officials, who have more prestige in the English community. Miller's model of community power includes a layering of influential persons, distinguishing between "potential influentials" and "key influentials." The key influentials actually took part in community decision making, while potential influentials could have done so but did not.

Belief in the elite model of community power is widespread. In an opinion poll about community power in the Philadelphia metropolitan area, approximately three-fourths of the respondents perceived community decision making in an essentially elitist fashion.[24] In response to the question —"In your judgment, do you feel that the big community decisions tend to be made by the same small crowd of people or do these people change

[22] Robert O. Schultze, "The Role of Economic Dominants in Community Power Structure," *American Sociological Review*, 23 (February, 1958), 3–9; see also Robert O. Schultze, "The Bifurcation of Power in a Satellite Community," *Community Political Systems*, Morris Janowitz, ed. (Glencoe: Free Press, 1961).

[23] Delbert C. Miller, "Industry and Community Power Structure," *American Sociological Review*, 23 (February, 1958), 9–15; and "Decision-Making Cliques in Community Power Structures," *American Journal of Sociology*, 64 (November, 1958), 299–310.

[24] Thomas R. Dye, "Popular Images of Decision-Making," *Sociology and Social Research*, 47 (October, 1962), 75–83.

according to the issue confronting the community?"—residents overwhelmingly responded that the "same small crowd" made all the decisions. In response to the question—"Are important issues usually quietly solved without the public knowing what they are or are they usually brought out into the open?"—a majority of respondents believed that most issues were resolved privately. Respondents were more or less equally divided over whether or not community decision makers acted in a socially responsible manner. The question was, "Do you feel that the people involved in making decisions have a broad sense of community responsibility or are they more concerned with protecting or furthering their own interest?" Interestingly, when elected public officials were asked the same questions, they responded in a completely different fashion from their constituents. Elected public officials did not feel that "the same small crowd" decided things, but instead adopted the pluralist view that decision makers changed according to the issues confronting the community. They strongly asserted that decisions were made openly and that decision makers were motivated by a broad sense of community responsibility. There is also evidence to suggest that elitist and pluralist images of community power are related to socio-economic status. Well educated, prestigiously employed, high income respondents tend to view community power in a pluralist fashion and have much more favorable attitudes toward decision makers. In contrast, poorly educated, low income respondents are much more likely to see "a small clique" running things and to have unfavorable attitudes toward decision makers.[25]

The Pluralist Model of Community Power

Political science had largely ignored the study of community power prior to the publication of Floyd Hunter's *Community Power Structure*. While sociologists had been developing an important body of literature on community power even before the Lynds' safari to darkest Indiana in the 1920's, community politics remained a "lost world" for political scientists.[26] Political science had been preoccupied with the municipal reform movement, the structure of local government, and administrative problems of economy and efficiency; they had largely ignored informal structures of power and decision making. Hunter's findings were very discomforting. They suggested that in reality American communities were not governed very democratically. Hunter's research challenged the notion of popular participation in "grassroots" democracy, and raised doubts as to whether or not the cherished values of Jeffersonian democracy were being realized

[25] See also John Haer, "Social Stratification in Relation to Attitudes Toward Sources of Power," *Social Forces*, 35 (December, 1956), 137–42.

[26] See Lawrence J. R. Herson, "The Lost World of Municipal Government," *American Political Science Review*, 51 (June, 1957), 330–45.

in community life. While admitting that "none of us [political scientists] has moved in with such a structure in dynamics of power in a metropolitan community," political scientists Herbert Kaufman and Victor Jones were willing to assert on the basis of their own "administrative experience" that Hunter's study was "at best . . . incomplete; at worst . . . invalid." [27] These political scientists believed that much more competition, access, equality, and popular participation occurred in community politics than the work of the Lynds, Warner, Hollingshead, Hunter, and others implied.

Modern pluralism does not mean a commitment to "pure democracy," where all citizens participate directly in decision making. The underlying value of individual dignity continues to motivate contemporary pluralist thought, but it is generally recognized that the town meeting type of pure democracy is not really possible in an urban, industrial society. The modern pluralist is aware of the rise of giant industrial and financial organizations and the threat they pose to individual liberty. (Historically, liberals perceived the threat to individual liberty to be the concentration of government power; but after the Industrial Revolution, liberals became more concerned with business power and often turned to the government to protect individual rights.) But it is the hope of modern pluralists that "countervailing" centers of power can help to offset corporate power and protect the interests of the individual. Hopefully competition between big business, big labor, and big government will keep each interest from abusing its power. Pluralism accepts strong government as protection against economic dominance. Likewise pluralism accepts the growing importance of organized group activity in politics, since it is recognized that the unorganized individual is no match for industrial bureaucracies. A central value in liberal political thought has always been individual participation in decision making. Historically, this meant voting, interest and activity in public affairs, information about public issues, and knowledge about democratic procedures, on the part of individuals. But to modern pluralists, individual participation has come to mean membership in organized groups. In an age of organization, meaningful participation and decision making is said to take place through the individual's membership in groups that make their influence felt in decision making. Interest groups become the means by which individuals gain access to the political system. Government is held responsible not directly by individuals, but by organized interest groups and political parties. Pluralists believe that competition between parties and organized groups, representing the interests of their citizen members, can protect the dignity of the individual and offer a viable alternative to individual participation in decision making.

The pluralist model of community power stresses the fragmentation of

[27] Herbert Kaufman and Victor Jones, "The Mystery of Power," *Public Administration Review,* 14 (Summer, 1954), 205–12.

authority, the influence of elected public officials, the importance of organized group activity, and the role of public opinion and elections in determining public policy. Who rules in the pluralist community? "Different small groups of interested and active citizens in different issue areas with some overlap, if any, by public officials, and occasional intervention by a large number of people at the polls." [28] Citizen influence is felt not only through organized group activity but also through leaders anticipating the reactions of citizens and endeavoring to satisfy their demands. In addition to the elected public officials, leadership in community affairs is exercised by interested individuals and groups, who confine their participation to one or two issue areas. What are leaders? "Leaders are activists. More precisely they are the most active activists." [29] The pluralist model sees interest and activity rather than economic resources as the key to leadership. Competition, fluidity, access, and equality characterize community politics.

Perhaps the most influential of the pluralist community studies was Robert A. Dahl's *Who Governs?*, a detailed analysis of decision making in New Haven, Connecticut.[30] Dahl chose to examine 16 major decisions on redevelopment and public education in New Haven and on nominations for mayor in both political parties for seven elections. Dahl found a polycentric and dispersed system of community power in New Haven, in contrast to Hunter's highly monolithic and centralized power structure. Influence was exercised from time to time by many individuals, each exercising power over some issues but not over others. When the issue was one of urban renewal, one set of individuals was influential; in public education, a different group of leaders were involved. Business elites, who were said by Hunter to control Atlanta, were only one of many different influential groups in New Haven. According to Dahl, "The economic notables, far from being a ruling group, are simply one of many groups out of which individuals sporadically emerge to influence the politics and acts of city officials. Almost anything one might say about the influence of the economic notables could be said with equal justice about a half dozen other groups in the New Haven community." [31] The mayor of New Haven was the only decision maker who was influential in most of the issue areas studied, and his degree of influence varied from issue to issue. "The mayor was not at the peak of a pyramid but at the center of intersecting circles. He rarely commanded. He negotiated, cajoled, exhorted, beguiled, charmed, pressed, appealed, reasoned, promised, insisted, demanded, even threatened; but he most needed support and acquiescence from other leaders who simply could

[28] Aaron Wildavsky, *Leadership in a Small Town* (Totawa: Bedminster Press, 1964), p. 8.

[29] *Ibid.*, p. 282.

[30] Robert A. Dahl, *Who Governs?* (New Haven: Yale University Press, 1961).

[31] *Ibid.*, p. 72.

not be commanded. Because he could not command them, he had to bar-gain." [32]

Aaron Wildavsky's study of Oberlin, Ohio revealed, if anything, an even more pluralist structure of decision making than Dahl found in New Haven.[33] Wildavsky's study of Oberlin was a reaffirmation of small town democracy, for in Oberlin, "The roads to influence . . . are more than one; elites and non-elites can travel them, and the toll can be paid with energy and initiative as well as wealth." [34] Wildavsky studied 11 community decisions in Oberlin, including such diverse issues and events as the determination of municipal water rates, the passage of the fair housing ordinance, the division of United Appeal funds, and a municipal election. Wildavsky set out to resolve once and for all the dispute between elitist and pluralists:

> If (after examining these issues) we find that the same participants exercise leadership in nearly all significant areas of decision, that they agree, and that they are not responsible to the electorate, we conclude that a power elite rules in Oberlin. . . . If we find that the leaders vary from one issue to another with such overlap as there is between issue areas concentrated largely in the hands of public officials, we must conclude that there is a pluralist system of rule in Oberlin.[35]

Wildavsky found "that a number of citizens and outside participants who exercise leadership in most cases is an infinitesimal part of the community," but no person or group exerted leadership in *all* issue areas. To the extent that overlap among leaders in issue areas existed, this overlap involved public officials—the city manager, the mayor, and city councilmen—who owed their positions directly or indirectly "to expressions of the democratic process through a free ballot with universal suffrage." In addition to public officials, leadership was exercised by individual "specialists," who confined their participation to one or two issue areas. Leaders very often competed among themselves and did not appear united by any common interest. Persons exercising leadership were of somewhat higher social status than the rest of the community, but it was not status or wealth that distinguished leaders from nonleaders, rather it was their degree of interest and activity in public affairs.

A team of Syracuse University social scientists provided additional support for the pluralist interpretation of community power.[36] They compiled a long list of community decisions in Syracuse and identified individuals who participated formally or informally in these decisions. Not one leader-

---

[32] *Ibid.,* p. 204.

[33] Aaron Wildavsky, *op. cit.*

[34] *Ibid.,* p. 214.

[35] *Ibid.,* p. 253.

[36] Frank J. Munger, *Decisions in Syracuse* (Bloomington: Indiana University Press, 1961); see also Linton C. Freeman, *et. al., Metropolitan Decision-Making* (Syracuse: Syracuse University Press, 1962).

ship group, but many, were revealed, each one dealing with issues in a separate field, such as health or education. In summing up the results of this massive study, Frank Munger writes:

> Only three overall conclusions seem warranted by the materials examined. First, the myth that significant decisions in Syracuse emanate from one source does not stand up under close scrutiny. Second, there tend to be as many decision centers as there are important decision areas, which means that the decision making power is fragmented among institutions, agencies, and individuals, which cluster about these areas. Third, in reality, there appear to be many kinds of community power, with one differing from another in so many fundamental ways as to make virtually impossible a meaningful comparison.[37]

In many ways New York City is in a class by itself, not only with regard to size but also in the complexity of its government. New York is simply too big, too diverse, to be dominated by a single family, a single industry, or even a small group of business and financial leaders. It came as no surprise when Wallace Sayre and Herbert Kaufman in their monumental *Governing New York City* concluded:

> No single ruling elite dominates the political and governmental system of New York City. . . . Most individual decisions are shaped by a small percentage of the city's population—indeed by a small percentage of those who engage actively in politics—because only the participants concerned have the time, energy, skill, and motivation to do much about them. The city government is most accurately visualized as a series of semi-autonomous little worlds, each of which brings forth programs and policies through the interactions of its own inhabitants. . . . New York's huge and diverse system of government and politics is a loose-knit and multi-centered network in which decisions are reached by ceaseless bargaining and fluctuating alliances among the major categories of participants in each center, and in which the centers are partially but strikingly isolated from one another.[38]

Edward Banfield's excellent description of decision making in Chicago also fails to reveal a "ruling elite," although the structure of influence is much more centralized than in New York City.[39] But Banfield finds that Mayor Daley's political organization is at the center of Chicago's influence structure, rather than a business or financial elite. According to Banfield: "Civic controversies in Chicago are not generated by the efforts of politicians to win votes, by differences about ideology or group interest, or by the behind-the-scenes efforts of a power elite. They arise, instead, out of the

---

[37] *Ibid.*
[38] Wallace Sayre and Herbert Kaufman, *Governing New York City,* Paperback Edition (New York: W. W. Norton & Co., Inc., 1965), pp. 710, 715–16.
[39] Edward Banfield, *Political Influence* (Glencoe: Free Press, 1961).

maintenance and enhancement needs of large formal organizations. The heads of an organization see some advantage to be gained by changing the situation. They propose changes. Other large organizations are threatened. They oppose, and a civic controversy takes place." [40] It is not usually business organizations that propose changes but "in most of the cases described here the effective organizations are public ones, and their chief executives are career civil servants." While Banfield acknowledged that business and financial leaders played an important role in Chicago politics, they did not really amount to a ruling elite. After studying seven major decisions in Chicago, Banfield concluded that political heads, such as Mayor Daley, and public agencies and civic associations employed top business leaders to lend prestige and legitimacy to policy proposals. The "top leaders" of Chicago—the Fields, McCormacks, Ryersons, Swifts, and Armours —and the large corporations—Inland Steel, Sears-Roebuck, Field's Department Store, and the Chicago Title and Trust Company—were criticized less for interfering in public affairs than for "failing to assume their civic responsibilities." Few of these top leaders participated directly in the decisions studied by Banfield. Banfield admits that this is not proof that the top business leadership did not exercise a great deal of influence behind the scenes. And Banfield acknowledges that the belief in the existence of a ruling elite is widespread in Chicago; he quotes the head of a Negro civic association as saying: "There are a dozen men in this town who could go into City Hall and order an end to racial violence just like you or I could go into a grocery store and order a loaf of bread. All they would have to do is say what they wanted and they would get it." [41] And Banfield states that top business leaders in Chicago have great "potential for power": "Indeed, if influence is defined as the *ability* to modify behavior in accordance with one's intentions, there could be little doubt that there exist 'top leaders' with aggregate influence sufficient to run the city." [42] However, Banfield maintains that these top leaders do not in fact run the city, for several reasons. First of all, there were many fundamental conflicts of interest and opinion among business leaders. Business leaders do not have sufficient unity of purpose in community politics to decide controversial questions. Secondly, top business leaders have no effective communication system among themselves which would enable them to act in concert. Thirdly, the top business leaders in Chicago did not have the necessary organization to carry out their plans even if they could agree on what should be done. (This is why the top business leaders in Philadelphia formed the Greater Philadelphia Movement, and the Allegheny Conference on Community Development was formed in Pittsburgh.) Banfield concludes: "The notion that 'top leaders' run the

[40] *Ibid.,* p. 263.
[41] *Ibid.,* p. 289.
[42] *Ibid.,* p. 290.

city is certainly not supported by the facts of the controversies described in this book. On the contrary, in these cases the richest men of Chicago are conspicuous by their absence. Lesser business figures appear, but they do not act concertedly: some of them are on every side of every issue." [43]

Comparative Study of Community Power

Only by comparing structures of power and decision making processes in a wide variety of communities can social scientists learn the actual extent of elitism or pluralism in American community life. Some communities may have concentrated, pyramidal structures of power, while others have diffused, multi-centered power arrangements. For example, it is very likely that decision making in Atlanta is much more centralized than in Chicago, and that decision making in Chicago is more centralized than in New York City or New Haven, Connecticut. Community power structures probably range from monolithic elites to very dispersed pluralistic patterns.

The key to understanding community power lies in identifying different types of community power structures and then relating these to social, economic, and political conditions in communities. For example, we may find that large communities with a great deal of social and economic diversity, a competitive party system, and a variety of well organized competing interest groups tend to have pluralist decision making systems. On the other hand, small communities with a homogeneous population, a single dominant industry, nonpartisan elections, and few competing organizations, may have power structures resembling the elite model.

One of the most important comparative studies of community power is *The Rulers and the Ruled* by Professors Robert Agger, Daniel Goldrich, and Bert Swanson, an intensive study of "power and impotence" in four American communities over a 15-year period. [44] These scholars identified four types of power structure, based upon the degree of citizen participation and influence and the degree of competition and conflict among political leaders. If many citizens shared political influence and there were two or more competing leadership groups, the community was said to have a "competitive mass" power structure. If many citizens shared political influence and there was little disagreement or conflict among leaders, the community's power structure was termed "consensual mass." If few citizens shared political influence and there was little disagreement among leaders, the power structure was said to be "consensual elite." If few citizens shared political influence, but leaders divided into competing groups, it was said to be "competitive elite" structure.

---

[43] *Ibid.,* p. 288.
[44] Robert Agger, Daniel Goldrich, and Bert Swanson, *The Rulers and the Ruled* (New York: John Wiley & Sons, Inc., 1965).

The "consensual elite" structure in *The Rulers and the Ruled* most closely resembles the elite model described earlier, since citizen influence is limited and leaders share a single ideology. The "competitive mass" structure most closely resembles our pluralist model, since many citizens share power and there are competing leadership groups. Of course the "ideal" community is probably the "consensual mass" type, where influence is widely shared among the citizens and there is little conflict among leaders. The municipal reform movement envisions such a community, where democracy prevails and "reasonable men" agree to govern in "the public interest."

The authors also proposed a typology of community "regimes" based upon the recognized "rules of the game" in community politics and the degree to which people believed they could be politically effective. If the rules of the game were adhered to by political leaders, and citizens believed they could influence policy, the regime was labeled a "developed democracy." If the rules of the game were adhered to by political leaders, but citizens felt politically ineffective, the regime was an "underdeveloped democracy." If leaders frequently resorted to illegitimate means to curtail political participation or free expression—including loss of employment, discrimination, or severe social ostracism—a regime was labeled either a "guided democracy," if public confidence remained high, or an "oligarchy," if people no longer felt they could affect policy.

The power structures and regimes in all four communities were described and classified at 15 different time periods from 1946 to 1961. This enabled the authors not only to compare different communities but also to see changes in communities over time.

The Rulers and the Ruled studies produced many interesting findings about community power. First of all, a "competitive mass" type of power

FIGURE 12.1

TYPES OF POWER STRUCTURES

Distributions of Political Power Among Citizens

		Broad	Narrow
Political Leadership	Convergent	Consensual Mass	Consensual Elite
	Divergent	Competitive Mass	Competitive Elite

SOURCE: Robert Agger, Daniel Goldrich, and Bert Swanson, *The Rulers and the Ruled* (New York: John Wiley & Sons, Inc., 1964), p. 73. Reproduced by permission.

FIGURE 12.2

TYPES OF REGIMES

Probability of Illegitimate Sanctions Being Used

		Low	High
Sense of Political Effectiveness	High	Developed Democracy	Guided Democracy
	Low	Underdeveloped Democracy	Oligarchy

SOURCE: Robert Agger, Daniel Goldrich, and Bert Swanson, *The Rulers and the Ruled* (New York: John Wiley & Sons, Inc., 1964), p. 83. Reproduced by permission.

structure (pluralist) is related to a "developed democracy" regime. A sense of political effectiveness among citizens and adherence to the rules of the game by leaders is essential for the development of broad citizen participation in community affairs and the emergence of competitive leadership groups. A lack of political confidence among residents, and a widespread belief that political activity is useless often results in a monopoly of political leadership and a "consensual elite" (elitist) power structure.

If leadership changes from competitive to consensual over time, the distribution of power tends to change from mass to elite. In other words, with the disappearance of competition among leadership factions, citizen participation declines, fewer issues are submitted to popular referendum, and the power distribution becomes more elitist. Conversely, when the distribution of power changes from elite to mass, that is, when an increasing number of people begin to "crack" the power structure, political competition is likely to increase.

A competitive mass (pluralist) type of power structure will be more stable over time if the competing leadership groups represent high and low socio-economic classes than if the competitors represent the same socio-economic class. Pluralism depends in part upon socio-economic cleavages in the community being represented by separate leadership groups. When competitive leaders represent the same socio-economic class, competition can easily disappear over time and the power structure becomes "consensual" rather than "competitive."

The authors found that developed democracy regimes and competitive mass power structures were less likely to occur in communities where the major industries were home-owned. Economic leaders of home-owned industries tended to be members of a single group of political leaders in the respective communities, which discouraged political competition. The prominence of these people influenced some groups in their communities to refrain from political activity because they feared illegitimate political sanctions, even though the actual use of these sanctions was relatively infrequent. Interestingly, the authors found no relationship between community size or growth rate and either the type of regime or the nature of the power structure in their four communities.

13

POLITICS, CIVIL RIGHTS, AND PUBLIC ORDER

The States and School Desegregation

The 14th Amendment declares:

> All persons born or naturalized in the United States, and subject to the jurisdiction thereof, are citizens of the United States and of the State wherein they reside. No State shall make or enforce any law which shall abridge the privileges or immunities of citizens of the United States; nor shall any State deprive any person of life, liberty, or property, without due process of law; nor deny to any person within its jurisdiction the equal protection of the laws.

The language of the 14th Amendment and its historical context leaves little doubt that its original purpose was to achieve the full measure of citizenship and equality for the American Negro. Some Radical Republicans were prepared in 1867 to carry out the revolution in southern society that this amendment implied. But by 1877, it was clear that Reconstruction had failed and that the national government was not prepared to carry out the long, difficult and disagreeable task of really reconstructing society in the 11 states of the former Confederacy.[1] In what has been described as the compromise of 1877, the national government agreed to end military occu-

---

[1] C. Vann Woodward, *Reunion and Reaction: The Compromise of 1877 and the End of Reconstruction* (Boston: Little, Brown and Co., 1951).

pation of the South, give up its efforts to rearrange southern society, and lend tacit approval to white supremacy in that region. In return, the southern states pledged their support of the Union, accepted national supremacy, and, of course, agreed to permit the Republican candidate to assume the Presidency after the disputed election of 1876.

The Supreme Court adhered to the terms of the compromise. The result was an inversion of the meaning of the 14th Amendment so that by 1896 it had become a bulwark of segregation. State laws segregating the races were upheld so long as persons in each of the separated races were treated equally. The constitutional argument on behalf of segregation under the 14th Amendment was that the phrase "equal protection of the laws" did not prevent state-enforced *separation* of the races. Schools and other public facilities that were "separate but equal" won constitutional approval. This separate but equal doctrine became the Supreme Court's interpretation of the Equal Protection Clause of the 14th Amendment in Plessy *v*. Ferguson:

> The object of the [14th] Amendment was undoubtedly to enforce the absolute equality of the two races before the law, but in the nature of things it could not have been intended to abolish distinctions based upon color, or to enforce social, as distinguished from political, equality, or a commingling of the two races upon terms unsatisfactory to either. Laws permitting, and even requiring, their separation in places where they are liable to be brought into contact do not necessarily imply the inferiority of either race to the other, and have been generally, if not universally, recognized as within the competency of the state legislatures in the exercise of their police power. The most common instance of this is connected with the establishment of separate schools for white and colored children, which has been held to be a valid exercise of the legislative power . . .[2]

As a matter of fact, of course, segregated facilities, including public schools, were seldom if ever equal, even with respect to physical conditions. In practice, the doctrine of segregation was "separate and *un*equal." The Supreme Court began to take notice of this after World War II. While it declined to overrule the segregationist interpretation of the 14th Amendment, it began to order the admission of individual Negroes to white public universities, where evidence indicated that separate Negro institutions were inferior or nonexistent.[3]

Leaders of the newly emerging civil rights movement in the 1940's and 1950's were not satisfied with court decisions that examined the circumstances in each case to determine if separate school facilities were really equal. Led by Roy Wilkins, Executive Director of the National Association for the Advancement of Colored People, and Thurgood Marshall, Chief

---

[2] 163 U.S. 537 (1896).
[3] Sweatt *v*. Painter, 339 U.S. 629 (1950); McLaurin *v*. Oklahoma State Regents, 339 U.S. 637 (1950).

FIGURE 13.1

SEGREGATION LAWS IN THE STATES, 1954

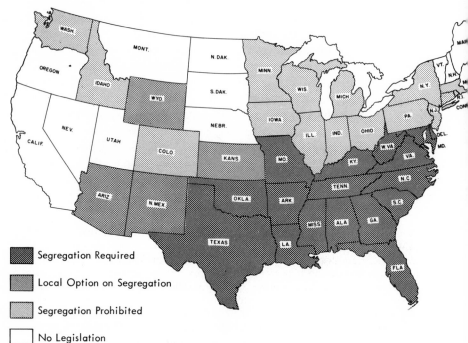

■ Segregation Required

▨ Local Option on Segregation

▧ Segregation Prohibited

□ No Legislation

SOURCE: *The New York Times,* May 17, 1954. Reproduced by permission.

Counsel for the NAACP, the civil rights movement pressed for a court decision that segregation itself meant inequality within the meaning of the 14th Amendment, whether or not facilities were equal in all tangible respects. In short, they wanted a complete reversal of the "separate but equal" interpretation of the 14th Amendment, and a holding that laws *separating* the races were unconstitutional.

The civil rights groups chose to bring suit for desegregation in Topeka, Kansas, where segregated Negro and white schools were equal with respect to buildings, curricula, qualifications, and salaries of teachers, and other tangible factors. The object was to prevent the Court from ordering the admission of a Negro because *tangible* facilities were not equal, and to force the Court to review the doctrine of segregation itself.

On May 17, 1954, the Court rendered its decision in Brown *v.* Board of Education of Topeka, Kansas:

> Segregation of white and colored children in public has a detrimental effect upon the colored children. The impact is greater when it has the

sanction of law, for the policy of separating the races is usually interpreted as denoting the inferiority of the Negro group. A sense of inferiority affects the motivation of a child to learn. Segregation with the sanction of law, therefore, has a tendency to retard the educational and mental development of Negro children and to deprive them of some of the benefits they would receive in a racially integrated school system.

Whatever may have been the extent of psychological knowledge at the time of Plessy v. Ferguson, this finding is amply supported by modern authority. Any language in Plessy v. Ferguson contrary to this finding is rejected.[4]

The Supreme Court had spoken forcefully in the Brown case in 1954 in declaring segregation unconstitutional. From a constitutional viewpoint, any state-supported segregation of the races after 1954 was prohibited. Article VI of the Constitution declares that the words of that document are "the supreme law of the land . . . anything in the constitution or laws of any state to the contrary notwithstanding."

From a political viewpoint, however, the battle over segregation was just beginning. Segregation would remain a part of American life, regardless of its constitutionality, until effective political power was brought to bear to end it. The Supreme Court, by virtue of the American system of federalism and separation of powers, has little formal power at its disposal. Congress, the President, state governors and legislatures, and the people have more power at their disposal than the federal judiciary. The Supreme Court must rely largely on the other branches of the federal government, on the states, and on private individuals and organizations to effectuate the law of the land.

Yet in 1954 the practice of segregation was widespread and deeply ingrained in American life. Seventeen states required the segregation of the races in public schools. These seventeen states were:

Alabama	North Carolina	Delaware
Arkansas	South Carolina	Kentucky
Florida	Tennessee	Maryland
Georgia	Texas	Missouri
Louisiana	Virginia	Oklahoma
Mississippi	West Virginia	

The Congress of the United States required the segregation of the races in the public schools of the District of Columbia.[5] Four additional states— Arizona, Kansas, New Mexico, and Wyoming—authorized segregation upon the option of local school boards.

Thus, in deciding Brown v. Topeka, the Supreme Court struck down the

---

[4] Brown v. Board of Education of Topeka, 347 U.S. 483 (1954).

[5] The Supreme Court also ruled that Congress was bound to respect the equal protection doctrine imposed upon the states by the 14th Amendment as part of the "due process" clause of the 5th Amendment. Bolling v. Sharpe, 347 U.S. 497 (1954).

TABLE 13.1

PUBLIC SCHOOL DESEGREGATION, FALL, 1964

	School districts			Negro school enrollment		Negroes in school with whites	
	Total	With Negroes and whites	Deseg-regated	Numbers	Percent of total enroll-ment	Numbers	Percent of total Negro enroll-ment
Ala.	118	118	8	293,476	34.8	94	0.03
Ark.	412	228	24	114,651	25.6	930	0.8
Fla.	67	67	21	246,215	19.7	6,524	2.6
Ga.	196	180	11	354,850	32.0	1,337	0.4
La.	67	67	3	321,000	28.4	3,581	1.1
Miss.	150	150	4	295,962	49.0	58	0.02
N.C.	171	171	84	349,282	29.7	4,918	1.4
S.C.	108	108	16	260,667	41.2	260	.1
Tenn.	152	141	61	173,673	19.3	9,265	5.3
Tex.	1,380	862	291	344,312	12.4	25,000	7.3
Va.	130	128	81	234,176	24.2	11,883	5.1
SOUTH	2,951	2,220	604	2,988,264	26.6	63,850	2.1
Del.	78	43	43	19,497	19.0	11,267	57.8
D.C.	1	1	11	123,906	87.6	106,578	86.0
Ky.	204	165	164	56,000	7.7	35,000	62.5
Md.	24	23	23	166,861	22.8	86,203	51.7
Mo.	1,542	212*	203*	102,000	10.0	44,000	44.1
Okla.	1,118	242	200	48,954	7.5	13,925	31.7
W. Va.	55	44	44	21,000	4.5	18,500	88.1
BORDER	3,022	730	678	533,218	14.8	315,471	59.2

*estimated
Source: Southern Education Reporting Service, *Southern School News*, Vol. 10 (Dec., 1964).

laws of 21 states and the District of Columbia in a single opinion. Such a far-reaching decision was bound to meet with difficulties in implementation. In an opinion delivered the following year regarding the question of relief for Brown and others similarly situated, the Supreme Court said:

> Full implementation of these constitutional principles may require solution of varied local school problems. School authorities have the primary responsibility for elucidating, assessing, and solving these problems; courts will have to consider whether the action of school authorities constitutes good faith implementation of the governing constitutional principles.[6]

Thus, the Supreme Court did not order immediate nationwide desegregation, but instead turned over the responsibility for desegregation to state

[6] Brown *v.* Board of Education of Topeka, 349 U.S. 294 (1955).

and local authorities under the supervision of federal district courts. The way was open for extensive litigation, obstruction, and delay by states that chose to resist desegregation.

The six border states with segregated school systems—Delaware, Kentucky, Maryland, Missouri, Oklahoma, West Virginia—together with the school districts in Kansas, Arizona, and New Mexico which had operated segregated schools, chose not to resist desegregation formally. The District of Columbia also desegregated its public schools the year following the Supreme Court's decision. Progress in desegregation in the border states is shown in Table 13.1; by 1964 over half of the Negro children in these states were attending integrated schools.

Resistance to school integration was the policy choice of the 11 states of the Old Confederacy. Refusal of a school district to desegregate until it is faced with a federal court injunction is the most common form of delay. Segregationists pressed for state laws which would create an endless chain of litigation in each of the nearly 3000 school districts in the South, in the hope that integration efforts would drown in a sea of protracted court controversy.

Other schemes have included state payment of private school tuition in lieu of providing public schools, amending compulsory attendance laws to provide that no child shall be required to attend an integrated school, requiring schools faced with desegregation orders to cease operation, and the use of pupil placement laws to avoid or minimize the extent of integration.[7] State officials have also attempted to prevent desegregation on the grounds that it would endanger public safety. State officials have themselves precipitated and encouraged violent resistance through attempts to "interpose" and "nullify" federal authority within their states.[8]

On the whole, those states which chose to resist desegregation were quite successful in doing so during the ten year period from 1954 to 1964. Table 13.1 indicates that in late 1964 only about two per cent of the Negro school children in the 11 southern states were attending integrated schools. Only 604 of the South's 2220 school districts which encompassed Negro students, were officially desegregated; and most of these 604 districts experienced only token desegregation. The effectiveness of state policy up to 1964

[7] State laws which were obviously designed to evade constitutional responsibilities to end segregation were struck down in federal courts. See Aaron v. Cooper, 261 F. 2d 97 (1958); Harrison v. Day, 106 S.E. 2d 636 (1959). However, federal courts have upheld pupil assignment laws, including the so-called "freedom of choice" plan, which permit parents to request school assignments and school authorities to assign pupils on an individual basis according to nonracial criteria—space available, etc. Pupil assignment laws were not held to be invalid on their face, although they give school authorities great discretion and it is difficult to prove that race did not influence pupil assignment. See Shuttlesworth v. Birmingham Board of Education, 358 U.S. 101 (1958); Bush v. Orleans Parish School Board, 308 F. 2d 491 (1962).

[8] The Supreme Court declared that the threat of violence was not sufficient reason to deny constitutional rights to Negro children, and again dismissed the ancient interposition arguments. Cooper v. Aaron, 358 U.S. 1 (1958).

in resisting the policy of the federal court is an important, although regrettable, comment on the powers of the states in our federal system.,

The decision of 11 southern states to resist desegregation was, of course, a product of the total cultural history of the region. The roots of racial attitudes in the South are too deep to examine here. However, progress in desegregation is not uniform throughout the southern states, and it is therefore possible to contrast the characteristics of those states that have made some progress toward integration with those that have not. For example, desegregation has been slow and painful in Mississippi, Alabama, and South Carolina, while changes have been somewhat easier in Texas, Tennessee, Virginia, and Florida. How do these states differ? What accounts for differences among southern states in their degree of resistance to desegregation?

Does a large proportion of Negroes in a state's population strengthen the integration movement or does it strengthen the resolve of segregationists to resist integration? The nonwhite population percentages in the 11 southern states in 1960 were as follows: Alabama, 30.1; Arkansas, 21.9; Florida, 18.0; Georgia, 28.6; Louisiana, 32.1; Mississippi, 42.3; North Carolina, 25.4; South Carolina, 35.0; Tennessee, 16.6; Texas, 12.6; Virginia, 20.8; The evidence is very strong that a large Negro population strengthens the position of segregationists. States with large Negro populations have made less progress toward desegregation than states with smaller proportions of Negro residents.

While large Negro populations appear to stimulate resistance to desegregation, wealth and urbanization appear to have the opposite effect. These variables are not as influential as Negro population percentages in explaining progress toward desegregation. However, the wealth and urbanism of Texas, Florida, and North Carolina do help to explain their somewhat more progressive posture toward desegregation. The ruralism and poverty in Mississippi, Alabama, and South Carolina help to explain their less progressive policies.

In the Civil Rights Act of 1964, Congress finally entered the civil rights field in support of court efforts to achieve desegregation. Among other things, the Civil Rights Act of 1964 provided that every federal department and agency must take action to end segregation in all programs or activities receiving federal financial assistance. It was specified that this action was to include termination of financial assistance if states and communities receiving federal funds refused to comply with federal desegregation orders. Thus, in addition to court orders requiring desegregation, states and communities faced administrative orders, or "guidelines," from federal executive agencies, particularly the U.S. Office of Education, threatening loss of federal funds for noncompliance. Acting under the authority of Title VI, the U.S. Office of Education required all school districts in the 17 formerly segregated states to submit desegregation plans as a condition of federal assistance. "Guidelines" governing the acceptability of these plans were frequently unclear, often conflicting, and always changing, yet progress toward desegregation was speeded up. In fact, Table 13.2 indicates that the U.S. Office of Education has been a great deal more successful than federal courts in ending segregation. In two years of administering federal grants according to Title VI of the Civil Rights Act, the percentage of Negroes in southern states attending schools with whites increased from 2 to 16, an eight-fold increase in only two years. By August of 1967 federal funds to 90 school districts had been terminated for noncompliance with federal executive-ordered desegregation guidelines.

Donald R. Matthews and James Prothro systematically examined the environmental and political factors associated with desegregation policy in 997 southern counties.[9] Their dependent variable was simply the presence

TABLE 13.2

DESEGREGATION SPEED-UP, 1964 TO 1966

	1964 Negroes in school with whites		1966 Negroes in school with whites	
	Number (in thousands)	Per cent of total Negro enrollment	Number (in thousands)	Per cent of total Negro enrollment
Southern states				
Alabama	–	0.03	12	4.4
Arkansas	1	0.8	18	15.1
Florida	7	2.6	65	22.3
Georgia	1	0.4	34	8.8
Louisiana	4	1.1	11	3.4
Mississippi	–	0.02	7	2.5
North Carolina	5	1.4	55	15.4
South Carolina	–	0.1	15	5.6
Tennessee	9	5.3	53	28.6
Texas	25	7.3	159	44.9
Virginia	12	5.1	62	25.3
Total	64	2.1	490	15.9
Border states				
Delaware	11	57.8	21	100.0
Kentucky	35	62.5	55	90.1
Maryland	36	51.7	127	65.3
Missouri	44	44.1	108	77.7
Oklahoma	14	31.7	31	50.8
West Virginia	19	88.1	21	93.4
Total	315	59.2	466	75.7

[9] Donald R. Matthews and James W. Prothro "Stateways versus Folkways: Critical Factors in Southern Reactions to Brown *v.* Board of Education," *Essays on the American Constitution,* Gottfried Dietze, ed. (Englewood Cliffs: Prentice-Hall, Inc., 1964), pp. 139–58.

or absence of some school desegregation in each county in 1960. The environmental variables that correlated most closely with this rough measure of desegregation were as follows:

1. Per cent of population urban;
2. Nonwhite median income;
3. Nonwhite median school years completed;
4. White median income;
5. Per cent of population Negro;
6. Per cent of population increase in 1940–50;
7. Per cent of church members Roman Catholic;
8. Per cent of church members Baptist;
9. Per cent of nonwhite labor force in white collar jobs;
10. Per cent of labor force in agriculture.

These variables are presented in the order of their strength of association with school desegregation. Matthews and Prothro concluded that desegregation is most likely in an urban environment in which Negroes and whites receive relatively high incomes and Negroes are relatively well educated. In addition, a large Negro population was a distinct barrier to desegregation. Apparently the presence of a large number of Negroes in a county tends to stimulate white resistance to desegregation, rather than provide effective positive support for it.

Matthews and Prothro found that political variables were much less influential in accounting for school desegregation policy than environmental variables. Their political variables were as follows:

1. Per cent states' rights presidential vote in 1948;
2. Per cent Republican presidential vote;
3. Highest per cent Republican in race for statewide office 1950–59;
4. Presence-absence of Negro race organization;
5. Presence-absence of white race organization;
6. Per cent of voting age Negroes registered to vote.

Further analysis by Matthews and Prothro indicated that most of the correlation between these political variables and school desegregation policy was really a product of the relationship between political variables and environmental variables. In other words, environmental variables rather than political variables appear to be most influential in shaping desegregation policy.

"De Facto" Segregation in Cities

In Brown v. Board of Education of Topeka, Kansas, the Supreme Court stated that segregation had "a tendency to retard the educational and mental development of Negro children and to deprive them of some of the benefits they would receive in a racially integrated school system." The U.S. Civil

Rights Commission reported that even when the segregation was *de facto,* that is, a product of segregated housing patterns and neighborhood schools rather than direct discrimination, the adverse effects on Negro students were still significant.[10] In northern urban school districts the Commission reported that predominantly Negro schools were less likely to have good libraries or advanced courses in sciences and languages than predominantly white schools and more likely to have overcrowded classrooms, poorly trained teachers, and teachers who were dissatisfied with their school assignments. Negro students attending predominantly Negro schools had lower achievement scores and lower aspiration levels than Negroes from similar economic backgrounds attending predominantly white schools. When a group of Negro students in class with a majority of advantaged whites was compared with a control group of Negroes attending school with a majority of disadvantaged Negroes, the difference in achievement amounted to more than two grade levels. On the other hand, the Commission contended that the achievement of white students in classes which were roughly half white was no different than that of a control group of white students in all white schools. Therein lies the essential argument for ending de facto segregation in northern urban school systems.

However, ending de facto segregation would require drastic changes in the existing concept of "neighborhood schools." Schools would no longer be a part of the neighborhood or local community but part of a larger citywide or metropolitanwide school system. Students would have to be bussed on a large scale into and out of the ghettos. In several large cities where Negroes comprise the overwhelming majority of public school students, desegregation would require city students to be bussed to the suburbs and suburban students to be bussed to the core city. Such a program would require the cooperation of independent suburban school districts, which seems very unlikely. Many suburbanites moved out of the central city in order to get their children out of city schools, and they are not likely to look with favor upon proposals to bus them back to the ghettos. Finally, the ending of de facto segregation would require school districts to classify students on the basis of race and use racial categories as a basis for school placement. Although this is supposedly a benign form of racial discrimination, it represents a return to government sponsored racial classification and the differential application of laws to the separate races. This would conflict with the traditional idea that the Constitution and laws of the United States should be "color blind."

To date, the federal government has taken no action to reduce de facto segregation in northern schools. In fact, an amendment to the 1964 Civil Rights Act specifically forbade government agencies from issuing any order

[10] United States Commission on Civil Rights, *Racial Isolation in the Public Schools,* 2 vols. (Washington: U.S. Government Printing Office, 1967).

to achieve racial balance in any areas that did not have legally separate schools for Negroes in the past. This meant that the U.S. Office of Education was forbidden to issue desegregation guidelines to school districts outside of the southern and border states.

While the Supreme Court has shown its distaste for color or racial classifications under the Constitution, those classifications that have been declared unconstitutional under the 14th Amendment have all been harmful to the minority race. It is very unlikely that the Supreme Court would hold that racial classification and "bussing" for the purpose of achieving integration is unconstitutional, since the racial classification is aimed at helping rather than harming the minority race. Thus, there is no constitutional barrier to "bussing." To date, federal courts have *not* held that there is any affirmative duty to correct de facto racial imbalances in the schools.[11] In other words, as yet there is no constitutional *duty* to eliminate de facto segregation, so long as school attendance lines were drawn with no real intention of segregating the races.[12] However, the Supreme Court, on more than one occasion, has altered its interpretations of the duties imposed on states and school districts by the 14th Amendment, and the Court may someday require school districts in both North and South to integrate student bodies consciously.

The extent of de facto segregation in the public elementary schools of the nation's 20 largest cities is shown in Table 13.3. It is easier to achieve desegregation when the Negro percentage of school enrollment is low; obviously desegregation is difficult if not impossible when there are few white students in public schools with whom to integrate Negro children. Thus, Washington, D.C. is virtually unable to achieve desegregation.

Desegregation in Philadelphia, Chicago, Detroit, Baltimore, Cleveland, St. Louis, and New Orleans is also made difficult by the fact that a majority of the students in the cities are Negro. Note, however, that there are important differences between cities with less than a majority of Negro students in the degree to which segregation exists. New York has only 20.7 per cent of its Negro students attending predominantly (90–100 per cent) Negro schools, while Milwaukee, with proportionately fewer Negro students, sends 72.4 per cent of them to predominantly Negro schools. Buffalo also has a large proportion (77.0 per cent) of its Negro students in predominantly Negro schools. Most of the southern cities continue to send heavy proportions of the Negro students to predominantly Negro schools: Houston—93.0 per cent; Dallas—82.6; New Orleans—95.9; San Antonio —65.9.

With the exception of Washington, D.C., no city as yet has so few white

[11] See Fuller *v.* Volk, 230 F. Supp. 25 (1964).
[12] Bell *v.* School City of Gary, 213 F. Supp. 819, aff'd, 324 F. 2d 209, cert. denied, 377 U.S. 924 (1964).

pupils that it is physically unable to bring an end to segregation, if we define segregation as schools with more than 90 per cent Negro pupils. Over 60 per cent of the public elementary pupils in Richmond, Baltimore, and St. Louis were Negro in 1965–66; these are the highest Negro enrollments of any large city in the nation, and there are still enough white pupils to abolish 90–100 per cent Negro schools, if the white pupils were spread around. (If a segregated school is defined as one with a *majority* of Negro students, there are about a dozen large cities which would be unable to desegregate, owing to a lack of white pupils.) Of course it is true that the greater the Negro proportion of the school population, the more extensive the policy change required to accomplish desegregation. But it is not impossible. The U.S. Civil Rights Commission has suggested several policy options for school districts wishing to desegregate: the "pairing" or merging of attendance areas of two or more schools; the establishment of cen-

TABLE 13.3

SEGREGATION IN PUBLIC ELEMENTARY SCHOOLS OF LARGE CITIES IN
1965--1966

	Negro students as a percent of total students	Percentage of Negro students in schools 90-100 percent Negro	Percentage of Negro students in schools 90-100 percent white
New York	31.0	20.7	56.8
Chicago	52.8	89.2	88.8
Los Angeles	19.2	39.5	94.7
Philadelphia	58.6	72.0	57.7
Detroit	55.3	72.3	65.0
Baltimore	64.3	84.2	67.0
Houston	33.9	93.0	97.3
Cleveland	53.9	82.3	80.2
Washington	90.9	90.4	34.3
St. Louis	63.3	90.9	66.0
Milwaukee	26.4	72.4	86.3
San Francisco	28.8	21.1	65.1
Boston	28.9	35.4	76.5
Dallas	27.5	82.6	90.1
New Orleans	65.5	95.9	83.8
Pittsburgh	39.4	49.5	62.3
San Antonio	14.3	65.9	89.4
San Diego	11.6	13.9	88.7
Seattle	10.5	9.9	89.8
Buffalo	34.6	77.0	81.1

Source: U.S. Civil Rights Commission, *Racial Isolation in the Public Schools* Vol.
I (Washington: Government Printing Office, 1967), p. 4.

tral "educational parks" integrating students from throughout the school district; and the closing of predominantly Negro schools and the dispersal of their students among other schools in the community.[13] The only technological innovation these policies call for is the school bus, and since 75 per cent of all public school children in the nation already ride buses, the feasibility of the bus seems beyond question.

The political problems of "bussing" far exceed its physical dislocations in creating obstacles to school desegregation. Yet several states have made more or less official policy pronouncements against de facto segregation. Massachusetts has taken the strongest policy stand of any state in its Racial Imbalance Act of 1965. This provides that a school district, upon notification by the state board that one of its schools is racially imbalanced (50 per cent or more Negro pupils), must prepare and file with the board a plan to eliminate the imbalance. If the school district fails to show progress within a reasonable time in eliminating racial imbalances, the Commissioner of Education must refuse to certify all state school aid for that school district. In New York, New Jersey, and Illinois, there are general laws guaranteeing equal educational opportunity, which have been construed by state boards and commissioners as mandating the elimination of racial imbalance in the selection of school sites and the drawing of attendance lines. However, the sanctions available to enforce these policies are vague and ill-defined.

Negro Population Trends

While Negroes constitute only 11 per cent of the total population of the United States, they are rapidly approaching a numerical majority in many of the nation's largest cities. Negroes already constitute a majority of the population of Washington, D.C., and by 1970 they will make up more than 40 per cent of the population of Detroit, Baltimore, St. Louis, New Orleans, Atlanta, Newark, Oakland, Birmingham, and Gary. They will make up nearly a third of the population of Chicago, Philadelphia, Cleveland, Memphis, Columbus, and Cincinnati. These population trends are bound to have an impact on politics and public policy in these cities.

The two outstanding trends in Negro population migration in recent decades has been the tendency of Negroes to leave the South and to move from rural to urban areas. Census figures show, for example, that while 87 per cent of the nation's Negroes lived in the South in 1900, only 56 per cent did so in 1960. While only 27 per cent of the nation's Negroes lived in urban areas in 1910, a full 73 per cent did so in 1960. Moreover, in leaving rural areas, Negroes tended to concentrate heavily in the central cities of metropolitan areas, rather than in small towns or in metropolitan suburbs. This concentration of Negroes in large central cities is a product

[13] United States Commission on Civil Rights, *op. cit.*, vol. I, pp. 140–84.

TABLE 13.4

NEGRO POPULATION OF NATION'S LARGEST CITIES
(*Figures are percentages*)

	1940	1950	1960	1970 est.
New York	6	9	14	19
Chicago	8	14	23	32
Los Angeles	4	9	14	23
Philadelphia	13	14	26	32
Detroit	9	16	29	47
Houston	22	21	23	27
Baltimore	19	24	35	47
Cleveland	10	16	29	38
Washington, D.C.	28	38	54	68
Milwaukee	2	3	9	18
Dallas	17	13	19	25
San Francisco	1	6	10	17
St. Louis	13	18	29	46
Boston	3	5	9	13
New Orleans	30	32	37	45
San Antonio	7	7	7	10
San Diego	2	4	6	10
Pittsburgh	9	12	17	21
Seattle	1	3	5	9
Memphis	41	37	37	39
Buffalo	3	6	13	22
Phoenix	6	5	5	10
Atlanta	38	37	38	39
Denver	2	4	6	10
Columbus, Ohio	12	13	16	32
Indianapolis	13	15	21	29
K.C., Mo.	11	12	17	24
Cincinnati	12	15	22	31
Minneapolis	1	1	2	5
Newark, N.J.	11	17	34	46
Fort Worth	14	13	16	20
Louisville	15	16	18	24
Long Beach	1	2	3	7
Portland, Ore.	1	3	4	7
Oklahoma City	9	9	12	18
Oakland, Calif.	3	12	23	39
Birmingham	41	40	40	40
Norfolk, Va.	32	29	26	23
Miami, Fla.	22	16	22	28
Omaha	5	6	8	12

Source: The National Advisory Commission on Civil Disorders, *Report* (Washington: Government Printing Office, 1968).

353

of the availability of low-priced rental units in older, run-down sections of central cities and of discriminatory housing practices of private owners and developers. Of course, underlying the concentration of Negroes in run-down sectors of central cities is often a lack of sufficient income to purchase housing in suburbs or in better city neighborhoods. This poverty and unemployment that contributes to the concentration of Negroes in "ghettos" is in turn a product of inadequate training and education, low aspiration levels, and often a lack of motivation. And problems in education and motivation are themselves related to a breakdown in family life, delinquency, and crime. Thus, urban Negroes face a whole series of interrelated problems in addition to discrimination: poverty, slum housing, undereducation, lack of job skills, family problems, lack of motivation, delinquency, and crime. It is difficult to talk about any one of these problems without reference to them all.

In recent years the migration of Negroes into cities, particularly in the North, has been accompanied by a heavy out-migration of whites fleeing to the suburbs for a variety of reasons. The total populations of many large central cities have remained stagnant in recent years or even declined slightly; Negro population percentages have increased because Negro in-migration has been equalled by the white out-migration. Negro birth rates in urban areas have also tended to be slightly higher than those of whites.

Politically, these population trends mean that there will be an increase in organized Negro participation in urban politics and increasing Negro importance and power in city administrations. The election of Negro mayors in Cleveland and Gary in 1967 provides evidence that there will be a rise in the number of Negro officeholders. Negro city councilmen, state legislators, and congressmen are likely to become commonplace in the next few years and evoke little comment from the news media. The number of Negroes in the U.S. House of Representatives—six in 1967—may rise to 12 within the next few years. The election of a Negro, Edward W. Brooke, to the U.S. Senate from Massachusetts, suggests that Negroes may also win important statewide elections. This increase in Negro officeholding can be attributed in a large measure to the concentration of Negro voters in large cities.

However, increasing Negro percentages in central cities are not likely to lead to Negro "takeovers," in the sense that Negro officeholders can afford to ignore or override the interests of white city dwellers. In the first place, whites are going to continue to constitute a majority of the population in most central cities. Secondly, Negro candidates are likely to find that there is more political mileage in appealing to white votes by pledging impartiality and promising to be "mayor of *all* of the people." There is little incentive in a strict racist appeal by Negro candidates, as long as whites remain a substantial proportion of the city voting population.

The growing percentages of Negroes in the central cities will continue to intensify some of the nation's most difficult social and economic problems. For city administrations, the continued in-migration of low income Negroes and out-migration of middle income whites can mean further erosion of the city's tax base, as commerce and industry follow the more affluent whites to the suburbs. The continued concentration of poverty and unemployment in central cities will create great strains on city budgets. Without increasing federal or state aid, cities will face a lack of funds to pay for welfare programs, housing programs, improved schools, vocational training, and other programs needed to improve Negro life. Without compensatory government action, the continued concentration of Negroes in big city ghettos will increase the risk of major riots, such as those which occurred in many cities in the summers of 1965, 1966, and 1967.

Yet even while these Negro population trends may suggest the intensification of many serious social and economic problems in cities, there are, nevertheless, some counteractive forces at work. For one thing, ghetto problems have now come to the surface in American politics and a whole web of federal programs have been developed to ease the problems of cities. In 1968 nearly $6 billion of federal money was earmarked for spending in urban areas for the following programs: Economic Opportunity Act, Model Cities, Rent Supplements, Urban Renewal, Urban Mass Transit, Urban Research, Neighborhood Facilities, Home Rehabilitation, Family Relocation, Rat Extermination, Elementary and Secondary Education, Manpower and Development Training, Foodstamps, School Lunches, and Community Health Services. Secondly, the growing political power of Negroes in cities may force local administrations to give far more attention and emphasis to Negro problems in the ghettos—poor schooling, poor housing, and lack of jobs. Local authorities who have not come to grips with Negro problems in the past will now be forced to do so. While cities and even states may not have the resources needed to aid the Negro poor, increased Negro power in cities and states will result in a corresponding increase in pressure upon the federal government to initiate massive aid programs in Negro ghettos.

The Making of Ghettos

Housing in America is becoming more, not less, segregated. Not only do population figures show that Negroes are being concentrated in central cities while whites are fleeing to the suburbs, but even *within* central cities Negro housing is highly segregated. (Figure 13.2, showing the distribution of Negro population in St. Louis by census tract in 1960, is typical of the distribution of the Negroes in most large cities.) This separation of racial groups between cities and suburbs, and within cities, is enforced by the

FIGURE 13.2

DISTRIBUTION OF NEGRO POPULATION IN ST. LOUIS BY CENSUS TRACT, 1960

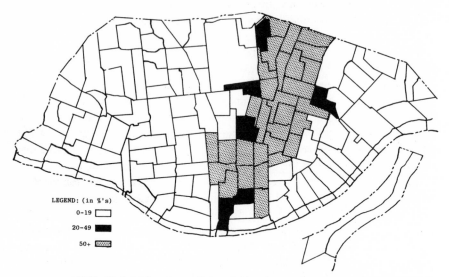

LEGEND: (in %'s)

0-19 ☐

20-49 ■

50+ ▨

SOURCE: U.S. Civil Rights Commission, *Racial Isolation in the Public Schools,* I (Washington: U.S. Government Printing Office, 1967), 33.

practices of the private housing industry—builders, mortgage lenders, landlords, and real estate brokers. While the housing industry contends that it is merely reflecting the preferences and financial resources of its customers, in 1958 the Commission on Race and Housing concluded that, "It is the real estate brokers, builders, and mortgage finance institutions which translate prejudice into discriminatory action." [14] The typical housing development concentrates homes in a single price bracket, so that most homeowners live on a street in which the price of homes do not vary in price more than $2000 or $3000. Real estate developers contend that the alternative pattern of building high and low income houses in the same neighborhood does not appeal to their customers. The result of this practice of building neighborhoods with uniformly priced homes is the creation of social class homogeneity within neighborhoods. This homogeneity even means that whites at different income levels live in different neighborhoods, and of course, it also means that less affluent Negroes are concentrated in areas where low priced housing is concentrated. Thus, social class segregation of neighborhoods leads to de facto segregation of Negroes in residential housing.

But in addition to economically imposed de facto housing segregation,

[14] U.S. Commission on Race and Housing, *Where Shall We Live?* (Washington: U.S. Government Printing Office, 1958), p. 27.

Negroes also face a great deal of direct discrimination in the sale and rental of housing. Until recently a large proportion of private housing in America carried racially restrictive covenants in deeds: "No part of the land hereby conveyed shall ever be used, or be occupied by or sold, demised, trans- ferred, conveyed unto, or in trust for, leased, or rented or given to Negroes, or any other person or persons of Negro blood or extraction, or to any person of the semitic race, blood, or origin, which racial description shall be deemed to include Armenians, Jews, Hebrews, Persians, and Syrians." [15] Not until 1948 was the judicial enforcement of such covenants held un- constitutional, and not until 1953 was enforcement by way of money dam- ages held unlawful.[16] Although racially restrictive convenants are no longer judicially enforceable, they are still used and the pattern they helped to create still exists.

Government policies have also contributed to housing segregation in America. Under Federal Housing Administration and Veterans Adminis- tration housing practices until the late 1950's, some $150 billion in mort- gage loans, representing more than 15 million housing units, were insured or guaranteed under the "homogeneous neighborhood" policies then in effect.[17] These FHA and VA housing programs were largely responsible for the flight of the white middle class to the suburbs by making home ownership easily available to the middle class. But in addition to the de facto segregation resulting from suburban growth, the FHA and VA also engaged in direct discrimination. The result was the creation of many all white suburbs around major urban centers, such as the Levittowns of Long Island, Pennsylvania, and New Jersey; Lakewood near Los Angeles; and Park Forest outside of Chicago. Negroes were systematically barred when these communities were built and sold. Equally important is the fact that federal housing programs have not made an investment in the housing needs of lower income families anywhere comparable to the FHA and VA investment in middle income housing. Since Negroes make up a dis- proportionate share of low income housing clientele, the result has been that Negroes have not had the same opportunity as whites to acquire homes under government insured programs.

Low rent public housing has been an important source of housing for Negroes, but public housing has been confined almost entirely to central cities. Of the public housing authorities in the nation's 24 largest metro- politan areas, in only one, Cincinnati, has the city housing authority been permitted to build outside of the central city. The effect of the public hous-

---

[15] *Hearings Before the U.S. Commission on Civil Rights on Housing in Wash- ington D.C.* (1958), p. 58; also cited U.S. Commission on Civil Rights, *op. cit.,* vol. I, p. 21.

[16] Shelley *v.* Kraemer, 334 U.S. 1 (1948); Barrows *v.* Jackson, 346 U.S. 249 (1953).

[17] U.S. Commission on Civil Rights, *op. cit.,* vol. I., pp. 22–24.

ing program, therefore, has been to intensify the concentrations of the poor and nonwhite in the central city. Moreover, even within central cities, local public housing authorities, instead of locating projects on small sites scattered throughout the city, have concentrated public housing projects in large blocks located in particular areas of the city, and most frequently in areas of already existing Negro concentrations.

In the Civil Rights Act of 1968 Congress banned racial discrimination in the sale or rental of homes or apartments. Real estate dealers, apartment developers, and mortgage lenders were specifically prohibited from discriminating on the basis of race; the only exception in the law dealt with private homeowners who sold their home themselves or rented an apartment which was attached to their house.

Despite this Congressional action, it is not yet clear whether a majority of Americans are really prepared to ban discrimination in housing and eliminate racial ghettos. Congress only acted on the fair housing legislation after the murder of Dr. Martin Luther King, Jr. in Memphis, Tennessee; in the absence of national remorse, Congress might not have acted on this legislation. Fair housing bills had consistently floundered in Congress prior to 1968. Moreover, mass opinion never seemed to favor fair housing laws. While it is true that fair housing laws have been passed by about half of the states, the California experience suggests that these laws have less than overwhelming support among voters. After the California legislature passed a fair housing law in 1964, the state's voters replied by overwhelmingly supporting a state constitutional amendment, known as Proposition 14, which prohibited the legislature from abridging the right of citizens to sell, lease, or rent to the persons of their choice. The effect of the constitutional amendment was to nullify the state's fair housing law; it was passed by a two-to-one margin of voters! (However, in a surprising decision which was later upheld by the U.S. Supreme Court, the California Supreme Court held that Proposition 14 was in violation of the 14th Amendment to the United States Constitution. The Court held that such a state constitutional provision lent state support to racial discrimination and hence violated the Equal Protection Clause of the 14th Amendment.[18]

There is reasonable doubt as to whether fair housing laws—federal, state, or local—would ever succeed in breaking up America's ghettos. A crucial problem is the enforcement of fair housing laws. These laws may eliminate overt discrimination, but it is very difficult to detect discrimination when a seller or his agent chooses to mask his prejudice. But perhaps the most important obstacle to the success of fair housing legislation is the economic inability of many Negroes to take advantage of it and purchase homes in affluent neighborhoods. Until the income levels of Negroes are raised suffi-

[18] Mulkey *v.* Reitman, 413 F. 2d 825 (1966).

ciently to enable them to buy suburban homes, fair housing legislation will remain largely a paper commitment.

There is, as yet, no evidence that cities with fair housing laws are any less segregated than those without such laws. This suggests that the economic constraints upon Negroes may be more effective in creating ghettos than any direct discrimination that can be eliminated through legislation. Finally, it should be pointed out that established residential patterns are very difficult to reverse. Many Negroes and whites become accustomed to prevailing residential patterns. Even if the housing market were open, so that housing choice could be freely exercised, there is some question as to whether there would be immediate significant changes in racial patterns of residence.

State and Local Antidiscrimination Laws

States and communities in America were active in antidiscrimination legislation long before the federal government got around to its Civil Rights Act of 1964.[19] In 1945 New York passed the first state antidiscrimination law dealing with private employment; this law was similar to Title VII of the federal Civil Rights Act passed 19 years later. Connecticut and New Jersey passed laws preventing discrimination in public accommodations in 1949; these laws were similar to Title II of the Civil Rights Act. By 1966 a total of 33 states had fair employment practice laws; 28 of these states strengthen their laws with commissions whose responsibility is to secure enforcement. Thirty-five states had public accommodation laws. Even more noteworthy is the fact that in 1966, 22 states had legislation outlawing discrimination in the sale or rental of housing. Thus, the record of states and communities in fighting discrimination in America is not wholly a negative one.

The typical state fair employment law operates as follows: after a complaint has been filed by an individual, an investigator from the commission tries to determine whether there is probable cause to believe that there is some "unfair" or "unlawful" practice relating to discrimination or segregation in employment; if probable cause is found, informal conciliation is attempted between the commission and the employer; if conciliation is unsuccessful, a formal complaint is issued and a hearing is held, at the conclusion of which the employer may be issued an order requiring him to cease the practice in question; if he refuses to comply, the commission may ask for a court order requiring compliance; if a court order is issued, of course, continued failure to comply would result in contempt of court proceedings with resultant fines or jail sentences. The problem with this ap-

---

[19] See Duane Lockard, *Toward Equal Opportunity* (New York: The Macmillan Company, 1968).

TABLE 13.5

STATE ANTIDISCRIMINATION LAWS
1966

	Fair Employment		Fair Housing		Open Public Accomodations	
	Commission	Statute Only	Commission	Statute Only	Commission	Statute Only
Alaska	X		X		X	
Arizona	X				X	
California	X		1			X
Colorado	X		X		X	
Connecticut	X		X		X	
Delaware	X				X	
Hawaii	X					
Idaho		X		2		X
Illinois	X			2		X
Indiana	X		X		X	
Iowa		X				X
Kansas	X				X	
Kentucky	X				X	
Maine				3		X
Maryland	X				X	
Massachusetts	X		X		X	
Michigan	X		X		X	
Minnesota	X		X		X	
Missouri	X				X	
Montana				4		X
Nebraska	X					X
Nevada		X				
New Hampshire	X		6		X	
New Jersey	X		X		X	
New Mexico	X					X
New York	X		X		X	
North Dakota						X
Ohio	X		X		X	
Oklahoma		5				
Oregon	X		X		X	
Pennsylvania	X		X		X	
Rhode Island	X		X		X	
South Dakota						X
Utah	X					X
Vermont		X				X
Washington	X			4	X	
Wisconsin	X		X			X
Wyoming						X
Totals	28	5	16	5	21	14

1. The Rumford Fair Housing Act in California was nullified by the Proposition 14 Amendment to the State Constitution adopted in November 1964, but Proposition 14 was subsequently declared unconstitutional by the California Supreme Court presumably leaving the Rumford Act intact.

2. Applies only to public housing or publicly assisted housing, including urban renewal housing.

3. Applies to rental housing only.
4. Applies only to housing associated with urban renewal programs.
5. Applies only to public employment.
6. In 1965 the New Hampshire legislature passed an act establishing a commission with jurisdiction over employment, housing, and public accomodations, but it included no appropriations for operation, leaving the new agency in a doubtful status.
Source: Duane Lockard, *Toward Equal Opportunity: A Study of State and Local Anti-Discrimination Laws* (New York: The Macmillan Company, 1968).

proach is that it requires individuals to make complaints before action is taken, and the commission must proceed with one case at a time. Employers are given many opportunities at various stages of proceedings to cease discrimination in the particular case in question and thereby avoid penalty. The case-by-case approach does not necessarily result in the opening of whole fields of employment to Negroes. There are instances in which a single Negro has been aided in getting employment by a commission order, but few other Negroes were subsequently hired. And occasionally, employers may be threatened into hiring less-than-qualified Negroes out of fear that a refusal to do so would result in costly, time-consuming, and embarrassing legal proceedings.

In 1957 the City of New York adopted a fair housing law that became a model for subsequent laws in 16 states and a number of cities. (The states are listed in Table 13.5, and the cities include New York, Philadelphia, Pittsburgh, Schenectady, St. Louis, St. Paul, and Washington, D.C.) Fair housing laws are enforced in much the same manner as fair employment laws: each proceeds on complaint, investigation, conciliation, formal notice and hearing, commission orders, and ultimately court sanctions to force compliance. However, most fair housing laws exclude certain housing from their coverage, for example, the rental of rooms within a residence or owner-occupied building (the "Mrs. Murphy" clause) or an even more significant exclusion—sales or rental of single-family homes. Only Alaska and Michigan bar discrimination in all housing without exception. Mrs. Murphy clauses are in effect in Colorado, Connecticut, Indiana, Massachusetts, New Jersey, and New York. Exceptions for single-family homes are in effect in Minnesota, Ohio, Pennsylvania, and Rhode Island. Oregon law applies only to businesses and New Hampshire and Maine only to rentals and not sales. Procedural delays are a particularly difficult problem in the enforcement of fair housing laws, since often the home in question is already sold to someone else and taken off the market before a complaint can be processed. The long-term effectiveness of fair housing laws in breaking up America's ghettos is still a question mark. Even Duane Lockard, a strong supporter of such laws, admits:

> Only an exuberant optimist would claim that the fair housing laws, which after all are of very recent origin, have dramatically opened up many

formerly white neighborhoods to Negroes. . . . The significance of fair housing laws lies in the future, not in their brief history. As a way of forcing
open doors that otherwise would remain shut, as a way of encouraging
Negroes to venture forth, the fair housing law has a considerable potential
effect. Granted that alone such laws can accomplish little, taken with
other social change they could have an impact on the housing market,
especially because they provide a means to break the resistance of the
hard core objector. Evasion of the law will undoubtedly be common, as
the subjective factors in the renting and sale of housing leave many loop-
holes for the evader, but the blatant discriminator can be reached by
imaginative, resourceful, adequately staffed and supported enforcement
agencies.[20]

Life in the Ghettos

It is not easy for white, middle class Americans to understand what ghetto
life is all about. As Roger Kahn, a white journalist who has tried to understand life in the ghettos, reports:

> Harlem is strange and dark and frightening, and if your skin is white,
> you are a marked alien. It doesn't matter whether you are a Quaker full
> of compassion, or a Jew, full of sympathy, or a Baptist, full of guilt, or
> a Roman Catholic, full of missionary zeal. 'Man,' they say in Harlem,
> 'long as you white, you ain't one of us, and what you doin' roun' here
> anyway, white man? Get on back downtown where you belong.' [21]

Poll takers and interviewers have a difficult time: "Man, you know why
I run first time you come? I thought you was fuzz, man, and I was a
hustlin' to stash my '45." [22] It is unlikely that many whites, liberal or conservative, understand the full extent of frustration, bitterness, and hatred
in America's Negro ghettos. White conservatives may be shocked to learn
that many middle class values about thrift, hard work, and the sanctity of
property are not universally shared with ghetto residents. White liberals
may be shocked to learn that racial prejudice is not the monopoly of the
white man.

Figures can only reveal the bare outline of the Negro's position in
American society. Yet figures make it very clear that, on the whole, Negroes do not enjoy the same affluence as white Americans. The average
income of a Negro family is only half the average white family's. Nearly
half of all Negro families are below the recognized poverty line of $3000
annual income. Twice as many Negroes live in substandard housing as
whites. Negro unemployment rate is twice as high as white. The average

[20] *Ibid.*, pp. 131–32.
[21] Roger Kahn, "White Man, Walk Easy," *Saturday Evening Post* (June 13, 1964);
also reprinted in Thomas R. Dye and Brett W. Hawkins, *Politics in the Metropolis*
(Columbus: Charles E. Merrill Books, Inc., 1967).
[22] *Ibid.*

Negro does not acquire as much education as the average white. Negroes are far less likely to hold prestigious white collar jobs in professional, managerial, clerical, or sales work. They do not hold many skilled craft jobs in industry, but are concentrated in operative, service, and laboring positions. Negro women not only have more children but have them earlier. And too many children too early make it most difficult for parents to finish school. Thus a cycle is at work in the ghettos: low education levels produce low income levels, which prevents parents from moving out of the ghettos, which deprives children of educational opportunities, and so repeats the cycle.

Daniel P. Moynihan has argued effectively that one of the worst effects of slavery and segregation has been its impact on Negro family life.[23] It was the Negro male who was most humiliated by segregation. The submissiveness which segregation implies is surely more destructive to the male than to the female personality. Keeping the Negro "in his place" usually means keeping the Negro *male* in his place; the female is not a threat to

TABLE 13.6

ECONOMIC CHARACTERISTICS, NEGRO AND WHITE POPULATIONS IN THE UNITED STATES, 1960 CENSUS

	Negro	White
Median family income	$2,520	$5,088
Per cent families less than $3,000	39.6	18.6
Unemployment rate	12.7	5.9
Median school completed by adults	8.2	10.9
Fertility rate	2,002	1,712
Per cent female headed families	22.4	8.7
Male occupations in per cent		
Professional	3.9	11.0
Managerial	2.3	11.5
Clerical	5.0	7.1
Sales	1.5	7.4
Farmers	4.4	5.6
Craftsmen	10.2	20.5
Operatives	23.5	19.5
Service	13.7	5.2
Farm labor	7.1	2.3
Labor	19.4	5.6
Not reported	8.4	4.2

Source: U.S. Bureau of the Census, *Statistical Abstract.*

[23] See Daniel P. Moynihan, *The Negro Family: The Case for National Action* (Washington: U.S. Government Printing Office, 1965); portions of the Moynihan Report are reprinted in Dye and Hawkins, *Politics in the Metropolis.*

anyone. The female-headed Negro family emerges as one of the striking features of life in the ghetto. Almost 25 per cent of all Negro families are headed by women. For the male offspring of a matriarchal ghetto family, the future is often depressing, with defeat and frustration repeating itself throughout his life. He may drop out of school in the ninth grade as a protest to his lack of success. If he fails his armed forces qualification test (and a majority of young men from the ghetto do so), he may never again have an opportunity for further education or job training. Lacking parental supervision, and with little to do, he may get in trouble with the police. A police record will further hurt his chances of getting a job. The ghetto male with limited job skills enters the job market seriously handicapped. His pay is usually not enough to support a family and he has little hope of moving up. He may tie up much of his income in installment debts for a car, television set, or other conveniences, which he sees in widespread use among middle class Americans. Because of his low credit rating, he will be forced to pay excessive interest rates, and sooner or later his creditors will garnish his salary. If he marries, he is likely to have at least five children, and he and his family will live in overcrowded, substandard housing. As pressures and frustrations mount, he may decide to leave his family, either because he has found his inability to support his wife and children humiliating, or because only in this way will his wife and children be eligible for welfare payments. Welfare policy again strengthens the role of the female in the Negro family, because she can get the family on welfare (particularly aid to families with dependent children) while the male cannot. In fact, his remaining with the family is an obstacle to receiving welfare payments.

Civil Rights and the New Militancy

The initial objective of the civil rights movement in America has been to prevent discrimination and segregation as practiced by or supported by *governments,* particularly states, municipalities, and school districts. But even while important victories for the civil rights movement were being recorded in the prevention of discrimination by governments, particularly in the Brown case, the movement began to broaden its objectives to include the elimination of discrimination in all segments of American life, private as well as public. Civil rights was redefined to mean not merely a legal, but an actual, possibility of developing human capacities and sharing in the goods a society has produced and the way of life it has built. This was a more positive concept of civil rights. It involved not merely restrictions on government, but a positive obligation of government to act forcefully to end discrimination in public accommodations, employment, housing, and all other sectors of private life.

As long as the civil rights movement in America was combating *government* discrimination, it could employ the Constitution as a weapon in its struggle for liberty, for the Constitution by definition governs the activities of *governments*. Since the Supreme Court and federal judiciary is charged with the responsibility of interpreting the Constitution, the civil rights movement could concentrate on Court action to serve their objective of preventing government discrimination. But the Constitution does not govern the activities of private individuals. It is the laws of Congress and the states which govern the conduct of private individuals. When the civil rights movement turned to combating private discrimination, it had to carry its fight into the legislative branch of government. The federal courts could help restrict discrimination by state and local governments and school authorities, but only Congress, state legislatures, and city councils could restrict discrimination practiced by private owners of restaurants, hotels and motels, private employers, and other individuals who were not government officials.

Yet Congress, prior to 1964, was content to let the President and the courts struggle with the problem of civil rights. In 1957 and 1960, Congress passed weak civil rights bills which made it illegal for any person to interfere with the exercise of rights under a federal court order, or to use interstate commerce for the purpose of burning or bombing any building. So strong was the reluctance of Congress to enter the field of civil rights that even those bills were extensively debated and compromised before final passage. Yet by 1964 the demand for strong civil rights legislation was so great that Congress could no longer ignore the nation's most pressing domestic issue.

A new militancy, expressed in Martin Luther King's call for nonviolent direct action, appeared in the civil rights movement in the mid-1950's. Between 1941 and 1954, Negro protests were primarily in the form of legal cases brought by the NAACP to federal courts; negotiation and bargaining with white businessmen and government officials, often by the National Urban League; and local lobbying on behalf of Negro constituents by Negro political leaders in northern communities. But in 1955 the Negro community of Montgomery, Alabama, began a year-long boycott with frequent demonstrations against the Montgomery city buses over segregated seating practices. The dramatic appeal and the eventual success of the boycott in Montgomery brought nationwide attention to a local Negro minister, Martin Luther King, and led to the creation in 1956 of the Southern Christian Leadership Conference. In 1960, Negro students from the North Carolina Agricultural and Technical College began a "sit-in" demonstration at the segregated Woolworth lunch counter in Greensboro, North Carolina. Soon, "sit-ins" in restaurants, "read-ins" in libraries, "pray-ins" in white churches spread throughout the South, generally under the leadership of the Southern Christian Leadership Conference, which followed "nonviolent" techniques. The Congress of Racial Equality (CORE), which at this time was also committed to the philosophy of nonviolence, initiated a series of "freedom rides" into the South, in which groups of white and Negro bus travellers attempted to desegregate travel and terminal facilities. Years before, the Supreme Court had held that segregation of interstate travel facilities was unconstitutional, but throughout the South, travel facilities remained segregated. The freedom riders underwent arrest and mob violence in many southern communities. Often police looked on while freedom riders were attacked by white segregationists. In 1961 President Kennedy was obliged to send 400 federal marshals to Montgomery, Alabama, to protect the freedom riders.

Perhaps the most dramatic confrontation between the civil rights movement and southern segregationists occurred in Birmingham, Alabama, in the spring of 1963. In support of a request for desegregation of downtown eating places and the formation of a biracial committee to work out the integration of public schools, Martin Luther King led several thousand Birmingham Negroes in a series of orderly street marches. The demonstrators were met with strong police action, including fire hoses, police dogs, and electric cattle prods. Newspaper pictures of Negroes being attacked by police and bitten by dogs were flashed all over the world. More than 25,000 demonstrators, including Dr. King, were jailed.

The year 1963 was probably the most important for nonviolent direct action. The Birmingham action set off demonstrations in many parts of the country; the theme remained one of nonviolence, and it was usually whites rather than Negroes who resorted to violence in these demonstrations. Responsible Negro leadership remained in control of the movement and won widespread support from the white community. The culmination of the nonviolent philosophy was a giant, yet orderly march on Washington, held on August 28, 1963. More than 200,000 Negroes and whites participated in the march, which was endorsed by many labor leaders, religious groups, and political figures. It was in response to this march that President Kennedy sent a strong civil rights bill to Congress, which was later to be passed after his death as the famous Civil Rights Act of 1964.

Again, in 1965, Martin Luther King led a successful nonviolent voting rights march from Selma to Montgomery, Alabama. This march was a protest against a refusal of local southern registrars to register Negro voters. The hostility of southern segregationists and the failure of state and local authorities to protect the marchers led President Johnson to federalize the national guard and order them to protect the demonstrators. After the march, President Johnson sent another historic civil rights measure to the Congress—the Voting Rights Act of 1965.

The Civil Rights Act of 1964 passed both houses of Congress by better than a two-thirds favorable vote; it won the overwhelming support of both Republican and Democratic Congressmen. It was signed into law on July 4, 1964. It ranks with the Emancipation Proclamation, the 14th Amendment, and Brown *v.* Topeka as one of the most important steps toward full equality for the Negro in America.

The Civil Rights Act of 1964 provides:

I. That it is unlawful to apply unequal standards in voter registration procedures, or to deny registration for irrelevant errors or omissions on records or applications.

II. That it is unlawful to discriminate or segregate persons on the grounds of race, color, religion, or national origin in any place of public accommodation, including hotels, motels, restaurants, movies, theatres, sports areas, entertainment houses, and other places which offer to serve the public. This prohibition extends to all establishments whose operations affect interstate commerce or whose discriminatory practices are supported by state action.

III. That the Attorney General shall undertake civil action on behalf of any person denied equal access to a public accommodation, to obtain a federal district court order to secure compliance with the act. If the owner or manager of a public accommodation continued to discriminate, he would be in contempt of court and subject to peremptory fines and imprisonment without trial by jury. This mode of enforcement gave establishments a chance to mend their ways without punishment, and it also avoided the possibility that southern juries would refuse to convict persons for violations of the act.

IV. That the Attorney General shall undertake civil actions on behalf of persons attempting orderly desegregation of public schools.

V. That the Commission on Civil Rights, first established in the Civil Rights Act of 1957, shall be empowered to investigate deprivations of the right to vote, study and collect information regarding discrimination in America, and make reports to the President and Congress.

VI. That each federal department and agency shall take action to end discrimination in all programs or activities receiving federal financial assistance in any form. This action shall include termination of financial assistance.

VII. That it shall be unlawful for any employer or labor union with 25 or more persons after 1965 to discriminate against any individual in any fashion in employment, because of his race, color, religion, sex, or national origins, and that an Equal Employment Opportunity Commission shall be established to enforce this provision by investigation, conference, conciliation, persuasion, and, if need be, civil action in federal court.

Opponents of the Civil Rights Act of 1964 argued that Congress unconstitutionally exceeded its delegated powers when it prohibited discrimination and segregation practiced by *privately owned* public accommodations and *private* employers. Nowhere among the delegated powers of Congress in Article I of the Constitution, or even in the 14th or 15th Amendments, is Congress specifically given the power to prohibit discrimination practiced by *private* individuals. In reply, supporters of the Act argued that Congress has the power to regulate interstate commerce. Instead of relying upon the 14th Amendment, which prohibits only *state-supported* discrimination, Congress was relying on its powers over interstate commerce. In unanimous opinions in Heart of Atlanta Motel *v.* United States [24] and Katzenbach *v.* McClung [25] in December of 1964, the Supreme Court upheld the constitutionality of the Civil Rights Act. The Court held that Congress could, by virtue of its power over interstate commerce, prohibit discrimination in any establishment that serves or offers to serve interstate travelers or that sells food or goods previously moved in interstate commerce. This power over commerce included not only major establishments, like the Heart of Atlanta Motel, but also the family owned Ollie's Barbecue serving a local clientele.

The Negro revolution in the 1960's meant a turning away from the slowly moving machinery of the federal courts and the slow evolution of public law. The civil rights movement invented new political techniques for minorities in American politics. In 1963 a group of Alabama clergymen petitioned Martin Luther King, Jr. to call off mass demonstrations in Birmingham. King, who had been arrested in the demonstrations, replied in his famous "Letter from Birmingham Jail": [26]

> You may well ask, 'Why direct action? Why sit-ins, marches, etc.? Isn't negotiation a better path?' You are exactly right in your call for negotiation. Indeed, this is the purpose of direct action. Nonviolent direct action seeks to create such a crisis and establish such creative tension that a community that has constantly refused to negotiate is forced to confront the issue. It seeks to so dramatize the issue that it can no longer be ignored. . . .
>
> You express a great deal of anxiety over our willingness to break laws. . . . One may well ask, 'How can you advocate breaking some laws and obeying others?' The answer is found in the fact that there are two types of laws: There are *just* laws and there are *unjust* laws. I would be the first to advocate obeying just laws. One has not only a legal but a moral responsibility to obey just laws. Conversely, one has a moral responsibility to disobey unjust laws. . . .
>
> All segregation statutes are unjust because segregation distorts the soul and damages the personality. It gives the segregator a false sense of superiority and the segregated a false sense of inferiority. . . .
>
> In no sense do I advocate evading or defying the law as the rabid segregationist would do. This would lead to anarchy. One who breaks an unjust

---

[24] Heart of Atlanta Motel *v.* United States, 379 U.S. 241 (1964).
[25] Katzenbach *v.* McClung, 379 U.S. 294 (1964).
[26] Martin Luther King, Jr., *Letter from Birmingham City Jail,* April 16, 1963; reprinted in full in Dye and Hawkins, *op. cit.*

law must do it openly, lovingly (not hatefully as the white mothers did in New Orleans when they were seen on television screaming 'nigger, nigger, nigger') and with a willingness to accept the penalty. I submit that an individual who breaks a law that conscience tells him is unjust, and willingly accepts the penalty by staying in jail to arouse the conscience of the community over its injustice, is in reality expressing the very highest respect for law. . . .

The Special Tactic of Civil Disobedience

Mass demonstrations, sit-ins, and other militant tactics often involve violations of state and local laws. For example, remaining at a segregated lunch counter after the owner orders one to leave may violate trespass laws. Marching in the street may involve the obstruction of traffic, "disorderly conduct," or "parading without a permit." Demonstrations may involve "disturbing the peace" or refusing to obey the orders of a police officer. Even though these tactics are nonviolent, they involve disobedience to civil law. Needless to say, violence, rioting, stoning, looting, and burning also violate the law, regardless of the causes of such activity.

Civil disobedience is not new. It has played an important role in American history, from the Boston tea party, to the abolitionists who hid runaway slaves, to the suffragettes who paraded and demonstrated for women's rights, to the labor organizers who picketed to form the nation's major industrial unions, to the civil rights marchers of recent years. Civil disobedience is a political tactic of minorities. Since majorities can more easily change laws, they seldom have to disobey them. It is also a tactic for groups who wish to change the social status quo in some way.

The political purpose of disobedience is to call attention, or "bear witness" to the existence of injustice. Punishment is actively sought, rather than avoided, since punishment will help to emphasize the injustice of the law. The object is to stir the consciences of an apathetic majority. Punishment inflicted for violation of an unjust law can shame a majority and make it ask itself how far it is willing to go to protect the status quo.

Clearly the participation of the mass news media, particularly television, contributes measurably to the success of civil disobedience. Breaking the law makes news, the news calls the attention of the public to the existence of unjust laws or practices. The public's sympathy is won when injustices are spotlighted, the willingness of the disobedients to accept punishment is evidence of their sincerity, and the whole drama lays the groundwork for changing unjust laws or practice. Cruelty or violence directed against civil disobedients by policemen, or other defenders of status quo, plays into the hands of the civil disobedients by further emphasizing the injustices they are experiencing.

Is it ever right to break the law? It would be difficult to argue that civil disobedience is *never* justified.[27] To do so would be to say that those who carried out Hitler's orders to murder millions of people were acting justly in following his orders. The Nuremberg trials held that individuals had a legal and moral duty to refuse to perform criminal acts even when ordered by government authorities to do so. When people are denied the right to participate in lawmaking, through free elections and representative governments, it is difficult to argue that they are morally bound to obey laws they had no share in making.

But it becomes more difficult to justify breaking the law in a democratic society, because such a society provides its members with legal means for the redress of their grievances—courts, legislatures, elections, political activity, and peaceful persuasion. However, in defense of civil disobedience in democratic countries, it can be argued that it is often necessary to convince an apathetic majority of the need to correct an evil suffered by a minority. There is also the argument that democratic processes work slowly; often decades are required to achieve even modest progress. If the suffering of a minority is particularly serious, long waits may be quite painful and cry may go up for "Freedom Now," with the emphasis on "Now." Civil disobedience can jolt democratic processes into motion.

Yet civil disobedience cannot be lightly undertaken. It can arouse extreme passions on either side, excite and provoke thoughtless masses, and make disrespect for law a commonplace and popular attitude. Leaders of the civil rights movement may talk of nonviolence, yet the risk of violence is very great. Mass followers may not always understand the distinction between nonviolent demonstrations directed against injustice, and rioting, looting, and vandalism directed against society itself.

Violence in American Cities

Civil disorder and violence are not new on the American scene. On the night of December 16, 1773, a group of "agitators" in Boston, Massachusetts destroyed 342 chests of tea. And violence as a form of social protest has continued intermittently in America to the present day. The nation itself was founded in armed revolution. In 1786 farmers who were in debt forceably stopped the trials of debtors in many Massachusetts cities and laid seige to the courthouse in Springfield, Massachusetts. The state militia was required to put down Shay's rebellion. Nat Turner's slave insurrection in 1831 resulted in the death of 51 white persons and the later execution of Turner and his followers. On July 13, 1863, New York City was the scene of the nation's first major draft riot. Foreign-born laborers protesting conscription and the ability of rich men to buy their way out of the

---

[27] See Charles Frankel, "Is It Ever Right to Break the Law?" *New York Times Magazine* (January 12, 1964); reprinted in Dye and Hawkins, *op. cit.*

service, rioted for four days, and there were more than 1000 casualties and extensive property damage. Negroes were the objects of much of the rioters' wrath, since many attributed conscription to Lincoln's attempt to free the slaves. Federal troops finally restored order. Violence was the constant companion of the early labor movement in America. In Pittsburgh, Pennsylvania, on July 22 and 23, 1877, respectively, an estimated 16 and 50 strikers were killed, and more than 125 locomotives, 2000 freight cars, and other property were destroyed. The famous Homestead Strike of 1892 turned Homestead, Pennsylvania, into an open battlefield. The Pullman Strike of 1893 in Chicago resulted in 12 deaths and the destruction of a great deal of railroad property. Again, troops were required to suppress the disorder. On April 20, 1914, Ludlow, Colorado, was the scene of the famous Ludlow massacre where company guards burned a miners' tent city and nearly 100 persons including women and children were killed. Race violence has also been common to the American scene. On June 20–21, 1943, racial violence erupted in Detroit, resulting in 35 deaths, 530 injuries, and about 1300 arrests.

Federal troops have been used to maintain order in America on many occasions. Article IV, Section 4 in the U.S. Constitution authorizes the federal government to protect the states against domestic violence "on application of the legislature, or of the executive when the legislature cannot be convened." But Presidents have used federal troops to quell domestic disorder even when they were not requested by a state governor or legislature. Federal troops were duly requested by local authorities to quell railroad strikes in 1877 in Pennsylvania and Illinois and mining riots in Idaho in 1892, to defeat "Coxey's Army" in Montana in 1894, to quell mining riots in Nevada in 1907 and again in 1914, in race riots in Washington and Omaha in 1919, to battle coal miners in West Virginia in 1921, to drive off the "bonus army" in Washington, D.C. in 1932, and to quell Detroit race riots in 1943 and 1967. President Eisenhower used federal troops to desegregate Central High School in Little Rock, Arkansas, in 1957. President Kennedy sent in federal troops to desegregate the University of Mississippi at Oxford in 1962. And President Kennedy federalized the Alabama National Guard in 1963, but did not use them, when Governor George C. Wallace capitulated in the desegregation of the University of Alabama at Tuscaloosa, Alabama. In 1965 President Johnson federalized the national guard and ordered them to protect the voting rights marchers from Selma to Montgomery, Alabama. Federal troops were not used in the Watts riots in 1965, although the federally trained and equipped California National Guard played a major role in quelling the disturbance. Again in Newark in 1967, it was National Guardsmen rather than federal troops who were primarily responsible for restoring order.

Yet even though domestic violence has played a prominent role in

America's history, the urban riots of the 1960's shocked the nation with the most massive and widespread civil disorders ever to face the nation. In city after city, Negro ghettos were racked with looting, burning, sniping, and rioting. Negro violence flared in cities as diverse as Los Angeles, Des Moines, Cleveland, Buffalo, Milwaukee, New York, Atlanta, Chicago, Tampa, Cincinnati, Erie, Detroit, and even New Haven, Connecticut. Over 100 major riots were reported in American cities from 1965 to 1967; all these riots involved Negro attacks on established authority—policemen, firemen, National Guardsmen, whites in general, and property owned by whites. Three of these riots—Watts, California, in 1965 and Newark and Detroit in 1967—amounted to major insurrections.

The Watts riot from August 11–17, 1965, was set off when a white motorcycle officer arrested a Negro youth for drunken driving in a Negro district of Los Angeles known as Watts. In the words of the McCone Commission report of the Watts violence:

> In the ugliest interval . . . perhaps as many as 10,000 Negroes took to the streets in neurotic bands. They looted stores, set fires, beat up white passersby whom they hauled from stopped cars, many of which were turned upside down and burned, exchanged shots with law enforcement officers, and stoned and shot at firemen. The rioters seemed to have been caught up in an insensate rage of destruction. By Friday, disorder spread to adjoining areas, and ultimately, an area covering 46.5 square miles had to be controlled with the aid of military authority before public order was restored. . . .
>
> When the spasm passed, 34 persons were dead, and the wounded and hurt numbered 1032 more. Property damage was about $40 million. Arrested for one crime or another were 3952 persons, women as well as men, including over 500 youths under 18. Lawlessness in this one segment of the metropolitan area had terrified the entire county and its 6 million citizens. . . .
>
> Of the 34 killed, one was a fireman, one was a deputy sheriff, and one a Long Beach policeman. . . .
>
> More than 600 buildings were damaged by burning and looting. Out of this number, more than 200 were completely destroyed by fire. The rioters concentrated primarily on food markets, liquor stores, furniture stores, clothing stores, department stores, and pawn shops. . . . We note with interest that no residences were deliberately burned, that damage to schools, libraries, churches, and public buildings was minimal, and that certain types of business establishments, notably service stations and automobile dealers, were for the most part unharmed.[28]

Newark's riots were set off when police arrested a Negro cab driver for reckless driving and resisting arrest. Fellow Negro cab drivers led a crowd to the police station in the overwhelmingly Negro central ward of Newark.

---

[28] John A. McCone, ed., *Violence in the City: An End or a Beginning.* Office of the Governor, State of California, Sacramento, 1965; reprinted in Dye and Hawkins, *op. cit.*

Soon rocks and bottles were clattering against the station house walls. For four consecutive days and nights, snipers held police and firemen at bay, while looters made off with the entire inventory of scores of stores, and arsonists set fire to a large portion of commercial property in the Negro section of Newark. New Jersey's governor proclaimed Newark a "city in open rebellion," declared a state of emergency, and called out the National Guard. More than 4000 city police, state troopers, and Guardsmen were required to bring order. Before the riot was over 25 persons were killed. Of those dead by racial violence only two were white—a policeman and a fireman. Among the Negro dead two were children and six were women.

In the violent summer of 1967, Detroit became the scene of the bloodiest racial uprising of the 20th century. A week of rioting in Detroit from July 23–28 left 41 known dead, more than 1000 injured, and 35,000 arrested. Fires left some 5000 persons homeless when whole sections of the city were reduced to charred smoke and ruins. Over 1300 buildings were totally demolished and 2700 businesses sacked. Damage was estimated at $500 million. Detroit's upheaval began when police raided a Negro after-hours club and arrested the bartender and several customers for selling and consuming alcoholic beverages after authorized closing hours. For five days Negro mobs looted, burned, and killed as a force of 15,000 city and state police, national guardsmen, and finally federal troops, fought to quell the violence. Most of the looted stores were groceries, supermarkets, and furniture stores. Many Negro merchants scrawled "Soul Brother" on their windows to warn the mobs off. Eventually homes and shops covering a total area of 14 square miles were gutted by fire. When police and National Guardsmen proved unable to bring order, Michigan's governor, George Romney, asked the President for reinforcements in the form of federal troops.

Assessing the Causes of Riots

Many factors have converged to bring violence to the nation's cities. Undoubtedly conditions in America's Negro ghettos provided the necessary environment for violence. Racial imbalance, de facto segregation, slum housing, discrimination, unemployment, poor schools, and poverty provide excellent kindling for the flames of revolutionary action. The conditions for Negro violence will continue to exist as long as there are Negro ghettos in the cities, as long as Negro unemployment is higher than white unemployment, as long as Negro incomes are lower than white incomes, and as long as there are discrimination, distrust, and hatred between the races.

Yet these underlying conditions for violence have existed for decades in America, and the nation never experienced simultaneous violent uprisings in nearly all of its major cities before the mid-1960's. What new ingredients were added to the incendiary conditions in American cities, which touched off this explosion?

The civil rights movement made many Negroes acutely aware of discrimination in American society and reduced their tolerance for injustice. The movement increased the aspiration levels of Negro masses and inspired impatience and hostility toward the "white establishment." The civil rights movement had to awaken Negroes to their plight in American society, before progress could be made in eliminating discrimination; but the price of this awakening was a major increase in aspiration levels and the risk of frustration and bitterness when these new aspirations went unfulfilled.

Responsible Negro civil rights leaders can understand and live by a philosophy of nonviolent direct action in which only unjust laws are disobeyed, in which disobedience takes place openly, lovingly, and without violence, and in which the protester willingly accepts the penalty of law in order to arouse the conscience of the community over injustice. But elements of the Negro masses in the ghettos may not understand or may reject this philosophy of nonviolence. The established Negro civil rights leadership may not carry great influence with the Negro poor in urban ghettos. The breakthroughs which the established civil rights movement made in public accommodations, employment, voting and officeholding may have opened new opportunities for the educated Negro middle class, but the undereducated Negro poor, living in the ghetto environment, cannot really take advantage of the many opportunities won in the civil rights movement.

The President's National Advisory Commission on Civil Disorders, perhaps in an attempt to shock the nation's white majority into action on urban problems, asserted that "white racism" is responsible for urban rioting. According to the Commission, the "bitter fruits of white racial attitudes" are:

> *Pervasive discrimination and segregation.* The first is surely the continuing exclusion of great numbers of Negroes from the benefits of economic progress through discrimination in employment and education, and their enforced confinement in segregated housing and schools. The corrosive and degrading effects of this condition and the attitudes that underlie it are the source of the deepest bitterness and at the center of the problem of racial disorder.
>
> *Black migration and white exodus.* The second is the massive and growing concentration of impoverished Negroes in our major cities resulting from Negro migration from the rural South, rapid population growth and the continuing movement of the white middle-class to the suburbs. The consequence is a greatly increased burden on the already depleted resources of cities, creating a growing crisis of deteriorating facilities and services and unmet human needs.
>
> *Black ghettos.* Third, in the teeming racial ghettos, segregation and poverty have intersected to destroy opportunity and hope and to enforce failure. The ghettos too often mean men and women without jobs, fami-

lies without men, and schools where children are processed instead of educated, until they return to the street—to crime, to narcotics, to dependency on welfare, and to bitterness and resentment against society in general and white society in particular.[29]

However, later in a more reflective passage, the Commission admitted that "these factors alone—fundamental as they are—cannot be said to have caused the disorders." The Commission recognized "powerful ingredients" which "catalyze the mixture":

> *Frustrated hopes.* The expectations aroused by the great judicial and legislative victories of the civil rights movement have led to frustration, hostility and cynicism in the face of the persistent gap between promise and fulfillment. The dramatic struggle for equal rights in the South has sensitized Northern Negroes to the economic inequalities reflected in the deprivations of ghetto life.
>
> *Legitimation of violence.* A climate that tends toward the approval and encouragement of violence as a form of protest has been created by white terrorism directed against nonviolent protest, including instances of abuse and even murder of some civil rights workers in the South; by the open defiance of law and federal authority by state and local officials resisting desegregation; and by some protest groups engaging in civil disobedience who turn their backs on nonviolence, go beyond the constitutionally protected rights of petition and free assembly, and resort to violence to attempt to compel alteration of laws and policies with which they disagree. This condition has been reinforced by a general erosion of respect for authority in American society and reduced effectiveness of social standards and community restraints on violence and crime. This in turn has largely resulted from rapid urbanization and the dramatic reduction in the average age of the total population.
>
> *Powerlessness.* Finally, many Negroes have come to believe that they are being exploited politically and economically by the white "power structure." Negroes, like people in poverty everywhere, in fact lack the channels of communication, influence and appeal that traditionally have been available to ethnic minorities within the city and which enabled them—unburdened by color—to scale the walls of the white ghettos in an earlier era. The frustrations of powerlessness have led some to the conviction that there is no effective alternative to violence as a means of expression and redress, as a way of "moving the system." More generally, the result is alienation and hostility toward the institutions of law and government and the white society which controls them. This is reflected in the reach toward racial consciousness and solidarity reflected in the slogan "Black Power." [30]

However, to say that the riots were unplanned, undisciplined, and unled is not to say that they have no purpose or that they were "senseless." The riots expressed a general hostility many Negroes feel toward white people,

[29] *Report of the National Advisory Commission on Civil Disorders* (Washington: Government Printing Office, 1968), pp. 203–24.
[30] *Ibid.,* pp. 204–205.

and toward established authority. They expressed the outrage many Negroes feel at their condition in American society. The riots, then, were an act of social protest.

This interpretation of the riots as purposeful social protest is supported by evidence which indicates that a large percentage of the Negro population in the ghettos supported the riots. Evidence compiled from many sources indicates that the rioters were not "a tiny minority," nor were they just "agitators," "criminals," or "riff-raff." Post-riot survey information indicates that roughly 20 per cent of the Negroes in the Watts area actually did participate more or less actively in the riot, and that more than half supported the activities of the rioters. Interviewers found that 58 per cent of the Watts residents felt that the long-run effects of the riots would be favorable; 84 per cent said that whites were now more aware of Negro problems; 62 per cent said that the riot was a Negro protest.[31] In summary, the riots are looked upon favorably by a large proportion of ghetto residents.

There is also evidence that the active rioters were not necessarily the poorest of the ghetto residents. In Detroit, the Commission on Civil Disorders reported that 61.4 per cent of the persons identified as rioters had annual incomes over $5000; 67.4 per cent of the rioters in Newark enjoyed such incomes.[32] Approximately 70 per cent of the rioters in both Detroit and Newark held jobs. Persons with some high school education were more likely to participate in riots than those with only grade school educations. In short, rioters were not necessarily poor, unemployed, and uneducated. Violent protest originates among those who have enjoyed some measure of affluence and want more, rather than among those who have never perceived how their life could be improved.

To be sure, this form of social protest is a criminal one. And it may be irrational and self-defeating. The great majority of the casualties of the riots—the dead, the injured, and the arrested—were rioters themselves. Much of the property destroyed belonged to the ghetto residents. Many businesses and other conveniences will never again go into the ghetto. The riots may have changed the attitudes of some whites toward the civil rights movement from sympathy to opposition. And, of course, violence itself cannot solve complicated social problems facing ghetto residents.

Nearly all riots are accompanied by charges of "police brutality." Incidents involving police action have often been the trigger for riots. Police–Negro tensions are always high in ghetto areas. Police themselves are not immune to social prejudice. The policeman's attitude toward ghetto residents is often affected by the high crime rate in ghetto areas. He is suspi-

[31] President's Commission on Law Enforcement and Administration of Justice, *Crime and Its Impact—An Assessment* (Washington: Government Printing Office, 1967), p. 116.

[32] *Report of the National Advisory Commission on Civil Disorders*, p. 131.

cious of ghetto residents because crime rates tell him that his suspicion is often justified. Moreover, experience from the riots clearly suggests that police and National Guardsmen are not well trained in riot control. Nor were mayors and other political officials well prepared to deal with riots. Often in the initial stages of rioting, the soft line toward rioters—police withdrawal, negotiations with leaders, promises of new public programs, and so on—resulted in an increase in violence rather than a lessening of it. When police were finally ordered to quell rioters and to use their weapons when necessary, their initial restraint often gave way to abandon. Heavy and undisciplined firing by police and National Guardsmen often led to unnecessary deaths. The riots suggested the need for better riot control training for police and National Guardsmen.

The Congressional Quarterly obtained responses from 130 mayors regarding the causes of riots.[33] A majority of the mayors identified "joblessness and idleness, especially among young Negroes," as the primary cause of the riots. The emphasis on this cause decreased however among mayors of smaller cities. Mayors of smaller cities more frequently chose "outside Negro agitators" as a primary cause of riots. Mayors of middle sized cities saw joblessness and Negro agitation as almost equally important. Few mayors of big cities said outside Negro agitators was a cause of "great importance."

In terms of solutions to the riot problem, mayors again split sharply along big-city, small-city lines. All mayors emphasized "traditional church and family values." But small-city mayors were more likely than big-city mayors to call for "greater penalties for rioters and those who incite to rioting." Most mayors seemed responsive to the idea of a massive "Marshall Plan" for the cities using federal funds, with big-city mayors more enthusiastic about this idea than small-city mayors.

Negroes and whites disagree sharply on the causes of the riots and ways to prevent future trouble. Public opinion surveys provide evidence of this. A Lou Harris survey released August 14, 1967, showed that 45 per cent of the whites interviewed contended that violence was provoked mainly by "outside agitators," "minority radicals," or "communist backing." Only 7 per cent of the Negroes interviewed took this view. Negroes cited frustration from lack of progress on jobs, education, and housing as the prime causes of ghetto riots. More than two-thirds of the Negroes questioned felt that police brutality contributed to the riots, but only one white in six acknowledged the existence of police brutality.

The reaction of federal officials to the rioting was mixed. It was not until July, 1967, that President Johnson publicly acknowledged the extent of civil disorder and condemned rioting. "Let there be no mistake about it—

[33] Congressional Quarterly Service, "Urban Problems and Civil Disorders," *Special Report* (September 8, 1967).

the looting, arson, plunder, and pillage which have occurred are not part of the civil rights protest. There is no American right to loot stores or to burn buildings, to fire rifles from rooftops. This is a crime. . . . Criminals who committed these acts of violence against the people deserved to be punished—and they must be punished." [34] Later the President cited the riots as additional reason why Congress should pass administration-backed urban programs to alleviate the ills of cities. In a letter to the Senate Majority Leader, President Johnson itemized 23 administration-backed programs, together with the appropriations requested for 1968, which he felt represented "an all-out commitment to the safety and well-being of our cities and to the citizens who live in them." Following is the list of programs and funds cited by the President: [35]

Program	Funds Requested
Crime Control	50 million
Firearms Control	—
Civil Rights Act of 1967	—
Juvenile Delinquency	25 million
Economic Opportunity Act	2.06 billion
Model Cities	662 million
Rent Supplements	662 million
Urban Renewal	40 million
Urban Mass Transit, advance appropriation	230 million
Urban Research	20 million
Neighborhood Facilities	42 million
Home Rehabilitation	15 million
Family Relocation Assistance	62 million
Rat Extermination	20 million
Elementary-Secondary Education Act	1.6 billion
Manpower Development and Training Act	439 million
Food Stamps	195 million
Child Nutrition and School Lunch Program	348 million
Community Health Services	30 million
Mental Health	96 million
Mental Retardation	25 million
Hospital Modernization (Hill-Burton)	50 million
Maternal and Infant Care	30 million

But many congressmen were concerned with any large-scale increase in federal expenditures in ghettos that might appear to reward rioting. Congress reacted by passing overwhelmingly a bipartisan anti-riot bill making it

[34] President Lyndon Johnson. From a speech on national television networks, July 27, 1967.
[35] Congressional Quarterly Service, *Weekly Report* (August 21, 1967), p. 1632.

a federal crime to cross state lines to incite a riot. The administration had opposed the bill as repressive and unlikely to contribute a solution to the underlying causes of riots. No new federal programs were devised by the President or passed by the Congress in direct response to the riots. Nor were already existing federal programs greatly expanded, despite suggestions for a massive multi-billion dollar "Marshall Plan" for America's ghettos. Perhaps the financial pressures of the Viet Nam war made such a course of action unfeasible at the time. Or perhaps neither the President nor Congress had any really new ideas about how to solve the complex problems of the ghettos.

The Commission on Civil Disorders recommended a "massive and sustained" effort on the part of national government to solve urban problems. However, its recommendations were noticeably lacking in innovation. The Commission recommended massive federal aid programs in employment, education, welfare, and housing, but it suggested no new departures from traditional programs in these areas. The Commission called for the creation of two million new jobs in ghettos, the elimination of de facto segregation, the construction of six million new units of public housing, and more liberal welfare benefits. In the Commission's words: "These programs will require unprecedented levels of funding and performance, but they neither probe deeper nor demand more than the problems which called them forth. There can be no higher priority for national action and no higher claim on the nation's conscience." [36]

[36] *Report of the National Advisory Commission on Civil Disorders,* p. 10.

14

THE POLITICS

OF EDUCATION

Directions in Educational Policy

Next to national defense, education is the nation's largest public undertaking. Over $20 billion a year is spent on public schools in the United States. While this is less than Americans spend on alcohol and tobacco, it is more than is spent for highways, welfare, police and fire protection, agricultural subsidies, public health, space research, or any other governmental function outside of the national military establishment. The primary responsibility for public education rests with the 50 state governments and their subdivisions. It is the largest and most costly of state functions.

It was in 1647 that the Massachusetts colonial legislature first required towns to provide for the education of children out of public funds, and by 1850 every state except Arkansas authorized the spending of tax monies for public schools. The rugged individualists of earlier eras thought it outrageous that one man should be taxed to pay for the education of another man's child. They were joined in their opposition to public education by those aristocrats who were opposed to arming the common man with the power that knowledge gives. But the logic of democracy led inevitably to public education. The earliest democrats believed that the safest repository of the ultimate powers of society was the people themselves. If the people make mistakes, the remedy was not to remove power from their hands, but to help them in forming their judgment through education. Congress passed the Northwest Ordinance in 1737 offering land grants for public schools in the new territories and giving succeeding generations words to be forever etched on grammar school cornerstones: "Religion, morality, and knowledge being necessary to good government and the happiness of mankind, schools and the means for education shall ever be encouraged." When American democracy adopted universal manhood suffrage, it affected every aspect of American life, and particularly education. If the common man was to be granted the right of suffrage, he must be educated to his task. This meant that public education had to be universal, free, and compulsory. Compulsory education began in Massachusetts in 1852, and was eventually adopted by Mississippi in 1918.[1]

Technological advances have changed the relationship between education and the economy. Many economists have come to classify education as a capital goods expenditure.[2] The National Education Association presses this point with legislators:

> There is an intimate relationship between schooling and the economic health of a nation and its citizens. Prosperity demands productivity and productivity demands trained talent. Education develops the intellectual and manual skills which underlie the productive abilities of individuals and nations today. Nations with the highest general level of education are those with the highest economic development. Schools, more than natural resources, are the basis of prosperity.
>
> The modern economy demands not muscle but skill and intellect. As energy is produced increasingly by mechanical means, the man who has only his energy to sell is increasingly dispensable. . . .
>
> Education does not guarantee health, wealth, or civic virtue; but sickness, unemployment, and crime are most prevalent among the undereducated segments of the population, and all undermine prosperity. Their cost is expressed in human and social decay and in public expenditures for police, relief, and treatment of preventable illness. Where ignorance generates poverty, poverty perpetuates ignorance, and the whole nation is the weaker. . . .
>
> A similar relationship appears in draft rejections. . . . Rejection rates cannot be attributed to lack of schooling alone, but they correlate highly with lack of education and with low expenditures for schools. . . .
>
> The ability of American society to conduct its essential affairs—political, economic, and military—depends directly on education.[3]

In the last six decades, public educational policy has responded dramatically to the new demands placed upon it by our nation's rapid economic de-

[1] See Thomas R. Dye, *Politics, Economics, and the Public* (Chicago: Rand McNally & Co., 1966), chap. 4.

[2] Harold M. Groves, *Education and Economic Growth* (Washington: National Education Association, 1961).

[3] Educational Policies Commission, National Education Association, *National Policy and the Financing of Public Schools* (Washington: National Education Association, 1962), p. 1.

velopment. Public elementary and secondary schools enroll over 43 million students. Public expenditures for education now amount to over $28 billion, more than 3 per cent of the nation's total personal income. Over $550 per year is spent on the public education of each child. Teachers' salaries have risen dramatically, and although the average teacher's salary is still lower than most other professions, it is more than the average industrial worker and a vast improvement over the salaries of even a few years ago. Teacher-pupil ratios have been lowered on the average to one teacher for every 23 pupils. State governments have undertaken a greater direct share of the responsibility for public education than ever before. Over 40 per cent of the costs of public schools are paid for directly with state, rather than local, revenues. School administration has been streamlined. School district consolidation has eliminated two out of every three school districts in the past 30 years.

This impressive record of progress in public education is a tribute to the capabilities of our 50 states. Yet national averages can obscure as much as they reveal about the record of the states in public education. Our federal system provides for the decentralization of educational policy making. Fifty state school systems establish policy for the nation, and this decentralization results in variations from state to state in educational policy. Only by examining public policy in all 50 states can the full dimensions of American education be understood.

The Cost of Teaching Johnny to Read

In the 1966–67 school year, public school expenditures for each pupil ranged from Mississippi's $315 to New York's $912. The nationwide figure for per pupil expenditures was $564.[4] Why is it that some states spend more than twice as much on the education of each child as other states? Economic resources are an important determinant of a state's willingness and ability to provide educational services. Urbanization, industrialization, and, especially, income correlate significantly with variations among the states in per pupil expenditures for public education. The results are the same even if the southern states are excluded from analysis. Clearly, wealth is the principal determinant of the amount of money to be spent on the education of each child. (See Figure 14.1)

Expenditures per pupil measure both the willingness and ability of a state to spend money for education. The next problem is to separate "willingness to spend" from "ability to spend," in order to roughly determine the sacrifice a state is making for education. The desire for education can be expressed in terms of school expenditures relative to some measure of a state's ability to spend money. In this way, states that spend more or less

---

[4] National Education Association, *Rankings of the States, 1967* (Washington: National Education Association, 1967).

relative to their ability can be identified. Public school expenditures, as a per cent of total personal income, really hold constant for ability to spend and more directly measure a state's willingness to sacrifice personal income for public education. This is referred to as a state's "educational effort."

FIGURE 14.1

THE FIFTY STATES ACCORDING TO MEDIAN FAMILY INCOME AND PER PUPIL EXPENDITURES, 1962

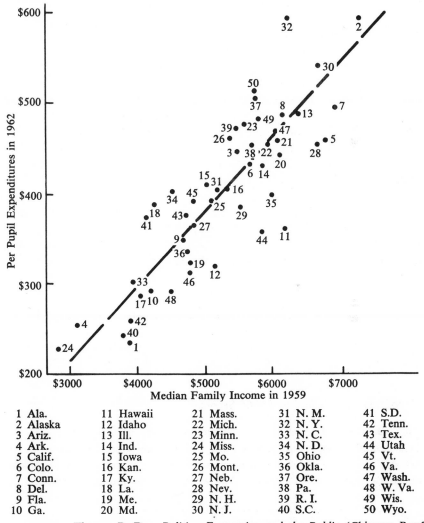

1 Ala.	11 Hawaii	21 Mass.	31 N. M.	41 S.D.
2 Alaska	12 Idaho	22 Mich.	32 N. Y.	42 Tenn.
3 Ariz.	13 Ill.	23 Minn.	33 N. C.	43 Tex.
4 Ark.	14 Ind.	24 Miss.	34 N. D.	44 Utah
5 Calif.	15 Iowa	25 Mo.	35 Ohio	45 Vt.
6 Colo.	16 Kan.	26 Mont.	36 Okla.	46 Va.
7 Conn.	17 Ky.	27 Neb.	37 Ore.	47 Wash.
8 Del.	18 La.	28 Nev.	38 Pa.	48 W. Va.
9 Fla.	19 Me.	29 N. H.	39 R. I.	49 Wis.
10 Ga.	20 Md.	30 N. J.	40 S.C.	50 Wyo.

SOURCE: Thomas R. Dye, *Politics, Economics, and the Public* (Chicago: Rand McNally & Co., 1966), p. 83. Reproduced by permission.

It is interesting to note that in the last few years America's "educational effort" has remained relatively constant. The nation as a whole has been spending about 3.9 per cent of its total personal income for public education. However, two states, Massachusetts and Rhode Island, spend less than 3 per cent of their total personal income for public schools, while two states, Arkansas and Wyoming, spend over 6 per cent.

It is interesting to note that increased industrialization, urbanization, and income actually result in a reduction in education effort. This is in striking contrast to the effect of these economic resources on per pupil expenditures: while per pupil expenditures increase with increasing income levels, school expenditures, as a percent of personal income, decline. This means that the poorer, less industrialized, rural states are actually putting forth a *greater effort* in the educational field relative to their resources than the wealthy, urban, industrial states. But so great are the inequalities among the states in wealth, that the poorer states, despite their greater effort, are unable to approach the wealthier states in per pupil expenditures. In 1966, even Mississippi's meager $315 per pupil expenditure (4.3 per cent of that state's personal income) represented a greater *effort* than New York's expenditure of $912 per pupil (only 3.9 per cent of that state's personal income spent on education). In short, wealthier states can provide better educations for their children with less of an economic sacrifice than that required of poorer states to provide an inferior education education for their children.[5]

The National Education Association has been cognizant of this situation for some time and has used these conditions to support appeals for federal aid to education. It is argued that federal aid will help to equalize educational opportunities throughout the nation:

> The operation of a national industrial economy appears to insure that average per capita incomes will be unequal among the states. The poorest states, if left to their own resources, have no reasonable prospect of raising the funds to provide adequate education. Some form of equalization is needed, because it is vital to the nation that the children in the poorest states also be well educated. Therefore, Federal participation in the financing of their schools is essential.[6]

Organizing and Financing Public Schools

The 50 state governments, by means of enabling legislation, establish local school districts and endow them with the authority to operate public schools. These laws create local school boards and provide a means for choosing their members, usually, but not always, by popular election. State

[5] Dye, *Politics, Economics, and the Public,* pp. 82–85.
[6] Educational Policies Commission, *op. cit.,* p. 23.

laws authorize boards to lay and collect taxes, to borrow money, to engage in school construction, to hire instructional personnel, and to make certain determinations about local school policy. Yet, in every state, the authority of local school districts is severely circumscribed by state legislation. State law determines the types and rates of taxes to be levied, the maximum debt which can be incurred, the number of days schools shall remain open, the number of years of compulsory school attendance, the minimum salaries to be paid to teachers, the types of schools to be operated by the local boards, the number of grades to be taught, the qualifications of teachers, and the general content of curricula. In addition, many states choose the textbooks, establish course outlines, fix styles of penmanship, recommend teaching methods, establish statewide examinations, fix minimum teacher-pupil ratios, and stipulate course content in great detail. Some states outlaw the mention of communism in the classroom or the teaching of evolution. In short, the responsibility for public education is firmly in the hands of our state governments.

State responsibility for public education is no mere paper arrangement. At one time there was no effective way that state governments could insure that local school districts conformed to state policies; there were no enforcement agencies or devices to guarantee that state regulations were enforced. But in recent years, two devices have been utilized effectively by the states to help insure that local districts do not deviate from state standards. The first device is the statewide administrative agency sometimes called the state board of education, state department of education, or the superintendent of public instruction. All states except Michigan, Illinois, and Wisconsin have established these agencies and given them general supervisory authority over the administration of state educational programs. In the 47 states with state boards of education, 31 are appointed by the governor. The number of popularly elected boards has increased from three to nine in the past decade. The central task of these state administrative agencies is to oversee local school districts and insure that state policies are being implemented. While there are some variations among the states in the power vested in these agencies, one trend is common to all of the states: state educational agencies are centralizing state control over education.

The operating head of these state agencies, generally called commissioner or superintendent of education, may exercise the most forceful influence over educational policy in the state. In 23 states these chief school officers are appointed by their boards, in 22 states they are directly elected, and in five states they are appointed by the Governor. The department that this officer oversees provides specialized technical services and information to local school officials; more importantly, it establishes and enforces statewide minimum standards in curriculum, teacher certification, school construction, and many other aspects of school policy and administration.

A second device for insuring the implementation of state educational policies is state grants of money to local school districts. Every state provides grants in one form or another to local school districts to supplement locally derived school revenue. This places the superior taxing powers of the state in the service of public schools operated at the local level. In every state, an equalization formula in the distribution of state grants to local districts operates to help equalize educational opportunities in all parts of the state. Equalization formulas differ from state to state as do the amounts of state grants involved, but in every state, poorer school districts receive larger shares of state funds than wealthier districts. This enables the state to guarantee a minimum "foundation" program in education throughout the state. In addition, since state grants to local school districts are administered through state departments of education, state school officials are given an effective tool for implementing state policies, namely, withholding or threatening to withhold state funds from school districts that do not conform to state standards. The growth of state responsibility for school policy was accomplished largely by the use of money—state grants to local schools.

Increasing state participation in school finance, then, is an indication of increasing centralization of education in the states. In 1900, the state proportion of total public school expenditures in the nation was only 17 per cent. By 1964, however, state governments contributed over 40 per cent of total funds spent for the public schools.

One of the most dramatic reorganization and centralization movements in American government in this century has been the successful drive to reduce, through consolidation, the number of local school districts in the United States. By 1967 this number had been reduced to 23,000. In a 30-year period, three out of every four school districts had been eliminated through consolidation. The one room school house, so glorified in song and story, yet so inadequate by today's educational standards, had been reduced by 1964 to less than 13 per cent of all schools. Support for school district consolidation has come from state school officials in every state. Opposition to consolidation has been local in character.

The extent of state participation in financing public schools and the success of the school district consolidation movement are both important indices of educational centralization in the states. While it is clear from national trends in both of these indices that the states on the whole are centralizing education, nonetheless, these trends are by no means uniform throughout the states. In Nebraska, New Hampshire, and South Dakota, the state government still provides only about 10 per cent of school revenues, while in Delaware, Louisiana, and North Carolina, the state pays over 70 per cent of the cost of the public schools. There is also considerable variation among the states in the success of the school district consolidation movement. The extent of consolidation can be measured by the average size of school districts in pupils. The larger the average district in a state, the further the movement toward consolidation has progressed. The average school district in the nation in 1962 enrolled 1073 pupils. However, the average school district in Florida, Hawaii, Louisiana, and Maryland had over 10,000 pupils, while the average district in North and South Dakota, Montana, and Nebraska had fewer than 200 pupils.

These two indices of centralization—the percentage of total school revenues from state sources and the average size of school districts in pupils— are related. States that pay the largest proportion of the public school bill have been the most successful in consolidating local school districts.

There is a slight tendency toward increased centralization in the poorer states and the states with lower adult education levels.[7] It is in these states that the state governments have played a greater role in the financing of public schools and the school consolidation movement has made the greatest progress. State participation in school finance decreases among the more wealthy states and the states with educated adult populations. Apparently, the lack of economic resources is a stimulus toward state participation in school finance and school district consolidation. Affluence, on the other hand, enables smaller local school districts to function more effectively, reduces the need for state aid, and delays the movement toward school consolidation.

States and School Teachers

Traditionally the public thought that teachers needed to know only a little more than the children they taught. Only recently have states begun to limit recruitment to persons with a bachelor's degree. Many persons without college degrees remain on teaching staffs in the public schools, and in addition, many states grant provisional, temporary, or emergency certificates to persons with little preparation for teaching. Approximately three-quarters of the nation's elementary school teachers are reported to hold bachelor's degrees, while about one-third of the nation's secondary school teachers hold master's degrees. Let us assume that the proportion of elementary teachers with a B.A. or B.S. degree and the proportion of secondary school teachers with a M.A. or M.S. degrees are rough measures of the adequacy of teacher preparation in a state school system.

The states that apparently placed little emphasis on elementary teacher preparation were not necessarily the poorer states, but they were the more rural and agricultural states.[8] The reliance of many midwestern, agricul-

---

[7] Dye, *op. cit.*, pp. 85–91.
[8] *Ibid.*, p. 92.

TABLE 14.1

RANKINGS OF THE STATES, 1968

Per Pupil Expenditures		Average Teachers Salary		Graduation Rate		Selective Service Mental Failures	
1. Alaska (3-$725)	$967	Alaska (24-$7083)	$9,444	Minn.	92.0%	Wash.	3.2%
2. New York	918	Calif.	8,900	Calif.	89.5	Mont.	3.5
3. N.J.	745	N.Y.	8,300	Iowa	89.4	Iowa	3.7
4. Conn.	707	Hawaii	7,914	Wisc.	89.1	Utah	3.9
5. Montana	656	Illinois	7,903	S.D.	88.4	Oregon	4.2
6. Calif.	653	Conn.	7,900	Hawaii	88.1	Minn.	4.4
7. Oregon	647	Maryland	7,857	N.D.	86.4	Wisc.	4.4
8. Maryland	631	N.J.	7,845	Wash.	86.1	Nebr.	4.5
Wyoming	631	Indiana	7,825	Neb.	85.6	Wyoming	4.5
10. Delaware	625	Nevada	7,825	Utah	85.2	N.H.	5.4
11. Arizona	623	Mich.	7,750	Mass.	84.4	Ver.	5.4
12. Minn.	621	Wash.	7,750	Mont.	83.8	N.D.	5.6
13. Hawaii	614	Delaware	7,625	N.J.	83.8	S.D.	5.6
14. Rhode Island	613	Arizona	7,610	R.I.	82.6	Kansas	6.0
15. Wisconsin	611	Mass.	7,550	Oregon	82.0	Mich.	6.4
16. Vermont	605	Oregon	7,550	Ohio	81.6	Idaho	6.6
17. Penn.	604	Minn.	7,465	Idaho	81.4	Okla.	7.2
18. Nevada	601	R.I.	7,400	Penn.	81.4	R.I.	7.2
19. Michigan	583	Ohio	7,300	Del.	80.8	Calif.	7.5
20. Washington	579	UNITED STATES	7,296	Col.	80.5	Mass.	7.6
21. Massachusetts	573	Wisconsin	7,274	Ver.	80.1	Ohio	8.0
UNITED STATES	573	Louisiana	7,238	Conn.	79.9	Colo.	8.5
22. Illinois	572	Penn.	7,225	Mich.	79.2	Ind.	8.5
23. Kansas	565	Iowa	7,208	N.H.	79.0	Nev.	8.8
24. Indiana	564	Florida	7,200	Maine	78.6	Penn.	9.1
25. Colorado	553	Wyoming	7,052	U.S.	77.8	Mo.	9.3
26. Louisiana	549	N.M.	6,981	Nev.	77.6	N.M.	9.7
27. Iowa	529	Colorado	6,900	Ind.	77.2	Maine	10.0
28. New Hampshire	524	Utah	6,640	Alaska	76.9	Alaska	10.3
29. South Dakota	519	Missouri	6,623	Md.	76.9	Hawaii	10.4
30. New Mexico	512	Virginia	6,600	N.Y.	76.9	Ariz.	10.9
North Dakota	512	Georgia	6,595	Mo.	76.8	Texas	11.1
32. Florida	504	Kansas	6,507	Ill.	75.9	Ill.	12.2
33. Ohio	502	Texas	6,500	Wyo.	75.7	U.S.	12.4
34. Virginia	496	Montana	6,375	Kans.	75.5	Md.	12.6
35. Missouri	492	N.H.	6,325	Va.	73.6	N.J.	13.2
36. Utah	479	N.C.	6,219	N.M.	73.2	Conn.	13.9
37. Idaho	478	Maine	6,150	Okla.	73.0	N.Y.	14.8
38. Nebraska	463	Kentucky	6,100	Ariz.	72.8	W. Va.	16.1
39. Oklahoma	453	Oklahoma	6,095	S.C.	72.2	Va.	16.2
40. Georgia	450	Nebraska	6,068	Fla.	71.9	Del.	17.0
41. Maine	442	Idaho	6,045	W. Va.	71.0	Ark.	17.3
Texas	442	Tennessee	6,000	Texas	70.2	Fla.	17.9
43. Kentucky	438	Vermont	5,950	Tenn.	70.0	Ky.	18.7
44. W. Virginia	437	W. Virginia	5,800	Ark.	69.4	Tenn.	18.8
45. N. Carolina	421	Alabama	5,725	La.	67.5	Ala.	24.1

Per Pupil Expenditures		Average Teachers Salary		Graduation Rate		Selective Service Mental Failures	
46. Tennessee	408	S. Carolina	5,630	N.C.	66.6	N.C.	24.8
47. Arkansas	398	Arkansas	5,596	Ala.	66.0	La.	25.6
S. Carolina	398	N. Dakota	5,580	Miss:	66.0	Ga:	28.0
49. Alabama	392	S. Dakota	5,100	Kentucky	65.8	Miss.	32.0
50. Mississippi	339	Mississippi	4,611	Ga.	64.9	S.C.	34.5

Source: National Education Association, *Rankings of the States, 1968.*

tural states upon the two-year normal school for teacher preparation may have retarded the development of four-year teachers colleges, which even the poorer states of the South have been able to provide. Apparently midwestern farm communities did not feel that their elementary teachers needed to be college graduates.

The average teacher's salary in the nation in 1966 was $6506 per year.[9] School teachers in Alaska, Connecticut, California, Hawaii, and New York were the best paid teachers in the nation in 1967, with average annual salaries in excess of $7500 per year. School teachers in Arkansas, South Carolina, North Dakota, and Mississippi were the lowest paid in the nation with average annual salaries in that year below $5200. The range of differences among the states in teachers' salaries were striking: California paid its teachers almost twice the annual salary paid to teachers in Mississippi.

Economic development is an important determinant in teachers' salaries. Income differences among the states explain almost 80 per cent of the variation among the states in average teachers' salaries.

Another important measure of the professionalization of teaching is the percent of total classroom teachers who are men. In 1967 the proportion of men among classroom teachers in the nation was 31.7 per cent.[10] The steady rise in the male proportion of teachers since 1910, when only 10.5 per cent were men, attests to the growing professionalization of public education.

Economic development is positively related to the proportion of male teachers, although the relationship is less direct than the relationship between economic development and salary levels. Wealthy, urban states, with well educated adult populations, attract more men into their public educational systems than states lacking in these attributes.

One final measure in instructional quality available for all 50 states is the pupil-teacher ratio, or the number of pupils enrolled per member of instructional staff. Two indices of economic development, family income and adult educational level, correlated significantly with teacher-pupil ratios in all

[9] National Education Association, *Rankings of the States, 1967.*
[10] *Ibid.*

states. Urbanization and industrialization appeared to have little independent effect on teacher-pupil ratios.

The Federal Role in Education

Prior to 1965 large-scale federal aid to education plans consistently floundered in the Congress; however, the federal government did contribute to public education through a number of specialized programs.[11] The total financial contribution of the federal government to public elementary and secondary education through these programs was quite small. Federal funds amounted to only about 4 per cent of the total public school revenues in 1962. With the passage of the Elementary and Secondary Education Act of 1965, the role of the federal government in education finance was greatly expanded. The Act, among other things, pledges important federal aid to "poverty impacted" schools, those schools which enroll children from low income families. The federal government commits itself in Title I to pay up to one-half of the average statewide per pupil expenditure for every enrolled child from a family earning less than $2000 per year. The formula results in larger proportions of federal aid going to poorer states. The Act, then, will tend to equalize educational opportunity throughout the nation and eliminate educational disparities among the states. The passage of the Act brought about a doubling of federal funds for public schools in a single year; federal school funds jumped from about 4 per cent of total school revenues to about 8 per cent. For the time being, of course, over 90 per cent of cost of public education is still borne by the states and their local subdivisions, and this means there are marked disparities among state educational systems. But if federal aid to education continues to increase, the disparities among state school systems may disappear. Centralization in school finance at the national level will doubtlessly bring about greater uniformity in school policy in the states and equalization of educational opportunity throughout the nation.

[11] In 1962 these programs included: (1) National Defense Education Act financial assistance to the states to strengthen public school instruction in science, mathematics, and foreign languages, to strengthen guidance counseling and testing in secondary schools, and to improve the statistical services of state agencies (begun in 1958); (2) Aid to school districts in federally affected areas, where federal activities create a substantial increase in school enrollments or a reduction in taxable resources because of federally owned property. Federal funds can be used for construction, operation, and maintenance of public schools in such districts (begun in 1950 but related to defense programs in World War II); (3) National school lunch and milk programs providing cash grants and commodity donations for nonprofit lunches served in public and private schools (begun in 1946); (4) Federal funds for the purchase of educational materials for the blind (begun in 1879); and (5) Federal grants for vocational education to help states and school districts provide training in agriculture, home economics, trades, and industries (begun in 1917). See U.S. Department of Health, Education, and Welfare, *Handbook of Programs,* 1963 edition (Washington: Government Printing Office, 1963).

TABLE 14.2

FEDERAL AID TO ELEMENTARY AND SECONDARY SCHOOLS:
MAJOR LEGISLATION

---

1. *Elementary and Secondary Education Act, 1965:* Cash grants for construction,
   operation, and maintenance of schools in poverty impacted public school districts
   on the basis of the number of children enrolled from poverty stricken families and
   grants to public and private schools for the support of specialized educational
   facilities.
2. *National Defense Education Act, 1958:* Financial assistance to states and public
   school districts to improve instruction in science, mathematics, and foreign languages, to strengthen guidance counseling and testing, and to improve statistical
   services. Amended in 1963 to include assistance in history, English, civics, geography, remedial reading, and library sciences. (Also included loans to undergraduates,
   fellowships to graduate students, and funds to colleges to improve training of
   teachers.)
3. *Federally Impacted Areas Aid Program, 1950:* Where federal activities create a
   substantial increase in school enrollments or reduction in taxable resources because
   of federally owned property, federal funds can be used for construction, operation,
   and maintenance of schools in public school districts. This program is an outgrowth
   of defense impacted area aid legislation in World War II.
4. *National School Lunch and Milk Programs, 1946:* Federal grants and commodity
   donations for nonprofit lunches and milk served in public and private schools.
5. *Smith Hughes Vocational Education Act, 1917:* Federal grants for vocational
   education to help states and public school districts provide training in agriculture,
   home economics, trades, and industries.
6. *Federal Aid to Colleges and Universities:* Although not direct aids to elementary
   and secondary schools, federal aid to colleges and universities indirectly helps
   elementary and secondary education by improving the educational climate of the
   nation. Major sources of federal aid include:
   a. "The G.I. Bill," providing federal grants for tuition and subsistence for veterans
      attending institutions of higher education.
   b. Morrill Land Grant Act of 1862, providing states with federal land, the proceeds
      from which were used to establish land-grant colleges and universities.
   c. Higher Education Act of 1965, providing federal funds for construction of col-
      lege facilities and to upgrade college libraries.
   d. Medical and Dental Education Program, providing federal funds for construction
      of facilities and loans to medical and dental students.

Drop-outs and Mental Failures

Given conflicts over the objectives of public education, it is difficult to
make any overall evaluation of educational output in the states. Is the
goal of public education college preparation, vocational skill, emotional
happiness, psychological adjustment, academic excellence, the reduction of
automobile accidents, the inculcation of spiritual values, the cultivation of
patriotism, the production of engineers and scientists, the training of competent homemakers, or winning the Olympics? How can we tell whether

FIGURE 14.2

THE FIFTY STATES ARRANGED ACCORDING TO ADULT EDUCATION LEVELS
AND HIGH SCHOOL DROPOUT RATES, 1963

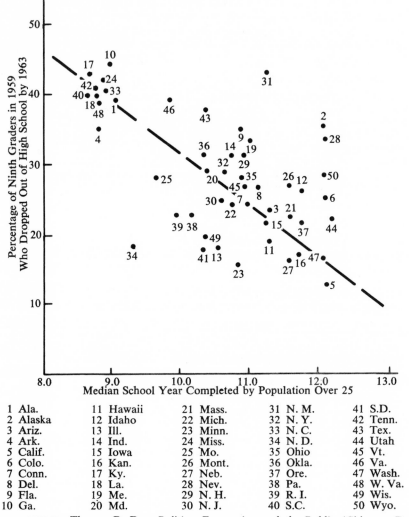

1 Ala.	11 Hawaii	21 Mass.	31 N. M.	41 S.D.
2 Alaska	12 Idaho	22 Mich.	32 N. Y.	42 Tenn.
3 Ariz.	13 Ill.	23 Minn.	33 N. C.	43 Tex.
4 Ark.	14 Ind.	24 Miss.	34 N. D.	44 Utah
5 Calif.	15 Iowa	25 Mo.	35 Ohio	45 Vt.
6 Colo.	16 Kan.	26 Mont.	36 Okla.	46 Va.
7 Conn.	17 Ky.	27 Neb.	37 Ore.	47 Wash.
8 Del.	18 La.	28 Nev.	38 Pa.	48 W. Va.
9 Fla.	19 Me.	29 N. H.	39 R. I.	49 Wis.
10 Ga.	20 Md.	30 N. J.	40 S.C.	50 Wyo.

SOURCE: Thomas R. Dye, *Politics, Economics, and the Public* (Chicago: Rand
McNally & Co., 1966), p. 99. Reproduced by permission.

the failure to achieve any one of these objectives is a product of our educational policies or an outgrowth of other national problems?

Two measures seemingly reflective of public education, which are available on a state-by-state basis, are the proportion of high school students
who drop out of school before graduation and the proportion of selective

service registrants who fail the mental examination prior to induction. Certainly the child who does not complete at least 12 years of education in a highly technological society represents a national liability, and so does the young man so feebly equipped with mental faculties that he is of no use to the armed services of the nation. On a nationwide basis, only about 759 out of every 1000 children who were ninth graders in 1961 managed to graduate from high school in 1965; some 241 of these 1000 children dropped out of school before graduation. These figures are an improvement over comparable figures for high schoolers during the 1956–1960 and 1946–1950 periods. The drop-out rate per 1000 ninth graders from 1956–1960 was 379, and the drop-out rate from 1946–1950 was 495 per 1000 ninth graders. There is considerable variation among the states in drop-out rates. In 1965, California graduated all but 111 of each 1000 ninth graders in 1961; while in Maine and South Carolina, the drop-out rate during that same period was 400 out of every 1000 ninth graders.

In 1964, before selective service qualification standards were lowered, 29.9 per cent of all selective service registrants given examinations failed the mental test. (An additional 22.7 per cent were medically disqualified to bring the total disqualifications to over half of all examinees.) In North Carolina, South Carolina, and Mississippi, over 50 per cent of the selective service examinees failed the mental test, while in four states—Minnesota, Washington, Iowa, and Utah—less than 10 per cent failed the mental test.

Among the 50 states, wealth and adult education levels are directly related to drop-out rates and mental failures.[12] Wealthy states with well educated adult populations are the same states that spend more per pupil on their public schools, pay higher teachers' salaries, attract more male teachers, and have better teacher-pupil ratios; and these same states tend to experience fewer high school drop-outs and selective service mental failures. In contrast, the less wealthy states with poorly educated adult populations, spend less per pupil on their public schools, pay lower teachers' salaries, attract fewer male teachers, and have poor teacher-pupil ratios; and these same states experience more drop-outs and mental failures.

Schools and Communities

Local control over public schools has been an article of faith for most Americans for many years. Responsibility for many basic decisions in public education lies with the 31,000 separate school districts in America. In theory, these school districts are subject to local control. The people of the local school district are supposed to exercise that control through an elected school board, and the board appoints a superintendent to act as the chief executive of the community schools. There is some variation to

[12] Dye, *op. cit.*, pp. 96–100.

that pattern—in approximately a quarter of the nation's school districts, the boards are appointed rather than elected, usually by city councils, county commissions, mayors, or even judges. In theory, these school boards exercise control over curriculum (that is, what should be taught in the schools), buildings and facilities, personnel, including both administrators and teachers, and perhaps most important of all, financing. These school districts are separate from city or county government. Education is independent of other local governmental responsibilities. In theory, separation of education from municipal government was meant to eliminate "politics" from education.

The formal structure of local school districts often obscures the realities of educational politics in communities. First of all, we have already seen that the concept of local control over education is circumscribed by both state and federal acts. Secondly, the concept of popular control over the schools through elected boards of laymen is challenged by the increasing professionalization of education. Finally, the idea that politics could be separated from education was never a reality. School districts are governmental units and there has always been conflict between individuals and groups over what should be done in the public schools. School board members, school superintendents, and teachers are engaged in political activity whether they like it or not. School administrators may call this activity "community relations," but in any other profession outside of education it would be called "politics."

School politics will differ from one community to another, but it is possible to identify a number of political actors who appear on the scene in school politics in almost every community.[13] There is, first of all, that small band of voters who turn out for school elections. It is estimated that, on the average, only about one-third of the eligible voters bother to cast ballots in school elections. Voter turnout at school bond and tax elections shows no ground swell of public interest in school affairs. Perhaps even more interesting is the finding that the larger the voter turnout in a school bond referendum, the more likely the defeat of pro-educational proposals.[14] In general, the best way to defeat a school bond referendum is to have a large turnout. Proponents of educational expenditures are better advised to work not so much for a large turnout as for a better informed and more educationally oriented electorate.

School board members constitute another important group of actors in school politics. School board members are generally better educated than their constituents. However, school board members are selected largely

[13] See Thomas H. Eliot, "Toward an Understanding of Public School Politics," *American Political Science Review,* 52 (December, 1959), 1032–50.

[14] See Patricia Sexton, "City Schools," *Annals of the American Academy of Social and Political Science,* 352 (March, 1964), 95–106.

from among business owners, proprietors, and managers. There is some evidence that people who are interested in education and have some knowledge of what the schools are doing tend to support education more than do the less informed citizens. Yet the occupational background of school board members suggests that they are sensitive to tax burdens placed upon businessmen and property owners.

Professional educators are much less restrained in their enthusiasm for the public schools. Many professional educators are distrustful of the laymen who compose the school boards; they often feel that educational policy should be in the hands of professional educators. They may feel that important decisions about curriculum, facilities, personnel, and finances should be the special province of persons trained in education. They view the school board's role as one of defending the schools against public criticism and persuading the community to open its pocketbook. Professional educators often support the idea that "politics" should be kept out of education; to them, this means that laymen should not interfere with decisions that professional educators wish to make for themselves. For example, on the critical question of what should be taught in the public schools, the American Association of School Administrators says: "Curriculum planning and development is a highly technical task which requires special training. . . . Board members do not have and cannot be expected to have the technical competence to pass on the work of expert teachers in this field." [15] School boards and voters (those who supply the money for the public schools and therefore feel that it is their legitimate right to control them) believe that citizen control of education is a vital safeguard of democracy. But professional educators sometimes feel that school board members are often uninformed about school problems or either unwilling or unable to support the needs of education. For example, school board members throughout the nation were much less likely to support federal aid to education than professional educators; many school board members felt that the federal government would strip them of their local power over the schools. Professional educators, on the other hand, were less fearful of dictation from Washington.

The professional educators can be divided into at least three distinct groups. Numerically the largest group, yet politically the least significant, are the school teachers. The most powerful group are the professional school administrators, particularly the superintendents of schools. A third group are the faculties of teachers colleges and departments of education at universities, who often have contacts with state departments of education and who influence requirements for teacher certification within the states. State and local chapters of the National Education Association (NEA) represent both teachers and administrators, but often they are dominated by

---

[15] Eliot, *op. cit.,* p. 1036.

professional administrators.[16] The participation of administrators in the National Education Association is one of the major criticisms of that organization made by the American Federation of Teachers (AFT). The AFT has emerged as an important voice of teachers in the nation's largest cities. The American Federation of Teachers is a labor union representing classroom teachers, and it employs all the recognized techniques of labor organizations to achieve its goals. The AFT advocates collective bargaining for teachers and, whenever necessary, the strike. In the past, the much larger NEA viewed these techniques as unprofessional, and it criticized the AFT for its connection with labor unions through the AFL-CIO. However, the growing membership of the AFT in large cities has brought about a greater degree of militancy by the NEA and its local and state chapters. The NEA has formed a Department of Classroom Teachers in order to avoid the charge that it is administrator-dominated. While it has never officially gone on "strike," it has invoked "professional sanctions" against states and school districts. Occasionally, professional sanctions have included a collective refraining from signing of teachers' contracts and a refusal to resume work at the opening of school in the fall. More recently in Florida, professional sanctions took the form of simultaneous mass resignation of all the state's teachers.

Schools within metropolitan areas are the scenes of particularly deep conflict within American society.[17] For in metropolitan areas, underlying disputes over curriculum, facilities, personnel, and finances, there are deep cleavages between haves and have-nots—suburbanites and central city dwellers, and ethnic and racial groups—which are reflected in struggles over public schools. The abandonment of the central city by middle class, white, child-rearing families has meant heavier and heavier concentrations in central city public schools of children from low income, racial minorities. Racial groups claim that they are underrepresented on big city school boards even though their children may constitute more than half of the school population in many large cities. They argue that there is an "equality lag" in schools in Negro areas—where schools do not measure up to those in white residential districts in terms of quality of teaching, the adequacy of facilities, and the availability of extra services. They also object to the "ability grouping" of children, which places many have-not children into lower tracts and separates them from more advantaged children from middle class families. They argue that with proper attention, the abilities of have-not children may prove roughly equal to those of more advantaged children and that, therefore, they should not be separated into different tracts at an

[16] See R. Joseph Monsen, Jr. and Mark W. Cannon, *The Makers of Public Policy* (New York: McGraw-Hill Book Co., 1965), chap. 6.

[17] See James B. Conant, *Slums and Suburbs* (New York: McGraw-Hill Book Co., 1961).

early age. Among the newer racial demands in urban schools are: (1) compensatory treatment involving vast expenditures for schools in low income areas in order to balance past inequities; (2) the elimination of racial imbalance in the schools and the bussing of whites into Negro schools and Negroes into white schools; and (3) the elimination of "neighborhood schools" and the scattering of Negroes and have-not groups in educational parks throughout the city. Of course there is strong opposition to these demands. Many parents argue for the continuation of "neighborhood schools," which means that, so long as housing is segregated in large cities, the public schools will be de facto segregated. (This problem is discussed at length in Chapter 13.)

Much of the recent concern in education for "culturally deprived" and "disadvantaged" students reflects the growing concern with the problem of low income, central city, racial minorities in the public schools. The influx of federal aid into city school districts may help to alleviate some of these problems. Federal aid under the Elementary and Secondary Education Act of 1965 is allocated disproportionately to poverty-impacted school districts. Moreover many of the programs under the Economic Opportunity Act of 1964 (the "War on Poverty") emphasize educational programs for disadvantaged groups, particularly "Operation Head Start," which attempts to better prepare the children of have-not families for a successful career in the public schools.

Reading, Writing, and Religion

The First Amendment to the Constitution of the United States contains two important guarantees of religious freedom: (1) "Congress shall make no law respecting an establishment of religion . . . ," and (2) "Or prohibiting the free exercise therof." The Due Process Clause of the 14th Amendment made these guarantees of religious liberty applicable to the states and their subdivisions as well as to Congress. Most of the debate over religion in the public schools centers around the "no establishment" clause of the First Amendment rather than the "free exercise" clause. However, it was respect for the "free exercise" clause that caused the Supreme Court in 1925 to declare unconstitutional an attempt on the part of a state to prohibit private and parochial schools and to force all children to attend public schools. In the words of the Supreme Court: "The fundamental theory of liberty upon which all governments in this Union repose excludes any general power of the state to standardize its children by forcing them to accept instruction from public teachers only. The child is not the mere creature of the state." [18] It is this decision that protects the entire structure of parochial schools in this nation.

[18] Pierce v. The Society of Sisters, 268 U.S. 510 (1925).

A great deal of religious conflict in America has centered around the meaning of the "no establishment" clause, and the public schools have been the principal scene of this conflict. One interpretation of the clause holds that it does not prevent government from aiding religious schools or encouraging religious beliefs in the public schools, so long as it does not discriminate against any particular religion. Another interpretation of the "no establishment" clause is that it creates a "wall of separation" between church and state in America, which prevents government from directly aiding religious schools or encouraging religious beliefs in any way.

The Catholic Church in America enrolls over six million students from kindergarten through the 12th grade (over 90 per cent of all private school students in the nation), and the Catholic Church has led the fight for an interpretation of the "no establishment" clause that would permit government to aid religious schools. As Catholic spokesmen see it, Catholic parents have a right to send their children to Catholic schools, and since they are taxpayers, they also expect that some share of tax monies should go to the aid of church schools; to do otherwise, they argue, would discriminate against parents who choose a "God-centered" education for their children. Those who favor government aid to parochial schools frequently refer to the language found in several cases decided by the Supreme Court, which appears to support the idea that government can *in a limited fashion* support the activities of church related schools. In the case of Pierce *v.* The Society of Sisters (1925), the Court stated that the right to send one's children to parochial schools was a fundamental liberty guaranteed to all. In Cochran *v.* the Board of Education (1930), the Court upheld a state law providing free textbooks for children attending both public and parochial schools on the grounds that this aid benefited the *children* rather than the Catholic Church and hence did not constitute an "establishment" of religion within the meaning of the First Amendment.[19] In Everson *v.* Board of Education (1947), the Supreme Court upheld the bussing of parochial school children to and from school at public expense on the grounds that the "wall of separation between church and state" does not prohibit the state from adopting a general program which helps *all* children, regardless of religion, to proceed safely to and from schools.[20] In McCollum *v.* Board of Education (1948), the court declared *un*constitutional religious instruction in the public schools given during school hours by representatives of Protestant, Catholic, and Jewish faiths.[21] However in Zorach *v.* Clauson (1952), the court upheld a religious "released time program," where the schools released children during school hours for religious instruction conducted *outside* of the public schools.[22] In this case the Court

[19] Cochran *v.* Board of Education, 281 U.S. 370 (1930).
[20] Everson *v.* Board of Education, 330 U.S. 1 (1947).
[21] McCollum *v.* Board of Education, 333 U.S. 203 (1948).
[22] Zorach *v.* Clauson, 343 U.S. 306 (1952).

stated, "We are a religious people whose institutions presuppose a supreme being." These cases suggest that the Supreme Court is willing to permit some forms of aid to parochial school *children* that indirectly aids religion, so long as this aid is not directly used for the teaching of religion.

Religious controversy was instrumental in the defeat of federal aid to education bills prior to 1965.[23] For many years supporters of federal aid to education outnumbered opponents, but supporters were badly divided over the question of whether or not federal aid should go to parochial schools. Bills that failed to provide aid to parochial schools lost the crucial support of Catholics in Congress, and bills that provided aid for parochial schools lost the necessary support of Protestants, who favored a strict separation of church and state. For example, in 1961, President Kennedy's federal aid to education bill was strongly opposed by a Catholic hierarchy when he stated: "In accordance with the clear prohibition of the Constitution, no elementary or secondary school funds are allocated for constructing church schools or paying church school teachers' salaries, and thus non-public school children are rightfully not counted in determining the funds each state will receive for its public schools."[24] Francis Cardinal Spellman of New York rallied Catholic opposition to Kennedy's bill:

> I believe that these recommendations are unfair to most parents of the nation's 6,800,000 parochial and private school children. Such legislation would discriminate against the multitude of America's children because their parents chose to exercise their constitutional right to educate them in accordance with their religious beliefs. . . . I cannot believe that Congress would enact a program of financial assistance and secondary education unless all children were granted equal educational privileges, regardless of the school they attend.[25]

Many Protestant spokesmen were equally opposed to any bill including aid to parochial schools. In a leading Protestant publication, an editorial read:

> Cardinal Spellman has not changed his mind. His aim is still to compel Protestants, Jews, and others to support a wholly controlled function of the Roman Catholic Church. The compulsion lies in the use of the taxing powers of the federal government to raise funds for Catholic schools. He has given us fair warning, so he should have our answer. American Protestants will never pay taxes to support Catholic schools. We will oppose enactments of laws which require such payments. If Congress is pressured into enacting such laws, we will contest them in the courts. If the courts reverse themselves and declare such laws constitutional, we will still refuse to pay these taxes, paying whatever price is necessary to preserve religious liberty in a pluralistic society.[26]

[23] See Hugh D. Price, "Race, Religion and the Rules Committee," *The Uses of Power*, Alan F. Westin, ed. (New York: Harcourt, Brace, & World, Inc., 1962).

[24] *Ibid.,* p. 24.

[25] *Ibid.,* p. 23.

[26] *Ibid.,* pp. 36–37.

As a result of these sharp religious divisions, federal aid to education floundered in Congress until 1965. In the Elementary and Secondary Education Act of that year, President Johnson compromised the religious issue. The largest share of federal money distributed under this Act goes to poverty-impacted *public* school districts, but the Act also includes federal grants for the purchase of specialized educational services and facilities, such as laboratories, textbooks, and instructional materials. Federal funds for these specialized educational facilities and services may go to both public and private schools. Presumably federal aid to a church school for the purchase of a specialized educational facility would not violate the constitutional prohibition against the "establishment" of a religion so long as the federal aid was not directly used for the teaching of religion.

While the Supreme Court has consented to government programs aiding the child in parochial school, it has also voiced the opinion that the no establishment clause of the First Amendment should constitute a wall of separation between church and state. In the words of the court:

> Neither a state nor the federal government can set up a church. Neither can pass laws which aid one religion, aid all religions, or prefer one religion over another. Neither can force nor influence a person to go to or to remain away from church against his will, or force him to profess a belief or disbelief in any religion. No person can be punished for entertaining or professing religious beliefs or disbeliefs, for church attendance or nonattendance. No tax in any amount, large or small, can be levied to support any religious activities or institutions, whatever they may be called, or whatever form they may adopt to teach or practice religion. Neither a state nor the federal government can, openly or secretly, participate in the affairs of any religious organizations or groups, and vice versa.[27]

Religious conflict in public schools also centers around the question of prayer and Bible reading ceremonies conducted by public schools. The practice of opening the school day with prayer and Bible reading ceremonies is widespread in American public schools. Usually the prayer is a Protestant rendition of the Lord's Prayer and Bible reading is from the King James version. In order to avoid the denominational aspects of these ceremonies, the New York State Board of Regents substituted a nondenominational prayer, which it required to be said aloud in each class in the presence of a teacher at the beginning of each school day:

> Almighty God, we acknowledge our dependence upon Thee, and we beg Thy blessings upon us, our parents, our teachers, and our country.

New York argued that this prayer ceremony did not violate the no establishment clause, because the prayer was denominationally neutral and be-

---

[27] Hugo Black, Majority Opinion in Everson *v.* Board of Education, 330 U.S. 1 (1947).

cause student participation in the prayer was voluntary. However, in Engle *v.* Vitale (1962), the Supreme Court stated that "The constitutional prohibition against laws respecting an establishment of a religion must at least mean in this country it is no part of the business of government to compose official prayers for any group of the American people to recite as part of a religious program carried on by government." [28] The Court pointed out that making prayer voluntary did not free it from the prohibitions of the no establishment clause; that clause prevented the establishment of a religious ceremony by a government agency, regardless of whether the ceremony was voluntary or not:

> Neither the fact that the prayer may be denominationally neutral, nor the fact that its observance on the part of the students is voluntary can serve to free it from the limitations of the establishment clause, as it might from the free exercise clause, of the First Amendment, both of which are operative against the states by virtue of the 14th Amendment. . . . The establishment clause, unlike the free exercise clause, does not depend on any showing of direct governmental compulsion and is violated by the enactment of laws which establish an official religion whether those laws operate directly to coerce nonobserving individuals or not.[29]

One year later in the case of Abbington Township *v.* Schempp, the Court considered the constitutionality of Bible reading ceremonies in the public schools.[30] Here again, even though the children were not required to participate, the Court found that Bible reading as an opening exercise in the schools was a religious ceremony. The Court went to some trouble in its opinion to point out that they were not "throwing the Bible out of the schools," for they specifically stated that the study of the Bible or of religion, when presented objectively as part of a secular program of education, did not violate the First Amendment, but religious *ceremonies* involving Bible reading or prayer, established by a state or school district, did so.

[28] Engle *v.* Vitale, 370 U.S. 421 (1962).
[29] *Ibid.*
[30] Abbington Township *v.* Schempp, 374 U.S. 203 (1963).

15

THE POLITICS

OF TRANSPORTATION

Public Highway Policy

Few inventions have had such a far-reaching effect on the life of the American people as the automobile. Henry Ford built one of the first gasoline driven carriages in America in 1893, and by 1900 there were 8000 automobiles registered in the U.S. The Model "T" Ford was introduced in the autumn of 1908. By concentrating on a single unlovely but enduring model, and by introducing the assembly line processes, the Ford Motor Company began producing automobiles for the masses. By 1921, there were over 20 million cars in existence, and the auto industry was established in the United States. Today there are over 90 million registered motor vehicles in the nation, almost one for every two persons living in the country; and the automobile population is increasing faster than the human population. The automotive and trucking industry ranks as the largest and wealthiest in the United States. It represents 10 per cent of the gross national product, it employs nearly 12 million persons, buys 22 per cent of the steel output, 61 per cent of the rubber, and 44 per cent of all of the radios produced in the nation. Automobiles and superhighways have radically changed the life style of Americans. They have helped to create mushrooming suburbs, which have drained white, middle class Americans from the nation's central cities, and threaten both to suffocate cities with polluted air and to strangle them with massive traffic jams. Automobiles and superhighways have made Americans more mobile, more travel conscious, more able to move about the country in search of opportunity. Freeways have reduced travel time and brought the farm closer to the city, and they have also contributed to the economic stagnation and decline of small towns and rural areas in the nation.

In addition to the economic and sociological significance, the invention of the automobile has had an important impact on politics and government. The provision of public highways is the second most costly function of state and local governments. Highway politics are of interest not only to the automotive industry and the driving public, but also to the oil industry, the American Road Builders Association, the cement industry, the railroads, the trucking industry, farmers, the outdoor advertising industry, county commissioners, taxpayer associations, conservationists, and neighborhood improvement associations. These political interests are concerned with the allocation of money for highway purposes, the sources of funds for highway revenue, the extent of gasoline and motor vehicle taxation, the regulation of traffic on the highways, the location of highways, the determination of construction policies, the division of responsibility between federal and state and local governments for highway financing and administration, division of highway funds between rural and urban areas, and many other important outcomes in highway politics.

Governments spent very little for public roads at the beginning of the century. The only hard surface roads to be found then were provided by city governments. But the automobile brought an insatiable demand for bigger and better highways. The automobile owner provided the broad base of political support for highway construction, but the leadership has come from the automotive and oil industries, the construction industry, the cement and equipment manufacturers, the organized farm interests seeking farm-to-market roads, and the trucking industry. The railroad industry has provided the only substantial opposition to highway building, but all the battles have been won by the supporters of highway transportation. Today, there are over two million miles of surface roads in America, and state and local expenditures for highways total over $12 billion annually. Highway expenditures account for about 18 per cent of all state and local expenditures, making highways second only to education in costs to states and communities.[1]

At the beginning of the century, most road expenditures were made by local governments, particularly cities. Cities had very early created hard surfaced street networks, which proved capable of servicing motor vehicles

[1] For a complete description of highway policy in the United States see Phillip H. Burch, *Highway Revenue and Expenditure Policy in The United States* (New Brunswick, N.J.: Rutgers University Press, 1962).

reasonably well. But rural areas were, to say the least, unprepared for the advent of the automobile. State after state established state highway departments charged with the task of constructing highways in rural areas. State highway systems came into being, and state governments assumed direct responsibility for the construction and maintenance of a large proportion of the public roads. States also began to distribute aid to local governments for highway purposes. Many state highway departments tried to distinguish between a "primary" state highway system, which was to connect cities and towns, and a "secondary" highway system, which would connect primary highways with local service routes and streets that provided direct access to farms and homes. Such a classification provided a logical division of responsibilities between state and local governments. But since the states generally financed the primary system, communities often pressured state highway departments to classify more roads as "primary" state highways, in order to shift the burden of finance onto the state. As a result, the proportion of roads designated as primary state highways gradually increased. The assumption of direct state responsibility for a "primary highway system" heavily favored rural areas; the goal of many state primary highway systems was to connect every county seat. The rural bias of state highway departments lingers even today.

Federal Highway Policy

It was in the Federal Aid Road Act of 1916 that the federal government, through its Bureau of Public Roads, first provided regular funds for highway construction under terms that gave the Bureau considerable influence over state policy. For example, if states wanted to get federal money, they were required to have a highway department, and to have their plans for highway construction approved by the Bureau of Public Roads. In 1921, federal aid was limited to a connected system of principal state highways, now called the "federal aid primary highway system." Uniform standards were prescribed and even a uniform numbering system added, such as "US 1," or "US 30." Federal aid was limited to a maximum of 7 per cent of the total mileage of the state and was only to connect major cities. The emphasis of the program was clearly rural. The federal aid formula appropriated funds, one-third on the basis of population, one-third on the basis of area, one-third on the basis of total mileage of postal routes in the states. States were required to match federal monies dollar for dollar.

The Federal Highway Act of 1944 designated a federal aid "secondary" system of farm-to-market roads, and provided for "urban extensions" of primary roads, in addition to the federal aid for the primary highway system. Federal funds for primary and secondary and urban extension roads, commonly called "ABC funds," are determined by three separate formulas, but all take into account area, population, postal routes, and mileage. These federal ABC funds are matched 50–50 by the states. In the use of their federal funds, states make the surveys and plans, let the contracts, and supervise the construction, but only with the approval of the U.S. Bureau of Public Roads. All ABC roads remain under the administrative control of the states, who are responsible for their operation and maintenance. In 1961, ABC federal funds amounted to about $700,000. All payments to contractors for work done on any federal aid project are made from state revenues; the Bureau of Public Roads makes very few direct payments.

The Federal Highway Act of 1944 also authorized the national system of interstate and defense highways ("I" highways)—now the most important feature of the federal highway policy. However, prior to 1956, only modest funds were provided by Congress for the "I" highway system, and these were provided on a 50–50 matching basis. It was not until the Federal Highway Act of 1956, under the Eisenhower administration, that Congress became serious about the "I" highway system. At that time, Congress provided for its completion by 1972, and changed the matching basis to 90 per cent federal and 10 per cent state. The Federal Highway Act of 1956 authorized 41,000 miles of highway, designed to connect principal metropolitan areas and industrial centers, thereby shifting the emphasis of federal highway activity from rural to urban needs. Figure 15.1 shows the "I" highway system as it will look upon its completion. Although the system will constitute less than 2 per cent of the total surface in the nation, it is expected to carry over 20 per cent of all highway traffic. The Bureau of Public Roads has been given strong supervisory powers, including the selection of routes (it can even transfer interstate mileage and funds out of a noncooperative state), but administration and execution are still left to state highway departments. Federal monies are paid to the states, not to the contractors, as the work progresses. The Federal Highway Trust Fund in the Bureau of Public Roads is responsible for orderly scheduling of federal aid and the phasing out of reimbursement requests for the states. A state can proceed in a more rapid rate building its "I" highways if it chooses to do so without federal reimbursement for a period of time; in practice, however, this does not happen. The Bureau makes the real determination of who gets what, when, and how in the interstate highway program. The 1956 Act has established uniformity in construction and engineering specifications and the maximum size and weight limits for "I" highway users. It is also agreed to reduce by 0.5 per cent the state's share of the cost of "I" highways if a state prohibits advertising on "I" highways. However, with only garden clubs available to battle the powerful billboard industry, only 16 states had adopted the ban by 1962, despite the federal monetary incentive to limit advertising.

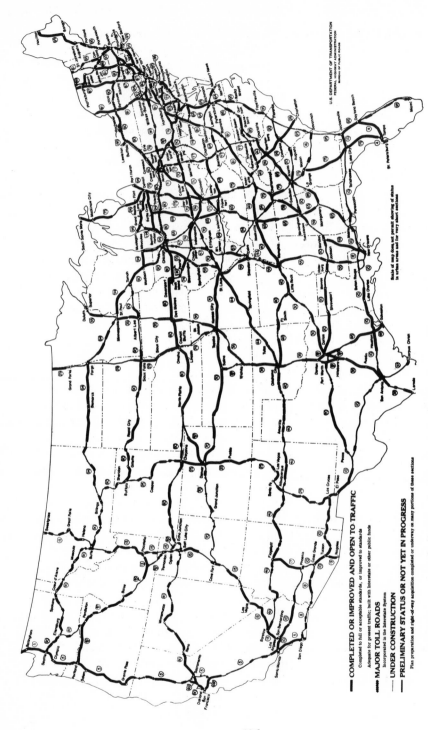

FIGURE 15.1   THE NATIONAL SYSTEM OF INTERSTATE AND DEFENSE HIGHWAYS, JUNE, 1968

SOURCE: U.S. Department of Transportation.

The federal interstate highway program reasserted federal interest in the highway field. Federal funds for highway construction now amount to about one-third of all state highway revenue.

State Highway Organization and Finance

The political importance of highway construction and the millions of dollars spent on highway building contracts each year have resulted in a tendency in some states to set highway departments and highway funds apart from the other functions of state government. Interests favorable to highway construction (road builders, oil and gas companies, automobile associations, and so on) have generally argued for the organization of independent highway departments or commissions, free from direct control by the governor. They have also supported a system of earmarking certain state revenues, generally gasoline taxes, motor vehicle registration fees, and other highway user revenues, for use on highways only. Of course, not all states have been willing to remove highways from the regular channels of public control, and the pattern of highway organization and finance varies from state to state.

Robert S. Friedman has classified 50 states according to their degree of organizational independence from the governor in highway policy.[2] He has defined a "dependent" highway department as one in which the governor is free to name, without restrictions, his own highway department head, who would serve at the pleasure of the governor. In contrast, an "independent" department is governed by a multi-member board or commission, which chooses the department head. The board may be chosen by the governor under certain restrictions: their terms of office would not coincide with that of the governor and its members could not easily be removed from office. Very often these board members or commissioners are chosen to represent geographic areas of the state, in formal recognition of the pork barrel character of much highway work. This localism is opposed by proponents of coordinated planning for state highways. States with independent boards or commissions spend slightly more per capita on highways than states with dependent highway departments. However, many of the states with gubernatorial control are the most urban, industrial states in the nation. It may be that ruralism produces both increased highway spending per capita and independent highway boards.

The principle source of highway finance is highway user revenue. Federal highway aid constitutes about 30 per cent of all highway funds, but most of the remaining 70 per cent comes from taxes and fees levied upon highway users. In only a few states are general revenues used for highway

<hr />

[2] Robert S. Friedman, "State Politics and Highways," *Politics in the American States,* Herbert Jacob and Kenneth Vines, eds. (Boston: Little, Brown and Co., 1965).

TABLE 15.1

COMPARATIVE STATE AND LOCAL HIGHWAY EXPENDITURES

State*	Rank according to ratio of highway expenditures to all governmental expenditures	Per cent highway expenditures of all state and local expenditures 1958-62 average	Rank according to per capita highway expenditures	Per capita highway expenditures 1958-62 average	Rank according to per vehicle highway expenditures	Per vehicle highway expenditures
South Dakota	1	33.24	3	$ 99.52	5	$199
Vermont	2	32.54	2	107.95	1	313
Wyoming	3	32.42	1	144.59	2	229
New Hampshire	4	30.60	7	84.17	3	219
North Dakota	5	28.64	4	98.80	6	196
Iowa	6	27.22	8	79.40	13	173
Montana	7	27.10	6	89.29	-	176
Idaho	8	27.00	10	75.10	22.5	148
Nebraska	9	26.64	14	69.25	18	155
Maine	10	26.56	16	67.93	7	189
Kansas	11	25.40	9	76.14	25	146
Tennessee	12	24.36	31	52.01	28.5	143
Kentucky	13	24.26	32	51.68	40.5	123
Mississippi	14	23.76	29.5	52.32	8	187
Arkansas	15	23.02	40	45.71	30	141
Texas	16	22.96	24	56.58	31	136
Virginia	17	22.80	36	49.95	37	127
Wisconsin	18	22.74	15	68.02	26	145
Alabama	19	22.42	39	47.84	17	157
New Mexico	20	22.00	12	69.43	14	169
Nevada	21	21.98	5	94.68	33.5	132
West Virginia	22	21.48	41	45.62	11	183
South Carolina	23	20.86	48	32.15	38.5	124
Connecticut	24	20.78	11	73.22	24	147
Ohio	25	20.28	27	54.40	23.5	143
Oregon	26	20.24	13	69.30	19	154
Minnesota	27	20.10	29.5	52.32	22.5	148
Louisiana	28	19.76	19	63.47	4	204
Oklahoma	29	19.68	25	56.03	47	105
Illinois	30	19.44	26	55.54	16	158
Utah	31	19.40	20	59.24	35	130
Delaware	32	19.38	18	63.81	9.5	185
Missouri	33	19.10	42	45.55	33.5	132
Georgia	34	18.70	44	42.98	38.5	124
Maryland	35	18.28	35	50.41	20.5	150
Arizona	36	17.92	23	57.51	20.5	150
Florida	37	17.86	37	48.98	32	134
North Carolina	38	17.82	46	35.19	45	108
Michigan	39	17.36	28	53.90	27	144
Indiana	40	17.28	17	66.51	43	116
Rhode Island	41	17.04	43	44.91	40.5	123
Washington	42	17.02	21	59.22	36	128
Colorado	43	16.76	22	57.52	44	109

State*	Rank according to ratio of highway expenditures to all governmental expenditures	Per cent highway expenditures of all state and local expenditures 1958-62 average	Rank according to per capita highway expenditures	Per capita highway expenditures 1958-62 average	Rank according to per vehicle highway expenditures	Per vehicle highway expenditures
Pennsylvania	44	16.48	45	$40.44	42	$118
Massachusetts	45	15.88	38	48.49	15	162
New York	46	13.92	33	51.47	9.5	185
New Jersey	47	13.00	47	34.60	46	107
California	48	12.82	34	50.49	48	100

*Alaska and Hawaii are excluded because they were not states during the entire period covered.
Sources: U.S. Bureau of the Census, *Governmental Finances in the United States, 1958-1962*; and U.S. Bureau of Public Roads, *Highway Statistics, 1963*.
Source: Robert S. Friedman, "State Politics and Highways," in *Politics in the American States,* eds. Herbert Jacob and Kenneth Vines, (Boston: Little, Brown, & Co., 1965), p. 432.

purposes. The state gasoline tax alone accounts for approximately half of all highway receipts. State gasoline tax rates are surprisingly uniform from state to state. All states levy gasoline taxes of 5–7½¢ per gallon. (The federal government now collects 4¢ per gallon.) The second most important highway revenue source is the motor vehicle registration fee. In some states, particularly in the South, this fee is primarily a regulatory device, with yearly charges running from only $3–$5. In other states, fees for passenger cars are $15 or more, with higher fees for heavier vehicles, particularly trucks and buses. Toll road receipts constitute another major highway revenue source in some states. Tolls exact revenue from *through* traffic, which has originated in another state and is destined for still another state. New York, New Jersey, and Pennsylvania collect about half of all the toll receipts in the nation.

The segregation of highway user revenues from general state revenues is an article of faith among highway interests. Prior to the rise of the automobile, highway expenditures came out of general revenue. But automobile travel has made it possible to place heavy reliance on highway user revenues as a source of highway funds. The theory is that such taxes insure that the cost of highways is paid by the user. As highway revenues have grown, highway interests have pressed for legal and even constitutional principles preventing the use of these revenues for anything except highway purposes. Today, more than half the states have constitutional provisions restricting the diversion of highway user revenue to nonhighway purposes, and many other states restrict diversion by statute or administrative practice. This policy guarantees a continued flow of road building funds and, in effect, gives highways preferential treatment over other public programs.

Urban industrial states are far more likely to divert highway receipts to nonhighway purposes than the rural agricultural states.[3] If success in preventing the diversion of highway receipts to other public programs is a valid measure of the strength of the highway interest groups, these interest groups have been significantly more successful in rural than in urban states.

A Comparative View of State Highway Politics

Interstate comparisons in highway policy are complicated by differences in area, geography, soil, and terrain among the states. Large but thinly populated states must maintain more miles of highway in relation to their populations than smaller, heavily populated states. It is relatively cheap to put highways in deserts, but expensive to do so in mountains. Highways built in climates that are subject to freezes, snowfalls, and rainfalls require more maintenance and repair than highways located in less rigorous climates. In short, natural factors, as well as economic and political factors, contribute to variations in highway policy among the states.

Highway expenditures do not guarantee a good highway system, but they do provide a rough index of the extent to which supporters of highways have succeeded in obtaining public funds for their objectives. Per capita state-local highway expenditures in the states in 1966 ranged from highs of $229 in Wyoming and $273 in Alaska to lows of $45 in North Carolina and $48 in New Jersey and Illinois. (Since federal funds flow through state highway departments, these state expenditure figures include federal highway money.) Per capita highway expenditures in the states are significantly related to urbanization: increases in urbanization result in a *decrease* in per capita highway expenditures.[4] In other words, rural agricultural states spend more per capita on highways than urban industrial states. Not only do rural farm states spend more per capita on highways, but they also spend more in relation to their personal income. The federal government relieves some of the burden of highway financing in rural states by giving them proportionately more funds than it gives to urban states. But federal monies notwithstanding, rural states still expend more effort for highways than urban states. Whether one prefers to measure highway efforts in per capita expenditures or in relative terms, the tendency for rural agricultural states to emphasize highways is unmistakable.

Quite clearly, rural politics are much more highway oriented than urban politics. Part of the reason for this may be the problems of rural politics a few years ago. Rural roads disturb relatively few individuals, while metropolitan highways involve uprooting thousands of outraged residents and

[3] See Thomas R. Dye, *Politics, Economics, and the Public* (Chicago: Rand McNally, 1966), chap. 6.
[4] *Ibid.*, pp. 157–61.

irate businessmen. Freeways are a good idea when they run through some-body else's back yard. Mileage is much cheaper and faster to build in rural areas; urban highways require more years and more money per mile. As Phillip H. Burch points out, "Urban highways are poor politics for a governor when his successor will be cutting all the tapes." [5] Finally, it may be that urban dwellers have come to accept traffic jams as facts of life. They have never known anything better, so they fail to fight for highways with the same zest as their country cousins.

Not only do rural states spend relatively more for highways than urban states, but the distribution of highway funds within states generally favors rural areas. Phillip H. Burch argues effectively that "the American city is being woefully shortchanged in the allocation of state highway department money." [6] It is difficult to measure the extent to which rural and urban areas are not receiving a fair share of state highway expenditures. But Burch notes that U.S. Bureau of Public Roads data show that about 44 per cent of all traffic occurs in urban areas, while state highway departments spend only about 25 per cent of their highway funds in urban areas. The most flagrant discrimination in the allocation of state funds occurs in rural states, and the fairest ratios occur in urban states.

All but two states offer some form of grants-in-aid to local governments for highway purposes. The justification for state grants-in-aid to localities centers on the need for minimum road conditions throughout the state, the inadequacy of local revenue sources, and the desire to equalize financial burdens throughout the state. Here again, the evidence seems quite conclusive that across the nation, urban areas are heavily discriminated against in state highway grants-in-aid to local communities. The U.S. Bureau of Public Roads reports that in 1961 71 per cent of all state grants to localities went to county and township roads and only 29 per cent went to municipal streets.

It is important to note, however, that in recent years discrimination against urban areas in highway expenditures has been somewhat modified. In recent years urban areas in most states have made significant gains in the percentages of state highway funds they receive. The federal interstate highway program has also improved the relative position of urban areas in highway fund allocations.

Partisanship and Highway Policy

Republican states appear to spend more for highways than Democratic states.[7] This relationship does not seem to depend upon socio-economic

---

[5] Burch, *op. cit.,* p. 173.
[6] *Ibid.,* p. 165.
[7] Dye, *op. cit.,* pp. 171–74.

factors, but appears to be a product of party approaches to highway policy. Apparently, Republican legislators are more prone to spend public money for highways in lieu of spending it for education, health, welfare, or other public programs. Democratic legislatures may not give as much priority to highway expenditures relative to other public programs. It should be noted, however, that Democratic and Republican party control of state government is not nearly as influential in determining highway policy as the rural or urban character of the state. The degree of urbanism or ruralism is a more important determinant of highway policy than party affiliation, but the effects of partisanship can still be observed.

One of the most frequent explanations of discrimination against urban areas in state highway policy is the underrepresentation of urban areas in malapportioned state legislatures. There is little doubt that in the past malapportionment has indeed underrepresented urban areas. Many political scientists predicted that reapportionment would bring about a fairer distribution of state highway funds between urban and rural areas. But whether or not discrimination against urban areas in highway policy is really a product of malapportionment remains an interesting question. There is little evidence that malapportionment itself is the cause of discrimination against urban areas in highway policy. In the past, both well apportioned and malapportioned legislatures have discriminated against urban areas to the same degree.[8]

In short, there is no real evidence that a rural "conspiracy" is involved in the allocation of highway funds. Highway construction and right-of-way acquisition in urban areas is very expensive. Urban dwellers do not always welcome highways the way rural dwellers generally do. Highway construction in urban areas means a dislocation of people, businesses, and neighborhoods, as well as the removal of property from tax rolls. Thus an increase in urban representation in state legislatures through reapportionment is not likely to solve the problem of urban transportation.

The Metropolitan Transportation Mess

To date, expressways have failed miserably in alleviating the transportation problems in large cities. Multi-million dollar freeways designed to unsnarl traffic become snarled themselves at rush hours almost as soon as they are completed. Automobiles funneled into downtown areas slow city traffic to a crawl, create giant parking problems, pollute the air, and slowly bring about economic strangulation of the central city. The result is to speed the exodus to the suburbs of residents, businesses, and industries, which tends to threaten the very survival of the nation's central cities.

City planners, transportation specialists, and nearly all who have studied

[8] *Ibid.*, pp. 174–77.

the modern city's traffic picture readily agree that the only way to relieve traffic congestion and preserve central cities is to get people out of private automobiles and into public transit, that is, "to move people, not vehicles." [9] Technological and economic evidence points to rail transit as the only reasonable way to move persons in and out of the central city at rush hours. Automobiles on expressways can move about 2000 people per lane per hour, buses can move between 6000–9000, but rail systems can carry up to 60,000 persons per hour. In other words, one rail line is estimated to be equal to that of 20 or 30 expressway lanes of automobiles in terms of its ability to move people.

Of course, as most commuters know all too well, privately owned commuter railroads are in generally deplorable operating condition and even worse financial condition. The average citizen has a tremendous investment in his automobile; the automobile has become a status symbol and even a way of life for the nation's suburbanites. Few Americans want to see their heavy financial investment sit in a garage all day. Americans clearly prefer private automobile transportation and costly expressways to mass transit, regardless of the arguments of transportation experts. The result is that existing private mass transit facilities have been steadily losing customers over the last two decades. As their operating costs increase and their patronage declines, many private bus and rail carriers resort to raising fares, reducing service and putting off maintenance—all of which simply drives away more customers and accelerates the downward spiral. Very often service is poor and equipment is dirty and uncomfortable. Spokesmen for commuter railroads insist that the fault is not theirs—that they must compete with automobiles operating on publicly subsidized, multi-million dollar expressways. The individual American cannot be lured away from his beloved automobile and the privacy and status he thinks it gives him.

It is virtually impossible for the nation's major cities to continue to rely upon automobile transportation over expressways to handle projected increases in transportation needs. Most of our cities are already experiencing expressway traffic jams at rush hours and a resulting increase in time and cost to the average automobile commuter. Needless to say, the cost of mass transit facilities on a per capita basis is infinitesimal compared to the cost of expressway building. Some pilot projects in New York, Philadelphia, San Francisco, and Boston found that it was necessary to provide public subsidies to commuter rail companies or to have city governments acquire these facilities at a loss if commuter service was to be restored. The cost of such public subsidies is very small in comparison with the cost of building and maintaining expressways. Thus, mass transit is a considerable saving to most cities, even if fares do not meet operating expenses. Moreover,

[9] See Francis Bello, "The City and the Car," *The Exploding Metropolis* (New York: Fortune Magazine, 1957).

these pilot projects indicated that new, speedier, more comfortable, air conditioned, high capacity trains with fewer stops and more frequent time schedules, together with an expensive advertising campaign, could lure many riders back to public transportation.

Mass transit facilities, while cheaper than expressways, are still quite costly, particularly for cities that do not already have commuter rail service. Requests for federal financial assistance for cities recently resulted in congressional enactment of the Urban Mass Transportation Act of 1964. The Act provided for federal grants for mass transportation facilities and equipment, for expanded research and demonstration programs, for the relocation of businesses and families displaced by mass transit projects, and for the planning of urban mass transportation facilities. Thus far, federal spending for mass transit under this Act has been very limited, a few hundred million dollars compared with nearly $3 billion per year for highways. Political support for this bill came from the nation's mayors, together with some assistance from railroad and transit car manufacturers. Political opposition to federal spending for urban mass transportation came, predictably, from the nation's rural areas. The American Farm Bureau Federation was assisted by conservative groups, which oppose the expansion of federal activities in another area of American life. Suburban interests have played an ambiguous role in urban mass transit debate: presumably, mass transit will make it easier for suburbanites to get in and out of the central city, but suburban commercial and industrial enterprises and real estate developers are not wholly in favor of strengthening the economic role of central cities.

Proponents of federally assisted mass transit argue that cities and states do not have sufficient resources to build mass transit facilities. They argue that mass transit is cheaper than expressway construction and that expressways can never handle predicted traffic increases anyhow. They emphasize the costs of traffic jams in time and wages lost and their economic impact on central cities. They point out that privately owned mass transportation facilities fail to show profits and that, therefore, these companies are not in a position to make improvements in equipment, facilities, and services at fare levels which would attract riders. Rural (and often Republican) opposition, stresses the increased centralization at the federal level that would be involved in federally aided mass transit. They object to the idea that the entire nation, including rural areas, should be asked to contribute to solving transportation problems of the nation's cities. Although the federal government contributes heavily to the expressway construction, they believe that states and communities should bear the cost of mass transit by themselves. Moreover, they express doubt about the feasibility of convincing Americans that they should give up the convenience of their automobile for mass transit.

To date, federal activity under the Urban Mass Transportation Act of 1964 has been limited largely to financing urban mass transportation planning. For the most part, pleasant, rapid, convenient, and efficient mass transit continues to be a planner's dream, and federal, state, and local policy continues to emphasize automobile transportation and expressway construction.

16

THE POLITICS OF WELFARE,

HEALTH, AND HOUSING

Development of Health and Welfare Policy

Concern for public health and welfare has been a recognized responsibility of government in English-speaking countries for almost 400 years. In the Poor Relief Act of 1601, the English parliament established principles of public welfare, which were to influence governments in England and the United States for centuries. This early "Elizabethan" welfare policy tended to view poverty as the product of moral or character deficiencies in individuals. Care of destitute persons was supposed to be minimal, to discourage all but the most desperate of the poor from seeking aid. Primary reliance was placed upon institutional care—county work houses, poor houses, or alms houses. The "able-bodied poor," those we call the unemployed, were sent to county work houses; while the "worthy poor," widows, aged, orphans, and handicapped, were sent to poor houses. Indigent persons who were mentally or physically ill were often kept in the same institutions. Destitute children were kept in county orphanages or sent to foster homes. Thus, public welfare was limited almost exclusively to institutional care; the distribution of food or clothing or other aid to homes of the poor was left to private charities. Whatever relief was provided by the public could never exceed the value of the income of the lowest paid person in the community who was not on relief. Poor rolls were made public, and relief was

416

forthcoming only if there were no living relatives who could be legally required to support a destitute member of their family.

Under Elizabethan law, the care of the poor was the responsibility of the local governments rather than the state and local governments. The parish in England, and the township and county in the United States, had to care for their poor out of their general tax funds. Since local governments wished to make certain that they were not caring for the poor of other communities, residence requirements were established for welfare care, and communities generally limited their support to those who had been born in the area or who had lived there for some time. By the late 19th century, state governments began to build and operate institutions for the insane, the deaf, the blind, and the orphaned. By 1931, all but five state governments had a special department concerned with public welfare and the administration of state institutions. The federal government provided only for needy veterans, Indians, and merchant seamen; most people felt that the federal government had no legitimate interest in public health and welfare.

The Great Depression brought about significant changes in attitudes toward public welfare and in the policies and administration of welfare programs. No longer were many people willing to believe that poverty was a product of the individual's moral or character faults. Millions who had previously considered welfare recipients to be unworthy of public concern now joined in the breadlines themselves. One out of four Americans was unemployed and one out of six was receiving some sort of welfare care. This widespread experience with poverty changed public attitudes toward welfare and led to a change away from Elizabethan policy.

The Great Depression quickly drained local governments of financial resources to aid the poor. The states rapidly increased their welfare activities and a majority of states distributed money to local relief agencies. But state governments themselves were also running out of money. Frantic appeals for help from the national government were made by states and communities. Even Herbert Hoover was forced into approving limited federal relief programs. The Roosevelt administration plunged into several large-scale emergency relief public works programs. After a while, these emergency programs were abandoned by the New Deal, but the precedent of federal responsibility for public welfare had been established.

Federal, State, and Local Responsibilities in Welfare

The Great Depression significantly influenced the nation's total welfare effort. The total amount expended for all welfare programs, including social insurance, public assistance, and public health, increased substantially. But it is also important to note the shift in responsibility from local and state governments to the national government. Today, the federal government finances three-fourths of the cost of social insurance programs; these federal costs in social insurance stem primarily from the Social Security program (OASDI). State expenditures in the social insurance field include expenditures for unemployment compensation, workmen's compensation, and state and local retirement systems. In the public assistance field, which includes welfare payments to the aged, the blind, the disabled, dependent children, and those who need general assistance, the federal government pays about half of the costs and the states and localities the other half. The states have continued to carry the largest share of the cost of institutional care, listed in Table 16.1 as "other welfare." The federal government's share of "other welfare" expenditures increased noticeably after the passage of the Economic Opportunity Act of 1964, with nearly $2 billion per year going to federal "anti-poverty" projects.

In the Social Security Act of 1935, the federal government undertook to establish the basic framework for welfare policies for all levels of government. State and local welfare activities are greatly influenced by federal policies begun in the Social Security Act of 1935.

The Social Security Act placed great reliance on *social insurance* to supplement and, it was hoped, eventually to replace *public assistance*. The distinction between a *social insurance* program and a *public assistance* program is an important one, which has on occasion been a major political issue. If the beneficiaries of a government program are required to have made contributions to it before claiming any of its benefits, and if they are entitled to the benefits regardless of their personal wealth, then the program is said to be financed on the *social insurance* principle. On the other hand, if a program is financed out of general tax revenues, and if the recipients are required to show they are poor before claiming its benefits, then the program is said to be financed on the *welfare* principle. One of the key features of the Social Security Act is the Old Age Survivors Disability Insurance (OASDI) program; this is a compulsory social insurance program financed by regular deductions from earnings, which gives individuals a legal right to benefits in the event of certain occurrences that causes a reduction of their income: old age, death of the head of the household, or permanent disability. OASDI is based on the same principle as private insurance—the sharing of a risk of the loss of income—except that it is a government program that is compulsory for all workers. OASDI is not public *charity,* but a way of compelling people to provide *insurance* against a loss of income. OASDI now covers about nine out of every ten workers in the United States. Both employees and employers must pay equal amounts toward the employees' OASDI insurance. Upon retirement, an insured worker is entitled to monthly benefit payments based upon his age at retirement and the amount he has earned during his working years.

TABLE 16.1

HEALTH AND WELFARE EXPENDITURES OF FEDERAL, STATE AND LOCAL GOVERNMENTS 1929 - 1965

	Social insurance			Public assistance			Other welfare			Health		
	Total	Federal percent	State and local percent	Total	Federal percent	State and local percent	Total	Federal percent	State and local percent	Total	Federal percent	State and local percent
1929	340	.21	.79	500	.01	.99	---	---	---	455	.10	.90
1935	384	.26	.74	2998	.79	.21	139	.01	.99	544	.11	.89
1940	1,216	.29	.71	3599	.63	.37	114	.09	.91	697	.14	.86
1945	1,388	.53	.47	1031	.41	.59	195	.45	.55	1937	.64	.36
1950	4,911	.42	.58	2496	.44	.56	402	.42	.58	2344	.28	.72
1955	9,845	.65	.35	3003	.50	.50	580	.42	.58	2914	.33	.67
1960	19,292	.74	.26	4101	.52	.48	1161	.35	.65	4342	.36	.64
1962	22,357	.72	.28	4441	.53	.47	1248	.35	.65	4757	.38	.62
1963	25,570	.76	.24	5275	.52	.48	1751	.31	.69	5596	.44	.56
1964	26,922	.77	.23	5614	.52	.48	1943	.32	.68	6050	.45	.55
1965	28,098	.78	.22	6259	.51	.49	2703	.47	.53	6651	.48	.54

Source: U.S. Department of Health, Education, and Welfare, *Health, Education and Welfare Trends 1963* (Washington: Government Printing Office, 1963), pp. 106-8; up-dated.

However, average monthly payments are really quite modest: in 1966 the average monthly amount for a retired worker with a wife age 65 was only $165.10. So OASDI has not eliminated poverty from the ranks of the retired in America.

OASDI also insures benefit payments to survivors of an insured worker, including his widow if she has dependent children. But if she has no dependent children, her benefits will not begin until she herself reaches retirement age. Finally, OASDI insures benefit payments to persons who suffer permanent and total disabilities that prevent them from working more than one year. However, on the whole, payments to survivors and disabled workers are just as modest as those provided retired workers.

OASDI is a completely federal program, administered by the Social Security Administration in the Department of Health, Education, and Welfare. But OASDI has an important indirect effect on state and local welfare programs, by removing people in whole or in part from welfare roles. By compelling people to insure themselves against the possibility of their own poverty, social security has doubtlessly reduced the welfare problems which state and local governments would otherwise face.

The second feature of the Social Security Act was that it induced states to enact unemployment compensation programs through the imposition of the payroll tax on all employers. A federal unemployment tax is levied on the payroll of employers of four or more workers, but employers paying into state insurance programs that meet federal standards may use these state payments to offset most of their federal unemployment tax. In other words, the federal government threatens to undertake an unemployment compensation program and tax, if the states do not do so themselves. This federal program succeeded in inducing all 50 states to establish unemployment compensation programs. However, the federal standards are flexible and the states have considerable freedom in shaping their own unemployment programs. In all cases, unemployed workers must report in person and show that they are willing and able to work in order to receive unemployment compensation benefits, and states cannot deny workers benefits for refusing to work as strike breakers or refusing to work for rates lower than prevailing rates. But basic decisions concerning the amount of benefits, eligibility, and the length of time that benefits can be drawn are largely left to the states.

A third major feature of the Social Security Act was its public assistance provisions. The OASDI and unemployment compensation programs were based upon the insurance principle, but the federal government also undertook to provide matching funds to the states, to provide public assistance to the aged, blind, disabled, and dependent children. Federal contributions are in the form of grants-in-aid to the states. The federal share is determined by a formula that attempts to equalize welfare efforts among the states by having the federal government pay a larger share to states with higher needs and less wealth. The federal aid formula influences the size of welfare benefits by authorizing the federal government to pay a large share of minimum benefits and a lesser share of benefits above the minimum, up to a maximum amount, above which the federal government pays no share. The federal government also pays half of the cost of administering the programs.

All of the states divide welfare assistance among the four categories of recipients aided by the government—the aged, the blind, the disabled, and dependent children. Within broad outlines of the federal policy, states retain considerable discretion in their welfare programs, in terms of the amounts of money appropriated, benefits to be paid to recipients, rules of eligibility, and rules of the programs. Each state may choose to grant assistance beyond the amounts supported by the national government, or it may choose to have no welfare programs at all. Each state establishes its own standards to determine "need." Later we shall examine variations in average benefit payments in these categorical assistance programs.

It is important to note that the federal government aids only four categories of welfare recipients. Only persons who are aged, blind, disabled, or dependent children fall within the categories of recipients eligible for federal support. Aid to persons who do *not* fall in any of these categories but who, for one reason or another, are "needy" is referred to as *general assistance*. General assistance programs are entirely state financed and state administered. Without federal participation, these programs differ radically from state to state in terms of the persons aided, the criteria for eligibility, the amount and nature of benefits, and financing in administration. Many of these programs continue to resemble Elizabethan welfare policy. The average general assistance payment is lower than comparable payments in federally supported programs.

States also continue to maintain institutions to care for those individuals who are so destitute, alone, or ill that money payments cannot meet their needs. These institutions include state orphanages, homes for the aged, and homes for the ill. They are, for the most part, state financed as well as state administered. Persons living in these tax supported institutions normally are not eligible for federal assistance, although they may receive old age payments for medical care received in a nursing home. This feature of federal welfare policy has provided incentive for the states to turn their indigent institutions into nursing homes. The quality of these homes and of the people employed to care for their residents varies enormously from state to state.

Federal standards for state public assistance programs, which are established as a prerequisite to receiving federal aid, allow considerable flexibility in state programs. Federal law requires the states to make financial contributions to their public assistance programs and to supervise these programs either directly or through local agencies. Whatever standards a state adopts must be applicable throughout the state, and there must be no discrimination in these welfare programs. The Social Security Administration demands periodic reporting from the states, insists that states administer federally supported programs under a merit personnel system, and prevents the states from imposing unreasonable residence requirements on recipients. But in important questions of administration, standards of eligibility, residence, types of assistance, and amounts of payments, the states are free to determine their own welfare programs. In 15 states, public assistance is administered directly by a state agency; in 19 states, by local agencies under state supervision; and in 26 states, by local agencies operating under city, county, or township governmental control.

Politics of Welfare

Political support for welfare programs is provided not so much by the poor themselves, but by civil rights groups, labor organizations, public and private social agencies and charitable organizations, and liberal journals and political groups. Large taxpayers, business organizations, and many individuals and groups who cling to rugged individualism and the traditional morality that held the individual responsible for his own misfortunes are generally less enthusiastic about welfare programs. An interesting illustration of political conflict over public assistance occurred in Newburgh, New York, in 1961 and attracted national attention.[1] City Manager Joseph M. Mitchell, backed by a Republican council and opposed by a Democratic mayor, publicly announced that he intended to remove all "chiselers," "loafers," and "social parasites" from the city's welfare rolls. Public assistance expenditures accounted for about one-third of the city's budget, and there were many Negro migratory workers who had settled in Newburgh in recent years. To many taxpayers, Newburgh's welfare administration had been a "soft touch" for too many people for too long. Mitchell announced a comprehensive "get tough" policy: all able-bodied men on welfare would be required to work a 48-hour week for the city; anyone who refused to accept a job offer was to be denied relief; applicants for relief who had left a job voluntarily rather than being fired or laid off were to be denied relief; no family on relief could receive more than the take home pay of the lowest paid city employee; all aid, except to the blind, the aged, and the disabled, was to be limited to a maximum period of three months within any one year; and finally, mothers of illegitimate children who were

---

[1] See Gilbert Y. Steiner, *Social Insecurity: The Politics of Welfare* (Chicago: Rand McNally & Co., 1966), pp. 110–12.

supported on relief were informed that they would be refused relief if they had any more children.

The New York State Department of Public Welfare immediately ordered Newburgh to drop this plan and bring its program back into conformity with the rest of the state. It accused Newburgh of "psychological warfare against the needy and the helpless." Mitchell replied that the New York Department of Public Welfare was destroying "home rule." Mitchell appeared to have the support of most of the city's taxpayers. Local opposition came from the Mayor, Newburgh's welfare commissioner (who was later replaced), the city's NAACP, the ministerial association, Catholic charities, and some local unions. But most of the community's "power structure" appeared to support Mitchell's program; this included most of the city's prominent business leaders. And *The Wall Street Journal* editorialized on behalf of the Mitchell program.

Eventually, the New York State Department of Public Welfare obtained court injunctions against the plan, largely on the grounds that it violated statewide policies and threatened the loss of federal support. Liberal journals and professional social workers argued that welfare abuses were quite minimal and that the Newburgh plan was degrading of human dignity and self-respect.[2] Widespread support for the Newburgh plan in the nation's press appeared to threaten public welfare programs throughout the nation. Newsmen pointed out that not a single case of fraud in Newburgh was ever substantiated, that only one able-bodied welfare recipient was found in Newburgh to begin work for the city, that a lack of uniform standards among communities would lead them to compete with each other in expelling their impoverished citizens, and that punishing unwed mothers would inflict hardship on their innocent children.

After its initial publicity, the Newburgh plan appeared to fade from prominence and no other communities adopted it. City Manager Mitchell eventually left Newburgh to become a paid organizer for the John Birch Society. However, the battle of Newburgh is a vivid illustration of the latent conflicts in public assistance policy. The taxpayers' cause rarely wins when the image of the welfare recipient is that of a respectable, aged, white, literate, "senior citizen" in his golden years. However, when the image of the public welfare recipient changes to that of an uneducated, unmarried, Negro mother and her illegitimate offspring, support of the white middle class community tends to wane. The idea of "toughening up" welfare policy is a popular one. Often it is argued a tough policy will drive out the cheaters, put the lazy to work, promote chastity among unwed mothers, and save money. However, there is no concrete evidence to support these hopes. It is believed that Clermont County, Ohio, was the first

---

[2] See Meg Greenfield, "The 'Welfare Chiselers' of Newburgh," *The Reporter,* Vol. 25 (August 17, 1961).

county in the nation ever to cut off all relief programs because of financial difficulties.[3] This occurred in 1961. But welfare recipients did not suddenly become self-sufficient as a result of this action. Instead, the burden of support was shifted from the public to unpaid landlords, unpaid grocers, unpaid physicians, churches, schools, and charitable organizations. A special study of the effect of terminating relief in this county showed a tremendous increase in the debts owed to landlords, grocers, physicians, and hospitals during the shut-off period. Charitable organizations were also called upon to deplete their scanty treasuries. Nor did the recipients go elsewhere to get their relief checks; most were long time or native born residents of the county, who clung to their homes and communities regardless of the deprivations.

Gilbert Steiner reports another illustrative case in the politics of welfare.[4] In 1962, Governor Otto Kerner of Illinois faced a state budget deficit, which he attributed to excessive welfare costs, particularly in the city of Chicago. Kerner was unwilling to raise taxes to meet rising welfare costs and suggested instead a toughening up of administration, eligibility, and benefits in welfare programs. Kerner proceeded to announce a reduction in welfare payments and a plan to report cases of ADC illegitimate births to the Attorney General for possible prosecution under adultery and fornication statutes. These proposals won very little support from Kerner's fellow Democrats, particularly in Chicago, where Democratic officeholders depended upon the votes of many low income, minority group members. Mayor Richard Daley maintained icy silence, but it was clear that he did not relish Kerner's proposals. Interestingly, Republicans from the downstate rural areas of Illinois welcomed Kerner's proposals and attempted to place ceilings on welfare payments by legislative enactment. Unwelcome praise came from the downstate Republicans, who argued that reduced allowances for Chicago relief recipients "won't hurt them at all." So great were the Republican proposed cuts, and so hostile was the reaction of Kerner's own party, that the governor was forced to reverse his position and undertake to oppose Republican cuts in the legislature. The governor and the legislature deadlocked, and appropriations for ADC ran out. In lieu of welfare checks, federal surplus food was to be distributed, but there was great disorganization in this plan. After considerable debate, a compromise was reached providing for new standards that cut welfare allowances.

As a result of this action, public assistance "hunger marchers" paraded to the state office building in Chicago in protest. The Welfare Council of Metropolitan Chicago protested "a picture of stark, thread-bare existence" for the poor. The Chicago chapter of the National Association of Social

[3] Steiner, *op. cit.*, p. 9.
[4] *Ibid.*, pp. 205–37.

Workers protested "a systematically imposed program of grinding want." The state public aid commissioner protested "the President of the United States has declared war on poverty and the state of Illinois has declared war on the poor." And *The Chicago Daily News* observed, "Illinois Values: Whole Milk for Convicts, Powdered Milk for Children on Relief."

To further complicate matters, Governor Kerner accepted the "resignation" of his old Commissioner of Public Aid, and appointed a new commissioner, who promptly advised that the solution to the welfare problem was the provision of birth control information and devices to the welfare recipients. Commissioner Arnold Maremont argued that his proposal was "intelligent, economic, and humanitarian." Yet no other proposal could be as politically disruptive as this one. Public hearings were held where Catholic groups and individuals argued that publicly supported birth control services would foster promiscuity. Catholic charitable organizations and Catholic politicians generally supported welfare care, but they vigorously objected to a plan that they thought would facilitate premarital and extramarital sexual intercourse. Both Governor Kerner and Mayor Daley backed away from the new commissioner on this touchy political question. Maremont argued that Gallup Polls had shown that most Catholics interviewed said that they were in favor of birth control, regardless of the official position of the Church.

Democrats began to fear that if Maremont alienated enough Catholics by continuing to push birth control, and if enough middle class voters were alienated by the high cost of relief for Chicago Negroes, both the welfare program of the state and perhaps even the Democratic party would suffer immeasurably. So they silently assented to the removal of Maremont and the elimination of the Public Aid Commission, replacing it with an executive department. They also assented to the cutback in welfare allowances mentioned above. The use of birth control information in welfare agencies remains highly restricted in Chicago, as well as throughout the nation.

Public Health Politics

Public health and sanitation are among the oldest functions of local government. Keeping clean is still one of the major tasks of cities today, a task which involves many different local governmental agencies in street cleaning, sewage disposal, garbage collection, and the provision of clean water supply. Very often these services are taken for granted in the United States, but in underdeveloped countries of the world, health and sanitation are still major tasks. Local public health departments are directly concerned with the *prevention* of disease. They engage in compulsory vaccination, immunization, and quarantine, as well as regulatory activity in the processing of milk and the safeguarding of water supplies. In more recent years, these agencies have become concerned with the difficult problems of air and water pollution. In addition to the preventive activities of the public health departments, state and local governments also provide extensive, tax-supported hospital care. State and local governments provide both general and specialized hospitals, health centers, and nursing homes, and very often subsidize private hospitals and medical facilities as well. New York City operates 22 hospitals, 27 health centers, employing over 40,000 people with a budget of over $300 million per year. This is the nation's largest city hospital system, but almost every community subsidizes hospital facilities in some way. City and county hospitals and heavily subsidized private hospitals are expected to provide at least emergency care to indigent patients.

Health and hospital care are also supported by state governments. State health departments generally supervise local health departments, distribute state grants to local health departments, and provide health services in areas where there are no local health facilities. Generally, local health departments need state monies in order to operate effectively. But perhaps the states' greatest impact on public health is the provision of specialized state hospitals for tuberculosis, mental illness, and so on. These specialized hospitals are managed directly by the states and are supposed to supplement local hospital care by providing facilities that local governments could not afford.

In nearly every community, decision making in health and hospital matters is firmly lodged in the hands of leaders of the local medical associations. These local physicians, men of prestige and influence in community leadership structures, believe that questions of public policy should be determined predominantly by the doctors as a group, through their local medical society. Often professional social workers and health workers have chafed under the reins of the physicians; they sometimes contend that the doctors insist on a private practice approach where public measures are critically needed.

America's problem in health and medicine are severe and national in character. Although the United States is the richest nation in the world, it ranks well down on the list of nations in medical care provided the average citizen, number of physicians available, infant death rates, average life span, and other indicators of national health and medical care. One particularly difficult problem is the small number of physicians graduated by the nation's medical schools. Moreover, as professional specialization becomes of more interest to doctors, the result is shortages in the ranks of general practitioners. It is ironic that the United States, the richest nation in the world, must turn to graduates of foreign medical schools for more than one-fourth of its hospital residents and interns. In many states, and particularly state institutions, this ratio is even higher.

The federal government is becoming increasingly involved in public health. The U.S. Public Health Service, now part of the Department of Health, Education, and Welfare, is one of the oldest agencies of the federal government, having been created in 1798 to provide medical and hospital care for merchant seamen. Today, the Service provides medical care and hospital facilities to many categories of federally aided patients; enforces quarantine regulations; licenses biological products for manufacture and sale; engages in and sponsors medical research; and, most important of all, administers federal grant-in-aid programs to states and communities for the improvement of health and hospital services. Federal grants-in-aid are available to promote the construction of hospitals, nursing homes, diagnostic centers, rehabilitation centers, medical schools, and other medical centers. Federal grants for hospital construction began in earnest with the passage of the Hill-Burton Act in 1946; these funds are usually made available on a matching basis of approximately two-to-one, with local communities carrying the heavier burden. The federal government's Veterans Administration also provides extensive medical and hospital care.

It is important to note, however, that despite federal efforts in the field of health, state and local governments continue to spend over twice as much as the federal government for health and medical care. Table 16.1 indicates that with the exception of the years of heavy postwar expenses for veterans' care, the federal government has always spent less in the health field than the states.

Even before the Social Security Act of 1935, persons concerned with the state of the nation's health, and particularly the medical care problems of the poor and the aged, had urged the federal government to undertake a broad national health care program. Proponents of the national health program generally shunned the English system of government-owned and operated hospitals and government-employed doctors, in favor of a compulsory medical *insurance* program closely linked to the Social Security Act. They envisoned a program in which all Americans would be required to insure themselves against the possibility of their medical indigency; the program would resemble private medical and hospital insurance, except that it would be compulsory. Individuals would continue to choose their own doctors, but their bills would be paid in whole or in part through their government medical insurance policy. Opponents of a national health program, led by the prestigious American Medical Association representing the nation's physicians, strongly opposed a national health program linked to social security. They deemed it "socialized medicine" and argued that it would interfere with the "sacred doctor-patient relationship." They argued that a large proportion of the population was already covered by voluntary private medical insurance plans, and that charity hospitals and charitable services of doctors were readily available to the poor. Basically the physicians worried that if the Social Security Administration paid insured persons' doctors bills, the Social Security Administration would begin to set maximum prices for physicians' services; the AMA feared that this would lead to the subservience of physicians to a government agency. Proponents of national health care waged a war of statistics, arguing that the poor and the aged were not receiving adequate medical care and that private insurance companies did not enroll these segments of the population.

This debate took place largely in Congress, but it had important ramifications for the states. In 1961, the American Medical Association, in the hopes of warding off a "medicare" national health insurance bill, supported the passage of the Kerr-Mills Act. This Act offered the states, on a roughly three-to-one ratio, federal funds to be spent on medical care of needy persons over 65 years of age. These funds were supposed to encourage states to provide medical care to their indigent aged, including hospitalization, nursing homes, medical fees; states were free to determine the character of their own program. The Kerr-Mills Act was a public assistance program, not a social insurance program; recipients need not show that they had made prior payments into the program, but they had to show that they were "needy." States have been notably unenthusiastic about the Kerr-Mills program; by 1966 only half of the states reported expenditures for the needy aged under Kerr-Mills provisions.

In 1965, after more than 30 years of unsuccessful efforts, Congress finally enacted an historic comprehensive medical care act for persons over 65, which became known as "Medicare." Passed over the opposition of the American Medical Association, Medicare provided for prepaid hospital insurance for the aged under social security, and low cost voluntary medical insurance for the aged under federal administration. Medicare includes: (1) a compulsory basic health insurance plan covering hospital costs for the aged, which is financed through payroll taxes collected under the social security system; and (2) a voluntary but supplemental medical program that will pay doctors' bills and additional medical expenses, financed in part by contributions from the aged and in part by the general tax revenues. It is not yet clear what the impact of this act will be at the local level, in terms of reducing state and local burdens of providing for charitable hospital and medical care. Social security never eliminated the need for welfare rolls and it is doubtful that Medicare will ever eliminate the need for tax-supported hospitals and health care. So far only aged persons are covered by Medicare provisions; the medical problems of the poor are still a responsibility of state and local governments and private charities.

In 1965, Congress also passed a Medical Assistance Program (Medicaid) which provided federal funds to enable states to guarantee medical services to all public assistance recipients. Each state operates its own Medicaid program. Unlike Medicare, Medicaid is a welfare program designed for needy persons; no prior contributions are required, but recipients of Medicaid services must be welfare recipients. States can extend coverage to other medically needy persons if they choose to do so. The cost of this program has far exceeded all original estimates, which suggests that the poor in America require much more medical attention than they have received in the past.

Passage of Medicare and Medicaid means a significant increase in the role of the national government in the health field. It may be that in the years ahead the national government, through these programs, will come to spend as much or more than state and local governments for health care for hospital purposes. But to date, state and local governments continue to carry the heaviest responsibility for the nation's health and hospital care.

A Comparative View of State Health and Welfare Policies

While the federal government plays a major role in shaping the state health and welfare programs, states continue to exercise major responsibilities in determination of health and welfare policy. States retain the right to determine whether they will participate in federal programs. Within broad federal regulations, the states determine the benefits to be allocated to recipients, the eligibility requirements, the extent of state financing, and the ways in which the programs are to be administered. For example, in 1966, the average weekly benefits per recipient of unemployment compensation ranged from a low of $24 in North Carolina to a high of $44 in Wyoming. Monthly old age assistance payments range from a high of $124 in Wisconsin to a low of $41 in Mississippi; aid to dependent children payments from a high of $218 in New York to a low of $51 in Mississippi. Similar variations and benefits are reported for other welfare programs. Wide variations among the states in per capita health and welfare expenditures can also be observed. In addition, states have different eligibility requirements and different standards of determining need; as a result, states will vary considerably in the number of welfare recipients per 10,000 population. States also vary with respect to the medical and hospital facilities available. Finally, states differ in the extent to which welfare services are state, rather than locally, financed and administered.

What accounts for differences among the states in health and welfare policy? All available evidence indicates that economic development is significantly related to health and welfare policy in the states.[5] Economic development, urbanization, income, and industrialization are closely related to benefit levels in all major programs. A state's income is the single most

[5] Thomas R. Dye, *Politics, Economics and the Public* (Chicago: Rand McNally & Co., 1966), pp. 115–48.

TABLE 16.2

AVERAGE MONTHLY PAYMENTS

Old Age		Aid to dependent children		Unemployment compensation		General assistance		Public assistance plus employment, security, health, and other welfare services	
1. Wis.	$124	N.Y.	$218	Wyo.	$44	N.J.	$120	La.	$56
2. N.H.	110	Ill.	214	Colo.	44	N.Y.	92	Okla.	53
3. Cal.	107	Wis.	203	Wis.	43	Haw.	92	Ark.	46
4. Haw.	105	N.J.	203	Mass.	41	Wis.	91	W. Va.	43
5. N.D.	101	Haw.	198	Nev.	41	Mich.	83	Ala.	40
6. Ill.	100	Conn.	197	N.Y.	40	Ill.	82	Ky.	39
7. R.I.	98	N.H.	188	Haw.	40	Minn.	82	Alas.	38
8. Iowa	98	Cal.	188	N.J.	40	Wyo.	77	Miss.	38
9. N.Y.	96	Mass.	188	Kan.	39	Md.	77	R.I.	37
10. Okla.	96	Minn.	188	Ohio	39	Mass.	74	Vt.	35
11. Neb.	96	N.D.	185	Del.	39	Conn.	74	N.M.	35
12. Mass.	96	R.I.	172	Conn.	39	R.I.	73	Colo.	34
13. Colo.	95	Kan.	168	Mich.	39	Kan.	72	Mo.	33
14. Minn.	94	Iowa	167	N.D.	39	Wash.	70	Cal.	33
15. Mich.	94	Ore.	165	Ill.	39	Ohio	69	Wash.	32
16. Md.	94	Md.	159	Wyo.	39	N.H.	69	Ga.	32
17. Kan.	94	Wash.	153	Alas.	39	Pa.	69	N.Y.	29
18. Ind.	93	Idaho	152	Idaho	38	Mo.	66	Mass.	29
19. Alas.	93	Utah	151	Utah	38	Utah	63	Utah	29
20. Vt.	92	Colo.	150	Ariz.	37	N.D.	61	N.D.	29
21. S.D.	92	Pa.	148	Md.	36	Cal.	59	N.C.	28
22. N.J.	90	Mich.	147	Neb.	35	Ore.	57	Tenn.	27
23. Ohio	90	Wyo.	144	Ore.	35	Mont.	56	Idaho	26
24. Wyo.	86	Mont.	144	Vt.	35	Me.	53	Tex.	26
25. Me.	84	Neb.	139	N.H.	34	Nev.	52	Minn.	26
26. Nev.	83	Ohio	138	Mo.	34	Del.	52	Me.	26
27. Mont.	83	N.M.	137	Ky.	33	Ariz.	52	Ariz.	25
28. Wash.	82	Okla.	136	Pa.	33	La.	52	S.D.	25
29. Pa.	82	Ind.	131	R.I.	33	Alas.	51	Haw.	24
30. La.	82	Nev.	131	La.	33	Va.	51	Pa.	24
31. Conn.	81	Alas.	130	W. Va.	32	Colo.	49	Ore.	24
32. N.M.	79	Del.	128	Iowa	31	N.M.	44	Iowa	23
33. Idaho	77	W. Va.	123	Mont.	31	W. Va.	36	Fla.	23
34. Utah	74	S.D.	122	S.D.	31	Ky.	35	Ill.	23
35. Ore.	73	Ariz.	121	Ind.	31	Ga.	32	Kan.	22
36. Mo.	70	Me.	114	Minn.	30	S.C.	31	Del.	22
37. Va.	69	Vt.	113	N.M.	30	S.D.	27	S.C.	22
38. Tex.	69	Va.	110	Tex.	30	N.C.	25	Mich.	20
39. Ala.	68	N.C.	106	Va.	30	Tenn.	24	Wyo.	20
40. Fla.	66	La.	102	S.C.	29	Miss.	18	Conn.	20
41. Del.	65	Mo.	100	Ga.	29	Ark.	16	Ohio	20
42. Ark.	65	Ky.	99	Tenn.	28	Ala.	13	N.H.	20
43. N.C.	63	Tenn.	98	Fla.	28	Okla.	11	Mont.	20
44. Ariz.	63	Ga.	92	Ala.	27	Fla.	NA	Nev.	19
45. Ky.	62	Tex.	91	Okla.	27	Tex.	NA	Neb.	18

Old Age		Aid to dependent children		Unemployment compensation		General assistance		Public assistance plus employment, security, health, and other welfare services	
46. Tenn.	$ 60	Ark.	$ 72	Ark.	$27	Ind.	NA	Wis.	$18
47. Ga.	59	S.C.	64	Me.	25	Vt.	NA	Md.	18
48. S.C.	56	Fla.	60	W. Va.	25	Neb.	NA	N.J.	17
49. W. Va.	55	Ala.	48	Miss.	25	Idaho	NA	Va.	15
50. Miss.	41	Miss.	33	N.C.	24	Iowa	NA	Ind.	14

Source: U.S. Bureau of the Census, *Statistical Abstract, 1966.*

important variable determining the level of welfare benefits. In terms of welfare payments, it is far better to be poor in a wealthy state than in a poor one.

Poorer states have larger proportions of their populations on public assistance rolls, and poorer states have lower welfare benefit payments. This means they pay smaller amounts of money to larger numbers of people. It is not surprising that economic development levels are closely related to benefits paid to recipients of *general assistance,* since relief in this area is paid for exclusively from state and local fiscal sources. But it is surprising that economic development in the states has such a great impact on benefit programs in which the federal government bears part of the cost. We would expect federal participation to reduce inequalities among the states. Actually the federal government does make larger health and welfare grants to the poorer states, and therefore helps offset disparities among the states based upon levels of wealth. However, the reason federal participation does not equalize welfare payments among the states is to be found in the formula that allocates federal money to the states for public assistance. The federal government, under its public assistance formula, pays a larger share of minimum benefits and a lesser share of additional benefits up to a certain maximum benefit level, after which the federal government pays nothing. The object of this formula is to help poorer states provide a minimum level of welfare service. However, since the formula results in a higher proportion of federal support to states with lower welfare benefits, the federal government actually rewards states for low payments per recipient. Poorer states can get the most federal aid by paying smaller amounts of money to large numbers of people.

Even though the federal formula does not offset disparities among the states in welfare payment levels, it does offset disparities among states in the burden of welfare costs. The federal government pays a larger share of public assistance costs in poorer states, while requiring richer states to share a greater portion of their public assistance costs. Federal percentages

FIGURE 16.1

THE FIFTY STATES ARRANGED ACCORDING TO MEDIAN FAMILY INCOME
AND AVERAGE OLD AGE ASSISTANCE PAYMENTS

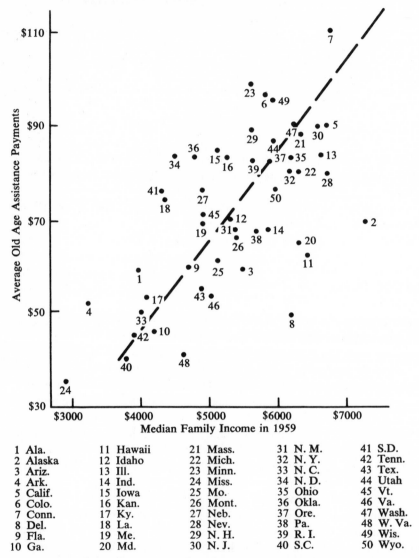

1 Ala.	11 Hawaii	21 Mass.	31 N. M.	41 S.D.
2 Alaska	12 Idaho	22 Mich.	32 N. Y.	42 Tenn.
3 Ariz.	13 Ill.	23 Minn.	33 N. C.	43 Tex.
4 Ark.	14 Ind.	24 Miss.	34 N. D.	44 Utah
5 Calif.	15 Iowa	25 Mo.	35 Ohio	45 Vt.
6 Colo.	16 Kan.	26 Mont.	36 Okla.	46 Va.
7 Conn.	17 Ky.	27 Neb.	37 Ore.	47 Wash.
8 Del.	18 La.	28 Nev.	38 Pa.	48 W. Va.
9 Fla.	19 Me.	29 N. H.	39 R. I.	49 Wis.
10 Ga.	20 Md.	30 N. J.	40 S.C.	50 Wyo.

SOURCE: Thomas R. Dye, *Politics, Economics, and the Public* (Chicago: Rand
McNally & Co., 1966), p. 126. Reproduced by permission.

FIGURE 16.2

THE FIFTY STATES ARRANGED ACCORDING TO MEDIAN FAMILY INCOME
AND THE FEDERAL PERCENTAGE OF PUBLIC ASSISTANCE FUNDS

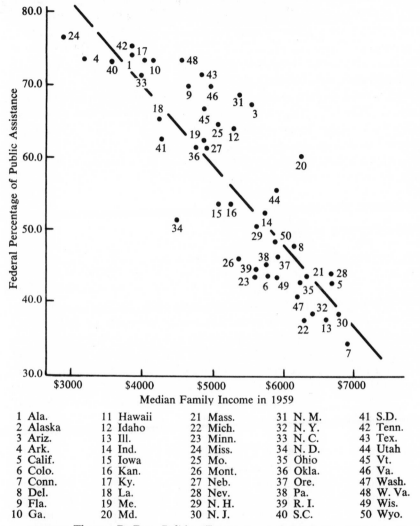

Median Family Income in 1959

1 Ala.	11 Hawaii	21 Mass.	31 N. M.	41 S.D.
2 Alaska	12 Idaho	22 Mich.	32 N. Y.	42 Tenn.
3 Ariz.	13 Ill.	23 Minn.	33 N. C.	43 Tex.
4 Ark.	14 Ind.	24 Miss.	34 N. D.	44 Utah
5 Calif.	15 Iowa	25 Mo.	35 Ohio	45 Vt.
6 Colo.	16 Kan.	26 Mont.	36 Okla.	46 Va.
7 Conn.	17 Ky.	27 Neb.	37 Ore.	47 Wash.
8 Del.	18 La.	28 Nev.	38 Pa.	48 W. Va.
9 Fla.	19 Me.	29 N. H.	39 R. I.	49 Wis.
10 Ga.	20 Md.	30 N. J.	40 S.C.	50 Wyo.

SOURCE: Thomas R. Dye, *Politics, Economics, and the Public* (Chicago: Rand McNally & Co., 1966), p. 137. Reproduced by permission.

of total public assistance expenditures declined with increases in state income levels.

Finally, it might be interesting to consider for a moment the pattern of private, in contrast to public, welfare effort. Complete information on private charitable activity, is, of course, impossible to obtain. However, per capita Community Chest donations clearly show that increased private charitable activity is related to high levels of income, urbanization, and industrialization in the states. Community Chest activity is particularly well organized and well financed in states with larger incomes. In contrast, poorer states have very weak charitable efforts. This means that if welfare services were left completely in private hands, inequalities among the states based upon income levels would be very great. While the effect of federal involvement in the case of the needy is to reduce somewhat the inequalities among the states, the effect of private donations is just the opposite, that is, it tends to accentuate inequalities of the states based upon the availability of wealth.

Politics of Public Housing

The problem of slum housing is an ancient one. Governments have always interested themselves in housing, primarily to secure maximum conditions of health, sanitation, and safety. Local governments in America bear the major responsibility for insuring adequate housing. Building codes and inspections of all sorts, covering electrical wiring, plumbing, materials, workmanship, and so on, are still a major concern of cities. Occasionally, building codes, zoning regulations, codes of health and sanitation, and fire prevention measures have succeeded in improving housing conditions in a limited fashion. But, on the whole, these approaches have been notable failures. In 1960 the U.S. Census Bureau reported that almost 19 per cent of the housing units in the nation were "dilapidated or without plumbing facilities"; another 8 per cent were "deteriorating." This means that over a quarter of the nation's housing is listed as substandard. It seems clear that local governments have been unable to cope with the problem of slums.

Typically, cities attempting to cope with housing problems have been beset with weaknesses of city administration, duplication of inspection procedures, lack of coordination, and tradition-bound approaches of many municipal inspection officials. Generally, inspection procedures have stressed minimal conditions for public safety rather than improvement of housing and living environment. Moreover, government regulations and administration must of necessity be framed in a political environment, in which private owners of land and houses are vocal enough and well organized enough to limit the degree to which private housing can be regulated. Slum owners often carry more political weight than slum dwellers.

But perhaps the most important obstacle to the elimination of slums is the economic problem of providing *low cost* yet *adequate* housing. If housing regulations were severe and rigidly enforced, private builders would probably be prevented from developing low cost housing, simply because it would not be profitable. Private enterprise can only be expected to provide housing that would make a profit; the only way private enterprise can provide low cost housing for the poor is to lower its own costs, and this in turn creates "slums."

As incomes and standards of living in America have risen, most Americans have been able to provide themselves adequate housing on the private market, many by acquiring their own homes in the suburbs. Suburban governments, through the use of planning, zoning, and subdivision control regulations, have been more successful in shaping land use than cities, in part because they are dealing with more affluent citizens. Suburban communities have been able to use zoning and subdivision regulations to help keep out "undesirable" influences, and to attract "desirable" ones to the community, as the local political system defines these terms. For example, some suburban governments have established subdivision control regulations requiring minimum lot sizes of five acres (thus assuring that only expensive homes can be built); or have required that each house differ in design from its immediate neighbors (thus discouraging mass housing developments); or have acquired vacant land for public purposes (thus controlling the rate of growth); or have even set minimum costs that citizens must pay for home construction. Zoning ordinances have been used to set aside large tracts of land in industrial and commercial development, so that these tax-producing businesses can help offset the costs of government for the suburban dweller. Occasionally, builders and developers may be required to pay special taxes or donate land for schools, parks, and other facilities, before they can build large developments in a community. All these regulatory policies go beyond adequate health and safety standards and attempt to shape the social, economic, and life style character of the suburban community. Many suburbs in a large metropolitan area will compete with each other for expensive residences or for industrial or commercial uses, which are both pleasant and profitable for the community and its local government. This competition among suburbs for high income residents and profitable business and commercial developments, together with the availability of large tracts of undeveloped land, combine to make the housing conditions in central cities even more desperate.

The failure of local government to adequately cope with housing problems led to the federal government's intervention in the housing field, with the passage of the Housing Act of 1937. Three major programs were inaugurated in the Housing Act of 1937—mortgage insurance, public housing, and urban renewal. First of all, the national government undertook, through its Federal Housing Administration (FHA), to guarantee private mortgages against default and thereby enable banks, savings and loan associations, and other lending agencies to provide long term, low interest, low down payment mortgages for Americans wishing to purchase their own homes. FHA was extremely successful in promoting homeownership among the middle class. FHA-insured mortgages enabled millions of American families to acquire their own homes, often in the suburbs. In fact, the success of FHA might even be one of the many factors contributing to the deterioration of central cities, for it enabled many middle-class residents to acquire their cherished home in the suburbs and leave the city behind. FHA is an entirely federally administered program, but its impact on city and suburban governments cannot be underestimated.

The Housing Act of 1937 also established a Public Housing Administration, in recognition of the need of public subsidies to secure adequate low rent facilities for the poor who could not afford homeownership even with the help of FHA. The Public Housing Administration does not build, own, or operate any of its own housing projects; rather it provides the necessary financial support to enable local communities to provide public housing for their poor if they choose to do so. The Public Housing Administration makes loans, contributions, and public grants to *local* housing authorities established by *local* governments to build, own, and operate low cost public housing. Local housing authorities must keep rents low in relation to their tenants' ability to pay. This means that local housing authorities operate at a loss and the federal government reimburses them for this loss. No community is required to have a Public Housing Authority; they must apply to the Public Housing Administration and meet federal standards in order to receive federal financial support.

Public housing has always been involved in more political controversy than FHA. Real estate and building interests, which support FHA because it expands their number of customers, have opposed public housing on the grounds that it was socialistic and wasteful. While, in theory, public housing serves individuals who cannot afford private housing, private real estate interests contend that public housing hurts the market for older homes and apartments. In addition, owners of slum dwellings seldom welcome competition from federally supported housing authorities. Political difficulties have also been encountered in the location of public housing units. Many Americans will support public housing for low income persons, so long as it is not located in their neighborhood. A large proportion of public housing occupants are Negroes, and this automatically involved public housing in the politics of race.

In recent years, many of the earlier supporters of public housing, including minority groups, labor, social workers, charitable organizations, and big city political organizations, have expressed doubts about the effect of public housing. Public housing, while providing improved living conditions, failed to eliminate poverty, ignorance, family disruption, juvenile delinquency, crime, and other characteristic troubles of slums. Very often, the concentration of large numbers of poor persons with a great variety of social problems into a single, mass housing project compounded their problems. Huge housing projects were impersonal and bureaucratic, and often failed to provide many of the stabilizing neighborhood influences of the old slums. Removing thousands of people from neighborhood environments and placing them in the institution-like setting of large public housing developments very often increased their alienation or separation from society and removed what few social controls existed in the slum neighborhood. Furthermore, Negro groups often complained that public housing was a new form of racial segregation, and indeed, the concentration of Negroes among public housing dwellers does lead to a great deal of de facto segregation in housing projects. Finally, it should be noted that rural interests are at best indifferent to public housing; even though rural areas contain just as much substandard housing as city areas, the dispersal of rural dwellers over large land areas makes the public housing approach unfeasible.

Political opposition to public housing has succeeded in Congress over the years in reducing federal appropriations for public housing construction. Requests by communities for federal aid for public housing have far exceeded the amount of money appropriated by Congress. The result in most communities is a long list of those persons who are eligible for public housing for whom no space is available. To alleviate this shortage and to correct some of the problems involved in large-scale housing projects, the Johnson administration obtained authorization from Congress for two programs to supplement public housing—a rent subsidy program and a dispersed public housing site program. The rent subsidy program authorizes federal grants to local housing authorities to provide cash grants to families living in substandard housing, thus enabling them to rent decent private housing facilities. The dispersed public housing site program will provide federal grants to local housing authorities to enable them to purchase single homes or apartment buildings throughout the community for operation as public housing units. The purpose of both of these programs is to speed up the availability of public housing units and, perhaps more importantly, to eliminate dependence upon large, institution-like public housing facilities and achieve more dispersal of public housing residents throughout the community. Opponents of these programs argue that the federal government is subsidizing "block busting" tactics in its attempt to disperse public housing dwellers, mostly Negroes, throughout the community. It is, they argue, a subtle form of open housing legislation, aimed at de facto housing segregation. As we noted in Chapter 13, opponents of "open housing" are politically potent in all sections of the country, and as a result both the rent subsidy and the off-site housing programs of the federal government have yet to receive much implementation at the local level.

Urban Renaissancemanship

In the Housing Act of 1937, the idea of urban renewal was closely tied to public housing. Slum residences were to be torn down as public housing sites were constructed. But in the Housing Act of 1949, the urban renewal program was separated from public housing, and the federal government undertook to support a broad program of urban redevelopment to help cities fight a loss in population and to reclaim the economic importance of the core cities. After World War II, the suburban exodus had progressed to the point where central cities faced slow decay and death if large public efforts were not undertaken. Urban renewal could not be undertaken by private enterprise because it was not profitable; suburban property was usually cheaper than downtown property and it did not require large-scale clearance of obsolete buildings. Moreover, private enterprise did not possess the power of eminent domain, which enabled the city to purchase the many separately owned tracts of land to insure an economically feasible new investment.

To save the nation's central cities, the Urban Renewal Administration was authorized to match local monies to acquire blighted land, clear off or modernize obsolete or dilapidated structures, and make downtown sites available for new uses. The federal government does not engage in these activities directly, but makes available financial assistance to local urban renewal authorities for renewal projects. When the sites are physically cleared of the old structures by the local urban renewal authority, they can be resold to private developers for residential, commercial, or industrial use, and two-thirds of the difference between the costs of acquisition and clearance and the income from the private sale to the developers is paid for by the federal government. In other words, local urban renewal authorities sustain a loss in their renewal activities and two-thirds of this loss is made up by federal grants; the rest must come from local sources. However, the local share may include non-cash contributions in the form of land donations, schools, streets, or parks.

No city is required to engage in urban renewal, but if they wish federal financial backing, they must show in their applications that they have developed a "workable program" for redevelopment and the the prevention of future blight. They must demonstrate that they have adequate building and health codes, good zoning and subdivision control regulations, proper administrative structures for renewal and other government services, sufficient local financing and public support, and a comprehensive plan of development with provisions for relocating displaced persons.

Political support for urban renewal has come from mayors who wish to make their reputation as rigorous proponents of progress by engaging in large-scale renewal activities that produce impressive "before" and "after" pictures of the city. Businessmen wishing to preserve downtown investments and developers wishing to acquire land in urban centers have provided a solid base of support for downtown renewal. Mayors, planners, the press, and the good government forces have made urban renewal politically much more popular than public housing.

Originally, liberal reform groups and representatives of urban minorities supported urban renewal as an attack on the slum problem. However, recently they have become disenchanted with urban renewal, complaining that urban renewal has not considered the plight of the slum dweller. Too often, slum areas have been cleared and replaced with high income residential developments or commercial or industrial developments that do not directly help the plight of the slum dwellers. Urban renewal authorities are required to pay landowners a just price for their land, but slum dwellers who rent their apartments are shoved about the city with only a minimal amount of support from the "relocation" division of urban renewal authority. Downtown areas have been improved in appearance, but usually at the price of considerable human dislocation. Thus, slum dwellers and the landlords who exploit them often join forces to oppose urban renewal.

Politics and Poor Folks—The Office of Economic Opportunity

There are about 35 million people, one-fifth of the nation's population, living in families whose income is less than $3000 per year. Poverty in the midst of a rich society is the most bitter kind of poverty to be experienced. Why is there poverty in a nation so rich? John Kenneth Galbraith, in his book, *The Affluent Society,* makes a useful distinction between "case poverty" and "area poverty." [6] Case poverty is largely a product of the personal characteristics of affected persons. Some persons have been unable to participate in the nation's prosperity because of old age, illiteracy, inadequate education, lack of job skills, poor health, inadequate motivation, or racial discrimination. Area poverty is a product of economic deficiency relating to a particular sector of the nation, such as West Virginia or much of the rest of Appalachia, and large parts of rural America. Urbanization, industrialization, and technological development appear to have passed up many of these areas, creating high rates of unemployment and large numbers of low income families. The decline in employment in the coal industry, the exhaustion of iron-ore mines, the squeezing out of the small farmer from the agricultural market, and other such economic factors create "pockets of poverty" or "depressed areas" throughout the nation. People in these

[6] John K. Galbraith, *The Affluent Society* (Boston: Houghton Mifflin Co., 1958).

areas suffer many of the problems of case poverty, because the two types of poverty are not mutually exclusive. But both case poverty and area poverty differ from the "mass poverty" of the 1930's or the mass poverty predicted for capitalist societies by Marxian doctrine. Today's poverty afflicts only a minority of Americans, and it does not disappear even when the economy expands and the nation is prosperous.

The federal government launched its campaign against area poverty with the Area Redevelopment Act of 1961.[7] This was a four year program of assistance for depressed areas, in which the Area Redevelopment Administration in the Department of Commerce provided long term loans at low interest to attract businesses to these areas, loans and grants to local governments for public facilities needed to attract businesses, and support for other community economic development and worker retraining programs. The Act was essentially a "trickle-down" approach to poverty, with most of the direct benefits going to businesses rather than the poor. Republicans charged that the program was a pork barrel to help elect Democrats, and many specific ARA projects were criticized for failing to alleviate poverty. In 1965, President Johnson requested Congress to replace ARA with an expanded and broadened program for depressed areas under the Economic Development Act of 1965. It authorized grants and loans for public works, development facilities, technical assistance, and other activities to help economically depressed areas and to stimulate planning for economic development. In this Act, the responsibility is placed upon local and state governments to apply for economic development assistance from the Economic Development Administration and to create multicounty and multistate development areas and districts for the purposes of planning economic development. The Economic Development Administration can make direct grants to communities for such projects as water systems, waste disposal plants, industrial development parks, airports, or other facilities that will improve employment opportunities in a depressed area; but it insists on regional planning and requires any community proposal to "substantially further the objectives of the war on poverty."

As an approach to case poverty, the federal government passed the Manpower Training and Development Act of 1962, which authorizes federal grants to state employment agencies and private enterprise for on-the-job training programs to help workers in depressed areas, or elsewhere, acquire new job skills. Originally, the act called for matching funds on a 50-50 basis by state governments after the first two years of the program; but when it appeared certain that states would drop the program altogether

[7] See James E. Anderson, "Poverty, Unemployment, and Economic Development: the Search for a National Antipoverty Policy," *Journal of Politics,* 29 (February, 1967), 70–93.

rather than share its costs, the federal government amended the act to authorize 100 per cent federal financing. It seems safe to conclude that state and local governments would not undertake manpower training programs for unskilled workers without full federal financial support.

The most important legislation in the "war on poverty" is the Economic Opportunity Act of 1964. Originally a great deal of stress was placed on local initiative and leadership and voluntary participation in communities. The Office of Economic Opportunity (OEO) was established with authority to support varied and highly experimental techniques for combating poverty at the community level. The focus was upon case poverty and the objective was to help the poor and unemployed become self-supporting and capable of earning adequate incomes, by bringing about changes in the individuals themselves or in their environment. The strategy was one of "rehabilitation, not relief." OEO was given no authority to make direct grants to the poor as relief or public assistance. All of its programs were aimed, whether accurately or inaccurately, at curing the causes of poverty rather than alleviating its symptoms.

The only program operated directly by OEO, without state or local initiative, is the Job Corps; this program is designed to provide education, vocational training, and work experience in rural conservation camps for unemployable youth between the ages of 16 and 21. All other programs require the initiation and cooperation of local community groups, either public or private. A Neighborhood Youth Corps program provides vocational training and work experience for youth while living at home. A Work-Study program helps students from low income families remain in school by giving them federally paid part time employment with cooperating public or private agencies. But the core of the Economic Opportunity Act was a grassroots "Community Action Program" to be carried on at the local level, with federal financial assistance, by public or private nonprofit agencies. Communities were urged to form a "Community Action Agency," composed of representatives of government, private organizations, and most importantly, the poor themselves. It was originally intended that OEO would support any reasonable antipoverty program devised by the local community action agency. Projects might include (but were not limited to) literacy training, health services, homemaker services, legal aid for the poor, neighborhood service centers, manpower vocational training, and childhood development activities. The Act also envisioned that a community action agency would help organize the poor so that they could become participating members of the community and avail themselves of many public programs already in existence. Finally, the statute established a domestic service corps—Volunteers in Service to America, or VISTA— to recruit volunteer workers for antipoverty projects, slum areas, Indian reservations, hospitals, migratory labor camps, and the like.

The Appalachian Regional Redevelopment Act in 1965 was another federal approach to the problem of area poverty. The name "Appalachia" denoted an 11-state region centering around the Appalachian mountains from southern New York to mid-Alabama. It was generally conceded to be the largest economically depressed area in the nation, although it did contain "pockets of prosperity." The focus of the Appalachia Act is upon highway construction, which was believed necessary to open up the region to economic development, although it may make it even easier for the residents to leave. Programs under the Appalachia Act will be carried out by existing national and state agencies, such as the U.S. Bureau of Public Roads and state highway departments. However, the entire program is coordinated by the Appalachian Regional Commission, which is comprised of the governor of each state in the region, or his representative, and a federal representative chosen by the President. This arrangement was designed to secure state participation and better adaptation of programs to local conditions. Needless to say, the Appalachian program stirred the interest of congressmen from other regional areas.

What are the political bases for the support and opposition to the war on poverty? Certainly the poor themselves are, in the words of Michael Harrington in *The Other America,* "politically invisible." "The people of the other America do not, by far and large, belong to unions, to fraternal organizations, or to political parties. They are without lobbies of their own; they put forward no legislative program. As a group, they are atomized. They have no face; they have no voice." [8] How then does one account for antipoverty legislation?

No doubt Presidents Kennedy and Johnson were motivated at least partly by the desire to be recognized as great Presidents, which of course requires important accomplishments. Writers such as Galbraith and Harrington helped to focus attention on poverty. Thirdly, the growing political power of the Negro and the success of the civil rights movement have contributed. Poverty is much higher among Negroes than among whites, so as Negro political strength grows, it tends to focus attention on the poor.

Organized group support for poverty programs has come from labor, liberal, welfare, civil rights, charitable, and professional organizations. Among these groups were the AFL-CIO, National Grange, National Farmers Union, National Urban League, National Council of Churches, National Education Association, General Federation of Women's Clubs, and so on. Opposition has come from the Chamber of Commerce, National Association of Manufacturers, the American Farm Bureau Federation, and some rightwing groups. The poverty program runs counter to the conservative ideology and it is criticized as unnecessary, or improperly

[8] Michael Harrington, *The Other America* (New York: The Macmillan Company, 1963), p. 13.

and hastily prepared, or as an improper activity for the national government. In Congress, antipoverty bills have been supported by northern Democrats almost unanimously, and by a half to two-thirds of the southern Democrats. Some eastern and urban Republicans have supported the program, but more than two-thirds of the Republicans in Congress have opposed most antipoverty bills.

At the local level, community action agencies were supported by, and sometimes even organized by, civic and charitable organizations, United Fund agencies, Catholic charities, civil rights groups, labor organizations, agricultural extension workers, school officials anxious to share in Head-Start funds, and to some extent, even the poor themselves. Opposition is weakened by the fact that one who opposes an antipoverty program appears to be in favor of poverty. Critics usually attack some peripheral aspect of the program rather than the program itself, such as the high salaries for the administrative officials, waste and extravagance, or immorality and delinquency, which occur at any of the program sites. But the poverty program has also had some difficulties with its friends as well as its enemies. Welfare departments sometimes feel that the community action agency is usurping its functions with the poor. State employment service and vocational rehabilitation agencies object that the OEO programs duplicate their own services. School adminstrators have insisted that preschool development programs, such as Operation Head-Start, must be administered by the schools and not by community action agencies; this has led to separation of Head-Start programs from community action agencies and their administration being placed in the hands of local school districts. Local political figures often object to community action agencies organizing the poor, for they see this as an attempt to give the poor political power. Once organized, the poor have often made uncomfortable demands upon local governments for adequate street cleaning, garbage disposal, housing code enforcement, courteous police treatment, and so on, in slum areas. In short, organizing the poor threatens to upset established power relations in communities. City officials have often objected to the fact that community action agencies do not come directly under the control of city governments, but instead are usually nonprofit, private corporations, in which government officials must share power with representatives of private organizations and of the poor. Finally, the poverty program is beset with all of the difficulties associated with the problem of race. Since Negroes constitute such a large proportion of the poor in most communities, the poverty program is seen by many as a program for Negroes. Thus it is possible to express hostility against Negroes in a more socially acceptable fashion by opposing poverty programs.

Another problem has been the policy of Congress and of the Washington offices of the OEO to restrict local discretion in the nature of their antipoverty activities. Congress has increasingly "earmarked" antipoverty funds for specific programs, such as Head-Start and manpower training, which are more politically acceptable than community organization and social service programs. And the Washington office of OEO has developed "canned programs" for certain kinds of antipoverty activities, which it "suggests" to the local community and gives priority to in community applications.

17

THE POLITICS OF

BUDGETING AND TAXATION

State-Local Tax and Revenue Policies

Federal, state, and local governments in the United States take about 37 per cent of the nation's income in taxes and revenues. The largest share of this total tax bite, about two-thirds, goes to the federal government, principally to pay for the costs of past, present, and future wars. But states and communities collect over one-third of all government revenues, and revenue-raising presents states and communities with important political choices. Decisions must be made about how much revenue is to be raised, how it will be raised, from whom it will be raised, and how great a financial burden will be imposed. These decisions often embroil states and communities in their most important political battles.

The U.S. Constitution places very few restrictions on the power of the states to tax: it prohibits states, without the consent of Congress, from levying taxes on imports and exports; and by implication it prohibits states from using the taxing power to deny to citizens equal protection of the law or due process of the law. State constitutions, however, restrict state taxing powers far more than the federal constitution. These state constitutional restrictions often include maximum rates, prohibitions on income or sales taxes, prohibitions on progressive rates, and prohibitions on classification schemes. These restrictions, of course, are generally the product of politi-

TABLE 17.1

TOTAL GOVERNMENT REVENUES, 1902-1966

	Amount in billions	Federal percentage	State-local percentage	Percentage of national income
1902	1.7	38.5	61.5	8.2
1913	3.0	32.3	67.7	8.6
1922	9.3	45.7	54.3	14.7
1932	10.3	21.6	78.4	24.2
1940	17.8	39.3	60.7	21.8
1950	66.7	80.3	19.7	27.6
1960	153.1	65.2	34.8	36.7
1961	158.7	63.8	36.2	37.2
1965	202.9	62.0	38.0	39.4
1966	225.6	62.5	37.5	37.0

Source: U.S. Bureau of the Census, *Statistical Abstract.*

cal victories by large taxpaying groups who have succeeded in writing their views on local taxes into state constitutions. In addition to taxes, states and communities also derive revenue from compulsory insurance payments, income from public businesses, fines, rents, and charges, and more importantly, grants-in-aid from the federal government. As we shall see, these non-tax revenues are an important part of state and local government finance.

Important changes have occurred in tax and revenue policies in America in the last few decades. In 1902 total government revenues amounted to only $1.7 million. States and communities collected more revenue than the national government: 61.5 per cent of all government revenues were raised in the states, while the federal government accounted for only 38.5 per cent of all revenues. And total government revenues amounted to only 8 per cent of the nation's income. Five decades later, public revenue collections in the United States had risen to over $225 billion. Perhaps more important than dollar increases is the fact that governments now take about 37 per cent of the national income. This means that the burden of government finance has grown much faster than the nation's income. Another important change is the change in the relative position of federal versus state-local revenue collections. Wars, depressions, and threats of war have resulted in the shifting of financial emphasis from the states and communities to the national government. The national government in 1965 collected 62 per cent of all revenues, while states and communities collected the remaining 38 per cent. However, it is interesting to note that in very recent years, state-local revenues have gained back some ground vis-à-vis the federal government. In the early 1960's, states raised tax and expenditure levels faster than the federal government.

There have also been some important changes in the sources of state and local revenues over the past few decades. In 1902, local revenues far surpassed the state revenues and the federal government provided very little help to states or communities. Today, state governments have assumed direct responsibility for many public programs, previously left to local communities, that were not undertaken at all. This trend towards centralized state government has meant that the states collect an increasing share of the total state and local revenue. States and communities now share total state-local revenues on an approximately equal basis. A major share of state-local revenues now comes from the federal government. Federal grants constitute nearly 20 per cent of the revenue of state governments and about 2 per cent of the revenue of local governments. And local governments receive over 25 per cent of their revenue from state grants-in-aid. This dependence of local governments upon state governments for revenue arose during the depression years. Today, intergovernmental payments are a vital source of revenue for both state and local governments. In 1962, 27 per cent of all local revenues came from either state or federal governments, and 20 per cent of all state revenues came from the federal government.

In recent years, both state and local governments have also received substantial incomes from various public enterprises and insurance programs. Today, many municipalities provide electric power, gas, recreational facilities, transit and transportation facilities, as well as water supply, on a commercial basis. Liquor store revenues have become a major source of state revenues. Today, payments into state unemployment compensation funds, workmen's compensation funds, and employee retirement funds are another important source of state government revenue, even though these payments are made to special funds. These insurance premiums, utility receipts, and liquor store receipts amount to over 16 per cent of all state-local revenue. Charges and miscellaneous general revenue have remained a relatively constant percentage of total state-local revenues over the years. These include everything from children's school lunch fees and text book charges, to interests from public investments, highway tolls, sewerage charges, and public hospital service fees.

Important changes have also occurred in the last 50 years in the types of taxes relied upon by state and local governments. At the turn of the century, general property tax reigned as the only really important source of state and local revenue. In theory, at least, all property within a community was assessed at market value and a single uniform rate of tax was applied. In practice, however, property assessments fell far below true market value, and they were not uniform from one county or municipality to the next; assessments varied from as high as 75 per cent of fair market

TABLE 17.2

A COMPARISON OF STATE AND LOCAL SOURCES OF REVENUE, 1902-1965

State government revenue by source

	Amount in billions of $	From federal government	From local government	Income taxes	General sales taxes	Motor fuel taxes	Alcohol and tobacco taxes	Other taxes including property	Charges	Insurance and utilities stores
1902	0.2	1.6	3.1	---	---	---	---	71.3	13.0	1.0
1913	0.4	1.6	2.7	---	---	---	0.5	79.5	15.7	0.0
1922	1.4	7.3	2.0	7.4	---	1.0	---	61.3	13.3	7.8
1934	2.5	8.7	1.8	6.0	0.3	20.7	0.7	46.6	10.5	4.6
1940	5.7	11.6	1.0	8.0	8.7	14.6	5.1	21.3	6.0	23.6
1950	13.7	16.4	1.1	8.4	12.0	11.1	6.0	18.5	6.5	19.0
1960	32.8	19.9	0.6	10.3	13.1	10.2	4.8	16.6	7.9	16.7
1961	34.6	19.0	0.6	10.5	13.0	9.9	4.9	16.7	8.2	17.1
1965	53.8	20.3	0.9	11.5	20.7	8.8	2.7	11.3	9.2	16.2

Local government revenue by source

	Amount in billions of $	From federal government	From state government	Income taxes	Excise and sales taxes	Property taxes	Other taxes	Charges	Utility receipts
1902	0.9	0.4	5.7	---	---	68.3	8.8	10.3	6.5
1913	1.8	0.3	5.2	---	0.2	67.9	6.4	13.2	6.8
1922	4.1	0.2	7.5	---	0.5	71.7	1.8	11.5	6.8
1932	6.2	0.2	12.9	---	0.4	67.2	1.4	9.8	8.1
1940	7.7	3.6	21.4	0.2	1.7	54.0	2.3	66.6	10.2
1950	16.1	1.3	26.1	0.4	3.0	43.7	2.4	9.9	13.2

Local government revenue by source

	Amount in billions of $	From federal government	From state government	Income taxes	Excise and sales taxes	Property taxes	Other taxes	Charges	Utility receipts
1960	37.2	1.8	25.0	0.7	3.6	42.5	1.9	13.0	11.6
1961	40.5	2.0	25.0	0.6	3.5	42.9	1.8	12.8	11.3
1965	53.8			0.8	3.9	41.3	1.5	13.3	10.5

Source: U.S. Bureau of the Census, *Historical Statistics of the United States* (Washington: Government Printing Office 1960), pp. 727, 729.

value to as low as 10 per cent. Some property was specifically exempted from property taxation—for example, the property of government agencies and religious institutions. Some property, especially personal property such as furniture and automobiles and intangible property such as stocks and bonds, was simply hidden from the tax assessors. The property tax on real estate provided most state and local revenue.

The awkwardness of the property tax, with its many inequalities and opportunities for evasion, eventually led to its disuse as an important source of *state* revenue; however, this tax continues to be the major source of revenue for *local* governments. Intangible property, such as stocks and bonds and personal property, has gradually been dropped from the local tax property rolls, either legally or illegally, but real estate is relatively easy to find and it cannot be easily moved about. A local sales tax can result in merchants moving beyond city boundaries, and a city income tax can speed the population exodus to suburbia. Because of the dependence of local governments on property taxation, the role of this tax in the total state-local revenue system in America remains significant. States that turn over governmental functions to communities will have a total tax structure that is heavily dependent on property taxation. States that assume more direct responsibility for public services will depend somewhat less on property taxation.

When prohibition ended, alcohol, and later tobacco, became important sources of revenue. It was relatively easy to win political support for taxes that penalized a recognized vice. The advent of the automobile and the heavy demand for public road construction made gasoline a natural object of taxation: the gasoline tax first adopted in 1919 spread to all states within ten years. This tax still supplies about 10 per cent of all state revenue. Under political pressure from the automotive and trucking industries, revenues from this tax are usually segregated from other revenues for use on highways only.

While the property tax is the most important source of revenue for local communities, the general sales tax is now the most important source of tax revenue for state governments. Consumers are a notoriously weak pressure group, and opposition by retailers can usually be squelched by state kickbacks of a certain percentage of a tax for the retailers' efforts in collecting it. It is difficult for taxpayers to count pennies dribbled away two or three at a time; the tax does not involve obvious payroll deductions, as in income taxation, or year-end tax bills as in property taxation. The burden of the sales tax is not as visible as the income or property taxes even when large items are purchased, and the purchaser usually considers the tax as part of the item's cost. By 1966, a total of 40 states had imposed a general sales tax.

Perhaps the popularity of the sales tax with state legislators is due to the fact that the federal government has "pre-empted" income taxation and

TABLE 17.3

STATES WITH SALES AND INCOME
TAXES IN 1966

States with both sales and income taxes	*States with sales tax but no income tax*	*States with income tax but no sales tax*	*States with neither sales nor income taxes*
Ala.	Conn.	Alaska	Neb.
Ariz.	Fla.	Del.	N.H.*
Ark.	Ill.	Minn.	
Calif.	Maine	Mont.	
Col.	Mich.	N.J.	
Ga.	Nev.	Ore.	
Haw.	Ohio	Ver.	
Idaho	Pa.	Va.	
Ind.	R.I.		
Iowa	S.D.		
Kansas	Tenn.*		
Kent.	Texas		
La.	Wash.		
Md.	Wyo.		
Mass.			
Miss.			
Mo.			
N. Mex.			
N.Y.			
N.C.			
N.D.			
Okla.			
S.C.			
Utah			
W. Va.			
Wis.			

*Taxes levied on individual income from interest and dividends only.

communities have "pre-empted" property taxation. There seems to be nothing left for the states to tax except consumption. It seems natural that the three levels of government should have three separate sources of revenue. Of course, the notion of "pre-emption" involves a value judgment— that property taxes should go no higher and that the federal government is now taking as much income as should be spared for public purposes.

In 1911, Wisconsin passed the first modern, enforceable, state income tax. Many states fell in line after the national government began taxing income in 1913. Like the general sales tax, the income tax can produce a great deal of revenue. But most of the states that adopted income taxation did so before World War II. In recent years the popularity of income taxes in the states has ebbed, perhaps as a result of the heavy federal income tax levies. Since income taxation significantly affects corporations and other large taxpayers, it is generally opposed by the business community; while business interests can generally be depended upon to oppose tax increases in general, if taxes must be raised, business interests seem to prefer sales taxation to income taxation. The opposition of the business community to income taxation has made states that were concerned with their competitive economic position afraid of taxes that might drive industry away. State legislators are always concerned with what neighboring states are doing. Although economists assert that taxes are far down the list of locational considerations of industry, the idea that an income tax discourages industry remains a widespread belief among state legislators.

In 1966, 34 states levied individual income taxes. (Two other states, New Hampshire and Tennessee, tax individual income from investments only.) Thirty-eight states levied corporate net income taxes; 26 levied both sales and income taxes; 14 levied sales but not income taxes; 8 levied income but not sales taxes. In 1966, only Nebraska and New Hampshire had neither a sales nor an individual income tax.

A Comparative View of State Tax Systems

What accounts for differences in tax and revenue policy? In 1964–65, for example, total state and local revenues amounted to $384 per person. Total state-local revenues varied from a high of over $500 per person in California, Nevada, and Wyoming, to a low of $244 in South Carolina. This means that per capita revenue levels of some states are over twice as high as those of other states. Some states rely heavily on their local governments and upon property taxation to supply needed revenue. Some states rely heavily on grants-in-aid. Tax burdens, that is, taxes in relation to personal income, also vary considerably among the states. Available evidence suggests that a state's level of economic development is the most important influence on state-local revenue policies.[1]

First of all, let us examine the effect of economic development on levels of taxation in the states.[2] In 1964–65, per capita state-local tax levels among the states ranged from a high of $379 (California) to a low of $159 (Arkansas). There is little doubt that the ability of the states to raise taxes

[1] Thomas R. Dye, *Politics, Economics, and the Public* (Chicago: Rand McNally & Co., 1966), chap. 7.

[2] Levels of *revenue* refer simply to amounts of money per person raised from all sources. Levels of *taxation* refer to amounts of money per person raised through taxation and excludes monies from federal grants-in-aid, insurance premiums, rents and charges, and utility and store receipts.

TABLE 17.4

TAXES AND REVENUES IN THE STATES, 1964-65

Per capita total revenue state-local		Per capita taxes state-local		State-local taxes as percent of personal income	
1. Alaska (1-$636.17)	$848.22*	1. California	$379.29	1. California	11.8%
2. Wyoming	619.22	2. New York	372.10	2. Vermont	11.8
3. Nevada	556.91	3. Nevada	321.82	3. Arizona	11.5
4. California	528.99	4. Wisconsin	309.53	4. Wisconsin	11.4
5. New York	481.35	5. Delaware	302.05	5. New Mexico	11.3
6. Hawaii	466.38	6. Massachusetts	302.03	6. New York	11.3
7. New Mexico	462.49	7. Minnesota	299.25	7. Minnesota	11.2
8. Delaware	461.23	8. Hawaii	297.91	8. Wyoming	11.2
9. Oregon	460.78	9. Washington	294.06	9. South Dakota	11.1
10. North Dakota	460.44	10. Colorado	291.93	10. Colorado	10.9
11. Washington	459.50	11. Connecticut	291.04	11. Montana	10.9
12. Montana	456.57	12. Michigan	289.66	12. North Dakota	10.9
13. Colorado	454.28	13. Oregon	280.72	13. Utah	10.8
14. Minnesota	437.06	14. Vermont	277.84	14. Louisiana	10.7
15. Vermont	430.61	15. Wyoming	277.76	15. Mississippi	10.6
16. Utah	420.71	16. Iowa	275.94	16. Hawaii	10.4
17. Arizona	414.52	17. Kansas	273.34	17. Iowa	10.3
18. Michigan	410.00	18. New Jersey	268.65	18. Kansas	10.3
19. South Dakota	404.86	19. Arizona	266.45	19. Maine	10.3
20. Wisconsin	403.81	20. Illinois	266.30	20. Idaho	10.2
21. Massachusetts	396.80	UNITED STATES	266.11	21. Washington	10.2
22. Idaho	395.92	21. Montana	264.87	22. Oregon	10.0
23. Kansas	392.72	22. Rhode Island	262.74	23. Massachusetts	9.9
24. Connecticut	389.43	23. Maryland	261.06	24. Nevada	9.9
25. Iowa	388.95	24. Indiana	257.19	UNITED STATES	9.7
26. Louisiana	385.71	25. Utah	254.61	25. Florida	9.6
UNITED STATES	383.56	26. Alaska (44-$187.35)	249.80*	26. Oklahoma	9.6
27. Oklahoma	368.11	27. North Dakota	248.32	27. Michigan	9.5
28. Rhode Island	365.97	28. Idaho	245.27	28. West Virginia	9.5
29. Illinois	361.24	29. Pennsylvania	245.05	29. Rhode Island	9.3
30. Maryland	360.34	30. New Mexico	243.15	30. North Carolina	9.2
31. Indiana	357.76	31. South Dakota	240.71	31. Indiana	9.0
32. New Jersey	351.36	32. Maine	233.18	32. Delaware	8.9
33. Florida	350.30	33. Florida	233.01	33. Pennsylvania	8.9
34. Nebraska	334.53	34. Ohio	225.26	34. Georgia	8.8
35. Pennsylvania	333.77	35. Missouri	222.67	35. Tennessee	8.8
36. Missouri	328.33	36. Louisiana	222.04	36. Texas	8.8
37. Maine	326.41	37. New Hampshire	220.95	37. Alabama	8.7
38. Texas	323.44	38. Nebraska	219.75	38. Arkansas	8.7
39. Ohio	322.69	39. Oklahoma	215.93	39. Maryland	8.7
40. New Hampshire	321.11	40. Texas	207.05	40. South Carolina	8.7
41. West Virginia	309.68	41. West Virginia	191.97	41. Connecticut	8.6
42. Georgia	306.51	42. Georgia	190.74	42. Kentucky	8.6
43. Virginia	297.93	43. North Carolina	188.30	43. New Hampshire	8.6
44. Alabama	293.06	44. Virginia	188.18	44. Nebraska	8.5
45. Kentucky	288.91	45. Tennessee	178.24	45. Missouri	8.4

Per capita total revenue state-local		Per capita taxes state-local		State-local taxes as percent of personal income	
46. Mississippi	$282.66	46. Kentucky	$174.89	46. New Jersey	8.3%
47. Tennessee	281.79	47. Mississippi	169.89	47. Illinois	8.1
48. North Carolina	276.88	48. Alabama	167.55	48. Ohio	8.0
49. Arkansas	269.28	49. South Carolina	160.82	49. Virginia	7.8
50. South Carolina	244.98	50. Arkansas	159.47	50. Alaska	7.4

Source: U.S. Bureau of the Census, *Statistical Abstract.*

is a function of their level of economic development. Figure 17.1 is a scatter diagram, showing the closeness of the relationship between tax revenues and median family income among the states. It shows that as family incomes go up, per capita taxes collected by state and local governments also go up.

The concept of tax *burden* generally refers to taxes paid in relation to personal income; because of differences among the states in income levels, states with the highest *levels of taxation* are not necessarily the same states with the highest tax burdens. The total tax burden in a state is measured by "total state and local tax revenues as a percentage of personal income." In 1964, the state-local tax burden averaged 9.7 per cent of personal income in the United States. Among the 50 states, high levels of industrialization usually reduced the burdens of taxation; industrialized states can collect a great deal of tax monies without taking a very large percentage of personal income.[3] Apparently the way to lower the tax burden in a state is to attract industry.

High tax burdens are not necessarily a product of high tax levels, although, of course, there is some relationship between these variables. Yet, high tax levels in an urbanized, industrialized, high income state may not necessarily be accompanied by a heavy tax burden. It is possible to have low tax levels that, because of the lack of industry and low income levels, may be very burdensome—that is, quite high in relationship to low incomes. In Figure 17.2, all states above the solid horizontal line can be designated as states with high tax levels. In those states in the upper right, high tax levels are accompanied by high tax burdens, but those states in the upper left (Delaware, Nevada, Connecticut, Illinois, and New Jersey) can collect high taxes per capita without imposing high tax burdens; they have sufficient industrial resources or other special tax sources (for example, gambling and entertainment in Nevada) to enable them to collect high per capita taxes without taking a large share of personal income. Even California and New York, which have the highest tax *levels* in the nation, rank below a number of other states in their tax *burdens,* because of their sur-

[3] Dye, *op. cit.,* pp. 188–91.

FIGURE 17.1

THE FIFTY STATES ARRANGED ACCORDING TO TAX REVENUE AND MEDIAN
FAMILY INCOME

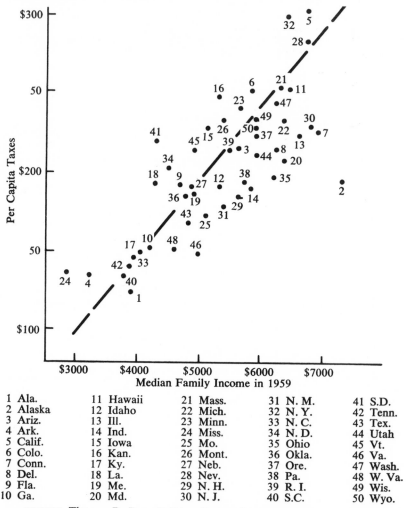

1 Ala.	11 Hawaii	21 Mass.	31 N. M.	41 S.D.
2 Alaska	12 Idaho	22 Mich.	32 N. Y.	42 Tenn.
3 Ariz.	13 Ill.	23 Minn.	33 N. C.	43 Tex.
4 Ark.	14 Ind.	24 Miss.	34 N. D.	44 Utah
5 Calif.	15 Iowa	25 Mo.	35 Ohio	45 Vt.
6 Colo.	16 Kan.	26 Mont.	36 Okla.	46 Va.
7 Conn.	17 Ky.	27 Neb.	37 Ore.	47 Wash.
8 Del.	18 La.	28 Nev.	38 Pa.	48 W. Va.
9 Fla.	19 Me.	29 N. H.	39 R. I.	49 Wis.
10 Ga.	20 Md.	30 N. J.	40 S.C.	50 Wyo.

SOURCE: Thomas R. Dye, *Politics, Economics, and the Public* (Chicago: Rand
McNally & Co., 1966), p. 189. Reproduced by permission.

plus of taxable economic resources. In contrast, states at the lower right
(Mississippi, North Dakota, Louisiana, and Idaho) are in the unhappy
position of having high tax burdens, despite the fact that per capita taxes
are low. Their economic resources are so limited that even though per capita
taxes and public service levels are low, tax burdens are still quite high.

Poorer states also differ from richer states in their reliance upon intergovernmental revenues. Federal monies are an important and growing source of revenue for state and local governments. In some program areas, federal grants-in-aid help to overcome economic inequalities among the states, but by no means has federal action eliminated disparities among the states in revenues or the impact of these disparities on state programs. In earlier chapters, we observed that federal formulas for the distribution of grants-in-aid in many education and welfare programs provided propor-

FIGURE 17.2

THE FIFTY STATES ARRANGED ACCORDING TO TAX REVENUES AND TAX BURDENS

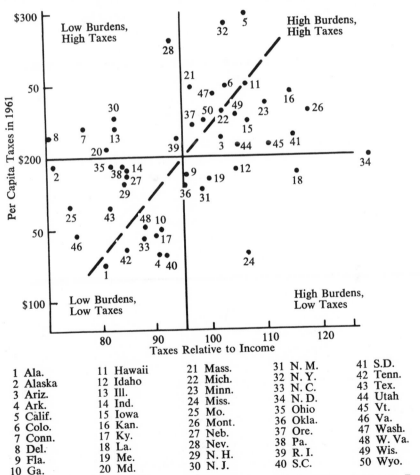

SOURCE: Thomas R. Dye, *Politics, Economics, and the Public* (Chicago: Rand McNally & Co., 1966), p. 190. Reproduced by permission.

1 Ala.	11 Hawaii	21 Mass.	31 N. M.	41 S.D.
2 Alaska	12 Idaho	22 Mich.	32 N.Y.	42 Tenn.
3 Ariz.	13 Ill.	23 Minn.	33 N.C.	43 Tex.
4 Ark.	14 Ind.	24 Miss.	34 N.D.	44 Utah
5 Calif.	15 Iowa	25 Mo.	35 Ohio	45 Vt.
6 Colo.	16 Kan.	26 Mont.	36 Okla.	46 Va.
7 Conn.	17 Ky.	27 Neb.	37 Ore.	47 Wash.
8 Del.	18 La.	28 Nev.	38 Pa.	48 W. Va.
9 Fla.	19 Me.	29 N. H.	39 R. I.	49 Wis.
10 Ga.	20 Md.	30 N. J.	40 S.C.	50 Wyo.

tionately larger amounts of money to poorer states and communities. The result is that poorer states and communities rely much more heavily upon federal grants-in-aid as sources of revenue.

Another important difference between richer and poorer states is in the degree of decentralization in state and local finance and administration. Local governments tend to play a greater role in the collection of taxes and the provision of public services in urban, high income states, while state governments collect a greater portion of revenue and provide more services in rural, low income states. Earlier, we observed that state governments in poorer rural states undertake more direct responsibilities in education, welfare, and highways. Low levels of economic development tend to force centralization upon these states. Wealthy urban states can afford to let local governments shoulder more responsibilities. This also means, of course, that the property tax—the chief source of income for local governments—is a relatively more important source of revenue in the wealthier urban states, which rely heavily upon their local governments for the provision of public services.

Types of Taxes and the Incidence of Taxation

The politics of taxation center about the question of who actually bears the burden or "incidence" of a tax, that is, which income groups must devote the largest proportion of their income to taxes. Taxes that require high income groups to pay a larger percentage of their incomes in taxes than low-income groups are said to be *progressive,* while taxes that take a larger share of the income of low income groups are said to be *regressive.*

Economist George Bishop estimates that, in general, state and local tax systems are regressive.[4] Certainly the revenue systems of state and local governments are much more regressive than that of the federal government, which relies heavily upon the highly progressive individual and corporate income tax. This means that, in general, if a particular governmental function is financed through state and local revenue systems rather than federal revenues, it is being financed on a regressive rather than progressive revenue basis. Thus, much of the political debate over "federalism," that is, over which level of government, state or federal, should provide a particular governmental service, concerns the fact that the federal government tax structure is generally progressive, while the state and local tax structures are generally regressive. If the federal government pays for a particular governmental program, it is being paid for out of progressive taxes, whereas if state and local governments pay for a particular governmental program, it is being paid for out of largely regressive taxes. There

---

[4] George A. Bishop, "Tax Burdens by Income Class," *National Tax Journal,* Vol. 14 (1961).

are many other factors to be considered in the allocation of responsibilities between states and the federal government, but the incidence of federal and state tax systems should not be overlooked.

According to Bishop, the income group under $2000 per year was estimated to have paid, in 1958, 11.4 per cent of its personal income into state and local taxes, while the income group over $15,000 paid only 5.8 per cent of its personal income into these taxes (see Table 17.5).

Bishop also estimates the incidence of the various types of state and local taxes. Property taxes are quite regressive. This conclusion is based on the assumption that the renter actually pays his property taxes through increased rentals levied by the landlord, and the further assumption that high income groups have more wealth in untaxed forms of property. Since the property tax is the foundation of local tax structures in every state, it is reasonable to conclude that states that rely largely upon local governments for taxes and services are relying more upon regressive tax structures. Yet, in defense of property taxation, it is often argued that no other form of taxation is really feasible for local governments. Local sales and income taxes force individuals and businesses to leave the communities levying them; real estate, on the other hand, is less easy to move about and hide from local tax assessors. Real estate taxes are the only type of taxes that can be effectively collected by relatively untrained local tax officials.

The burden of property taxes depends upon the ratio of assessed value of property to the fair market value of the property; the rate at which assessed property is taxed, which is usually expressed in mills, or tenths of a per cent; and, finally, the nature and extent of tax exemptions and reductions for certain types of property. The ratio of assessed value to full

TABLE 17.5

STATE AND LOCAL TAX BURDENS BY INCOME IN 1958

Source	Family personal income							
	Under $2,000	$2,000-$3,999	$4,000-$5,999	$6,000-$7,999	$8,000-$9,999	$10,000-$14,999	$15,000 and Over	Total
Individual income	0.5	0.8	0.6	0.2	0.3	0.3	0.7	0.5
Corporation income	0.2	0.2	0.1	0.1	0.2	0.2	0.4	0.2
Excises and sales	4.8	3.9	3.7	3.6	3.2	3.2	2.1	3.3
Estate and gift	–	–	–	–	–	–	0.5	0.1
Property	5.9	4.6	4.1	3.7	2.8	2.8	2.1	3.5
Total, excluding social insurance	11.4	9.5	8.5	7.6	7.3	6.5	5.8	7.6

Source: George A. Bishop, "Tax Burden by Income Class," *National Tax Journal*, XIV (1961), quoted in staff report of the Advisory Commission on Intergovernmental Relations, *Measures of State and Local Fiscal Capacity and Tax Effort* (Washington: Government Printing Office, 1962), p. 23.

market value may be quite low, sometimes less than 10 per cent, and it may vary from one community to the next, even in those states requiring uniform assessment ratios throughout the state. The failure of communities to have periodic and professional tax evaluation studies performed means that taxes continue to be levied on old assessment figures, even while market values go up. The result, over time, is a considerable lowering of assessment ratios, and therefore taxes, on older homes and businesses and industries. Newer residents, whose sale price is generally known to tax assessors and who must therefore pay taxes on the uniform assessment ratio, are generally much more favorable toward re-evaluation of property for assessment purposes. There are very few communities in which a suggestion of a re-evaluation will not set off a heated debate between those who are enjoying a low assessment and those who are not. When a community tampers with re-evaluation or a change in the ratio of assessed to market value, it threatens to change the incidence or distribution of tax burdens within a community. If new tax revenues are needed, it is much easier to simply increase the rate or millage to be applied against the assessed value of property. Many communities face state restrictions on maximum tax rates, or they are required to submit any proposed increase in tax rates to the voters in a referendum. These restrictions are usually favored by low tax forces, which have succeeded in obtaining legislation at the state level that impairs the taxing abilities of local governments.

Some categories of property are exempt from taxation; these usually include properties that are used for nonprofit, charitable, religious, educational, and other public purposes. Occasionally such exemptions are attacked by those who feel that they are, in effect, subsidies to the exempted organizations; this is particularly true regarding exemptions for religious property. Occasionally, exemptions for educational or public properties work a hardship on communities in which large public facilities or educational institutions are located. But the exemptions that arouse the greatest controversy are usually those given by state or local governments to new business and industry, in an effort to induce them to locate in the state or community granting the exemption. Competition among states and communities for industry sometimes results in flagrant abuse of tax exemptions as inducements to business and industry.

State governments have generally given up trying to revise property taxes and have turned to individual and corporate income taxes, general sales taxes, and excise taxes on gasoline, alcohol, and tobacco. Bishop has estimated that state and local sales and excise taxes are generally regressive, but not as regressive as property taxes.[5] The regressivity of sales taxation is based upon the assumption that low income groups must devote most, if not all, of their income to purchases, while high income groups

[5] Bishop, *op. cit.*

devote larger shares of their income to savings. Many states exclude some of the necessities of life from sales taxation, such as packaged food bought in supermarkets, in order to reduce the burden of sales taxation on the poor. Yet, on the whole, sales taxation remains more regressive than income taxation.

The choice between a sales and an income tax represents one of the most important policy choices facing a state government. The yield from both types of taxation can be quite large, and both sales and income taxes can feasibly be collected at the state level. Conservatives argue that the broad base of sales taxation insures that those who benefit from public services share in the cost of them. In other words, sales taxation insures that low income groups will share in the cost of government. Income taxes are said by conservatives to discourage savings and reduce investment incentives. Conservative views toward property, sales, and progressive income taxation were succinctly summarized by Barry Goldwater:

> Government has a right to claim an equal percentage of each man's wealth and no more. Property taxes are typically levied on this basis. Excise and sales taxes are based on the same principle—although the tax is levied on a transaction rather than on property. The principle is equally valid with regard to incomes, inheritances, and gifts. The idea that a man who makes $100,000 a year should be forced to contribute 90 per cent of his income to the cost of government, while the man who makes $10,000 is made to pay 20 per cent, is repugnant to my notions of justice. I do not believe in punishing success.[6]

Moreover, sales taxes are not as visible as income or property taxes, since sales taxes are paid pennies at a time. Generally, the consumer considers the sales tax as part of the price of the item. Moreover, state sales taxes are useful in reaching mobile populations, that is, tourists, commuters, and transients—persons who derive benefits from a host state but who would otherwise not pay for these benefits.

In contrast, progressive state income taxes are defended upon the principle of the ability to pay; that is, the theory that high income groups can afford to pay a larger percentage of their income into taxation at no more of a sacrifice than that required of lower income groups to devote a smaller proportion of their income to taxation. The principle of a graduated income tax based on ability to pay, a principle accepted at the federal level

[6] Barry Goldwater, *The Conscience of a Conservative* (Copyright 1960, Victor Publishing Company, Inc., used by permission of MacFadden-Bartell Corporation, New York), p. 3. The quotation is used to illustrate conservative opinion. The misleading figures were supplied by Goldwater. In 1960 the actual federal income tax on $100,000 net taxable income was about 60 per cent, while the tax on $10,000 net taxable income was about 24 per cent. Following the federal income tax reduction of 1964, the actual federal tax on $100,000 net taxable income was 48 per cent, while the tax on $10,000 was still about 24 per cent.

in 1913 with the passage of the 16th Amendment, together with the convenience, economy, and efficiency of income taxes are generally cited by proponents of income taxation. Sales taxes are very difficult to administer, and some retailers may pocket tax funds, unless a state has a considerable force of auditors to oversee sales tax collection.

Most of the states which adopted income taxation did so before World War II. Perhaps this has resulted from the heavy federal income tax levied during and after the war. Perhaps the opposition of the business community to income taxation has dissuaded states from levying such taxes in their effort to attract new industry. Perhaps liberal opposition to sales taxation is crumbling, as the result of widespread affluence in postwar America. Or perhaps liberals have accepted the arguments of John K. Galbraith that their past opposition to sales taxation tended to reduce the amount of public funds available to support public improvements.[7] Galbraith argues effectively that the benefits to low income groups which result from increased public expenditures outweigh whatever burdens are imposed on them by the regressivity of sales taxation. The sales tax seems to be emerging as the major source of state revenue in urban as well as rural states and in high as well as low income states.

The Politics of Budgeting

Too often we think of budgeting as the dull province of clerks and statisticians. Nothing could be more mistaken. Budgets are political documents which record the struggles of men over "who gets what." The budget is the single most important policy statement of any government. There are few government activities or programs which do not require an expenditure of funds, and no public funds may be spent without budgetary authorization. The budget sets forth government programs, with price tags attached. Determining what goes into a budget, that is, the budgetary process, provides a mechanism for reviewing government programs, assessing their cost, relating them to financial resources, making choices among alternative expenditures, and determining the financial effort that a government will expend on its programs. Budgets determine what programs are to be reduced, increased, initiated, or renewed. The size and shape of the budget is a matter of serious contention in the political life of any state or community. Governors, mayors, administrators, legislators, interest groups, and citizens all compete to have their policy preferences recorded in the budget. The budget lies at the heart of the political process.

Budget making authority is formally placed in the hands of the governor

[7] John K. Galbraith, *The Affluent Society* (Boston: Houghton Mifflin Co., 1956), chap. 22.

in all but seven states: Arkansas, Florida, Indiana, Mississippi, North Dakota, South Carolina, and West Virginia. The actual task of preparing the budget is carried out by an agency or official under the supervision of the governor, variously designated as the director of finance, budget director, or secretary of administration of finance. In those states where the governor does not have central control over budget making (generally regarded as "weak" governor states), budget making is often the responsibility of a budget commission. Such commissions are ordinarily composed of a group of state officials—governor, chief budget officer, comptroller, treasurer, attorney general, secretary of state, and perhaps the commissioner of agriculture and superintendent of schools. In addition to these executive officers, often a budget commission will include important legislative leaders, such as the chairmen of the finance and appropriations committees in both houses of the legislature. Most large cities place formal budget making authority in the hands of the mayor, who in turn relies upon a budget director or finance director to prepare the city's budget under his supervision.

The budgetary process begins with the governor or mayor's office sending to each governmental agency and department a budget request form, accompanied by broad policy directives to agency and department heads about the size and shape of their requests. Very often these budget requests must be made six to twelve months prior to the beginning of the fiscal year for which the requests are made; governmental fiscal years usually run from July 1 to June 30. After all requests have been submitted to the budget office, the serious task of consolidating these many requests begins. Individual department requests are reviewed, revised, and generally scaled down; often departments are given more or less formal hearings on their budget request by the budget director. The budget agency must also make revenue estimates based upon information it obtains from the tax department. Finally, budget requests and revenue estimates must be prepared. A great many decisions may already have been made by the time the budget director submits the tentative budget to the governor or mayor for his approval. But a governor or mayor must decide whether his budget is to be balanced or not; whether particular departmental requests should be increased or reduced, in view of the programs and promises important to his administration; whether economies should involve overall "belt-tightening" by every agency or merely the elimination of particular programs; or finally, whether he should recommend the raising of new taxes or the incurring of additional debt, and if so, what kinds of taxes or debts should be requested. These decisions may be the most important that a mayor or governor makes in his term of office, and he generally consults both political and financial advisors—budget and tax experts, party officials, interest group representatives, and legislative leaders. Ordinarily, these difficult decisions must be made before the governor or mayor presents his budget message to the legislature. This budget message explains and defends the final budget presented by the chief executive to his legislative branch.

The governor's budget generally appears in the lower house of the legislature as an appropriations bill and it follows the normal path of any bill. It is assigned to a ways and means committee or appropriations committee, which often holds hearings on the bill and occasionally reshapes and revises the executive budget. After the house committee reports the appropriations bill and it is passed by the lower house, it is then sent to the upper house where it repeats essentially the same steps. How a governor's budget fares in the legislature generally depends upon his general political power, public reactions to his recommendations, the degree of support he receives from department heads, who are often called to testify at legislative budget hearings, his relationships with key legislative leaders, and the effectiveness of interest groups that favor or oppose particular expenditures. After it is passed in identical form by both houses, the final appropriations measure is sent to the governor for his signature. If the governor has an item veto, he can still make significant changes in the budget at that time; however, most governors are obliged to accept the final appropriations measure, which provides basic authority to spend money for the fiscal year. Of course, agencies granted the authority to spend a particular amount are not required to do so, and if the funds are not available, agencies may be forced to spend less than their appropriation. However, no agency may spend more than its appropriation for particular programs.

What forces are actually involved in the budget making process? First of all, there is ample evidence that budgeting is a very *conservative* process—that is, if one defines the term conservative to mean preservation of the status quo.[8] Invariably the forms provided by the budget office require departments to prepare budget requests alongside of last year's expenditures. Decision makers generally consider last year's expenditures as a base. Consequently, active consideration of budget proposals is generally narrowed to new items or requested increases over last year's base. The attention of governors and legislators, and mayors and councils, is focused on a narrow range of increases or decreases in a budget. A budget is almost never reviewed as a whole every year, in the sense of reconsidering the value of existing programs. Departments are seldom required to defend or explain budget requests, which do *not* exceed current appropriations; but requested increases in appropriations require extensive explanation, and they are most subject to downward revision by higher political officials. The "incremental" nature of budgeting creates some interesting informal

[8] For a discussion of the budgetary process at the federal level see Aaron Wildavsky, *The Politics of the Budgetary Process* (Boston: Little, Brown and Co., 1964).

rules of the budget game. Thomas Anton summarizes some of these budgetary folkways:[9]

1. Spend all of your appropriation. A failure to use up an appropriation indicates that the full amount was unnecessary in the first place, which in turn implies that your budget should be cut next year.
2. Never request a sum less than your current appropriation. It is easier to find ways to spend up to current appropriation levels than it is to explain why you want a reduction. Besides, a reduction indicates your program is not growing and this is an embarrassing admission to most government administrators.
3. Put top priority programs into the basic budget, that is, that part of the budget which is within current appropriation levels. Budget offices, governors and mayors, and legislative bodies will seldom challenge programs which appear to be part of existing operations.
4. Increases that are desired should be made to appear small and should appear to grow out of existing operations. The appearance of a fundamental change in a budget should be avoided.
5. Give the budget office, chief executive, and the legislature something to cut. Normally it is desirable to submit requests for substantial increases in existing programs and many requests for new programs, in order to give higher political authorities something to cut. This enables them to "save" the public untold millions of dollars and justify their claim to promoting "economy" in government. Giving them something to cut also diverts attention away from the basic budget with its vital programs.

Budgeting is very *political*. As Aaron Wildavsky was told by a federal executive, "It's not what's in your estimates, but how good a politician you are that matters." [10] Being a good politician involves (1) the cultivation of a good base of support for one's requests among the public at large and among people served by the agency; (2) the development of interest, enthusiasm, and support for one's program among top political figures and legislative leaders; and (3) skill in following strategies that exploit one's opportunities to the maximum. Informing the public and one's clientele of the full benefit of the services they receive from the agency may increase the intensity with which they will support the agency's request. If possible, the agency should inspire its clientele to contact governors, mayors, legislators, and councilmen and help work for the agency's request. This is much more effective than the agency trying to promote for its own requests.

Budgeting is also quite *fragmented*. In at least 31 states, there is some form of constitutional earmarking of funds. Eleven states dedicate over one-third of all their revenues to particular funds and purposes, thus placing these outside of the budget making process. Federal and state laws

[9] For an excellent description of budgetary politics in a state, see Thomas J. Anton, *The Politics of State Expenditure in Illinois* (Urbana: University of Illinois Press, 1966).
[10] Wildavsky, *op. cit.,* p. 19.

severely limit the alternatives to decision makers involved in the budgetary process at the local level. Finally, as we have already seen, socio-economic conditions further reduce the alternatives for budgetary action. Very often, local governments *begin* the budgetary process by estimating the amount of revenues that can reasonably be expected from the existing tax base, various service charges, and intergovernmental revenues; this estimate then becomes the ceiling for all budget requests. This practice, together with the conservative tendency of accepting past expenditure levels, seriously curtails policy change. This may be part of the reason why governors and mayors have a difficult time bringing about significant policy changes, and it contributes to the public's view of "politics as usual" and a feeling that nothing can be done, regardless of who is elected.

Fragmentation also occurs in the consideration of budget requests by the governor and the legislature. In theory, the budget office is supposed to bring together budget requests and fit them into a coherent whole, while at the same time relating them to revenue estimates. But often budget offices do little more than staple together the budget requests of individual departments, and it is very difficult for a governor or mayor, and almost impossible for a legislature or council, to view the total policy impact of a budget. Wildavsky explains that the fragmented character of the budgetary process helps to secure agreement to the budget as well as reduce the burden of calculation.[11] Some budgets *must* be agreed upon by the executive and the legislature if the government is going to continue to function at all, and this pressure to agree often means that conflicts over programs must go unresolved in a budget. Calculations are made in small segments, often by legislative subcommittees, and must be accepted by the legislature as a whole. If each sub-committee challenged the result of the others, conflict might be so great that no budget would ever be passed. It is much easier to agree on a small addition or decrease to a single program than it is to compare the worth of one program to that of all others.

Finally, budgeting is *nonprogrammatic*. For reasons which accountants have so far kept to themselves, an agency budget typically lists expenditures under the ambiguous phrases: "personnel services," "contractual services," "travel," "supplies," "equipment." Needless to say, it is impossible to tell from such a listing exactly what programs the agency is spending its money on. Obviously such a budget obscures policy decision by hiding programs behind meaningless phrases. Even if these categories are broken down into line items (for example, under "personnel services," the line item budget might say, "John Doaks, Assistant Administrator, $15,000"), it is still next to impossible to identify the costs of various programs. Reform-oriented administrators have called for budgeting by programs for many years; this would present budgetary requests in terms

[11] *Ibid.*, p. 59.

of end products or program packages, like aid to dependent children, vocational rehabilitation, administration of fair employment practices laws, highway patrolling, and so on. Chief executives generally favor program budgeting because it will give them greater control over the policy. But very often administrative agencies are hostile toward program budgeting; it certainly adds to the cost of bookkeeping, and many agencies feel insecure in describing precisely what it is they do. Wildavsky points out that there are some political functions served by nonprogram budgeting. He notes that:

> Agreement comes much more readily when the items in dispute can be treated in dollars instead of basic differences in policy. Calculating budgets in monetary increments facilitates bargaining and logrolling. It becomes possible to swap an increase here for a decrease there or for an increase elsewhere without always having to consider the ultimate desirability of the programs blatantly in competition. . . . Party ties might be disruptive of agreement if they focused attention on policy differences between the two political persuasions. . . . Consider by contrast some likely consequences of program budgeting. The practice of focusing attention on programs means that policy implications can hardly be avoided. The gains and the losses for the interests involved become far more evident to all concerned. Conflict is heightened by the stress on the policy differences and increased still further by an inbuilt tendency to an all-or-nothing, "yes" or "no" response to the policy in dispute. The very concept of program packages suggests that the policy in dispute is indivisible, that the appropriate response is to be for or against rather than bargaining for a little more or a little less. Logrolling and bargaining are hindered because it is much easier to trade increments conceived in monetary terms than it is to give in on basic policy differences. Problems of calculation are vastly increased by the necessity, if program budgeting is to have meaning, of evaluating the desirability of every program as compared to all others, instead of the traditional practice of considering budgeting in relatively independent segments.[12]

Program budgeting also provides the opportunity for the introduction of performance standards in the budgeting process. "Performance budgeting" usually involves the designation of some unit of service, for example, one pupil, one hospital patient, or one welfare recipient, and the establishment of standards of service and costs based upon a single unit of service. A common example of performance budgeting is found in school systems, where pupils are designated as a basic unit of service and standards for numbers of teachers, supplies and materials, auxiliary personnel, building floor space, and many other cost items are calculated on the basis of the number of pupils to be served. Thus, standards may allocate teachers on the basis of one to 25 students, or a full time principal for every 250 students, or a psychologist for every 1000 pupils, or $20 worth of supplies

[12] *Ibid.,* pp. 136–38.

TABLE 17.6

DECISIONAL HISTORY OF SELECTED AGENCY APPROPRIATIONS IN ILLINOIS, 1963

	Last biennial appropriation	Budget request	Budgetary commission	Governor	Appropriations bill	General assembly	Approved
Dept. of Public Aid	$615,707,478	$701,556,483	$-63,433,337	- - - - - - - -	$638,123,146	$+1,881,255	$640,004,401
Federal	280,586,446	302,721,006	- 254,716	- - - - - - - -	302,466,352	+4,141,700	67,851,934
State	335,121,032	398,835,415	-63,178,621	- - - - - - - -	335,656,794	+4,414,840	433,090,000
Supervisor of Public Instruction							
Operating Distribution Grants	51,810,149	77,948,344	-20,988,110	$+ 6,750,000	63,710,234	+3,689,154	160,481,521
Common School Fund	393,396,000	534,250,000	-85,160,000	-16,000,000	433,090,000	+ 879,765	58,450,317
University of Illinois	133,741,170	194,387,740	- 4,427,319 -14,925,200*	-18,968,540*	156,066,681	+9,808,715	65,043,951
Southern Illinois University	41,986,941	102,545,444	- 6,878,475 -23,950,000*	-16,955,806*	54,761,163	- 4,030,484	247,702,925
Teachers College	47,475,140	71,089,029	- 853,756	- 6,071,087*	64,164,186	+5,991,046	36,744,312
Dept. of Mental Health	206,136,237	258,057,410	- - - - - - - -	-17,625,000 - 2,538,200*	237,894,210		18,223,116
Dept. of Public Safety	42,286,783	63,258,383	- 300,000	650,000 -21,533,587*	40,774,746		
Dept. of Public Works	14,939,056	14,146,390	- 328,820	- 1,585,000*	12,232,070		

*Capital Item

Source: Adopted from Thomas Anton, *The Politics of State Expenditures in Illinois*, (Urbana: University of Illinois Press, 1966), pp. 266-68.

for every student, and so on. These formulas are used to determine the allocation of resources at budget time. One political consequence of the use of formulas in performance budgeting is the centralization of budgetary decision making. Departments are merely asked to provide the number of pupils or patients or recipients or other units of service they expect to serve in the coming fiscal year. A central staff of budget analysis then determines allocations through the application of formulas to the service estimates provided by the departments. Many departments, accustomed to less bureaucratic procedures, feel that the use of formulas is mechanical and inflexible. But it is not surprising in a large and complex bureaucracy to see the search for equitable patterns in the distribution of resources leading to the use of formulas applied throughout the system. Often, however, once a formula has been established, it is difficult to change or adjust the formula even from one year to the next. H. Thomas James, in a study of educational expenditures in large cities, reported that the traditional inflexibility of formulas could only be adjusted under severe political pressures: "In Chicago, a selected district was provided with extra remedial teachers; in New York the 'more effective school' plan substituted a 'saturation' for a 'normal' staffing pattern; in St. Louis a slum district was given an increased allotment of teachers." [13] Performance budgeting places great power in the hands of the staff personnel budget offices who devise the formulas. Performance budgeting is generally favored by economy-minded groups, particularly businessmen who are familiar with the application of unit cost procedures to manufacturing enterprises.

Thomas Anton has examined the respective roles of the governor, state agencies, the budgetary commission, and the legislature in the development of the Illinois budget in 1963.[14] Agency budget requests are generally much higher than last year's appropriations. The executive budgetary commission makes heavy cuts into agency requests. The governor makes additional cuts to bring his budget into balance. But the general assembly proceeds to restore many of the cuts in agency requests. The final budget is much higher than last year's appropriations, but much lower than agency requests.

Federal Grants-in-Aid

Federal grants-in-aid are money payments made by federal agencies to state and local governments for the purpose of carrying out programs of interest to the federal government. Federal grant-in-aid programs are estab-

[13] For an excellent description of the budgetary process in big-city school systems, see H. Thomas James, *Determinants of Educational Expenditures in Large Cities of the United States* (Stanford, Cal.: Stanford University, School of Education, 1966).

[14] Thomas J. Anton, "Roles and Symbols in the Determination of State Expenditures," *Midwest Journal of Political Science*, 11 (February, 1967), 27–43.

lished by Congress under its power to "tax and spend for the general welfare." We have already described federal grant programs in education, welfare, housing and urban renewal, and highways and mass transit, but there are more than 200 federal grant-in-aid programs currently in operation, which cover a tremendously wide variety of programs (see Table 2.5 in Chapter 2). It is true that states and communities administer these programs, and generally match federal funds from their own fiscal sources, but federal grants-in-aid usually involve federal intervention in policy making, through minimum standards and "guidelines." Federal agencies retain the right to approve or disapprove grant applications submitted by states and local governments.

Federal grant-in-aid programs are growing at a very rapid rate. In 1964, federal grants-in-aid to state and local governments totalled $10 billion, but in 1967, this figure had grown to over $15 billion, an increase of 50 per cent in three years. These federal grants-in-aid now make up about 15 per cent of all state and local revenues. The rate of expansion of federal grant-in-aid spending suggests that states and communities are becoming increasingly dependent upon the federal government every year.

Of course, not all the states share equally in federal aid programs. Each state's share of federal revenues will vary according to its population, needs, fiscal resources, and formulas which Congress develops for the distribution of funds for federally assisted programs. In addition, a state's share of federal aid will depend upon the extent to which the state and its communities decide to participate in federal programs. Overall, federal grant-in-aid payments in 1966 constituted more than 25 per cent of state-local revenues in Arizona, Alaska, Arkansas, New Mexico, Vermont, West Virginia, and Wyoming, and less than 10 per cent in New York.

We have already seen that federal programs in education, welfare, health, housing and urban renewal, and highways still leave considerable policy discretion to the states in these areas. Proponents of the present federal grant-in-aid system argue that it does not undermine the role of states and communities in the American federal system, but in fact strengthens federalism. They have referred to a sharing of federal, state, and local responsibility in program areas as "creative federalism" and have defended it as a pragmatic approach to many of the nation's most pressing problems. Federal grants-in-aid, in general, are defended on three important grounds: (1) the states and communities have either ignored or been unable to cope with the problem for which the federal grant-in-aid program is intended; (2) only the federal government has sufficient financial resources to deal effectively with the particular problem involved; or (3) federal aid programs help to equalize state-local opportunities to deal with major problems by giving more aid to poorer states. Problems in education, welfare, health, housing, civil rights, and other major domestic areas are said to be national responsibilities which are too large and too complex to be dealt with effectively at the state and local level without federal assistance. It is also argued that the federal government, with its progressive and individual corporate income tax, is the only level of government with the fiscal resources to deal effectively with these domestic issues.

Actually, the argument that federal assistance helps to equalize opportunities in the 50 states deserves closer study. While it is true that in some programs—education, for example—federal funds are allocated to poorer states and communities, there is no actual correlation between wealth and total per capita federal grants.[15] In other words, the federal government does *not* hand out more dollars per capita to poorer than to richer states. However, poorer states *rely* on the federal dollars that they receive to a greater degree than richer states. Federal grants-in-aid constitute a larger *percentage* of the total revenues of poorer, rural states; [16] these states need their federal dollars more than richer urban states. Only in this way can it be said that federal grants help to equalize opportunities in education, welfare, health, and housing throughout the 50 states.

Opponents of federal aid programs see them as a threat to the American federal system and to the independence of states and communities. They believe that federal grant-in-aid programs give the federal government undue influence over policies and programs of state and local governments. While it is true that state or local government participation in federal grant programs is voluntary, they believe that states and communities join federal aid programs because they fear to let other states and communities receive federal dollars to which their citizens have already been forced to make contributions. Other critics of federal grant-in-aid programs point to the uncoordinated and bureaucratic character of the more than 200 grant-in-aid programs currently administered by the federal government. They charge that the federal government has never set any meaningful priorities among its hundreds of grant programs. The result is that too few dollars chase too many goals. Domestic problems of inadequate education, crime, poverty, slum housing, and so on, continue to persist and grow despite federal grant programs. Many states and communities neglect their responsibilities while waiting for federal funds to solve their problems, in the manner of prospective heirs anticipating the deaths of rich uncles while ignoring other possibilities of improving their own lots in life. Federal funds are addictive, and states and cities allow projects well within their means to become stalled once federal money is imbedded in their plans and thinking. Opponents of federal aid programs also argue that the failure of states

[15] See George F. Break, *Intergovernmental Fiscal Relations in the United States* (Washington: The Brookings Institution, 1967), pp. 120–28.

[16] Dye, *op. cit.*, p. 193.

TABLE 17.7

FEDERAL GRANTS-IN-AID IN THE STATES

	Per càpita federal aid to state and local governments, 1965	Federal aid as percent of state local revenues 1966
United States	$ 79	15.8%
Ala.	90	27.6
Alas.	420	44.4
Ariz.	92	20,3
Calif.	72	16.4
Col.	120	19.4
Conn.	60	12.6
Del.	78	14.9
Fla.	56	14.1
Georgia	79	20.5
Hawaii	103	20.3
Idaho	146	19.8
Ill.	66	12.4
Ind.	62	11.7
Iowa	131	14.3
Kansas	153	14.9
Kent.	88	24.2
Louisiana	105	21.7
Maine	71	19.4
Maryland	56	12.5
Mass.	77	13.6
Mich.	57	12.7
Minn.	108	16.1
Miss.	90	23.7
Mo.	96	20.1
Mont.	202	24.7
Neb.	173	16.2
Nev.	141	22.3
N.H.	67	16.6
N.J.	40	10.4
N. Mex.	138	29.6
N.Y.	57	8.6
N.C.	60	17.7
N.D.	269	18.2
Ohio	55	14.6
Okla.	129	23.5
Ore.	119	22.3
Pa.	55	13.8
R.I.	88	18.2
S.C.	58	18.8
S.D.	211	21.6
Tenn.	84	22.8
Texas	75	16.8
Utah	131	24.6
Ver.	131	26.8
Vir.	74	19.2

United States	Per capita federal aid to state and local governments, 1965	Federal aid as percent of state local revenues 1966
Wash.	$ 93	16.5%
W. Va.	98	27.1
Wis.	58	10.4
Wy.	262	33.9

Source: U.S. Bureau of the Census, *Statistical Abstract 1967.*

and communities to deal with some of their problems is a product of the fact that their financial resources have been dried up because of heavy federal taxation. Critics believe that sending tax dollars to Washington to have them returned in federal grant programs is inefficient because a great deal of money disappears along this route in overhead and administrative costs of the federal government. (Actually, the U.S. General Accounting Office reported in 1957 that the average administrative expenses in tax collection and administration of all federal grant programs amounts to only 1.6 per cent of grants paid out.) [17] And of course, there are always specific complaints with particular federal standards or guidelines, such as the complaints by southern school systems (and some northern city school systems) about the racial integration guidelines of the U.S. Office of Education.

As a result of widespread dissatisfaction over the administration of federal grant-in-aid programs, several proposals have been made for a system of unrestricted federal grants to states with no strings attached. These grants assume the form of block grants to states or communities for a stated purpose, such as education, health, or welfare, but the way in which the money would be spent is to be determined by the state or community itself. These block grants would avoid the excessively detailed grant-in-aid applications, and would enable each state and community to apply its federal aid to its most compelling problems. Unrestricted federal grants might assume the form of revenue sharing, with a certain percentage of federal income tax collections turned back to the state and local governments for use as they see fit. These shared revenues would presumably replace earmarked and controlled, conditional grants-in-aid by the federal government. It would follow the pattern of states that allocate to their political subdivisions a share of their tax receipts. This would give states and communities some access to the fiscal resources of the federal government, yet at the same time insure state and local control over the use of these funds.

[17] See Break, *op. cit.,* p. 84.

Block grants and shared revenue proposals are generally supported by those groups who fear centralization of power at the federal level. They are joined in their opposition by those who oppose directions in federal domestic policy in recent years. Groups who oppose federal policy naturally welcome the opportunity to shift decision making from the federal level to states and communities. Interests that are in the minority in national politics, but who constitute majorities in certain states or communities, obviously would support proposals to transfer policy making from the national level to the state and local level. The Republican party has been less enthusiastic about federal grant-in-aid programs and has tended to provide the bulk of support for block grant and revenue sharing proposals. Considerable support for these proposals should also be forthcoming from the southern states, so long as the formula for the distribution of unconditional federal funds recognizes inequalities among the states in financial resources and provides larger shares of federal money to poorer states. Southern states and communities object to federal policy, not federal money, and certainly not to equalization formulas.

INDEX